# Business in Action

## An Introduction to Business

### THIRD EDITION

**Lester R. Bittel**
Professor of Management
College of Business
James Madison University

**Ronald S. Burke**
Chairperson
Management Planning Services Company

**Charles P. Bilbrey**
Associate Professor and Department Head
Information and Decision Sciences Department
James Madison University

Gregg Division
## McGRAW-HILL BOOK COMPANY
New York • Atlanta • Dallas • St. Louis • San Francisco
Auckland • Bogotá • Guatemala • Hamburg • Lisbon
London • Madrid • Mexico • Milan • Montreal • New Delhi
Panama • Paris • San Juan • São Paulo • Singapore
Sydney • Tokyo • Toronto

*Sponsoring Editors:* Edward Byers, Phyllis Kurzer, and Lawrence Wexler
*Editing Supervisor:* Nicola von Schreiber
*Design and Art Supervisor and Cover Designer:* Nancy Axelrod
*Production Supervisors:* Priscilla Taguer and Mirabel Flores
*Photo Editor:* Rosemarie Rossi
*Text Designer:* Gail Schneider
*Cover Photographer:* Wolfson Photography, Inc.


**Library of Congress Cataloging-in-Publication Data**

Bittel, Lester R.
  Business in action.

  Includes index.
  1. Business enterprises—United States.  2. Industrial management—
United States.  I. Burke, Ronald S.  II. Bilbrey, Charles P.  III. Title.
HF5343.B57  1988      658      87-3134
ISBN 0-07-005565-3

## PHOTO CREDITS

Page 3: Mel DiGicomo/Image Bank; page 6: Morton Beebe/Image Bank; page 30: Grafton Marshall Smith/Image Bank; page 56: Peter Arnold, Inc.; page 74: PepsiCo, Inc.; page 97: Arthur d'Arazien/Image Bank; page 100: International Stock Photo; page 118: Hank Morgan/Rainbow; page 139: The Bravo Group, Young & Rubicam, Inc.; page 142: Will Faller; page 166: D. McDonald/The Stock Shop; page 190: Jules Allen; page 216: Ford Motor Co.; page 235: Steve Dunwell/Image Bank; page 238: Burt Glinn/Magnum; page 264: Ted Kawaleski/Image Bank; page 290: Walter Bibikon/Image Bank; page 314: Jules Allen; page 333: Stan Pak/International Stock Photo; page 336: Richard Hackett; page 356: Richard Hackett; page 382: Bruce Davidson/Magnum; page 405: Michael K. Nichols/Magnum; page 408: Richard Hackett; page 432: Burt Glinn/Magnum; page 460: Kilian/Image Bank; page 483: Frank Whitney/Image Bank; page 486: Alex Webb/ Magnum; page 508: Marvin E. Neuman/Image Bank; page 530: Richard Hackett; page 556: Eli Reed/Magnum.

## Business in Action:
### An Introduction to Business, Third Edition

1 2 3 4 5 6 7 8 9 0  VNHVNH  8 9 4 3 2 1 0 9 8 7

ISBN 0-07-005565-3

# Contents

*Unit 5*

*Unit 6*

*Unit 7*

# Preface

This third edition of *Business in Action* further refines its uniquely flexible, adaptive approach to the study of business. The textbook has been expanded and enhanced for its use as a fully comprehensive, independent study resource. It now can be supplemented by adopting either a traditional student *Activity and Study Guide* or an experiential business model and student activity guide entitled *SSweetco: Business Model and Activity File*. This has as its core element a simulated model of a realistic company (SSweetco, the Shenandoah Sweets Company). A comprehensive package of instructional resources is also available to help the instructor achieve his or her course objectives.

## THE TEXTBOOK

The uniquely designed textbook is especially easy to read and comprehend. Each chapter systematically enumerates and links its learning objectives and chapter overviews with its major descriptive sections and summary highlights. These are arranged in an easy-to-follow outlining structure to help students in their study. Extensive business examples, case studies, news reports, role models, and end-of-chapter review questions make this textbook, by itself, a complete and well-rounded teaching and learning resource.

## Organization and Contents

The textbook has been carefully reorganized into 7 major units and 24 chapters. Each unit is an independent entity. Therefore an instructor can tailor the sequence of units and contents to match his or her own course of study.

The textbook has been substantially revised and updated. Chapter 4, on small business, has been expanded, providing more in-depth coverage of entrepreneurship and franchising. Unit 3, "Marketing of Products and Services," now includes a separate chapter (Chapter 10) on "Pricing Strategies for

Profit." The importance of computers and technology in our rapidly changing information economy is recognized in Chapter 12 titled "Information and Computer Systems." Chapter 15 dealing with human relations now includes an expanded discussion of productivity.

## Textbook Features

Each chapter of the textbook integrates a set of learning devices that promote an understanding of how business operates.

**PICTOGRAPHS.** Pictographs are previews, or advance summaries, of the chapter presented in pictures and words. They are used to simplify and speed up the absorption of complex ideas. Similar illustrations are widely used in news magazines, such as *U.S. News and World Report*, to convey ideas readily and save readers precious time.

**LEAD ARTICLES AND PHOTOGRAPHS.** Each chapter is introduced by an article and related color photograph dealing with an issue, trend, company practice, or development in business. Each article, rewritten from popular business sources, serves as a springboard and dramatic lead-in to the subject matter and issues raised in a chapter.

**KEY TERMS.** Significant terms are highlighted in bold type at their point of definition in the textbook. They are also listed in the Review Questions at the end of each chapter with convenient cross-referencing to the pages on which they are defined.

**TABLES AND FIGURES.** Tables presenting arrays of data, and figures that illustrate concepts and ideas, are widely used throughout the text.

**ACTION BRIEFS.** Short anecdotes are interspersed in the margins of the text, providing a representative sampling of business practices, commendable or otherwise. There are over a hundred Action Briefs throughout the text; most are new to this edition.

**BILLBOARDS.** These features are found in specially chosen chapters of the text. Billboards are divided into two parts: readings that focus on business issues, and Profiles. The readings are based mainly on current events. They focus primarily on thought-provoking, business-related social issues and aim to stimulate students to form their own opinions about those issues. Profiles are vignettes that highlight the role, characteristics, and contributions of men and women who are succeeding in the business world.

**KEY CONCEPTS.** At the end of each chapter, the ideas presented in the pictographs and main headings are summarized. The concepts are keyed by number to the pictographs, objectives, and the major text headings—a system that helps link all major learning elements together.

**REVIEW QUESTIONS.** Each chapter concludes with a list of questions testing students' understanding of text material.

**CASE CRITIQUES.** Each chapter is supplemented with two documented and/or hypothetical case studies illustrating practical applications of key concepts and key terms. These case studies are designed to encourage students to develop critical judgments in assessing business actions.

**TECHNOLOGY IN THE WORKPLACE.** Also, at the end of each unit is another special feature: Technology in the Workplace provides a sampling of how careers and work are changing because of the development of new technologies, such as robotics, electronic mail, compact disks, and, of course, computers.

## SUPPLEMENTS AND INSTRUCTIONAL RESOURCES

The following ancillaries are available with *Business in Action*, Third Edition.

## SSweetco: Business Model and Activity File

Using this simulation and practicum, students can become involved in the creation, operation, and growth of Shenandoah Sweets Company (SSweetco), a candy manufacturer and retailer. Assignments in the practicum—which are completely correlated with the textbook—enable students to experience firsthand how the concepts presented in the text are put to work in the real world. Students assume 32 career roles for the simulated business. Assigned activities require students to answer questions, solve problems, make calculations, complete typical business forms, and analyze and make deci-

sions in case studies involving SSweetco and Valleyville, its associated business community.

## Activity and Study Guide

For instructors who favor traditional teaching approaches, this self-study guide offers chapter-by-chapter learning objectives, summaries of key concepts, and vocabulary and concept review questions. It also includes cases for analysis and interpretation, and supplementary readings. Self-check answer keys are provided for the student.

## Computer Applications for Introduction to Business, IBM PC

These are easy-to-use, easy-to-operate, computer-based applications. Students assume the roles of employees and managers for SSweetco and help it solve typical business problems. At a basic, easy-to-follow level they learn to use modern productivity tools—spreadsheet, database, and graphics—to make decisions in such areas as marketing, production, finance, and human resources management. No previous background in computers is needed. A booklet containing the narrative and background information for the computer activities is available for the student. A preformatted IBM data disk with the programs for the computer applications is also available with the specific computer decision-making applications. To run the software, adopters must separately order the McGraw-Hill Integrated Software, IBM Version, the program disks that interact with the data disk to make the applications fully operational. Instructors who use either experiential or traditional approaches can make effective classroom use of these applications.

## Computerized Test Bank, IBM PC

This microcomputer test bank with over 1,400 objective questions provides a quick and easy means of generating tests. Instructors have the option of adding or deleting questions to the test bank. Thus the test bank can be tailored to the instructor's particular classroom needs.

## Course Management Kit

This boxed set of instructional resources provides course management materials in a "unitized" format that makes them easy to use. An introductory booklet includes suggestions for teaching the course,

course schedules, a bibliography, and a list of suggested audiovisual materials. Seven additional booklets—one for each unit of the text—offer text-management and enrichment suggestions, printed tests, readings, and strategies for integrating text chapters with the student study supplements. A set of overhead transparencies is also provided as a further aid to instruction.

**Lester R. Bittel**
**Ronald S. Burke**
**Charles P. Bilbrey**

# Acknowledgments

The authors acknowledge the invaluable advice and guidance provided by those people in the academic ranks who served as reviewers or consultants for this and other editions of the work. Their ideas and suggestions have profoundly shaped the pedagogy, format, features, and content of the text and the various components of the *Business in Action* teaching and learning system.

Special thanks are extended to **Professor Abu Selimuddin of Berkshire Community College** for any number of his creative ideas that have found their way into the text; **Professor A. H. Friedman of J. Sargeant Reynolds Community College** for his considerable advice on economics content; **Gregory C. Dellinger** for his library search for technological and computer-related materials; **Professor W. L. Safford of Rowan Technical College;** and **R. Lawrence LaForge,** who contributed so much as a coauthor of the second edition of this program.

## List of Reviewers/Consultants

**James Alston**
*Rappanock Community College*

**Teresa Kay Avila**
*College of Business*
*Ball State University*

**Dr. Robert S. Bulls**
*J. Sargeant Reynolds Community College*

**Dr. Helen Diamond**
*Citrus College*

**Frieda Ford**
*Indiana Vocational Technical College*

**Marvin Keefer**
*Academic Dean,*
*Commonwealth College*

**Margaret Knight**
*Dean,*
*Rutledge College*

**Richard M. Kotz, Jr.**
*American Institute of Business*

**Susan W. McClure**
*Tri-County Technical College*

**Andrew M. McKee**
*North Country Community College*

**Donald Park**
*American Institute of Commerce*

**Glenn S. Smith**
*Eastern Arizona College*

**Charles Trester**
*Northeast Wisconsin Technical Institute*

**William J. VanDeVeer**
*Mohave Community College*

**Kenneth D. Wagner**
*The Bradford School*

# To The Student

## Guidelines for Study With Business in Action

The following steps constitute an effective way to study the materials in each chapter. The key to effective study is making maximum use of the numbers that identify each pictograph, objective, major text heading, and key concept. If you are not already familiar with these features, you should read the discussion of "Textbook Features" starting on page v of the Preface.

**STEP 1.** Study the pictograph. Spend two or three minutes to be sure you get the whole picture. Then read the learning objectives that precede each chapter.

**STEP 2.** Now skim through the entire chapter reading only the main headings and subheadings. These headings provide an outlining structure for each chapter. They reinforce and extend the ideas presented in the pictograph. (These headings also may be used as your outline structure for notetaking from the text.)

**STEP 3.** Read the Key Concept summaries and glance at the list of key terms at the end of the chapter. Be alert for definitions of these terms as you read the chapter.

These first three steps, which make up a "three-part linked learning system," will help you quickly summarize the basic concepts in a chapter by skimming it in about 10 to 15 minutes. You are now prepared to read the chapter for details that will help you flesh out the Key Concepts.

**STEP 4.** Read the chapter carefully for detail. Devote an hour or more to this. Keep notes of important facts. Write down the definition of any terms that are necessary for understanding the topics under discussion. Key terms are in bold type for ease of identification.

As you read each chapter for detail, be certain to study each table and figure to be sure of its meaning. Also read the Action Briefs in the margins of the text to get a feel for what *actually occurs* in business as opposed to what *ought* to happen.

**STEP 5.** Answer the Review Questions. It is a good idea to make a note of the pages on which the answer appears.

**STEP 6.** Read each of the Case Critiques. Try to make a connection between what has occurred in the cases and what you have just read in the text. Answer the questions associated with each case.

If your instructor has assigned the *Activity and Study Guide,* move to the corresponding chapter in that supplement and complete the assignments provided there. Be sure to self-check your answers to identify content areas that require further study.

*Only if your instructor has assigned material from the student supplement, SSweetco: Business Model and Activity File for Business in Action, Third Edition, should you continue with Steps 7 and 8 in the study plan as described below.*

**STEP 7.** If your instructor has included the SSweetco supplement in your course materials, move to the corresponding chapter in the activities section of *SSweetco: Business Model and Activity File.* Read the performance objectives that precede the two levels of achievement. Then complete the exercises and activities for the first level of achievement, the "Application Level."

**STEP 8.** Proceed to the next, higher level of achievement, "Analysis and Interpretation," by completing the decision-making and case problem assignments.

Rigorous follow-through on these study procedures will lead to good study habits that can have a positive effect on what you learn in this introductory business course and may, as a result, help to improve your grades.

# UNIT 1

# *The Business System in the United States*

Unit 1 establishes what American business is all about. It lays the groundwork for understanding how an idea or concept can be transformed into a viable product or service for sale in the marketplace.

## CHAPTER 1

Business is a creative, competitive activity that has always played an important part in shaping American society. By satisfying the needs and wants that people are not able to satisfy for themselves, business helps to improve the quality of their lives.

## CHAPTER 2

The purpose of business is to combine resources such as land, labor, and capital in such a way that it will make them more valuable. Operating in a political and economic climate that supports individual rights, American business has as its guiding principle the right to private ownership and capital along with a responsibility to respect the environments upon which it depends.

## CHAPTER 3

Businesses can take many different forms. Each offers its own set of advantages and drawbacks. The choice of ownership form is dependent upon how the owners of a business perceive these conditions.

## CHAPTER 4

There has been a revival of the entrepreneurial spirit in America. With it has come a surge of newer, smaller, more innovative companies. Operation of these small companies, especially franchising, while similar in many ways to that of larger ones, takes on a unique character of its own.

## CHAPTER 1

# The Roles of
# Business Enterprise
# in Society

## Learning Objectives

*The purpose of this chapter is to define business in the United States, describe its characteristics and the conditions under which it operates, and summarize its development.*

*As evidence of general comprehension, after studying this chapter you should be able to:*

1. *Define a business enterprise and distinguish among private, nonprofit, and public enterprises.*

2. *Discuss the three major functions of business in society.*

3. *Explain the process of converting resources and adding utility.*

4. *Recognize the threefold classification of business enterprises by type and activity, and identify the groupings under the Standard Industrial Classification system (SIC).*

5. *Explain the meaning of risk and uncertainty in business.*

6. *Recall the major stages in the development of modern American business.*

7. *Identify the five environments in which the business system operates.*

*If your class is using SSweetco: Business Model and Activity File, see Chapter 1 in that book after you complete this chapter. There you will find exercises and activities to help you apply your learning to typical business situations.*

## 1 DEFINITION

Business is an activity that satisfies human needs and wants by providing goods and services for private profit.

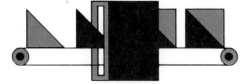

## 2 VALUES

Business provides individuals and society with . . .

Means of exchange
Wealth
Employment

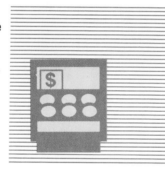

## 3 PROCESS

Business processes convert input resources—by creating or adding utility of form, place, time, or possession—into more valuable outputs or end products.

## 4 VARIETY

Businesses occur in a variety of sizes and classifications.

Production:
Manufacturing of consumer and industrial goods

Distribution:
Transportation, storage, and retailing

Services:
Personal, professional, financial, and communications

## 5 DYNAMICS

The business environment is characterized by:

Risk/Uncertainty
Gain/Loss
Success/Failure
Stagnation/Growth
Change/Opportunity

## 6 HISTORY

American business has gradually shifted its emphasis:

| | |
|---|---|
| Agriculture | Industry |
| Transportation | Production |
| Communication | Services |
| Banking | Marketing |

 1770s

 TODAY

## 7 ENVIRONMENT

Businesses exist within and react with five interdependent environments.

economic
legal-political
social-cultural
physical
technological

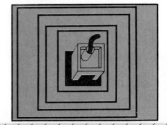

# NEW HOUSE FOR SALE!

*You see it happen every day. A bulldozer clears an empty lot. A masonry crew arrives to build a foundation. Carpenters erect a framework of posts and beams. A roof goes into place, and the house is closed in. The electricians, plumbers, and painters go to work. The lot is graded and the lawn is seeded. A real estate agent puts up a "For Sale" sign. A family falls in love with this house. They make a trip to the bank to arrange a mortgage. Finally, the deal is closed and the house is theirs.*

*This process takes place over 500,000 times each year in the United States. It causes more than $100 billion to change hands. It creates more than 875,000 jobs, for which nearly $25 billion is paid in wages. Each home will require up to 12,000 board feet of lumber; it may come from as far away as Idaho or Georgia. Some 99 square feet of glass may make up the windows, and these may come from Tennessee or New Jersey. There will be one or two bathtubs, three sinks, and two toilets, and these may come from Texas or Wisconsin. The 33 gallons of paint for each home can come from just about any state in the Union. And that's not all. For each home there will be over 7,000 square feet of drywall, more than 3,000 cubic feet of insula-*

*tion, 15 doors, 230 running feet of gutters and downspouts, and dozens of electrical switches and lighting outlets.*

*The process of building and buying and selling goes far beyond the products you see, like bricks and mortar. It involves surveyors and architects, truckers and warehouse handlers, drapery salespeople and interior decorators, real estate agents and credit managers, bankers and lawyers, file clerks at the county courthouse and classified advertising clerks at the local newspaper, small businesses, and giant corporations. They are all part of a vast and interrelated network of purposeful activity that makes up the business system of America. It is a network of individuals in literally thousands of industries, from computers to carpet sweepers, from high tech to dirty hands. These are the millions of individuals who labor or who buy and sell, the countless businesses and labor unions, the millions of citizens and consumers, and the long line of government agencies. Together, they represent the powerful force that transforms the nation's resources into trillions of dollars of goods and services that satisfy the material needs and wants of our society.*

# 1 THE BUSINESS ENTERPRISE
*A private, profit-motivated means of satisfying human needs*

An activity that satisfies human needs and wants by providing goods or services for private profit is called a **business enterprise.** From a cookie-vending cart in Los Angeles to General Motors in Detroit, every business (1) satisfies needs, (2) provides goods and services, and (3) does so with the intention of making a profit. A fundamental characteristic of American business is that it uses private money and resources, or capital, to pay for the costs of setting up and running commercial enterprises. The willingness of private investors to risk their capital in the hope of gaining profit distinguishes the American system from those in which the government supplies the resources.

## SATISFYING NEEDS AND WANTS
*The guiding principle*

All human beings have certain basic needs—things that they must have in order to survive. In addition to these basic needs, there are many things that people want to make their lives more comfortable or satisfying. A business must provide its customers—whether they are individuals, other companies, or the government—with something that they need or want. Otherwise, the business will have no sales, no income, and no profit and will be forced to close its doors. The idea that success in business depends on fulfilling consumer needs and wants is fundamental to the American business system.

Human needs and wants shift with the advance of civilization. Yesterday's demand for horse collars and horse carriages has been replaced today by an even greater demand for automobiles and motorcycles. In like manner, the manual typewriter has given way to the electronic word processor, and the tape deck is replacing the phonograph record. Specific consumer demands change constantly, but there will always be a wide range of human wants and needs to encourage business to operate, whatever the circumstances.

## GOODS AND SERVICES
*The means to satisfy human needs and wants*

In meeting human needs and desires, businesses provide goods and services to consumers. **Goods** are physical products and include both necessities like food and shelter and luxuries like television sets and motor boats. **Services** are activities that help people or organizations without directly creating a physical product. Services can be classified as personal, professional, or financial. In the modern world, services range from home and office maintenance and repair to financial operations and highly complex communications and research activities. Lawn mowing, auto repair, television programs, and banking are other examples. Thousands of different kinds of services make up this rapidly growing business segment.

There are additional subcategories of goods and services. Goods made and sold to meet the needs and wants of manufacturers are called industrial goods. They normally undergo a process of conversion as they are utilized in the fabrication of the final product. Goods made and sold to meet the needs and wants of consumers are known as consumer goods and do not require processing by their ultimate users. Services may also be subdivided into those that are business-oriented, such as office maintenance, and those that are consumer-oriented, such as hairstyling. Nonprofit organizations also provide services, usually related to education, health care, and social welfare.

## PRIVATE PROFIT

### The payoff for satisfying consumer needs

The primary goal of business is to make money. In a sense, it is the businessperson's payoff for satisfying human needs and wants. In simplest terms, **profit** is the amount of money left from income made by selling goods and services after all costs of producing, marketing, and distributing the goods and services have been paid. Said another way, persons enter business with the hopes that they will take in more money than they spend. (See Table 1-1.) Obviously, sometimes there is no money left over, or costs turn out to be higher than income. If that unhappy outcome occurs, the business either breaks even or takes a loss. The intention in business, however, is to operate in such a way that profits will be as high as possible, consistent with social responsibility. The incentive to make money is called the **profit motive.**

The profit motive is that which most clearly distinguishes business from other kinds of enterprises in the United States. There are other organizations that also meet some of the wants and needs of people. They provide goods and, particularly, services. These enterprises differ from business in several ways, but the principal difference is that they do

**TABLE 1-1
PROFIT OR LOSS?**

*How One Company Makes a Profit*

| | |
|---|---|
| Company A adds up the revenues each year from sales of its products or services (like this). | $100,000 |
| It deducts the costs each year for its materials, labor, rent, utilities, etc. | − 90,000 |
| What's left is its *profit.* | $ 10,000 |

*How Another Company Doesn't Make a Profit*

| | |
|---|---|
| Company B adds up its revenues for the year (like this). | $100,000 |
| It deducts its expenses for the year (like this). | −105,000 |
| And it ends up with a *loss* (like this). | − $5,000 |

*Moral*

To make a profit, a business must generate revenues that are greater than its expenses.

not seek a profit. The most important kinds of enterprises of this kind are private nonprofit enterprises and public enterprises.

## NONPROFIT ENTERPRISES
*Voluntary contributions or taxes provide capital*

**PRIVATE NONPROFIT ENTERPRISES** *Private nonprofit organizations* are financed, established, and operated in much the same way as business. Their goal, however, is not to make a profit, but to meet needs that are not or cannot be effectively or fully satisfied by business. Among private nonprofit enterprises are hospitals, museums, research and charitable organizations, colleges and universities, and professional associations. Financing for these organizations is provided by voluntary contributions from individuals, businesses, and, in part, the government.

**PUBLIC ENTERPRISES** *Public enterprises,* organizations operated by units of government and financed with taxes or service charges to the public, are increasingly important in American society. Many of these organizations—like highway departments, public health services, local sewage disposal plants, and water systems—are operated just as if they were businesses. They have the same management problems, the same kinds of budgets, similar physical plants and personnel, and often the same concerns with income and costs. The difference is that a public enterprise is not financed with private capital and does not expect to make a profit. Funds to establish public enterprises usually come from taxes. The enterprises generally are operated so that income and expenses will be equal. If a profit does occasionally result, this surplus belongs to the sponsoring government body rather than to private investors.

## 2 VALUES
### Business contributes certain values to society

Although the main motivation for establishing and operating a business is to make a profit for investors, business serves important social functions beyond this. Our society supports and encourages business because it makes these contributions. American business provides individuals and society as a whole with a means of exchange, with wealth, and with employment. It is not the only institution in the United States that makes such contributions to society, but it is probably the most important.

## MEANS OF EXCHANGE
*Buying and selling*

Few societies have ever endured where each individual or family produced all of the essentials of life for private use. Even in pioneer America, specialization existed in the production of tools and weapons, household implements, and certain other goods, including agricultural products. The fact that certain people and groups had goods that others needed and did not or could not produce for themselves created a need

---

### Action Brief

#### WHO EARNS WHAT FROM YOUR JEANS?

*If you pay $18.96 for a pair of blue denim jeans, who really gets your money? Lots of people besides the retail shop where you bought them. The cotton farmer, for instance, gets $1.63 off the top. The mill that cleans, or "gins," the raw cotton gets 41 cents. Another 4 cents goes for miscellaneous handling. The textile mill that weaves and dyes the fabric takes $3.30 for its contribution. The actual garment manufacturer, such as Levi's, gets another $5.13. That means that the cost of your jeans as they leave the factory is about $10.51. Between the wholesaler and the retailer, another $8.45 is shared. Remember: These two businesses provide the jeans with utility of place and time. That is, you could get those jeans right now, without waiting, and at a store right in your own neighborhood.*

for trade. The trade—or exchange—of goods and services is a basic function of business. In a highly technical, specialized society such as ours, this aspect of business predominates. Today, if you wished to have a Sony Walkman, for example, you would mow a lawn for wages or make an item for sale, and exchange that money with a retailer for the Walkman. The retailer, in turn, would exchange the money with the manufacturer to obtain the Walkman. A modern family directly produces virtually none of the necessities of life. Food, clothing, shelter, and the means of transportation and communication are all supplied by the buying and selling processes that are part of business.

# WEALTH
*More than money*

Business creates wealth that would not otherwise exist. Although **wealth** is commonly interpreted to mean the possession of a super abundance of money, the term embraces everything that money can buy as well. More specifically, wealth also includes material goods, services, and leisure, all of which have been made available to us by business. Consider again a family attempting to produce everything for its own needs. One or two people working with handmade tools can produce only the most rudimentary goods—and barely enough of them to fill even the family's needs. No matter how skilled these people may be, the demands made on their time are enormous. They must, for example, grow and preserve food, build and maintain shelter, deal with medical problems, and find fuel. Such diverse activity does not leave them free to accumulate wealth of any kind. Business allows the accumulation of wealth by providing economical manufacturing and efficient distribution of goods and services. This is not possible in a subsistence society.

Most people seem to strive for a life that is more than a hand-to-mouth existence, but not everyone pursues wealth with equal fervor. The business system in America serves the ambitious as well as the satisfied, but it tends to encourage earning and spending.

# EMPLOYMENT
*Rewarding occupations*

One of the greatest social contributions of business is to provide employment. An obvious benefit of employment is that it gives people the money needed to buy goods and services in a business-oriented society. Employment serves a greater function, however. In today's society, jobs and careers can be among the most important paths to personal satisfaction. Useful, productive, and rewarding employment can give meaning to people's lives by providing them with a sense of purpose, a feeling of accomplishment, and an outlet for creativity. In a relatively free and open business environment, such as ours, the opportunity to advance as the result of improved skills and abilities is a great incentive to personal growth. As a society is the sum of its citizens, personal growth contributes to social and economic growth.

As society's needs and wants change, so do employment opportunities change. Only a few years ago, most jobs in business involved making goods; today most jobs in business are concerned with providing services. (See Figure 1-1.)

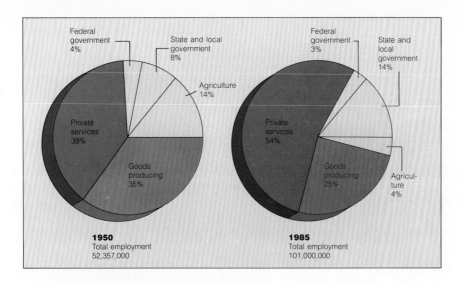

Figure 1-1 The shift in employment from the goods-producing sector to the services sector.

## 3 THE BUSINESS PROCESS
*Converts resources to useful goods and services*

Business performs its many functions mainly by converting available resources into products or services for which there is a demand. The **conversion process** creates or adds value or usefulness to resources. This is achieved by giving resources utility of form, place, time, or possession—or of some combination of these.

## CONVERTING RESOURCES
*Transforms input into output*

Of the **resources** used by business, the most familiar may be the physical raw materials used in manufacturing. The conversions of iron ore and other materials into steel, and of steel into farm implements, are clear examples of creating a useful product from a raw material of little apparent value. Soil and seeds are familiar resources too. The farmer combines them in the agricultural process to produce vegetables, grains, and fruit. Resources may themselves be manufactured goods as they are for retail camera or clothing stores. Human skills or knowledge, particularly in the modern world, may also be considered business resources. For an advertising agency, a newspaper, or a research organization, human abilities and creativity are the chief resources.

Conversion of resources takes place on a far broader plane than the manufacture of shoes and sunglasses. It is inherent in every business. Banks convert money into loans and interest. Department stores convert goods into sales. Movie theaters convert film into entertainment. Restaurants convert foodstuffs into meals. Insurance companies convert premium payments into protection. Motels convert furniture and fixtures into shelter for travelers. Construction firms convert concrete into highways. Airlines convert fuel and planes into transportation. A doctor converts the knowledge of medicine into health.

In summary, the business process converts **inputs,** resources that go into a production or operation process, into **outputs,** end products or services which have value and utility. (See Figure 1-2.)

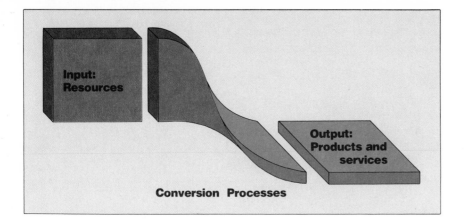

Figure 1-2 How businesses add value to resources.

## ADDING UTILITY
*Makes output more useful than input*

If businesses are to sell their goods or services for a profit, they must change their resources in some way to make them more useful or desirable to consumers. A business may give these resources **utility of form** by physically changing them in a way that increases their value. A sheet of plastic, for example, is shaped into a Frisbee. **Utility of place** is given to resources by moving them into a location where they are available for immediate use by customers. In this way, a transportation company creates utility of place by conveying goods and raw materials to where they are needed. For instance, fuel oil stored at the refinery cannot be used by consumers; the oil is valuable for heating a house only after it has been delivered there. **Utility of time** is given to a resource or product by making it available to consumers without delay. Thus retailers who invest their money to maintain a stock of goods that is always available on their shelves provide their customers with utility of time. These stocked goods are more valuable to consumers because they can be readily obtained. **Utility of possession** is created by advertising and promotion. These activities increase the value of goods and services by increasing public demand for them. Since advertising and promotion stimulate the feeling or awareness of desire to possess and use, they are essential aspects of the American business system. Utility of possession, place, and time are closely related to marketing activity, as you will see in Unit 3, for the major goal of marketing is to get products to those who need them, in places where they are needed, at the time of such need.

## 4  KINDS OF BUSINESSES
*An endless variety*

The many functions of business and the endless possibilities for carrying out the conversion processes have resulted in remarkable diversity in American business, from single-owner welding shops to multinational manufacturing companies like General Electric, employing hundreds of thousands of people. Products range from electrical circuit systems nearly too small to see with the naked eye, to an entire chemical plant prefabricated for export. Businesses can be classified by type: production, distribution, or services. Businesses may also be grouped into standard industry classifications.

## PRODUCTION ENTERPRISES
*Emphasize physical conversion*

Companies that manufacture materials or goods are engaged in **production.** The production may be on a basic level—such as mining, farming, or forestry (often called the extractive industries)—or it may use already-manufactured materials to produce higher-level goods. The final manufacture of a television set, for example, is the end result of a long chain of processes usually performed by many different companies.

## DISTRIBUTION ENTERPRISES
*Emphasize transportation and selling*

The process of moving goods from their point of production to consumers is called **distribution.** The most obvious example of distribution is physical transportation: railroads, shipping and trucking companies, and airlines. Packaging and grading operations (of bulk foods, like bagging potatoes for example) belong to this category. So do companies that store goods in warehouses and those merchants engaged in wholesale distribution and retailing.

## SERVICE ENTERPRISES
*Provide assistance rather than goods*

**Service enterprises** comprise the fastest growing area of business activity, which includes firms that do not directly create or distribute goods. The communications industry—including the press, radio and television, and the telephone and telegraph system—is a service industry. Services to individual consumers, such as repair and maintenance, are also included, as are hotels and restaurants, barbers and hairdressers, private educators, doctors and dentists, and hospitals. Financial institutions such as banks and savings and loan companies, insurance companies, and computer service organizations also provide services and are included in this classification.

## CLASSIFICATION BY INDUSTRY
*Federal designations*

A somewhat more detailed and useful breakdown of businesses by type is offered by the federal government. It is widely used for reporting and analyzing statistical data on business. This approach classifies and groups individual businesses into large industry designations. Thus, an **industry** is a collection of all businesses that perform similar operations to provide the same kinds of goods and services. All companies that process textiles, for example, make up the textile industry.

The **Standard Industrial Classification (SIC)** is the numerical system devised by the U.S. Office of Management and the Budget. SIC (as shown in Table 1-2) places each company in a major industrial classifi-

**TABLE 1-2**
**STANDARD INDUSTRIAL CLASSIFICATION SYSTEM (SIC)**

*Major Classification Divisions**

A. Agriculture, Forestry, and Fisheries

B. Mining

C. Contract Construction

D. Manufacturing

E. Transportation, Communication, Electric, Gas, and Sanitary Services

F. Wholesale and Retail Trade

G. Finance, Insurance, and Real Estate

H. Services (Hotels, Amusements, Auto Repairs, Medical, Legal, and Educational)

I. Government

J. Nonclassifiable Establishments

*Each major division is further broken down into subclassifications indicated by numbers: for example, 2521 for manufacturing of wooden office furniture. There are 99 major groups in all, with Manufacturing having nearly 450 individual (or four-digit) classifications.

*Source: Standard Industrial Classification Manual,* Executive Office of the President, Office of Management and the Budget, U.S. Government Printing Office, 1972.

cation. There are 99 of these. The company may then be classified into one of hundreds of smaller classifications within that industry. That way, each company that is classified as a member of SIC 2385, Raincoats and Other Waterproof Garments, for example, can compare its production, sales, employment, and financial data with that of others in the same industry.

# 5 THE DYNAMICS OF BUSINESS
## Business is dominated by uncertainty and change

The activities of business take place in a turbulent, dynamic environment. Business itself changes as social and economic conditions change. Forecasting the overall performance of business is difficult; precisely determining the outlook for any individual business is nearly impossible. Uncertainty underlies all business activity. It is this uncertainty, coupled with the element of change, that creates an environment of risk for business while at the same time presenting business with major opportunities for reward and success.

## RISK
### A basic feature of American enterprise

Risk is a fundamental feature of American business. People are free to invest their capital and make a profit, but at the same time, they must face the possibility of loss. This is the risk that they take. The expectation of gain is the major driving force of business, but there is always the chance that a decrease in the demand for products, ineffective management, government regulation, social change, or dozens of other factors may cause a loss. If this loss is only temporary, a business may recover. If, however, the expenses of the business continually exceed its income, the business will be insolvent, no longer able to pay its debts. Though the possibility of loss and failure is a problem, it is also a great incentive to careful management and aggressive competition.

## GROWTH, STABILITY, OR STAGNATION
### Describes the level of economic activity at a given time

A certain amount of inertia enters into every human enterprise. Although growth appears to be the healthiest state for people, businesses, and the economy in general, periods of stagnation have always interrupted this process. Stability is an intermediate stage that seems only to be maintained by the promise of future growth. The government has attempted to counteract national economic stagnation, and good business managers make a concerted effort to prevent slumps in their company or industry, but performance uncertainty continues.

## OPPORTUNITY AND CHANGE
### An impetus for growth

The continual change in the business world creates conditions ripe for opportunity. Risk of loss and failure may threaten survival in the business world. Within the last two decades, firms that were household names like Addressograph-Multigraph, Grant's variety stores, and Iowa Packing have passed from the scene, but dozens of other companies like Apple Computer, Family Dollar Stores, and Louis Rich packaged foods have sprung up to take their places. Without the freedom that results in risk, however, opportunity is lost. Shifting markets, management and personnel problems, and a changing social environment all present the owner or manager with opportunities to implement new practices and operations. It is only through the exploitation of opportunities presented by change that growth and profits occur.

## 6 AMERICAN BUSINESS HISTORY
### From exploitation to regulation

In the beginning, the business of America was mainly farming. Most manufactured goods were imported from Europe. As the population migrated westward, however, the need arose for an efficient means of transporting goods between cities. Railroads were built by business speculators in the 1800s to fill this need. In turn, the railroads spurred the growth of business beyond the pioneers' wildest dreams. They also made possible telegraph lines along the rights of way. This fast new method of communication linked buyers and sellers across great distances, creating a network of business markets across the nation. Banks, then run by unregulated groups of investors, supported these flourishing markets by supplying capital. Population growth was stimulated by an influx of immigrants attracted by expanding employment opportunities in the growing American economy.

## RAPID INDUSTRIAL GROWTH
*From agriculture to industry*

The vastness of American resources—land and minerals, a cohesive transportation and communication system, capital, and an eager labor force—gradually shifted the focus of business from agriculture to industry. Small shops were incorporated into large factories. Product parts were standardized so that the unskilled labor market could be tapped. New sources of power—steam and electricity—turned the wheels and did the work faster. Business growth spurted ahead in the late 1800s. This was a period of rapid industrialization that caused business to run rampant in its haste to make profits. Lack of restraints resulted in capricious, often unfair business practices.

Workers were exploited. Labor unions were pushed aside. The little investors were duped. The interests of the general public were ignored. As a response to this exploitation, there began a trend in 1889 and 1890 that continues to some extent today. The public called upon its government to pass laws regulating and limiting business operations. Chief among these laws were the Interstate Commerce Act, which is a law to regulate transportation, and the Sherman Antitrust Act, which is a law designed to discourage anticompetitive business practices. (These, as well as other important regulatory laws, will be discussed in more detail in later chapters.)

## TOWARD A SERVICE ECONOMY
*From products to services*

Nothing held back the growth of business for long. American business soon took worldwide leadership in production capabilities. By the middle of the twentieth century, however, a subtle shift took place in consumer demand. The public, with its newfound leisure, began to demand services as well as products. These purchased services came in the form of hotel and motel rooms, meals served in restaurants, extensive health care, vacation trips to faraway places, and entertainment of all kinds. The business entrepreneur proved to be just as eager to provide services as goods, as long as there was a possibility of profit.

## MARKETING EMPHASIS
*From production to marketing*

In the rush to produce either goods or services, business had a tendency to make something available first, and then to sell it. When the public displayed indifference toward these products and services, this practice often led to great waste. Goods were sold at a loss, and services went begging. To avoid this outcome, the emphasis in American business has swung since World War II from production to marketing. Successful business firms now first try to assess what the market wants—or will buy—and then try to match their production efforts to that demand.

## THE MODERN OUTLOOK
*A balanced approach*

Maintaining a balance between what is good for business and what is good for the public at large is a major concern in America. Each decade, of course, introduces new problems. Today, we are concerned with such matters as decent wages and rising prices, industrial pollution and protection of the environment, the need to create more jobs and to make jobs more satisfying, equal employment opportunities, and business ethics. The American approach is to seek resolution of these issues two ways— in the marketplace and in the legislature. Business generally will do everything in its power to make a profit; consumers usually will do their best to buy only what they feel is a bargain. When the marketplace fails to provide mutual satisfaction, both parties are likely to seek government aid.

## 7 TODAY'S BUSINESS ENVIRONMENT
*An interaction with society and nature*

Business cannot and does not exist in a vacuum. Each business firm operates within a web of external conditions that both nurture and restrain its survival and growth. This web, or network, is often called the business system. A *system* is a group of related parts that work together in an organized way for some specific purpose—or purposes. A particular firm also has its own unique internal system. This usually consists of people working together to convert or transform the company's resources into useful products or services for sale. The stock clerks in a supermarket, for example, receive canned goods and place them on the shelves. Other clerks operate the checkout counters. Still other employees come in at night to sweep and clean. The store manager tries to tie this system together by making sure that the goods are ordered on time, that the employees fulfill their job duties, and that money flows in from customers and flows out to pay suppliers and employee wages. Regardless of how well this internal system may function, the firm is at the mercy of other factors in the outside environment that make up the business system. This environment is made up of five major, interacting influences or conditions. (See Figure 1-3.)

## A COMPANY'S INDUSTRY
*Others who fish in the same pond*

Every business firm operates within, or in competition with, a family of similar firms. They may be smaller or larger, but they have in common similar products or services, similar processes and technology, and similar

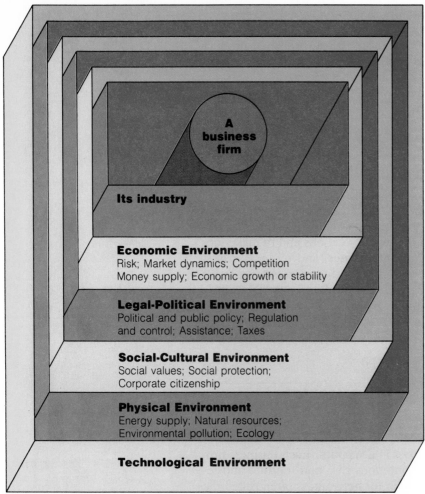

Figure 1-3 Five environments
surround a firm and its industry.

markets. A dressmaker who hand sews a silk blouse for a person in Yank-ton, North Dakota, for example, is in the same industry (the apparel industry) as Liz Claiborne, Inc., which produces thousands of blouses of every imaginable style and sells them to millions of customers in thousands of retail shops all over America. Both the one-person firm and the giant corporation buy the same kind of fabrics, perform the same kinds of production processes, and sell to the same kind of customers. They compete in the same industry, although their bases of operations may be thousands of miles apart.

# THE ECONOMIC ENVIRONMENT

*It provides the basic setting*

The economic environment sets the basic rules by which business operates. In the United States, the economic setting is guided by the principles of modified capitalism, as described in Chapter 2. Business functions in an environment where entrepreneurs are free to risk their money with the hope of creating profits, and where a free market exerts the ultimate control over business decisions. The supply of money available in the economy is also a part of the economy and profoundly affects business decisions. Periods of economic growth and recession also affect business operations.

■   The environment of the marketplace has become increasingly changeable as styles and fashions affect the sale of a wider range of goods. Consumer tastes in clothing, for example, are continually shifting. It is not uncommon for a particular style of men's ties or women's skirts to last for only a year or less. This same unstable pattern of consumer preferences extends to automobiles, electronic equipment, foods, and other goods.

■   The total amount of money in the economy for use by customers and by businesses presents another critical point. Businesses need money to operate. Much of the money is borrowed. When the cost of borrowing (interest rates) is low, businesses are encouraged to expand their facilities because their total costs will be lower. When interest rates are high, businesses tend to hold back, as do consumers, and wait for cheaper money.

■   General economic conditions tend to swing up and down in cycles of growth followed by stagnation followed by growth. When the economy is strong and growing, businesses grow and prosper. In periods of economic stagnation or decline, business tends to suffer and so does employment. These variations tend to vary in intensity. In "boom" periods profits and employment may be very high: in a "recession," profits may be poor or nonexistent, businesses fail, jobs become scarce, and unemployment rises. Such variations in the health of the economy create what is called the ***business cycle*** (see Figure 1-4), where business activity and employment alternately rise and fall. The duration of a business cycle may be as little as 5 years or more than 15 years.

## THE LEGAL-POLITICAL ENVIRONMENT
*It provides the regulatory framework*

The legal-political environment is shaped by the interaction between business and government at the federal, state, and local levels. The main job of the government is to protect the property rights and civil rights of its citizens. In performing this role, our government's activities impinge solidly on business.

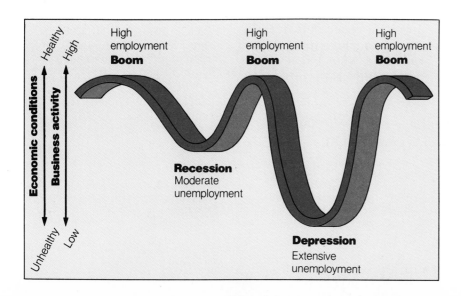

Figure 1-4 The business cycle affects business activity and employment.

# BILLBOARD

## TOWARD A HAMBURGER ECONOMY?

In what businesses should America try to grow? In the traditional manufacturing industries such as autos and tractors, bicycles and television sets, washing machines and toasters? Or in the service industries such as fast-food restaurants, retail and wholesale trades, travel and entertainment, banking and insurance? Chrysler chair Lee A. Iacocca answers the question this way: "We can't afford to become a nation of video arcades, drive-in banks, and McDonald's hamburger stands." He goes on to suggest that America should try to rebuild its basic industries through improved quality and productivity.

Other economists observe that it is the new, high-technology businesses like computers, office automation, and robotics that will replace the jobs in the traditional industries. Unfortunately, the actual job growth seems highest in soft drinks and other beverages, tobacco, health care, and publishing—along with banking and other financial institutions. The trouble is that as sales in the newer,

---

### In what businesses should America try to grow?

---

high-tech, computer-related industries grow, the number of jobs does not grow in the same proportion. To many Americans, the issue comes down not so much to economics, but to where they'd like to work and what kinds of jobs they would like to occupy.

### QUERIES

**1.** Based upon your own judgment and experience, which way do you think the United States should try to move now—toward more service-type jobs or toward more basic factory jobs?

**2.** How important do you think it is for America to try to regain or maintain world leadership in the manufacture of autos?

**3.** If you had your choice, which kind of job would appeal to you most—working to serve people or working to produce a product? ■

---

SOURCE: Peter Behr, "Shift Toward Service Continues," *The Washington Post*, January 13, 1985, p. F1.

# PROFILE

JANE EVANS has been called "The Girl Wonder" by *Working Woman* magazine. And with good reason. At age 25, she was the president of I. Miller, a major manufacturer of women's shoes. From there, she bounced upward to General Mills, where she became executive vice president of its fashion group. In that job she managed the fortunes of Izod, Ltd. (clothing with the alligator trademark), Ship 'n' Shore (blouses), Footjoy (athletic shoes), and Lark (luggage). Not bad for an interim job! From General Mills she moved ever upward to the presidency of another national firm, Monet Jewelers.

How did Evans find this pathway to the sky? She started as a management trainee with I. Miller and quickly moved into a slot as an assistant buyer of shoes, then on to merchandise buyer within a year, almost unheard of advances in retailing. She did her job well, but says:

*I think it was my enthusiasm that gave me the opportunity to handle the top spot. I sort of grew up with instincts about*

**JANE EVANS**

*business. I also feel a desire to accomplish. I even spent my time off in retail stores that received our merchandise, so I learned more about the job than required.*

*I had some good ideas about what needed to be done strategically. I also had a team of competent buyers, managers, and merchants that believed in my ideas. I. Miller made its first profit in ten years when I was president. By the time I finished at I. Miller, I was pretty much on the road to becoming a skilled, professional manager.* ∎

SOURCE: Melissa Sones, "Girl Wonder Comes of Age," *Working Woman*, March 1985, pp. 122–125.

■ The government regulates business in order to promote free competition. In the past, large groups of powerful companies forced competitors out of business through unethical means. They then raised prices to create huge profits. The Sherman Antitrust Act of 1890 was the first of a number of laws passed to prohibit such conspiracies.

■ The government regulates business to protect consumers. In the past (and sometimes today), products were sold that were harmful to users. Our government has repeatedly passed laws (like the Food and Drug Act) to outlaw such products and to protect consumers from false advertising and other fraudulent marketing practices.

■ The government sometimes controls prices—in periods of war or possibly runaway inflation. In recent years, the government has stepped in to regulate the prices of vital services like medical services, rent, and commodities, such as gasoline.

■ The government protects inventors and other creative people by issuing patents, trademarks, and copyrights, which prohibit unrightful use by others.

■ The government promotes health and safety. It regulates the work of pharmacists and optometrists, for example, by making them obtain certification licenses. Legislation also requires that businesses maintain minimum standards of health and safety to protect workers and the general public from danger. Other laws restrict the amount of pollution a business may excrete into air or water.

■ The government levies taxes on businesses. These taxes range from taxes on profits to taxes for the privilege of operating and storing goods in a particular state or community. Businesses also pay employment taxes covering employment pay and social security benefits. The tax system, however, is often relaxed to encourage businesses to expand their facilities (and, hopefully, to create jobs), to explore for scarce minerals, and to conserve energy.

■ The government also stimulates and supports business ventures. It is far from true that the government's only role is that of regulation. It strongly supports many industries, but primarily transportation and agriculture, by providing aid in the form of financial subsidies. It protects other industries by placing a special tax (called a tariff) on goods that are imported for sale in competition with domestic products.

# THE SOCIAL-CULTURAL ENVIRONMENT
*It is the people's way of living* ▬▬▬▬▬▬▬▬▬▬

The total collection of a people's beliefs, customs, and ways of living makes up their **culture.** It exerts a powerful influence on the way a business operates and, in the long run, on how profitable it will be.

■ In the United States, the belief in the importance of physical goods and services that provide comfort and convenience is called **materialism.** It is the basis for our business system. If people did not desire wealth, there would be no profit motive, and there would be no private enterprise. Business, in turn, influences the values of society. The marketing emphasis, for example, has changed the ordinary person's concept of necessity. Advertising and promotion stimulate the demand for many products, like automatic coffee-brewing pots, once considered luxuries, as valuable and justifiable necessities of life.

■ The values of business and society often come into conflict. The unrestrained right to make a profit has led to the sale of shoddy products and dangerous services to a poorly informed and materialistic public. Society, however, when abused or threatened, will seek to protect itself. As a consequence, a persistent and potent social force has emerged in America. It helps to protect individuals from unreasonably high prices or low quality or unsafe merchandise. It is made largely of consumers who unite formally or informally to protect their interests. This movement is called **consumerism.** Its efforts have led to significant changes in the laws that regulate business. More important, perhaps, consumerism has served to alert American business to the power to buy or not to buy that exists in the marketplace.

■ Enlightened businesses try to become better corporate citizens. A small local retailer or service company, which is in direct daily contact with its customers, is very vulnerable to consumerism. Such companies cannot survive for long if they ignore the concerns and wishes of their customers. Large, centralized corporations, however, are more insulated from complaints about quality or service or from local irritation about noise or pollution. In the face of the potential and concerted consumer pressures, however, the more progressive firms are learning that it is less costly to take the initiative in becoming more reliable suppliers and good neighbors.

## THE PHYSICAL ENVIRONMENT

### It sets nature's boundaries

The interdependence of business and its various environments is further demonstrated by its relationship with the physical environment. Many of the resources used to create products come from the physical environment—from the land and seas. The use of these resources is a legitimate concern of the economic system, of government, and of the entire society. Some of the gravest problems faced by business have arisen from conflicting interests in the use of natural resources and from the depletion of raw materials.

■ All production requires energy. Manufacturing, transportation, farming, mining, communications, and all other business activities are impossible without a reliable source of power. Over the years, energy in the United States has become more and more dependent on petroleum products like oil and natural gas. Now, business and society are beginning to realize that the amount of petroleum remaining in the ground in the United States is not sufficient to meet our long-term needs. (See Figure 1-5.) Having to rely on oil produced in other countries is a serious problem because the demand for oil is increasing all over the world with the spread of industry.

■ Many other natural resources that once seemed inexhaustibly abundant are in danger of depletion. We are facing shortages of iron, copper, and other minerals, as well as of petroleum. Reforestation programs have not kept up with the demand for timber. Water—which is essential for irrigation, manufacturing, and domestic use—is in short supply in many areas. And there is not enough land to meet the demand for residential and commercial development.

The challenge business must confront is to find ways of making

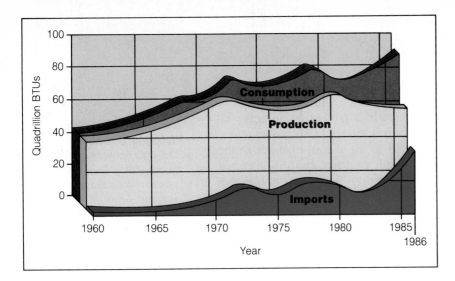

Figure 1-5 Energy for America: a declining dependence on imports.

production more efficient and less wasteful of scarce, and increasingly expensive, raw materials. Recycling of paper products and reprocessing of water for industry are examples of more efficient use of resources.

■ Any efforts to solve the shortages of energy and raw materials have to be evaluated in terms of their potential effect on the environment. Often, there is a high price to be paid in terms of polluting the air, soil, or water, or permanently damaging the land. On the other hand, efforts to safeguard the environment can involve an even greater expenditure of energy, as exemplified by automobile air pollution controls, which cut down on gasoline mileage.

■ Many thoughtful people believe that the best approach to solving the problems of business growth and depletion of natural resources is to strike an ecological balance. *Ecology* is the science that studies the interaction between living organisms and their environment. Ecologists generally view the natural world as a complex, interrelated system in which the actions and behavior of every part affect every other part. A concern for ecology on the part of business is being stimulated by all of its environments—the economic system, the government, social and cultural forces, and the physical world. It has become increasingly important to consider all of the possible results of business decisions, good and bad. Maturity, it is said, is reached when a person understands and accepts the consequences of his or her actions. The same appears true of business.

## THE TECHNOLOGICAL ENVIRONMENT
*Bursting with change and opportunity*

Lord Kelvin, the great scientist of the nineteenth century and discoverer of the principle of artificial refrigeration, lamented that with the knowledge of modern chemistry and physics there would be no more scientific frontiers. In his view, society knew all there was to know about nature and its physical environment. Little did Kelvin anticipate the discovery of the atom and its fission into atomic power. Nor did he foresee the invention of the transistor in the 1950s, which first made possible the miracle of miniature radios and, later, the incredible speeds of data calculation and manipulations of the modern computer. In your lifetime, probably no other technological advance has made or will make a greater impact upon business than computers and computerized information systems. They have radically changed the way businesses operate. And they have greatly changed the nature of jobs—and job opportunities—at all levels of employment.

# Key Concepts

1. Business is an enterprise that satisfies the needs and wants of consumers by providing goods and services to make a profit.

2. Business serves important social functions by providing wealth, employment, and a means of exchange.

3. **a.** Business operates by converting resources into more valuable end products.
   **b.** Business makes resources more valuable by giving them utility of form, place, time, or possession.

4. The many varied businesses in the United States are often classified by their type of operation: production, distribution, or services.

5. Risk, growth or stagnation, change, and opportunity characterize the business environment and business cycle.

6. The development of the business system in the United States demonstrates:
   **a.** Its basic dependence on transportation, communications, and banking services.
   **b.** Its need for some regulation and control to protect the public interest from the business abuses of the few.
   **c.** Its emergence from an industrial preoccupation with products and production to an emphasis on services and marketing.

7. Business functions in a complex environment, influenced by interdependent economic, legal-political, social-cultural, physical, and technological forces. Successful businesses tend to adapt well to an ever-changing environment.

# Review Questions

1. Define, identify, or explain each of the following key terms and phrases found on the pages indicated.

*business cycle (p. 19)*
*business enterprise (p. 7)*
*consumerism (p. 23)*
*conversion process (p. 11)*
*culture (p. 22)*
*distribution (p. 13)*
*ecology (p. 24)*
*goods (p. 7)*
*industry (p. 13)*
*inputs (p. 11)*
*materialism (p. 22)*

*outputs (p. 11)*
*private nonprofit organization (p. 9)*
*production (p. 13)*
*profit (p. 8)*
*profit motive (p. 8)*
*public enterprise (p. 9)*
*resources (p. 11)*
*service enterprise (p. 13)*
*services (p. 7)*
*Standard Industrial Classification (p. 13)*
*system (p. 17)*
*utility of form (p. 12)*
*utility of place (p. 12)*
*utility of possession (p. 12)*
*utility of time (p. 12)*
*wealth (p. 10)*

2. Name the three types of enterprises discussed in the text. How do the three differ in their sources of financing, reasons for operating, and goals?

3. How does business contribute to society other than by providing profits to investors?

4. Describe and give examples of some of the resources that business uses in creating its end products for sale. Is it likely that new resources will be exploited in the future? Why or why not?

5. What is meant by giving resources utility of form, place, time, and possession? Give an example of a type of business that increases or creates each kind of utility.

6. Why is risk a basic fact of any business undertaking in the United States? Is this good or bad? Why?

7. What four conditions does the text identify as helping to shift the focus of business from agriculture to industry? Can you think of others?

8. What role did labor unions and government regulation play in the development of American business as we know it today?

9. Name the five business environments. What is the relationship among the five? Are any of the environments subordinate to any of the others?

10. What is a system? Give an example to show that small systems often are organized into larger systems for more generalized purposes.

# Case Critique 1-1
# From a Damper Flapper and a Clock to Mainframe Computers

The thermostat that regulates the temperature in your home or office got its start over 100 years ago in Minneapolis when Albert Butz invented a way of connecting a thermometer with a metal flapper placed in the chimney flue of a coal furnace. About the same time in Elmira, New York, Schuyler B. Post invented a similar mechanism. Post's device, however, was attached to a clock. When the hour hand passed six in the morning, for example, it would trigger the damper flapper to open so that the fire in the furnace would burn hotter. The clock could also turn down the damper at night. Since neither Butz nor Post was great shakes as a salesperson or had money to invest in these ideas, they sold their inventions to two different companies. Eventually, the two companies got into a legal dispute as to which had the original patent. The case was settled out of court in favor of the eastern company, with the western company paying a royalty of $10 for each thermostat it manufactured. Fifteen years later, the Honeywell Heating Specialties Company bought the patent rights from both the eastern company *and* the western company. Thus, the Minneapolis-Honeywell Regulator Company, now simply Honeywell, Inc., was created.

The thermostat did not at first succeed. It had little public demand, since few people knew about it. And when they did, a home owner still had to go to the cellar anyway to put coal on the fire. To make matters worse, few furnaces were equipped with a flue and damper that could accommodate Honeywell's thermostat. It soon became clear to the manufacturer that what was needed was a way of telling the public about this device, a way of influencing furnace manufacturers to change their dampers, and someone to go out and sell. Beginning in 1908, Honeywell mounted a nationwide advertising campaign in the home magazines of the day. A typical ad read: "Whew! It's Hot! and Boo! It's Cold! These are expressions never heard in homes equipped with the Minneapolis Heat Regulator." Supported by these ads, Honeywell sent door-to-door salespeople to comb the land to sell thermostats to home owners. The company next expanded into office and industrial temperature controls. The clumsy clock arrangement was replaced by electric and then electronic systems. When the transistor was born in the 1950s, the thermostat utilized the new integrated circuits—in reality, miniature computers are now controlling home temperatures. From that tiny device, Honeywell took a giant step forward in 1970 to form a division to design, manufacture, and distribute a full line of commercial computers under the Honeywell name. Today, the company has over 10,000 customers with over $12 billion worth of computer systems installed.

1. What kind of business process—or processes—is Honeywell involved in?
2. Which of Honeywell's products are consumer goods and which are industrial or commercial goods?

3. Who eventually took the risk of making and selling the thermostats—the inventors or a business enterprise? Why do you suppose it was done that way?
4. In what ways did Honeywell's success reflect the history of business in the United States?

SOURCE: Judith Yates Borger, *Honeywell: The First 100 Years*, Honeywell, Inc., Minneapolis, 1985.

# Case Critique 1-2
## Survival of the Clothespin King

In a small town in Maine, the Penley Corporation makes 175 million clothespins a year. These are wooden ones, not metal or plastic. They continue to be used in large numbers in spite of stiff competition with gas and electric clothes dryers. Dick Penley, who owns and operates this company, is known as the Clothespin King because his is the largest such business in the world—$5 million a year in sales. At times, he feels as if the new technology will put him out of business. But then he comes up with other ideas for using clothespins, like selling them to craftspeople who make them into little red- or green-coated reindeer. The use of clothespins for crafts now represents 10 percent of his business. Penley can also use his woodworking machinery to turn out related products like cutlery handles, duck calls, and honey dippers.

Like the automobile business, the clothespin industry faces difficult foreign competition. A few years ago, 50 percent of all wooden clothespins used in the United States were imported. The industry went to Washington to ask for protection and got it. The federal government imposed a quota on imports limiting them to 25 percent of all wooden pins sold here. The quotas were lifted in 1986, however, and the industry must find a way to survive without further help from the government. It does so by introducing new machinery to cut the pins faster and trimmer and to shape automatically

the springs for the clip-type pins. And where the pins have been traditionally counted and bagged by hand, this, too, is now done automatically.

In comparison to the wood-products industry as a whole, just how big is the business of transforming 4-foot logs into 4-inch clothespins? America's $15 million clothespin industry supports only four domestic firms, with Penley the largest. This makes the industry just a tiny fraction of the $55 billion wood-products industry. In the face of competition from all sides—plastic and metal pins and automatic clothes dryers—will this tiny industry survive? Says the Clothespin King, "If I didn't think we had a future, I wouldn't be here."

1. What factors in the technological environment are tending to make the wooden clothespin obsolete?
2. Where does competition for Dick Penley's clothespins come from?
3. In what way does the legal-political environment help the wooden clothespin industry?
4. If the wooden clothespin industry is so small, what other kinds of products do you think make up the rest of the sales in the wood-products industry as a whole?

SOURCE: Kathy Rebello, "Clothespin Makers Hang On," *USA Today*, December 5, 1983, p. 7B.

## CHAPTER 2

# The American
# Free Enterprise
# Economic System

## Learning Objectives

*The purpose of this chapter is to outline the resources common to all economic systems, define capitalism as it operates in the United States, and provide an understanding of other economic systems so that you may compare their effectiveness.*

*As evidence of general comprehension, after studying this chapter, you should be able to:*

1. *Identify the four features that are common to all economic systems and distinguish between producers and consumers.*

2. *Relate the concept of supply and demand to a business situation.*

3. *Recognize the elements of a private enterprise system and the presence of a monopoly or an oligopoly.*

4. *Understand the role of government regulation in modified capitalism.*

5. *Compare and contrast socialism, communism, and capitalism.*

6. *Outline the various kinds of measurements for gauging the effectiveness of these economic systems.*

*If your class is using SSweetco: Business Model and Activity File, see Chapter 2 in that book after you complete this chapter. There you will find exercises and activities to help you apply your learning to typical business situations.*

# 1 FEATURES IN COMMON

These economic resources are common to all economic systems:

Land

Labor

Capital

Technology

# 2 LAW OF SUPPLY AND DEMAND

Economic systems try to balance

Supply          Demand

# 3 PRIVATE ENTERPRISE: THE MARKET SYSTEM

A private enterprise system is an unplanned, demand, market economy which adds entrepreneurship to other economic resources and is called "pure capitalism," when characterized by . . .

Private ownership

Private profit

Free markets
and Free choice

Free competition without
monopoly or oligopoly

# 4 MODIFIED CAPITALISM: THE AMERICAN WAY

In the United States there is modified capitalism because the system includes limited government regulation.

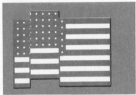

# 5 SOCIALISM AND COMMUNISM

Other economic systems are planned, command economies.

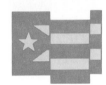

Socialism:
Centralized planning
Extensive government
    regulation
Government ownership of
    basic industries

Communism:
Centralized planning
Extensive government
    regulation
Total government ownership

# 6 ECONOMIC MEASUREMENTS

These are measurements of the effectiveness and growth of an economic system:

Standard of living
Disposable income
Personal spending

Gross national product
(GNP)

Capital supply
Inflation

Productivity
Employment
Quality of life

# SHARING THE PIE OR MAKING IT BIGGER?

*People in the United States enjoy the fruits of a $4 trillion a year economy. That means—on average—every man, woman, and child delivers more than $16,000 a year in products and services for the common good. The catch, of course, is that this is an average figure. Many people contribute nothing. Some, like rock music stars and computer program designers, create hundreds of thousands of dollars of product or service annually. The great majority of the population tends to contribute significantly more than the $16,000 national average.*

*An even bigger catch in these figures, however, is that the $4 trillion of benefits is not shared equally among the American public. Here again, some people get, if not nothing, very little. In recent years, others—like T. Boone Pickens ($22.8 million), chairperson of Mesa Petroleum Company, and Michael Jackson ($35 million), a popular entertainer—have received millions of dollars each year in salary and bonuses. Most people, however, work for wages that just about equal the $16,000 that they contribute to the economy in the production of goods and services. In addition to the extremely high and low beneficiaries, there is a significant segment of the population still to be recognized. This group—not necessarily millionaires—draws what may seem like a disproportionate share of income from the $4 trillion economy. These are the people associated with successful businesses as owners, investors, managers, and employees with scarce skills that are in high demand.*

*This economic situation is unique to the United States and other nations that operate under a business system that encourages each individual to strive for the most he or she can get, without assuring anyone that the rewards will necessarily be distributed according to either contribution or need. This system, while not without flaws, has worked very well for the United States. There are other economic and political systems that operate under different premises and rules, and with varying results. In England and Sweden, for example, the government exercises a great deal of control over the way individuals and businesses may compete for their share of the benefits. These, and other countries like them, also try to see that the benefits are shared in such a way that all of their citizens are assured of a reasonably decent economic life, regardless of their contributions to the economy.*

*In the Soviet Union, the People's Republic of China, and Cuba, for example, the governments exert even stronger control over how jobs are obtained. Furthermore, almost all businesses in these countries are run by the government. In turn, however, these governments go to great lengths to try to assure their citizens that the rewards of their economy will be shared rather equally, both in good times and bad.*

# 1 FEATURES COMMON TO ALL SYSTEMS
## *Limited resources and unlimited needs*

When it comes to running its economy, each nation faces a universal problem: What is the best and fairest way to divide up the country's resources—its pie, so to speak? Some countries have a bigger and better pie than others: they have more to go around in the first place. This is true of the United States. Many other countries have fewer and less valuable resources. Unfortunately, for many of these countries there are often more people who need and want to share these resources. This leads many countries to approach their economic problems from a point of view different from that of the United States.

The test of the effectiveness of an economy, however, is not only how fairly it distributes its wealth. It is also important that a nation find a way of extracting the maximum amount of goods and services from its resources. In this sense, an effective economy will help to make a nation's pie larger each year than the year before. Thus, there will be more to go around. The generally accepted belief in the United States is that the economic system should first assure growth in the amount of wealth; only after that is accomplished should the nation be concerned with the equitability of the distribution of its wealth. Many other nations approach their economic problems the other way around. (See Figure 2-1.)

Over the course of history, different societies have developed widely varying solutions to their economic problems. They vary, for example, as to who has access to resources (government or private individuals, and businesses or a combination of the two) and who allocates the products and services derived from these sources (the government or private individuals through free choice, or some combination of the two). An examination of these differences in some of the world's major economic systems will point out the distinctive nature of the modified private enterprise business system as practiced in the United States.

There are no perfect economies. Some do perform better than others however. For this reason, people seeking to improve the economic performance of their countries study economics. **Economics** is the study of how the goods and services a nation wants get produced, and how they get distributed among the people of that nation. Economics is also the study of how a country can make the system of production and distribution work better. Increasingly, however, it becomes difficult to separate the economic system of one country from that of another because the pattern of worldwide distribution makes them interact and become dependent upon each other.

Every economic system operates under two constraints: (1) the limitations of its economic resources and (2) the counteracting forces of supply and demand.

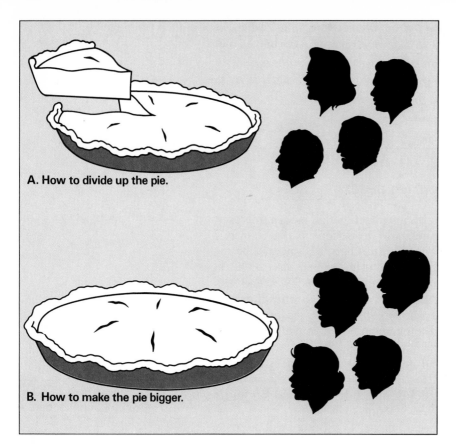

A. How to divide up the pie.

B. How to make the pie bigger.

Figure 2-1 Two basic economic problems.

## ECONOMIC RESOURCES
*These are always limited*

All economic systems begin with the same basic resources: land, labor, capital, and technology. These are limited in extent at any given time, both in the world at large and in a specific country. Using these limited resources for the good of society is the chief task of any economic system.

**LAND** All real property is a basic economic resource. **Land** includes the open fields used by farmers, urban factory sites, and backyards. The oceans, also a resource, are considered part of the land. The physical raw materials used by manufacturers, such as iron ore and petroleum, are products of the land. The basic industries of agriculture, forestry, and fishing depend directly on the land. Land as a resource is clearly limited in extent and in the amount of raw materials it contains.

**LABOR** All of the men and women who are available to do work of any kind make up the country's **labor force.** The hundreds of millions of people worldwide who are employed by business organizations are part of the labor force, as are the self-employed. The president of a corporation is as much a part of labor as a materials handler on the loading dock.

**CAPITAL** Wealth that is available to support the activities of producing goods and services is **capital.** Capital may be cash that has been accumulated to start a business, to cite a simple example. A woman who has saved $10,000 from her salary managing a retail store might use it to buy equipment and merchandise to open her own store. The $10,000 is capital. Capital may be in any form; it may be money, material goods, or talent. Any kind of wealth qualifies as capital if it is used to create more wealth.

**TECHNOLOGY** *Technology* refers to the methods used in producing goods and services. Although technology is usually thought of as involving machines and electronics, it is the applied science or knowledge behind the machines and is a most important and useful economic resource.

## PRODUCERS AND CONSUMERS
*Makers and takers*

In every type of economy there are two sets of people—or enterprises—that make the system work. These are producers and consumers.

**PRODUCERS** Producers are the people who perform the work that provides goods and services for society. This group includes not only those people who work with their hands, but also those who start up and/or manage a business. It also includes the investors who supply the money to initiate and sustain a business. In the economic sense, a baseball player is a producer, as is the person who changes your auto tires and the fry cook in a fast-food restaurant. Producers, taken as a whole, supply the products and services that are demanded by consumers.

**CONSUMERS** Consumers are the people (often the same people who are producers, only now wearing different hats) who buy the products and services provided by the producers. Consumers are made up of individuals, families and households, businesses, and also government purchasers. Consumers play an important role in most societies since they decide what they will buy, where they will buy it, when, and from whom. Their decisions about how they will spend their incomes greatly affect what the producers will supply.

## A SYSTEM OF EXCHANGE
*In one pocket and out the other*

Oddly enough, almost all producers are also consumers. That is, a person who works in a factory making shoelaces is a producer; when that same person spends the money received for working to buy food, he or she is a consumer. Similarly, the factory that produces shoelaces is also a consumer—of yarn for the laces and metal for the tips. In a way, the continual exchange of money between producer and consumer is what makes an economy function. (See Figure 2-2.)

## 2 THE LAW OF SUPPLY AND DEMAND
*It is a perpetual balancing act*

The central function of every economic system is to allocate its limited resources to satisfy the needs and desires of its people. The amount

*Action Brief*

### YES, WE GOT TOO MANY BANANAS!

That was the cry of Castle & Cooke, Inc., a couple of years ago. Better known for its Dole pineapple products, in 1980 Castle & Cooke got deeply into the banana business. It soon found that the banana industry was plagued by a worldwide oversupply. Unfortunately, the company had contracted with growers in Central America to buy, at a prearranged price, all they could grow. And grow them, they did! At times, Castle & Cooke had so many bananas that they lost $2 on every box they couldn't sell (and which, consequently, spoiled) and $1 on every box they could sell. This continued for over 2 years to the tune of losses of $126 million. Enough was enough; so Castle & Cooke got out of the banana business as quickly as it could.

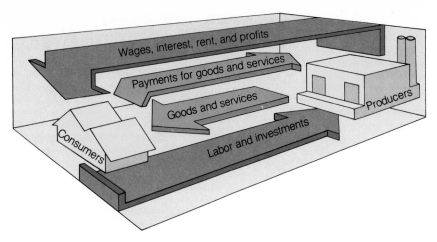

Figure 2-2 Circular flow of income between producers and consumers.

of goods produced depends upon the amount of resources available and on many other factors. At the same time, the people in a society have a great variety of needs and wants. Some of these, such as the need for food and shelter, always exist. Others, such as the desire to own a particular style of clothing, continually change. Economies generally try to maintain a balance between the goods and services available from their producers (the supply) and the needs and wants of their consumers (the demand).

Supply and demand also have more precise meanings. These meanings are essential to an understanding of economic systems.

**SUPPLY** *Supply* may be defined as the quantity of an economic good that is made available for sale by all the producers of that particular product or service. Figure 2-3 shows, for example, what the supply of digital-calculator pens might be at a particular time. In its simplified format, it shows that producers are ready to provide only 100,000 pens at a price of $5 each. They are willing to make increasingly larger quantities available at higher prices, however. For $10 each, the quantity would be another

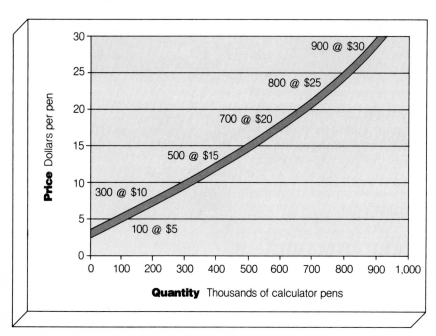

Figure 2-3 Simplified producer supply curve for calculator pens showing the number of pens that will be made available by manufacturers at each given price.

200,000 pens, or 300,000 in all. And so on up to a price of $30, where 900,000 would be available. In other words, producers are likely to make more goods available at higher prices and fewer at lower prices.

**DEMAND** *Demand* may be defined as the quantity of an economic good that consumers will buy at a specific price. Figure 2-4 shows, for example, what the overall demand for pens might be at a particular time. Consumers are ready to purchase only 100,000 pens at $30 each. But they stand ready to purchase increasing amounts at lower prices. Their viewpoint toward prices is in direct contrast with that of the producers.

**LAW OF SUPPLY AND DEMAND** The conditions of (1) supply and (2) demand for a particular good, like the calculator pen, at a particular time work together to determine the price of the good and the amount that will be exchanged. This relationship is called the *law of supply and demand.* It is best illustrated by placing the demand curve (from Figure 2-4) on top of the supply curve (from Figure 2-3) as shown in Figure 2-5. The point where the two curves intersect determines for both producers and consumers what quantity of goods will be produced and what price they will sell for. In the case of the pens at this particular time, 500,000 will be available at $15 each. This point of intersection is sometimes called the *equilibrium point,* or *equilibrium price.* This is an ideal condition. It does not always work out this way in practice. It does represent, however, the kind of thinking on the part of producers and consumers that enables them (collectively) to arrive at a point of exchange that will satisfy the greatest majority of both.

Conditions of supply and/or demand change constantly. As a consequence, the supply curve of Figure 2-3 may move to the right or the left on the price versus quantity chart, according to many factors that may affect producers' attitudes, motivations, and ability to compete. When this happens, the supply curve will intersect the demand curve at a different point. As a result, the quantity available and its price at that particular

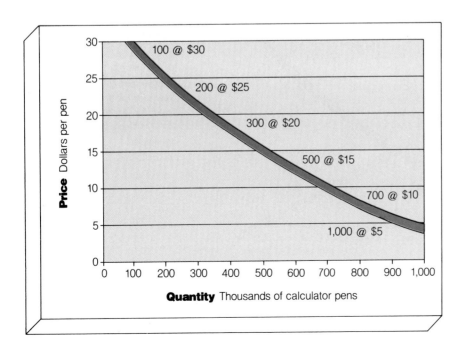

Figure 2-4 Simplified consumer demand curve showing the number of calculator pens that will be bought at each given price.

time will change. Similarly, the demand curve (or condition) shown in Figure 2-4 may shift to the right or left, according to factors that affect consumers as a whole, such as the amount of money they have to spend. When this happens, the demand curve will intersect the supply curve at a different point, with a resultant change in the quantity and price of goods available and purchased.

## GOVERNMENT'S ROLE
### Arbitrating of supply and demand

All economies must make fundamental decisions about supply and demand. Often these are political decisions, since they define the government's role. At one extreme, a government can regulate and control the sources of supply, making available for consumption only those products that government sees fit for a society; similarly, it can regulate the distribution system so that individual demand receives little consideration. At the other extreme, a nation may allow any and all of its people to scramble for available resources, supplying whatever products and services in any quantity they wish; in like manner, this kind of economic approach stands back and lets the demand of each consumer determine what will be bought and what will not. Many economies fall somewhat in between the two extremes.

The role of government, history has shown, becomes a major factor in distinguishing one economic system from another. The three most important aspects of a government's role are:

■ *Planning:* the scope of central economic planning undertaken and implemented by the government. Centralized planning has never been popular in the United States. It is extensively used in nations like Sweden, Italy, and the Soviet Union.

■ *Regulation:* both (1) the extent to which a government regulates supply and (2) the degree of control it exercises over the exchange system

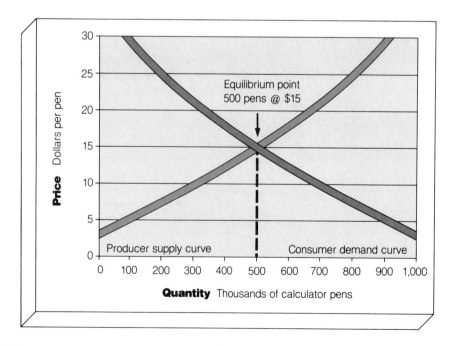

Figure 2-5 How supply and demand conditions determine price and quantity sold.

between producer and consumer. In the United States, such regulation is held to a minimum needed to protect its citizens from exploitation by business. In nations like the People's Republic of China, the Soviet Union, and many small, developing nations of Africa, regulation is the way of economic life.

■ *Ownership:* the degree to which a government owns, or controls, capital, economic resources, and the means of production. Here again, government ownership in the United States is limited to properties like national forests, seashores, and, to a minor degree, the postal service. In Sweden, many of the basic industries like power generation and transportation are owned and operated by the government. The same is true in countries like France, England, and Japan. In Cuba, the People's Republic of China, and the Soviet Union, government ownership is absolute.

## 3  THE PRIVATE ENTERPRISE SYSTEM
### *Depends upon demand in the marketplace*

Government plays the smallest role under a system of private enterprise. **Private enterprise** allows businesses to pursue their operations without repressive central government planning or control. It depends on stimulating and satisfying consumer demand rather than on planning supplies and then trying to control demand. Control over how resources are used and what goods and services are produced is determined by the operation of a free market.

A *free market* exists whenever one person wishes to sell something, another wishes to buy it, and they determine the price of sale by negotiation without outside interference. This concept of a marketplace is central to a private enterprise economy. It describes the free behavior of buyers and sellers. This occurs even in a very complex society where there are many sellers with the same or similar goods and many buyers with different amounts of money and motivation. Thus a **market economy** can be regarded as a system in which buyers and sellers exchange goods and services at prices mutually agreed upon.

The marketplace controls a private enterprise economy by automatically allocating resources to meet consumer demands. Goods that consumers do not want or need will not sell and will not continue to be produced. Goods for which there is a great demand will sell well, and producers will increase the supply. The free market operates on all transactions in a true private enterprise system. It not only affects the cost and supply of goods and services produced by businesses but also applies equally to wages paid to employees, costs of factories and production equipment, interest on borrowed money, and every other transaction between individuals or companies.

The main distinguishing features of the private enterprise system, then, can be summarized in three terms: (1) it is *unplanned* because government controls neither the supply nor demand of goods and services, (2) it is a *demand economy* because the wants and needs of consumers determine the allocations of resources, and (3) it is a *market economy* because it responds to the effects of supply and demand operating in a free market.

# THE ENTREPRENEURIAL SPIRIT
## Individual, private initiative

To the four basic economic resources, private enterprise adds a factor that must be considered in itself—the entrepreneurial spirit. An **entrepreneur** is someone who uses personal initiative to organize a new business. The entrepreneurial spirit shows itself in the creativity and willingness to take risks displayed by those men and women who have made the free market system work. New consumer demands would remain unsatisfied if entrepreneurs did not recognize them and assemble the capital and organize businesses to provide the wanted products or services.

Most of the famous names of American business have been entrepreneurs: Rockefeller, Carnegie, Ford, Morgan, Mellon, and countless others. Steve Jobs and Steve Wozniak who created Apple Computer and Frederick W. Smith who started Federal Express are more recent examples. All those thousands of people who go into business for themselves to provide services on a local level are entrepreneurs, too. It is at the local level, perhaps, where the spirit of entrepreneurship is gaining its greatest energy. This will be explored further in Chapter 4.

# PURE CAPITALISM
## Unrestrained freedom to buy, sell, and compete

The system of true private enterprise is often called **pure capitalism.** It is based on the private ownership of business capital. Consumers and producers have a free choice of what to buy and what to sell. Profits from business operations go directly back to the people who invested their capital. Competition is free and is allowed to operate and evolve without regulation.

**PRIVATE OWNERSHIP** The ability to produce, buy, and sell goods for a profit is rooted in private ownership of property. Under capitalism, land and buildings, machinery, furniture, works of art, inventions, mineral and water rights, and all other kinds of property are privately owned.

The profit motive is based on this right to own and to dispose of property. Since individuals can use things they own as they see fit, they are free to use them for their own private gain, if they so choose. Also, any profits they make will be their private property as well, and they are motivated to make as much profit as possible.

**FREE CHOICE** Pure capitalism implies free choice for both consumers and producers. Consumers may decide to buy or not to buy a product and may buy it from any supplier they choose. Manufacturers and distributors are also free to produce or sell the goods they believe will be most profitable. This freedom of choice is a basic feature of a free market system.

Individual freedom extends further. Under pure capitalism, people are free to pursue any occupation they choose. They are free to become entrepreneurs and produce their own goods or services for their own use or for sale. They are also free to work for any person or company they choose or to work for no one at all.

**PRIVATE PROFIT** The hope of making private profit and of creating more personal wealth is the main reason businesses are started and continue to operate. Without private profit, entrepreneurs would not be encouraged to use their skill and creativity to meet consumer demands. Without private profit, investors would not take the sometimes substantial risk of providing the capital needed for business. Without private profit, buying and selling in a free marketplace would not take place. Capitalism depends on profit for its motive force.

**FREE COMPETITION** In an economic system with freedom of choice, competition will develop among producers of the same or similar products. If someone in town processes dairy products, an entrepreneur is free to open a similar plant and to attempt to sell the same kinds of goods to the same customers. This is direct competition. In pure capitalism, all buyers and sellers operate in competition with other buyers and sellers of the same goods and services.

Free competition has many advantages. Competitive enterprises usually sell at lower prices. If one firm tries to create maximum profits by selling goods at a very high price, another firm is very likely to gain a competitive edge by selling the same goods at a lower price. In a competitive situation, companies often try to attract customers by offering better service, warranties, financing, and other benefits. Competition encourages business managers to produce a better product for the same price. It also leads to efficiency in production and management because improvement in these areas will increase profits without driving customers to other firms. All of these benefits help individual consumers and, at the same time, improve the productivity of the whole economy. They help to produce the most and best goods and services for the least investment in capital, labor, and other resources.

In some cases, free competition is self-limiting, and this may be disadvantageous. Companies may compete so successfully, ethically or unethically, that they are able to eliminate other companies that sell the same goods and services. A company that operates with no competition in producing or marketing particular goods is a *monopoly.* If such a company makes a product that is in high demand, it can charge unreasonably high prices and act in other ways that are harmful to society. In some industries, there is a condition of "monopolistic competition." This is a situation where there are fewer firms than if free competition were perfect. These fewer firms, however, are able to produce or sell products that are slightly different or exert some control over the prices charged. A good example is in retailing where a large drug chain may compete with dozens of small drugstores and yet legally force down the prices of products like aspirin and toothpaste.

An *oligopoly* exists when there are only a few competitors supplying the same goods or services to the same market. This is a common situation in the United States today whether one looks at automobile manufacturers or at the florist shops in a small town. Oligopolies are not usually strongly competitive because managers are aware that all the competing firms can sell at higher prices to their mutual benefit. This can happen when a company is very familiar with its competitors' business practices and prices, even without deliberate price fixing (companies conspiring to set abnormally high prices industrywide).

Problems such as those caused by monopolies have resulted in changes in the private enterprise system in the United States. Most of these changes involve increased government regulation of business practices. Because of these changes, the United States economic system today may best be called modified capitalism.

# 4 MODIFIED CAPITALISM
*Imposes some government regulation*

The economic system in the United States was founded on the principles of private enterprise. The basic rights of capitalism—private property, freedom to buy and sell, private profit, and competition—are protected. Today, however, the government takes a much more active role in economic issues, mainly to protect individual consumers and society as a whole from abuses by business.

## GOVERNMENT REGULATION
*Laws protect the powerless*

Many kinds of business activity today are regulated by legislation. In many cases, it is illegal to knowingly sell products that are harmful to the public. Safety devices and special materials are required for many products. Fraudulent marketing practices are generally outlawed. Laws protect society from dangerous manufacturing processes and waste products. Other laws attempt to protect the environment from long-term destruction.

Unfair business practices, such as creating monopolies and price fixing, are prevented by federal legislation. Companies are required to provide their workers with safe working conditions, and most employers are required to pay a minimum wage. Activities of organized labor are controlled to some extent; certain restrictions on strikes are available to protect the national interest, for instance.

Government regulation of business in the United States is limited. Its intention is to allow private enterprise to operate to the greatest extent possible, while protecting the safety, health, property, and rights of individuals.

***OTHER GOVERNMENT INTERVENTION*** Government intervention manifests itself in other ways besides direct regulation. In recent years, there has been a growing acceptance of the belief that the government should try to protect citizens from the effects of business cycles. Historically, the economy has passed through periods of high production with full employment and increasing wages, followed by periods of recession accompanied by unemployment and falling output, as illustrated in Figure 1-4 in the previous chapter. Through various means and with varying success, the government has tried to stabilize the economy, restraining growth on the peaks and stimulating business in the valleys.

Even this kind of intervention in the free operation of business is very limited compared to that of other economic systems. Two systems of particular interest today—socialism and communism—are distinguished from modified capitalism by their strong reliance on government planning and control, as well as by other factors.

# 5 SOCIALISM AND COMMUNISM
*Alternative economic command systems*

Most other economic systems differ from private enterprise in their stress on government planning of economic activity. (See Table 2-1,

**TABLE 2-1**
**COMPARISONS BETWEEN CAPITALISM, SOCIALISM, AND COMMUNISM**

| Factor | American Capitalism | Socialism | Communism |
|---|---|---|---|
| Ownership of land and other productive assets | Private ownership with certain guaranteed rights as to ownership of its output. | State owns and operates certain basic industries such as utilities, transportation, and steel. | State owns all productive land and assets. |
| Incentives | Wages and profits directly related to one's ability to serve in the market. | Wages related to a judgment of the value of each person's contribution to society. | Publicly announced work standards with incentives of patriotism, public recognition, status, and awards. |
| Labor | Freedom to work where and at whatever job one chooses. | Free choice of work, but state encourages some and discourages other forms of employment. | Workers have some choice of occupation, but state prescribes the place of work and is the only employer. |
| Capital | Provided primarily by private investors and lending institutions. | Provided by individuals' investment in state's bonds and by prices paid for goods. | Provided by the state from taxes generated by production. |
| Risk and loss | The responsibility of private individuals, owners, investors, and creditors, with little or no help from the government. | Risk and losses of state-owned industries borne by citizens either through higher taxes or higher prices. | Government and, in turn, the people accept all risks; losses generally absorbed by a lower standard of living. |
| Technology | Generated privately and stimulated by government funding of research. | Stimulated largely by government intervention and funding. | Generated almost exclusively by state actions and funding. |
| Competition | Free choice to compete encouraged, protected, and regulated to some extent by law. | State-owned facilities operate according to master plan; private businesses may compete, but must accommodate themselves to master plan. | Generally prohibited and counter to dominant economic and political philosophy; under rigidly enforced state economic and political restrictions. |
| Government influence | Stimulates private and individual initiative; regulates business actions that are legally deemed to be not in the public interest. | State prepares master plan specifying most economic activity, including regulation. | State owns and operates virtually all productive assets in accordance with economic and political plans. |
| Products and services | Determined largely by consumer demand and profit potential for private business enterprise. | Basic products and services determined largely by central planning; other products by profit potential. | Commanded entirely by state economic and political plans. |
| Consumer choice | Extremely broad, and generally unrestricted except by an individual's income. | Generally unrestricted except by consumers' income. | Limited to planned supply and restricted by individuals' incomes. |

"Comparisons Between Capitalism, Socialism, and Communism.") In other systems, government planners assess resources and social needs and then direct the manufacturing and distribution facilities in their country toward certain goals. Since economic activity is controlled by government command or edict, these are called **command economies.** Socialism and communism will be considered here only in their economic aspects. The political and philosophical backgrounds of the systems are not essential to a general understanding of their functioning.

## SOCIALISM
*Government ownership of key industries* ━━━━━━━

*Socialism* is an economic system in which the major production and distribution industries are owned and operated by the government. Officials directly manage some or all of the extraction of raw materials, manufacturing, communications, and transportation. Government also plays a heavy regulative role in all other business activity. Some of the freedoms of capitalism, however, exist in modified form. Private ownership of small businesses, residences, and personal property is allowed. People are generally free to work where they wish, although the government encourages workers to enter industries where they are needed. A limited amount of private profit is available to small businesses, but most profits end up in government hands because of high taxation. Limited competition among some businesses is permitted, but every effort is made to eliminate competition in major industries. Proponents of socialism claim that the absence of large-scale competition results in increased efficiency. They believe that the presence of many small competitors in the same market causes duplication of effort and wastes resources.

In control of the major production facilities, socialist governments are able to plan the kinds of quantities of goods to be produced. The governments usually intend to use this power to distribute the goods and services of the economy more equally to the citizens. In theory, basic services like health care, employment, education, good housing, and transportation are available to everyone. Generally, consumers can buy what and where they want, although the prices of many commodities, like bread and milk, may be fixed by the government.

The economies of countries such as Sweden, Denmark, France, Great Britain, and many African and South American states are socialist to varying degrees. The long-term success or failure of these economies has yet to be determined, but problems have emerged. Government-run production facilities tend to develop large, nonproductive managerial bureaucracies resulting in less efficient provision of goods and services. Individual incentive to produce appears to wither under socialism. Creativity and initiative are not always rewarded, and socialist economies easily fall into stagnation because they imitate rather than innovate.

Many people in the United States think that its economy could be called "creeping socialism." That is, they think that the more the federal government provides in health care and welfare for the disadvantaged or the more it exerts regulation upon prices and/or the way that business can be conducted, the more the United States is gradually moving away from an economy of modified capitalism and moving toward socialism.

# COMMUNISM
*State ownership and operation of all resources*

*Communism* replaces the operation of a free market almost entirely with central government planning and control. Most of the rights enjoyed in a capitalist system are denied. Private ownership of business property is usually prohibited; the state owns resources and production and distribution facilities. Decisions about what goods and services will be available are made by state planners rather than by consumers in a free market. Individuals are not allowed to establish business enterprises. Private profit is not permitted. Citizens are expected to contribute their best for the good of the state and receive in return only what they need for a modest life. Competition has been almost eliminated.

Justifications for such a system are similar to those for socialism. Supporters believe that the wealth of the society can be more equitably distributed and that central planning and the lack of competition result in more efficient production.

The Soviet Union, the People's Republic of China, and Cuba have communist economies. In the Soviet Union, particularly, a considerable evolution from pure communism has begun to take place. Incentives for increased worker performance are now more common, and wealth is being distributed to some degree according to the abilities and contributions of the individual.

None of these economic systems exist in pure form. Just as capitalism allows government regulation and control of the economy, socialism and communism often introduce features of private enterprise. These adjustments are efforts to improve the functioning of these economies.

# 6 ECONOMIC MEASUREMENTS
*How well people live under a system*

In determining the effectiveness of an economy, a variety of measures are available. These center on how well people are able to live (standard of living, amount and type of employment, and access to the good things in life), the total production of goods and services, the efficiency of that production (gross national product and productivity), and the financial status of the economy. These measures contribute to an understanding of an individual economy and help us to compare economies.

# STANDARD OF LIVING
*Basics plus amenities*

A *standard of living* is the extent to which members of society are able to satisfy their basic needs such as food, adequate clothing, and shelter and are able to acquire the other goods and services that make life more comfortable and more enjoyable. Two specific measurements are (1) *disposable income,* the amount of income left to be spent after taxes have been withheld, and (2) *personal spending,* the amount of income actually spent and how it is spent. In some economies, workers are unable to obtain the necessities of life even after spending their entire income. In advanced economies, ordinary employees may have as much as 50 to 60 percent of their income left to spend on pleasurable goods and services after attending to basic necessities.

# GROSS NATIONAL PRODUCT
## *The sum of all economic output*

The **gross national product** (GNP) is the total market price of all the goods and services created by an economy. It is calculated over a year and reflects the total output of production facilities. The GNP in the United States has been increasing at a rapid rate: from $504 billion in 1960 to over $4,000 billion in 1987. The per capita gross national product is often used in comparing the economies of different countries. It is calculated by dividing the GNP by the country's total population. The per capita GNP for several nations is shown in Table 2-2.

Many experts believe that to talk about the GNP in dollars as they are totaled up each year can be misleading. That is, if the GNP were $2,000 billion in 1975 and $3,000 billion in 1984, the two numbers cannot be compared because the 1984 dollar is not worth as much as the 1975 dollar because of inflation. These experts calculate a "real" GNP which reduces both figures to what a dollar was worth in some base period, like 1972.

There is still another factor that affects the measurement of a nation's GNP. Increasingly, mainly because of the wish to evade taxes, citizens of many countries, including the United States, do not report their sales, wages, and other incomes to the government. Individuals and companies

**TABLE 2-2**
**GROSS NATIONAL PRODUCT\* PER CAPITA IN 15 NATIONS**

| U.S. Dollars* | Nation |
|---|---|
| 18,196 | Switzerland |
| 15,768 | United States |
| 13,864 | Sweden |
| 13,496 | Canada |
| 12,757 | Germany (West, Federal Republic) |
| 11,578 | France |
| 10,704 | Japan |
| 10,171 | United Kingdom (England) |
| 7,593 | Soviet Union |
| 2,336 | Mexico |
| 2,134 | Argentina |
| 789 | Egypt |
| 440 | China (People's Republic/Mainland) |
| 250 | India |
| 197 | Zaire |

\*Data has been adjusted to reflect 1986 dollars.

*Source:* Table No. 1472, "Gross National Product in Current and Constant (1982) Dollars Per Capita, 1975 to 1983," *Statistical Abstract of the United States,* 106th ed., 1986, U.S. Department of Commerce, Bureau of the Census, p. 843.

perform work "off the books," that is, without any record of the wages or goods exchanged. Individuals may not report tips, and there is a great deal of "bartering," by which individuals or companies exchange goods for services. The United States Department of Commerce estimates that this "underground economy" amounts to $88 billion a year or more that does not get counted in its GNP.

## CAPITAL SUPPLY
*Assets available for business and production*

The supply of capital in use and available for use by business can be estimated as an indication of present and potential business activity. Without adequate capital for business operations, other resources cannot be utilized to produce goods, resulting in a stagnating economy. Heavy capital investment in plant and production equipment, on the other hand, is a sign of a growing economy since it creates conditions for increased production.

Capital supply is also greatly affected by inflation. Inflation is an increase in the amount of money in circulation or available as bank credit. This causes a decrease in the value of money and a general increase in prices. Consumers' dollars become worth less than before. Investors hesitate to put money in new ventures. Producers, too, pay more for the products and services (such as labor and materials) that they consume. In turn, the producers raise prices. Such step-by-step raising of prices and wages has been dubbed "the wage-price spiral." Inflation is damaging to an economy and its people. In some nations of the world—like Canada, Israel, and Argentina—inflation has occasionally "run away" at rates of from 20 to more than 400 percent a year. In most countries of the world, including the United States, inflation often becomes a major problem with no easy or apparent solution.

## PRODUCTIVITY
*A measure of an economy's efficiency*

The amount and value of the goods and services produced from a given input of resources are a measure of **productivity.** The higher the relative productivity of an economy, the better that economy is judged to be. A business, or a nation, can improve productivity in two ways: (1) by producing more and better goods from the same amount of resources, or (2) by producing the same quantity and quality of goods from fewer resources. This concept is illustrated in Figure 2-6. In 1900, for example, it may have taken a cobbler 1 week to make a pair of boots. Today, the same cobbler, assisted by modern machinery acquired through the investment of capital, might produce 50 pairs of boots. The quantity and value of the cobbler's output (productivity) would have increased 50 times. The cost and value of the inputs, however, would also have risen because of the higher tool costs. Productivity improvement, like inflation, has become a major problem of most economies. The United States was once the indisputable leader in the world's productivity, but it is now in a neck-and-neck race with such nations as Japan, West Germany, and France.

# EMPLOYMENT

*How many share in the economy's fruits*

The number of people in a society who are employed or unemployed is a useful measure of the economy's success. A high unemployment rate means that many people are being excluded from at least some economic benefits. It also means that one of the basic economic resources—labor—is being underutilized and the output of the economy is not at its maximum.

The quality of employment is also an indicator of how well the economy is functioning and the extent to which economic benefits are being enjoyed. Societies in the early stages of growth have more people performing basic production activities and relatively few managers, white-collar workers, and professionals. This means, of course, that the work provided is generally dirtier, harder, less knowledge-oriented, and performed in less pleasant surroundings. As economies advance, more people find employment outside of basic production, particularly in those occupations that provide services. This is illustrated in Figure 1-1 in Chapter 1, which shows the shift in employment in the United States toward service occupations.

More important, healthy economies tend to create jobs. Unhealthy economies tend to suffer from unemployment. This condition is often masked in communist countries, where people are considered employed even though they may not be performing productive work. Nevertheless, it is typical of modified capitalism—and even of many forms of socialism—that the economic health varies from healthy to unhealthy and back again. (See Figure 1-4 in Chapter 1 for an illustration of how employment varies with the business cycle in the United States.) Variations in unemployment among economies take place with varying intensity too. (See Figure 2-7.) Unemployment also tends to strike hardest at the less privileged segment of a society. For example, during the 1980s in the United States, about 30 percent of the black population was below the poverty level compared with about 10 percent for whites. Unemployment fol-

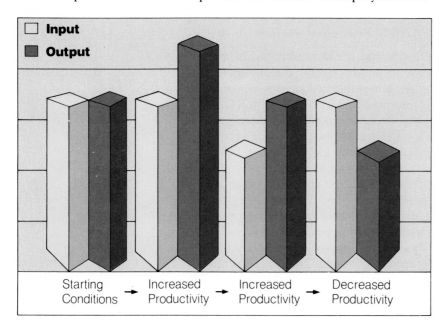

Legend:
☐ **Input**
■ **Output**

Starting Conditions → Increased Productivity → Increased Productivity → Decreased Productivity

Figure 2-6 Productivity compares output with input.

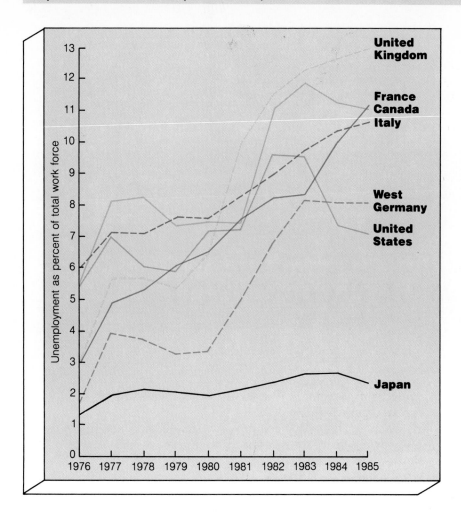

Figure 2-7 How unemployment varied over time in seven nations trading in the same markets.

lowed the same pattern, averaging around 15 percent among blacks and 6 percent for whites.

## QUALITY OF LIFE
*Nonmaterial benefits*

A final indication of economic success is the quality of life of the society's population. Although this is more difficult to measure, it may be the ultimate test, since the fundamental purpose of an economic system is to satisfy as many wants and needs as possible with its available resources. Leisure time, recreational and cultural facilities, adequate health care, physical safety, attractive surroundings, social cooperation, and thousands of other factors contribute to a worthwhile life. Providing this kind of life appears to be the highest challenge of an economic and social system. It is a challenge that is now being confronted by advanced nations such as the United States but that may, unfortunately, remain far beyond many other nations.

Many economies place greater value on providing health care and care for the aged than on providing entertainment, sporting diversions, and recreation. While statistics are hard to gather in this area, an insight can be gained into differing values and the benefits provided by different economies by examining Table 2-3. It shows, for example, that in some

# BILLBOARD

## WHICH COMES FIRST: JOBS OR PRODUCTIVITY?

As the United States turned the corner in the mid-1980s and headed back to a more healthy economy, a troubling fact became evident. Gains in productivity and profits were often at the expense of employment. A study of the 500 largest companies listed by *Forbes* magazine, for instance, showed that during 1 year alone these companies removed 840,000 employees from their payrolls. And productivity shot up by a solid 10 percent. Economists said this was good: the companies were more productive since they were generating greater sales and profits while using fewer people. Furthermore, some of the displaced employees found jobs elsewhere, since overall employment in the United States grew by 4 percent. An important reason for the productivity gains for these 500 companies was that they either backed up or replaced their employees with more and better tools and machines. In the

> **Gains in productivity and profits were often at the expense of employment.**

previous year, the capital invested per employee had been about $208,000; this grew 11 percent to $231,000, while employment among the 500 companies dropped by only 4 percent.

### QUERIES

**1.** Should productivity gains be made at the expense of people's jobs?
**2.** What measures does the United States government take to soften the impact of unemployment?
**3.** What circumstances might make it a good thing to replace people with machinery?
**4.** Would you rather see more or less government regulation of steps taken by private enterprise to improve productivity? ∎

SOURCE: "The Productivity Puzzle," *Forbes*, April 29, 1985, p. 231.

# PROFILE

WILLIAM A. LAMOTHE follows in the footsteps of one of business's most famous personalities, Will Keith Kellogg. Kellogg invented Corn Flakes and built what was to become a billion-dollar business from them. LaMothe came into the Kellogg Co. picture as a Corn Flakes salesperson. But by the time he had a chance to take over the top spot in the corporation in 1979, the giant cereal maker was on the brink of real trouble. For 6 years, the Federal Trade Commission, claiming a "shared monopoly" existed in the cereal industry, had been trying to break up Kellogg into several smaller companies. Meanwhile, growth in Kellogg's basic business had virtually stopped. Many analysts described it as a mature industry, one in which growth was no longer possible. Consumers, hit by the recession, were substituting generic brands and private labels for Kellogg's top four products: Kellogg's Corn Flakes®, Kellogg's Frosted Flakes®, Kellogg's® Raisin Bran, and Kellogg's® Rice Krispies®.

Instead of being discouraged, LaMothe struck back. He had attorneys mount an aggressive legal defense that led to dismissal of the FTC's case.

LaMothe then directed his attention to the core of Kel-

**WILLIAM A. LAMOTHE**

logg's business. He led his Board of Directors with a major commitment to reinvest heavily in Research & Development, advertising and promotions, and processing technology. This action doubled the company's pace of new product introductions, drastically increased advertising and promotion costs, and began the implementation of advanced cereal marketing technology throughout its worldwide infra-structure. LaMothe's strong financial commitment to the future growth of Kellogg's business was made at the expense of short-term profits.

The payoff: A new period of outstanding growth for Kellogg Company.

As to cereals being a mature market, LaMothe disagrees. "On average, Americans eat 9 pounds of breakfast cereal a year. But in Pittsburgh, they eat 13 pounds. We're going to make it the same all over the country. We have to be inventive enough to 'grow' the market." That's how aggressive businesses deal with economic, government, and market problems. ∎

SOURCE: Jack Willoughby, 'The Snap, Crackle, and Pop Defense," *Forbes*, March 25, 1985, pp. 82–83.

of the nations, where the economies range from modified capitalism to outright socialism to communism, health care (in the form of having fewer people share the nation's hospital beds) is more generous than in the United States. On the other hand, the economies of the United States, Japan, and Western Europe lead to significantly longer life spans than in Argentina, Egypt, India, and Nigeria. The amount of public money spent on education varies widely too. As a measure of an economy's effectiveness in providing luxuries beyond life's necessities, the figures on telephones, television sets, and radios are revealing. The United States leads by far with 765 telephones, 790 television sets, and 2,043 radios for every thousand people. Compare these three figures with those for other economies: People's Republic of China 50, 7, 67; Egypt 12, 44, 174; India 50, 3, 61; Poland 150, 234, 247; Sweden 890, 390, 858; and Japan 520, 556, 713. It follows, of course, that when comparing the effectiveness of one economy with that of another, many outputs must be examined. Even then, conclusions will be based upon the value an observer places on each of the outputs.

### TABLE 2-3
### COMPARISONS OF OUTPUTS OF DIFFERENT NATIONAL ECONOMIES*

| | Life Expectancy in Years | People Per Hospital Bed | Government Expenditures on Education as % of GNP | No. of Telephones Per 1,000 Population | Automobiles No. Persons Per Car | No. TV Sets Per 1,000 Population |
|---|---|---|---|---|---|---|
| United States | 75 | 171 | 6.8 | 765 | 1.8 | 790 |
| Argentina | 69 | 188 | N.A. | 104 | 8.4 | 199 |
| Canada | 75 | 129 | 8.0 | 664 | 2.3 | 463 |
| China [People's Republic] | 65 | 493 | 2.3 | 5 | 10,220.0 | 7 |
| Cuba | 73 | 246 | N.A. | 42 | N.A. | 168 |
| Egypt | 53 | 509 | 4.1 | 12 | N.A. | 44 |
| France | 74 | 170 | 5.1 | 541 | 2.6 | 375 |
| Germany [West-Federal Republic] | 74 | 89 | 4.6 | 571 | 2.7 | 360 |
| India | 53 | 634 | 3.2 | 5 | 740.0 | 3 |
| Japan | 76 | 84 | 5.7 | 520 | 4.5 | 556 |
| Mexico | 66 | 863 | 2.7 | 89 | 15.0 | 111 |
| Nigeria | 39 | 1,251 | 2.1 | 2 | 125.0 | 5 |
| Poland | 71 | 134 | 5.7 | 15 | 11.0 | 234 |
| Soviet Union | 73 | 80 | 4.1 | 98 | 26.0 | 308 |
| United Kingdom | 73 | 119 | 5.5 | 477 | 3.4 | 479 |

*Latest available data, ranging from 1978 to 1985.

*Source:* "Comparative International Statistics," *Statistical Abstract of the United States,* 106th ed., 1986, U.S. Department of Commerce, Bureau of the Census, Washington, D.C.

# Key Concepts

1. All economic systems have four basic resources for producing goods and services: land, labor, capital, and technology. They also have producers and consumers and some system of exchange between them.

2. Economic systems try to balance the supply of resources with the demand for them.

3. A private enterprise system is an unplanned, demand economy, controlled by a free market. It is based on private ownership, free choice, private profit, and free competition.

4. The United States economic system is called modified capitalism because it is rooted in private enterprise but permits limited government control to protect society from harmful business practices.

5. Other systems have highly planned command economies. Under socialism, the government owns some or all of the main production and distribution facilities, and competition is limited. In a communist system, most property is in government hands, and individual economic freedom and competition are held to a minimum.

6. A number of economic measures show how well citizens live, how many and how efficiently goods and services are produced, and how well economies function. These measures include the standard of living, gross national product, capital supply, level of productivity, level and distribution of employment, and the quality of life.

# Review Questions

1. Define, identify, or explain the following key terms and phrases found on the pages indicated.

    *capital (p. 32)*
    *command economies (p. 42)*
    *communism (p. 43)*
    *demand (p. 35)*
    *disposable income (p. 43)*
    *economics (p. 31)*
    *entrepreneur (p. 38)*
    *equilibrium point (equilibrium price) (p. 35)*
    *free market (p. 37)*
    *gross national product (p. 44)*
    *labor force (p. 32)*
    *land (p. 32)*
    *law of supply and demand (p. 35)*
    *market economy (p. 37)*
    *monopoly (p. 39)*
    *oligopoly (p. 39)*
    *personal spending (p. 43)*
    *private enterprise (p. 37)*
    *productivity (p. 45)*
    *pure capitalism (p. 38)*

    *socialism (p. 42)*
    *standard of living (p. 43)*
    *supply (p. 34)*
    *technology (p. 33)*

2. What are two important questions that each nation must ask about its economic system?

3. What three aspects of government involvement in economic matters are likely to determine its essential economic system as either a demand or command economy?

4. Distinguish between a producer and a consumer. In what ways are they similar?

5. What is the law of supply and demand? Give an example of a product or service for which the price has changed due to shifts in supply or demand.

6. What is the difference between a demand economy and a command economy? Which economic systems fall into these two categories?

7. Why is the economic system in the United States called modified capitalism?

8. What are some of the goals and purposes of government intervention in economic and business affairs in the United States.

9. How do private ownership and competition work under capitalism, socialism, and communism?

10. What is meant by gross national product? If productivity were to increase, but all other aspects of the United States economy remained unchanged, what would be the effect on the GNP? What effect do you think such a situation would have on the price of individual goods and services?

# Case Critique 2-1
## A Warehouse Full of Running Shoes

"Spectacular $1,400,000 Nike Close-Out! $20 Shoes for Only $6.88!" That's what ads for discount houses around the country read in 1985. Nike, Inc., creator of the famous waffle-bottom running shoe, just happened to find itself with 11 million extra pairs in its warehouses. No one was buying them. Why? The people who had made Nike rich by paying a premium for its upscale running shoes were now buying more stylish aerobic and leisure-wear shoes. The market for the more functional shoe had plunged 30 percent in the previous year. Despite the fact that Nike was selling one out of three running shoes in the United States, it had missed the boat on the fashion change. It kept on making expensive running shoes even if fewer and fewer people were buying them. This shortsightedness cost the company more than $2 million in losses as it unloaded these shoes at bargain prices. Some 400 employees lost their jobs, too, as a result of this oversupply. Belatedly, Nike introduced $40 leather shoes used in aerobics and bicycling and contracted to spend $2.5 million to stimulate demand.

1. What kind of an economy is Nike operating in? What economic principle does this case illustrate?

2. Why might the company be able to retail the running shoes at $6.88 when it couldn't sell them at $20?

3. In this situation, which party played the stronger role in the economy, the producer or the consumer? Why?

4. Should the government have gotten involved in this situation to protect Nike from losses and to protect employees from losing their jobs?

---

*SOURCE:* Cathy Hedgecock, "Can Nike Play Catch-Up Ball?" *Venture,* April 1985, p. 95.

---

# Case Critique 2-2
## A Heck of a Way to Run the Railroads

In England, crack express trains rip along at 100 miles an hour or better. Not only that, they run with the frequency of a typical inner-city bus line. The same is true of Japan. These trains are operated not by private enterprise, but by the government. When the Arab oil embargo was at its peak and public transportation suffered badly, the United States embarked on two programs of publicly owned railroads: Amtrak and Conrail. Amtrak was formed as a quasi-public (partly public, partly private) operation financed mainly by the federal government. Its objective was to restore fast, high-quality passenger rail service along routes between major cities. After a number of false starts, due mainly to underestimating how bad the railways and equipment were, Amtrak began to deliver on its service promises. The only problem, or the main problem, however, was that people did not flock to the new service. Some lines, like the one between New York and Washington, D.C., flourished, but passenger travel on most other lines languished. The government kept pouring millions of dollars into Amtrak to keep it in business, while closing down some of the least-traveled lines. By the mid-1980s, the public seemed to have had enough of government ownership and was clamoring for Amtrak to be shut down entirely.

Conrail was a similar quasi-public attempt to put together a number of bankrupt and near-bankrupt railroads into an efficient, interconnected freight service. Its fate pretty much followed the fortunes of Amtrak. Competition with other more efficient private railroads and with the newly deregulated trucking and airlines industries became too much of an obstacle to profitability. There were other difficulties, too, especially in trying to reach some sort of universally acceptable agreement with the dozens of labor unions which had represented the separate railroads. By the mid-1980s, Conrail, too, had exhausted the public's patience with government ownership. Instead of advocating its closing, however, Conrail was offered at a knockdown price to private investors, who thought they could find a way to make it profitable. The public rebelled at this, too. Finally, the government reconstituted Conrail as a private corporation and sold its shares on the open market to the general public.

1. Partial or complete government ownership of Amtrak and Conrail is more typical of other economies than that of the United States. What are they?
2. In what way do you think the law of supply and demand affected the prosperity of Amtrak?
3. Do you think that Amtrak and/or Conrail should be kept running regardless of how costly this is to the government? Why? What might private enterprise do to make these railroads more profitable?
4. To what extent should the government regulate ticket prices on public transportation, whether or not it is owned privately or by the government? What about schedules? What about employees' wages?

SOURCES: George S. Vozikis and Timothy S. Mescon, "Consolidated Rail Corporation (Conrail)," in W. P. Glueck and L. R. Jauch, *Business Policy and Strategic Management*, 4th ed., McGraw-Hill, 1984; Ken Bubenzer, "AMTRAK," in G. A. Steiner, J. B. Miner, and E. R. Gray, *Management Policy and Strategy*, 2nd ed., Macmillan, 1982.

## CHAPTER 3

# The Legal Forms of
# Business Ownership

## Learning Objectives

*The purpose of this chapter is to describe the three most common forms of private business ownership and assess their advantages and disadvantages, present the factors that influence the choice of ownership, and outline some of the less common forms of business ownership.*

*As evidence of general comprehension, after studying this chapter you should be able to:*

1. *Distinguish between public and private ownership.*

2. *Distinguish between the three major forms of business ownership.*

3. *List the main features and describe the advantages and disadvantages of a sole proprietorship.*

4. *List the main features and describe the advantages and disadvantages of a general partnership.*

5. *List the main features and describe the advantages and disadvantages of a corporation.*

6. *Recognize the factors that affect the choice of the form of ownership.*

7. *Identify and explain five other alternate forms of business ownership, especially franchising.*

*If your class is using SSweetco: Business Model and Activity File, see Chapter 3 in that book after you complete this chapter. There you will find exercises and activities to help you apply your learning to typical business situations.*

## 1 BUSINESS OWNERSHIP IMPLIES PRIVATE OWNERSHIP

KEEP OUT

## 2 THERE ARE THREE COMMON FORMS OF OWNERSHIP

They depend on the number of owners and the extent to which the owners share in the risks, liabilities, and profits of the business.

SMITH'S

SMITH & JONES

S&J INCORPORATED

## 3 PROPRIETORSHIP

(Ownership by one individual)

SMITH'S

## 4 PARTNERSHIP

(Ownership by two or more individuals)

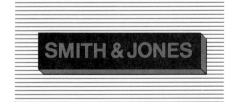
SMITH & JONES

## 5 CORPORATION

(Ownership by the shareholders)

S&J INCORPORATED

## 6 FACTORS THAT INFLUENCE CHOICE OF OWNERSHIP

Nature of the business:
- Type of business
- Scope of operations
- Extent of government regulation

Financial considerations:
- Funds required
- Degree of risk
- Extent of liability
- Tax vulnerability
- Division of profit

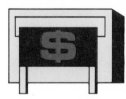

Attitudes of owners:
- Number of owners involved
- Life expectancy of business
- Kind of internal organization
- Degree of direct control desired

## 7 THERE ARE FIVE MORE ALTERNATE FORMS

| |
|---|
| Limited partnership |
| Joint venture |
| Joint stock company |
| Cooperative |
| Franchise |

# A RANGE OF OWNERSHIP FORMS

*In the recessionary doldrums of the late 1970s, Rhea Beckner had no job and couldn't find one in her part of Oregon, where unemployment was 13 percent. She was, however, a fast and accurate typist. So, with that skill and $2,000 of borrowed capital, she began a typing and word processing business in her home. Beckner, like millions of other enterprising individuals, had become the sole proprietor of a profit-making business. After she had paid off her loan, she found herself clearing a modest $600 a month. This was a little less than she would have made as a hired typist. The big difference, however, was that she was now working only a 25-hour week! This gave her a flexibility that fit her life-style. What's more, Beckner now feels that by running her own business she is in control of her own life.*

*James Bussey and Alice White run a highly successful florist business in Atlanta. It is, for example, the first black-owned outlet to be accepted for FTD wire service in Atlanta. Bussey and White got together to form a business partnership because Bussey has a knack with floral arrangements while White has a sharp grasp of modern business management methods. Like many partnerships, the two owners split the chores. Bussey handles the floral operations and the marketing aspects of the business, like making the rounds of local churches and calling on the Atlanta convention bureau for business leads. White applies her expertise to keeping the books, dealing with banks and creditors, and overseeing the computer operations.*

*Unlike Beckner, Bussey, and White, many businesses take a different form. They set themselves up as corporations. That is, they sell shares of their ownership to thousands of individual investors, who, in turn, depend upon hired managers to operate the business. Many of these corporations are very large. For example, International Paper Company employs more than 33,000 people, Quaker Oats 26,000, and Atlantic Richfield oil company 39,000. It takes huge sums of money to put so many employees into business, far more than any one person could raise.*

*There are ways to form a business other than the sole proprietorship, partnership, or corporation. As an intermediate stage between a partnership and a corporation, for example, there is the cooperative. During the 1960s and 1970s, many people joined together to form food-buying and food-selling cooperatives, like the Cincinnati Food Co-Op. It has 800 members. Each* *pays a one-time, refundable capital fee of $115 and $15 annual dues. In addition, each member must work 1.5 hours a month free. This co-op does about $500,000 in sales each year, and members make their purchases at about 25 percent below prices at other food stores.*

*Still other people, like Wayne Boggs of Richmond, Virginia, choose to combine their single-owner independence with big-corporation support. They do so by entering into a franchise arrangement. Boggs, for example, had run an independent burglar alarm business for years. Then the competition got rough. So he opted to link up as a franchisor with a national corporation, Security Alliance Corporation. It cost Boggs $10,000 at the time to get the local franchise, and he agreed to pay Security Alliance 6 cents on every dollar he takes in. In return, the Security Alliance connection gives Boggs additional purchasing power and nationwide advertising support. While the arrangement places restrictions on Boggs' independence, under the franchise form, his business grew by one-third. And with the management advice he gets from the corporation, Boggs finds the business as a whole operating more profitably.*

# 1 PRIVATE VERSUS PUBLIC OWNERSHIP
## *Business implies private ownership*

Under modified capitalism in the United States, nearly all businesses and property used by businesses are owned by private citizens, either individually or in groups. This is a basic requirement of a capitalist economy. In socialist and communist economies, significant portions of the resources and production facilities are owned by the government or some other public body. Even in our economy there is limited public ownership of certain business-type enterprises and of some natural resources. Some power and transportation companies are owned by local governments, and nearly all sewage and water services are publicly owned. Much of the timber and mineral resources in the country are owned by the government and sold or leased to industries for their use.

Government ownership of business property is, nevertheless, limited in the United States. Most property is privately owned, and private citizens have the right to decide how it will be used. This includes the right to receive and keep any profits that may be made from it. By law, the private ownership of business property may take a variety of forms.

**A MATTER OF CHOICE** Over 500,000 new businesses start up each year. Some begin on a shoestring: the corner hobby shop may have only a 6-month lease on a storefront and $1,000 in equipment and merchandise. Companies like General Motors, Exxon, and Sears are at the other extreme. They may have over $50 billion worth of assets and may count their revenues each year in the billions of dollars too. Regardless of size, however, all businesses use property in the form of capital, production equipment and facilities, raw materials, and other resources to create their goods and services. The tangible and intangible property the business uses in its operations belongs to the owners of a business. The laws prescribe a variety of possible forms business ownership may take. The different forms have advantages and disadvantages, depending on the size, type, and goals of individual businesses. Selecting the proper form of ownership is critical to the success of any business undertaking. It will partially determine how much capital is available, what kind of management techniques are needed, how easy it is to create new products and expand operations, and other issues fundamental to running the business.

# 2  FORMS OF BUSINESS OWNERSHIP
## *There are three common choices*

The most common kinds of business ownership are the sole proprietorship, the partnership, and the corporation. In a proprietorship, a single person owns and controls the business resources. A partnership splits ownership and management responsibility among two or more people in some way they privately agree upon. A corporation shares ownership among a group of investors and is often managed by professionals who may or may not also be owners.

The extent to which each form of ownership occurs in different kinds and sizes of businesses varies. As would be expected in a society that stresses the value of personal initiative and entrepreneurship, the largest number of businesses in the United States are sole proprietorships. About 70 percent of the total number of businesses in the country are organized in this way. Their receipts, however, make up only 6 percent of the total; their profits make up about 25 percent. Most of these businesses are small: local grocery stores, beauty salons and barbershops, motels and restaurants, repair shops, and small construction firms.

Partnerships are the least common form of business organization, making up about 8 percent of the total. Partnerships are common among businesses that provide professional services and in the finance, insurance, real estate, and the mining and quarrying industries.

Only about 20 percent of the businesses in the United States are corporations, but these produce about 90 percent of the nation's total business receipts and two-thirds of the profits. Figure 3-1 shows how the various forms of legal ownership compare in number of establishments and total revenues. Most of the large production and distribution firms are corporations. Many features of this form of ownership make it suitable to such companies, especially the ability to raise large amounts of capital and the ability of a corporation to continue to exist and grow even if particular individuals die or leave the firm.

# 3  SOLE PROPRIETORSHIP
## *One person assumes all risks and keeps all profits*

To expand the definition, a **sole proprietorship** is a form of business ownership in which a single individual assumes the risk of operating a business, owns its assets, and controls and uses any profits that are made. **Assets**, in this sense, are valuable property used for or resulting from the business: cash, money owed by customers, inventory on hand, real estate, office fixtures, machinery, and so forth.

In this form of ownership, the proprietor must accumulate enough capital to start and run a business from personal resources, loans secured

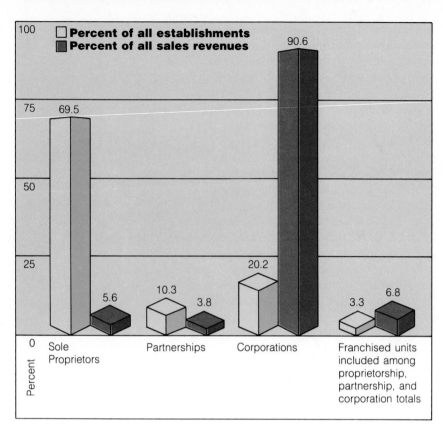

Figure 3-1 Comparisons between legal forms of business by number of establishments and sales revenues.

by personal credit, or a combination of the two. The capital is used to buy or rent a place of business, buy inventory for resale, install needed equipment, advertise products or services, pay employees, and purchase services from other companies and individuals. Rhea Beckner used her $2,000 capital to make a down payment for a computer and printer and to purchase an electronic typewriter and have a telephone line installed.

Proprietors have **unlimited liability:** they are personally responsible for paying all debts and charges that may arise from the operations. They may also keep all profits that are left after expenses are paid. This form of ownership is suitable for any small business: wholesale and retail trade, construction, plumbing contracting, movie theaters, restaurants, radio, television and automobile repair shops, and hundreds of others. The great majority of farms are owned and operated with unlimited liability as well.

## ADVANTAGES

### Ease of establishment and exclusive rights to profits

Sole proprietorships are so prevalent because they have four very important advantages: (1) ease of setting up, operating, and closing a business, (2) complete ownership of all profits, (3) high credit standing, and (4) tax advantages. For most small businesses, these advantages are great enough to outweigh any of the benefits of other forms of ownership.

Generally, a proprietorship is begun merely by deciding to undertake a lawful activity for profit. No state or federal charter is required, although in some places and for some kinds of businesses a local license may be needed. Rhea Beckner, for example, had to file a business name and get an official identification number in Oregon. Since all management control is usually in the hands of one person, a proprietorship is easy and flexible to run. The proprietor can make changes in operations quickly to take advantage of opportunities that might arise. In addition, government regulation of proprietorships is slight, and more freedom of action is possible. As long as debts and bills have been paid, a proprietorship can be dissolved as easily as it was begun, merely with a decision to stop operations.

Since the owner of a proprietorship assembles and controls all the assets used to start and run a business, he or she also has a right to all the profits that may result from its operation. In any kind of organization other than sole ownership, at least some, and sometimes all, of the profits must be shared with others. Being able to keep all the profits of a business is a great incentive to a proprietor. Careful management, skill, and hard work are usually the direct cause of profits, and the clear relationship between efforts and rewards is a strong motivation for most proprietors.

Banks and other lending institutions often give a somewhat higher credit rating to proprietorships than to businesses like corporations in which the owners are not personally liable for business debts. Since not only the assets of the business but also the proprietor's personal assets—a car, stocks and bonds, and real estate—may be used to satisfy business debts, the debts are more likely to be paid. The sole proprietor has a greater incentive to find ways to satisfy business debts in order to protect his or her personal assets.

A proprietorship usually receives tax breaks because there are generally no extra federal or state taxes on the business itself. A corporation, by contrast, must itself pay taxes on its earnings, and then stockholders must pay taxes a second time when the earnings are distributed to them. A sole proprietor pays only the same individual income tax that a person who is not self-employed would pay.

## DISADVANTAGES
*Unlimited liability, restrictions on size, and limited duration* ━━━

Many of the factors that create the advantages of sole proprietorship also result in disadvantages. The most serious of these are (1) unlimited liability, (2) restrictions on size, and (3) limited duration.

The same personal responsibility for business debts that often gives proprietorships an improved credit standing can be a heavy burden for the owner. Despite the efforts of owners, many small businesses fail. In a proprietorship, all of the assets of the owner, not just those invested in the business, may be sold to pay off creditors. A proprietor risks much more than does an investor in a corporation.

Although there are exceptions, few sole proprietorships have grown into large businesses. Since the capital used in the business is restricted to what a single person has or can borrow, the substantial amounts of resources needed for a large company are usually not available. In addition, a single manager is not normally capable of running a large business without the assistance of experts in management specialties such as marketing and finance. Because of the other limitations on size, particularly lack of adequate capital, proprietorships are often unable to compete effectively with corporations or partnerships for personnel with such management skills. The unlimited liability of the owner also restricts the business's ability to undertake large projects because the proprietor may be reluctant to risk losing both his or her business and personal assets.

Since a sole proprietorship exists through the efforts of a single person, the firm often is forced to shut down if the owner dies or becomes disabled. Major business activities, like large-scale manufacturing, are rarely attempted when there is such a threat to the continuity of the firm; the risk of losing the capital invested is too great. The assets of a proprietorship may often be sold to a new owner, but the highly personalized relationship between management and customer makes it difficult, in many cases, for a new owner to step in.

# 4 GENERAL PARTNERSHIP
## Two or more people assume all risks and share all the profits

When two or more people operate a business as co-owners, their form of ownership is a *general partnership.* The partners contribute their private capital, whether owned or borrowed, accept personal liability for all the debts of the business, and share the profits among themselves in some manner that is satisfactory to all involved. The contribution and share of the profits of each partner need not be equal. In a general partnership, however, the partners, individually and as a group, are equally liable for the business's debts, even if the partners must use their personal assets to satisfy them.

Any kind of business can be operated as a partnership—a garden supply store, a restaurant, a small manufacturing company—but partnerships are particularly common among businesses that provide professional services. Doctors, dentists, lawyers, accountants, brokers, and other professionals often use this form of ownership to reduce overhead costs for each partner and to take advantage of each other's expertise in various areas.

## ADVANTAGES
### Additional capital and diversity of skills

Many of the advantages of a partnership are the same as those of a proprietorship: ease of starting the business, good credit standing, and tax savings. Partnerships are not much harder to establish than proprietorships. At most, they require a written contract, called "articles of partnership," between the associates. The credit standing for a partnership generally is even better than for a proprietorship since all the personal and business assets of the partners may be liquidated to pay off business debts. Partnerships are not taxed separately from the individual incomes of the partners. Additional advantages of partnerships are that (1) more capital is available, (2) the diversity of management skills possessed by the partners can be useful, and (3) prospects for growth are better.

Although most partnerships have few members (two to four partners is most common), multiple ownership still provides considerably expanded financial resources when compared to a proprietorship. The personal wealth and credit of all the partners may be pooled to provide the capital needed for a larger operation or for a firmer financial base for a

## Action Brief

### A CENTURY AND A HALF OF PRIME RIBS

That's how long Boston's famous Durgin-Park restaurant has been serving up the biggest portions in the East. It all began in a waterfront warehouse in 1840. Three partners—John Durgin, Eldredge Park, and John Chandler—had the notion that hard-working people needed lots of food. And they started up what was to become one of the nation's most successful restaurants. The partnership dissolved, however, when both Durgin and Park died. Chandler continued to operate as a sole proprietorship, and he handed the restaurant down to his children and grandchildren until it was sold in 1945 to another sole proprietor, John Hallett. The restaurant continued to prosper under the new owner, but it was sold again in 1977 to another partnership, the Kelley brothers. Over nearly 150 years, Durgin-Park has had only four sets of owners, a record not likely to be matched in today's changing times.

small business. The formation of a partnership often means less risk for each individual partner.

Partnerships can provide a wider range of business and management skills than is available to a sole proprietor. Partners often have complementary abilities: one may be best in sales and marketing, another in financial management, another in production or services. This diversity can lead to a sounder business operation.

More capital and management skill allow partnerships to grow more easily than most proprietorships can. Expansion or the development of new products or services requires capital; partners generally have more combined assets than a single individual. The diverse management skills available to partnerships permit a wider range and larger scale of operations. The specialized employees that would be needed for a larger firm can often be attracted and kept in the company by including them in the partnership agreement.

## DISADVANTAGES
*Unlimited liability plus potential conflicts*

Some of the disadvantages of partnerships are similar to those of a proprietorship: limited duration, unlimited liability, and restricted growth potential. If one of the partners dies or becomes unable to continue in the business, the partnership must be dissolved or changed in some way. Such uncertainty about the duration of a partnership may interfere with making long-term commitments. The unlimited liability of each partner for the debts of the business is probably the single greatest disadvantage of this form of ownership. This can result in severe losses to one or more partners when the assets of other partners are not great enough to pay their share of debts. Even though a partnership has a greater capacity for growth than a proprietorship, it is still quite limited in the capital it can raise and the staff it can assemble compared with a corporation. There are other disadvantages that are especially common in partnerships: management conflict and the difficulty of recovering investments.

In a partnership, especially in a small business, all partners often have equal authority. This division of authority can result in conflict when two or more of the partners disagree. (See Table 3-1.) These conflicts can become very severe, on occasion, because each of the partners individually is legally and financially responsible for the business actions of the other partners, even if the actions were taken secretly.

Once an individual's resources are invested in a partnership, it is often difficult to recover them. The other partner or partners may not be able to afford to buy the assets of the person who decides to withdraw, and it may be hard to find another buyer with the right combination of capital and skills. If a partnership is forced to dissolve because of the wish of a partner to withdraw, assets often must be sold below market value, and a loss results for everyone.

**TABLE 3-1**
**CHECKING OUT A PARTNERSHIP**

Partnerships are like marriages. Both parties bring their unique expectations and contributions. Unless there is a mutual and continuing satisfaction with the other person's performance, a divorce may ensue. Accordingly, Gloria Gilbert Mayer, joint owner of a restaurant in St. Paul, Minnesota, offers this advice for minimizing partnership problems:

1. Investigate your partner beforehand, as thoroughly as you investigate the business you are undertaking. Be sure you know your partner in a business sense. What is your partner's work record? Is she or he reliable, prompt, knowledgeable, and flexible?
2. Identify your own abilities and liabilities. Make an inventory of your strengths and weaknesses and discuss them with your partner. Your partner should reciprocate. By so doing, you will be able to begin your business understanding where your best contributions can be made.
3. Mention the unmentionable. Secrets will eventually come out. For example, if banks are going to ask for loan guarantees, personal finances and fiscal responsibility should be discussed beforehand.
4. Be prepared to share the potential for loss equally. If the business does not do as well as expected, the amount of the loss may affect each individual differently. One partner may, for example, be willing to pitch in and make even greater sacrifices and contributions (especially financial ones), while the other partner may simply want to bail out and dissolve the partnership.
5. Establish a clear, legal, and binding method of setting work schedules and of settling disputes. This should be formulated at the start, while each party is friendly and can agree on policy.

Source: Gloria Gilbert Mayer, "The Ten Principles of Partnership," *Working Woman,* November 1984, p. 78.

# 5 CORPORATION

*Shared ownership with unlimited potential for future growth*

The predominant form of ownership for large businesses in the United States is the corporation. A **corporation** is an association of individuals created under authority of law which exists and has powers and liabilities independent of its members. A corporation may be created for many purposes: charitable, educational, governmental, and so forth. A business corporation, however, is organized for the purpose of providing goods and services for a profit.

Each part of the definition of a corporation has significance in terms of why this form of ownership is desirable for certain purposes. A corporation is made up of and owned by a group of people. The group may be small, such as a local land development company with four owners, or the group may be very large, like the millions of people who own shares of the General Motors Corporation or International Business Machines. The owners share in the total investment and risk and divide any profits that are made. A corporation is created under authority of law, and a charter must be obtained from one of the 50 states before a business corporation can be formed. A corporation exists separate from its owners as a legal entity. As such, it has certain rights granted by law: it may own and sell property, borrow money, manage its own affairs, enter into contracts, and sue and be sued in court. A corporation is liable for the payment of its own debts; individual owners are not responsible except to the extent that they have invested money in the corporation. Their personal assets cannot be seized to pay the debts of a corporation. Owners, thus, have **limited liability.**

## ADVANTAGES
*Limited liability and greater capital resources*

Many advantages of the corporation stem from its multiple ownership and its existence separate from its owners. The main advantages are (1) the ability to raise large amounts of capital, (2) limited liability of investors, (3) continuous existence, (4) ease of investing and withdrawing investment, and (5) specialized management.

Corporations account for nearly 90 percent of the business revenues in the United States. One reason is that a corporation has the capability of raising the tremendous amounts of capital needed for large manufacturing, transportation, and communications enterprises. Corporations can accumulate capital by selling shares in their ownership, or stock. Assets of the largest corporations run into the billions of dollars; no proprietorship or partnership has been able to amass such amounts. The limited liability offered by the corporate organization attracts larger numbers of investors than would otherwise be available. If a person invests $1,000 in General Motors Corporation stock, he or she would lose only that $1,000 if the corporation dissolved. Personal assets other than the amount invested are not risked.

Another feature of the corporation that has made it the predominant kind of ownership for large firms is its ability to survive independent of any particular investors or managers. Even if the owner of a significant amount of stock dies or wishes to withdraw, his or her portion of ownership ordinarily can be easily sold on the market, and the business activities of the corporation continue uninterrupted. The same independence from particular owners allows corporations to continue in existence for long periods of time, even forever, at least in theory. The fact that portions of ownership, in the form of stock, can be traded on the open market like any other commodity is an advantage in itself. This makes it easy for investors to acquire partial ownership and easy for them to withdraw from the corporation when they wish.

Organization as a corporation can solve the difficulty of providing adequate and diverse management. Except in very small corporations, most stockholders are not directly involved in the management of the company. The company is free to hire any employee it can afford and is thus able to get the specialized professional skills needed for sound management.

# DISADVANTAGES

*Higher taxation and more complex operations* ━━━━━━━━━

The main disadvantages of a corporation are (1) generally higher taxation, (2) the complexity and high cost of its establishment and operation, (3) legal restrictions on activities, and (4) somewhat lower credit standing. Other less important disadvantages are (5) the managers of a corporation do not have the strong personal motivation that results from personal ownership and liability, and (6) that, for companies with many stockholders, confidentiality of financial information becomes practically impossible to maintain.

One of the greatest objections to the corporate form of ownership for many businesses is that corporations are taxed more heavily than a proprietorship or a partnership. A corporation is a separate legal entity; its earnings are taxed directly and at a relatively high rate. The same earnings are taxed again as personal income when they are distributed to stockholders. In addition, states usually charge corporations annual registration or franchise fees. Because of the intricacy of federal tax laws, however, many large corporations have been able to avoid, or minimize, their tax contributions. For example, General Electric Company paid nothing in income taxes on sales of $28 billion in 1984.

The role of governments in authorizing the operations of corporations creates still another disadvantage: corporations are often expensive to establish and complex to run because of government regulation. Incorporation fees, sometimes amounting to tens of thousands of dollars for a sizable company, must be paid when the charter is secured. More government regulations apply to corporations than to any other form of ownership. Simply preparing the many reports required to show whether there has been compliance with government regulations can be a complex and expensive management task. Keeping track of the company's stock and who owns it is another job that is not necessary in a proprietorship or partnership.

When the charter is granted for a new corporation, the kind of business activities to be undertaken is specified. If the corporation wishes to engage in other activities, an amendment to the charter is required. Although this process is usually routine, it cost money in terms of management time and legal fees. The resulting delay sometimes interferes with the chance to take advantage of opportunities that might arise.

The limited liability of investors lowers the credit standing of the company somewhat. Lending institutions know that owners cannot be required to use their personal assets to pay off the corporation's debts. If a proprietorship and a corporation of the same size applied for a bank loan, the proprietorship would have a slight advantage because of the unlimited liability of the owner.

For corporations whose shares are sold openly to the public, an added problem is the possibility of a "takeover" of its operations by a group of "unfriendly" investors who purchase a majority of shares.

***Subchapter S corporations*** offer small business owners a unique choice. This option enables owners to retain the limited liability protection while avoiding the corporate income tax. Instead, owners may elect to pay these taxes as if they were individual partners. This usually results in a lower tax rate. There are a number of restrictions placed upon Subchapter S corporations, however. Among these are the following: there can be no more than 15 shareholders, 20 percent of the income must come from inside the United States, and no more than 20 percent can be from investments.

# 6 CHOICE OF OWNERSHIP FORM
## *Three factors influence choice*

Each of the three common forms of ownership has important advantages and disadvantages, and no form is ideal for all businesses. The special characteristics of each form, however, usually make one more suitable than another for a given business enterprise. Fortunately, the form of ownership can usually be changed as needs change. The major factors to be considered in choosing a form of ownership are the nature of the business, the financial effects on operation, and the attitude of the owners.

## NATURE OF THE BUSINESS
*Size and scope favor corporations*

The size of the business and the kind of goods and services it provides will influence the best form of ownership. The features of proprietorship are generally most beneficial to a small business, while one of the main advantages of a corporation is that it can provide the resources and management needed for a large company. The geographic scope of operations has a similar effect: proprietorships are more common in businesses with local markets, while corporations are more common for regional or nationwide operations. If the corporate form of ownership is chosen, the business will always be subject to more government regulation than proprietorships or partnerships.

## FINANCIAL ASPECTS
*Money matters plague unincorporated businesses*

The amount of funds needed by a business is one of the single most important factors in choosing a form of ownership. A proprietorship is limited to the resources of the owner, and partnerships are limited to the resources of its partners. Corporations, however, can assemble large amounts of capital from many different investors. The degree of risk and the extent of liability the owners are willing to accept will affect the choice of the form of ownership. A corporation usually has fewer tax advantages, and this must be weighed against other needs. The division of profits is usually quite simple in a corporation since earnings are distributed based on the number of shares owned. Some partnerships require complex earnings distribution schemes to allow for the varying contributions and portions of ownership held by partners.

## ATTITUDES OF OWNERS
*Independence through proprietorships*

The number of owners involved in a business venture has an obvious effect on the form of ownership. Often, an entrepreneur may wish to have complete control of operations and is unwilling to share profits; proprietorship is the clear choice if needs for capital and management can still be met. Where there are multiple owners, other factors must be considered. If a continuing operation is to be established, one that will outlast its founders, a corporation is most suitable. If the owners wish to retain a high degree of direct control of operations, a partnership will more often offer this than would a corporation. A partnership also generally gives owners more equal participation in management; corporate organization typically limits the authority of individuals to specific areas.

Table 3-2 summarizes the advantages and disadvantages of the three major forms of business ownership.

# 7  OTHER FORMS OF BUSINESS
## Alternate forms offer a variety of options

While the main forms of business ownership are sole proprietorship, general partnership, and corporation, there are numerous variations that may be used in certain instances. These variations include limited partnerships, joint ventures, joint stock companies, cooperatives, and franchises. Each form is advantageous under certain circumstances.

**TABLE 3-2**
**ADVANTAGES AND DISADVANTAGES OF DIFFERENT FORMS OF BUSINESS OWNERSHIP**

| *Sole Proprietorship* | *Partnership* | *Corporation* |
|---|---|---|
| *Advantages* | | |
| 1. Ease of setting up, operating, and closing. <br> 2. Complete ownership of profits. <br> 3. Higher credit standing. <br> 4. Lower tax rate. | 1. Relatively easy to set up. <br> 2. Partners own the profits. <br> 3. Even higher credit standing. <br> 4. Taxes applied to individuals, not to partnership. <br> 5. More capital is available. <br> 6. Greater diversity of operating skills. <br> 7. Better prospects for growth. | 1. Limited liability of investors. <br> 2. Ease of investing and withdrawing investment. <br> 3. Ability to raise large amounts of capital. <br> 4. Survival almost assured. <br> 5. Specialized management. |
| *Disadvantages* | | |
| 1. Unlimited liability for the owner. <br> 2. Restricted growth potential. <br> 3. Sickness or death of owner may mean end of business. | 1. Unlimited liability for the partners. <br> 2. Restricted growth potential. <br> 3. Sickness or death of partner may mean end of business. <br> 4. Potential conflicts between partners. | 1. Generally higher taxation. <br> 2. Complexity in starting up and in operating. <br> 3. Legal restrictions on activities. <br> 4. Lack of motivation toward company goals among its hired managers. <br> 5. Loss of financial confidentiality in corporations that offer their securities to the general public. |

# HYBRID PARTNERSHIPS AND JOINT VENTURES
*Special solutions for special needs*

The law makes it possible to establish a partnership in which one or more partners are granted limited liability, provided there is always at least one partner with unlimited liability. This form of ownership is a *limited partnership.* The partner or partners with limited liability are protected from losing more than the amount they have invested in the business because their personal assets cannot be seized. They are not, however, allowed to take an active part in managing the business. The main advantage of this type of ownership is that it allows a partnership to acquire capital from investors who do not wish to be active in the business.

A partnership set up to carry out a temporary short-lived business project is called a *joint venture.* This form of ownership is often used in real estate transactions and is sometimes the initial form new corporations take when they are first being set up. A joint venture is different from ordinary general partnerships in that it usually terminates after its specific, one-time function has been accomplished. Some joint ventures may last indefinitely if the partners agree to renew the contract periodically. Two examples are when AT&T and Olivetti formed a joint venture with AT&T marketing Olivetti's computers, and when the General Motors Chevrolet division got together with Toyota Manufacturing Inc. to form New United Manufacturing Inc. to build Chevy Nova's.

Partnerships may be established that raise capital by selling portions of ownership on the open market in the form of stock certificates. Such an organization is called a *joint stock company.* It combines features of a partnership and a corporation. Although this form is legal in most states and provides a means of assembling capital, it is seldom used today because stockholders have unlimited liability for the financial obligations of the company.

# COOPERATIVE
*Sharing economies of scale*

Small producers of goods or consumers of goods and services sometimes wish to band together to achieve the competitive advantage of larger size in the marketplace. Such groups may form a *cooperative* in which production, marketing, or purchasing facilities are jointly owned and are operated mainly to provide a service to members rather than to make a profit. Fruit growers, dairy farmers, and other producers have formed marketing cooperatives and many have nationally known trademarks. *Sunkist, Sun-Maid,* and *Sun-Sweet* are the brand names for citrus fruits, raisins, and prunes marketed by three different fruit-grower cooperatives. Consumer cooperatives (like Cincinnati Food Co-Op) attempt to achieve lower prices by buying in quantity and by eliminating the profit in the final selling of goods. In a cooperative, any profit made is usually distributed to members as a rebate. Members of a cooperative usually have one equal vote in running its affairs, no matter what share of ownership they may have. Today, excluding credit unions, there are nearly 13,000 cooperatives in the United States.

# FRANCHISING

## *A protected form of proprietorship* _____

A very popular and rapidly growing form of business ownership is the *franchise.* This is a licensing arrangement that permits an individual to own his or her business while benefiting from the use of the trademark, know-how, and reputation of an established firm. In return, the individual owner—the *franchisee*—pays the parent company—the *franchisor*—a royalty from part of the business's profits.

There are several different kinds of franchising agreements, but the most popular is for a major firm to franchise an entire retail network. This method is used by companies in such diverse fields as fast foods (McDonald's Corp.), sewing machines (Singer Co.), temporary help (Manpower, Inc.), auto repair shops (Midas-International Corp.), and motels (Holiday Inn Motel). (See Chapter 4 for more on franchising.)

# *Key Concepts*

1. Nearly all business facilities and resources in the United States are privately owned. The ownership may take a number of legal forms.

2. The most common forms of ownership are sole proprietorships, general partnerships, and corporations. Most businesses (about 70 percent) are proprietorships, but most revenues (about 90 percent) are generated by corporations. Partnerships are the least common form of business organization, making up about 8 percent of the total of all business organizations in the United States.

3. In a proprietorship, assets and profits are owned by one individual who has unlimited liability for the legal and financial obligations of the business.

4. In a general partnership, assets and profits are owned by two or more persons who each have unlimited liability for business debts.

5. Stockholders own the assets and share the profits of a corporation. Their risk and liability are limited to the amount of their investment. Corporate enterprises enjoy many important advantages, including the ability to raise large amounts of capital, continuous existence, ease of investing and withdrawing an investment, and specialized management.

6. The choice of the best type of ownership for a business is based on the nature of the business, the financial effects on operations, and the attitudes of the owners.

7. In addition to the three common forms of ownership, there are five alternative forms which can provide special solutions to special business problems and needs. These alternate forms include the limited partnership, the joint venture, the joint stock company, the cooperative, and the franchise.

# *Review Questions*

1. Define, identify, or explain each of the following key terms and phrases, found on the pages indicated.

*assets (p. 58)*
*cooperative (p. 68)*
*corporation (p. 63)*
*franchise (p. 69)*
*franchisee (p. 69)*

*franchisor (p. 69)*
*general partnership (p. 61)*
*joint stock company (p. 68)*
*joint venture (p. 68)*
*limited liability (p. 68)*
*limited partnership (p. 68)*
*sole proprietorship (p. 58)*
*Subchapter S corporation (p. 65)*
*unlimited liability (p. 59)*

2. Why is such a large part of business revenue in the United States earned by corporations when the great majority of businesses are proprietorships?

3. What is the difference between unlimited and limited liability? Which of the three main forms of ownership have limited liability and which have unlimited liability?

4. Assuming a proprietorship, a general partnership, and a corporation were all the same size, which do you think would pay more taxes on earnings? Which would probably have the highest credit standing? Explain your answer.

5. Like proprietorships, partnerships are easy to start, have a good credit standing, and result in tax savings. In what ways are partnerships superior to proprietorships?

6. What are the main points of the definition of a corporation?

7. What are the five important advantages of the corporate form of ownership?

8. In what ways might the attitude of an owner affect his or her choice of a business form? Describe the kind of person who is most likely to choose a sole proprietorship.

9. How is a limited partnership different from a general partnership? How is a joint venture different from other partnerships?

10. Why do small producers sometimes form cooperatives? How are profits distributed in a cooperative? In what industries might one find cooperatives in operation?

# Case Critique 3-1
## From Auto Buff to Auto Parts Magnate

Like lots of teenagers, Fran LaBrecque was crazy about cars. In 1965, the year he got his first driver's license, he owned 13 of them. He bought most of them for $50 or less. This led him to his first job out of high school as an auto mechanic in his home in a Boston suburb. LaBrecque didn't see much future with his head buried all day long under an auto hood, though. Selling cars had a lot more appeal. And he found that he was a natural at it. Along the way, however, LaBrecque stumbled on an interesting fact: a new sedan that you had just bought for $8,885 would cost you $32,548 in parts—plus your labor—if you were to build it yourself. With those figures in mind, Fran moved to a job with a small auto parts jobber. And there he discovered another interesting fact: more and more of the people fixing cars were not auto mechanics in garages but individuals doing it as a hobby. LaBrecque sold his boss on the idea of bankrolling him to the tune of $10,000 in a retail, discount auto parts store. He called it American Discount Auto Parts (or ADAP). This business grew from a loose sort of general partnership, with his former boss as the major partner, until in the early 1980s its 38 regional stores were doing more than $45 million a year in sales. Growth during a 5-year period was at the rate of 37.5 percent a year!

Much of ADAP's success was attributed to LaBrecque's management skill. He had quickly discovered still another interesting fact: the profit on "hard parts" like carburetors, shocks, and mufflers is no greater than that on "soft parts," or "junk," as they are known in the trade—like flashlights, cans of air freshener, and sheepskin seat covers. Anyone who comes into an ADAP store is a likely customer for "soft parts," while you might wait a long time, for example, for a person wanting to buy a carburetor for a 1976 Chevy. Accordingly, LaBrecque set up his inventory system so that half of what ADAP carries is "junk" and the other half, "hard parts." He then designed his own computer control system to keep track of how many of each of 11,000 parts each store sells per day. The fast movers get inventory priority, while the slow movers are chosen very carefully.

LaBrecque and his two partners sold ADAP to Rite Aid Corporation in 1984 for $28 million. They could have built ADAP into a national chain by making it a publicly owned corporation, but they chose to let an established national retailer take over. The new owner, Rite

Aid, however, chose to retain millionaire Fran LaBrecque as manager of ADAP. "He is a very capable manager," said Rite Aid's president, "and what's more, he's developed a staff of good managers." With Rite Aid, the key issue is the bottom line—profits. And Fran LaBrecque has shown that he knows how to deliver them, regardless of what kind of company he works for.

1. What form of business ownership did Fran LaBrecque choose to begin his own business? Why?

2. As a partnership, what problems would ADAP encounter when trying to establish itself on a national basis?

3. When LaBrecque sold his company, could he keep all the profits for himself? Who would he have to share them with?

4. After selling ADAP to Rite Aid, LaBrecque was retained as the manager. Was he now an employee or an owner or both? Why?

*SOURCE:* Joseph Dalton, "Do-It-Yourself Dynasty," *Esquire,* December 1984, pp. 338–344.

# Case Critique 3-2
## $150 Million Down the Drain

One of the great corporate collapses of the last decade was the failure of AM International. Once known as Addressograph-Multigraph Corporation, this manufacturer of old-fashioned duplicators and addressing machines had been marginally profitable for over 50 years. With the advent of copying machines, its technology became rapidly obsolete. The company changed its name to AM International and went all out to develop the new technology of word processing.

For a while, in the late 1970s and early 1980s, it looked as if the company would fly very high again. Hundreds of thousands of investors purchased over 10 million shares of its stock. They paid prices ranging from $9 to $21 a share. Then, suddenly, everything went wrong for AM. In 1981, it lost $245 million on sales of $857 million. This means that for every dollar the company took in, it lost 29 cents! A close look at the way the company was being run showed that its managers were careless and inefficient. By early 1982, the company was $250 million in debt to banks and suppliers. Its net worth to the stockholders dropped to a paltry $14 million, or about $1.40 a share.

The company kept losing money so fast that its creditors pressed it into bankruptcy. The stockholders, who had invested over $150 million in the company, were left holding a company whose principal assets were owed to its creditors. AM's stockholders were unhappy, of course. But, unlike the company's creditors who were still clamoring to be paid, the stockholders' losses were limited to exactly what they had invested in the corporation. There was no legal way the creditors could collect any money from the shareholders. If there was not enough money left after the sale of the company's plants and equipment to pay all the creditors, that was no concern of the stockholders.

1. Under corporate law, what privilege did AM's stockholders enjoy when the company failed? What is the significance of this privilege in the corporate form of business organization?

2. What was the advantage to AM International, in the first place, of forming a corporation rather than a single proprietorship?

3. How much control did AM's owners (stockholders) have over the way the company was managed?

4. In spite of its ultimate collapse, AM, under one name or another, had stayed in business for over 50 years. What corporate feature does this longevity stem from?

*SOURCE:* "AM International: When Technology Was Not Enough," *Business Week,* January 25, 1982, p. 62.

# *Entrepreneurs,*
# *Small Business,*
# *and Franchising*

## *Learning Objectives*

*The purpose of this chapter is to emphasize the similarities and differences between small and large businesses and to discuss the various factors that influence the success of entrepreneurs and of small businesses.*

*As evidence of general comprehension, after completing this chapter you should be able to:*

1. *Recognize the kinds of people who create small businesses and explain the strengths and weaknesses of their approach.*

2. *Define a small business and compare its operations, advantages, and disadvantages with larger businesses.*

3. *Compare the ease of entry into capital-intensive and labor-intensive fields and recognize the ways in which operating emphasis differs among such businesses.*

4. *Explain the need for a definite market for a firm's products or services, the need for having sales revenues equal or exceed operating expenses, and the value of a business plan.*

5. *Identify the major ways in which the federal government tries to provide special assistance to small businesses.*

6. *Describe the elements of a typical franchising arrangement and its advantages and disadvantages.*

*If your class is using SSweetco: Business Model and Activity File, see Chapter 4 in that book after you complete this chapter. There you will find exercises and activities to help you apply your learning to typical business situations.*

## 1 ENTREPRENEURS PREVAIL

Innovative, energetic, and freedom-loving
. . . but often narrow-gauged

## 2 SMALL BUSINESS MUST DO EVERYTHING THAT BIG FIRMS DO . . .

but with fewer resources.

## 3 DIFFERENT KINDS OF OPERATIONS REQUIRE SPECIAL EMPHASIS

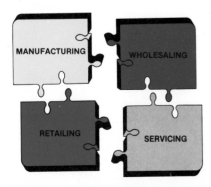

## 4 MARKETING AND FINANCIAL KNOWHOW ARE ESSENTIAL

Genuine market

Plan for reaching it

MONEY IN
EQUALS
MONEY OUT

Smart management

## 5 THE GOVERNMENT TRYS TO HELP

Financial help

SOLD

SBA

Vendor's advocate

Management counselling

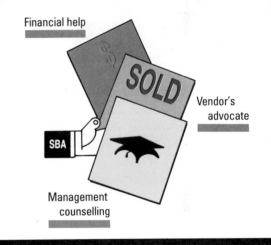

## 6 FRANCHISING CAN PROVIDE A HEAD START

Know-how

Trademark

Reputation

# THE LURE OF SMALL BUSINESS

*Sales of rerun albums, rejected songs, and* The World's Worst Records *make impressive profits for a couple of West Coast entrepreneurs. In the 1970s, Harold Bronson and Richard Foos were going nowhere in a small retail record shop in Santa Monica, California. Then they got the bright idea of buying the license rights of musical turkeys from the big record companies that own the master tapes. They then rerelease them under their own label, Rhino Records. Bronson and Foos generally pay a $2,500 to $5,000 advance against royalties and make a gross profit of about 25 percent an album. Their biggest success to date was* The Turtles Greatest Hits, *which sold 50,000 albums. Rhino Records started with $4,000 in cash and released seven albums in its first year of operation. By the mid-1980s, its sales had topped $1 million.*

*Hundreds of thousands of other enterprising young—and older— people are shifting the attention of American consumers away from the large, traditional corporations to small, innovative, exciting new businesses. It is the dream of many job-locked individuals that some day they will break the bonds and open their own small businesses. Thousands do each year. And thousands fail. The opportunity glows like a rainbow, nevertheless. Liz will start up her own tailor shop. Joe, Frank, and Marian will form a partnership for a balloon business. Sybil's idea for a diet center will start on a shoestring and mushroom 20 years later into 1,300 franchises. Anthony will form his Spaghetti Pot, not to serve meals to sit-down customers, but as a take-out service. David grows his own grapes and operates a marginally profitable winery. John and his family incorporate to sell the flowers they grow at a roadside stand. In Alabama alone, 500 small business people are growing Christmas trees for sale. Elsa and Peter run a unisex hairstyling parlor. Linda operates a small firm that provides accounting services for other small businesses. Charlie mowed lawns in high school; his incorporated firm now performs contract gardening for over 200 home owners, restaurants, banks, and shopping malls.*

*What does it take to start up and run a small business profitably? Six areas of expertise predominate: (1) an entrepreneurial spirit, (2) the capability of operating on limited resources, (3) a sense of what makes or breaks a particular kind of business, (4) financial awareness and a sound business plan, (5) a little bit of help from the government, and—for some—(6) the ease of entry provided by a franchise opportunity.*

# 1  A REVIVAL OF THE ENTERPRISING SPIRIT
## *Energetic, innovative, freedom-loving people*

The bureaucracy and decay associated with so many large companies have had a beneficial side effect upon the United States economy: they rekindled the enterpreneurial spirit among hundreds of thousands of Americans. Between 1979 and 1986, the number of new businesses started each year grew by more than one half. What's more important is that these new, smaller businesses—those employing under 100 people—created more than half of the new jobs generated by new business formations during the period. (See Figure 4-1.)

## ENTREPRENEURS
### *Special kinds of individuals*

Many people can start or join a small business. Those who start them up, however, are characterized by unusual energy and the willingness to take risks. Typically, these entrepreneurs see an opportunity that has been overlooked by, or that is too small to attract, a larger business. A major construction firm, for example, may not want to take on small jobs, like renovating an old house or putting in a dormer window. To entrepreneurs, jobs like these represent opportunity. They are willing to risk their capital and their jobs to take advantage of them.

Many entrepreneurs seek independence. They have a maverick streak in them that urges them to try to go their own way. They like the freedom of choosing their own work methods and setting their own work hours. Often, these small business operators find out that such independence is illusionary. They discover that instead of having to knuckle

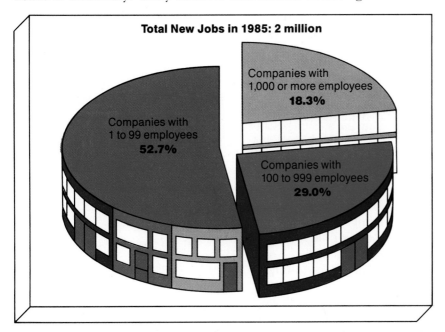

Figure 4-1 Small companies are creating most of the new jobs.

under to a boss in a large corporation, they must accommodate the whims and demands of their customers. In general, hours of employment for operators of small businesses tend to be very long. Sixty-hour weeks are not unusual.

**PROFILE OF AN ENTREPRENEUR** Observers describe entrepreneurs as energetic, freedom-loving, and risk-taking. This is probably true, although generalizations can't include every type of individual. *Venture* magazine, however, surveyed 2,700 successful entrepreneurs to find out more about them. This is what they found. Entrepreneurs, typically:

- Are the first-born child (44 percent for men; 47 percent for women).
- Held three or more jobs before age 15.
- Started their first business before they were 20.
- Are hard-working (31 percent are at work by 7:30 a.m.).
- Are demanding bosses.
- Are college graduates (64 percent).
- Believe themselves to be self-directed.

---

*SOURCE:* Nancy Madlin, "The *Venture* Survey: Probing the Entrepreneurial Psyche," *Venture*, May 1983, p. 24.

---

It has also been thought that since entrepreneurs have to handle all aspects of a fledgling business, they are broad-gauged individuals. In many instances, this has not been the case. Dun and Bradstreet, a firm that specializes in examining the credit worthiness and financial strengths of businesses, regularly reports that the major cause of small business failures lies in the weakness of its management. Women and men who create a new business often excel in one particular line of work. Because of this single-specialty background, many entrepreneurs fail to recognize the importance of other aspects of the business. Don Valentine, an investor who helped to fund Apple Computers, observes that it is important for an entrepreneur "to know what he doesn't know. Many entrepreneurs have incredible blind spots. They are often insensitive to the importance of sales, or manufacturing, or how to price their goods profitably."

**THE DARKER SIDE OF OWNERSHIP** Job busting, as some call the act of breaking away from employment by others and setting up one's own business, isn't always as happy a venture as it appears to be. There are formidable risks. An individual's nest egg or life's savings can be lost, often very quickly. Or, if the entrepreneur has left an attractive, secure position in a larger company, the job may no longer be available if the venture goes down the drain. There is also a very real difficulty in being a boss of one's own. Without a boss or other support, the entrepreneur has no one to listen to complaints about long hours, poor pay, irritating customers or clients, and insensitive management. Sick days and vacations are often nonexistent, at least at the start. And, if things go wrong, there is usually no one to blame except yourself.

Finally, there is rarely an opportunity that is a "sure thing." Seemingly foolproof ventures almost always contain weak spots that can only be detected after the business is launched. Consumer or marketing fads are notorious fields to invade. The list of them is long and tragic: Hula

Hoops, suntan booths, video game arcades (like Chuck E. Cheese's Pizza Time Parlors), and wood stoves. Typically, either the market fades away, or it becomes viciously price-competitive. Merchandise on the retailer's shelf grows obsolete. Powerful competitors force the small business to offer larger and larger discounts. The cost of the product or service offered begins to exceed the price that can be charged for it. Unanticipated expenses mount as additional advertising and services are required to keep the business afloat. All too often, the entrepreneur is not equipped with the skills or financial resources needed to make the business survive.

**HELP FROM OUTSIDE** Many entrepreneurs and inventors have good business ideas but not enough money to get their ventures under way. Accordingly, many have found that another kind of entrepreneur, called a venture capitalist, can be of great help. A *venture capitalist* is an individual (sometimes a group of individuals or a corporation) who will provide funds to start up a new enterprise. They do so on the condition that the owner of the business assign a significant share of ownership to the investor. Venture capitalists are usually investors who have ready money, or access to it. They rarely get involved in operating the business. They are willing to take unusual risks in return for potential profits that are much larger in proportion to the capital they have risked.

## 2  SMALL FIRMS DO EVERYTHING THAT LARGE FIRMS DO
### And they must do it with less

The excitement about the revival of entrepreneurship should not lead you to believe that small businesses are different in concept from large businesses. A small business, regardless of what legal form it chooses to take, must raise capital and produce and market its goods and services, just like big businesses do. When it comes down to size, however, "small" is a relative term. About 99 out of every 100 firms in the United States have annual sales of less than $1 million. The great majority of businesses—typified by the entrepreneurs you just read about—are very, very tiny by comparison. The giant companies draw your attention by their advertising and the ever-present availability of their products. More than 500 of them do more than $1 billion in sales each year. A few—like Exxon, General Motors, and IBM—have sales of over $50 billion. Sears, Roebuck does $40 billion, Procter & Gamble $15 billion, and Eastman Kodak more than $11 billion! Down a notch in sales from the top 500 are another 1,000 or so firms that seem small only when compared with the giants. These firms, although their names and brands may be nationally known, count their sales only in the tens of millions of dollars. Companies with brands like Wham-O, Crayola, and Tabasco are examples.

Below these 1,500 to 2,000 companies lies the large mass of small businesses. For example, 8 out of 10 of the more than 11 million businesses in the United States take in less than $100,000 a year. That means that nearly 9 million companies are so small that they can support only two or three adult owners or employees. They can do that only under the most favorable conditions. Most small businesses do not do nearly so well. And most small businesses remain small; only a few grow up to be big businesses.

## SMALL VERSUS LARGE OPERATIONS
*They differ in scale and resources*

It is true that the operation of a small business is fundamentally the same as a large one. Regardless of size, every business has to perform the same managerial and operational functions. Every business must find a way of competing in the social, political, physical, and economic environment. Nevertheless, there are significant differences. These differences are mainly a matter of scale and resources.

The scale of operations in a small business is often crude and in miniature. The owner of a small manufacturing company, for example, must plan production (although it may be done on the back of an envelope), engage in research and development (if only in the back room over a hot plate), arrange for operating materials and supplies (perhaps picking them up in the trunk of a car), and exercise control (such as checking accounts on the kitchen table at midnight).

It is legendary, too, that managers of small businesses wear a number of hats as they fulfill various functions. Their businesses are not large enough to afford the hiring of specialists. The heart of the matter is that small businesses operate without the resources of larger ones. To begin with, they do not have as much money. And it is money that provides the financial support needed to obtain all the other essential operating resources of a business—facilities, equipment, materials, and labor. In spite of this, small business operators can find a way to survive and succeed. They do so by cutting everything down to size and by applying their limited resources to the most pressing, immediate problems. Rarely, however, are the resources of a small business ample enough so that it can afford to take the long view of its operations.

## DEFINITION OF SMALL
*It is a relative term*

Agencies of the federal government have taken pains to try to define "small business." The purpose of their definitions is to guide the government in its efforts to provide support and encouragement to small business operators. These definitions of **small business** can be summarized as follows:

1. It is small relative to other firms in its industry.
2. It is independently owned.
3. Its operations are typically local in nature.
4. Its owners are likely to be its operators.
5. For federal interest and support purposes, certain upper limits have been set on size according to the nature of the class of business: At their largest, (1) a small retailing firm will have less than $1 million in annual receipts; (2) a wholesaling firm, less than $9.5 million; (3) a service firm, less than $2 million; and (4) a manufacturing firm, fewer than 250 employees.

---

## Action Brief

### BANKROLLING A START-UP

*A common question from would-be entrepreneurs is, How much money do I need to get started? Obviously this varies from business to business. The best guess about capital requirements for a number of popular businesses is: telephone answering service, $28,800; health food store, $53,400; yogurt bar, $46,200; plant shop, $30,000; pet shop, $61,200; and dating service, $33,000. If you really want to try a low-entry-capital business, there is always janitorial service, $3,000; street vending, $1,080; and parking lot striping service, $1,440. These are average figures required to move a business from start-up to the break-even point.*

As you can see, "small" can be quite large, even under the federal specifications. In this chapter, however, the focus of the discussion is on the 9 million or so firms whose businesses fall far below the federal limits.

Finally, ownership of small businesses can, and does, take any form of legal ownership. Small businesses are mainly single proprietorships, but they may also be partnerships. A great many are in the form of small, family-style or closely held, corporations.

## WHERE THE MONEY GOES
*Only a little left for the owner*

To get a better sense of the challenge to small business operations, consider a business that has sales at the top of the range, or about $100,000 a year. That figure sounds like a lot, doesn't it? A closer examination of the numbers, however, is revealing. (See Figure 4-2.)

■ Most businesses spend 20 to 50 cents of each sales dollar for materials and supplies. Let's be generous and earmark only $20,000 for this expense. (That leaves $80,000.)

■ Businesses typically spend another 20 percent for rent, heat, light, telephone, insurance, and taxes. We will earmark $20,000 for these. (That leaves $60,000.)

■ It is a rare firm that does not incur 20 to 50 percent for labor costs. We will use the lower figure and take away only $20,000. (That leaves $40,000.) We are not through yet.

■ Many companies must consider an auto or truck for transportation,

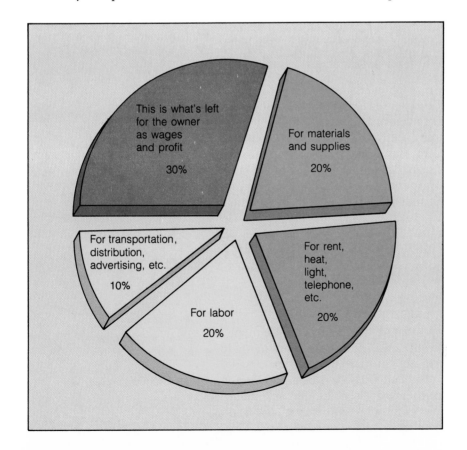

Figure 4-2 Where the money goes in a small business.

advertising expenses, and commissions to salespeople or distributors. This eats up another 10 percent, or $10,000. (That leaves $30,000 for the owner-operator—before taxes—to compensate for the risk involved and his or her own labor.)

A profit of $30,000 a year on $100,000 sales is exceptional. In the great majority of cases, the profit figure is much lower than that—more nearly $10,000 or less. Why do owners choose to stay in business under these circumstances? The answer is often quite simple. The major portion of their labor costs is paid not as wages to outsiders, but to the owners themselves, or to employees who are members of their families.

## SMALL BUSINESS ADVANTAGES
*Faster response and lower overheads*

People who operate small business often find that they have several advantages over larger ones. If a business succeeds, an owner may find himself or herself deriving far more income from profits than he or she might earn otherwise as an employee of a larger company. It is a fact that hundreds of people become millionaires each year by starting up their own businesses.

Small firms can act faster than larger firms. They are like small motor boats that can turn quickly in the water to avoid a collision. A large ocean liner may take a mile or more to alter its course.

Decisions are made more rapidly in small firms, because there are fewer people whose opinions must be considered. There are fewer levels of bureaucracy and considerably less red tape. A local retail store, for example, can detect the appeal of the latest clothing fad and put merchandise on its shelves, while the potential for that fad is still being discussed in product committee meetings of a large department store chain.

Finally, overhead, in a small firm, is far less than in larger companies. *Overhead* is the term applied to the expenses incurred by activities that do not add visible value during the conversion process. A large manufacturing firm, for example, may employ a full-time nurse to take care of employees' minor ailments. While this may be a desirable service to the employees and to the organization, a smaller firm may not offer the same kind of service. As a consequence, it spends less money on medical care and many other desirable, but not indispensable, overhead activities.

## 3  EACH KIND OF BUSINESS HAS ITS DISTINCT OPPORTUNITIES AND CHALLENGES
*Labor is often more vital than capital*

Small businesses are usually those that require relatively little money to start up. This means that they are not capital-intensive. They are more likely to be labor-intensive, in that labor, usually the owner's, is the prime resource. Inner-city people who start their own businesses often describe the assets they build from their own labor as "sweat equity." Businesses that require little in the way of capital, equipment, and facilities to begin are described by economists as having **ease of entry**. Capital-intensive and labor-intensive businesses, however, have their own special problems, as shown in Figure 4-3.

## FOUR COMMON FIELDS ATTRACT
*Each presents its own particular challenge*

Certain kinds of industries attract small business because of their relatively low capital requirements and their ease of entry.

**RETAILING** All that is required in the way of facilities is a rented store and some shelving. Merchandise may often be bought on credit. Location, however, is critical. Rent for a good business location, such as a shopping mall, can run as high as $3,000 a month for a 20- by 30-foot store. Retailing can be intensely competitive. As a consequence, profit margins are very slim. Grocery retailing is a case in point. The most successful supermarkets average less than 3 percent net profit on sales. This fact often surprises people who enter this business, since the price a customer typically pays is from 20 to 40 percent higher than the actual cost of the product to the retailer. Labor, rent, and overhead costs account for the difference.

Merchandising sense—the knack of knowing what to carry in stock and how to price it profitably—is particularly important in retailing. In recent years, a sensitivity to the needs of local consumers has helped small, independent supermarket operators to succeed in many instances where a supermarket giant has failed.

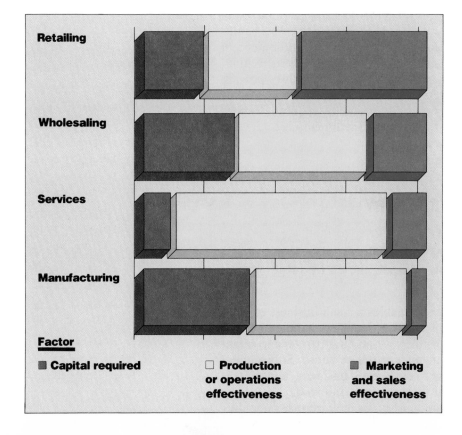

Figure 4-3 Relative importance of various factors to small business operations.

**WHOLESALING** Despite the criticism from consumers that "middlemen" or "intermediaries" occasionally attract, the United States economy would not survive without them. There always seems to be a place for the entrepreneur who is willing to assume the burden of helping to distribute someone else's products. The wholesaler does this by either (1) buying from a manufacturer and reselling to retailers or industrial users or (2) acting in some way or another as a go-between. Wholesaling profit margins are almost always less than those in retailing. The profit a wholesaler makes depends greatly upon the value the manufacturer and the retailers, or industrial users, place on the service that is rendered. As a consequence, wholesalers often find themselves in a profit squeeze between the two.

**SERVICES** Here, again, small businesses may provide services directly to consumers or to other firms. The firms that buy this service may be other small businesses or very large ones. Opportunities to create a small service business are everywhere. To begin with, there are those services that are relatively capital-intensive, like dry cleaning, self-service laundries, and photo finishing, of course. There are a greater number of services that are labor-intensive, however. These include accounting and tax preparation, hairdressing and barbering, window washing and floor waxing, lawn mowing and gardening, painting and carpentering. Many of these small businesses exist by performing, for a fee, a portion of the work *(subcontracting)* of a larger firm. This helps to lessen the need for marketing skills, since the larger firm often obtains the business through its own sales force or advertising programs before passing a portion along to the small subcontractor.

**MANUFACTURING** Small business operators look for manufacturing opportunities that are relatively low in capital requirements. As a result, many small manufacturing companies use secondhand equipment or engage in labor-intensive operations. Leather working, silversmithing, weaving, and other small craft operations have been especially popular in the last decade. Small manufacturers often keep their capital needs low by purchasing semifinished components rather than by acquiring expensive equipment to make the parts themselves. Small manufacturers also do a great deal of subcontracting work for larger firms so as to minimize marketing expenses.

## TWO POPULAR AVENUES OF ENTRY
*Provide a quick start and low overhead* ━━━━━━━━━━━

In addition to franchising, which is discussed in Section 6 of this chapter, two popular forms of easy entry are chosen by small business operators.

**SUBCONTRACTING** This approach enables a small business to get a share of a larger job that it could not afford to finance or handle by itself. A couple of individuals working together as a roofing partnership might never be able to manage the building of a complete house. Subcontracting the roofing portion of the larger contractor's business, however, is attractive to them. Their financial investment is minimal. They have little marketing to do. They get paid quickly for their efforts, since they do not have to wait until the house is sold. On the other hand, they may be forced to take on work that has only minimal profitability, since the house builder also expects to make a profit from the subcontractor's work.

**DIRECT MAIL** In the last two decades, many a person has started a part-time business based upon direct mail operation. Direct mail is the solicitation of customer orders by mail (telephone, television, or magazine advertisements may also be used) and fulfillment of these orders by postal or commercial delivery. This is a special form of retailing, of course. It has the advantage of enabling a business to begin on a very small base. The business, if it succeeds, can be built little by little. Direct mail is very risky, however. To be profitable, 2 out of every 100 mailings must be converted to sales. This takes unique marketing and cost control efforts. Postal rates keep rising. Catalogs and mailing prices are increasingly expensive. In its early stages, direct mail operation is very labor-intensive. It requires a great deal of careful record keeping and market analysis.

Inventory costs for direct mail operations can be minimized through the use of **drop shipments.** Using this method, the direct mail operator does not stock the items that are promoted. In effect, he or she acts like a manufacturer's agent. When a customer makes a purchase, the direct mail operator notifies the manufacturer, distributor, or retailer who, for a fee, ships the product directly from its inventory.

# 4 MARKETING AND FINANCIAL KNOW-HOW ARE ESSENTIAL
*They lay the foundation for a good business plan*

It takes more than a good idea to start and operate a small business. A knowledge of marketing principles and financial fundamentals is essential. From these, an entrepreneur can construct a plan that may lead the new business along the path to success. In addition, the small business owner must be a good manager, one who is able to put the plan into action and keep it on course.

## A GENUINE MARKET
*Substance, not wishful thinking* ▬▬▬▬▬▬▬

Good ideas are surprisingly easy to come by. The world seems to be full of ingenious people who can think up new ways to peel an orange, polish your teeth, or keep the rain out of chimneys. The trick is to invent a product or conceive of a service that people (1) want in sufficient quantity and (2) are willing to pay a price for that makes it all worth your while. Small businesses succeed only if there are enough people or companies nearby (or who can be reached economically by mail or other means) who want this service. Experience shows that a business should not be launched without first getting assurance that these conditions exist. It is not enough to ask a friend or relative. Hard facts and opinions must be gathered from people who really know the business, from government sources of economic data, and from information collected by local chambers of commerce and other business associations. Unless there is convincing evidence of a genuine market, a new venture is best left on the drawing board.

## FINANCIAL LITERACY
*Two unforgiving principles*

The need for small business operators to understand the principles of accounting and finance cannot be overstated. All too often, a business either fails to get off the ground or fails later on because of money matters. The money needed to sustain a business during the start-up period may be insufficient, or the owner may fail to control its finances during its operation. There are many accounting practices and financial principles to be observed, but two demand critical attention:

**1.** *Over the long haul, more money must flow into the business than is paid out in expenses.* A coffee shop, for example, may have days when business is so good that the cash register is ringing constantly. There are other days, however, when business is not only slow but the bills come due from the food supplier, the landlord, and the telephone company. The day's receipts may fall far short to cover the checks written on that day. Over a period of time, say a week or a month in most cases, the total dollars coming into a business must be great enough to pay all the expenses incurred during that period. (See Figure 4-4.) Many owners fail to keep track of this relationship between cash inflow and outgo. They mistakenly think of daily receipts as profit, rather than what these revenues really are—a source of money to pay expenses. It is only after the bills are fully paid that a profit may remain.

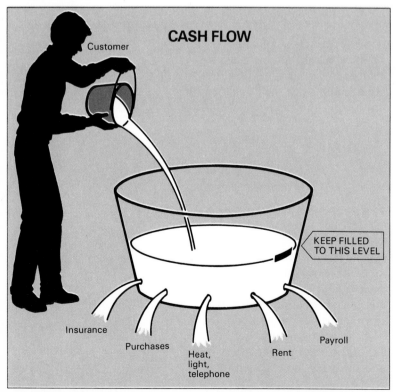

Figure 4-4 Cash flow: The money flowing into a business must at least equal the money going out.

**2.** *An enterprise must have a good idea of how much business it must do to break even.* That is, the owner of the coffee shop must know how many meals she must serve in a week, for instance, to pay for all the costs of purchasing the food and preparing and serving the meals. Not only that, the owner must also figure in the overhead—or on-going—costs of rent, heat, insurance, telephone, and the like. These costs must be apportioned to the cost of each meal too. By making these calculations, the owner will know in advance that the coffee shop must serve 1,250 meals a week to break even. A new coffee shop may only serve 500 meals its first week of operation. Neverthe-less, the new owner may believe that through advertising and word of mouth, the business will keep building at the rate of 50 meals a week. That way, the owner can predict that the business will break even (or reach the 1,250 meals a week target) in 15 weeks, or at the end of the 16th week.

It is especially important to know when the break-even point will occur because the business loses money until it breaks even. (See Figure 4-5.) If the owner has enough capital (over and above the receipts from each meal sold) to be able to pay the expenses of operating for the 15 weeks, then the business has a chance of succeeding. But if the owner has only enough capital to make up the difference between receipts and expenses for 10 weeks, the business may fail prematurely. (It should be clear that the lower a company's break-even point, the better off it is, since it makes a profit sooner and on a lesser amount of sales. This is true

Figure 4-5 Breakeven: A company must sell enough goods or services to break even on its expenses.

of large companies as well as small. One of the major secrets of the revival of Chrysler Corporation is that under Lee A. Iacocca the company cut its break-even by more than one-half, from 2.4 million automobiles a year to 1.1 million.) Most businesses do not grow as quickly as was hoped for at the start. Many businesses take 3 or more years to break even. For that reason, to be on the safe side, the owner of a new venture should have enough capital on hand at the start to carry the business for 3 years.

## A SOUND BUSINESS PLAN
*Road map to profits*

Before funds can be obtained from most investors, the small business operator must provide a written plan of what she or he intends to do and how this will be accomplished. This brief, but comprehensive, document is called a ***business plan.*** The business plan may take many forms, but it usually includes the following five elements:

**1.** A description of the product or service to be provided. This should include a description of its unique features and the owner's patents, trademark, or copyright.

**2.** An analysis of the size and nature of the market for which the product or service is intended. For example, if the entrepreneur is preparing to offer a window-cleaning service to local home owners, the market might be described as "800 single-family homes and 200 multiple-dwelling units within a 12-mile radius." Identification of the number and size of the competitors would also be mentioned here.

**3.** A plan for placing the service or product on the market. The plan should specify how the product will be sold—directly to consumers or through wholesalers or retailers.

**4.** A plan for the location and layout of operating facilities. This portion of the plan also covers what will be needed in the way of equipment and labor. The plan should answer questions about how fast and accurate the operating procedures should be, what kind of equipment will be required, how much it will cost, and the kind and number of employees needed for operations. The person starting the window-cleaning business, for instance, might estimate that one panel truck is needed, three kits of tools, one large and two small ladders, and two healthy, energetic helpers.

**5.** Basic financial information. At the minimum, this requires (1) an estimate of the capital needed to get the business started and to sustain it until it breaks even, (2) a forecast of the sales revenues and estimates of expenses over a period of time, and (3) a plan for managing and controlling the company's financial affairs.

## SMART MANAGEMENT
*Someone to pull it all together*

It is an owner or manager who breathes life into business plans. The owner or entrepreneur must have the ability to raise the money and assemble the tools and equipment of operation. This is only the beginning, however. It will still take a vigorous, ongoing effort to see that the right people are hired and that they are given clear directions for what they are supposed to do. After all, it is a company's employees who really operate the business. The owner must coordinate these activities to ensure that the product or service is provided in the prescribed fashion. He or she must also see that the products and services are brought to market persuasively and priced in a profitable way. The owner must keep a watchful eye on both sales and expenses, pushing one ever upward while trying to hold down the other. These coordinating, directing, and controlling activities are the really critical responsibilities of the small business operator. They require what are known as management skills. A small business will survive and succeed when its owner or managers have the "right managerial stuff." Without good management, the business will falter and fail.

## 5 THE GOVERNMENT TRIES TO HELP
### Federal agencies aid small business operators

Several agencies of the federal government offer support and guidance to small businesses. Principal among them is the **Small Business Administration (SBA)**. The SBA was created by the Small Business Act of 1953. Its headquarters are in Washington, D.C., and it operates a number of vital programs from 10 regional and over 100 field offices. Because many citizens believe that small business should be treated no differently than big business, there is occasional political pressure to abolish the SBA. Despite these viewpoints, the SBA continues to exist and provide a variety of useful, specialized services.

**FINANCIAL ASSISTANCE** The SBA helps small businesses to find financing when other credit sources are denied them. In addition, it licenses two privately owned types of companies that help provide such financing. They are the Small Business Investment Corporation (SBIC) and the Minority Enterprise Small Business Investment Company (MESBIC). The latter facilitates loans for socially or economically disadvantaged owners.

**VENDOR'S ADVOCATE** The SBA establishes procedures to help small businesses obtain a fair share of the enormous government purchases. The procedures establish avenues of approach, either through direct sales or by obtaining subcontracts from major contractors to the government.

**MANAGEMENT ASSISTANCE** The SBA offers training and counseling to new business entrepreneurs as well as to experienced owners. This is accomplished in many ways. It is done through volunteer groups, like the Service Corps of Retired Executives (SCORE), and through activities like the Small Business Institute (SBI), which assigns faculty-guided college students to study a business's operating problems. Firms that operate with SBA guaranteed loans often must utilize this service. The SBA also manages the Office of Business Women's Ownership, which helps women-owned businesses to make maximum use of generally available government assistance. One of the SBA's most useful aids is a series of publications dealing with the specific operating problems of small businesses.

In the long run, however, most small businesses must start up and survive on their own. Informed operators, of course, seek out and accept every kind of assistance that they can get from federal sources.

# 6  FRANCHISING PROVIDES A UNIQUE ENTRY OPPORTUNITY

## *Ready-made reputations for purchase*

As indicated in Chapter 3, franchising is a form of business that combines many of the aspects of small business proprietorship with the know-how, trademarks, and reputation of an established, often very large, corporation. To repeat the earlier definitions—a *franchise* is usually a licensing agreement that permits an individual to own his or her business while benefiting from the know-how, trademarks, and reputation of the established firm. In return, the individual owner—the *franchisee*—pays the licensing company—the *franchisor*—an initial start-up fee, a royalty from part of the business sales or profits, and sometimes an additional royalty for a share in national advertising programs.

**FRANCHISING ARRANGEMENTS** The skills required in starting a business from scratch are so varied that the opportunity to purchase a franchise appeals to many would-be entrepreneurs. The franchisor usually provides all the financial, production, and market planning for the business, along with a location and the equipment needed to start up. The franchisee pays a flat sum of money for this comprehensive head start (called a *turnkey arrangement,* as shown in Figure 4-6.) Typically, the franchisee also continues to pay the franchisor a percentage of sales revenues so long as the franchise exists. The advantages of obtaining the varied know-how and assistance are often offset by the fees charged by the franchisor. Franchise operation, like most small businesses, usually requires hard work and long hours from the owners with no guarantee of success.

**OPPORTUNITIES** There are nearly one-half million franchised establishments in the United States with more still on the way. (See Figure 4-7.) They account for sales of nearly $500 billion each year. The traditional franchisors—automobile dealers, gasoline service stations, and soft drink bottlers—still dominate the field. They make up about 75 percent of all franchised sales, although the number of these establishments has dropped dramatically in the last 15 years. Newer franchised products and

Figure 4-6 Turnkey arrangements provided by some franchisors are designed to get the franchisee off to a comprehensive headstart in operating a business.

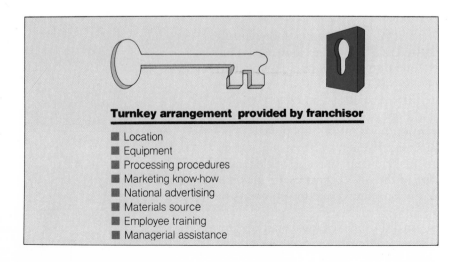

**Turnkey arrangement  provided by franchisor**

- Location
- Equipment
- Processing procedures
- Marketing know-how
- National advertising
- Materials source
- Employee training
- Managerial assistance

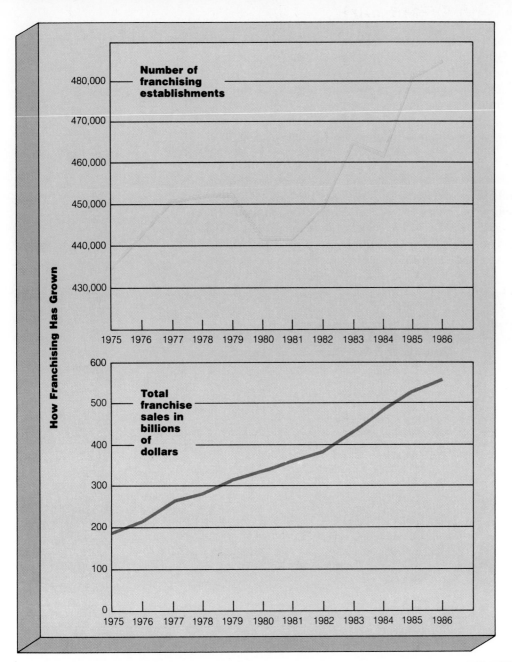

How Franchising Has Grown

Number of franchising establishments

480,000
470,000
460,000
450,000
440,000
430,000

1975 1976 1977 1978 1979 1980 1981 1982 1983 1984 1985 1986

Total franchise sales in billions of dollars

600
500
400
300
200
100
0

1975 1976 1977 1978 1979 1980 1981 1982 1983 1984 1985 1986

services account for the remaining 25 percent of sales. This group includes fast-food restaurants, automotive services, convenience stores, and business aids and services. One-third of all retail sales in the United States is now generated by franchised units. Franchised fast-food operations showed the greatest gain in sales volume during the 1970s, and they now account for more than one-fourth of total sales among eating and drinking establishments.

**EMPLOYMENT** Many high school and college students have found their first jobs as employees of a retail franchise, especially fast-food outlets. Typically, these jobs prove to be less than satisfactory to most young people. The work is generally part-time, and it is not unusual for the employee to be asked to work only during the peak dining hours. Em-

Figure 4-7 How franchising has grown: Sales has grown steadily while number of establishments has fluctuated.

ployees are paid the minimum wage, and even this compensation is becoming more and more of a burden for the franchisee. Jobs are learned in an hour or two, often with the aid of filmstrips or other visual aids. Supervision is provided by unit managers, who are usually in their early twenties, and by assistant manager trainees, who are often only slightly more experienced than the employees they supervise. The trainees work long hours and are not highly paid, although those who remain in the industry may eventually draw annual incomes of $25,000 to $50,000.

**OWNERSHIP** The franchise offers persons who are relatively inexperienced in a particular field a chance to own and operate a business. In effect, it is a form of sole proprietorship. The franchisor provides the franchisee with a facility, operating advice, and marketing support. In return, the franchisee can be expected to make an initial cash outlay of anywhere from $10,000 to $150,000 for the right to buy into the business. (See Table 4-1.) The total capital commitment required may be as high

**TABLE 4-1**
**EXAMPLES OF FRANCHISE OPPORTUNITIES OFFERED BY FRANCHISORS**

| Type of Franchise | Trademark or Trade Name | Nature of Product or Service | Initial Cash Requirement* |
|---|---|---|---|
| Home improvement and maintenance | Winterizing Systems of America | Residential and commercial building winterizing | $ 34,500 |
| Nonfood retailing | Koenig Art Emporium | Art supplies, picture framing | 45,000 |
| Business aids and services | Alphagraphics | Printing and electronic graphics (full-scale) | 225,000* |
| | Budget Instant Printing Centers | Printing and copying | 12,500 |
| | Todays Temporary | Temporary office help | 40,000 |
| | Huntington Learning Centers | Continuing education; remedial instruction | 54,000 |
| | General Business Services, Inc. | Financial management counseling and business advice | 22,000* |
| | CelluLand | Cellular car phones | 140,000* |
| Health and physical care | Health Force | Health care center management and operation | 50,000 |
| | Physicians Weight Loss Centers | Weight control center management and operation | 12,500 |
| | BodyComp Weight & Wellness Systems, Inc. | Computerized fitness analysis; weight control programs | 30,000 |
| Automotive products and services | Mr. Transmission | Auto transmission installations | 35,000+* |
| Equipment sales | Machinery Wholesalers Corp. | New and used equipment sales | 10,000 |
| Restaurant | Ponderosa | Fast-food steak house | 125,000 |
| | Blimpie | Fast-food sandwiches | 75,000* |

*1987 figures; all other figures, 1985 data.

as $1 million for a first-class franchise (like McDonald's) in a prime location. Franchise ownership usually demands hard work and long hours, and, in most instances, financial rewards are modest, although there are franchisees who have become millionaires. Like all businesses, franchising is risky. Additionally, there have been notable cases of unscrupulous franchisors who were more interested in selling franchises (pyramiding) than in supporting them.

**ADVANTAGES AND DISADVANTAGES OF FRANCHISES** For the parent firm, or franchisor, a franchise provides several advantages. It gives the parent firm greater control over its distribution network, limited liability, reduced investment requirements, and sometimes faster growth. For the franchisee, the system enables him or her to get into business quickly, employ proven operating methods, and benefit from mass purchasing. There are drawbacks for both sides, however: (1) increased buying power does not necessarily assure a profit, (2) corporate control by the parent company tends to stifle initiative at the local level, where marketing flexibility is so necessary, (3) financial rewards to the individual are usually small in proportion to the time and effort required, and (4) profit margins for both the franchisor and franchisee tend to be so small that parent firms may be encouraged to buy back franchises, putting them in competition with other remaining franchises.

# Key Concepts

1. Entrepreneurs and people who start up and operate small businesses derive advantages from their characteristic initiative, energy, and desire for independence. There is a great deal of risk involved, however. Resources are typically limited, and the specialist who starts up a business must learn how to become more of a generalist so that he or she can handle all aspects of the business.

2. Small firms must do everything that large firms do, although they have fewer resources and operate on a smaller scale. A major advantage of a small business is its low overhead, but this implies that the owner must wear many hats. On the other hand, decisions can be made quickly and red tape can be held to a minimum.

3. Each kind of business poses a different kind of start-up and operating problem, according to how capital-intensive or labor-intensive it is. Emphasis in retailing and wholesaling is on marketing skills; in services and manufacturing, emphasis is on production and operations excellence.

4. Small business operators must comprehend the basic principles of marketing and finance. In particular, they must be certain that there is a genuine market for their product and that they have a grasp on their revenues and costs so that they acquire and maintain enough capital to survive and succeed. This knowledge must be translated into a business plan to guide the management and control of the business.

5. The federal government offers special assistance to small businesses in the form of loan guarantees, help in obtaining government business, and management advice and guidance. Much of this assistance is provided through the Small Business Administration (SBA).

6. Franchising provides a unique way for starting up and owning your own business under a licensing arrangement with an established company. The small business owner benefits from the trademarks, know-how, and reputation of the larger corporation, but pays a relatively high price for these privileges and also gives up some independence.

# Review Questions

1. Define, explain, or identify each of the following key terms or phrases found on the pages indicated.

> business plan (p. 86)
> drop shipment (p. 83)
> ease of entry (p. 80)
> franchise (p. 88)
> franchisee (p. 88)
> franchisor (p. 88)
> overhead (p. 80)
> small business (p. 78)
> Small Business Administration (p. 87)
> turnkey arrangement (p. 88)
> venture capitalist (p. 77)

2. Describe a typical entrepreneur. What kinds of characteristics would you expect him or her to have? What might be a principal shortcoming?

3. Compare a venture capitalist with a typical entrepreneur. What is a major difference between them?

4. How is a small business distinguished from a large business? List some of the advantages and disadvantages of a small business.

5. Refer to Figure 4-3 and give some reasons for (1) manufacturing needing more capital than retailing, (2) services requiring greater operating effectiveness than retailing, and (3) retailing needing greater marketing or sales expertise than manufacturing.

6. What makes subcontracting attractive to small businesses? What are some of the possible drawbacks about it?

7. Explain why it is so important for a small business to take in more money than it spends. How does this relate to its need for adequate start-up capital?

8. Why might a potential investor in a small business want to see its business plan?

9. List three kinds of services that the federal government offers small businesses through the Small Business Administration.

10. Why might a person who wishes to own a small business be attracted to a franchising arrangement?

# Case Critique 4-1
## Subcontracting in Reverse

Subcontracting the work of a principal contractor or company is a proven way for a small company to start up a business or to get its share of a bigger one. Larger companies are aware of this interest on the part of smaller firms. Consequently, almost every major corporation asks smaller companies to perform selected work or services for them on a subcontracting basis.

An occasional small company also seizes upon this technique to set itself up in a larger business than its capital might otherwise support. This was true of So What! of California, a manufacturer of women's budget clothing. Its owner, Ron Dickey, started working at 17 for a national clothing firm ($500 million or more a year in sales). His first job was sweeping the floors, but he advanced to cutter, to sewing

supervisor, and finally to production manager. Then, with $25,000 raised from a second mortgage on his home, Dickey started So What! If he had completely equipped his own shop, he would have needed $100,000. Instead, he contracted out the production of his garment designs to dozens of smaller firms. He had to pay a little more than if his shop had manufactured them. And he had to inspect the subcontracted work carefully to make sure that it measured up to So What!'s quality standards. But, by doing it this way, So What! cut down on overhead. Furthermore, Dickey could leave the manufacturing headache to the smaller subcontractors while he devoted his efforts to design and marketing on a national scale. Today, with sales running to $15 million, and employment under

100, So What! still contracts out the majority of its production.

The trend toward subcontracting is very strong in labor-intensive industries like the garment trades. It is also an indicator of a more general trend toward smaller factories. Overall, the average size (judged by employment numbers) of factories in the United States has been declining. The reason is that more and more larger companies try to shift their costly labor-intensive functions to subcontractors, while an increasing number of entrepreneurs choose subcontracting as an easy way to enter competitive fields.

1. What are the advantages of subcontracting for the company that lets out the contracts? For the subcontractor?
2. What disadvantages do you see for either party?
3. Does So What! qualify as a small business by federal standards? Why or why not?

*SOURCE:* Joel Kotkin, "Unlimited Partners," *INC*, May 1985, pp. 117–118.

# Case Critique 4-2
## Up—Then Down—and Out

Marilyn Gordon and her family opened the first videocassette rental store in Little Rock, Arkansas, in 1979. Videocassette players, now nearly as common as television sets, were a rarity. Taped movies rented at $5 a night. It was a good business for Gordon, and it was to get even better. By 1983 there were 17 million videocassette player units in the United States, and the numbers were to double by 1985 and keep on growing. Where the videotapes themselves had once been scarce, these were available in growing numbers too. Manufacturers were releasing them at the rate of 150 or more a month, or about 1,800 a year.

By 1985, however, the movie rental business had begun to change. In the beginning, the Gordon shop had been one of a kind in Little Rock. Now, other small firms were attracted to the business. The number of competitors in Little Rock moved to 7 in 1983 and jumped to 38 in 1985. Not only that, supermarkets and drug chains began offering videocassettes for rent. Rental prices for many tapes dropped to $2 a night. Some stores offered mid-week bargains as low as $1 a night.

A rental shop typically paid $50 for a new cassette. If a store were to stock all the new releases, it would have to spend as much as $100,000 a year on them. Gordon figured that a small independent like herself would need a revenue of $3.95 a tape if she were to make a profit. This was an average figure. Some tapes

rented two or three nights a week and stayed "alive" for months. Some tapes rented only occasionally and quickly became obsolete. Competitive advertising for the rental of tapes also increased. This meant that if a store were to survive, it would have to get into the advertising game too. Some stores in Little Rock budgeted as much as $2,000 a month for newspaper or radio advertising.

Some customers didn't want to pay cash. Instead, they wished to use their credit cards, which added to the cost of operations. Other customers wanted to screen tapes before renting, and this required additional help.

The squeezes got so tight in movie rentals that in 1985 Gordon chose to shut down her business in Little Rock. She sold most of her tapes to an out-of-state wholesaler. The wholesaler, in turn, sold them at reduced prices to secondary outlets like dry cleaners and trailer parks. Said Gordon, "It got to the point where it wasn't profitable anymore. The business was just breaking even, and I don't work for a breakeven." Nevertheless, larger rental shops and those that were part of a chain of national stores continued to stay in business and survive.

1. Over the years, what happened to the amount of capital required to open and operate a videocassette rental business? Why?
2. Nationally, the number of people renting movie tapes was increasing by leaps and

bounds. What happened to make the movie rental business in Little Rock less attractive—and less profitable?

3. Why do you think that some stores could offer lower prices than others and still make a profit?

4. What did Gordon mean when she said she wouldn't work for a breakeven? Why was her medium-sized business unable to compete profitably, while the larger chains and the smaller secondary outlets were able to stay in business?

SOURCE: Michael Cieply, "Despite Movie Rental Boom It's 'The End' for Many Shops," *The Wall Street Journal*, April 1985, p. 25.

# Technology IN THE WORKPLACE

## What it will take to succeed

Recent studies have concluded that at no time in history has there been a greater range of new technologies and inventions posed for commercial development. In my own industry—the automobile industry—we know that within the next decade every single function in the motor vehicle will be under computer control. Electronics will govern *everything!*

In our manufacturing facilities, we'll see a similar change: every device and function in our plants—from material handling to machining, assembly, inspection, and maintenance—will be under computer control. The power of the computer will migrate down to lower processes. We'll have sophisticated machines at all levels, not just the high-powered computer at the top and the "dumb" machines at the bottom. Machines will interact more with other machines than they will with their operators. Everyone in the industry will use a computer on a daily basis.

Employees will have to be trained to think in terms, not just of a single function but of a whole system of functions, because everything will be interconnected. More than ever before, business will need outstanding people. We will need people, not just with high grades, but also with drive, dedication, and determination. We will need people with judgment—with the ability to know the right things to do at the right time.

*Roger B. Smith, chairman of General Motors Corp., Detroit, Michigan*

SOURCE: Roger B. Smith, "What Will It Take to Be Successful During the Rest of This Century?" Spring High Tech '85 Supplement, King Features, *The Washington Post,* May 5, 1985, p. 5.

## Robot labor: $1 an hour

Some 10 to 15 million jobs are forecast to be replaced by automation, such as robots, by 1990. The reason is an economic one. By 1990, projections are that skilled human labor in goods-making industries will be approaching $25 an hour. On the other hand, robot labor costs will drop to $1 an hour. Robots—which now cost, on average, $40,000 each—will cost only $10,000 by 1990. And they will last for at least 5 years before needing replacement.

SOURCE: Senator Gary Hart, "Endangered People and the Individual Training Account," *Computers and People,* May–June 1983, p. 14.

# UNIT 2

# Management and Organization of Business

Unit 2 describes the contributions of management to the prosperity of a business and the ways in which internal relationships of jobs and people are structured for optimum effectiveness.

## CHAPTER 5

Once a business has been created, it is the quality of its management that determines its ultimate success or failure. Effective managers must perform a number of vital functions, not the least of which is decision making, in order to sustain a business in the face of ever-competitive environments. Those companies whose managers plan realistically and follow through with sound organization, direction, and control are most likely to succeed.

## CHAPTER 6

The fate of a company is also deeply affected by the productivity of the people involved and the logic and harmony of their relationships. It is critical, therefore, that the internal structure of these relationships be appropriate to a company's goals, plans, and resources, especially its human resources.

## CHAPTER 5

# The Functions That Management Performs in a Business

## Learning Objectives

*The purpose of this chapter is to define the nature and purpose of management and explain three widely accepted approaches to management, describe the four key functions that managers perform, and outline some of the qualities and skills needed by professional managers.*

*As evidence of general comprehension, after studying this chapter you should be able to:*

1. *Define management and managers in general terms.*

2. *Differentiate between management as an art and as a science.*

3. *Distinguish between the classical, behavioral, and quantitative approaches to management.*

4. *Identify and be able to apply the four functions of the management process: planning, organizing, directing, and controlling.*

5. *Explain the role of managerial decisions in a business and describe the decision-making process.*

*If your class is using SSweetco: Business Model and Activity File, see Chapter 5 in that book after you complete this chapter. There you will find exercises and activities to help you apply your learning to typical business situations.*

## 1 MANAGEMENT

Management is the process of planning, organizing, directing, and controlling the use of a firm's resources so as to attain its objectives effectively and economically.

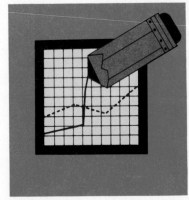

## 2 MANAGEMENT IS BOTH AN ART AND A SCIENCE

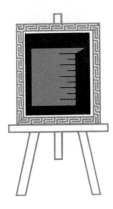

## 3 APPROACHES TO MANAGEMENT

Management may be approached from a variety of standpoints:

Classical (Rational)

Behavioral (Human Relations)

Quantitative

## 4 THE FOUR KEY FUNCTIONS OF MANAGEMENT

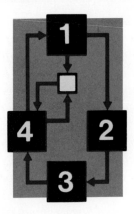

**1** Planning

☐ Objectives
☐ Strategic plans
☐ Operating plans

**2** Organizing resources, activities, and people

**3** Directing and coordinating

**4** Evaluating and controlling

## 5 MANAGERS ARE DECISION MAKERS

They choose specific plans of action from among several alternates.

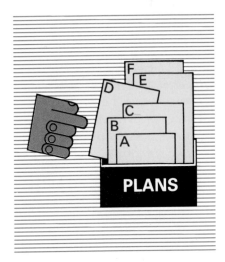

PLANS

# ILLUSTRATING WHAT MANAGEMENT IS ABOUT

The annual report of a major insurance company, CIGNA Corporation, illustrates what business management is mostly about: planning, organizing, directing, and controlling. For example, the opening pages of the report headline the corporation's priorities and basic objective: In unequivocal terms, it says, "Our primary objective is to improve the company's financial performance." That means that the company intends to make a bigger profit than the year before.

Its statement continues: "Our aim is to provide a level, quality, and price of service that will make it attractive for customers to renew existing business and to purchase additional products and services." OK, so how does CIGNA intend to accomplish this? The report then describes its plans. In part, they are: "The development of innovative products . . . enhancement of our communications systems . . . use of new technologies." Specifically, the company said it will spend "$200 million to expand telecommunications systems."

The report then outlines how the company will organize and direct its 47,000 employees toward the attainment of these goals: "We are deeply committed to the continued development of a positive working environment that enhances individual effort and encourages employees to use their talents to the fullest." Next, the report speaks of management's efforts to control corporate performance: "The company has closely examined its cost structure and has taken actions to reduce costs while maintaining the highest possible level of service. . . . We have introduced tighter underwriting standards, a smaller and more productive agency plant, and improved expense controls." Finally, CIGNA looks ahead to its long-term strategy and related objectives: "The company's long-term business direction is to expand as a premier financial services company, providing a broad range of insurance and other financial products and services to commercial customers of all sizes domestically and in selected commercial financial markets internationally." In its 1986 annual report, CIGNA was able to say, "Our consolidated operating income of $534 million established record earnings for the year."

SOURCE: 1984 and 1986 Annual Reports, CIGNA Corporation, Philadelphia.

# 1 MANAGEMENT DEFINED
*Attaining results with the help of others*

The managers of all businesses, small as well as large, must perform the same functions as the managers of CIGNA. As compared with the millions of employees everywhere who perform the actual day-to-day work of a business—working at machines and desks and sales counters—managers make a uniquely different contribution to the business. They are charged with planning, overseeing, and coordinating the work activities of other people. To succeed in business, it is essential for you to understand the difference between the work of managers and the work of nonmanagers.

The process of planning, organizing, directing, and controlling the use of a firm's resources to effectively and economically attain its objectives is called *management*. A business can be viewed as a system: a group of related parts organized to work together for some purpose. Management is the function that integrates the parts of this system and makes sure that they work together toward a desired purpose. *Administration* is another term with nearly the same meaning, though it is more often used to refer to the management of institutions, such as schools or hospitals. It may, however, also be applied to business firms, particularly to the functions of higher-level management.

## MANAGERS
*Perform common duties although exact roles differ*

**MANAGER** A person who performs the unique work of management is called a manager. That is, a *manager* plans, organizes, directs, and controls a company's business.

An important characteristic of managers is that they do their jobs by working with and through *other people*. If the manager of a furniture plant wishes to manufacture a thousand coffee tables, he or she does not go to the plant and start producing them. The manager directs other employees to do the work. When directly creating products, a manager is not performing the management function.

In many small businesses, managers work only part-time at management. They then devote the rest of their time to selling, production, or some other business function. A carpenter who heads a crew of workers for a construction company has a similar role. Half of the carpenter's time may be spent actually using the tools of the trade, while the remainder of the time may be spent telling others what to do and checking the quality of their work. The latter exemplify the true management functions.

**TYPES AND LEVELS OF MANAGEMENT** Small businesses usually have one or two managers who are responsible for the diverse management duties needed to keep the business running. Typically, the owners of a small company are the direct managers. The range of a manager's function extends from deciding to buy new stationery for $30 to deciding to buy a new store for $500,000. Large companies, on the other hand, have staffs of professional managers who specialize in particular facets of the overall operation. One person may be responsible for production, another for sales, another for advertising, and so forth. All of these functions must then be integrated and evaluated by top management. Typically, managers in larger companies are ranked according to their level

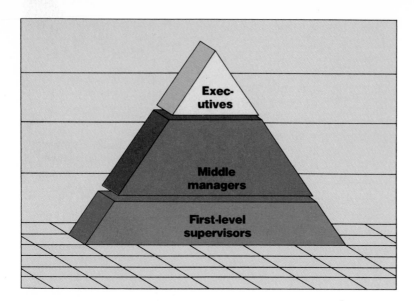

Figure 5-1 Levels of management.

within the company, as shown in Figure 5-1. Managers at the highest levels are usually called executives. They may also carry titles like president, chairperson, vice president, or general manager. Managers at the lowest levels are usually called supervisors. In between the highest and the lowest levels, managers are usually called managers, although their titles may also bear a prefix (like *marketing, sales, production,* or *accounting*) to show what type of managers they are. All managers, however, regardless of the size of the company or their level within it, try to achieve the same thing: to work effectively with people so that the business achieves its objectives.

## 2  MANAGEMENT AS ART AND SCIENCE
### *A combination of instinct and logic*

The goal of management is to integrate the diverse elements of a business—people, machinery, money, buildings, and raw materials—and direct them toward a common purpose. To do this well, a manager must combine the intuitive abilities of art with the rational methods of science.

Nearly everything a manager does is accomplished through other people. Although psychology and sociology are making progress in describing human behavior scientifically, most facets of personal interactions remain unclear. Basically, successful personal interactions in a business setting are dependent on the sensitivity of the manager. Intuition and sensitivity are also useful in the many business decisions that must be made with incomplete data. If an executive must decide whether to introduce a new product, he or she will have a variety of data and the opinions of others. Nevertheless, much, even most, of the relevant data will not be available. In order to make such decisions, experienced executives must have a feel for the market and for the behavior of consumers.

Rational and quantitative approaches are becoming ever more common and successful in business. These scientific aspects of management stress the use of data gathered and measured according to certain orderly principles. These methods are widely used not only in production and distribution but also in the people-oriented management functions, such as supervision and sales. In spite of the growing importance of these techniques, however, management will probably continue to function as both an art and a science.

# 3 APPROACHES TO MANAGEMENT
## Three prevailing schools of thought

It has been clear from the emergence of modern business that effective management will produce higher profits. Accordingly, managers have been highly motivated to understand the nature of their job and to improve their performance. From the last half of the nineteenth century to the present, three theories of management have achieved popularity. These are the classical, the behavioral, and the quantitative approaches to management. Today, management combines features of all of these in a balanced approach.

## CLASSICAL APPROACH
### Features rational analysis

The central belief of the **classical school of management** (sometimes called the traditional school) is that by applying rational analysis to the production and management functions of a business, worker and equipment productivity can be increased, resulting in higher profits. This idea was first introduced around the turn of the century by Frederick W. Taylor in the United States, and Henri Fayol in France, among others. They put forth the view that a logical study of procedures was required in order to improve the efficiency of the increasingly complex businesses that had begun to spring up at that time. Fayol divided the manager's job into specific functions in the belief that this systematic breakdown of responsibilities would promote effectiveness. Taylor was particularly interested in what is now called industrial engineering. His time-and-motion studies, as well as other job studies in the 1880s and 1890s, prepared the way for the mass production and assembly line system of today.

## BEHAVIORAL APPROACH
### Emphasizes human relations

The classical, rational approach to management tended to ignore the human element. Its originators, especially Taylor, believed that higher productivity would permit higher wages and salaries. They made little allowance, however, for other human needs. In the 1930s, there arose a new approach to management stressing the human factors in business. This approach became known as the **behavioral**, or **human relations, school.** Its adherents believed that an organization's goals could be met only by first understanding and then consciously dealing with human needs and interactions. Great emphasis was placed on human motivations and on group dynamics. In more extreme expressions of this view, managers were expected to act as psychological counselors for their workers.

# B·I·L·L·B·O·A·R·D

## ARE MANAGERS REALLY WORTH WHAT THEY ARE PAID?

**S**alaries paid to the chief executive managers of America's largest companies are staggering. In 1985, for example, they soared to unheard of levels. In broadcasting, Tom Murphy of Capital Cities made $612,000; Leonard Goldenson of ABC, $973,000; Thornton Bradshaw of RCA, $1.7 million; and Thomas Wyman of CBS, $1.18 million. Harry Gray of United Technology got $2.17 million, but David Jones of Humana (health care) got $17.9 million! Donald Trautwein of Bethlehem Steel, whose company lost money that year, was paid $502,000. Famed Lee Iacocca of Chrysler received $5.5 million as his company topped all profit records. Retailer Edward Telling of Sears, Roebuck was rewarded with $2.13 million. Not only

that, most of these men got other perquisites of office—chauffeur-driven limousines and a company plane at their disposal. Most worked long hours and made the key decisions for their companies. Interestingly, of the 785 best-

---

### Salaries paid to executives are staggering.

---

paid executives in America that year, only two were women. They were Katherine Graham of The *Washington Post* with $742,000 in compensation and Marion Sandler of Golden West Financial with $374,000. Furthermore, the

best-paid executive in a particular industry headed that industry's most profitable company only one quarter of the time.

#### QUERIES

**1.** What do you think these managers should do to justify these salaries?
**2.** How can the difference in salaries between executives in different industries be explained?
**3.** What is your reaction to the fact that so few women reach the top salary ranges? What would you suggest to increase their numbers? ■

---

SOURCE: "Who Made What at the Top in U.S. Business," *Forbes*, June 3, 1985, pp. 114–145.

# PROFILE

RONALD GOLDSBERRY grew up on the impoverished side of Wilmington, Delaware. He was the top manager at Parker Chemical Company. He's now the general manager of Ford Motor's Plastics Division. Goldsberry put himself on the managerial track by graduating fifth in a high school class of 400, then moving on to advanced degrees in chemistry and business. "My scientific training," he says, "gave me discipline. It showed me how to tackle a problem . . . thinking it through and experimenting with ideas." Associates describe him as an amiable, yet driven manager. Goldsberry, however, says he can "play hardball when necessary." He showed this characteristic during difficult negotiations with the company's labor union and in enforcing safety rules. After first proving himself as a first-rate chemist, Goldsberry took time off to get an MBA. He observes, "I saw a number of talented specialists embark in business and fail because they didn't have management expertise. I knew that if I integrated management skills with my technical

**RONALD GOLDSBERRY**

expertise, I would be a more proficient and confident business person." Now as the general manager for an important division of a major company, he can testify to his judgment. ∎

SOURCE: Derek T. Dingle, "Turning Chemicals Into Gold," *Black Enterprise*, June 1984, pp. 193–198.

## QUANTITATIVE APPROACH
*Stresses numbers and systems* ━━━━━━━━━━━━━━

In the 1960s, another emphasis in the study of management began to emerge. A *quantitative approach* stressing the use of numbers, and largely derived from systems theory, began to be applied to business management and its associated activities. *Systems theory* is a group of verbal and mathematical principles that describe how the related parts of a system may be organized. Such an arrangement permits management to predict how changes in one part will affect the other parts. This approach allows the use of statistical studies of groups of workers, consumers, or managers for making certain decisions. Mathematical models are often constructed to predict the results of alternative management actions. A new field of study, *decision sciences,* analyzes the methods by which business activities are carried out and proposes changes for increased efficiency. The difference between this kind of analysis and the classical approach is that the quantitative method emphasizes (1) the overall system in which work is being done and (2) the statistical study of groups of operations rather than a close analysis of a particular worker or job. The development of the computer and its ready availability have made the systems approach a reality for almost every kind of business, although practical limitations are ever present.

## TODAY'S APPROACH
*Toward optimization and balance* ━━━━━━━━━━━━━━

The main effort among managers today is to take the best of these approaches and use each where it will do the most good. Some call this the *contingency,* or *situational, approach.* The functional analysis of the classical school is still useful in improving efficiency and in organizing management tasks. The human relations school is influential in many personnel decisions and contributes greatly to the understanding of leadership, motivation, and other human characteristics. The quantitative tools of systems theory and operations research are only now beginning to be used confidently by large numbers of managers to improve decision making. These various approaches to management, combined with intuitive ability and with common sense and experience, help to make modern business management increasingly effective, humane, and flexible.

## 4  MANAGEMENT FUNCTIONS
*Managers have four basic responsibilities*

Managers typically perform four key functions for their businesses: (1) planning, (2) organizing and staffing, (3) directing and coordinating, and (4) evaluating and controlling. Each of these functions is continuous, and all are interrelated, as shown in Figure 5-2. The functions can be seen as a process continuously repeated in a cycle. Managers make plans to solve the problems and to take advantage of the opportunities presented to their companies. People are recruited to carry out the plans. Some kind of organization, indicating who works for whom and what each person's responsibilities are, is set up. The manager oversees the

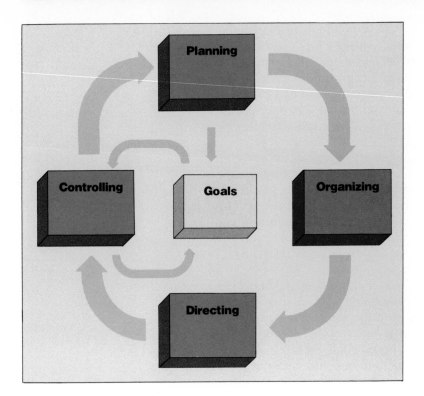

Figure 5-2 Management functions.

operation of this organization. He or she directs and coordinates the activities of those who work in it. Evaluations of how well the organization is working toward its goals partially determine plans for future operations.

These managerial functions overlap and affect one another. While one plan or group of plans is being carried out, other plans are being made. The results of one effort influence the results of others. The evaluation of results leads to control, which influences other functions.

## PLANNING
*Setting goals and establishing procedures*

Planning is the backbone of every management effort. **Planning** is a process of systematically making decisions about what will be done in the future and how it will be done. Managers must decide *what* their organization will do, *where* and *when* it will be done, *how* to do it, and *who* will do it.

**PLANNING OUTPUTS** Planning has a specific purpose along with a number of associated outputs. The primary purpose of planning is to create a plan. A **plan**, to a business manager, is an explicit statement of the business's future objectives combined with a step-by-step description of the actions that will be necessary to reach those objectives. The planning process centers on the two main requirements of this definition: clear goals and specific actions to reach them. (See Figure 5-3 for their relationships.)

The terms **goals** and **objectives** can be used interchangeably. They represent the targets, or end points, toward which business efforts are directed. At a given time, a company may have hundreds of overlapping and interconnected objectives. It may want to make a profit of $5,000 for which it must meet sales goals of $100,000 and production goals of 100 units a day and quality goals of fewer than 2 complaints for each 1,000 units shipped. Some goals are general and long-range, such as maintaining an annual corporate growth rate. Many others are very specific and detailed, such as those calling for a maintenance crew to repair six leaking valves on Tuesday.

Organization objectives exist in a hierarchy. The overall goal of a business might be to make a profit on investors' capital. Other specific goals should support this main goal—and others on the same level. The company may establish a goal of generating $25 million in revenues. This will require lower-level goals of a specified amount of production and sales during the year. Lower-level goals, such as keeping machinery in operation 80 percent of the time or making sales calls on five customers a day, help to meet the production and sales goals.

Planning helps establish policies; in fact, policies *are* a kind of plan. A *policy* is a general guide as to how managers and workers should make decisions on issues that may come up in future situations. A company may have a policy of always buying from the lowest of three bidders. The policy does not specify from whom, but it does guide the decision. Policies do not absolutely specify what decision is to be made; they direct the process, but the ultimate choice is made by the decision maker. Policies help make decisions consistent from person to person and department to department so that a difficult decision process does not have to be repeated every time there is a recurring problem.

Planning also develops the lower-level guides as to how a company operates. Workable procedures result from planning. A *procedure* is a defined way of performing an activity. A procedure, for example, might specify how incoming materials are to be checked for quality.

Rules are even more specific than procedures. A *rule* prescribes a particular action that ought to be taken—or not taken—by employees. Rules allow no room for decision making. Examples are the prohibition of personal calls on company telephones and the requirement that all incoming mail be immediately stamped with the date and time.

A *program* is another kind of operating plan. Programs combine all of the goals, methods, work assignments, budgets, and other guides and resources needed to complete a segment of work. For instance, a company might institute a program to automate its production facilities.

A *budget* is an operating plan that is expressed in concrete numbers. The most common kinds of budgets are financial. These show expected or allowable expenditures. Many other kinds are possible, however. Budgets may show working hours, materials, shipping time, or almost any other factors that can be expressed numerically. Budgets and budgeting are further discussed in Chapter 14.

**STRATEGIES AND OPERATING PLANS** Plans are generally classified according to their level of immediacy. That is, long-range plans force a company to look into the future. Shorter-range plans provide a close-up view of what should happen. Long-range plans are generally called strategies, while short-range plans are called operating plans. A *strategy* is an overall guide to courses of action to be followed to meet long-range objectives. Strategies serve as long-range guides and are determined by high-level management. A paper manufacturer might decide that it could best maintain high sales by providing faster delivery than its competitors. It might then adopt the strategy of always delivering sooner than the other paper companies.

*Operating plans* are specific planned actions needed to support strategies. They usually concentrate more on short-term goals and are often developed by lower-level managers. The paper manufacturer might make changes in its shipping room, use different shipping methods for certain orders, change package sizes or shapes, or make any number of other moves to support its strategy of quick delivery.

The key terms related to planning all bear a relationship to one another, as illustrated in Figure 5-3.

**ADVANTAGES OF PLANNING** Planning of some sort must take place; otherwise there would be chaos as everyone did his or her own thing. Planning should precede all other activity, since order and meaning depend on knowledge of the plan into which one's own efforts fit. A production shop can do nothing, for example, unless someone has decided what product to make, has ordered the materials, and has decided on the production method. Whenever there is business activity, there is some kind of planning. Planning methods differ mainly in the extent to which they are systematic, thorough, adequately long-range, and based on sound information and methods. There are important advantages to systematic planning:

■ Good planning minimizes risk and uncertainty. Although neither can be eliminated, both risk and uncertainty can be reduced by making estimates of future events and problems and by systematically making changes to improve future performance.

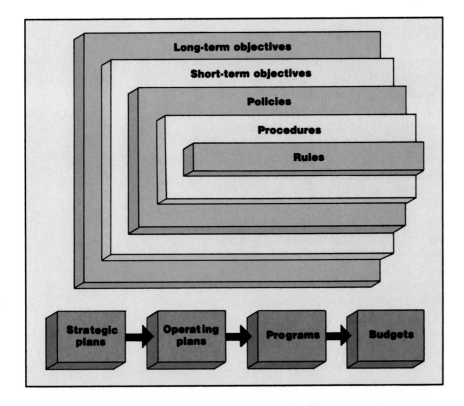

Figure 5-3 Relationships of planning terms and planning activities.

■ Planning focuses attention on goals. Successful planning forces managers to decide what an organization's goals are. It helps eliminate irrelevant activities.

■ Planning helps to make organizations operate economically. It can eliminate expensive mistakes. It allows enough time to develop the most efficient designs and work methods. It allows managers to anticipate—and take advantage of—economic and social changes.

■ Planning is essential to effective control. Plans, and the information on which they are based, provide the measure of success by which a company's actual operations may be judged.

## ORGANIZING
### *Arranging resources, activities, and people*

Plans specify the actions to be taken; the way in which these actions will be carried out is determined by the organizing function of management. **Organizing** is the process of setting up the structure and rules to control the way resources—workers, material, machinery, and money—work together to reach objectives. Organizing determines what authority each employee has, who will do what job, what methods and equipment will be used, and other specific rules which determine how the work will be done. Chapter 6 describes the organizing function of management in greater detail.

## DIRECTING
### *Putting plans and people in motion*

Outstanding plans and an excellent organization will accomplish nothing unless people are actually put to work, doing the right job and doing it correctly. **Directing** is the process of guiding and motivating people in the organization to do the work needed to accomplish the company's goals. It includes telling and showing subordinates what jobs to do and how to do them and detecting errors and seeing that they are corrected. Effective directing requires the kind of sensitivity and leadership that will motivate subordinates and fellow workers.

Another aspect of directing an organization is the coordination of effort that all good managers try to achieve. In management, **coordinating** is largely a process of assuring communication between parts of the organization—individuals, departments, and levels of management—to make sure that they are working together on appropriate efforts toward mutual goals. Business systems are so complex today that many managers must depend heavily upon computers to provide the information and communications needed for coordination. Coordination attempts to avoid duplication of effort or omission of some essential activity. It ensures that various parts of a total effort will take place at the right time and in proper sequence.

Directing requires the ability to influence other people so that they will work toward the goals of the company. It requires the ability to motivate others to do their best work. It requires the ability and willingness to communicate and to get others to communicate.

# CONTROLLING
## *Evaluating and correcting performance*

The final function of management is ***controlling***. It requires evaluating the performance of the firm and its parts and making changes to improve operations. This function is clearly related to all of the other things management does, but it is most intimately connected with planning. The evaluations that are made as part of controlling the business operation serve to determine whether plans are being carried out and objectives met. This information is, in turn, used to formulate new plans so that there is a constant interaction between the two functions.

Controlling compares actual results of operations—sales, production output, costs, product quality, and employee performance—with performance goals or standards. (See Figure 5-4.) These ***standards*** describe what will be considered desirable results. They should be established as the first step in control. Ideally, the standard should be set as part of the planning process.

In the controlling process, the results of current operations are measured in some way, quantitatively if possible. Statistical reports for product quality control, sales reports showing quantities of goods or services sold, budget variance reports showing costs of operations, and numerous other statistics on clerical activity, inventory, plant maintenance, and personnel provide a great deal of the information necessary for effective control.

This operating data is then compared with performance standards, and variances are identified. Investigation is necessary at this point. Many factors may cause variances between performance and standards. The standards themselves may be out of line and need adjustment.

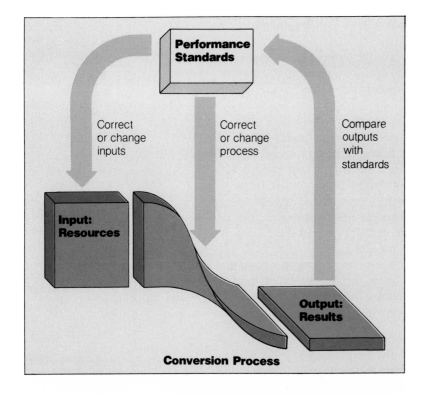

Figure 5-4 Management controlling process.

Faults in the way a company or department is organized may contribute, for example; or directing and coordinating efforts may have been inadequate. Factors in the business environment—such as an economic slump, a drop in consumer confidence, or government action—may also account for unexpected results.

After identifying the problems and contributing causes, management must take action to correct them. The control function then gives way to the planning function. Control procedures may show that product quality is slipping so that new machinery or better supervision may be needed. Costs may be too high in certain departments so that more efficient procedures or restriction of operations may be called for. Sales for a certain product may not be as high as expected so that sales commission rates may have to be increased or more advertising and promotion or product improvements may be required. All of these questions, in the typically successful business, will begin yet another turn of the continuing management cycle or system of planning, organizing, directing, and controlling.

# 5  MANAGERS ARE DECISION MAKERS
## *The courage and insight to make choices*

Almost every function that managers perform requires a decision, often many of them, dozens of times a day. Some decisions must be made on the spur of the moment, as when an employee asks whether or not to accept returned merchandise from a customer. Other decisions may be deliberated over long periods of time, as when a company must choose between erecting a new facility in a new location or remodeling an existing building. As you might conclude, a manager's ability to make decisions is an important part of what makes him or her valuable to an organization.

*Decision making* is the selection of one course of action from among a number of possible courses of action. The alternatives may be immediately obvious, or they may be purposely developed as part of the process of deciding.

Decision making is difficult and often requires a good deal of courage. The reason is that the outcome of choosing a particular course of action is not certain. It involves risk. The decision maker may be right or wrong. If a manager knew for sure that the company would make a $50 million profit by introducing a new product, the decision would be easy. However, a manager almost never knows that. The actual result of bringing out the new product may be a $5 million loss followed by the firing of the manager by the board of directors. Uncertainty about the future always exists and causes risks to decision makers.

In making a decision, managers must have expectations about the results of actions and about what will happen in the future. These expectations are always tested against actual events. The closer the expectations are to reality, the better the decisions that can be made.

**THE DECISION-MAKING PROCESS** Decision-making is not the exclusive responsibility of managers. Increasingly, employees at all levels are invited to share this process with their bosses so that the organization can benefit from each person's view of problems to be solved and actions to be taken.

Most people can make better decisions in complex situations if they approach problems systematically. Although different paths may be used to reach the same goals, a good approach to decision making involves six important steps first suggested by the ancient Greek philosopher Aristotle:

■ *Identify and define the problem.* Answer the questions, Why is a decision needed? What is the exact problem to be solved or issue to be settled?

■ *Establish objectives.* Decide what outcome is desired once the decision is made. How will the success of the chosen course of action be determined? Business objectives may be defined monetarily, by improved personnel morale, by better company reputation, and in countless other ways.

■ *Gather, classify, and study information.* Become well-informed about every possible aspect of the problem. Try to understand the relationships among different forces and factors.

■ *Develop possible alternative courses of action.* Creatively work out a number of possible courses of action that might help you reach the desired objectives.

■ *Evaluate each alternative.* Determine the advantages and disadvantages of each possible action. Decide whether returns will exceed costs, whether each action is suitable to expected business situations, and how successful each will be in meeting objectives.

■ *Make a choice.* Use the results of the evaluations to pick the best alternative.

# *Key Concepts*

**1.** Management is the process of planning, organizing, directing, and controlling the use of a business's resources so as to effectively and economically attain the business's objectives.
**2.** Effective management requires a combination of the intuition and sensitivity characteristic of art and the rationality typical of science.
**3.** Modern managers usually try to use the best features of the classical, behavioral, and quantitative approaches to management.
**4.** The major management functions are:
   **a.** Planning specific actions in order to meet future objectives
   **b.** Organizing people and other resources to accomplish the actions
   **c.** Directing members of the organization in performing their jobs
   **d.** Evaluating results and exercising control by making needed improvements
**5.** Perhaps above all else, managers are decision makers who take the major responsibility for choosing, among alternatives, the course of action a business will follow, from day to day and over the long term.

# Review Questions

1. Define, identify, or explain each of the following key terms found on the pages indicated.

*administration (p. 101)*
*behavioral (human relations) school of management (p. 103)*
*budget (p. 108)*
*classical school of management (p. 103)*
*contingency (situational) approach (p. 106)*
*controlling (p. 111)*
*coordinating (p. 110)*
*decision making (p. 112)*
*decision sciences (p. 106)*
*directing (p. 110)*
*goals (p. 107)*
*management (p. 101)*
*manager (p. 101)*
*objectives (p. 107)*
*operating plans (p. 109)*
*organizing (p. 110)*
*plan (p. 107)*
*planning (p. 107)*
*policy (p. 108)*
*procedure (p. 108)*
*program (p. 108)*
*quantitative approach (p. 106)*
*rule (p. 108)*
*standards (p. 111)*
*strategy (p. 108)*
*systems theory (p. 106)*

2. What is the main contribution of management to a business?

3. Distinguish between managers and non-managers.

4. Today's managers must be skilled at applying methods from three main schools, or approaches, to management. What are these three approaches, and what is the main emphasis of each?

5. The four basic functions of the management process are referred to as a cycle. What are these functions? Why is each important? Why are they said to occur in a cycle?

6. Why are plans so vital to a business operation?

7. How are plans, goals, and standards related?

8. What element links controlling to planning?

9. Why is it said that decision making is related to all four functions of management?

10. When a manager makes a decision, what five things must she or he consider before making a choice of the appropriate action?

# Case Critique 5-1
## When Apples try "bluebusting"

The success story of the computer age was Apple Computer, Inc. Born in a garage in the "silicon valley" of California, it took off like a rocket and made its two young founders millionaires. Both were inventive types. Steve Wozniak took his millions and set out in another direction. Steven Jobs, however, stayed with the company. His intent was to make the Apple and Macintosh computers into formidable competition for the biggest computer company of them all—IBM. IBM's trademark color is blue, so Jobs nicknamed his staff "bluebusters."

As Apple chairperson, Jobs ran a California life-style type of operation. Employees at all levels came to work in T-shirts, jeans, and running shoes. Large audio speakers blasted rock music at night and played classical music during the day. The staff was young, unorthodox, self-motivated, and enthusiastic. In the early days, this talented group of innovators could do almost nothing wrong. New product introductions were gobbled up by the public. Sales soared to more than half a billion dollars a year. But a strange thing was happening. IBM kept increasing its share of the small computer market, while Apple's share kept shrinking.

Somewhere along the line, Jobs made a critical planning decision. He would split Apple into two divisions, one chasing its personal computer market and the other trying to break into the commercial computer market. The plan ran into trouble. Jobs then went outside the company to find a business manager with greater marketing know-how than he. Jobs brought in John Sculley, a former PepsiCo (soft drink) executive as president. No sooner had Sculley arrived when the bottom began to fall out of Apple's staple, the personal computer market. Profits in both divisions shrank. Sculley discovered that the free-swinging staff could spend money faster than it came in. New product developments were not hitting their delivery deadlines. Before long, Sculley had to get tough. He announced a "period of austerity." He shut down unprofitable operations, put a freeze on hiring, and got rid of several top executives who he figured were excess baggage. Sculley stopped the fiscal bleeding, but even with massive advertising programs, he was still unable to get the company's products moving ahead again profitably. Next, he reorganized the company, merging the two divisions again along functional lines to "create a more effi-cient organization." He vowed that he would "leave no stone unturned in our effort to return to significant profitability." Finally, in a move that shocked insiders and outsiders as well, Sculley did the unthinkable. He removed chairperson Jobs from all direct responsibilities for running the company. Not a single person reported to him any longer. Jobs was very unhappy, but the company's board of directors thought it was for the best to remove Jobs from a position of influence for day-to-day operations.

1. What management functions does Steven Jobs seem to be very good at?
2. What management functions has John Sculley had to emphasize since joining Apple?
3. What shortcomings probably led to the removal of Steven Jobs from control over the company he founded?

SOURCES: Deborah Wise and Catherine Harris, "Apple's New Crusade," *Business Week*, November 25, 1984, pp. 146–156; Michael Schrage, "Apple Sets Corporate Reshuffling," *The Washington Post*, June 1, 1985, p. C-1–2.

# Case Critique 5-2
## Open a Store a Year—Forever!

When Chuck Sims—chief executive officer of Remco Enterprises, Inc., a Houston-based television, stereo, and appliance rental chain—was starting up, he had big ideas for the future. Growth was what he had in mind. His basic plan was simple: "Let's open one rental store a year—forever!" How did he decide where that store would be? "We used to say—that's a big city; let's go there. There's got to be a lot of business there; look at all those folks." Following this plan, Remco exploded from a hole in the wall to a company with 20 stores doing $3.6 million annually. The problem was that Chuck Sims no longer had a good idea of where the company was going. He asked himself, "How far into the future should we plan? Two years? Three years? Five? Maybe we should flip a coin," says Sims. "I still had only vague goals in the back of my head, nothing I ever communicated to anyone. I wanted things like a store in the country, a nice office—all that ego stuff."

1. What was wrong with Chuck Sims' planning process.
2. What was a prime missing ingredient in Sims' plans and planning process?
3. When Sims tried to decide how far he should look ahead, what kind of plan was he concerned about? What kind of a plan was the one for opening a store a year?
4. What do you think of the way in which Sims picked new store locations? How would you improve the process?

SOURCE: Lucien Rhodes, "He Learned You Can't Do It All Alone," *INC*, March 1980, p. 41.

# How Businesses Organize Internally

## Learning Objectives

*The purpose of this chapter is to define the internal organizational structure of business and the organizing process, delineate the principles of good organization, and identify the predominant organizational structures of business enterprise.*

*As evidence of general comprehension, after studying this chapter, you should be able to:*

1. *Differentiate between organizing and organization.*

2. *Distinguish between formal and informal organizations.*

3. *Explain the principle of division of labor and how tasks and activities are typically divided up into departments within a business organization.*

4. *Define authority and responsibility, and explain the importance of delegating each.*

5. *Understand and apply the four principles of good organization.*

6. *Recognize the three basic organization structures.*

*If your class is using SSweetco: Business Model and Activity File, see Chapter 6 in that book after you complete this chapter. There you will find exercises and activities to help you apply your learning to typical business situations.*

## 1 INTERNAL ORGANIZATION

It prescribes the tasks and activities to be carried out, establishes the relationship between them, and assigns each individual certain roles in order to meet planned objectives.

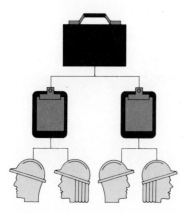

## 2 TYPES OF ORGANIZATION

Organization may be formal or informal.

## 3 DIVISION OF LABOR

The organizing process involves the division of tasks and activities among individuals and departments.

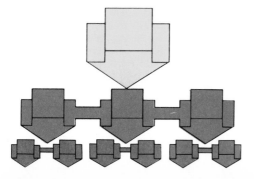

## 4 DELEGATION OF AUTHORITY

Distribution of authority along with responsibility assures that tasks and activities are carried out.

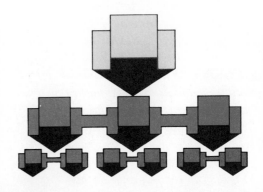

## 5 PRINCIPLES OF ORGANIZATION

An organization should be set up in accordance with well-established principles.

| | |
|---|---|
| Service of planned objectives | ✔ |
| Form to fit size and function | ✔ |
| Clearly defined duties | ✔ |
| Limited number of subordinates | ✔ |

## 6 TYPICAL ORGANIZATION STRUCTURES

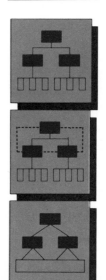

Three forms predominate.

Line organization

Line-and-staff organization

Functional organization

# A MODEL FOR BUSINESS ORGANIZATION

*For over 60 years, American companies have modeled their organizational structure after General Motors Corporation. In the early 1920s under the legendary Alfred P. Sloan, Jr., the giant corporation broke itself into several parts, each operating almost like an independent company. There was a separate division for Chevrolet, Buick, Pontiac, Oldsmobile, and Cadillac. Each division had its own manufacturing and its own sales department. The only central control from headquarters in Detroit was financial. Sloan liked to keep a tight hold on the purse strings, but otherwise he encouraged each division to compete with the others. That kind of organization was immensely successful, until the Germans and Japanese invaded the United States with small cars.*

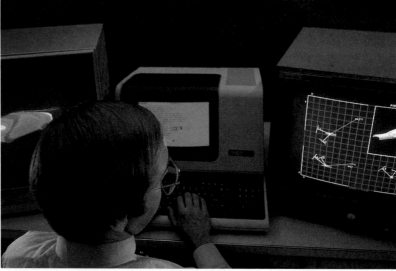

*Each of the GM divisions viewed small cars as unprofitable. Each division wanted another division to protect the corporation on the small-car front. So, for many years, GM simply did nothing. And when it did introduce the Chevy Nova, it turned out to be less than a resounding success. While GM was able to maintain its leadership in the automobile industry throughout the small-car era and into the 1980s, the management of the company was aware that there was something unsound about the way the corporation was organized. . . .*

*In 1983, GM finally changed its organizational structure. Under a new head man, Roger Smith, the company consolidated its auto divisions. Where there had been five divisions, there would now be only two. One would make large cars; the other would make small cars. The brand names might remain the same (Chevrolet, Buick, etc.), but there would now be only two sets of manufacturing and sales departments instead of five. Duplication of effort would be minimized, and central headquarters would exert stronger control.*

*The recentralization of control at General Motors proved to be only the first of several moves to change the nature and internal structure of the corporation. The company bought a high-technology firm (Hughes Aircraft) and a giant computer services company (Electronic Data Systems). Using these as a springboard, the company began to form new divisions, each with a completely different purpose from the others and from GM's traditional business. There was one important exception—the Saturn project. . . . The Saturn division was charged with developing a completely new way to design and manufacture the car of the future. . . .*

*The organizational changes at General Motors were unusual, in light of the company's history and nearly 750,000 employees. It is not unusual, however, for a company to continually seek new ways to structure its businesses so that its activities are better coordinated and more effective.*

*SOURCE:* Barry Stavre, "Dealing With the Doubters," *Forbes,* March 25, 1985, pp. 39–42.

# 1 ORGANIZATION DEFINED
## *Organizing is the process; organization is the structure*

Whenever individuals come together for a common purpose, their separate activities must be coordinated to achieve maximum effectiveness. A professional football team, for instance, is divided up into three groups—offense, defense, and special teams. The responsibility for the actions of each group rests with an assistant coach or group captain. The combined actions of all three groups are coordinated under the direction of the head coach. The same principle operates in business. The work performed in a restaurant, for example, is divided among three functions—food purchasing, food preparation, and food service. Each group of employees that performs these functions has its own supervisor or manager. The efforts of all three groups are coordinated under the direction of a general manager or owner.

The term "organization" has come to acquire a number of meanings. A group of people who meet and have some sort of formal relationship—such as a civic club, a political party, or an athletic team—may be called an organization. A business enterprise—with all its resources, personnel, equipment, and methods of production and distribution—is typically called an organization. The term "organization," however, has its most proper meaning in a managerial context when it refers to the outcome of the organizing function described in Chapter 5.

In the **organizing process,** management sets up the structure and rules that control the way a company's resources will interact to reach objectives. The resulting internal structure is the **organization.** This structure prescribes the tasks and activities to be carried out, the relationship between these activities, and the role each individual in the company will play in meeting planned objectives. Thus management is responsible for the organizing function or process and the organization itself. The organization forms the framework within which all other activities take place. A poor organization causes confusion, waste, and dissatisfaction. A good organization allows employees to do their best work in meeting company goals.

# 2 FORMAL AND INFORMAL ORGANIZATION
## *One is planned; the other occurs mainly as a matter of chance*

Organizational relationships within a business may be formal or informal. **Formal organizations** are consciously planned. They are arranged according to rational principles which are usually set down in writing. *Informal organizations* exist without specific planning. Small businesses, especially proprietorships, usually have a minimum of formal organization. Decisions about what work will be done and by whom are generally made by the owner. Large companies, however, almost always have complex and detailed formal organization plans. These describe exactly the jobs to be done. They define each employee's responsibilities and the rights and powers employees have in carrying out their work. The purpose of these formal organizations is to control the routine activities and decisions that keep the company running.

**AWARENESS OF INFORMAL ORGANIZATION** Even in large companies with comprehensive formal organization, informal relationships exist and remain important. This informal organization develops from the social likes and dislikes of employees. Much of the communication in a business takes place within this informal organization, as workers tell each other things they have heard and done. Many employees with special know-how and skills in persuasion can affect the way work is done even though they are not given the formal authority. These spheres of influence overlap the formal structure and can either reinforce it or work against it. Personal friendships and conflicts are another force in the informal organization. People will usually try to work with other people they like and will try to avoid those they dislike. These patterns can have a significant influence on the way projects are actually executed, regardless of the specifications of the formal organization.

Advocates of the behavioral school of management have shown that the way people behave in small groups largely affects the performance of the entire organization. These factors are discussed further in Chapter 16.

**EMPHASIS ON FORMAL ORGANIZATION** Although managers must be aware of the existence and influence of informal relationships in their firm, their main concern is supervising the process of formal organization. The process involves defining and allocating the work to be done and establishing the responsibilities and authority associated with each job.

# 3  ALLOCATION OF WORK
## Dividing up tasks and responsibilities

One of the manager's first tasks, when organizing, is to divide up all the activities involved in operating the business into specific jobs and departments. This is called the *division of labor.* It is based upon the premise of all formal organizations that every employee should have a clearly defined job with specific activities and duties to perform. Ideally, a particular routine of activities should always be done by the same person or job classification. All of the specific jobs are then grouped, for management purposes, into sections, departments, or divisions, or some other designation. The process of creating such groupings is called *departmentalization.*

**DEPARTMENTALIZATION** The distribution of jobs and activities into departments may be based on many factors.

---

*Action Brief*

**"HOT SITE" MANAGEMENT**

*When General Electric Company became worried about the security of its computer systems, it established a separate organization—Disaster Recovery System (DRS)—to watch over the "hot sites" within the company. That is, at each place where GE stored massive banks of information, there was a local manager to oversee it. DRS managers then got the idea that they might try to sell the excess data storage capacity to other firms as a service. GE thought about that for a while and decided to move control of its hot sites back to the company's headquarters. It said that the centralizing of this function had nothing to do with lack of cooperation between the various site managers. "Some things are just done better centrally," the company stated. But others wondered whether the company was dissatisfied because it had lost control over the hot sites when they were separately managed.*

■ *By function.* Most companies define jobs and departments by function: shipping, purchasing, accounting, selling, advertising, maintaining machinery, and so forth. Managers generally believe that it is best for a single job to lie wholly within one functional area whenever possible. Jobs within a larger department or division may be grouped by the requirement for certain skills or by the use of similar working methods. In a department responsible for maintaining the machinery in a large plant, there might be sections or individuals specializing in caring for fluid systems or making electrical repairs.

■ *By geography.* Some companies split activities along geographic lines. A large retailing company may have four sales managers performing nearly the same job in different regions of the country.

■ *By product or customer.* Departments or individual jobs may also be established to deal with particular products or to sell to special customers, such as the government.

Many large companies combine these methods of allocating work and responsibility, as shown in Figure 6-1.

## 4  DELEGATION
### *Distribution of responsibility and authority*

The division of labor creates individual jobs with particular, defined responsibilities—along with certain rights and restrictions.

**RESPONSIBILITY** The responsibilities of a job are the duties an employee is obligated to fulfill while performing the job. ***Responsibilities*** are prescribed by the activities to be performed combined with standards

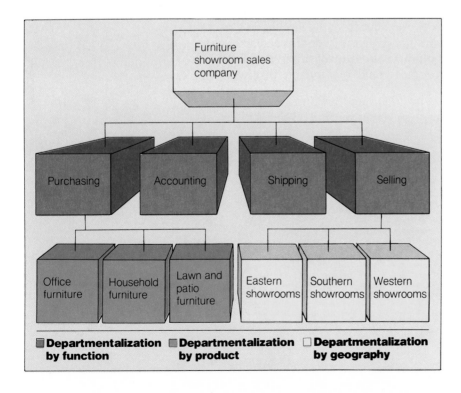

Figure 6-1 Different methods of departmentalization combined in the same company.

for correct performance. For example, a production worker may have the responsibility of installing the control panel frame on an electric stove, using the right number and size of bolts, and adequately tightening the bolts without damage to surrounding parts. An advertising manager might be responsible for supervising a staff of people and planning and carrying out advertising campaigns for a wide range of markets within a specific budget. The president of a corporation is usually responsible for the smooth operation of the entire company, for making an adequate profit now and in the future, for planning and managing expansion, and for avoiding internal developments that may harm the company.

**AUTHORITY** When accepting a job, an employee is obligated to meet its responsibilities. To do this, employees at any level must have adequate authority. *Authority* has two main aspects: (1) the right to take certain actions, such as spending company funds or sending out news releases, in the performance of a job and (2) the right to require subordinates to perform duties they are assigned. Authority allows employees to make decisions and take actions needed to carry out their jobs. Authority involves the right to commit company resources to meet goals. A production worker might have the authority to use expensive machinery, to reject faulty assemblies, or to stop operations if a malfunction or dangerous situation arises. Higher-level jobs in the organization have increased levels of authority, extending to the right to commit millions of dollars to a new product or to company expansion. It is essential that responsibility and authority be equitable, or balanced, as shown in Figure 6-2. That is, there should be neither too little nor too much authority assigned to the job to be done.

The authority to direct the work of others is basic to the operation of a formal organization. If the division if labor in a company is to function smoothly, managers must have the authority to require their subordinates to perform the work specified in the organization plan and to work according to planned standards. This does not eliminate the likelihood that subordinates will have considerable influence on the decisions and activities of their managers. But without ultimate authority of supervisors over subordinates, most organized companies could not remain that way.

**DELEGATION** Authority is said to be "delegated" within an organization. *Delegation,* in this sense, means assigning specific responsibilities

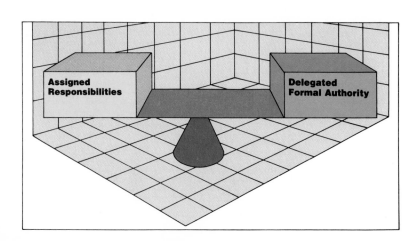

Figure 6-2 Responsibilities balanced with authority.

along with related rights and authority to individuals and groups. The chief executive officer of a corporation, with the concurrence (approval) of the board of directors, usually has broad responsibilities and the authority to make decisions and direct others in the company. It is not possible, however, for the president or chairperson to personally attend to all management issues. The chief executive delegates some tasks to others. They perform certain duties and make specific kinds of decisions. They, in turn, will delegate responsibilities and related authority to others, down to the lowest level of workers in the firm. The belief that clear-cut lines of authority should be established to connect the top to the bottom of the organization is called the *scalar principle.*

One other aspect of the delegation of authority and responsibility deserves consideration. A manager may delegate responsibility to a subordinate—and grant him or her sufficient authority to carry it out—but the manager never escapes the *accountability* for the proper completion of the task that has been delegated. If things go wrong, the superior is the one who is held to be at fault, not the person to whom the task was delegated.

# 5 PRINCIPLES OF ORGANIZATION
*Four guidelines help to create a sound internal structure*

Every business firm has its unique organizational requirements. There are, however, certain principles that help to establish a sound internal structure. By following these principles, management creates an organization that is planned, suitable to its purpose, well-defined, and as uncomplicated as possible.

## ORGANIZATION FOLLOWS PLANNING
*Structuring the organization to meet company objectives*

The organization process should always follow the planning process. In the management cycle described in Chapter 5, organization is described as one of the steps used to meet objectives set in the planning process. An important measure of the effectiveness of an organization is the extent to which it allows and helps its members to work for the goals of the company. Therefore, a clear definition of the goals is essential to setting up a good organization. Planning should also provide the performance standards and evaluation methods needed to make improvements in the organization. The close relationship between planning and organization also implies that an organization must be flexible. Through the planning process, new objectives will be generated as problems and opportunities arise. An organization must have the capacity to adjust itself to these new objectives. A manager who imposes a completely rigid organization on a company's operations is not making the best use of the company's resources.

*Action Brief*

**I'M IN CHARGE NOW!**

When Josephine Richardson—president of a 125-employee security-guard service in California—went out of town for a couple of weeks on business, she left her second in command in charge. When she came back, Richardson realized that the No. 2 person had turned the company upside down in her absence. "He tried to give the impression that he was totally in charge. He alienated the employees until it was like 'mutiny on the ship,'" said Richardson. She vowed this would never happen again. In the future she would choose her second in command carefully. She didn't want an imitation of herself. But she did want to delegate major responsibility to a person "who does not compete with the boss or make decisions that disrupt the flow of business." It seems to be a fact, when delegating, that the next in charge often has to learn to take a backseat and forgo glory and attention. Says one expert on the subject, "A strong right hand shouldn't be your clone, but it should be someone who complements and supports your management style when you're in and out of the office."

## STRUCTURE FITS SIZE AND FUNCTION
*Determining whether a complex or simple structure is most suitable*

The organization must deliberately be made suitable to the size and function of a company. A proprietorship with two or three employees requires little formal organization. A large manufacturing firm with thousands of workers cannot operate at all without a formal and sophisticated organization plan. Imposing a sophisticated organization on a small company, however, is inefficient. The functions a company performs must also partly determine the best kind of organization. Manufacturing firms need complex structures to manage the intricacies of production, while a department store needs a different structure to generate income by stocking and selling goods. Companies with many unskilled workers need supervisory patterns different from those of firms with highly trained professional or technical personnel.

## DUTIES AND RELATIONSHIPS ARE CLEARLY DEFINED AND SPECIFIED
*Clarifying and unifying the chain of command*

The flow of delegated responsibility and authority and channels of communication should take place in a carefully specified **chain of command.** The chain of command is directly related to the scalar principle, which establishes who reports to whom from the bottom to the top of the organization. This requires that every job be clearly positioned in the organizational structure with a specified superior and subordinates, if there are any. As a consequence, every person will know exactly what his or her duties are as well as have the authority to perform them. Additionally, the principle of **unity of command** advises that every employee should have only one superior. Such unity avoids conflicting commands and instructions and confusing divisions of authority.

As another general rule, it makes sense to keep the number of levels of authority to a minimum. Unnecessarily long chains of command slow down the communications and the decision-making processes.

## NUMBER OF SUBORDINATES IS LIMITED
*Restricting the span of control to promote effective supervision and coordination*

The **span of control** (also called the span of management), or the number of employees directly supervised by one person, must be restricted. Supervision mainly involves assigning work, stimulating motivation, locating errors and inadequate work, and seeing that corrections are made. Effective supervision requires involvement with subordinates; this limits the number of direct subordinates a supervisor should be assigned. Six to eight direct subordinates is a frequently mentioned maximum. Actually, the number of subordinates will depend on the type of work they do, the amount of authority given to them, and other factors. In certain kinds of activities, like an automobile assembly line for example, 50 employees under a single supervisor is not unusual.

***CENTRALIZATION VERSUS DECENTRALIZATION*** Organizations can also vary in the extent to which authority is distributed down the chain of command to middle and lower levels of management. A ***centralized organization*** is one in which almost all of the authority is concentrated in a few positions at the top. In a company with centralized organization, nearly all important operating decisions will be made by top management. The main task of those below is to carry out their decisions efficiently. A ***decentralized organization*** delegates much more authority to the managers who are closer to actual operations. First-level supervisors and department heads have maximum responsibility and authority to make decisions concerning their work. Top management devotes its attention to general company goals and policies and to monitoring and handling exceptional conditions that arise.

Centralized organizations usually give managers a limited but tighter span of control, with each manager having fewer subordinates. This often adds additional—and cumbersome—levels of authority, which create a taller organizational structure as shown in Figure 6-3. Managers in decentralized organizations often have a larger span of control (creating a flatter organizational structure) since subordinates are given more authority and freedom to act and may receive less direct supervision from above.

## 6 TYPICAL ORGANIZATIONAL STRUCTURES
### Three types predominate

In the long history of business management, three major kinds of internal structures have evolved: line, line-and-staff, and functional. Most companies use one or more of these forms today. All of these structures are ways of delegating authority and assigning responsibility to achieve a manageable division of labor. Patterns of delegation differ in each case.

Managers view some positions in a company as line positions and others as staff positions. Line positions are the direct chain of command

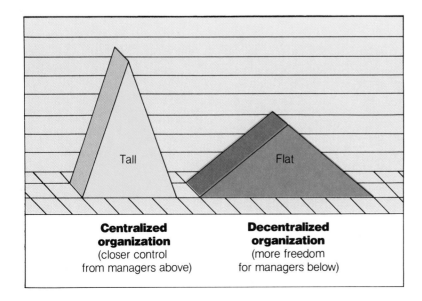

Centralized organization
(closer control from managers above)

Decentralized organization
(more freedom for managers below)

Figure 6-3 Differences in organization structures according to degree of centralization.

that carries out the company's business. Production, sales, financing, and all of the other jobs directly related to generating income for the company are usually considered line positions. Positions that assist the line employees with specialized abilities and activities—such as an attorney, a market researcher, and a public relations specialist—are called staff positions. The different functions of the positions result in differences in their authority relationships. Line positions have a direct supervisor-subordinate relationship; the supervisor is authorized to direct the work of the subordinate, and the subordinate is obliged to accept the direction. Staff positions usually have an advisory relationship with other managers and workers in the company. As advisers, they may offer expert guidance and analysis for any level of management but their recommendations do not usually have the force of authority.

## LINE ORGANIZATION
*Simple and direct*

An internal business structure in which every employee is a member of a direct chain of command from the top executives down through the levels of management is called a *line organization,* illustrated in Figure 6-4. In this structure, every person is directly responsible to a single supervisor who is superior in the organization. It is called a line organization because authority flows in a direct line from the top of the organization to any individual worker at any level. A production worker may report directly to a supervisor, the supervisor to a plant superintendent, the plant superintendent to a production manager, the production manager to a general manager, and so on. Each department or division is relatively independent of other departments or divisions and concentrates on its own role.

The line organization has a distinct advantage in its simplicity; every employee can understand the organization and know where he or she stands. Line organizations afford clear and distinct distribution of author-

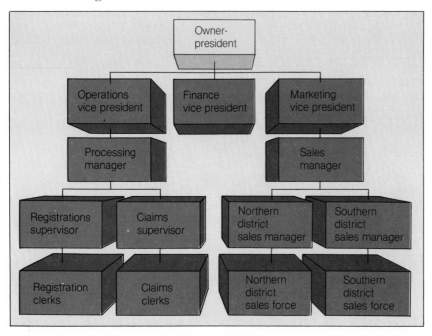

Figure 6-4 Example of basic line organization in an insurance company.

ity, and allow every employee to answer directly to only one supervisor. The direct supervisor-subordinate relationship makes it easier to maintain discipline and quality of work. The direct line relationship also aids faster decision making and makes individuals more accountable for their actions.

A great disadvantage of the line organization is that it is sometimes not capable of handling the complex management and technical needs of a large, modern company. For this reason, relatively "pure" examples of this structure are generally found in smaller companies. Another disadvantage is that there are often insufficient formal means for communication and coordination between departments. Also, since managers are responsible for all of the work of their subordinates, they are often burdened with decisions about details.

## LINE-AND-STAFF ORGANIZATION
*Adds specialists*

As the complexity and size of a company increase, managers usually find it necessary to modify the line organization by adding staff specialists to handle certain specific duties. This is called *line-and-staff organization* and is illustrated in Figure 6-5. It is the most common internal structure today, especially for large companies. The staff specialists perform technical services and provide expert guidance to line managers. They may also assume part of the planning and communicating functions of line managers. The staff specialists advise line managers but do not normally have direct authority over the positions they advise.

The great advantage of the line-and-staff organization is that it allows specialists to handle highly technical or complex functions while the company retains many of the benefits of line organization. Many typical staff functions—purchasing, personnel, data processing, and engineering and design work, for example—can be performed by experts in these areas while the company continues to maintain the clear chain of responsibility and authority of a line organization.

The disadvantage of a line-and-staff organization is that conflict often arises between line positions and staff positions. Line managers and workers may consider staff specialists as expensive extra baggage. Staff workers may resent managers who do not take their advice. Staff workers may try to exert authority over line operations. The cost of staff specialists increases the company's overhead for management as well. Line personnel may come to rely too heavily on the services of staff experts. Thus decisiveness may be sacrificed and authority diluted.

Line employees and staff employees may be organized in many combinations. For example, a company may set up separate divisions to handle different products, different customers, or different geographic regions. Each division may be organized as a line-and-staff structure, and the overall organization of the company may also reflect this structure.

## FUNCTIONAL ORGANIZATION
*Specialization dominates*

An alternative way to organize a business is to assign managers the responsibility for all activities and decisions in certain defined functional areas of operations. This is called *functional organization,* and is illus-

# B·I·L·L·B·O·A·R·D

## A BETTER WAY TO MAKE A PIN

Our economic growth has been based on specialization. A prime example of production specialization is the division of labor, which is the very foundation of the factory system.

Adam Smith describes in *The Wealth of Nations*, published in 1776, a British pin factory:

*One man draws out the wire, another straightens it, a third cuts it, a fourth points it, a fifth grinds it at the top for receiving the head; to make the head requires two or three distinct operations; to put it on is a peculiar business, to whiten the pins is another; it is even a trade by itself to put them into the paper; and the important business of making a pin is, in this manner, divided into about eighteen distinct operations. . . . I have seen a small manufactory of this kind where ten men only were employed. . . . Those ten persons . . . could make . . . upwards of forty-eight thousand pins in a day. . . . But if they had all wrought (worked) separately and independently . . . they certainly could not each of them have made twenty, perhaps not one pin in a day.*

---

### Division of labor is the very foundation of the factory system.

---

The goal of establishing the internal structure of a business is to create a smoothly coordinated division of effort such as this. The work of every part of the organization—management, sales, production, warehousing, and all the rest—is broken down into subordinated units. The many units are then connected with a flow of materials and information.

### QUERIES

**1.** Do you think that the principle of division of labor has really increased the productivity of individuals? of groups of individuals?
**2.** What are some of the disadvantages you can think of that might be associated with the division of labor?
**3.** In what ways might a computer system improve the effectiveness of a company using the principle of the division of labor? ∎

---

SOURCE: Adam Smith, *The Wealth of Nations*, Modern Library, New York, pp. 3–4.

# PROFILE

**D**ONNA KNOX has been called "Dallas's 30-Second Manager." She manages the Dallas Apparel Mart with its 4,000 tenants and half a million visitors each year. To get the job done, she relies on a dedicated staff, a strong pair of legs, and a walkie-talkie. She has a reputation for never being in one place in the immense Mart for more than 30 seconds. As executive vice president of the Mart (a job she acquired at age 34), Knox is responsible for leasing the various showrooms, overseeing building operations and security, registration of buyers, and food and beverage sales.

Knox describes her career path as "unconventional." One of seven children, she got used to work early in her life. She worked her way through college at a wide range of jobs, from cooking to selling. She tried teaching school, then got into her own barbecue restaurant business. This didn't pan out, but it led Knox into catering, and ultimately into selling showroom space for the Mart. Thereafter, she moved up quickly to her present position, quadrupling her salary in 6 years. ■

**DONNA KNOX**

SOURCE: Jacqueline Giambanco, "Dallas's 30-Second Manager," *Working Woman*, October 1985, pp. 143–145.

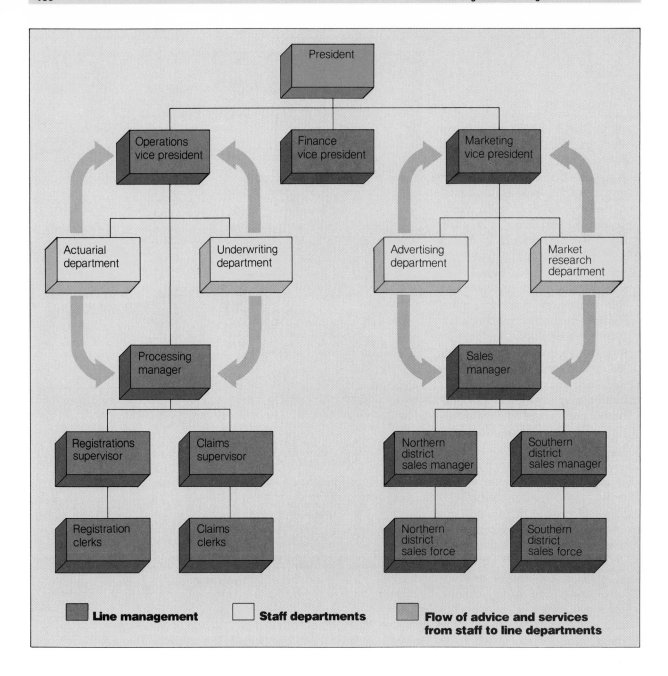

Figure 6-5 Example of the addition of staff departments to form a line-and-staff organization structure.

trated in Figure 6-6. This structure, for example, might have five managers supervising the workers who perform distinctly different functions in a bank, as shown in the figure. This form has the advantage of allowing managers and employees to specialize in one particular skill or area of operation. The functional organization is most commonly found in medium-sized organizations, where no divisionalization (see below) has taken place.

The functional organization is typically merged with the line and staff organization structure, as illustrated in Figure 6-5. In that figure, "operations" and "marketing" are line functions at the executive level of the organization. Similarly, "processing" and "sales" are line functions at

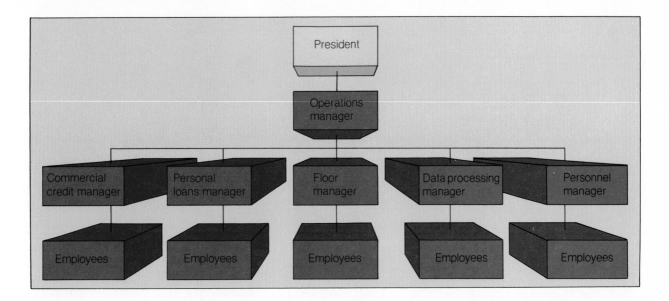

the middle-manager level. At the supervisory level, "registration" and "claims" are line functions reporting up the line to the processing manager.

Figure 6-6 Example of functional organization in a bank.

## DIVISIONAL ORGANIZATIONS

*Focus on products, customers, or geography*

As businesses grow, they often find it effective to divide up their organizations ever further. In so doing, they create a ***divisional organization.*** They may do so in three ways. They may do so by *product,* as in Figure 6-7. In this example, a firm that manufactures tractors for farmers, road graders for construction contractors, and lawn mowers for home use might "divisionalize" in order to make and sell each major product in its

Figure 6-7 Example of product or divisional organization structure for a manufacturing company.

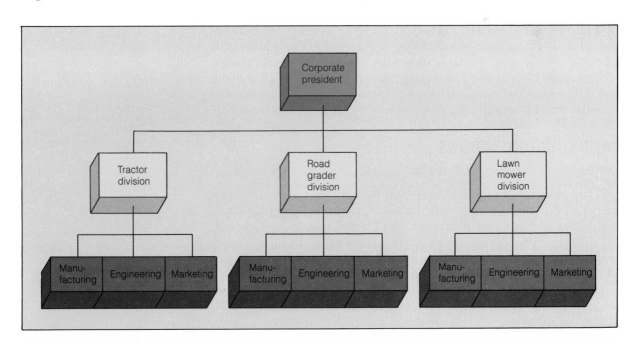

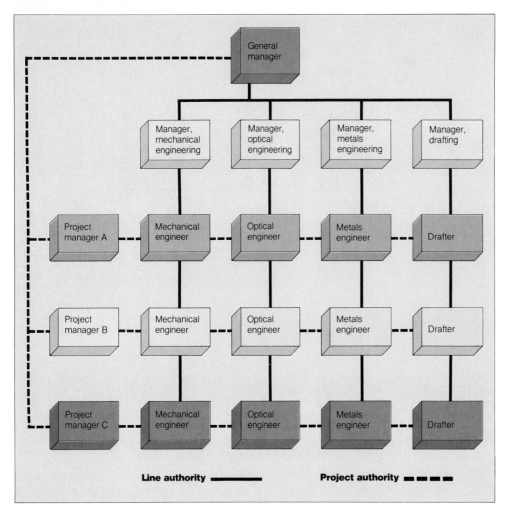

Line authority ━━━━━        Project authority ▬ ▬ ▬ ▬

product line. Note that under each division head, this organization is essentially a "functional" one, with manufacturing, engineering, and marketing functions shown. Following the same concept, a company may divide itself according to *customers* served (agricultural, industrial, and consumer) or by *geography* (with a west coast, central, and eastern division), with each division again having its own separate functions to serve it. In actual practice, many large companies combine functional and divisional structures in a variety of ways to suit their particular needs.

Figure 6-8 Example of a matrix organization.

## MATRIX ORGANIZATIONS
*Dual authority for special projects* ━━━━━━━

A unique kind of organization is used by firms that must manage a number of one-time projects—such as road, dam, or bridge building, construction of large aircraft or space exploration vehicles, or research investigations. These firms use a **matrix organization**, which allows a project manager to exercise temporary authority over a number of specialists who also must report to different line managers for supervision in their specialties. This enables specialists to be assigned to projects where they are needed, as shown in Figure 6-8. It has the disadvantage, however, of asking an employee to report to two different bosses.

The matrix form of organization, or some modification of it, is becoming increasingly popular. This is especially true in high-technology companies where there is great dependence of all the major functions (like production, operations, and marketing) upon information and services that can be provided by specialized departments. When this occurs, employees of the specialized departments are temporarily assigned to task forces associated with a particular major function or to project committees.

## COMMITTEES
*Combine varied viewpoints and expertise*

When a group of people are assigned to discuss, or to deal directly with, a well-defined matter, this group is called a **committee.** A committee's role may be strictly advisory, as when a cost reduction committee makes suggestions to a production manager as to where costs might best be reduced. Or a committee may be given power to act directly, as when a bank's loan committee decides whether or not to grant a large loan to a credit applicant. Committees have the advantage of bringing together many viewpoints to bear on a problem. They also have the disadvantage of tending to arrive at ineffective compromises so as to satisfy everyone.

# *Key Concepts*

1. The internal structure of a business determines the relationships between a company's activities and personnel, and it controls how they interact to achieve planned objectives.

2. Organization may be formal, consciously planned according to rational principles, or informal, occurring on the basis of personal influence and social likes and dislikes.

3. The first task in the organizing process is to divide all of the company's internal activities into defined jobs and to group these jobs in appropriate departments.

4. Every job in a business has certain duties or responsibilities that employees are obligated to perform. Authority, the right to make specific kinds of decisions and to direct the work of subordinates, is delegated to employees to allow them to meet their responsibilities.

5. Certain principles help managers establish organizations that are well-planned, suitable to

their purpose, well-defined, and as simple as possible:

   **a.** The organization should be structured to meet company objectives.

   **b.** Structure should fit the size and function of a company.

   **c.** Duties and relationships should be clearly defined and specified.

   **d.** The number of subordinates should be limited.

6. The most common organizational structures are line, line-and-staff, and functional. A company may also be separated into divisions according to product line, customer markets, or geography. A matrix form of organization is especially useful for handling one-of-a-kind projects. Committees, too, are useful for pooling the expertise of people who work in different departments.

# *Review Questions*

1. Define, identify, or explain each of the following key terms or phrases, found on the pages indicated.

>*accountability (p. 123)*
>*authority (p. 122)*
>*centralized organization (p. 125)*
>*chain of command (p. 124)*
>*committee (p. 133)*
>*decentralized organization (p. 125)*
>*delegation (p. 122)*
>*departmentalization (p. 120)*
>*division of labor (p. 120)*
>*divisional organization (p. 131)*
>*formal organization (p. 119)*
>*functional organization (p. 127)*
>*informal organization (p. 120)*
>*line-and-staff organization (p. 127)*
>*line organization (p. 126)*
>*matrix organization (p. 132)*
>*organization (p. 119)*
>*organizing process (p. 119)*
>*responsibility (p. 121)*
>*scalar principle (p. 123)*

>*span of control (p. 124)*
>*unity of command (p. 124)*

2. What is meant by the internal organization of a business?

3. How does formal organization differ from informal organization?

4. One of the first concerns of a manager, when establishing an organization, is dividing up a company's activities into specific jobs and departments. What are some of the bases on which work activities can be divided?

5. What is authority, and why must it be delegated within an organization?

6. What are some of the principles of organization mentioned in the chapter?

7. What is the difference between a centralized and a decentralized organization?

8. What is the main advantage of a line-and-staff organization over a line organization?

9. What is the main disadvantage of a functional organization?

10. From what two bosses is someone in a matrix organization likely to receive orders?

# *Case Critique 6-1*
## *Loosening the Reins*

When Tom Barrea, chief executive officer, set up an organizational structure for his company, he did it all by the book. The Thomas National Group would provide data processing services to other companies for a fee. The company would be relatively small, with about 100 employees. As chairperson, Tom had three vice presidents reporting to him. Each was in charge of a separate function—marketing, programming, and data processing. In turn, each of these vice presidents had a number of specialized managers reporting to them. Under this system, when someone down the line had a problem, the employee would bring it to his or her manager for an answer. If it couldn't be resolved at that point, the problem would be relayed up the line to the next level for solution.

Problems began, however, when this vertical system kept the company's relatively small staff of people from communicating with one another across functions. The company was also adding new services to be offered to its customers. Under the original organization, there would have to be a specialist for the new service in each department. Gradually, communications in the company broke down. Problems took forever to be solved. Management was increasingly indecisive.

Finally, Barrea changed the company's organizational structure. Instead of a narrow, vertical pattern, he created a broader, horizontal one. Now, in addition to the three functional vice presidents reporting to him, he has an executive vice president to coordinate administrative affairs and three vice presidents who head up the new special services. Each vice president has been given greater authority to deal with problems in his or her area. Barrea is in constant touch with all seven vice presidents. He encourages communications between departments. And even the lowest-ranking person in the organization has only a level or two to get to the top.

1. What is the name of the reporting system that Barrea originally set up for his company?
2. What was the form of departmentalization originally chosen? What were its drawbacks?
3. What new form of departmentalization was added to the old structure? Is the new organization structure more centralized or decentralized than before?

SOURCE: Thomas Barrea, "I Unchained My Chain of Command," *INC.*, October 1981, p. 129.

# Case Critique 6-2
## A Three-way Stretch

What would be simpler than making and selling weighing devices such as industrial scales? That was what Henry F. Henderson, president of H. F. Henderson Industries, thought when he struck out on his own after years as a manager for one of the nation's largest scale companies. Henderson soon found out.

Initially, Henderson marketed his products through manufacturer's representatives (reps), people who sell a number of different manufacturers' products on commission. As the business got more complex, Henderson found that he had to develop his own sales force.

As the business grew, Henderson found the company continuing to bid on, and get, various high-tech projects—including design and construction of special robots—many from the government. Almost all of these were one-of-a kind projects; the company performed them under contract, and when the project was completed, it was rarely repeated. To handle this kind of work, Henderson had to create a number of specialized departments in the company, such as software development, electrical engineering, mechanical engineering, and applications engineering. Selected members of these specialty departments work together in project groups under a project leader. The project leader has the responsibility for coordinating the work of the specialists.

The company now has 75 employees and revenues of more than $10 million a year. It is so effective that it was named *Black Enterprise* of the year in 1984. To keep the company's diverse activities on target, Henderson had to construct an internal organizational structure that was clear-cut yet offered great flexibility. The organizational structure is shown in Figure 6-9.

1. Henderson Industries combines the advantages of more than one basic organizational structure. Which particular structure, however, dominates?
2. Which parts of the organization work mainly on projects? What kind of organizational structure does that indicate, even though it isn't drawn on the organization chart?

SOURCE: Udayan Gupta, "B. E. Company of the Year: Henderson Industries," *Black Enterprise*, June 1984, pp. 106–114.

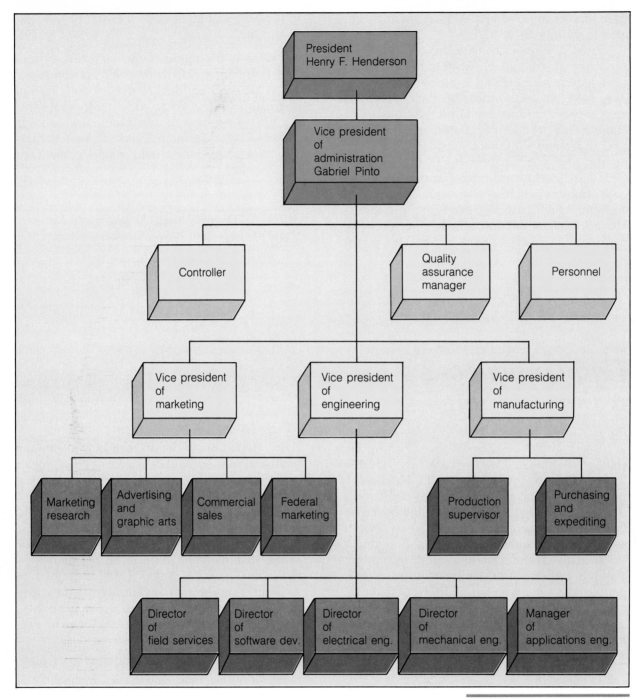

Figure 6-9 H.F. Henderson
Industries Organizational Chart

## New roommates in the executive suite

Managers everywhere are discovering that work once left to their secretaries and administrative assistants is often better done by themselves—on personal computers. Executives as highly placed as the president of Westinghouse Electric Corp. and a senior vice president for General Electric Company regularly use their personal computers as word processors for writing letters and memorandums to their staffs. "It doesn't take much more than junior high school typing capability," says Raymond Marshall, GE's head of technology operations, and he can send instant messages via the company's electronic mail system to his staff in Europe and Asia. Of course, that isn't the major reason that Marshall and other managers sit down at the keyboard of their personal computers. They use them because they can quickly calculate the effect on hundreds of financial alternatives. Using a typical "decision support" system, a sales manager, for example, can estimate the probable effect on profits of a change in sales commissions. An executive at R. J. Reynolds Industries can, within minutes, use a personal computer to coordinate production schedules for a variety of tobacco products. Not only that, the chart-drawing capabilities of the computer help to prepare graphics that make it easier for managers to communicate their ideas to their staffs.

SOURCE: Mike Lewis, "The New Roommates in Executive Suites," *Nation's Business,* March 1984, p. 37.

## Better than flipping a coin

Faced with a decision of which 20 or 30 of a possible 1,000 products to market, a marketing manager, using an off-the-shelf computer program, can get an immediate answer as to which are the best choices. Or take a production manager trying to choose among several manufacturing sites. The manager will figure in such variables as land costs, labor quality, transportation accessibility, etc., and ask the computer program to make the decision. Such computer systems are called "decision support" programs. The manager must establish beforehand what critical factors must be weighed. These factors compose a checklist of expenses and possible revenues and profits that can be matched against time. Once these criteria have been plugged into the computer, the program displays the best possible advice to the manager. What's the secret? The program has built into it the expertise of dozens of management consultants. When managers ask the questions, their criteria are matched against the experience and judgment of the consultants to calculate the best possible alternative.

SOURCE: Ellen Benoit, "Deus Ex Machina," *Forbes,* May 6, 1985, p. 100.

# UNIT 3

# *Marketing of Products and Services*

Unit 3 explains the vital importance of marketing to business and outlines the marketing mix. It describes how products and services are developed and the distribution system that places them in their markets. It also explains various ways in which goods and services are promoted, priced, and sold.

## CHAPTER 7

Marketing performs the functions that are concerned with the development of products that consumers want and need, and their distribution and promotion to consumers. Marketing's effectiveness depends upon a knowledge of markets and consumer motivations and the ability to divide markets into segments.

## CHAPTER 8

The distribution of goods to consumers is accomplished through a vast and complex network of marketing channels. A variety of intermediaries, mainly wholesalers and retailers, are employed by most producers for this purpose.

## CHAPTER 9

Marketing promotion combines the elements of personal selling, advertising, and sales promotion. These are essentially communication functions used to inform potential consumers and to get them to buy.

## CHAPTER 10

Sellers price their goods for a profit, but the free market itself exerts tremendous force in its balancing of supply and demand. A variety of pricing strategies and techniques are used by marketers to attract consumers.

CLIENT: Kentucky Fried Chicken Corp.
PRODUCT: Taste/Good Meal
TITLE: "Don Quijote"

LENGTH: 30 Seconds
COMM'L. NO.: KFC-85-30TV #06
DATE: March 1985

DON QUIJOTE: Sancho, ¿qué ves?

Sancho, What do you see?

SANCHO: ¡Molinos, Don Quijote!

Windmills, Don Quijote!

DON QUIJOTE: ¡No idiota, gigantes que vienen a atacarnos!

Nay mistaken one, they're giants coming to attack!

SANCHO: Mi Señor, necesitará una buena comida antes de la batalla.

Then my Master will need a good meal before battle.

JINGLE: ¿A dónde vas a ir?

Where are you gonna get it?

DON QUIJOTE: ¡Una comida que inspire mi espada!

A meal to inspire my sword!

JINGLE: ¿A dónde vas a ir?

Where are you gonna get it?

DON QUIJOTE: ¡Ah Kentucky Fried Chicken!... ¡el pollo soñado!...

Ah, Kentucky Fried Chicken!...the chicken I've been dreaming of...

SANCHO: Mmmmm....!

DON QUIJOTE: ¡Una comida digna de Don Quijote de la Mancha!

A meal worthy of Don Quijote de la Mancha.

SANCHO: ¿Mancha? Si no ha quedao ni "mancha" mi Señor.

Mancha? There isn't even a "mancha" (trace) left for my Master...

JINGLE: Kentucky Fried Chicken ¡El Pollo de Pollos!

Kentucky Fried Chicken The Chicken of Chickens!

CHAPTER
7

# Products, Services, and Markets

## Learning Objectives

*The purpose of this chapter is to explain the marketing concept, the marketing mix, and the functions of marketing as well as to distinguish among markets, identify consumer buying motives, and describe the processes of product development and market segmentation.*

*As evidence of general comprehension, after studying this chapter, you should be able to:*

1.  *Define the marketing concept.*

2.  *Identify the four elements of the marketing mix.*

3.  *Recognize the functions performed in managing the marketing process.*

4.  *Define a market and differentiate between the consumer market and the industrial market.*

5.  *Recognize some of the main consumer buying motives.*

6.  *Explain the product development process, recognize the stages in a product life cycle, and understand the importance of branding and packaging in product differentiation.*

7.  *Explain demography and market segmentation and the contributions of marketing research.*

*If your class is using SSweetco: Business Model and Activity File, see Chapter 7 in that book after you complete this chapter. There you will find exercises, activities, and cases to help you apply your learning to typical business situations.*

140

## 1 THE MARKETING CONCEPT

emphasizes profits derived from customer satisfaction.

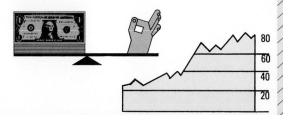

## 2 THE MARKETING MIX

has four main ingredients:

 Products or services planned to satisfy consumer needs.

Placement in the market for distribution.

 Promotion for sale and consumption.

Pricing according to consumer habits and purchasing power.

## 3 MARKETING FUNCTIONS

are many and varied.

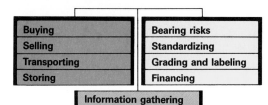

| Buying | Bearing risks |
| Selling | Standardizing |
| Transporting | Grading and labeling |
| Storing | Financing |
| Information gathering | |

## 4 TWO MARKETS PREDOMINATE

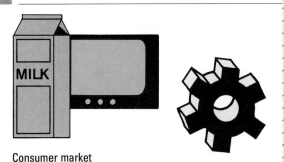

Consumer market

and Industrial market

## 5 CHARACTERISTICS OF THE CONSUMER MARKET

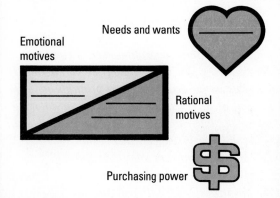

Emotional motives

Needs and wants

Rational motives

Purchasing power

## 6 PRODUCT PLANNING

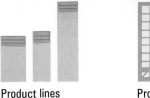

Product lines

Product life cycles

Brand names

Packaging

## 7 MARKET SELECTION

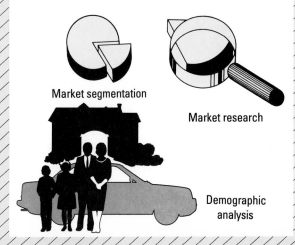

Market segmentation

Market research

Demographic analysis

# SUCCESS FOR A NEW PRODUCT

*It's a reasonably sure bet that 5,000 new products or services will be offered to the public this year. Only a handful will be original. Probably fewer than 500 will show a profit—ever. Fewer than 50 will stay on the market more than 10 years. Good marketing management helps a business to improve these odds on the acceptance and profitability of its products. Take the Aziza Polishing Pen, a felt pen-like device for coloring fingernails. The idea was born in the laboratories of the Prince Matchabelli division of Chesebrough-*

*Ponds. Two scientists were aware that many women wanted to color their fingernails but were generally dissatisfied with the traditional nail polishes because the process takes so long. A prototype of the new way to color nails eventually worked its way out of the research department and into the marketing department, which was enthusiastic about the pen's marketing potential. Instead of rushing the product to market, however, the marketers first spent $500,000 on marketing research. They did so to make certain whether or not enough women would really appreciate the value of this technique and, in fact, buy the pen in sufficient quantities and at a price to make it profitable for Prince Matchabelli.*

*The research was favorable. The product was produced in large quantities and was placed by Matchabelli's salespeople in the warehouses of a network of independent distributors who resell drugs and cosmetics to retailers. A major advertising campaign was launched in magazines and on television. Within weeks the product was displayed on cosmetic counters all over the country. Its attractive package featured the Aziza's unique qualities along with a price tag that matched what most buyers thought made the pen a good value. The product was an instant success in its marketplace. Its success can be attributed to the care and skill with which the company attended all the elements in the marketing process.*

## 1 THE MARKETING CONCEPT

*The marketing concept builds profits from corporate concern for consumer needs and interests*

In the modern world, marketing is a complex process involving a long chain of activities. It wasn't always this way. Two hundred years ago, it was common for every producer of goods to know his or her customers personally and to hand deliver products or wait for people to come into the workshop where the goods were made. Today, the practice of making products by hand for local customers has all but disappeared. It has been replaced by an extremely complex marketing system that moves goods and services of all types to diverse markets all over the country and the world.

Producers today are usually separated from consumers by a complicated chain of brokers, wholesalers, agents, and retail stores. Producers must make an effort to find out what kind of products and services consumers want and to create and offer these for sale. They also must make efforts—through advertising and other means—to inform consumers about the goods and services that are available. Product designs, distribution, advertising, and pricing all depend on knowing markets.

Successful products satisfy a consumer's needs or wants, or both. The rash of products and services aimed at helping Americans get, or remain thin, is an example. Thompson Medical Co. of New York had been selling an appetite depressant (Dexatrim) in drugstores for years, with some success. In the early 1980s, the company became increasingly aware that their market was broadening to include people who were as much concerned with health and fitness as they were with their weight. Accordingly, the company introduced Slim-Fast, a meal replacement product that could induce weight loss while providing proper nutrients. It wasn't a new idea. Products like Metrecal had been around for years. The big difference was that the public was now "ready" for meal replacements. Slim-Fast was introduced in 1980 and, by 1985, its sales were over $100 million a year, more than the company's original product.

**A CHANGE IN EMPHASIS** Early in this century most companies emphasized production efficiency as the means of creating and increasing profits. This may be called the "production concept." At the time, the manufacturing capabilities of industry were so limited, compared with the large demand, that any useful goods produced could usually be sold with little difficulty. As the years went by, however, production capacities increased faster than the population. Managers came to see that positive sales efforts would be needed if production and profits were to be maintained at a high level. Companies began to use sophisticated and expensive advertising methods and employed staffs of trained salespeople. This is typical of the "selling concept."

In the last 35 years, business has been influenced by the **marketing concept.** This concept rests on the belief that profits can be maximized by concentrating on the needs and wants of consumers and by creating products for which there is a known demand. One result of this belief is that more companies are using research to find out what kinds of goods and services consumers want before developing new products. The marketing concept has not eliminated earlier concerns with production efficiency or with selling, but has added to them. Most managers today believe that the evaluation of consumer desires for goods and services is as necessary to long-term success as are high-quality, low-cost production and persuasive selling techniques.

**MARKETING CREATES UTILITY** The marketing concept is consistent with the underlying proposition of American business (as explained in Chapter 1) wherein a business must create utility for its customers. Marketing creates utility of *form* (by shaping the product or service to conform to consumer demand), of *time* (the product or service is there when needed), of *place* (it is on hand conveniently), and of *possession* (title or ownership is arranged for transfer from seller to buyer). In the marketing process, product development is concerned with the utility of form; product distribution provides utility of time and place; product or service advertising, sales, and pricing promote the utility of possession.

## 2   MARKETING ELEMENTS

*Marketing requires a mix of four p's: product development, placement, promotion, and pricing*

Marketing is a major function of business management. **Marketing** is the process of (1) planning products or services that will satisfy specific wants and needs of consumers, (2) placing these products or services in the marketplace for distribution, (3) promoting the sale and use of products or services to consumers, and (4) pricing these products or services so that they will suit the buying habits and purchasing power of potential customers.

The four elements, or activities, of the marketing process are popularly referred to as the **marketing mix.** Take a moment to look more closely at each element. *Product planning* concentrates on learning which goods and services consumers want and then designing (or "developing") products to meet these desires. *Product placement* (or "distribution") involves decisions about warehousing and transportation and whether to sell directly to the public or through various chains of intermediaries, such as retailers. *Product promotion* is a vital function that includes not only personal selling but also advertising and direct-sales promotion, such as free samples, point-of-purchase displays, and discount coupons. *Product pricing* requires a critical decision since it ultimately determines whether the product will sell (or be bought) and, if so, whether it will be profitable.

All of these functions must be pursued on a continuing basis to improve sales. Marketing operations are especially apparent when new products are introduced. One of the best examples of this was the successful marketing of L'eggs pantyhose. The product was made of modern synthetic materials and was designed to sell at prices below those prevailing in the women's hosiery market. The lower price, combined with distinctive and convenient packaging (the hose are sold in a plastic egg-shaped container) and with an innovative distribution method, resulted in an immediately successful product. The distribution, in particular, contributed to success. L'eggs are sold from display racks in supermarkets, drugstores, and other outlets not specializing in women's apparel. The marketers created a large demand by making their product a convenience item for many women. The product, price, and distribution system were reinforced by an advertising campaign designed to create recognition of the unusual name and motivate impulse buying.

In the case of L'eggs, the marketers were able to create the right marketing mix, the right combination of product type, price, distribution, and promotion to tap strong consumer demand. Their efforts demonstrate the modern approach to management which uses the marketing concept to increase company profits.

# 3  THE FUNCTIONS OF MARKETING
*Marketing requires the performance of services beyond those of simple buying and selling*

While marketing focuses on the buying and selling exchange, its success usually depends upon offering or providing a number of related services. These services represent values that often are hidden from the general public. Without them, however, the utility that consumers expect would not materialize. Accordingly, marketing managers must be prepared to create and supervise a wide range of specific activities. The relative importance of each may vary with different companies, but nearly every business firm is concerned with buying, selling, transporting, storing, risk-bearing, standardizing, grading and labeling, financing, and gathering and using information. (See Figure 7-1.)

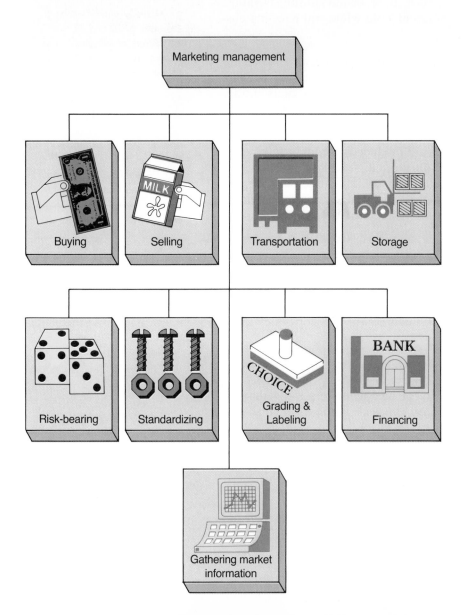

Figure 7-1 Functions of marketing management.

**BUYING** Buying is an extremely critical concern for wholesale and retail companies. The success of these firms is very directly dependent on their purchasing agents' ability to anticipate consumer demand for particular goods. They must be able to locate the best sources of supply for goods and to negotiate favorable terms in price and quality.

**SELLING** Selling is often seen as the core of the marketing function. All the other marketing activities ultimately aim at selling goods and services to produce income. Personal selling, sales promotion, advertising, demonstrations, and displays all contribute to this goal, as will be seen in Chapter 9.

**TRANSPORTING** Goods cannot be sold without transporting them to the point of sale and then to the ultimate consumer. Careful management of the transportation of products can bring significant savings in the cost of selling them. The vast network of transportation systems in the United States enables many firms to centralize their manufacturing facilities. This helps them to achieve economies of scale while still reaching customers in remote areas.

**STORING** Storing is required to keep goods until they are made available to consumers. Some goods, such as agricultural produce, must be stored because they are produced seasonally. Many wholesalers and retailers store goods near final buyers in order to avoid delays caused by transporting from the point of manufacture.

**RISK-BEARING** Whenever goods are produced or bought to be sold, there is the risk that they cannot be sold profitably. Risk-bearing, then, is an inevitable function in any marketing activity. Efficient management, including careful market and cost analysis, will reduce but not eliminate this risk. Other risks, such as fire and theft, can be reduced through insurance.

**STANDARDIZING** The modern system of producing goods in one location to be sold to buyers in a wide area requires that products be standardized. This way, customers know what to expect from a product wherever they buy it. Safety razors, for instances, have their heads all made the same size so that when customers buy razor blades, they know that the blades will fit.

**GRADING AND LABELING** Grading and labeling have a similar purpose, allowing buyers to know the quality of goods without inspecting them. Meat that is graded "U.S. Choice" by government inspectors will have nearly the same quality and characteristics regardless of which producer it comes from.

**FINANCING** Most companies must pay for the production or purchase of goods before they receive payment from customers. This requires financing. Money is often borrowed to pay for raw materials, transportation, or inventory. The loans are then repaid from income when the goods are resold to consumers. This system of financing production and inventory stabilizes the market, making goods available on a steadier basis.

**GATHERING MARKET INFORMATION** This is important to the management of all the other marketing activities. It may involve (1) sophisti-

## Action Brief

### AN "AVERAGE" CUSTOMER

Customers for a particular kind of product or service often project similar characteristics. Tenneco Inc. wanted to know more about an average customer who stops at their Food Mart chain of gasoline stations. Here's what their customer looked like:

■ Usually male, between the ages of 26 and 35.
■ Stops at the same store once or twice a week, usually in the early evening.
■ Purchases an average of $9 worth of gasoline and $2 worth of merchandise.
■ Lives either under 1 mile or over 5 miles away from the store.
■ Convenience is the main reason for buying, although low price may have attracted him originally.

cated research on the desires and buying habits of consumers, (2) automated systems giving frequent sales and inventory information, or (3) informal information gathering through contact with suppliers, dealers, and buyers. Without some means of gathering information, other marketing decisions cannot be made with any confidence.

# 4 MARKET CLASSIFICATIONS
## Markets are where the buyers are

Effective marketing focuses on an understanding of markets. A **market** has been defined as a means by which buyers and sellers exchange goods at a price they agree upon. Marketers concentrate on buyers: people with needs and wants that will cause them to buy products. To constitute a market, the people must have money to spend on goods and services and the willingness to spend it. To a marketing manager with a product to sell, the market also includes other sellers with products that compete for the satisfaction of the same consumer demands.

Such explanations make a market seem very abstract. To most businesses, however, markets are very specific and concrete. If not, they try to make them that way. Your local beauty salon can probably pinpoint its market very clearly, even to the point of describing exactly the kinds of persons, their living places, incomes, and preferences in styling. Nationwide distributors of frozen foods can do the same. Birdseye will count noses in its market by the millions, but will still try to nail down how many in cities and states and what kinds of potential customers according to purchasing habits and life-styles. Manufacturers of electric motors, too, who sell to appliance manufacturers, will also try to identify their markets in terms of specific customers by size, location, and purchasing volume.

**TWO MAJOR CLASSIFICATIONS** In the broadest sense, there are only two kinds of markets for goods and services: the consumer market and the industrial market. It has been popular to designate these markets by the kinds of goods sold to them. **Consumer goods** are bought and used by individuals and families without further processing. **Industrial goods** are bought by other businesses or institutions for use in making other products or for providing services. Both of these markets have their own characteristics. Both are shaped and influenced by the ability and willingness of their members to spend money to satisfy their wants and needs.

**OTHER OVERLAPPING MARKETS** The two major market designations do not tell the whole story. There are other important markets to which consumer and industrial goods are sold. (See Figure 7-2 for their relationship.) These markets are:

■ *Commercial market.* This market may be thought of as all the wholesale distributors and retailers who buy industrial and consumer goods for resale either to other businesses or directly to the consumer. A producer of bottled soft drinks may think of restaurants and vendors as a "commercial market," factory complexes as an "industrial market," and supermarkets as the "consumer market."

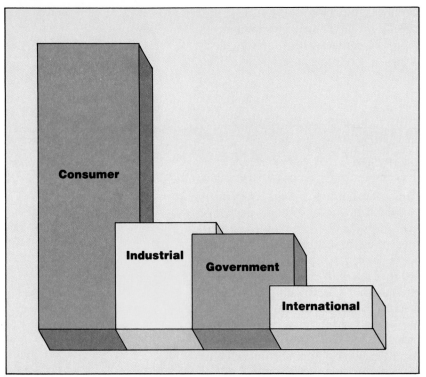

Figure 7-2 Size relationships of major U.S. markets.

■ *Institutional market.* These are the thousands of hospitals, churches, and educational institutions. Producers of industrial goods, like air compressors, who sell to hospitals would think of that market as the "institutional" one. A firm that offers consumer services, like rug cleaning, to a church might describe that segment of the market as "institutional."

■ *International market.* Goods and services (both industrial and consumer) that are exported to other countries make up a sizable market, nearly $400 billion annually.

■ *Government market.* The federal, state, and local governments spend nearly $800 billion each year on all manner of goods from water pipes and police officers' uniforms to military supplies. The federal government's portion runs to about 40 percent of the total.

As you can see, when it comes down to specific products and particular markets, business people are likely to use more descriptive terms for their market than the two broader designations.

**POPULATION CENTERS AS MARKETS** As a convenience to both industrial and consumer markets, the federal government also identifies certain large concentrations of population as markets. If an urban area has a city or county with 50,000 people or more, it is designated as a ***standard metropolitan statistical area (SMSA).*** There are 323 SMSAs in the United States and Puerto Rico. Almost all large companies and many smaller ones plan their marketing programs around these large markets.

# CLASSIFICATIONS OF CONSUMER GOODS
*Consumer goods fall into three classes*

Consumer goods are bought by individuals or families to satisfy their own needs and desires. Goods and services for consumers include thousands of different products manufactured and distributed by numerous firms. These products are divided into three types based on the buying habits of consumers: convenience, shopping, and specialty goods. (See Figure 7-3.)

**CONVENIENCE GOODS** *Convenience goods* include products and services that are selected because they are readily available, rather than because they compare favorably with other products. Consumers are familiar with these products and are usually willing to accept substitutes or pay a slightly higher price rather than go to another store. Consumers usually buy convenience goods at retail outlets near their homes. Unit prices are generally low. Products that are used frequently in the home are convenience goods: orange juice, milk, razor blades, cleaning products, nonprescription drugs, and flashlight batteries, for example.

**SHOPPING GOODS** The most important characteristic of *shopping goods* is that consumers not only buy them regularly but consider it worthwhile to devote effort to comparing prices, brands, and dependability. Shopping goods are almost always more expensive items than convenience goods, and buyers are often willing to do considerable shopping around before making a selection. Some examples of shopping goods are furniture, most home appliances, apparel, television sets, and automobiles.

**SPECIALTY GOODS** *Specialty goods* have unique characteristics, not shared by competing goods, that make consumers willing to exert considerable effort to locate and buy them. Buyers normally will not accept a substitute for a specialty product; they want a particular brand and no other. Consumers are familiar with the distinctive qualities of different brands of specialty goods, sometimes even to the extent of

Figure 7-3 Classifications of consumer goods puts them into three kinds of stores.

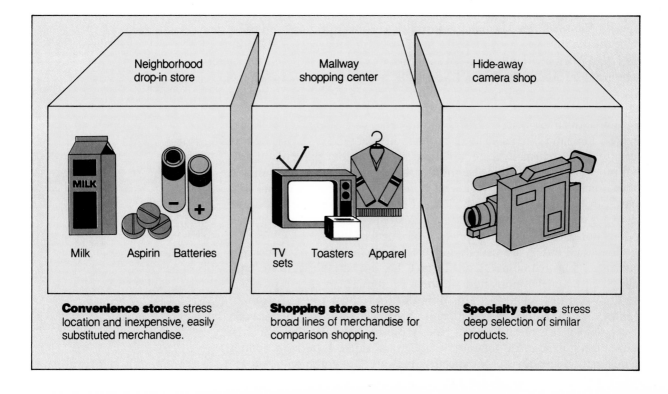

Neighborhood drop-in store

Mallway shopping center

Hide-away camera shop

Milk   Aspirin   Batteries

TV sets   Toasters   Apparel

**Convenience stores** stress location and inexpensive, easily substituted merchandise.

**Shopping stores** stress broad lines of merchandise for comparison shopping.

**Specialty stores** stress deep selection of similar products.

having sophisticated technical knowledge of them. This is often true of purchasers of stereophonic sound equipment, for instance. Many specialty goods have relatively high unit prices, but this is not always true. Many people will not accept substitutes for a particular brand of soft drink or chewing gum. For them, these products are specialty goods. Other more typical examples are automobiles, clothing, cameras, sports equipment, and some kinds of home furnishings.

The automobile is an example of a product that is both a shopping and a specialty good. Different shoppers may view products in different ways. Most people buy television sets as shopping goods; whenever they want to buy a new set, they will consider a number of competitors and then make a selection. Some people, however, consider a television set a specialty item and would be willing to drive to another town, if necessary, to buy a particular brand. Services vary in the same way. Many people consider having the oil changed in their car a convenience service and will have it done at the nearest gas station even at a slightly higher price. Others will compare the prices and services of a number of shops.

## THE INDUSTRIAL MARKET

*Industrial buyers: fewer in number, but they usually make bigger, more rational purchases*

Industrial goods are used to produce other goods or services or are consumed in the operations of a business or other organization. **Raw materials** are unprocessed natural resources—such as the products sold by mines, farms, and forestry operations—that are bought by other businesses for use in their manufacturing processes. Many companies process raw materials into intermediate materials that are usable by consumers only after further processing. Sheet metal for heating ducts and leather for shoes are two examples. The manufacture of **component parts** for sale to a manufacturer is a major industry. Sales of this sort are said to be made to the "original equipment manufacturer or market," or simply, the OEM market. Many companies produce machinery and equipment to be used by other companies. Expendable supplies, such as paper and typewriter ribbons, are bought for use in daily operations. All of these are examples of goods sold to the industrial market.

The industrial market differs in a number of ways from the consumer market. Demand fluctuates more in the industrial market. This is partly because there are usually fewer potential customers for a particular industrial product and partly because industrial buyers are more aware of and more quickly influenced by general economic changes. Industrial purchases are made to meet clearly defined needs; goods are rarely bought when not needed. Thus, demand for industrial goods is relatively stable; it does not vary much as the price of products changes.

Industrial orders are usually much larger than individual consumer purchases. This, combined with the fact that industrial buyers are typically more rationally motivated and better informed about the products they buy, creates selling patterns different from those in the consumer market. An exchange of considerable technical information between buyer and seller is often needed. Sales representatives for the industrial market often have broad technical training and skills. Extended periods of negotiation and revision of specifications are also common.

# 5 CHARACTERISTICS OF THE CONSUMER MARKET
## *How and why individuals and families buy*

People who purchase goods and services for their own or their family's use make up the consumer market. Numerous factors affect what people buy, in what quantities, and where. The most important of these are the nature of individual needs, buying habits, motivation, and purchasing power. These correspond almost directly to the needs, willingness to buy, and ability to buy that characterize every market.

**PRIMARY NEEDS AND SELECTIVE SATISFACTION** Every consumer requires the necessities of life: food, clothing, shelter, and some medical care. These are called *primary needs.* Consumers also want other kinds of goods and services based on their interests, goals, and individual characteristics. When they buy goods and services for this reason, this is called *selective purchasing.* The wish to buy a piece of jewelry, an antique pistol, a rare coin, or a trip to the Bahamas does not result from primary needs for sustenance and protection. Instead, it stems from higher-level needs such as esteem, mental stimulation, or physical attractiveness. Such needs operate in people of all economic classes. The Kaiser automobile, which had a very short market life, is a good example. As George Romney, an auto company executive explained: "The Henry J. (Kaiser) failed because they stripped it to make a car for the poor people, and the poor people didn't want a car made for poor people."

Since everyone must meet primary needs, marketing efforts in this area generally focus on inducing consumers to buy one particular brand rather than another. For the consumer, there is no choice as to whether to buy food or not, but there is a huge variety of competing brands and stores. Marketing efforts for selective purchases try to make the product itself attractive—and then call attention to the attributes of a particular brand or supplier.

**PARTICULAR PRODUCTS FOR THREE COMPELLING REASONS** Consumer motives for choosing to buy certain products and rejecting others may be rational or emotional. *Rational motives* involve reasoned judgments about the desirability of a product based on its value or quality compared with competing products. Choices based on cost—buying lower-cost goods of similar quality or buying at sales—usually result from rational motives. Buying one brand of lawn mower rather than another because of known facts about its good service record, or its ease of starting, is rational. Rational motives lead consumers to make a purchase only if the product is needed for a specific practical use.

*Emotional motives* spring from feelings. The emotions usually motivate purchases of products bought to provide physical pleasure: foods that taste good but have little nutritive value, phonograph records, art, and furniture that is expensive but attractive to look at. Consumers may be motivated to buy a certain kind of car or house or clothing because they feel these goods will boost their status or self-esteem. Pride in ownership is a powerful motive. The desire for personal attractiveness to others, socially and sexually, affects the selection of hundreds of products, from cosmetics to yachts. Fear—of financial loss, physical harm, or ill health—is a common motive for buying insurance, health care aids, safety devices, and similar products.

Consumers are influenced as to *where* they buy by **patronage motives.** These result from a complex of rational and emotional factors that make a particular store appear more desirable than another. The services offered by a store—such as delivery, extended credit, refunds, and exchanges—may make it more attractive to customers. A convenient location, adequate parking, ease of access, protection from weather, and other similar factors may make one store seem more desirable than another. A reputation for providing high-quality merchandise or service is a powerful draw for many customers.

Buying a particular product at a particular store usually results from a combination of rational, emotional, and patronage motives. Reasons for buying sports equipment, for instance, may be largely emotional, but usually also include some rational concern for fitness and health. Selecting a particular set of golf clubs almost always includes judgments about quality versus cost combined with emotional factors such as the desire to emulate expert golfers.

**THE WHEREWITHAL TO BUY** Besides the desire to buy, consumers must have the ability to buy before they can be considered part of a market. This ability to buy goods and services is called **purchasing power.** Purchasing power for some products depends on disposable income and for other products on discretionary income. **Disposable income** has already been defined (Chapter 2) as the amount of money left after federal, state, and local taxes and other fixed deductions have been withheld, it is the same as take-home pay. Disposable income has a direct effect on the type of housing, clothes, food, and other necessities a family can afford. Producers of those kinds of goods judge consumer purchasing power by disposable income. **Discretionary income** is the amount of money that is left after the basic needs of life have been obtained. It determines purchasing power for the thousands of products that may or may not be bought, at the consumer's discretion. Purchases made with discretionary income have received great attention from business in the last 50 years.

*Action Brief*

### RENEWED LIFE FOR COLOR TV

*Just when the experts had figured that the lifecycle of color TV sets had reached maturity, if not the decline, sales took off like it was spring again. Sales of color TV sets were flat during the 1970s. Then, with the introduction of videocassette recorders (VCRs), which use the TV set as a monitor, color TV sales rose sharply, from about 14,000 units a year to more than 24,000. Other factors contributed to the renewed life in color TV. Innovations in technology found a way for TV sets to produce sharper and more colorful pictures than before. The cable alternative to broadcasting delivered pictures with less distortion. VCRs deliver their pictures without commercial interference too. Add stereo sound, and the TV monitor has become the focal component in what is now a home entertainment system.*

## 6  PRODUCT PLANNING AND DEVELOPMENT
*Businesses must create and maintain products and services that are right for their markets*

The most difficult challenge to a business is to find or develop products or services that fit their markets. Even if a product is successfully launched, it takes constant vigilance to keep a product in tune with the preferences of the buyers in that market. This requires an ability: to predict customer demand and changes in it; to recognize the shifts in customer need for, or interest in, your product as it ages; and to make certain that a customer can tell—and prefer—the difference between your product or service and its competitors.

# PRODUCT DEVELOPMENT

*An innovative process dependent upon knowledge of the market to be served and the people in it*

Most people, when asked to describe a product, tell how big or heavy or fast it is. That is the wrong way to create a new product or to make an old one better. The most important characteristics of a product or service is the *function* it performs. Above all, people who buy products want to know what the product will do—*for them*. So, for marketers, a **product** can be described as anything that satisfies a person's (or company's or institution's or organization's) wants or needs. Using that definition, a product may be a person (like a popular entertainer), a place (like Hawaii, to visit), a physical object (like an alarm clock), an idea (like a course on self-awareness), a service (like hair fashioning), a government program, a charity, and so on. Buyers and potential buyers in any market place a value on each product that is made available to them. Even if they do so subconsciously, they always ask three sets of questions:

**1.** How good will that product be for me? How well will it fit my needs? What benefits will I derive from it?

**2.** What are the drawbacks of this product? Will it wear out quickly, require extra effort on my part, or cost too much?

**3.** Can I get a better deal from another product like it or one that might substitute for it?

In addition to fitting a product to the market, planners must also think about how well a new product fits the company's existing product line. A **product line** is a group of similar or related products that can be made using the existing production facilities and the same distribution and promotion methods. If a new product can be made on the same machinery that makes the existing products, can be sold by the same salespeople, and can be handled by the present advertisements, then it might be considered a good extension of the product line. As the market demand for more nutritious cereals increased, Kellogg's, for example, extended its line of Corn Flakes, Rice Krispies, and All-Bran by adding products like Cracklin Oat Bran, Fruitful Bran, and Rice Krispies Bars.

# PREDICTING DEMAND

*Needs must be strong and markets large enough*

If a company is in the business of selling shoes and it develops a serviceable, inexpensive disposable travel slipper, the new product must still clear two hurdles. First, there must be a strong need among travelers for such a convenience, and there may not be. There must also be enough travelers within reach of the company's distribution system—in its market—to make the new product sell in sufficient quantities. There are many ways of making estimates of needs and market size. The U.S. Department of Commerce and other government agencies have libraries of information about numbers of people, where they live, what they do, and how much money they have to spend. Other sources, like associations of similar companies in the same industry, can provide more specific information about market size and buying habits. Independent survey organizations often provide even greater detail. The chart in Figure 7-4 was prepared by one such company to indicate the extent of unfilled wants of a number of specific products.

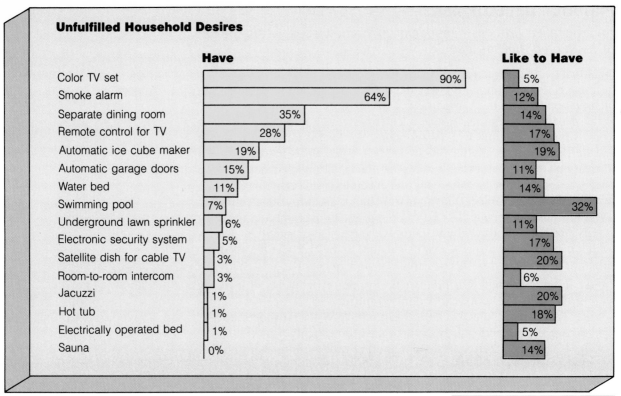

**Unfulfilled Household Desires**

| | Have | Like to Have |
|---|---|---|
| Color TV set | 90% | 5% |
| Smoke alarm | 64% | 12% |
| Separate dining room | 35% | 14% |
| Remote control for TV | 28% | 17% |
| Automatic ice cube maker | 19% | 19% |
| Automatic garage doors | 15% | 11% |
| Water bed | 11% | 14% |
| Swimming pool | 7% | 32% |
| Underground lawn sprinkler | 6% | 11% |
| Electronic security system | 5% | 17% |
| Satellite dish for cable TV | 3% | 20% |
| Room-to-room intercom | 3% | 6% |
| Jacuzzi | 1% | 20% |
| Hot tub | 1% | 18% |
| Electrically operated bed | 1% | 5% |
| Sauna | 0% | 14% |

In many markets, there are many competitors trying to sell similar products to the same people or the same industrial buyers. In such cases, the market begins to look like a pie of limited size over which each particular product must fight for a share. A number of companies, for instance, compete for their share of the soft drink market in the United States, as shown in Figure 7-5A. Typically, each one wants a larger share. Those who get a larger share of the market do so at the expense of other

Figure 7-4 Examples of unfilled consumer demand. Source: "Roper's America," prepared by the Roper Organization, *Ad Forum,* November 1984, p. 27.

Figure 7-5 How soft drink companies compete for markets.

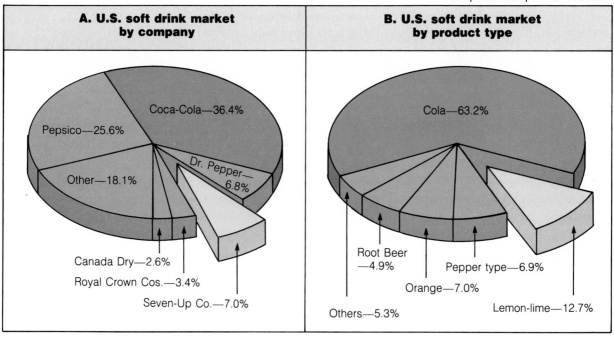

**A. U.S. soft drink market by company**

Coca-Cola—36.4%
Pepsico—25.6%
Other—18.1%
Dr. Pepper—6.8%
Canada Dry—2.6%
Royal Crown Cos.—3.4%
Seven-Up Co.—7.0%

**B. U.S. soft drink market by product type**

Cola—63.2%
Root Beer—4.9%
Orange—7.0%
Pepper type—6.9%
Lemon-lime—12.7%
Others—5.3%

companies that get a smaller share. When markets are limited in size, or are growing at a very slow rate, new product developments are likely to focus on ways to cut up the market differently, as shown in Figure 7-5B. A company that is unable to successfully introduce products in the cola segment, like Seven-Up's producer, may try to make the lemon-lime market segment larger. Or it may try introducing new products in the root beer and orange segments, where competition is less formidable.

**STRIVING FOR MARKET SHARE** Market share has increasingly become a dominant concern in marketing. A major study released in 1985 demonstrated the vital importance of a firm's having a large market share. Analysis of corporate earnings showed that unless a product was ranked fourth or higher in sales in its market, the chances of its making money were very slim. When a product has a large share of its market, a company's advertising goes much further. General Motors, for example, spends far less per auto sold than does Ford or Chrysler or American Motors. The result is that businesses tend to put their money and marketing efforts behind products that are in the lead. They are hesitant about introducing products into markets where other products are well established and have significant market shares.

*SOURCE:* Dick Stevenson, "One, Two, Three or Out: Brand Rank Is Everything," *Ad Forum*, February 1985, pp. 22–27.

# A CONCERN FOR AGING PRODUCTS
*Four phases of a product's life cycle*

The main reason companies must continually develop new products is because products have a life cycle. The four stages in the **product life cycle** are introduction, growth, maturity, and decline. (Their effects on sales and profits are shown in Figure 7-6.)

When a product is first introduced, there will have been no sales yet and there will be an accumulated loss resulting from development costs.

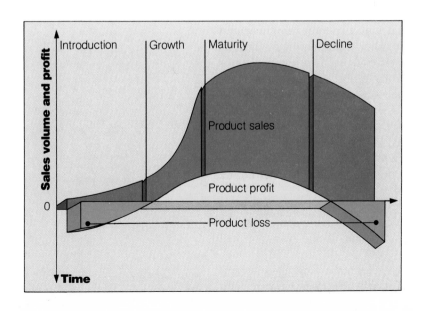

Figure 7-6 Stages in a product life cycle.

Initial promotion efforts must expose the product to consumers and publicize its unique features and value. If the introduction is successful and if there is a potential demand, the product will enter a period of growth, when sales increase, sometimes at a very rapid rate. It is generally during this phase that a product first becomes profitable. At this stage, other companies recognize the success of the product. They begin to compete by producing their own version of it. Maturity follows with sales growth reaching a plateau as the market demand becomes satisfied. Profits may remain satisfactory at the beginning of this stage, but they often dwindle as the increasing efforts of competitors begin to be felt. At some point in the maturity stage or even earlier, a new product aimed at the same market will probably have been introduced and the original product will enter the decline stage. Profits will fall rapidly because of intense compensation, and eventually sales will fall to a low level as the product is succeeded by a new and better one.

Sometimes, of course, a product or service simply outlives its demand, and if this happens, the product must die. This was true of the famous Flexible Flyer sled with steel runners. It was true of home floor-waxing services, too, where waxless floor coverings eliminated the need for waxing.

Aging also occurs to markets. The market for television sets, for example, is mature; it may, in fact, be in a stage of decline. (See Action Brief on page 152.) When the life cycle of a company's market approaches maturity and decline, prudent companies stop creating new products for that market. Instead, they seek to enter new and different markets with new products and product lines. The market for pureed baby food, for example, is mature. Gerber Products Co. maintains its market share, but it also entered the children's bedroom furniture market, the children's clothing market, and the child care market, the last of which appears to still be in the growth phase.

## BRANDS AND TRADEMARKS
*Brands help to identify products*

A trademark or brand is an important tool in differentiating products and creating buyer loyalty. A **brand** is some combination of words or symbols that identifies the goods or services of a specific producer and distinguishes them from the products of other manufacturers. **Trademark** has essentially the same meaning except that it refers to brands that are protected by law. The government prohibits the use of a trademark except with the permission of the company that registered it. Brands are important in marketing because they make it easy for consumers to tell one product from another. Buyers feel confident buying certain brands because they can be assured of consistent quality. Advertising depends on brands. Even if consumers were convinced about buying a company's product, they would not be able to identify it without a brand.

Trademarks should not be confused with patents, which protect the ownership of inventions or new and unique ways of doing something, or with **copyright,** which is a registered protection of the ownership of books, articles, poems, and music.

Marketers approach the use of brands differently. Kellogg's, for example, puts its trademark on everything it sells. So does Gillette with most of its product lines. On the other hand, Procter & Gamble lets its brand names—like Cheer, Citrus Hill, and Pringles—become the distinguishing feature of its products. General Foods, however, treasures its trademark so much that when it adopted its now-familiar leaflike GF, it spent $2 million to make the change. Consumers recognize a General Foods product, first by its brand name—like Jello, Maxwell House, and Post Toasties—and then by the GF logo.

## PACKAGING
*Often part of the product*

Packaging and labeling also add to the distinguishing characteristics of a product. With perfumes, for example, the dispenser and package may cost as much as or more than the contents. The same is true with unique dispensing devices, such as the popular pump for toothpastes. In many ways, the packaging of the product can become an essential part of the product itself. The booming fruit juice market in the mid-1980s saw marketers struggling to outdo one another with different packaging—from cans, bottles, and frozen cans to Del Monte's aseptic "punch boxes" and Tropicana's squeezable cartons. Aseptic packaging has extended the fruit juice market because of the preponderance of younger consumers. The coated paper package is safer for children than glass or metal, lighter to carry in school lunch boxes, and more appealing for children to drink from. Who can really say that the juice is bought for its content or package or both!

## 7  MARKET SELECTION
*Techniques for understanding and simplifying diverse markets*

The marketing concept stresses the tailoring of products and marketing efforts to consumers. Consumers, as you have seen, exist in all sorts of markets. These markets are overlapping and diverse. As a consequence, consumers are not all that easy to search out and service. Marketers try to make sense of this complexity through the statistical study of population characteristics. They also try to simplify markets and make them more approachable by means of a technique that divides large, complex markets into smaller, simpler ones.

## DEMOGRAPHIC ANALYSIS
*Statistical description of the consumer population*

As an aid to understanding market populations (in industrial as well as consumer markets), the study of demography is very useful. **Demography** is the analysis of population statistics and subgroups within that population. Demography provides marketers with data not only about the size of the population (number of companies, people, families, etc.) but also, and perhaps more important, about their characteristics. These include a wide range of basic information, such as age, sex, geographic location, personal income, and other factors that might affect spending

# B·I·L·L·B·O·A·R·D

## IS BRANDING JUST A COSTLY HOAX?

**S**ome consumers say that brand labels cover a multitude of sins. Others say that if food manufacturers were asked to "bare all," there would be a lot of embarrassed advertisers and surprised consumers.

*The Washington Post* claims that there is a lot of product swapping, label switching, and recipe imitating between brands, private labels, and generics. Here are a few examples:

- Some of Safeway's Town House brand canned fruits are packed by Del Monte. Safeway claims that its product is identical with the Del Monte brand, other than label and lower price.
- There are only three manufacturers in the business of producing instant breakfasts: Carnation, Pillsbury, and a company named Dean Foods. If an instant breakfast label says anything but Carnation or Pillsbury, it was manufactured by Dean, despite what the label says.
- Land O'Lakes manufactures an instant dry milk under its own Flash brand. Since there is so little variation in how dry milk is processed, the company also packs it in a plain black-and-white generic box. A con-

---

### Brand labels cover a multitude of sins.

---

sumer can buy the generic for about 15 cents less than the Flash brand.

Surprisingly, there are no stringent legal rules covering national versus store versus generic brands. Many national brands manufacturers pack a line of store brands, so in fact the two products may be identical. Some national brands pack a generic line that is in fact a lower-grade product. Some store brands are packed by private-label packers exclusively. Others are packed right in the store or in the store's warehouse.

### QUERIES

**1.** So long as the prices are lower, does it make any difference to you who packs the contents in the can?

**2.** Should manufacturers of brand items be required to prove that the difference in price is justified. How would they do so?

**3.** Do you feel that branding and the use of brands should be regulated by the federal government? Why? ■

---

*SOURCE:* Carol Sugarman, "What's in a Brand?" *The Washington Post,* March 10, 1985, pp. K1–K3.

patterns. Age, for example, is a factor and has received considerable analysis. Marketers wish to know as much as possible about teenagers, young adults, middle-agers, and, especially, "senior citizens." Demographic data on the United States population aged 65 and over, for example, pinpoints states where this particular age group is growing fastest (Nevada, Arizona, Hawaii, Alaska, and New Mexico during the 1980s). Marketers who wish to sell products appropriate for older citizens might want to target these states.

Demography can also provide a wide range of useful information other than age and geographic location. Further analysis can describe the population in terms of the following:

- *Activities* (how they spend their spare time), personal values (what they believe in or cherish), interests (such as hobbies), life-styles (recreational habits), and opinions (about politics, precooked meals, music, or just about anything)
- *Benefits*, such as the value they place on comfort, convenience, durability of a product, economy, health, safety, or prestige
- *Consumption*, especially how much of a product they buy and how, what sort of incentive it takes to make them buy, and how loyal they are to a particular brand or store

## MARKET SEGMENTATION
*Breaking large markets down into little ones*

The study of demography leads naturally to the technique of market segmentation. **Market segmentation** is the process of dividing the total population in a market into several subgroups or segments, each of which tends to have similar characteristics. A manufacturer of women's clothing, for example, may not wish to sell to the entire female population. Instead, it may choose to focus its marketing efforts on women who wear petite sizes, or on women 5 feet 10 inches tall or over. A hair stylist may try to segment a local market of people who can afford to pay $25 or more for a trim. One restaurant in town may cater to families, another to singles. Using any combination of the demographic variables mentioned above, marketers can segment larger markets any way they please. (See Figure 7-7.) The idea, of course, is to choose a market that is most appropriate for a company's particular line of products and services.

Increasingly in recent years, marketers have searched for segments that contain affluent people, such as Yuppies (young urban professionals). The conclusion is that consumers in these market segments will pay higher prices and, as a result, the profits will be higher. Haagen-Dazs ice cream is a good example. The manufacturer added more butterfat and packed in less air, but gave it a price double that of the most expensive nationally distributed brand. Not only that, the difference between selling price and cost to the retailer for the super-high-priced brand was 40 percent as compared with 30 percent for the lower-priced brand. For every half gallon sold, a retailer made a gross profit of around $2 rather than 75 cents!

Once a market segment has been targeted, all marketing efforts must be tuned to that market. This requires packaging and pricing that are most appealing to that segment. A distribution network must be established that can deliver goods to the target. It also means that the sales and promotion efforts must be "in sync." Advertising, in particular, is used to

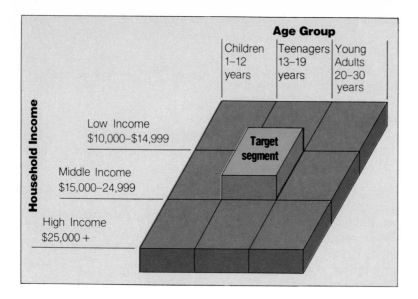

Figure 7-7 Example of market segmentation showing a segment for TV-computer games targeted at teenagers from middle-income homes.

"position" the product in the chosen market. The concept and technique for product positioning will be discussed in detail in Chapter 9.

## MARKET RESEARCH

*Information before, during, and after the sale*

Market (or marketing) research is a special branch of marketing. Its purpose is to provide useful information about markets and the marketing process. Such information leads to effective product planning and market segmentation. It helps to determine the right means of distributing a product, such as whether or not direct mail might be a better way to sell expensive leather handbags than through specialty shops. Such research can also gather a variety of information about the best ways to communicate with customers and how they react to a company's advertisements. Because this kind of research can study so many aspects of the marketing process, it is called marketing research.

*Marketing research* is the systematic gathering, recording, and analyzing of data about problems relating to the marketing of goods and services. This research, however, is costly and is typically used sparingly and on selected problems. Marketing research uses not only the techniques of demography and segmentation but also such methods as personal interviews, survey questionnaires, observation of shoppers' behavior in stores, and consumer test panels. A questionnaire survey uses a standardized set of questions to ask people about their preferences or their buying habits. A consumer test panel is a group of people gathered (by mail, by telephone, or in person) to get their reactions to new products and new product lines. Such techniques give information about what kind of products will sell, what kinds of advertising and packaging are effective, and what influence price has on buying decisions.

Marketing research may also be used to forecast future sales trends in markets. Information for this purpose typically comes from studying data and trends in the national economy (collected from the U.S. Department of Commerce and other government sources) and analyzing the past and present performance of a particular industry or firm.

# Key Concepts

1. The marketing concept rests on the belief that profits can be maximized by concentrating on the wants and needs of consumers and by marketing products for which there is a known demand.

2. The marketing mix involves the business activities (or elements) that are concerned with the planning, placement (distribution), promotion (advertising and sales), and pricing of products and services.

3. Management of the marketing process requires the performance of a number of functions in addition to buying and selling; these include transporting, storing, risk-bearing, standardizing, grading and labeling, financing, and gathering market information.

4. A market exists when people have wants and needs combined with the willingness and ability to spend money to satisfy them. The major markets for goods and services are the consumer market and the industrial market.

    **a.** The consumer market consists of people who buy products for their own use. Products for the consumer market are traditionally divided into convenience goods, shopping goods, and specialty goods.

    **b.** The industrial market consists of people and firms who buy goods and services that will be used to produce other products or that will be used in the daily operation of a business or institution.

    **c.** In addition, there are other important, often overlapping markets, including the commercial, institutional, international, and government markets.

5. Consumers who purchase goods and services for themselves do so to satisfy primary needs and also for selective (or pleasurable) satisfaction. They buy according to rational, emotional, or patronage motives. And the extent of their buying is affected by their personal purchasing power, which in turn is limited by their disposable and discretionary incomes.

6. Product planning is concerned with developing products and product lines, predicting demand, relating this demand to product life cycles, and differentiating products by brands, trademarks, and packaging.

7. Market selection depends upon the study of demographic characteristics of a market's population, segmentation of the market into smaller, more approachable units, and the prudent gathering and analysis of information through marketing research.

# Review Questions

1. Define, identify, or explain each of the following key terms or phrases, found on the pages indicated.

    *brand (p. 156)*
    *component parts (p. 150)*
    *consumer goods (p. 147)*
    *copyright (p. 156)*
    *convenience goods (p. 149)*
    *demography (p. 157)*
    *discretionary income (p. 152)*
    *disposable income (p. 152)*
    *emotional motives (p. 151)*
    *industrial goods (p. 147)*
    *market (p. 147)*

    *market segmentation (p. 159)*
    *marketing (p. 144)*
    *marketing concept (p. 143)*
    *marketing mix (p. 144)*
    *marketing research (p. 160)*
    *patronage motive (p. 152)*
    *primary needs (p. 151)*
    *product (p. 153)*
    *product life cycle (p. 155)*
    *product line (p. 153)*
    *purchasing power (p. 152)*
    *rational motive (p. 151)*
    *raw materials (p. 150)*
    *selective purchasing (p. 151)*

*shopping goods (p. 149)*
*specialty goods (p. 149)*
*standard metropolitan statistical area (SMSA)*
*(p. 148)*
*trademark (p. 156)*

2. How does the marketing concept differ from earlier approaches to creating profits?

3. Describe the four major elements of the marketing mix.

4. Give an example of grading and labeling and explain how this function can add utility to a product.

5. How does the industrial market differ from the consumer market?

6. Distinguish between a convenience good and a shopping good.

7. What is the difference between buying for primary needs and selective purchasing?

8. When are profits likely to be highest during a product's life cycle? lowest? Why?

9. Describe some of the ways to differentiate one product from another.

10. How are demography and market segmentation related?

# Case Critique 7-1
## A camera of the future today?

In 1986, Hitachi Ltd. of Japan introduced a new kind of camera to Americans. The camera does not use any film. Instead, it depends upon "electronic imaging." This is somewhat like the process used for making a television videotape. The camera records the image on a tiny magnetic disk, like the floppy disk used in a computer. The electronic picture can be viewed immediately on a television screen. The user can then make a print of the snapshot with a separate printer. The introductory cost of the electronic imaging camera was in the neighborhood of $2,000.

Americans didn't exactly jump at the chance of owning one of these newfangled picture takers. After all, they could always buy a Polaroid Instamatic camera. Or, or course, they could use their traditional cameras, take a set of pictures, and have their handy drugstore or photo shop develop the film roll for them.

One complaint about the new camera was that the actual print wasn't as clear as what appears on a standard film. The electronic image had 300,000 "dots" called pixels. By contrast, a Kodachrome slide contains more than 18 million pixels, and thus yields a sharper and more detailed picture. This wouldn't matter, said one observer. "The consumer of today is a television person. He doesn't know from the quality of the image. He knows from what he sees on television. If the camera is priced right, people will accept a lower quality of picture." An-

other expert agreed. He thinks that affluent people will gladly pay extra for a camera to save on film processing costs. "A lot of people are tired of plopping down a $10 bill and picking up a yellow bag of prints, only some of which are good enough to keep." Electronic photography, he says, while requiring a lot of complex equipment, will give the consumer a chance to "peek, pick, and print."

1. How ready do you think the American public is for the electronic camera? Why? What principle of marketing does the manufacturer appear to have ignored?

2. What advantages and disadvantages for the consumer can you see in this product?

3. What other things might Hitachi Ltd. have done before introducing the product in the United States?

4. Some camera experts felt that the camera would be attractive to news photographers, even if it didn't appeal to the average consumer. If this is true, what must Hitachi do to the camera market in order to reach these professionals and other potential consumers?

5. What phase of the product cycle does the traditional camera appear to be in? What phase do you think the instant camera *market* is in?

*SOURCE:* Alex Beam and Otis Port, "The Filmless Camera Is Here, But Will It Sell?" *Business Week*, April 15, 1986, pp. 151–153.

# Case Critique 7-2
## The Rise and Fall of Generics

As the recession of the late 1970s deepened, generic brands began to proliferate on supermarket shelves. Such nonbranded, no-frill products had long been popular in Europe. Americans, now, seemed ready to go for them in a big way. From 1 percent of all supermarket sales in 1980, generics reached an all-time high of 2.35 percent of supermarket sales in 1982 and 1983. Since then, sale of generics has declined gradually, but steadily.

Generics are defined as unadvertised, lower-grade, lower-priced "store" brands. Generally speaking, retailers make less profit on a generic sale than on the sale of nationally advertised brands. Some of the large supermarket chains do "brand" their generics. Ralph's Grocery chain of California offers its private-label "Plain Wrap" line and Jewel stores in Chicago its "No Name" label. In general, the quality of the generic brands is not as good as in the nationally advertised brands. Peas, for example, may be scrawny, yellowish-green, and slightly misshapened. Consumers often seem surprised to find this difference in quality. Repeatedly, they have asked that the quality of generics be improved. Supermarket operators reply that "price goes with quality. When you have high standards, you defeat the marketing purpose of generics."

All generics do not suffer equally from consumer disinterest. Generic foods have the most trouble. Nonfood items like paper goods, coffee filters, plastic trash bags, and disposable diapers continue to sell well. One supermarket manager explains this phenomenon, "People are very cautious when it comes to products they ingest. Paper goods work well because it's very easy to reduce the quality of paper without notice. If you reduce the quality of mayonnaise by putting in a lower grade of oil, you can immediately smell and taste it."

Many retailers have reduced the number of generic items they carry. They often do so selectively. Other supermarkets have raised the standards of quality on certain products. Pathmark stores of New Jersey, for example, carefully watches the quality of 53 of its 363 generic offsprings, especially whole-kernel corn, strawberry gelatin, and spaghetti sauce.

A few major retailers won't sell generics. They say that such products are not consistent with good quality. Nevertheless, only a few food retailers have given up on generics entirely. They agree that generics no longer sell very well and that their sale takes away from the sale of their higher-priced brands. They worry, however, that if a recession comes along, people will be clamoring for generics again.

**1.** Based on the statistical information in the first paragraph, from 1980 to 1982-1983 what phase in the product life cycle typified generic brands? What phase in the product life cycle has typified generic brands since 1983?

**2.** What changes in the economy are likely to affect the sale of generics and how?

**3.** Do you think it is a good idea for a supermarket to improve the quality of its generics while keeping their prices low?

*SOURCE:* Amy Dunkin, "No-Frills Products: An Idea Whose Time Has Gone," *Business Week*, June 17, 1985, pp. 64–65.

## CHAPTER 8

# Marketing

# Distribution Systems

## Learning Objectives

The purpose of this chapter is to explain the function of the marketing distribution process, discuss the role of wholesalers and retailers, physical distribution strategies, and describe modes of transportation in this process.

As evidence of general comprehension, after completing this chapter you should be able to:

1. Relate the purpose of the marketing distribution system.

2. Recognize and explain the various distribution channels.

3. Distinguish between wholesalers and retailers and identify the various kinds of wholesaling operations.

4. Identify the various ways by which retailing ownership and operations can be classified.

5. Explain physical distribution strategy as it applies to warehousing, handling, and transportation costs.

6. Identify various modes of transportation and explain the advantages and disadvantages of each mode.

If your class is using Ssweetco: Business Model and Activity File, see Chapter 8 in that book after you complete this chapter. There you will find exercises and activities to help you apply your learning to typical business situations.

## 1 DISTRIBUTION SYSTEMS PLACE PRODUCTS IN MARKETS

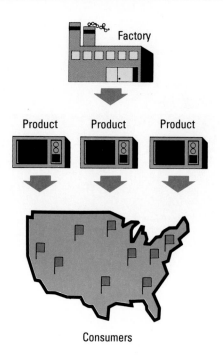

Factory

Product    Product    Product

Consumers

## 2 PRODUCTS FLOW THROUGH DISTRIBUTION CHANNELS

Indirect channels

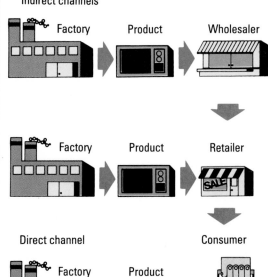

Factory    Product    Wholesaler

Factory    Product    Retailer

Direct channel

Factory    Product    Consumer

## 3 WHOLESALERS OPERATE BETWEEN PRODUCERS AND RETAILERS

Wholesaler

## 4 RETAILERS OPERATE BETWEEN WHOLESALERS AND CONSUMERS

Retailer

## 5 PHYSICAL DISTRIBUTION

Resolves storage, handling, and moving problems and places warehouses in optimum locations between producers and consumers.

## 6 DIFFERENT MODES OF TRANSPORTATION

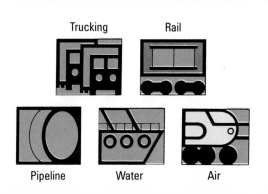

Trucking    Rail

Pipeline    Water    Air

# AN INDISPENSABLE ARTERY

*A Red Arrow Freight tractor-trailer rig hurtles out of Houston heading for Denver. It is carrying a load of electronic optical equipment manufactured in a plant in southern Texas. The truck will transfer the trailer to a G. I. Trucking Company tractor in Denver, which will haul the load to a huge warehouse complex in La Mirada, California. The trailer will be unloaded there, and its contents will be broken up into smaller lots. Some will be distributed to factories throughout California in less-than-truckload lots along with other merchandise heading for the same destinations. One lot, however, will be loaded into a huge boxlike container and shipped by ocean freighter to Hawaii where it will be delivered to the Hawaiian Pacific Freight Forwarding terminal in Honolulu. A local truck will bring the equipment to the receiving dock of an electronic assembly plant on the other side of the island. Meanwhile, back at the Red Arrow Freight Lines terminal in San Antonio, a container of wicker furniture that has just arrived from the West Coast is being marked for shipment via railroad to a Carolina Freight Carriers terminal in Cherry Hill, New Jersey. When it arrives there, the furniture will be uncrated and shipped by smaller truck to a fur-*

*niture wholesaler in Philadelphia. From there, the furniture will be delivered by the wholesaler's private carrier to various retail home furnishings shops in eastern Pennsylvania. This pattern of exchange will occur hundreds of thousands of times each day in America. The material being hauled will differ, so will the destinations, and so will the transportation companies. Red Arrow, G. I. T., Hawaiian Pacific, and Carolina Freight just happen to be part of a single corporate network of interlocking trucking companies. But, like so many other transportation companies, they help to provide the physical artery that connects the producers with the marketers that make up the distribution system of American business.*

## 1 PURPOSE OF DISTRIBUTION SYSTEMS
### *Distribution systems make manufactured products available for purchase*

Everything you buy when you go shopping has been made available through distribution systems. These systems include the wholesalers, distributors, agents, and retailers who buy and sell the goods. These agencies are coordinated with the transportation companies—truckers, railroads, and others—that physically move goods to the market. Production distribution, including physical distribution, is a marketing function that is fundamental to the functioning of business and to the economic well-being of the country. Businesses set up distribution systems to make their products available to consumers. Almost everything that people buy is made by a company that specializes in producing a limited range of similar products. Distribution systems physically move these products from the producer to the buyer. Thus they enable stores to stock many kinds of specialized products for convenient purchase.

Product distribution requires distribution channels and physical transportation. **_Distribution channels_** are the means producers use to put their goods on the market. This may be done through wholesalers, retailers, or by selling directly to consumers. Transportation systems determine how goods are to be stored and transported to where they will be sold and ultimately used.

Product distribution adds value to goods by creating utility of place. To a person with a blowout, a new tire is worthless in the manufacturer's warehouse. It becomes valuable only after it has been brought to where it is accessible to the consumer. Product distribution makes goods more valuable by placing them where they can be bought and used by people who need them. As a consequence, each intermediate person or firm who handles a product also expects to retain a portion of the sales price, which increases at each exchange, as a profit for his or her efforts. These profits come from the price increase that takes place at each exchange. These price increases—or markups—vary at each stage of exchange and also from product to product, as shown in Figure 8-1.

## EXTENT OF MARKET COVERAGE
### _Affects design of distribution networks_

Probably the first decision a producer of goods or services must make concerns how widely these products should be distributed in the market-

Figure 8-1 How intermediaries share the dollars consumers spend on food. _Source:_ "Food Marketing," _Agricultural Outlook,_ U.S. Department of Agriculture, March 1983, p. 14.

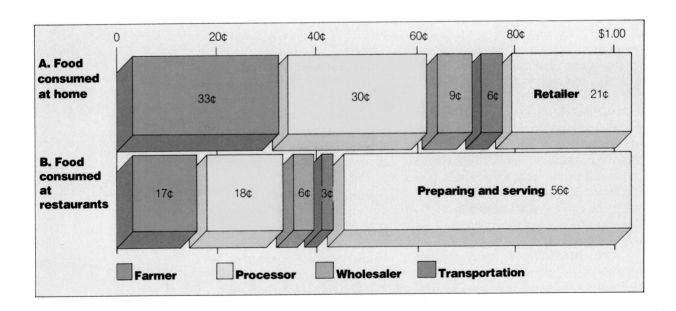

place. Consumers are made aware of this decision by the extent to which these products or services are made available to them. If you wish to buy a particular model automobile, say a Chrysler, you will probably find only one dealer in your neighborhood. If you like a certain brand of coffee, there is a very good chance you will be able to buy it in any number of local supermarkets, independent groceries, and convenience stores. If you want to buy a high-performance stereo system, you may find that there are only a couple of stores where you can buy them. Each situation reflects the producer's choice of how widely or deeply it wants to cover its markets.

If a producer wants to get its product into every possible nook and cranny of as many markets as possible, the producer chooses *intensive distribution*. Producers of soap, chewing gum, canned goods, orange juice, coffee, and almost every kind of everyday product used in the home set up a network of intensive distribution. At the other extreme are producers like the auto makers who try to limit their distribution to a particular wholesaler or retailer in a geographic region. The producer believes that this *exclusive distribution* approach will provide the product with maximum sales attention and service after the sale. In between these two approaches is the *selective distribution* network. Producers who choose this method do so in the belief that their product will also require a degree of skill and commitment on the part of the dealer if it is to be marketed properly. These producers don't want mass, or intensive, distribution, but they do want their product or service handled by a number of carefully selected outlets in as many areas as possible.

## 2  DISTRIBUTION CHANNELS

*Distribution channels: routes that products follow on the way to consumers*

Distribution channels are the routes that products follow as they are bought and sold on their way to final buyers. Many goods, especially those for the consumer market, are sold by the producer to intermediaries. *Intermediaries* are companies that perform the marketing functions of storing and selling in return for discounts from the producer or potential profits from markups when they resell the goods. These intermediaries perform an indispensable service for today's businesses. A manufacturer in Ohio may wish to sell shoelaces to shoe stores, shoe repair shops, grocery stores, sporting goods shops, department stores, and variety stores across the country. The shoelace maker probably could not profitably sell to, supply, and bill each of these stores individually, as the cost of maintaining an account is very high. The solution to this problem is for the manufacturer to sell to intermediaries. The manufacturer's marketers might sell to one wholesaler who supplies shoe stores nationwide. Sporting goods distributors might buy and resell to local shops. Chain stores might buy large quantities to reship to their many local outlets. All of these intermediaries take over some of the burden of marketing from the original producer.

The choice of the proper channel or channels to use presents an important marketing decision. The specific channel chosen will depend not only on the product or service to be sold but also on the size and the characteristics of the market to be reached. Figure 8-2 shows, for example, how complex the distribution channel is for the sale of a candy bar, since so many different routes are available. The Hollywood moviemakers were faced with a difficult problem when their typical route to the moviegoer began to thin out as more and more people stayed home to watch movies on cable or videocassettes. Whereas in the past the intermediary had been local movie theaters, now the movie producers sell their films to HBO or Showtime/The Movie Channel and the like and to major wholesalers of videotapes.

## CONSUMER CHANNELS
### *Intermediaries dominate consumer channels*

The most common channel for distributing consumer goods is the traditional path from manufacturer to wholesaler to retailer to consumer. This is called ***indirect distribution*** because intermediaries move the goods from producer to consumer. Some companies use ***direct distribution*** channels, selling their products to ultimate buyers with no intermediaries involved. This approach is less common for consumer goods than it is for industrial goods, but many companies combine it with traditional indirect distribution to reach specific market segments.

***DIRECT DISTRIBUTION*** The form of direct distribution most familiar to consumers is ***direct mail.*** Consumer goods are shipped directly to the customer's home. Sales are solicited either through the mail, television, telephone, or coupon advertisements in magazines. Books and records, in particular, have been successfully sold using this method. Selling and distribution costs are generally very high, however. This has not prevented the direct mail catalog business from flourishing. It should be noted, of course, that many catalog operations cannot really be classified as direct selling. Most of the consumer catalog sales are carried on by retailers, who act as intermediaries for hundreds of producers. A catalog, for example, that sells men's sport clothes is in all probability the work of

Figure 8-2 Example of distribution channels selected by a candy company to deliver goods to the candy bar market. *Source:* Philip Kotler, *Marketing Management: Analysis, Planning, and Control,* 2d ed., Prentice Hall, Inc., Englewood Cliffs, New Jersey, 1972, p. 32. Reprinted by permission.

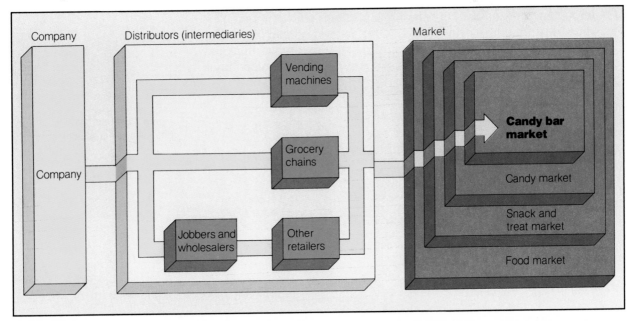

a retailer offering products from brand name manufacturers that consider the catalog merchant one of many important intermediaries.

Door-to-door selling is, of course, as old as the Fuller Brush man. For some companies, it remains a major means of direct distribution. It has been used with great success for vacuum cleaners, cosmetics, and encyclopedias. Salespeople may actually knock on doors, or they may contact customers directly at "parties" such as those that Tupperware and Mary Kay representatives hold. Direct selling costs are very high, but this has not deterred Avon Products, Inc. from selling $1 billion a year in cosmetics. Direct selling of this kind does become more and more difficult as salespeople become harder to find and potential women customers are at work rather than at home. It should be noted that many door-to-door salespeople—including most of Avon's more than 700,000 representatives—are, technically, independent retailers. They perform as if they are Avon's direct line to the consumer. In fact, Avon sells the merchandise to the sales representative, who in turn sells to the purchaser. In many cases, the manufacturer may make the shipment direct while the salesperson collects the money for the purchase.

Some manufacturers maintain retail stores that sell directly to customers. These are called **manufacturer's outlets.** They have the advantage of returning retail profits to the manufacturer and may sometimes generate a large volume of business. The disadvantage of these outlets are that they require a large capital investment, compared with other distribution methods, and they involve the manufacturer in the specialized management problems of retailing.

Figure 8-3 shows direct channels for distributing consumer goods.

**INDIRECT DISTRIBUTION** Many producers sell goods to retail stores that resell them to consumers. Automobile and home appliance manufacturers are good examples. This practice gives the manufacturer more control over the marketing of products, often provides faster distribution of new models or styles, and helps to ensure that the goods will be aggressively promoted. It also requires the manufacturer to deal directly with a large number of individual stores.

Important advantages of the manufacturer-wholesaler-retailer-consumer distribution channel account for its widespread use. The **wholesaler** saves both manufacturers and retailers the complications and expenses of dealing with large numbers of accounts. Wholesalers buy a

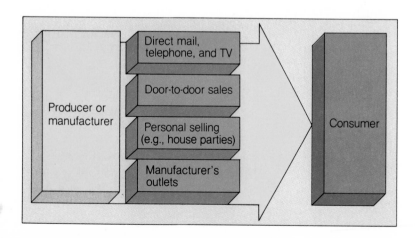

Figure 8-3 Direct distribution channels for consumer goods.

variety of goods in substantial quantities from different manufacturers. They then resell smaller quantities of different goods to individual retailers. As a result, manufacturers deal directly with fewer points of sale, and retailers work with fewer points of purchase. Wholesalers take up some of the marketing functions of manufacturers, and retailers can keep a smaller stock of goods since resupply from wholesalers is convenient and rapid.

Distribution through chain stores or buyer's **cooperatives** works in a similar way and has some of the same advantages. The chain provides central purchasing facilities and curtails expenses by buying in large quantities. Most chains have their own warehouses and sometimes their own transportation facilities.

The various indirect distribution channels for consumer goods are illustrated in Figure 8-4.

## INDUSTRIAL CHANNELS
*Direct selling predominates*

Goods for the industrial market also have direct and indirect distribution channels. Direct selling and distribution predominate in this market, however. Figure 8-5 shows the most often used direct and indirect channels for products for the industrial market. (It also illustrates the direct and indirect channels used for agricultural products.)

**DIRECT DISTRIBUTION** The flow of technical information between buyer and seller in the industrial market often makes it very difficult to use a wholesaler. The high price of many industrial goods—machinery

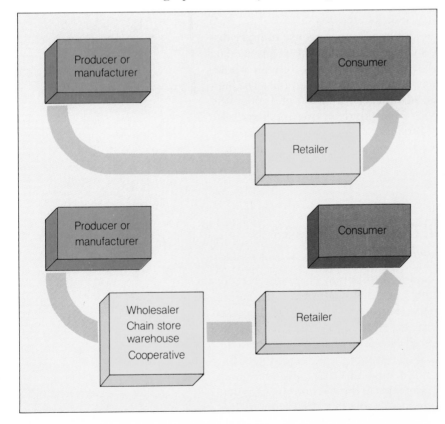

Figure 8-4 Common indirect distribution channels for consumer goods.

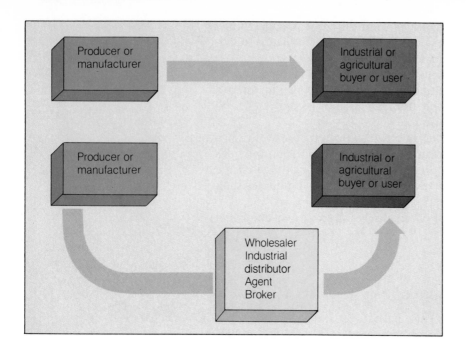

Figure 8-5 Distribution channels for goods sold to the industrial and agricultural markets.

and large quantities of raw materials, for example—also makes it practical for producers to devote more of their own staff's time to selling to individual accounts. Producers of industrial goods usually have a smaller number of potential customers. This makes it easier to deal with them without intermediaries. For these reasons, direct distribution is popular in the industrial market.

***INDIRECT DISTRIBUTION*** Some industrial suppliers use indirect distribution. Expendable supplies—such as paper, business forms, data processing supplies—as well as office furniture are sold through wholesalers. Tools, small parts, and electrical and plumbing supplies are handled by industrial distributors. The advantages for buyers and sellers are similar to those for consumer goods. Other kinds of intermediaries also operate in the industrial market. Brokers, agents, and manufacturers' representatives may perform various roles for buyers and sellers in setting up the final exchange of goods.

## DISTRIBUTION OF AGRICULTURAL PRODUCTS
*Specialized intermediaries prevail*

Farm products often have complex distribution channels. Farmers sometimes sell directly to consumers at "pick-your-own" orchards or roadside stands. More often, however, farm produce must be processed before it is used by consumers. Farmers sell to an intermediary such as a granary, dairy or fruit cooperative, or livestock buyer. The intermediaries then resell the goods to processors. The output of the processing of food is then distributed in much the same manner as other consumer goods. Brokers and agents often play the same roles in the distribution of agricultural produce as they do in the industrial market. (See Figure 8-5.)

# 3  WHOLESALERS
## Wholesalers link producers and retailers

Distribution for many companies is often wholly dependent upon the use of wholesalers and retailers. These two kinds of intermediaries are distinguished mainly by how their customers will use the goods they buy. Wholesalers sell to companies or individuals who will either directly resell the products or process them further and then resell them. Retailers, on the other hand, sell their goods almost entirely to the ultimate consumers. Wholesale and retail operations both can take a variety of forms. The wholesaling function is performed by merchant wholesalers, agents and brokers, assemblers, chain store warehouses, and cooperative wholesalers. They perform for the producer many of the marketing management functions described earlier in Chapter 7.

## MERCHANT WHOLESALERS
### They take ownership before reselling

Merchant wholesalers may best represent the true wholesaling process. They buy goods in quantity from many different manufacturers and generally resell them in different quantities at a profit to other wholesalers, to retailers, or to other companies. They simplify selling for the producer and buying for the retailer. Merchant wholesalers are often divided into categories according to the types of services they offer. *Full-service wholesalers* usually have a regular sales program, allow credit purchases, assist with transportation, and perform most of the other marketing functions. On the other hand, *limited-function wholesalers* perform few functions besides buying and reselling products. They may provide a specialized or limited range of goods on a cash-and-carry basis.

## AGENTS AND BROKERS
### They operate on commissions

Agents and brokers differ from merchant wholesalers in that agents and brokers do not actually purchase the goods they sell. They facilitate sales by personal selling. Agents and brokers help develop specifications, assist in negotiations, and sometimes set up transportation and financing. **Selling agents** handle nearly the entire marketing function for a company and sell its entire output. **Manufacturer's agents** sell only part of a company's output and engage in direct selling efforts while the company handles other marketing functions, including advertising, shipping, and billing. **Brokers** may represent either buyers or sellers. Their main function is as an intermediary in specialized or complex marketing situations. Brokers usually receive a commission for their services.

## OTHER KINDS OF WHOLESALERS
### Each serves a special purpose

Wholesalers who specialize in buying produce from individual farmers and putting together large quantities for processing and distribution are called **assemblers.** They make it possible for a cheese manufacturer, for example, to collect all of the milk needed for production without having to deal with hundreds of individual farmers. Assemblers also deal with forest products and certain other goods.

Many chain stores perform the wholesaling function for themselves by maintaining centralized warehouses. They save money by buying goods in quantity directly from the producer and then redistributing them in smaller quantities to the chain's retail outlets. To gain this kind of advantage for themselves, independent retailers sometimes band together to set up a wholesaling cooperative. As the member-owners of this cooperative, which functions much like the chain-store warehouses, the retailers are said to be part of a *cooperative chain.*

## 4 RETAILERS
### *Retailers sell directly to consumers*

The type of intermediary most familiar to consumers is the *retailer.* These are companies or individuals who buy products for resale to ultimate consumers. Retail outlets range in size from sidewalk stands to ten-story department stores and sell everything from candy bars to cabin cruisers. Retail outlets also sell services. Many deliver goods, allow purchases on credit, and give information and advice. For some retail businesses, such as restaurants, the service component—cooking and serving food—may be a very significant part of the retailer's contribution. The great diversity of retail outlets may be organized in several ways: by types of ownership, by types of operation, and by types of goods and services provided.

## TYPES OF OWNERSHIP
### *Most are independent proprietorships*

Most retail stores are sole proprietorships or partnerships that operate independently. They buy goods from wholesalers or manufacturers and resell them, providing whatever goods and services they believe will be profitable. A second important class of retail outlets is *chain stores.* These are companies, often corporations, with a number of retail stores at different locations. The central management of a chain store usually handles some or all of the purchasing for all of the outlets and manages storage and transportation of goods. Food supermarket chains like Safeway, A&P, and Kroger are, perhaps, the most visible of these. Individual stores have varying degrees of independence in different chains. Retailers that function both as independent stores and chains are called *voluntary chains.* Independent stores may band together, or join an existing group of similar stores, to gain certain advantages of chains, such as volume buying, without giving up their individual ownership.

Franchising, discussed in Chapter 4, has also become a major form of retail ownership.

## TYPES OF OPERATION
### *Five types prevail*

Perhaps the classic example of a retail store is the *general store,* so important during the early part of this century as a marketplace for con-

---

## Action Brief

### IF 1 IS GOOD, 49 MUST BE BETTER

It used to be that a mill or factory would open a side door and invite local customers to come in and buy its products at a discount. Some of these factories, especially the textile mills, made a big business of it, opening or franchising mill outlet stores all over the region. Today, the center for manufacturers' outlet stores is indisputably the Reading, Pennsylvania, area. Not only are there dozens of such outlets from factories all over the country, but there are even outlet malls. One of the biggest is MOM. It has 49 outlet shops (Johnston & Murphy shoes, Judy Bond blouses, Stauffer's frozen foods, Van Heusen shirts, among others). This mall even features a hotel to accommodate the bus loads of excursion shoppers that descend on the area from Philadelphia and New York.

sumer goods. Stores like this carried many different kinds of merchandise and served a local market. General stores still exist in many rural areas and in inner-city neighborhoods, but they have largely lost their economic importance. Stores that sell only one type of merchandise—such as food, hardware, books, and drugs—are called **single-line stores.** They usually have a wide selection within their particular line and often give extra services such as delivery and credit. A subcategory of the single-line store is the **specialty shop.** These are even more specialized and carry a narrow line of goods such as computers or stereo systems. Some stores, for instance, carry only knives but have a vast selection of hunting and camping knives, pocketknives, and all kinds of cutlery for the kitchen, often made by scores of different manufacturers. Other specialty stores may sell only denim clothes or hiking boots, citizens' band radios, or any of dozens of other specialized lines of goods. A **department store** may be viewed as a large version of the general store. Department stores try to carry a variety of different kinds of merchandise and offer many choices within each line. Most department stores stress service and offer a wide range of aids and conveniences to shoppers. **Variety stores** also offer a diverse range of goods. The selection, however, is not as great as in a department store. Variety stores often specialize in lower-priced merchandise.

Some retail outlets are not stores at all. **Mail-order houses** sell directly to consumers and are like retail stores except that contact is made by mail and the orders placed by mail or telephone. Goods are then shipped by mail, parcel service, or rail. Door-to-door selling does not use a store.

**Vending** is another form of retailing that is widely used. Machines may be placed in stores, but they are also commonly found in all manner of public places, offices, and factories too.

## TRENDS IN RETAILING
*High volume, minimum service, and low prices*

Retailers appear to be just as innovative as those who develop new products and services. The reason is clear. Retailing is extremely competitive. Owners and managers must continually strive for ways to make their operations more attractive to both producers and consumers. Producers prefer retailers who can distribute large volumes of their products. Consumers are attracted to retailers who offer low prices, since a comparative shopping advantage can easily be recognized. Consumers also like service, but it is a difficult value to assess. When given a choice between (1) a wide selection of merchandise at low prices and a help-yourself policy and (2) a limited selection at higher prices but with considerable help from salespeople along with other accommodations such as easy credit and installation and instruction after the sale, a significant majority of consumers choose the low-priced alternative. All the evidence points to a continuation of retailing operations that feature high volume, low prices, and minimum services. There are exceptions, of course, as creative retailers seek to open up market segments for themselves that are less competitive and more profitable. Nevertheless, the number of retailing approaches dependent upon mass appeal continues to grow. There are, for example:

■  *Mass discount retailers, like K mart.* These are essentially giant self-service variety stores. They are extending their appeal now by adding groceries to their traditional hard goods (appliances, home furnishings, etc.) and soft goods (clothing). This will increase their one-stop shopping appeal. They are becoming more like supermarkets.

■  *Warehouse showrooms.* These have been very successful for furniture and large appliances. They have grown in number because they allow consumers to see and touch the product, and yet get immediate delivery at a lower price than at a typical furniture store.

■  *Catalog showrooms.* They offer a line of merchandise similar to that of a department store, but use the warehouse-showroom approach. They grew rapidly in number, but now face serious competition from department stores and mass discount retailers as they encroach into their territories.

■  *Convenience stores.* These are really around-the-clock variations of the old general store, but with a highly selective, fill-in line of merchandise that is highly priced. They have had steady and impressive growth. (See Figure 8-6.) These retailers, too, continue to try to expand their lines by adding meals that customers can heat up in a microwave oven and video-tape rentals. The trend is also to offer more than just fill-in goods and to expand in size from a typical 4,000 square feet to as large as 60,000 square feet, which is larger than some supermarkets. Such expansion inevitably leads the convenience stores into direct competition with supermarkets and lessens the uniqueness of convenience—enabling customers to park their cars at the door, find what they want, and get out in a hurry.

■  *Deep discount stores.* They acquire "distress" merchandise (leftovers that manufacturers and other retailers are trying to get rid of) and sell at very low prices in barnlike warehouses with the minimum of customer

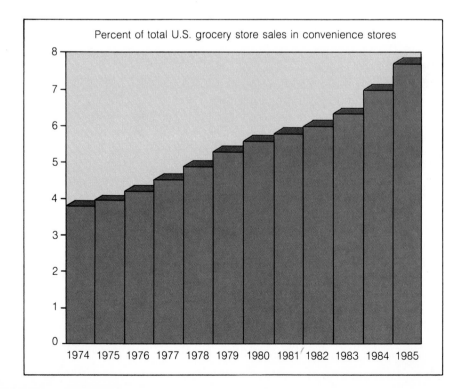

Figure 8-6 Growth of grocery sales in convenience stores.

accommodation. Some customers complain that this form of merchandising is like a large garage sale, but at prices 50 to 80 percent below retail, more of these deep discounters will be seen.

■ *Licensing of concepts, brand names, trademarks, and copyright.* Licensing has extended the entire concept of marketing intermediaries to producers and retailers. A company that holds a trademark or copyright licenses it for use to other producers or retailers. Strawberry Shortcake set the trend in this direction, followed by such popular items as ET. Licensing now is applied to a wide number of products, as illustrated in Figure 8-7. Estimates are that sales of licensed products in retail outlets have increased from $4 billion in 1977 to more than $50 billion in 1987.

■ *Shopping malls or centers.* They continue to grow in unabated fashion. The very large malls dominate retailing activity in many towns and cities, making it increasingly difficult for merchants in downtown areas to survive. The appeal of shopping malls is their assurance to the consumer of (1) a wide selection of merchandise, food service, and entertainment and (2) a broad range of quality and price with (3) the convenience of one-stop parking.

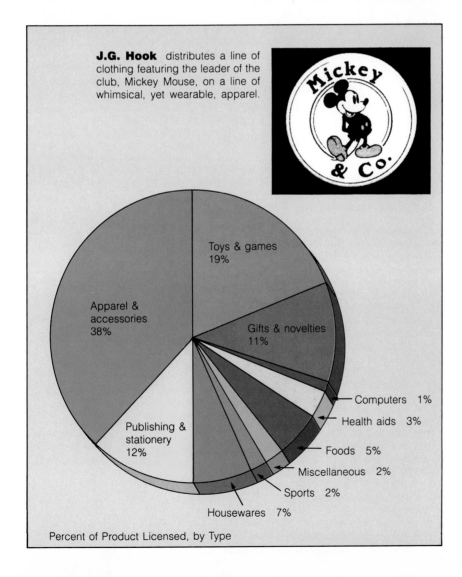

**J.G. Hook** distributes a line of clothing featuring the leader of the club, Mickey Mouse, on a line of whimsical, yet wearable, apparel.

Toys & games 19%

Apparel & accessories 38%

Gifts & novelties 11%

Computers 1%

Health aids 3%

Foods 5%

Miscellaneous 2%

Publishing & stationery 12%

Sports 2%

Housewares 7%

Percent of Product Licensed, by Type

Figure 8-7 Distribution of retail sales of license.

# 5 PHYSICAL DISTRIBUTION STRATEGIES
*Cope with problems of storage, handling, and transportation*

The design and maintenance of a physical distribution system for the effective means of moving goods within marketing channels are essential for marketing success. ***Physical distribution*** encompasses the physical flow of raw materials and component parts to, and within, the production process as well as the flow of finished goods and merchandise through the marketing channels from producer to consumer. Marketing management is particularly concerned with the design and selection of a system for (1) storing finished goods conveniently, (2) handling these materials carefully and economically, and (3) arranging the most effective, and least costly, means of transporting them.

## STORAGE OF GOODS AND MERCHANDISE
*Minimum inventory with maximum availability is the goal*

The first task involved in physical distribution is deciding where goods are to be stored while they are awaiting sale. Some will be held at intermediaries' storage facilities, some at the manufacturer's warehouse, and some at the point of manufacture. The distribution manager's goal is to maintain inventory levels of goods as low as possible without causing unfilled orders or delay to customers (see Figure 8-8). Inventory represents money that has been spent (by purchasing from the manufacturer) and not yet re-earned (by selling the goods). One important aspect of inventory control is warehouse location.

***WAREHOUSE LOCATION*** Managers have several alternatives when establishing a warehousing system. They may own and operate their own *private* warehouses at any number of locations; they may use *public* warehouses operated by other companies for profit; or they may use a combination of the two. The location of warehouses and the amount of inven-

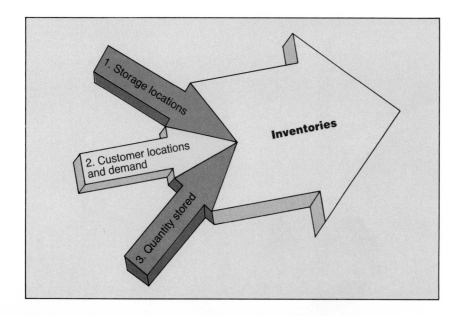

Figure 8-8 Three factors that must be balanced in inventory decisions by the physical distribution system.

tory to be kept in each are important. Managers must try to balance the costs of maintaining a high inventory with the costs of running out of goods and being unable to fill orders. Products must be stored at locations that will reduce delays caused by shipping. At the same time, marketers must avoid establishing so many distribution points that they become inefficient and difficult to manage.

## HANDLING OF MATERIALS
### Convenience and economy are desired

Considerable labor can be expended in picking up and moving materials within warehouses and into and out of trucks, railroad cars, barges, and ships. To this end, much attention has been given to mechanization and simplifying the process. Conveyor belts, industrial lift (or fork) trucks, and automatic systems for placing goods into and retrieving them from warehouse storage areas are much in evidence in warehouses and shipping and receiving areas. Two recent developments help to make the material-handling process even simpler and more efficient.

*Unitization* is a technique for combining as many packages as possible into one load, or unit. This is accomplished in many ways such as banding the packages together with steel strapping, holding them together with plastic shrink wrapping (a package of chicken parts is "unitized," for example, by shrink wrapping in the meat department of a supermarket), or nesting packages together in interlocking fashion on a wooden platform or pallet. When a load of packages has been unitized, it can be handled as a single unit by a forklift truck, crane, or other handling device.

*Containerization* takes unitization one step further. A number of packages or units are placed in an even larger container (a wooden or metal box) that can be sealed against theft and other damage. This method also saves on handling costs and insurance. A container can be loaded on a flatbed truck at a warehouse and delivered to a railroad terminal, where it is placed upon a flatbed railcar and shipped to a warehouse across the country. The container may also be delivered to a shipping dock and loaded onto an overseas freighter. This process is brought another step forward by "piggyback" and "fishyback" transportation arrangements. In these cases, the truck trailer itself becomes the container. The trailer is simply detached from the tractor and placed on a railcar or freighter for further shipment.

## 6  MODES OF TRANSPORTATION
### Proper selection can cut costs significantly

Many business managers believe that the transportation of goods is a major area in which operating efficiency can be significantly improved. Decades of emphasis on reducing production costs may have pushed manufacturing efficiencies to the limit. Accordingly, improvement in the efficiency of transportation is the next best target. Physical distribution accounts for as much as 10 to 40 percent of the total sales price of common goods. Savings in transportation costs can, therefore, have an important effect upon both prices and profits.

---

### Action Brief
### HANGING IN

In the shadow of Chicago's famed Wrigley Field, there is a vestige of times past. It is the Spotlight Groceries, a neighborhood food and convenience store run by Esther and Carmel Varella. They've hung in for over 20 years, in the face of supermarket and chain convenience-store (like 7-Eleven) competition. The Varellas say that customers are attracted to the personal service they can get from a family-owned retailer. "If there's a problem, they confront the owners, not just a salesperson. There's no permanent set of rules here. And if we know someone, we'll take their personal check." Surprisingly, most of these "corner stores" don't price as high as the convenience chains. The chains are higher-priced by choice; typically, they price at a 35 to 40 percent markup, with no flexibility. The real problem, of course, for the mom-and-pop operation is that they can't buy in large enough quantities to get good discounts, and they don't have the space to store a wide selection of merchandise. Nevertheless, many continue to hang in, working 15-hour days, 7 days a week, providing service that other intermediaries do not or cannot offer.

# BILLBOARD

## THE WHEEL OF RETAILING

A Harvard professor once observed that the temptation of retailers is to begin with a simple idea, and then increasingly complicate it until it is unwieldy and unprofitable. At that point, the professor said, an entrepreneur enters the field with a simple idea, similar to the original one. This "new" idea is so successful that the aging, complicated retailing operation gradually fails. And then the process repeats itself. The professor called this process "the wheel of retailing." One notable examples is the lodging business.

Hotels in the early 1900s prospered so much that they offered more and more services. Along came motels in the 1930s, which offered none at all. The motel idea caught on. Then in the 1960s and 1970s the motels added coffee shops and swimming pools. Soon they were so large that you needed someone to carry your bags again. And what happened next? An entrepreneur came up with the "new" idea of economy motels with no frills, no coffee shops, and no swimming pools.

Today's candidate for the wheel of fortune is the catalog showroom store. The concept is only two decades old. These outlets were born of the idea of carrying most of what a department store might, but with a significant difference. They provided very little sales help and virtually none of the amenities. Customers would look at a display case, select what they wanted from an in-store catalog, and wait to receive their merchandise. These stark showrooms pros-

### What will happen next?

pered because they offered name-brand products at prices lower than those of anyone else around.

By the 1980s, department stores and mass merchandisers like K mart were meeting the catalog showroom prices, head to head, while giving customers better service, and often in more attractive surroundings. What did the catalog stores do? They broadened

their product lines from hard goods to soft goods to match the department stores. They made their stores fancier, began advertising, and even added sales help. The catalog showroom began to look more and more like a department store. What will happen next? Will someone introduce a no-frills, limited selection drive-in, where you pick up your own merchandise?

### QUERIES

1. Which kind of retailer has the best chance of surviving in the 1990's: the mass-merchandise discount store, the department store, or the catalog showroom?
3. Which do you think is more important to consumers: a wide selection of products to choose from, low prices, or better service? ∎

SOURCE: Kimberley Carpenter, "Catalog Showrooms Revamp to Keep Their Identity," *Business Week*, June 15, 1985, pp. 117–120.

# PROFILE

STEWART LEONARD is a unique retailer. He conceived of, and operates, Stew Leonard's, a giant food market in Norwalk, Connecticut. What makes his place so different is that it has the trappings of both a carnival and a farm. In the dairy section, for instance, customers can watch as milk is pasteurized and packaged. In the produce section, they can see the unpacking of fruit and vegetable shipments as they arrive by truck. In fact, customers can buy the goods right off the conveyor belt. In addition, employees dress as cartoon characters to entertain children.

Leonard began as a farm boy and switched to retailing. He says that his inspiration was Walt Disney, and he tries to fashion his outlet after Disneyland. His underlying philosophy about business is, "What isn't good for the customers isn't good for me." He does it all so well that public television's *In Search of Excellence* show featured his operation as the largest single-store retailer in the United States. Stew's place attracts 10,000 shoppers a day and has annual sales in the $90 million range. How does Leonard feel about all this? He says, "You find something you love to do, and the reward is to find that you're good at it." ∎

**STEWART LEONARD**

*SOURCE:* Haya El Nasser, "Grocer Rings Up Good Will," *USA Today*, January 17, 1985, p. 2B.

## SELECTION OF MODES
*Advantages and disadvantages of each method*

Products can be transported by many means: rail, air, truck, pipeline, steamship, and barge. Table 8-1 summarizes some of the general advantages and disadvantages of different transportation modes. Decisions about how to ship goods are influenced by a number of important factors. The type of product is a basic determinant. Iron ore is too heavy and is needed in quantities that are too large to be shipped by air. Television sets cannot be transported by pipeline. Speed is often important because it reduces delays and may allow companies to keep a smaller inventory. The cost of shipping has a direct effect on selling price and on profits. A shipping method that has reliable schedules and nearby terminal facilities is desirable.

**TABLE 8-1**
**ADVANTAGES AND DISADVANTAGES**
**OF MAJOR MODES OF TRANSPORTATION**

| MODE OF TRANSPORTATION | ADVANTAGES | DISADVANTAGES |
| --- | --- | --- |
| Railroad | Low cost shipment of heavy goods over long distances. Reliable schedules. Little damage to goods. | Access to terminals sometimes difficult. No service in many small towns. Less suitable for small shipments and short distances. |
| Motor trucks | Provide door-to-door delivery. Can ship to and from nearly any point. Frequent service. Little damage to goods. | Less suitable for shipping very large quantities and for some bulky or large goods. More affected by weather than railroads. |
| Water transportation | Low cost. Can handle very large quantities. | Slow speed. Infrequent service. Not available in many places. Damaged goods more likely. |
| Airlines | High speed. Frequent service. Little damage to goods. | High cost. Access to terminals sometimes difficult. Not available in many small towns. Schedules affected by weather. |
| Pipeline | Low cost. Continual delivery. Not affected by weather. | Only suitable for liquids or gases. Slow delivery. |

*Action Brief*

**NEXT: A PEOPLE MOVER?**

*The principle of a distribution system is to bring producer and consumer together. Typically, the system focuses on moving the product from one to another as quickly, conveniently, and economically as possible. When you're in the service business, however, the distribution system may have to operate the other way around. The provider of the service remains in one place, and the customer is brought there. This is what happens when we use the telephone, of course. Now, however, airports are using computerized, conductorless trains to move passengers from the ticket counters to the boarding ramps. The concept seems to be spreading. The People-Mover Group, a builder of computer-programmed and computer-operated monorail systems, proposes their use in shopping malls and even to shuttle visitors between casinos in Atlantic City, New Jersey.*

An important consideration is how well a mode of transportation suits other features of a product's distribution system. A company that ships goods to only two or three intermediaries has far different requirements from one that ships directly to hundreds of individual retail stores in towns and cities. Even a feature so basic as transportation costs must be considered only as a part of the whole. A number of companies have found that the extra cost of shipping by air was justified by its speed. Rapid deliveries by air allow the elimination of many warehouses close to markets and mean that total inventory on hand can be reduced.

Transportation companies are called carriers. Carriers are classified legally three ways. **Common carriers** can haul just about anything, including people. Common carriers include trucklines, airlines, railroads, ships, and buses. They usually have to obtain permission from federal, state, and/or local governments to operate over specified routes. **Contract carriers** offer their services for hire to any kind of business. They are typically smaller operations than common carriers. Increasingly, the legal distinction between common and contract carrier is unclear and lacking in real significance. Competition within each type and between them is keen in terms of services offered and rates charged. After all, transportation companies, except for some urban bus and rail lines, are also businesses seeking to make a profit through providing a service.

**Private carriers** are those companies that own or lease their own fleet of trucks, barges, or tankers to haul their own products. A large petroleum company, like Exxon, for example, may operate its fleet of huge supertankers to transport crude oil to its refineries. Many other large and small firms also own and operate smaller fleets of trucks. For example, a manufacturer may transport its goods from a production site to an industrial customer, wholesaler, or retailer; or a wholesaler may ship goods regularly to retailers; or a retailer may use its only truck to deliver a product directly to a customer's home.

## FREIGHT RATES

*Weight and distance are major determinants* ===============

Freight rates for rail shipments, and to some extent truck and other transportation modes, follow a common principle: Rates are based upon weight of the load and how far it is to be shipped. The goods themselves, however, can also affect the rates charged. A bulkier product (like empty soda cans being shipped to a bottler) will be priced at a higher rate per pound than a more compact and dense good (like bottle caps or body-building weight bars). The reason is that the weight per cubic foot of shipping space occupied is lower for the former than for the latter, and the shipper has to compensate for using up a lot of space at a light weight. Shipping rates will also take into account such factors as the value of the merchandise (clock motors as compared with paper towels), the extra protection needed for damage or theft, and the load's perishability (tomatoes compared with bricks) as a premium for fast delivery. Other charges—such as loading, unloading, and insurance—will be added to determine the total cost of a shipment.

When price quotations are given for goods, it is common to specify who must pay the shipping costs, the buyer or the seller. **FOB factory**, or FOB city of origin, means that the buyer must pay shipping costs, but that the seller will load goods at their point of origin. FOB stands for "free on board." **FOB destination** means that the seller will pay transportation costs except for unloading at the destination.

## GOVERNMENT REGULATION
*Relaxed, but still complex*

For many decades transportation by common and contract carriers was intensely regulated by the federal and state governments. Since the early 1980s, the operation of trucklines and airlines has been "deregulated" by the federal government. Nevertheless, the Interstate Commerce Commission still maintains a certain amount of supervision over the selection and operation of the various truck routes. The Department of Transportation performs similar surveillance over airline operations. The states and local communities continue to regulate and license the various carriers. Railroads, shipment by water, and pipeline operation and rates are still regulated by the federal government, but not nearly so stringently as in the past. Table 8-2 lists the principal federal agencies that still regulate transportation.

**TABLE 8-2**
**MAJOR FEDERAL REGULATIONS OF TRANSPORTATION**

| REGULATORY AGENCY | AUTHORITY |
|---|---|
| Interstate Commerce Commission (ICC) | Regulates interstate railroads, bus companies, truckers, waterways, and pipelines. |
| Federal Marine Commission (FMC) | Regulates ocean shipping. |
| Federal Aviation Agency (FAA) | Licenses airline pilots, certifies airworthiness of aircraft, and sets safety standards for airports. |

# Key Concepts

1. Marketing distribution systems make products available to buyers by using distribution channels and various modes of transportation. Product distribution adds value to goods by giving them utility of place.

2. Distribution channels are the paths that goods follow on their way to markets. The channels are said to be direct when the goods pass straight from the producer to the ultimate consumer. The channels are said to be indirect when products pass through various intermediaries. Intermediaries may be wholesalers or retailers.

3. Wholesalers distribute goods to buyers who are not the final consumers, such as retailers, other wholesalers, and companies that will further process the goods.

4. Retailers buy goods to resell in the consumer market. Retail outlets differ in types of ownership, types of operation, and types of goods and services provided.

5. Physical distribution controls the way that goods are stored and moved from producer to points of sale and resale. Physical distribution systems try to optimize warehouse locations, inventory size, and transportation methods, and to minimize material handling in order to provide the best service at the lowest cost.

6. Choice of transportation methods depends on the type of product to be shipped and on other factors such as speed, cost, and accessibility of shipping modes. All of these must be considered in relation to other distribution elements like the number of wholesalers or retailers and the number and location of warehouses.

# Review Questions

1. Define, explain, or identify each of the following key terms and phrases, found on the pages indicated.

> assembler (p. 173)
> broker (p. 173)
> chain store (p. 174)
> common carrier (p. 183)
> containerization (p. 179)
> contract carrier (p. 183)
> cooperatives (p. 171)
> cooperative chain (p. 174)
> department store (p. 175)
> direct distribution (p. 169)
> direct mail (p. 169)
> distribution channels (p. 167)
> exclusive distribution (p. 168)
> FOB destination (p. 184)
> FOB factory (p. 183)
> general store (p. 174)
> indirect distribution (p. 169)
> intensive distribution (p. 168)
> intermediary (p. 168)
> mail-order house (p. 175)
> manufacturer's agent (p. 173)
> manufacturer's outlets (p. 170)
> physical distribution (p. 178)
> private carrier (p. 183)
> retailer (p. 174)
> selective distribution (p. 168)
> selling agent (p. 173)
> single-line store (p. 175)
> specialty shop (p. 175)
> unitization (p. 179)
> variety shop (p. 175)
> vending (p. 175)
> voluntary chains (p. 174)
> wholesaler (p. 170)

2. What are the two main decisions a marketing manager makes in setting up a distribution system?

3. What is the difference between a direct distribution channel and an indirect one?

4. Describe a typical distribution channel from farm to corner grocery store for a common product like packaged frozen corn.

5. How do wholesalers help producers and retailers with distribution channels?

6. What is the difference between a merchant wholesaler and a manufacturer's agent?

7. In what ways is a department store like a general store? a variety shop?

8. Describe some local examples of the trend of retailers toward obtaining a high volume of sales at low prices.

9. What is the general goal of marketers when deciding where to store inventories and what amount to keep at each location?

10. Compare the advantages and disadvantages of shipping by rail with shipping by truck.

# Case Critique 8-1
## One-Stop Fashion Merchandising

When apparel manufacturers, especially those in the fashion trades, want to get their goods to market, they usually sell first to a retailer. Typically, manufacturers display their designs at a fashion show. Retailers from all over the country attend the show and select the merchandise they wish to purchase. When the purchase is consummated, the manufacturer ships directly to the retailer, who in turn sells the clothing to the ultimate consumer.

It is a common practice also for manufacturers to use the services of another type of intermediary—wholesalers, agents, or brokers—to get goods to the market.

To facilitate the work of the manufacturer's own salespeople as well as wholesalers and other intermediaries, some very large cities, like New York and Chicago, provide special facilities, such as a merchandise market. A good example is the gigantic one in Dallas, called

The Apparel Mart. It is a six-story building that covers four city blocks (larger than 37 football fields). Inside, there is an immense showroom filled with display booths and a theater where fashions are modeled. Representatives of some 10,000 lines of clothing, western wear, and accessories for men, women, and children are typically on duty during a seasonal show. At shows, as many as 100,000 buyers from retail stores see the latest fashions and talk to designers, representatives of manufacturers, and wholesalers. Firms that exhibit or "write business" at the mart pay rent for their display space. All merchandise is shipped, as usual, from the manufacturer, either directly to a retailer or through a wholesaler to the retailer.

1. The Apparel Mart is part of a channel of indirect distribution. What service does it perform that makes it worth the cost of space rental for the manufacturer or wholesaler?
2. Why would a retail store buyer travel to a merchandise mart to make a purchase when it might be assumed that a manufacturer's salesperson should call on the retail store?
3. How does a person who buys his or her clothing at a retail shop benefit from the function performed by the merchandise mart?

---

*SOURCE:* Thomas W. Lippman, "Dallas Has Own 'Garment District' in Texas-Size Apparel Mart," *The Washington Post*, June 1, 1982, p. D–1.

---

# Case Critique 8-2
## The Beleaguered Supermarket Chain

A corporation like Kroger Co. that has annual sales of over $15 billion has a lot of weight to throw around. It also makes a big target for competitors. The giant supermarket chain's response has been to keep on the move, bobbing and weaving like a boxer, shucking off blows and striking some of its own. In Cincinnati, Kroger's home base, foreign competition entered the fray. Hyper Shoppes (a European-based firm) opened a Bigg's "megamarket" of more than 180,000 square feet. That's about four times larger than the average Kroger store! In the supermarket business, the trend is to make stores larger and larger.

All over the United States, Kroger's basic strategy has been to respond to the consumer's desire for around-the-clock convenience. So, at its "superstores," Kroger never closes. Kroger also responds to the consumer's interest in one-stop shopping. Its supermarkets feature not only a full range of groceries but also specialty shops with gourmet foods, photo-finishing services, and a drugstore. Its inside flower shops make Kroger the largest retail flower operation in the United States. Many of its markets even have banks (of which Kroger is a part owner) and insurance sales.

The strongest competition for Kroger comes from warehouse-store operations. Price wars are not uncommon, although Kroger claims that it must cut its prices (sometimes below cost) to stay alive when it is surrounded by warehouse-store operations. Kroger says that its pricing policy "reflects logical market conditions and customer preferences." Kroger wins some of these battles, and loses others. For instance, after building 28 new stores in the Pittsburgh, Pennsylvania, area, Kroger pulled out entirely, closing down all 43 stores. It has also closed more than 100 stores elsewhere, wherever it couldn't make the profit it seeks.

Kroger's latest strategy focuses on allowing each store to stock its shelves according to the ethnic and demographic characteristics of its neighborhoods. Thus, in south Texas, stores feature Mexican specialities; in Detroit and Milwaukee, Polish cold cuts; and in high-rent districts, expensive ready-to-eat food.

In some areas, Kroger acts as its own wholesaler, eliminating the intermediary between producer and retailer. Not only that, Kroger also operates an independent wholesale distributorship in a joint venture with a major grocery wholesaler. This operation offers groceries and general merchandise to independent retailers and to smaller supermarket chains.

**1.** What difference, if any, does it make to the grocery processors whether or not Kroger cuts prices of its merchandise?

**2.** How wise do you think it is for Kroger supermarkets to act as an intermediary, not only for groceries and related merchandise but also for banking and insurance? Does it make any difference to the consumer?

**3.** What are the advantages to Kroger of acting as its own wholesale intermediary? to the consumer? to the food processors? to the competition?

---

*SOURCE:* Rikki Danielson, "Kroger Dodging Volleys From All Sides," *Advertising Age,* April 18, 1985, pp. 20–22.

---

## CHAPTER 9

# Marketing Promotion: Selling, Advertising, and Sales Promotion

## Learning Objectives

*The purpose of this chapter is to explain the function and the objectives of marketing promotion, describe the role of personal selling, sales management, and advertising in promotion, and outline some of the methods used in sales promotion.*

*As evidence of general comprehension, after studying this chapter you should be able to:*

1. *Define the promotional mix and distinguish between pushing and pulling strategies.*

2. *Recognize the factors that influence promotion strategies.*

3. *Distinguish between selling and nonselling functions in the selling profession, and describe various sales jobs and positions.*

4. *Outline the five classes of advertising.*

5. *Recognize the factors that affect the choice of advertising media.*

6. *Explain six specific techniques utilized in sales promotion.*

7. *Identify the governmental agency that regulates advertising and debate the value of advertising for the economy and for society.*

*If your class is using SSweetco: Business Model and Activity File, see Chapter 9 in that book after you complete this chapter. There you will find exercises and activities to help you apply your learning to typical business situations.*

## 1 MARKETING PROMOTION

uses the promotional mix.

- ■ Advertising
- ● Personal Selling
- ▲ Sales Promotion

To push

and/or pull

products through distribution channels

## 2 PROMOTION STRATEGY

Sets objectives

and selects the mix

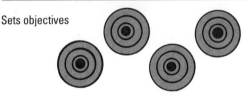

## 3 PERSONAL SELLING

Person-to-person persuasion

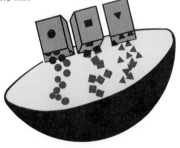

## 4 ADVERTISING

supports personal selling and influences buyers

BETTER! NEW MORE! BUY!

## 5 ADVERTISING MEDIA

stimulates in many forms.

Radio, television, billboards, print, etc.

## 6 SALES PROMOTION

complements personal selling and advertising

Samples,
Contests,
Coupons,
Etc.

## 7 SOCIETY

Regulates and challenges
the value of advertising

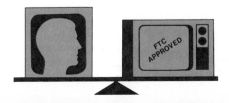

# THE VALUE OF ADVERTISING AND PROMOTION

*Three companies battle for the shaving-razor market. Two others are trying to steal it away. Gillette is top chopper, with 60 percent of the nearly $4 billion wet-shave market. Warner-Lambert's Schick ranks a poor second with 19 percent, and Bic is not far behind it with 18 percent. Wilkinson Sword, the company that started the switch to stainless steel blades, is all but out of the race. Victor Kiam's Remington electric shaver, along with Norelco, keeps trying to blindside the leaders. Their aim is to get American men—and women—to switch to shaving the "dry" way.*

*Some 61 million men, and 71 million women (that's right, more women in the total than men), choose the "wet-shave" method. Why do they choose this method over the dry approach? Why do they choose Gillette over the other two big competitors? It's largely a matter of how these products are advertised and promoted to the public. Wet shaving is promoted to men as the more masculine choice, a pleasing morning ritual. Women, who view shaving arms and legs as just another chore, are carried along because the bulk of advertising seen on television features wet-shaving devices. The electric razor, which is used by only one out of four people in the United States (compared with Europe, where half of all shavers use the dry method), suffers from the same problem. Three wet-shave companies dominate the airwaves. Gillette, for example, spent $7 million in just 6 months to introduce its Atra Plus. It then spent another $9 million on things like "three for the price of two," discount coupons, point-of-use displays, and retailer discount deals. While this was going on, Schick and Bic were fighting back hard, but not with as many dollars to spend. When you've got 60 percent of the market and each of your competitors has only about one-third of what you have, you can outspend them on advertising more than two to one. No wonder the electric shaver people, with much smaller budgets, have such a hard time making an impression on buyers. Nevertheless, Remington has crept into the viewers' minds. Most everyone can recall Mr. Kiam in his bathrobe telling viewers that he liked the electric razor his wife gave him so much that he bought the company.*

*Meanwhile the three wet-shave companies use their advertisements to try to differentiate themselves, one from the other. Gillette's Atra Plus talks about not only its pivoting head but also its "ultrasmooth lubricating strip that activates when wet." Schick promotes the idea that its razor provides "the longest shave around." Bic used John McEnroe, the tennis star, to tout its Bic Orange as not only inexpensive but "great for sensitive skin."*

*Advertising like this may amuse or entertain us and often test our credulity, but it is an important part of marketing promotion. It can be accused at times of wastefulness, but it—taken within the context of the American business system—performs an invaluable function in bringing about the satisfactory and economic exchange of goods.*

*SOURCE:* Bernice Kanner, "Nobody Knows the Stubble They've Seen," *New York Magazine,* May 27, 1985, pp. 22–24.

## 1 THE FUNCTION OF MARKETING PROMOTION
### *Promotion uses a three-part mix to move products through distribution channels*

If a club you belong to were to put you in charge of promoting an amateur variety show it is presenting, you would face a challenge. First, no one except the club members would know that the show is to be held. Second, even though people usually enjoy locally produced shows, they need persuasion to buy tickets. Several coordinated efforts would probably be necessary to approach the problem. You might send news releases or make personal visits to newspapers and radio and television stations in your area. These media might consider your event newsworthy, especially if it benefits a charity. They might also publish or broadcast general announcements of community events. You might place paid advertisements in the same media to inform people about the show and interest them in buying tickets. Advertising and publicity alone would sell some tickets through your ticket offices, but you would probably need to do some direct selling as well. Club members could sell tickets on downtown streets, at shopping centers, and door-to-door. Advertising would reinforce these personal selling efforts and make them more successful. You might also decide that door prizes would generate more interest or that offering free tickets as prizes on a radio contest would produce free publicity.

These efforts at promoting your club's variety show demonstrate the elements of promotion: selling, advertising, and sales promotion. Almost all successful organizations use some kind of promotion in their activities. Promotion is one of the essential marketing functions that allow businesses to operate.

It is helpful to think of marketing promotion as essentially a communications process. Its purpose is to stimulate and facilitate an exchange, first of information and then, as a consequence, of goods and services between producer and consumer. The distribution system provides the channels through which products move. The promotional effort is aimed at stimulating the movement of goods through those channels.

## PROMOTIONAL MIX
### *Three vital elements in the whole*

As in the example of the amateur variety show, professional marketers try to establish the right mix of promotion efforts to sell their products.

There are three major elements of this *promotional mix:*

■   *Personal selling,* which involves presenting goods or services to potential customers on a person-to-person basis

■   *Advertising,* which is a sales presentation delivered through communications vehicles known as the *media*

■   *Sales promotion,* which includes specialized techniques used to back up selling and advertising such as contests and store displays

## THE PUSH-PULL EFFECT

*Promotion pushes and/or pulls* ════════════════════

The promotion techniques described above may be combined in different ways for different products and markets. Two common strategies are to push goods through distribution channels and/or to pull them through.

In the *pushing strategy,* products are promoted strongly to wholesalers and retailers in an effort to persuade them to sell the products aggressively in the market. This approach stresses personal selling to intermediaries. Producers give trade discounts, help to pay for advertising (they give *cooperative advertising allowances*), and often provide selling materials, such as brochures, posters, and so forth. Selling to intermediaries is emphasized so as to ensure that the products will be widely available to consumers.

The *pulling strategy* attempts to stimulate a strong consumer demand which will, in turn, influence intermediaries to distribute products widely. This approach emphasizes advertising more than personal selling. The idea behind this strategy is that if direct consumer advertising convinces people that they want to buy a specific product, they will ask for it in stores. The stores will then order it from wholesalers to meet the demand. Products are thus pulled through distribution channels by strong consumer demand.

Most marketers use both strategies for common consumer goods. (See Figure 9-1.) They may, however, emphasize either pushing or pulling for a particular item. The pushing strategy, with its personal approach, is more common in promoting products to the industrial market.

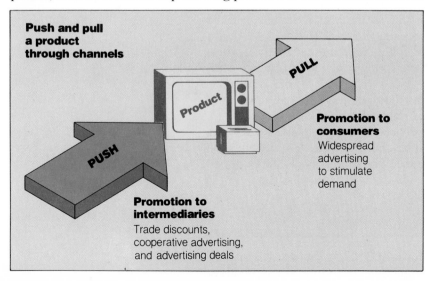

Figure 9-1 Tandem promotion strategy using both pushing and pulling techniques.

# 2  PROMOTION STRATEGY
## Sets objectives and integrates elements of the mix

To be successful, promotion efforts must be integrated. Advertising, selling, and sales promotion must work together and reinforce one another. The entire coordinated promotion effort for a product or group of products is called a *promotion campaign.* Campaigns try to maintain the right promotion mix for every product. In setting up campaigns, marketers use planning and analysis to suit promotion activities to the nature of the product and company. They specify objectives and devise promotion strategies to meet them.

The amount of money available for promotion limits a sales campaign. Advertising and personal selling are both very expensive, especially when carried on through a long campaign. This is one reason companies try to develop product lines. Promotion dollars can then be spread over a group of related products instead of spent on a single one.

## STRATEGIC OBJECTIVES
### Promotion must inform, tempt, and differentiate

Whichever promotional strategy is chosen, it will almost always have one or more of these goals:

■  Promotion tries to inform and educate the public about a company or its products. This kind of informational promotion may range from letting potential buyers know about the availability of products to sophisticated campaigns that present a company or industry in a favorable light.

■  Promotion attempts to increase or maintain sales volume or share of market. Increasing product sales and thus revenue is, of course, the fundamental purpose of promotion. Maintaining a stable sales pattern can also be important, however. A constant, predictable minimum sales volume can improve planning, budgeting, and distribution. Careful promotion can help achieve this.

■  Promotion helps to position products in the market and to differentiate them from competitors. *Positioning* refers to aiming a product at specific market segments which would be most likely to buy it. *Differentiation* means pointing out the unique features of a product that would make it appeal to the market segments chosen. Positioning and differentiation take place in all kinds of promotion. They are especially prevalent in the automotive industry. Some cars are promoted for their luxurious appearance, even though they may be costly to operate because of low gas mileage. Others are clearly differentiated as having good gas mileage, unusual safety features, a good service record, or other features that would appeal to certain segments of the total market. Figure 9-2 illustrates how differentiation qualities in two toothpaste products can be used to position a third.

## INFLUENCING FACTORS
### The product, its life cycle, and costs are determinants

The kind of product and the market to which it will be sold are important in choosing a promotion strategy. Generally, advertising rather

---

## Action Brief

### WOULD YOU RENT A CAR FROM THIS AGENCY?

*Most products or services have a number of features that help to differentiate one from another. The goal of a good advertising campaign is to (1) choose the feature or features that have the greatest pulling power and (2) try to show how that particular feature makes the product or service better than its competitors. When it comes to car rentals, what makes a person choose Avis or Hertz or National or whichever? Sometimes it is hard to tell the difference between them. Time magazine was interested in this problem so that it could help its car rental advertisers plan campaigns. It asked 2,000 customers to rank what was most important to them when picking a rental car. Can you guess? At the top of the list was the mechanical condition of the car (88 percent felt that was vital). Next was assurance that reservations would be honored (83 percent); then came speed at check-in (60 percent), clean cars (55 percent), speed at checkout (55 percent), and convenient locations (55 percent). Price was a poor last (38 percent). It makes you wonder why so many rental services stress price in their ads rather than features at the top of the customer want list!*

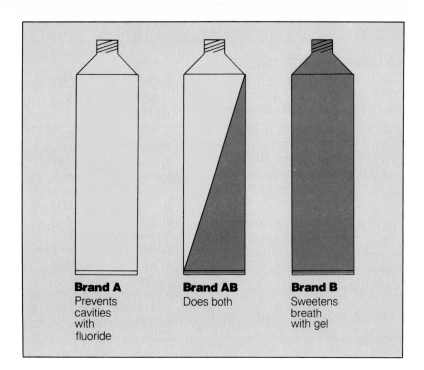

**Brand A**
Prevents cavities with fluoride

**Brand AB**
Does both

**Brand B**
Sweetens breath with gel

Figure 9-2 How product differentiation is used to position toothpastes.

than personal selling is used to promote consumer products, while the reverse is the case for the industrial market. Goods and services for the industrial market typically have promotion campaigns that emphasize personal selling. They use advertising and sales promotion only for support. Even for consumer goods, companies that produce high-priced goods often stress personal selling or use an expensive combination of selling and extensive advertising.

The present stage of a product in its life cycle also affects promotion needs. (See Figure 9-3.) The introduction of a product is usually accompanied by *informative advertising*. Its purpose is to generate an initial demand by describing the features of the product and making it recognizable to consumers. As a product reaches the growth and maturity stages, *persuasive advertising* may be used to improve its position relative to increasing competition. Persuasive advertising often compares a product with its competitors, and points out superior features of the advertised product. In their late maturity and decline phase, products are often given *reminder advertising*. This is intended to keep well-established products fresh in the minds of consumers. Products' life cycles affect personal selling and promotion the same way as they affect advertising.

# 3  PERSONAL SELLING
## *Person-to-person often makes the difference*

Personal selling often adds an invaluable ingredient to promotion strategy. It requires that a producer's representative make face-to-face (or telephone-to-telephone) contact with the potential buyer. During a sales

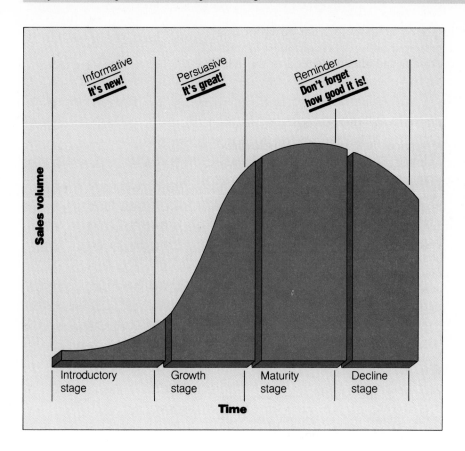

Figure 9-3 Different kinds of advertising for different stages of the product life cycle.

presentation, no matter how brief, the salesperson has a unique opportunity to *inform* potential consumers of the characteristics of a product or service and *persuade* them to buy. Personal selling involves not only the actual selling process but also a number of nonselling activities that support company relations with customers. This support may range in complexity from clerical order taking to sophisticated technical consulting, dependent upon the kind of product or service being offered.

## THE SALES PROCESS
*Locating, presenting, and closing*

All good salespeople engage in a process of communication with prospective customers. The purpose of the communication is to describe the product, stress its desirable qualities, and influence the prospect to buy.

Personal selling efforts may be divided into three progressive steps.

■ *Locating prospects.* It is useless and wasteful to make a sales presentation to someone who is not genuinely a potential customer. The main requirements for prospects are that they have a need or desire for the type of product being sold, that they have the money to buy it with, and that they have the authority to buy it.

■ *Making the sales presentation.* Many salespersons divide the presentation into (1) getting the prospect's attention, (2) stimulating the desire to buy, and (3) meeting objections. The presentation must include making a good initial impression, describing the product and its advantages, and answering questions.

■   *Closing* occurs when the salesperson actually asks for an order or a purchase. Closing techniques range from making a direct request to starting to write the order as if the customer had already agreed to the sale.

## NONSELLING FUNCTIONS
*Salespeople do much more than sell* ━━━━━━━━━

Sales personnel provide many services to customers. Wholesalers' representatives, for example, sell almost exclusively to intermediaries. Besides selling, they may help to arrange store and window displays, help to train retail clerks, handle adjustments and returns, help their customers to price goods for resale, and help to set up delivery schedules and methods. Retail salespeople handle complaints and returns and often give information unrelated to selling.

Salespeople also have a number of nonselling duties to perform for their company. They may be required to attend sales meetings and training sessions, help to train other salespeople, locate new customers or prospects, and collect credit information. Some retail clerks help to count inventory and stock display shelves. Most sales representatives and retail clerks must also keep sales records.

## THE SELLING PROFESSION
*Jobs range from the straightforward to the subtle* ━━━━━━━━━

Specific jobs in personal selling vary greatly in their complexity, skills required, and salaries. Many sales jobs, particularly at the retail level, are mainly clerical. They involve completing sales slips, making change, and recording credit purchases. Route salespeople, such as those who supply dairy and bakery goods to grocery stores, also mainly take orders and supply goods, without doing much actual selling. House-to-house salespeople spend most of their time actually making sales presentations or traveling, but they work in an environment where the percentage of successful presentations is rather low. Engineering and industrial sales require substantial technical ability and high-level creative selling skills.

Some salespeople concentrate almost entirely on opening new accounts, maintaining goodwill, and helping customers make good use of the products after purchase. These activities are called *missionary selling* and are very important in dealing with technical products like computers and manufacturing machinery.

Generally, intangible products are harder to sell than physical goods. Selling life insurance requires considerable skill in financial planning, for instance. Selling a product such as advertising space in a magazine, or a service like management consulting, requires subtle control of selling techniques, sensitivity to other people, and a command of technical knowledge.

**PLANNING AND PROSPECTING** Many people think of selling as an easy, congenial, independent way of life. For salespeople whose income is directly related to how much they sell, the job turns out to be one that requires a lot of personal discipline. A young computer sales representative with Sperry Corp. in Kansas remarked that he could leave nothing to chance. "If you want to make it in sales," said Joe Privitera after a few months on the job, "you must learn to make time work for you. The more organized I am, the more secure I feel." Research supports this view. It shows that in direct sales, results are critically linked to the number of contacts initiated with potential buyers. Figures vary according to product or service sold, but a good rule of thumb is that it takes about 25 contacts to get 12 meaningful responses. These result in an opportunity to make 5 sales presentations and 3 closed sales. A sales training expert, George W. Dudley, concludes that "as many as 80 percent of all salespeople who fail within their first year do so because of insufficient prospecting activity."

SOURCE: George W. Dudley and Shannon L. Goodson, "Fear of Prospecting," *Training*, September 1984, pp. 58–69.

Personal selling, no matter how effectively it is carried out, isn't everything there is to marketing promotion. It must support, and be supported by, other marketing efforts involving advertising and sales promotion.

## 4 ADVERTISING PRINCIPLES
*Media, not people, persuade*

Advertising is a type of promotion that does not use personal contact. Advertising presents informative and persuasive sales messages through communication media such as newspapers and television. Advertising stimulates interest in and demand for specific products, and thus supports sales promotion and personal selling. It is also often used to generate a favorable public attitude toward a company, industry, or other institution.

## OBJECTIVES OF ADVERTISING
*Advertising supports selling*

The main purpose of advertising is to help sell goods and services. Specific advertisements or advertising campaigns may try to meet this goal in different ways:

■ Advertising supports personal selling. At every stage of a distribution channel, products are more readily accepted if advertising has already informed the potential buyer of a product's features and has encouraged a favorable attitude toward it.

■ Advertising reaches people sales personnel cannot. It is rarely possible to have a sales force large enough to reach every potential customer. Effective advertising can motivate people to seek out salespeople or retail outlets on their own.

■ Advertising improves relationships with dealers. Retailers and wholesalers know that products that are advertised will be in greater demand and have a larger sales volume. A manufacturing company that advertises will increase not only its own sales but also sales for wholesalers and retailers who stock the producer's goods. Such results and the hope of sales encourage intermediaries to stock the producer's goods so that they are available when consumers want to buy them.

■ Advertising helps open new territories, tapping potential markets. When a company is trying to expand its sales territory, advertising can create the product and company recognition that will allow its sales force to start generating sales.

■ Advertising creates an initial demand for new products. When a new product or service is introduced, no demand exists because potential buyers do not even know the product is available. Advertising is usually the best way to inform enough people about new products.

■ Advertising increases sales volume. Keeping consumers constantly aware of a particular brand of product will make them more likely to buy it. Advertising can increase sales by popularizing goods or services among segments of the market that have not used them in the past. It can point out less familiar features to people who already use particular kinds of products.

■ Advertising can promote goodwill. Many advertising campaigns portray a company as being reliable, interested in the public good, and a good citizen. These advertisements focus on the company or organization itself rather than on a specific product. Advertisers benefit by creating public acceptance. Sales may increase if the company creates an image of providing good service or reliable products. Goodwill toward a company or industry may make higher prices more acceptable. Some companies have even tried to influence upcoming legislation that may affect them by presenting their case to the public through advertising.

■ Increasingly, advertising is being called upon to do the selling job alone. Direct mail advertising, aimed at completing the sale either by mail or telephone call to an order taker, continues to gain in usage. Mail-order houses, as described in the previous chapters, depend exclusively upon advertising. Of course, it is increasingly difficult with direct mail (or direct marketing through television, magazine, and newspaper ads) to separate advertising from sales promotion. The important point is that many producers look to advertising to replace or minimize sales effort because of the relatively small cost per "call" of advertising as compared with personal selling.

## HOW ADVERTISING WORKS

*It advances prospects from unawareness to action* ━━━━━━━━

The task of advertising is, like that of personal selling, to inform and persuade. Its goal, in most instances, is to have customers buy the products or services offered. To carry out these tasks and attain its goals, advertising tries to move potential customers from a stage where they are not aware that the product or service exists to the point where they actually buy the product, as shown in Figure 9-4. As the pyramid suggests, the task is most difficult at the lack of awareness stage and tends to get easier as the potential buyer is brought closer to the action stage. Not all advertising must start from the bottom. A person may be aware of a particular brand of clothing, for instance, and comprehend its good quality. If that is the case, its advertising must try to make the persuasion more convincing so as to stimulate greater desire for that brand. In situations where the product is well established and has already been bought once by the consumer, the task of advertising is to stimulate repurchases

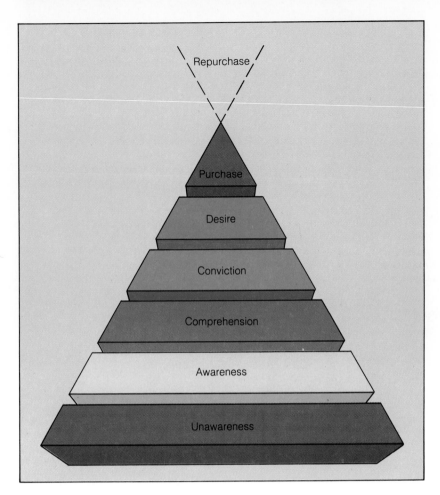

Figure 9-4 Advertising's tasks: to move potential customers from unawareness to purchase.

as with "reminder" advertising or by informing buyers of other things a product can do for them. When Arm & Hammer baking soda advertised that the product was good not only for baking but also for reducing odors in the refrigerator, that was an example of the latter.

## CLASSES OF ADVERTISING

*Advertising has five dimensions*

All advertising is intended to present an informative and persuasive message that will in some way help the advertiser to meet his or her goals. Within this general framework, however, advertising varies greatly. Types of advertising are usually classified by general objectives, content, intended market, geography, and media, as illustrated in Figure 9-5.

**GENERAL OBJECTIVES** Advertisements are classified generally by whether they are indirect or direct. Most advertising is *indirect,* as it does not attempt to close sales or directly generate orders. Instead, the intention is to increase product acceptance and preference in order to bring about more sales in the future. Some advertising is *direct,* however. It aims at getting people to actually place orders directly by mail or telephone. Familiar examples are advertisements for records on late-night television, and mail and coupon advertisements for magazine subscriptions.

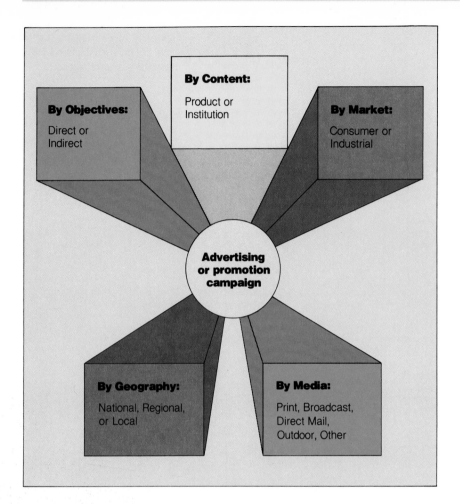

Figure 9-5 Different classifications of advertising are used to create an advertising or promotion campaign.

**CONTENT** *Product advertising* is designed to increase sales of specific goods or services. All of the familiar advertisements for television sets, automobiles, hair sprays, restaurants and motels, drugs and cosmetics, and hundreds of other products are meant to persuade people to buy the goods and services advertised. ***Institutional advertising*** presents the messages of a company, a group of companies, or other institutions without the intention of selling specific products. Companies often use institutional advertising to promote their reputation for providing good service or for showing concern for social interests. Industry organizations often advertise specific kinds of goods and services supplied by many individual companies. The wool, cotton, and railroad industries, for example, have used this approach. The federal government is another outstanding example of an institutional advertiser. Measured by total advertising expenditures, the government is one of the largest advertisers in the United States. For example, in one recent year the U.S. government spent over $190 million dollars on advertising. Advertising done by institutions in general constitutes a growing segment of this country's total advertising expenditures.

**ADVERTISING TO MARKETS** Advertising must be aimed at specific markets and can be classified that way. The largest general categories are consumer, trade, industrial, and professional markets. Of these, advertising to consumers is the most important type. Trade advertising is directed toward wholesalers and retailers; professional advertising is aimed at lawyers, doctors, and dentists; and industrial advertising promotes products for industrial use.

***GEOGRAPHIC CLASSIFICATION*** Advertising is often divided into national and local components. Many media, such as television networks and national magazines, can present sales messages nationwide. Others, such as local radio stations and newspapers, reach only a local audience. Major advertisers often combine the two kinds of exposure to reach the market segments they are aiming at. Businesses with local markets normally use only local media.

***ADVERTISING MEDIA*** Print, electronic broadcast, direct mail, and outdoor billboards are the most commonly used media for presenting advertising messages. Newspapers account for nearly one-third of total advertising revenues. Television is second, followed by direct mail, radio, magazines, and miscellaneous media. The large miscellaneous category is a collection of advertisements on public transportation, floor racks, window signs, matchbooks, and pens, to name a few examples. Although television is now in second place in advertising revenues, it is growing in importance. Magazines are capturing smaller shares of advertising revenues now than they did in the past. The percentage of total volume of advertising carried by different media is illustrated in Figure 9-6.

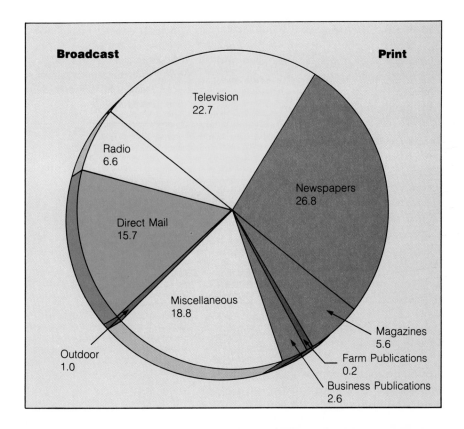

Figure 9-6 Advertising volume by media.

# 5  ADVERTISING MEDIA AND SELECTION
### The options are numerous; agencies help decide

Success in advertising requires careful selection of the most effective media for presenting sales messages. **Media** is the term applied to the means of transmitting an advertising message. The various popular commercial media each have their own particular advantages and drawbacks.

## POPULAR MEDIA
### Five forms dominate

Monthly magazines have different readers than do tabloid newspapers. Television advertisements reach different people at a different cost than do billboards on the expressways. An advertisement on the local radio station makes a different impression from one received in the mail. Many factors have to be considered in choosing a medium for any given purpose. The most important are the audience to be reached, cost, timing, and flexibility.

For an advertisement to be successful, it must reach enough people, and it must reach the right people. Media vary tremendously in the size of their audience or readership. A rural newspaper may be read by fewer than 5,000 people. Some network television events may be viewed by 50 million people. Media also differ as to the market segments that have exposure to advertisements. Some magazines, for instance, are read almost exclusively by affluent, well-educated urban and suburban readers. These usually contain many advertisements for restaurants, jewelry, and expensive home furnishings. Discount houses or manufacturers of low-priced goods prefer to advertise in some other medium that would reach more lower-income people.

Costs for advertising must be considered in relation to the size and type of audience reached. Most newspapers, magazines, and radio and television stations give potential advertisers estimates of the cost per thousand readers or listeners. This information can be used in comparing costs among the different media.

Media also differ in timing. Some magazines present a company's sales message only once a month, while radio stations can air sales messages every half hour. Timing also affects the preparation of advertisements and the extent to which they can be kept up to date. A complex filmed message for network television will have to be written, filmed, and scheduled months in advance and cannot easily be changed if the advertiser's plans change. A single advertisement for a newspaper can be revised up until the day before publication, and sometimes up until a few hours before the paper is printed. Magazine advertisements must usually be in final form by 4 weeks to 2 months before printing. Radio advertisements are normally fairly easy to keep up to date if they are locally produced.

Table 9-1 outlines some of the major advantages and disadvantages of the most important advertising media.

**MEDIA MIX** Rarely does a marketing promotion campaign rely upon a single media form. Instead, most producers will choose to distribute their advertising over a combination (or mix) of media forms. The amount of

---

## Action Brief
### ALWAYS KEEP THEM LAUGHING

*Do you want to be able to write good television commercials? Maybe you're not interested, but you may want to know which kinds score the best with television viewers. Commercials with humor are most certain to appeal. That was the conclusion of a study by a rating bureau of 1,000 viewers. If you want to lose the audience, hidden-camera testimony is the pits. In between, the second best appeal is a commercial with children, followed by portrayal of real-life situations and musical commercials. Advertisers start to lose viewers when they feature endorsements from experts, spots with celebrity sports figures, and product demonstrations. Next to the bottom are commercials that use "Mr. Big," the company president. Lee Iacocca for Chrysler was the exception!*

**TABLE 9-1**
**ADVANTAGES AND DISADVANTAGES OF THE MAJOR ADVERTISING MEDIA**

| Media | Advantages | Disadvantages |
|---|---|---|
| Newspapers | Can reach very large proportions of local markets. Cost per thousand people reached is often relatively low. Advertisements may be revised until day before publication. Special interest sections may be able to reach market segments. | Can be read quickly. Some pages or sections are often skipped. Difficult to reach national audiences. Market segmentation is not as precise as with some other media. |
| Magazines | Suitable for reaching national market. Can provide very precise market segmentation. Read more carefully than newspapers, and advertisements are more prominent. | Advertisements must be prepared up to 3 months in advance and cannot easily be changed afterward. Cannot reach specific local markets as easily as newspapers. Do not reach as large a national market as television networks. Advertisements are only published once a week or once a month. |
| Television | Advertisements can be lively and persuasive with sight and sound. Network television reaches a large national market. Local stations reach specific local markets. Advertisements can be repeated frequently. | Costs may be too high for small advertisers. Advertisements must be prepared far in advance and are difficult and expensive to change. Precise market segmentation usually cannot be achieved. |
| Radio | Similar to television except sound only. Costs may be lower. Exposure to local markets is often very good. | Advertisements are easily lost in program content. Network radio does not reach the large national market of television networks. |

**TABLE 9-1 (Continued)**

| Media | Advantages | Disadvantages |
|---|---|---|
| Direct Marketing | Directly solicits orders by mail, telephone, television, radio, magazine, and newspapers. Precise market segments can be reached. Can be used locally, regionally, or nationally. Can be used by any size and type of business. | Cost per sale can be high. Maintaining current and accurate mailing lists is difficult. Expensive to project high-quality image. |
| Outdoor | In areas of high traffic, billboards and other displays can effectively repeat simple sales messages. Total cost is competitive. | Not suitable for many products. Some objections on the grounds of taste. Difficult to keep messages up to date. |

money available for the campaign will limit, of course, how much can be spent on each medium. Some producers will allocate the lion's share of their money to newspapers, as illustrated in Figure 9-7. Others, such as a local restaurant, may balance the major shares between radio and newspapers, with a little bit for The Yellow Pages. A national advertiser introducing an orange drink may go all out for network television, with minor allocations in home magazines and local newspapers.

## ADVERTISING AGENCIES
*They produce the words and music*

*Advertising agencies* are companies that plan, produce, and place advertisements in the media. Business enterprises that perform these services are called agencies because they were once viewed as manufacturers' agents for newspapers and magazines, radio and television stations, and other advertising media. Agencies advise advertisers on their total marketing programs and help decide what part advertising will play. They write the advertising copy and produce artwork, films, songs, and other material. They then serve as contracting agents and buy newspaper and magazine space or broadcast time needed to display or present the advertisements. The work of an advertising agency is complex. It requires a wide range of different technical and creative skills combined with careful business and financial management.

Agencies are paid through a combination of commissions based on media billings and reimbursement for direct costs. An agency that prepares a series of newspaper advertisements for a department store, for example, will charge the store for costs of preparing artwork, typesetting, and other similar direct costs. Their main revenue, however, will come

---

*Action Brief*

### COUPONS: A PART OF THE NEW LIFE-STYLE

*The use of couponing by advertisers promoting the purchase of key products has become an American way of life. There are many varieties on the coupon theme. For example, you can get a second one of the same product with the coupon and a small additional payment; or you can get one of another companion product at a discount with the coupon; or you can get something free with a certain number of coupons. Most commonly used coupons are the simplest: a certain number of cents off on a specified purchase. The idea in the mind of the advertisers is to use coupons as incentives to stimulate sale of a new product or of one whose sale is slumping, or to clear factory and warehouse shelves in the slack season. An important survey showed that couponing is popular among consumers: 68 percent of all households claimed they used them. Where did they redeem them? In grocery stores, mainly—55 percent; then about equally distributed but in descending order of preference came fast-food chains (cents off on a hamburger or a free soda with a meal), discount stores (on a variety of hard and soft goods), and drugstores (on everything from cosmetics to proprietary medicines).*

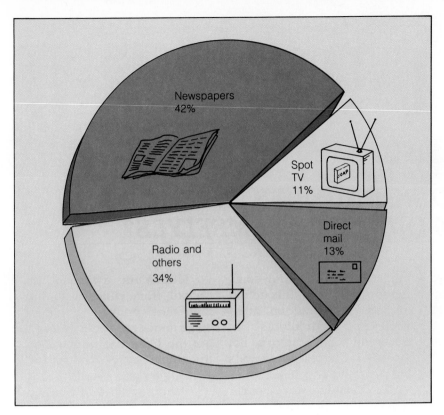

Figure 9-7 Media mix: Advertising expenditures by media in the grocery market.

from a commission deducted from the price of the newspaper space used in running the advertisements. The agency bills the department store for the full cost of the space. It then deducts its commission (usually 15 percent) and pays the remainder to the newspaper.

# 6 SALES PROMOTION
## *Everything that is not selling or advertising*

Sales promotion is the third type of promotion complementing personal selling and advertising. It includes a number of specific sales tools:

- *Point-of-purchase advertising (POP)* includes any kinds of sales messages presented at the place where goods are actually bought, especially in retail stores. These include store displays, in-store sales posters, and similar promotional devices intended to stimulate sales immediately.
- *Specialty advertising* refers to sales messages presented on small gift items such as matchbooks, pens, ashtrays, coasters, key rings, and balloons.
- *Trade shows* give producers the opportunity to show and sell their goods, mainly to intermediaries. Manufacturers or service companies present displays at trade shows that are attended by wholesalers, retailers, agents, or sometimes by the general public. This relatively low-cost promotion method is often a major pushing strategy.
- *Samples* are useful in getting consumers to try new products or different brands. Distribution of free samples is commonly integrated with advertising campaigns when new products are introduced.

# B·I·L·L·B·O·A·R·D

## SHOULD NONNUTRITIOUS FOODS SPEAK OUT FOR THEMSELVES?

At one time in the United States, it was good just to get enough to eat. That was before nutritionists discovered that many of the foods that satisfied appetites were loaded with things that weren't good for the body. As a consequence, this bad news has depressed the sale of many food products: butter, meat, sugar, eggs, potatoes, and coffee, to name a few. Sales of eggs dropped by 17 percent in 20 years; sugar dropped from 89.2 pounds a person in 1975 to 67.5 today; coffee dropped from a 33 percent share of the beverage market in 1962 to 18 percent today; potatoes dropped by 35 percent during a similar period. Candy sales hit an all-time low in 1983. Increasingly, however, the marketers of these maligned foods have struck back. Here are some samples of current-day advertising campaigns.

Kraft's ads have claimed that its Velveeta cheese is a "blend of natural cheeses, milk, and other wholesome ingredients." What this ad did not point out is that the "other wholesome ingredients" in processed cheeses are not cheeses at all. The key word is that Velveeta is a blend.

The Beef Industry Council, in defending charges that beef contains fats and cholesterols, advertised that "beef gives strength."

### Marketers of these maligned foods have struck back.

The Sugar Association launched a $2 million campaign urging that consumers "use real sugar if you know what's good for you."

The Coffee Association spent $20 million in a "coffee achievers" campaign presuming to tell coffee drinkers that it calms the nerves and perks up the spirits at the same time.

M&M/Mars switched its appeal from children to the idea that candy is a wholesome snack for adults. It even got the Mars bar adopted as the official snack food for the 1984 Olympics.

Potato Board ads claimed that potatoes were being given a bad reputation and that they were, of themselves, without latherings of butter and sour cream, nutritious.

### QUERIES

**1.** Do you think that marketers of foods of doubtful nutrition should be permitted to publish their points of view in paid advertisements, or should these ads be prohibited?
**2.** What might be done to make certain that the claims of advertisers are absolutely true and not misleading or deliberately confusing? ■

SOURCE: Christine Dugas, "Countermarketing: 'Bad' Foods Fight Back," *Ad Forum*, January 1985, pp. 18–22.

# PROFILE

ALEXANDER KROLL climbed the ladder from a stint in the U.S. Army's military police to all-American at Rutgers, to professional football player, to president and CEO of Young & Rubicam, the world's largest privately-held advertising agency. Along the way he was an analyst in the agency's research department, a copywriter, and head of the creative department. Associates say that Kroll's biggest assets are leadership, tenacity, grit, and energy.

Kroll says of American advertisers:

*We have, underlying everything else, a skill at using research and more unabashed salesmanship than in any other country. Advertising is a practical art; it's more like the building trades than fine art.*

*If you go back 15 years, the automobile industry, among others, wasn't particularly communications-sensitive. The power of the three major companies' distribution system was more critical; if you looked at their shares of market, there was an uncanny coincidence between distribution and share. But the distribution system doesn't carry the business anymore. With Europeans and Japanese competing now, the majors can't tell the factory to produce as many cars as they* want the public to order. The momentum has shifted to the consumer. Advertising communications mean more.

*Advertising is in some ways like the sports I used to play. It requires discipline and personal goal setting. Athletics is great training for advertising: you find out how hard it is to win and how good it feels to win.* ■

**ALEXANDER KROLL**

SOURCES: "Alex Kroll of Young & Rubicam on Creativity," an interview with *Ad Forum*, January 1985, pp. 30–31; Bernice Kanner, "Alex Kroll Plays to Win," *New York Magazine*, November 8, 1982, pp. 46–52.

■ Premiums and coupons are used similarly to samples. *Premiums* are small gifts offered with a purchase of the product being promoted. *Coupons* give buyers a discount when buying promoted goods. Both may make a product attractive enough for trial use by consumers.

■ *Promotional contests* offer prizes to participants in conjunction with the promotion of products. They sometimes help generate word-of-mouth advertising. Great care and specialized knowledge are needed for their use because of legal restrictions and high costs.

## 7  ADVERTISING AND THE PUBLIC
### Society regulates it and challenges its value

Most marketers make a good case for advertising. It helps to bring new ideas and comforts to many people who otherwise would not enjoy them. Economically, advertisers claim that the costs of distribution are lowered and mass production is made possible. The public at large has its doubts about these conclusions. Accordingly, society has seen fit to enact legislation regulating advertising in the United States and to engage in inconclusive debates about its social worth.

## REGULATION OF ADVERTISING
### The FTC holds the whip

Because of the effects of advertising on consumer buying habits, and because advertising clearly has the ability to deceive, the government has taken considerable interest in regulating advertising practices. The most general legal tool has been the Wheeler-Lea Bill of 1938. This gave the Federal Trade Commission (FTC) the responsibility of monitoring advertisements that fall under federal jurisdiction. The FTC goal is to eliminate advertisements that deceive the public about the nature of products or services advertised. The FTC tries to get advertisers to tell the whole truth about their products.

A number of federal laws also affect the labeling and advertising of certain products. The Wool Products Labeling Act, the Flammable Fabrics Act, and the Truth-in-Packaging Act are examples. Many states also have similar statutes aimed at specific industries or practices. Industry self-regulation, through such organizations as the Association of National Advertisers and the American Association of Advertising Agencies, also attempts to limit deceptive advertising.

## IMPLICATIONS FOR SOCIETY
### Its social value is challenged

The social value of advertising in the United States is controversial, but few would argue with its economic importance. Nearly $100 billion was spent on advertising in 1987, and the total has been increasing annually. Table 9-2 shows the top 25 national advertisers arranged by industry. It is clear that for many large companies, advertising their products is a major undertaking. Procter & Gamble Co., Philip Morris Companies, and RJR/Nabisco Companies spend in the billions. Certain industries—

---

### Action Brief

#### THE COURT OF MISLEADING ADVERTISEMENTS

*It's reassuring to know that somebody cares about whether or not the ads you see are really true. Not surprisingly, advertisers seek the same kind of assurance about their competitors' ads. The National Advertising Division (NAD) of the Council of Better Business Bureaus cooperates with the National Advertisers Regulation Board to investigate and rule on complaints. Here are two interesting cases.*

*Arm & Hammer challenged Airwick Industries' ad that said, "The noses have spoken, 93 percent of expert noses prefer Carpet Fresh." After exposing the product to an independent board of scientific experts, the study confirmed the claims, and the ads were continued.*

*Mattel, Inc. was queried about its ads for Rainbow Brite dolls. Its television commercial showed the dolls in an animated sequence without making it clear that the dolls couldn't really sing and dance. NAD recommended that "care should be taken not to exploit a child's imagination. . . . Fantasy should not create unattainable . . . expectations." Mattel discontinued the ad.*

**TABLE 9-2**
**LEADING ADVERTISERS**

| Company by Rank | Advertising Expenditures* | Percent of Sales Revenues Spent for Advertising | Product Lines |
|---|---|---|---|
| 1 Procter & Gamble | $1,600,000,000 | 14.3 | Soaps and cleansers |
| 2 Philip Morris Companies | 1,400,000,000 | 12.3 | Tobacco and beer |
| 3 RJR/Nabisco | 1,093,000,000 | 8.7 | Tobacco and food |
| 4 Sears, Roebuck & Co. | 800,000,000 | 2.0 | Retail and insurance |
| 5 General Motors Corp. | 779,000,000 | 8.8 | Automotive |
| 6 Beatrice Companies | 684,000,000 | 7.9 | Food |
| 7 Ford Motor Company | 614,600,000 | 1.4 | Automotive |
| 8 K mart Corp. | 567,000,000 | 2.5 | Retail chain |
| 9 McDonald's Corp. | 550,000,000 | 19.2 | Food service |
| 10 Anheuser-Busch Companies | 522,900,000 | 6.8 | Beer and entertainment |
| 11 American Telephone & Telegraph | 521,318,000 | 1.5 | Communications |
| 12 Ralston Purina Co. | 508,365,000 | 8.6 | Food |
| 13 Dart & Kraft | 489,349,000 | 6.7 | Food and pharmaceuticals |
| 14 General Mills | 484,146,000 | 10.6 | Food |
| 15 J. C. Penney Co. | 478,892,000 | 3.6 | Retail chain |
| 16 PepsiCo Inc. | 478,372,000 | 6.7 | Soft drinks and food service |
| 17 Pillsbury Co. | 473,220,000 | 8.8 | Food |
| 18 Warner-Lambert Co. | 469,339,000 | 28.4 | Pharmaceuticals |
| 19 Unilever U.S. | 413,623,000 | 9.9 | Soaps and cleansers |
| 20 Johnson & Johnson | 401,217,000 | 10.1 | Pharmaceuticals |
| 21 American Home Products Corp. | 399,516,000 | 11.0 | Pharmaceuticals |
| 22 Chrysler Corp. | 393,400,000 | 2.1 | Automotive |
| 23 Coca-Cola Company | 390,000,000 | 7.9 | Soft drinks and entertainment |
| 24 General Electric/RCA Corp. | 373,336,000 | 1.1 | Electrical machinery and electronics |
| 25 Kellogg Company | 364,299,000 | 17.5 | Food |

*Ranked by expenditures in the United States reported in 1986. Percentages are related to United States sales only.

*Source:* Reprinted with permission from the September 4, 1986, issue of *Advertising Age.* Copyright © 1986 by Crain Communications, Inc.

especially those heavily aimed at consumers, such as cosmetics and cleaning products manufacturers—spend significant portions of their total revenues on advertising. For example, Noxell Corp. in the early 1980s spent about 20 percent of its revenues for advertising.

There is little doubt, then, that advertising has a significant economic impact. But what does it accomplish? Does it really contribute to the good of society? There is widespread disagreement on these questions.

Proponents of advertising point out its benefits to business and society. Business gains from advertising because it helps sell products. It supports other promotion efforts, especially personal selling. It helps increase the strength of whole industries, as when railroad lines advertise as a group to improve their competitive position with respect to other modes of transportation. Advertising increases demand, both for the goods and services of particular companies and for products in general, thus benefiting business by increasing market size. It may also benefit society. Higher production creates more jobs and a higher standard of living. Extensive demand allows economical mass production so that goods can be manufactured at a lower unit cost. Advertising also helps to spread new ideas and innovations.

Nevertheless, many people are doubtful about the social value of advertising. The most common objection is that even if advertising has potential benefits for consumers, the benefits are not enjoyed by them. Manufacturers, they say, use mass production to make goods at a lower unit price but do not pass the savings on to consumers. Advertising may also interfere with free competition. Instead of competing on the basis of price or product quality, some companies are able to maintain and increase market shares merely by advertising more heavily. Some brands may be so strongly advertised as to gain a near monopoly in some segments of the market. Advertising may make these products almost immune to competition, even from a better product. In spite of government regulations, some advertising is deceptive. Even without making clearly false statements, advertising can mislead by implication. A person in a white laboratory coat promoting a pain remedy on television may suggest to viewers that doctors support the product even if they do not.

A fundamental objection to advertising that is often voiced is that advertising promotes materialism by constantly stressing the value of buying goods. According to this view, advertising encourages people to change their attitudes and ideas about life merely so that businesses can sell their products. Supporters of advertising reply that strong product promotion does not create materialism but merely operates within a society that was materialistic long before advertising gained its present importance.

---

# Key Concepts

1. Marketing promotion uses a combination of personal selling, advertising, and sales promotion to push or pull products through distribution channels.

2. Promotion campaigns establish a unified promotion effort appropriate to the product, company, and market and are designed to achieve planned objectives.

3. Personal selling is a major type of promotion using personally presented sale messages to persuade prospects to buy goods or services.

4. Advertising uses communication media to support personal selling, to stimulate buyers' interest in and demand for products, or to promote goodwill. It may be classified by its objectives, content, market, geography, and media.

5. The most effective media for specific advertising campaigns and messages must be chosen on the basis of costs, type and size of audience, timing, and flexibility. Advertising agencies specialize in coordinating campaign design and media selection.

6. Sales promotion complements personal selling and advertising with a variety of techniques such as point-of-purchase displays, specialty advertising, trade shows, samples, coupons, and contests.

7. The government, and in particular the Federal Trade Commission, regulates advertising to help prevent deceptive practices. Nevertheless, the public still has concerns about the value of advertising for society and the economy. Among the concerns is that advertising can interfere with free competition and may foster unbridled materialism.

# Review Questions

1. Define, explain, or identify each of the following key terms or phrases, found on the pages indicated.

*advertising (p. 192)*
*advertising agencies (p. 204)*
*cooperative advertising allowances (p. 192)*
*coupons (p. 208)*
*differentiation (p. 193)*
*direct advertising (p. 199)*
*indirect advertising (p. 199)*
*informative advertising (p. 194)*
*institutional advertising (p. 200)*
*media (p. 202)*
*personal selling (p. 192)*
*persuasive advertising (p. 194)*
*point-of-purchase advertising (p. 205)*
*positioning (p. 193)*
*premiums (p. 208)*
*product advertising (p. 200)*
*promotion campaign (p. 193)*
*promotional contests (p. 208)*
*promotional mix (p. 192)*
*pulling strategy (p. 192)*
*pushing strategy (p. 192)*
*reminder advertising (p. 194)*
*sales promotion (p. 192)*
*samples (p. 205)*

*specialty advertising (p. 205)*
*trade shows (p. 205)*

2. What are the three main kinds of promotion efforts and how do they work together in a campaign?

3. How is promotion related to a product's life cycle? What type of promotion is needed when a product is first introduced? in growth and early maturity? in late maturity and decline?

4. What are the important functions that must be performed as part of the personal selling process?

5. What are some of the most important objectives of advertising?

6. Give examples of product and institutional advertising.

7. What kinds of advertising media reach the largest national audiences? What kinds of media directly solicit orders?

8. Cite some commonly seen examples of sales promotion techniques.

9. What are some of the arguments used to defend the value of advertising, and what are some used to challenge it?

10. What major federal agency regulates advertising? Describe the kinds of advertising you find most deceptive and/or most objectionable.

# Case Critique 9-1
## Not for "Dishpan Hands"

Why don't women buy more computers? That was a question that marketers were asking during the computer-sales recession of the mid-1980s. A number of facts helped to shed some light on the subject, although the right direction to pursue wasn't exactly clear. At that time, research showed that 78 percent of the computers used in offices were bought by men. In light of the fact that women make up more than two thirds of office employment, this seemed strange. The figures on purchases for the home were a little better; 60 percent were bought by women. On the other hand, of those computers

bought for the home, men made up about 75 percent of the users. These figures were a little conflicting, especially when industry spokespeople were consulted. They estimated that of all personal computers bought, men outnumbered women buyers by a ratio of more than 8 to 1.

One observer suggested that the figures didn't tell the whole story: it might help to look at the way that computers were sold. One television commercial for a major company, for example, featured not a woman professional, but an office assistant. She was shown juggling a lot of balls, indicating how many things she was expected to do. The ad then had her look at the personal computer, getting the notion that it would simplify her job, with the suggestion, "Why not bounce the idea off your boss?" Apple computer seemed to try harder. It designed its personal computer line with women in mind. The company said it wanted it "to look as good on a kitchen counter or coffee table as in the office." Apple's advertising agency, too, said it tried to keep its commercials nonsexist. One commercial showed a female teacher preparing to leave the classroom at the day's end. She is approached by a little girl asking for help with her computer homework. The message, said the agency, is "that computers are not just for boys."

Some questions also arose about the appropriateness of the available software for home use. One research agency examined a major software display and concluded that it stressed the home economics side of a woman's life: rec-

ipe file and kitchen inventory programs. On the other hand, one software company was proud of its Barbie game. It said, "There's no reason for a young girl to play boys' games like GI Joe and Hot Wheels on a home computer."

1. What do you think is wrong with the advertising approach used to sell computers to women? How would you improve it?

2. If you were to rewrite the ad showing the woman assistant in the office, how would you change the "tag" line quoted in the case? Why?

3. How do you react to the software program prepared for women's use in the home? What suggestions can you make that might (1) provide better female-oriented programs or (2) help to sell male-oriented programs to women?

*SOURCE:* Karrie Jacobs, "The Gender Gap in Selling High Tech," *Adweek*, April 1985, p. 46.

# Case Critique 9-2
# Gold Doesn't Glitter for All

As the American athletes breezed across the winning line by the dozens in the 1984 Olympics, it appeared certain that many of them would become rich as a result. Not because of their athletic pursuits, but because they could now trade their names as gold medal winners for lucrative endorsements. It didn't work out that way. Only one or two really cashed in. Most of the rest got pretty slim pickings. Everyone by now has seen Mary Lou Retton's smiling face on a box of Wheaties or on a television commercial. Her prowess and pixielike charm made her a big winner in the advertising world. General Mills, McDonald's, and clothing stores like J. C. Penney and Sears have found her to have enormous customer appeal. But what about some of the others? Vidal Sassoon's hair products and Soloflex exercise machines tried gymnast Mitch Gaylord with some success. Carl Lewis, who won four gold medals, turned off his fans with his prima donna image, and the big advertisers walked away from him. For rea-

sons that aren't exactly clear, the advertisers also ignored the potential appeal of endorsements from Greg Louganis, a multimedal diver, and Valerie Brisco-Hooks, the super speedster with three gold medals. Winners in relatively obscure sports like shooting and synchronized swimming never really had a chance. Their appeal, at best, would be for narrow population segments rather than the mass appeal needed for television commercials.

The failure of the Olympic gold to glitter went even further. Companies like Eastman Kodak and Miller's High Life beer failed to make much capital of their endorsement and support of the Olympic theme. Kodak thought that "Ridin' Free in America" and Miller believed that "Made in America" would turn consumers toward them. Market research performed after the Olympics did not confirm this result.

The decision to choose and use a sports star for product endorsement is dependent upon

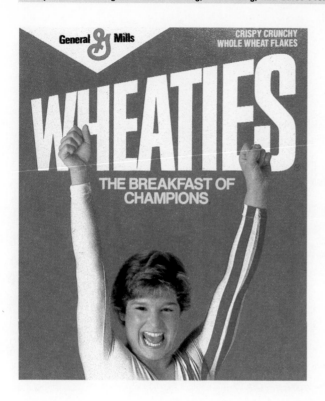

many things, of course. When it comes down to it, one authority commented, "It's fame that an athlete receives with the Olympic gold. It's Madison Avenue that awards the bankable gold."

1. Why do you think some Olympic medalists are chosen for endorsements and others are not?
2. Do you think that the use of popular sports figures and entertainers for product endorsement is an effective advertising technique? Why?
3. What is your reaction to the failure of companies who used their promotions to support the Olympics to gain any measurable advantage from it?

SOURCE: Kim Foltz and Linda Tibbets, "Olympic Gold's Lost Luster," *Newsweek*, July 1, 1985, pp. 46–47.

## CHAPTER 10

# Pricing Strategies
# for Profit

## Learning Objectives

*The purpose of this chapter is to explain the various factors that influence prices that are paid in the marketplace, to outline the various strategies and techniques used by sellers for setting prices, and to indicate the roles of consumers and government in this system.*

*As evidence of general comprehension, after studying this chapter, you should be able to:*

**1.** *Recognize the factors that enter into the determination of the break-even point and know how a chosen price affects that point.*

**2.** *Describe the effect of the conditions of supply and demand upon prices at which goods are sold.*

**3.** *Identify the four major pricing strategies and describe six common tactics used in setting prices.*

**4.** *Explain the markup pricing method and differentiate between markup based on purchase cost and markup based on selling price.*

**5.** *Define unit pricing and discuss the roles of consumers and government in the pricing system in the United States.*

*If your class is using SSweetco: Business Model and Activity File, see Chapter 10 in that book after you complete this chapter. There you will find exercises and activities to help you apply your learning to typical business situations.*

## 1 SELLERS TRY TO MAXIMIZE PROFITS

Producers' costs affect prices

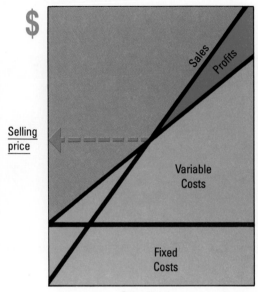

$

Sales

Profits

Selling price

Variable Costs

Fixed Costs

Sales Volume

## 2 SUPPLY AND DEMAND PLAY A BIG ROLE

Market prices strike the balance

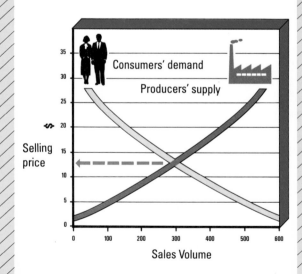

Consumers' demand

Producers' supply

Selling price

Sales Volume

## 3 PRICING PRACTICES ARE REALISTIC

Four main strategies

Follow-the-leader

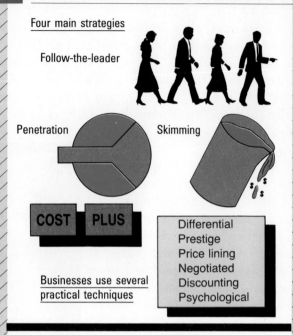

Penetration          Skimming

COST PLUS

Businesses use several practical techniques

Differential
Prestige
Price lining
Negotiated
Discounting
Psychological

## 4 RETAILERS APPLY MARKUPS

Selling price

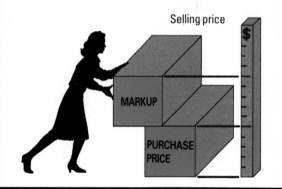

MARKUP

PURCHASE PRICE

## 5 PRICES ARE NOT REGULATED

Informed consumers benefit from unit pricing

69¢  BOX  = $1.38/lb.

and by casting economic votes

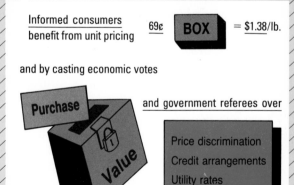

Purchase

Value

and government referees over

Price discrimination
Credit arrangements
Utility rates

# A PRICE-CUTTING TREND

When rental prices for videocassette tapes dropped from $3.95 a night to $1.95, a woman who ran a rental store in Little Rock gave up. "I can't break even at that price," she said. When the shakeout in videocassette players followed, prices for brand name units dropped out of sight, in some cases from over $699 to $299. A Sears catalog at the time featured a reduction in the price of Cheryl Tiegs T-shirts from $13.99 to $7.99. The operative word in the Sears catalog was "cut": "Washers and dryers—cut $90; Kenmore refrig-erator—cut $120; boat covers—cut 20 percent; stretch jeans—cut $4." And if it wasn't "cut," the words were "save!" "low," "less," or "1/2 price." A&P stores took out full-page ads announcing "over 5,000 new low prices." And if customers clipped the A&P coupon, they would get a dozen eggs free. A local furniture store adver-tised its 4th of July special: "Every-thing up to 1/2 price off!" Safeway's meat department listed its specials: Sirloin steak ("Safeway quality grade") $2.99 a pound, porterhouse $3.99, Holly Farms whole fresh fryers 59 cents a pound, Perdue whole fresh fryers 69 cents a pound. "Wait a min-ute," customers typically complain. "Can all this stuff really be on sale? What do these prices really mean?"

Price temptations surround consumers. Television, magazine, radio, and newspaper advertisements almost all claim that the prices cited are "re-duced" or the items are "on sale." Nichols, for example, a major variety chain, features an annual "Dollar Ganza." The range of products priced by Nichols for sale is wide. Does the customer want Kodak color-print film 2 for $5? misses' tank tops, 2 for $6? a 10-inch Regal silverstone frying pan for $5? Daiwa Jupiter spinning-reel fishing rod for $19, down from $24.99? or perhaps a choice of Gillette Good News! 5's, Aqua Net hair spray 12-ounce size, Soft Soap 15-ounce refill, VO-5 15-ounce shampoos, or Wet Ones 70's at $1 each? or a Huffy 10-speed bike, regularly $97.96 for only $79! The offers go on, more than 300 products, from garbage cans to nightgowns. In like fashion, every Thursday of the year, your local newspaper will feature page after full-page ads of sales at your national independent supermarkets. "It's incomprehensible!" say many consumers. "It all makes sense," say the producers and retailers of these products.

# 1  SELLERS' PRICES TRY TO MAXIMIZE THEIR PROFITS

## They set prices related to their costs

Pricing plays an important role in the American economy. The price placed on a good or service helps to determine who will have that particular product, without intervention from the government. If an individual or company needs or wants a product badly enough, it may pay the established price for it. If enough people want the product, other producers will enter the market and, in most cases, the price will be driven down so that more people who want the product can afford it. Pricing done freely in this manner saves the government from the difficulty of trying to tell producers what they should make and how much of it.

The other side of prices is that the consumers can choose to buy, or not to buy, at a given price. The better the bargain that consumers perceive at a given price, the greater the likelihood that they will buy at that price. When value doesn't appear to measure up to the price asked, people will go elsewhere. That's one advantage of having a Wendy's, McDonald's, Bonanza, Golden Corral, Burger King, and the like on the shopping strip when you're hungry for a hamburger. You can pay the price to whatever retailer offers what you believe to be the best combination of values—from bun, to beef, to pickle, and to cleanliness, service, and atmosphere.

In the American economy, several forces interact to determine prices. The producer of a product or service tries to set prices that will maximize profits. Consumers look for prices that give them the most for their money. Competing producers try to set prices that will give them a larger share of the market by enhancing the consumers' view of the value received. The federal government stands by as a referee to make sure that prices are reasonably fair; with some services, like electricity and telephone rates, approval must be secured from the government before a price is set. In general, though, a company is free to set its own prices.

A company that provides a product or service, however, would be foolish to just try to pick a price from the air. Whatever price a seller asks, whether high or low, it is usually based upon a knowledge of what it costs to produce and market that product. That is an essential starting point. With that knowledge in hand, the seller can then adopt price strategies that offer the best chances of maximizing profits.

## KNOWLEDGE OF THE BREAK-EVEN POINT

### The sales volume at a particular price where profits begin ━━━

The key for understanding the influence of costs on prices is a knowledge of a business's **break-even point.** This is the point at which the volume of goods sold at a chosen price will exactly equal the total cost of producing these goods. Below that sales volume, a company will lose money. Sales above that point will return a profit to the company.

In figuring the cost of making products for sale, companies must consider two different kinds of costs. Some costs are directly associated with the production of a specific item. A wooden table, for instance, may contain $12 worth of wood, glue, screws, and finishing materials and take

$14 worth of labor to construct. These costs are directly related to the number of tables made. One table will need $26 worth of materials and labor. One thousand tables will need $26,000 worth. (For the sake of simplicity, quantity discounts on materials are ignored.) Since these costs vary with the amount of output, they are called *variable costs.*

Other costs do not vary so directly with the amount of goods produced but remain relatively stable. These *fixed costs* include such items as rent, heat, light, insurance, and other overhead costs. They cannot be associated with any particular unit of output. It should be noted that fixed costs are not, in fact, entirely fixed. For instance, a machine that is used heavily on long production runs may need more repairs and replacements than one that is rarely used. More heat will be needed when a plant has full employment than when it is partly idle. Fixed costs are the general costs of keeping a business running. They do, nevertheless, affect the total costs of producing goods. In break-even calculations, they are considered fixed regardless of the amounts produced.

The break-even point is the quantity of goods or services that must be sold at a chosen price so that the total revenue from these sales will exactly equal the total costs (variable as well as fixed) incurred by the company for making that quantity of goods or services. The calculation of this point is done in three steps, as shown graphically in Figure 10-1.

### STEP 1 IS TO FIND THE TOTAL COST OF PRODUCING THE GOODS
The graph in Part 1 of Figure 10-1 assumes that the fixed cost of operating this particular company is $1,000. A straight line (the fixed-cost line)

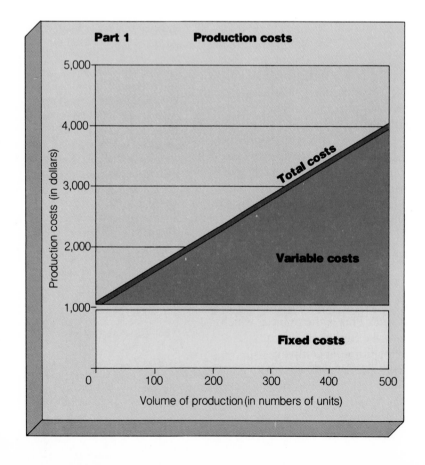

Figure 10-1 How a break-even point is determined. (See the explanation of Parts 1, 2, and 3 of the break-even chart.)

Part 1: Variable costs of production (labor and materials) are added to the Fixed costs to construct the Total costs line.

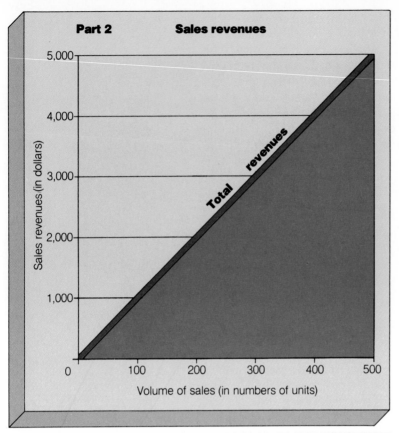

**Part 2**      **Sales revenues**

Part 2: Revenues from sales are plotted from 0 for no sales to $5,000 for sales of 500 units to construct the Total revenues line.

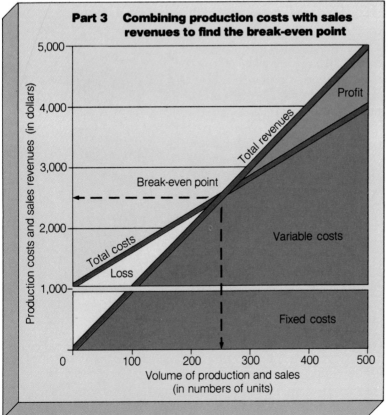

**Part 3**     **Combining production costs with sales revenues to find the break-even point**

Part 3: Charts from Part 1 (Production costs) and Part 2 (Sales revenues) are superimposed on one another to find the break-even point. This occurs where the Total cost line intersects the Total revenues line. Sales of fewer than 250 units will result in a loss; sales of more than 250 units will result in a profit. At sales of 250 units, the company will just break even.

is drawn at the $1,000 cost level, indicating that the company will have to spend that amount regardless of whether it makes no widgets or 500 of them. The variable cost for making this particular widget is known to be $6 each, to cover the cost of materials and labor. If the company makes 100 widgets, the variable cost will be $600 (100 × $6); if it makes 200, the variable cost will be $1,200; if it makes 300, the variable cost will be $1,800, and so on. The trick now is to find the total cost. This is done by adding the variable cost in each instance to the fixed cost. Thus, for 100 widgets, the total cost is $1,600 ($600 + $1,000); for 200, $2,200 ($1,200 + $1,000); for 300; $2,800 ($1,800 + $1,000); and so on. The graph shows the total cost by plotting 0 production at $1,000, 100 at $1,600, 200 at $2,200, and 300 at $2,800, and connecting the points.

**STEP 2 IN CALCULATING THE BREAK-EVEN POINT IS TO FIND THE TOTAL REVENUE FOR ANY LEVEL OF SALES** Here, the assumption is that the company will sell its widgets at $10 each. If it sells none, its revenue will be $0. That is the first point on the graph, shown on Part 2 of Figure 10-1. If it sells 100, the revenue will be $1,000 (100 × $10); if it sells 200, the total revenue will be $2,000 (200 × $10); if it sells 300, it will be $3,000 (300 × $10); and so on. These points are plotted on the sales revenue chart (Part 2 of Figure 10-1) and connected to form the total revenue line.

**STEP 3 IS TO PUT THE TWO CHARTS TOGETHER** The point at which the total sales revenue line intersects the total cost line is the break-even point (as shown in Part 3 of Figure 10-1). If you look closely, you can see that the company would lose money if it made and sold only 100 widgets (total revenue = $1,000; total cost = $1,600). Similarly, it would lose money at 200 widgets (total revenue = $2,000; total cost = $2,200). It will make a profit, however, if it makes and sells 300 widgets (total revenue = $3,000; total cost = $2,800). The point at which it will begin to make a profit, then, is somewhere between 200 and 300 widgets, the point at which the total revenue line crosses the total cost line. For this company, the break-even point is 250. (Total revenue for 250 widgets is $2,500 [250 × $10]; total cost for 250 widgets is $2,500 [250 × $6 + $1,000].)

The company in this example now knows that if it decides to make fewer than 250 widgets and sells them for $10 each, it will lose money even if it sells them all. If it decides to make more than 250 widgets, and is able to sell them all for $10, it will begin to make money. Based on this knowledge, a company can try to either raise its selling price or reduce its costs in order to lower its break-even point. In any event, the company will always know how many widgets it must sell to make a profit, regardless of how many it makes initially.

Service companies use the same principle in pricing and costing their units of service (such as the number of windows to be washed). Retailers and wholesalers apply the same analysis in determining how many units of merchandise must be sold at a given price to break even.

# HOW PRICE AFFECTS BREAK-EVEN
*The higher the price, the lower the break-even point;*
*and vice versa*

If fixed and variable costs remain the same, and only the price of the product or service is changed, the new price will have the effect of raising or lowering the break-even point. When the price is raised, this lowers the break-even point. The company will make a profit sooner at the higher price. When the price is lowered, this raises the break-even point. The company will have to sell more of its products before it starts making money. Figure 10-2 shows how price changes upward or downward affect the break-even point of the widget company.

Break-even points are notoriously high in the petroleum industry, where fixed costs are enormous. During the early 1980s, when the price of gasoline decreased, most of the large oil companies reported reduced profits. An industry spokesperson said at the time that "almost all refineries are operating in the red because of depressed prices for gasoline and heating oil." The individual attributed this to "weak demand and overproduction." Underlying it all, however, were the high fixed costs of the business. Lower demand was pushing prices below the oil companies' break-even point.

## 2  MARKET PRICES REFLECT SUPPLY AND DEMAND

*Consumer demand greatly influences prices that producers charge*

Back in Chapter 2, much was said about the way in which prices are affected by the law of supply and demand. That is, the market price of a product is the result of a balancing act between (1) the supply of goods placed in the market by all the producers in that market and (2) the degree of demand (what people are willing to pay) of all the potential consumers in that market.

Take a look at a specific, narrowed-down example—the market for hamburgers in a small town. People are very price-conscious there. Very few people (35) would buy hamburgers every day at $1.50. A great number of people (120) might buy hamburgers each day at 50 cents. This is the demand curve illustrated in Figure 10-3A. Note that as the price gets

Figure 10-2 How price changes the break-even point.

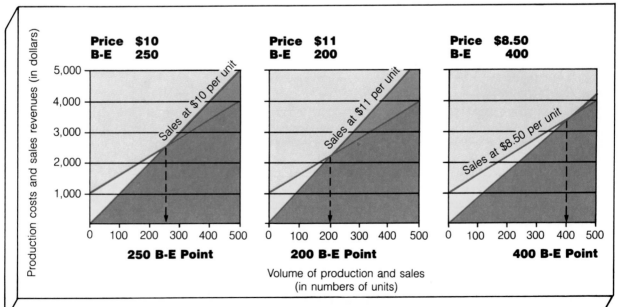

Figure 10-3 How supply and
demand establish market price.

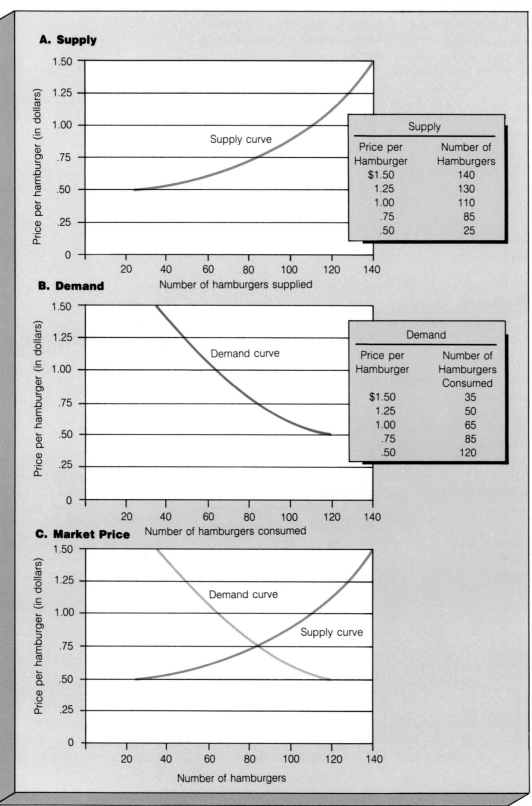

lower, the number of people that may buy a hamburger daily increases.

Now look at the restaurants in that town. There are only a few of them. Nevertheless, taken together, they might be willing to prepare 140 hamburgers a day at the $1.50 price. At 50 cents a hamburger, only 25 would hit the griddle. This is the supply curve illustrated in Figure 10-3B. Note that as the price increases, the number of hamburgers made available increases too. When the price drops, the number made available drops too.

What—in effect—the market does is to place the demand curve on top of the supply curve to find a balance point. That is the point in Figure 10-3C where the two curves intersect. The intersect point is the price (85 cents) at which hamburgers will generally be sold in that town.

**SURPLUS AND SHORTAGES.** The forces of supply and demand always strive to find a balance point. When prices appear attractive to producers and sellers, more of them come into the market. If too many come in, this often creates a surplus, and prices are dropped to a level where there are enough consumers to absorb the supply. If there are not enough suppliers to keep up with the demand, there is a shortage of supply. When this happens, the goods are typically sold at a higher price to a lesser number of consumers. When prices are set in response to shifts in consumer demand, the practice is called **demand pricing.**

The impact of supply and demand forces on prices is especially evident in commonly used products. The price of peanuts and, as a consequence, peanut butter is an example. When the peanut growers in Georgia had a bumper crop in 1984, the increased supply created a surplus and had the effect of driving prices down, since demand did not increase at the same time. An 18-ounce jar of peanut butter, which had been selling for $1.79 before the harvest in 1984, dropped to $1.59 by the end of the year. Gasoline prices also reflect supply and demand. Figure 10-4 shows what actually happens to prices and the consumption of gasoline as the supply varied from surplus to shortage to surplus during the years 1978 through 1984.

Competition counteracts the freedom to raise prices. Free competition tends to drive prices down for two reasons. First, the entrance of a competitor into the market will increase the supply of a product. This works against high prices because the immediate scarcity is reduced. Additionally, new competitors often purposely sell at a lower price in an effort to cut into the sales of an established producer or supplier.

# 3  PRICING PRACTICES ARE REALISTIC
## They temper objectives with market realities

The practical result of all this is that marketers have a choice to make when pricing products. They can establish high prices with the expectation of selling fewer units but with a greater profit on each unit. The other alternative is to set low prices in an effort to achieve volume sales even though the profit on each unit may be small. The typical response to this choice is to try to find exactly the right price that will maximize profits by balancing sales volume with profit per unit.

**Interrelation Between Gasoline Prices and Gasoline Consumption**

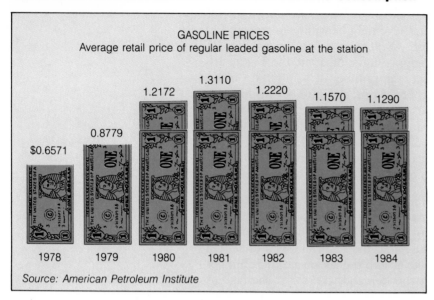

Figure 10-4 Interrelation between gasoline prices and gasoline consumption.

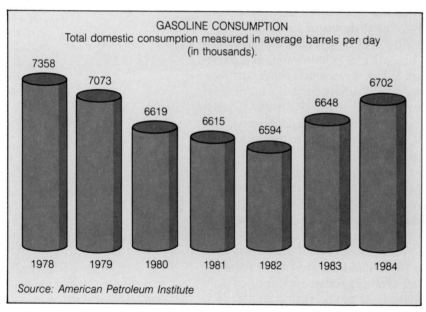

# PRICING STRATEGIES
*Four basic approaches*

Specific methods for setting prices usually depend on development costs, manufacturing costs, demand estimates, existing and potential competition, promotion and distribution plans, expected length of the product's life cycle, and other factors. Many of these pricing methods are complex. There are, however, certain general pricing practices that demonstrate the approaches that companies use. The four major methods are cost-plus, follow-the-leader, penetration, and skimming.

Probably the single most common pricing method is to set prices that are very close to those already established for similar products of competing firms. A major company in the industry, called a price leader, may determine what the new prices will be. Other producers usually adjust their prices to stay in line. This may be called *follow-the-leader pricing*. The advantage of this practice is that it limits excessive price competition that might result in lower profits for everyone. It also simplifies the pricing process. Companies do not have to perform all of the research and analysis involved with other pricing methods. At the same time, companies that use this kind of pricing do not have the assurance that they really are selling at the optimum price.

*Penetration pricing* is sometimes used when introducing new products. It involves setting as low a price as possible, considering manufacturing and other costs, with the expectation of achieving volume sales. Its main advantage is that it can result in high profits if market penetration is sufficient. It also discourages competitors from entering the field because a substantial part of the demand will already be met and because the profit margin on each unit will be slim.

A third alternative is to set the highest price consumers are likely to accept when the product is introduced and plan to lower prices later when competition makes itself felt. This is called *skimming*. The intention behind skimming is to recover the development costs of a product while the field is still relatively noncompetitive. This approach is more common with products that have a novelty value and for which there is a strong demand and few competitive suppliers.

*Cost-plus pricing* simply adds an arbitrary markup to the cost of producing the goods or service.

## PRICING OBJECTIVES
### Chosen with profits in mind

Producers, wholesalers, and retailers are rational in their price-setting practices, even though this may not always be apparent. Prices will be set first to cover costs and enable a company to exceed its break-even point, and then as high as the market will bear, consistent with a company's pricing objectives. A company may, for example, want to establish a pricing policy that will build not only one-time purchases but also repeat customers. Prices in such cases, and these are many, will be based upon long-term relationships and long-range profit objectives. Another company may be interested mainly in the immediate profit and set prices without regard to repeat business. In other instances, a company introducing a product may wish to place its price low enough to capture as large a share of the market for that product as possible; later on, it may raise the price. When Polaroid introduced its first instant color-print camera, it used that policy. In general, a company's pricing objectives will depend upon consideration of several factors, each of which has an impact on profits:

1. The cost of producing and marketing the product
2. How quickly the company wants to retrieve the money it has spent on developing the product
3. How big a profit it wants to make on that particular product
4. Whether or not the product will be sold only once or become regularly offered for sale
5. The relationship of that product's price to the price of others in the company's product line

## Action Brief

### YUGO, THE UNBELIEVABLE BARGAIN

Americans in 1986 weren't sure they would buy an automobile from a Yugoslavian importer at $5,000 a copy. The price was so low that consumers felt that there just had to be something wrong with it. There was no catch, however. Zastavia, one of the best but least-known European automakers, had decided to design and produce a car for the American market. Since its homeland was Yugoslavia, the car was to be called Yugo. After studying consumer behavior in the United States, the company concluded that persons earning less than $25,000 were not sharing in the current auto-owning boom. They could and would buy a new car for $5,000. So, with this target price in mind, the Yugoslavian manufacturer worked backward to design, produce, and market a car that could be sold for that price.

6. Whether the product is new in the market or is an established one

7. How unique the product is compared with others on the market

8. The phase of the product's life cycle

9. What kind of long-term relationship and pricing relationship the company wishes to establish with its customers

10. What kind of price comparison it wishes to make in the consumer's mind vis-à-vis the sellers of competitive products

11. The extent to which it wants to capture a commanding share of the market

12. The amount of inventory it has of that product and how badly it wants to reduce it—and how quickly

## PRICING PRACTICES
*Tactics vary for practical reasons* ━━━━━━━━━━━━━

Pricing policies and practices vary widely according to the preferences of the seller and the practices in a particular market. There are a number of tactics and techniques that are commonly practiced.

- **Differential pricing** sets different prices for various segments of the market. It is most apparent when applied to the seasonal rental prices for resort accommodations. In-season prices are usually dramatically higher than off-season rates.

- **Prestige pricing** tags a product with a price so high that its purchaser can assume that its quality is far and above all other products. Countess Mara ties and many other branded clothing, cosmetics, and perfumes are often priced out of all relationship with their costs, but these expensive products find a market among buyers who enjoy the prestige (real or assumed) associated with their ownership.

- **Price lining** is dependent upon a reseller's policy of segmenting merchandise into certain price lines. It is typical for a clothing store, for example, to classify men's suits as low-, medium-, and high-priced lines. If the established price lines are $100, $150, and $200, suit manufacturers must price their products so as to fit into the retailer's price line.

- **Negotiated prices** are those that are agreed upon after give-and-take by buyer and seller. Consumers are exposed to it somewhat in new-car purchases. The practice is very common in the sale of industrial goods and services.

- **Discounting** represents any reduction from an established, or **list**, price. Discounts are regularly offered for quantity purchases and for cash payments. Discounting is also used for **promotional pricing**. This occurs two ways. Prices may be marked down from list to encourage customers to buy a product that they might not otherwise buy, or at least not at that particular time. It is common practice in supermarkets to offer a **loss leader**, a product priced sharply below list price in order to attract customers into the store, where they make other purchases while they are there.

- **Psychological pricing** is a tactic that relies upon consumers' perception of a price's value. It often depends upon setting an odd-numbered price, just below the logical even-numbered price. An $8.00 tape album might be priced at $7.99, for example. The belief is that the price is registered in the consumer's mind as $7 rather than $8. One could argue that the retailer loses 1 cent on each sale, and if 10,000 tapes are sold each year, such pricing would lead to a loss of $100. This seems trivial in relation to the sales obtained by this tactic.

# 4 MARKUP IS THE KEYSTONE OF RETAIL PRICING

### The difference between price paid and selling price

When it gets down to the nitty-gritty of pricing, wholesalers and retailers are guided almost exclusively by two factors: gross margin and markup. The two terms are closely related. The **gross margin** is simply the difference between the price the retailer pays for the merchandise and the price he or she is able to sell it for. The gross margin is of vital concern to the intermediaries since it must cover all their fixed and variable operating costs and also provide them with a profit. Markup and margin are terms that are often used interchangeably. **Markup**, however, is a calculated difference between buying and selling price established by the technique of markup pricing. **Markup pricing** is based upon establishing beforehand how much higher—in terms of a percentage—the selling price should be than the cost price. Markups determined by markup pricing are expressed as percentages. They may be quoted as a percent of either the cost or the selling price, as shown in Table 10-1. The two different ways of expressing markup often lead to confusion, and it is important for people discussing markups to be certain of the method used before comparisons can be made.

Markup practices vary from industry to industry, from product to product, and from store to store. They are not established by law or by agreement between competitors, which would be illegal. They are usually the result of years of tradition. The traditions usually bear a relationship to production costs, marketing expenses, and consumer attitudes inherent in that particular market. Auto dealers, for example, traditionally mark up cars between 11 and 18 percent of the sales price. It is not uncommon for jewelry stores, however, to mark up some products by as much as 300 percent of cost. Grocery products typically carry a 20 percent

**TABLE 10-1**
**TWO WAYS OF CALCULATING MARKUP PERCENTAGES**

|  | Percentage of Cost (Purchase Price) | Percentage of Selling Price |
|---|---|---|
| Retailer's Cost | $ 6.00 | 6.00 |
| Markup | 4.00 | 4.00 |
| Selling Price | 10.00 | 10.00 |
| Percent Markup = | $\dfrac{\text{Markup}}{\text{Cost (Purchase Price)}}$ | $\dfrac{\text{Markup}}{\text{Selling Price}}$ |
|  | $= \dfrac{4.00}{6.00}$ | $= \dfrac{4.00}{10.00}$ |
|  | $= 66.66\%$ | $= 40\%$ |

markup. Mass discount stores, like K mart, have average markups of about 40 percent based on costs, compared with 50 percent for department stores. Within a particular retail store, some products, like small appliances, may have a much lower markup than the store's general, or "keystone," markup. Most small retailers and wholesalers establish their keystone markup for each type of product as a pricing policy. Then as each product is marked for sale, the keystone markup price is calculated (often using a computer program that makes the calculations and prints out the price tag) according to the preestablished percentage.

When a retailer or other business reduces its previously posted list price, such discounting is often referred to as **markdown.**

# 5 CONSUMERS MUST FEND FOR THEMSELVES
## Government regulation of prices is limited

Since the United States operates under a free market system, there is little price regulation provided by the government. Businesses may set prices with little restraint. Informed and progressive businesses, of course, are more likely to adopt pricing policies that attract and hold customers rather than exploit their patronage. There is no assurance, of course, that this will happen. Accordingly, the best assurance of fair pricing is an informed consumer population.

## INFORMED CONSUMERS
### Find bargains and protect themselves against unfair pricing

When it comes to prices, there is no free lunch. In the main, you get only what you pay for. The basic rule from the buyer's viewpoint is that *price should reflect value.* A price quoted in one store that is greatly lower than in another is suspect. Consumers must be on their guard against "hidden" costs. For example, does the price include delivery, installation, necessary spare parts? How good is the warranty and over how long a period does it last? Are the qualities comparable between Brand X and Brand Y? What do the financing charges really add up to? When in doubt, consumers are advised to compare prices and values at two or more competing stores. Where competition is intense among sellers, genuine bargains can be found.

One good way for consumers to know what value they receive at a given price is to look for **unit pricing.** Many states mandate it in larger stores; many large supermarkets provide it voluntarily. Unit pricing helps consumers compare the prices of similar items by giving the price in a standard unit, such as an ounce or a pound. It is much easier to compare a 10-ounce can at 45 cents with a 12-ounce can at 50 cents if the unit price is 4.5 cents an ounce on the first can and 4.2 cents an ounce on the second.

Consumers must also be alert to "sale" pricing that implies low prices when they may not, in fact, be low prices at all. A "closeout sale," for example, does not necessarily mean that the goods being closed out are high-priced merchandise that has been allowed to accumulate in inventory. It may simply mean that the merchant bought the stock of average merchandise a week ago and is closing it out this weekend. Other sales terms that can be questioned include "comparably priced," "priced elsewhere at," "never priced lower," "our lowest price," and—especially— "will never be priced this low again." All these terms may be used legitimately, but they often imply more than is actually delivered.

To become better informed, consumers can consult a number of consumer publications, such as *Consumer Reports* and *Consumers Digest*, which examine products, prices, and brands to provide estimates of comparative value. Local chambers of commerce and offices of The Council of Better Business Bureaus can often provide information about the reliability of companies doing business in a community, although these organizations may refrain from commenting on prices as such.

# GOVERNMENT REGULATION
*Provides some protection and selective controls*

The policy of the United States government is to keep its hands off pricing except in a few carefully selected areas. It does enforce a number of laws, however, that help to protect consumers from generally unfair business practices, and some of these impinge directly upon prices.

The Robinson-Patman Act of 1936 makes it a crime for a seller to sell at **predatory prices**—lower prices in one geographic area than in another in order to eliminate competition or to sell at unreasonably low prices to drive out competition. This law, which is intended to end **price discrimination,** is enforced by the Federal Trade Commission. For a number of years, various states enacted so-called fair trade laws, which protected small retailers from price competition from larger stores that could afford to set lower prices because of their volume. The Consumer Goods Pricing Act of 1975 repealed such laws.

The federal government and some states also regulate the prices (or rates) that are charged for certain public utilities such as electric power, natural gas, and telephone. Railroad freight rates and pipeline rates are also largely regulated by the federal government. Occasionally, in times of national emergencies due to war or economic conditions (like the gasoline shortage during the OPEC crisis), the government may also regulate, or "freeze," prices. On the whole, however, such actions have been greatly resisted by business and by Congress.

Of particular relevance to prices are the provisions of the various consumer-related laws such as the Consumer Credit Protection Act (Truth-in-Lending Law), the Fair Credit Reporting Act, the Fair Credit Billing Act, the Equal Credit Opportunity Act, and the Fair Debt Collections Act. Among other protections offered, these laws force a seller who urges a consumer to buy on credit to make a "full disclosure" of exactly what those terms entail. These laws, and some state laws, also provide for a 3-day "cooling off" period to protect consumers who have been pressured into signing a contract which they later find to be not as attractive as it appeared at the time.

The practice of "bait-and-switch" pricing and merchandising is prohibited by the Wheeler-Lea Amendment to the Trade Commission Act. Bait and switch occurs when a product is advertised at an unusually low price (the bait) and the salesperson switches the customer's interest to a higher-quality, higher-priced model. This is illegal if the intention was never to sell the low-priced model in the first place.

# Key Concepts

**1.** Sellers price their products or services with the intention of making a profit. The starting point in a seller's price-setting process is a consideration of the cost of developing, producing, and marketing the product and, especially, a knowledge of how the price chosen will affect the number of units needed to be sold to make a profit. The higher the price that can be obtained, the lower the break-even point, and vice versa.

**2.** The conditions of supply and demand in a particular market greatly influence the prices at which products are sold. When supply exceeds demand, there is a surplus and prices are likely to drop. When demand exceeds supply, there is a shortage and prices are likely to rise.

**3.** Producers and sellers typically choose among four major pricing strategies. *Follow-the-leader pricing* occurs when most sellers set prices in a similar range. *Penetration pricing* sets prices comparatively low so as to capture a large share of the market. *Skimming* relies upon a new product that is so unique that a very high price can be charged when it is introduced; this enables the producer to recoup development costs as quickly as possible. *Cost-plus pricing* adds an amount to the expenses incurred in developing, producing, and marketing the product in order to cover overhead and provide a profit. In addition, a wide variety of pricing practices are employed to fit a variety of objectives and marketing situations. These include differential, prestige, and psychological pricing; discounting; negotiated pricing; and price lining.

**4.** Markup pricing is a technique especially used by wholesalers and retailers. Markup, or gross margin, is the difference between what resellers pay for a product when they buy it and the price they get for it when they sell it. The principle of markup pricing is to compare the markup with either the purchase price or the selling price in order to establish a standard markup percentage.

**5.** In the free market system of the United States, informed consumers are a potent force in the determination of prices they pay. A knowledge of unit pricing, along with an active determination to make certain that the prices they pay reflect genuine value, helps make consumers more effective participants in the market system. The federal government tries not to intervene in pricing. It has, however, enacted laws against discriminatory pricing and laws for the protection of consumers who enter contracts or use financial credit. The government also regulates pricing of public utilities—such as electric power, natural gas, and telephone services—and rates for shipments by rail and water. Occasionally, in times of national emergency, the government may intervene to "freeze" prices.

# Review Questions

**1.** Define, explain, or identify each of the following key terms or phrases, found on the pages indicated.

*break-even point (p. 217)*
*cost-plus pricing (p. 225)*
*demand pricing (p. 223)*
*differential pricing (p. 226)*
*discounting (p. 226)*
*fixed costs (p. 218)*
*follow-the-leader pricing (p. 225)*
*gross margin (p. 227)*
*list price (p. 226)*
*loss leader (p. 226)*

*markdown (p. 228)*
*markup (p. 227)*
*markup pricing (p. 227)*
*negotiated price (p. 226)*
*penetration pricing (p. 225)*
*predatory prices (p. 229)*
*prestige pricing (p. 226)*
*price discrimination (p. 229)*
*price lining (p. 226)*
*promotional pricing (p. 226)*
*psychological pricing (p. 226)*
*skimming (p. 225)*
*unit pricing (p. 228)*
*variable costs (p. 218)*

2. A woman operates a word processing service and knows that she must prepare 25 pages a day at $3 each to break even. She moves to a smaller office building where her rent will be significantly lower. Will she have to prepare fewer or more pages now to break even? Why? Could she now reduce her page rate a little and still break even at 25 pages a day? Explain.

3. If a company lowers its selling price in order to attract more business, what effect will that have on its break-even point? Is it a good idea to cut prices to attract more business? Explain.

4. Discuss the difference between a surplus and a shortage and what might cause each of them. What is likely to happen to prices in each case?

5. Distinguish between penetration pricing strategy and skimming. When are these strategies most likely to occur?

6. Provide some examples of price lining.

7. Describe some of the uses or objectives of discount pricing.

8. How are gross margins and markup pricing related? If a retailer buys a pair of athletic shoes for $15 and fixes a selling price at a markup of 33 percent over the cost, what will the selling price be?

9. What does unit pricing tell a consumer about the value received at a particular price? Why is this important?

10. What sorts of prices is the federal government likely to regulate?

# Case Critique 10-1
## Halston: You Made Penney's Prices Too High

Roy Halston Frowick, the boy from Iowa, tried to bring high fashion to J. C. Penney in the early 1980s with his Halston III line of women's clothing. Observers regarded this as a brilliant move for both parties. Halston's reputation was associated with very high priced fashions usually found only in exclusive stores. Halston III would be a moderately priced line of women's sportswear, dresses, and accessories. The pricing strategy went something like this: Prices would be structured so that Halston III would be priced lower than designer fashions in department stores but higher than nondesigner styles that Penney and other competing stores carried. Two things immediately went wrong. First, department stores reduced the price of their designer fashions to below the Halston III price. Next, Penney's regular customers turned cool toward buying Halston III fashions since their prices were 15 percent higher than traditional Penney pricing for the top of its line. Within a very brief time, Penney had to mark down its list prices. Penney's retail store managers complained that markdowns moved from 20 to 30 percent and finally to 50 percent.

While all this was going on, Sears, Roebuck and Co., another mass merchandiser, took a different approach. It introduced its Cheryl Tiegs celebrity line of fashions. Sears' pricing strategy was to peg the price for the Tiegs line at a level that matched its existing prices. So, while Penney was trying to upgrade its present customers and attract additional customers who were used to paying, and who were willing to pay, higher prices, Sears had no problem selling the Tiegs line to its regular customers.

1. What pricing consideration had Penney tried to overcome in setting higher-than-usual prices for its top-of-the-line fashions?

2. Since the competing department stores reduced the prices of their designer lines so quickly, what does this tell you about the condition of supply and demand in the women's designer fashions market at that time?

3. At markdowns of up to 50 percent, what do you think of Penney's chances of making a profit on the Halston III line at that time?

4. What made Sears' pricing strategy more successful than Penney's?

*SOURCE:* Peggy Marion, "J. C. Penney and Halston: A Marriage on the Rocks," *Ad Forum*, May 1985, pp. 49–50.

# Case Critique 10-2
## What Kind of Way Is This to Set Prices?

There are more than a half dozen companies that make a business of competing with the U.S. Postal Service for fast overnight delivery of packages and documents. There are Federal Express, Emery Air Freight, DHL, and Purolator, for starters. An important segment of the industry is engaged in international shipments. Sales within that segment total over $1 billion annually. The field is very competitive. Thus, it is typical for the carriers not only to cut their prices but also to raise the package size allowance cutoff points. One company, however, takes a different pricing point of view. It is World Courier, Inc. of Greenwich, Connecticut. It refuses to be drawn into the price wars. In fact, it prices its services more than three times higher than the norm of its competitors. For example, when Emery was charging $27 for door-to-door service from New York to Paris and DHL $30 for transatlantic delivery between New York and London, World Courier was asking for, and getting, $99 and up for the same delivery. In fact, the company handles international deliveries so well and so often that its revenues regularly top $50 million a year.

The answer to this seemingly impossible difference in rates lies in two important factors. World Courier claims that it serves a different segment of the international market than its competitors. Says World's founder and chair, "Our customers are likely to be a grain shipper, or an international lawyer, a bank or other financial institution that stands to lose hundreds of thousands of dollars with each day's delay in the delivery of its documents. The documents might be a $50 million bundle of cancelled checks bound for the Federal Reserve piling up interest at $30,000 a day or a bill of lading for $20 million in grain."

A second point of differentiation has to do with the exact nature of the delivery service. World Courier promises delivery at the earliest possible time without regard to expense. Bigger shippers try to consolidate shipments, and this can cause minor delays at both sides of the ocean. By using the first available direct flight, even for one piece, World can guarantee not just next-day service, but delivery by 10 a.m. anywhere in the world.

1. Of the four basic pricing strategies, which comes closest to World Courier's pricing approach? Why?
2. How do you explain the company's ability to charge such high rates in comparison with its competitors?
3. How might a change in supply-and-demand conditions and a resulting change in the nature of competition affect World Courier's pricing policy?

SOURCE: Marie D'Amico, "World Courier Skims the Cream," *Venture*, April 1985, p. 100.

## Ad agencies join the computer revolution

Creative spirits in advertising agencies have long resisted the inroad of computers. They are gradually giving in, however, because the order and logic of computer systems shores up traditionally weak accounting and paperwork systems. Agencies are often paid according to the time each person spends on a particular account. Computerized timekeeping records make billing far more accurate than before. Another area that is often characterized by mass confusion is the issuance of ad-insertion orders to newspapers and magazines and to radio and television stations. Furthermore, insertions have to be verified after the ads have run before clients will pay for them. In many agencies, computers do all this instantly and reliably. Agency executives used to keep the books in whatever spare time they could find. "Now, by using computers," said the owner of one agency, "our productivity has increased drastically. We have as close to a paperless operation as you can."

SOURCE: Dylan Landis, "Computers Help Agencies Account for Business," *Ad Week,* April 29, 1985, p. 16.

## No more "telephone tag"

Now that Dollar General Corp. (Scottsville, KY) has a voice mail system, district managers no longer have to play "telephone tag" with store managers. Under the old, call-recording system, each of 100 district managers would call in on Sunday and leave a travel schedule for each day of the next week. These were typed up by a clerk and posted at headquarters. If the district manager had to change a schedule, this was telephoned in when it occurred. The purpose was to let each of Dollar General's 1,150 store managers know where and when they could reach their district managers when a decision was needed. The old system ate up $24,000 a month in credit card calls plus an operator and a WATS line working full time. At its best, the system often ran hours, if not days, behind actual travel schedules. Store managers constantly played the game of telephone tag trying to reach their bosses. With voice (electronic) mail, the store manager uses his or her own telephone to put the question directly into the district manager's voice mail box. When the district manager calls in, he or she gets the messages immediately and can reply immediately using the system in reverse to contact the store manager.

SOURCE: Henry Holtzman, "Voice Mail: Still an Infant Technology," *Modern Office Technology,* June 1985, pp. 77–90.

# Production and Operations Management and Controls

Unit 4 covers the essentials of production and operations management, information analysis, data processing and computer systems, and accounting. It also explains the use of budgets to plan and control business operations.

## CHAPTER 11

Production and operations management is concerned with physical conversion processes; layout and location of facilities; and the planning and control of production schedules, industrial purchasing, inventories, and quality.

## CHAPTER 12

Management information systems (MIS) provide managers with the knowledge needed for planning, operating, and controlling.

## CHAPTER 13

The accounting process provides a detailed record of business transactions involving money. These records enable managers to better direct and control operations.

## CHAPTER 14

Budgets help to control business operations. They are prepared from business forecasts, which are estimates of future sales, expenses, and profits. Managers compare actual performance with budgets to determine how well their businesses are doing, based upon its plans.

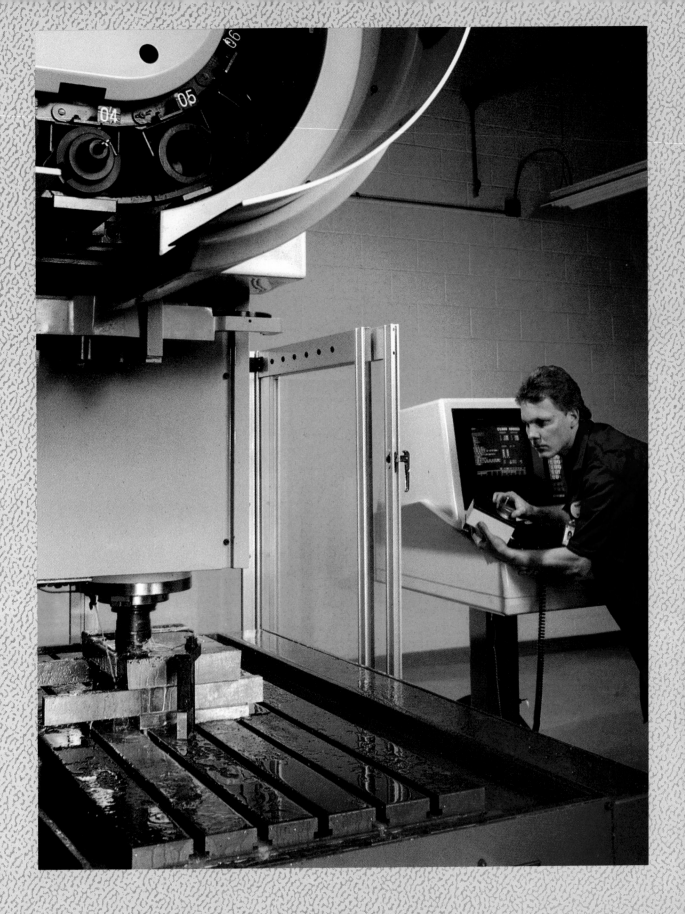

# Production and

# Operations

# Management

## Learning Objectives

*The purpose of this chapter is to define production and operations processes and describe the layout and selection of their facilities; and to outline the ways in which inventories, quality, and progress are controlled.*

*As evidence of general comprehension, after studying this chapter you should be able to:*

1. *Classify the various processes as either industrial or nonmanufacturing, and recognize the impact of automation, computers, and other technology on these processes.*

2. *Recognize and describe the advantages of the four major ways to lay out a business facility.*

3. *Identify the factors that affect the choice of a business site.*

4. *Outline the production and operations planning process and explain the use of Gantt charts and PERT networks.*

5. *Explain the role of industrial purchasing and the purposes of make-or-buy decisions and value analysis.*

6. *Describe the main features and techniques of inventory control, quality control, and progress control.*

*If your class is using SSweetco: Business Model and Activity File, see Chapter 11 in that book after you complete this chapter. There you will find exercises and activities to help you apply your learning to typical business situations.*

## 1 BUSINESS PROCESSES

fall into two major categories:

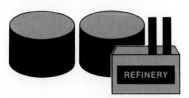

Industrial/Manufacturing
(those that produce goods)

Nonindustrial/Service
(those that provide services)

## 2 PHYSICAL LAYOUT

determines operational efficiency through orderly flow, minimum handling, and maximum space utilization.

## 3 LOCATION OF FACILITIES

must take into account five factors:

Markets
Resources
Utilities
Community
Process

## 4 PRODUCTION AND OPERATIONS PLANNING

decides what to make and how much, how to make it and in what sequence, and when to make it.

## 5 INDUSTRIAL PURCHASING

involves buying for conversion rather than resale.

## 6 PRODUCTION AND OPERATION CONTROLS

monitor . . .

Inventories to balance acquisitions with the demand for them

Quality to minimize defects and errors using motivational programs and statistical analysis

Zero Defects and Quality Circles

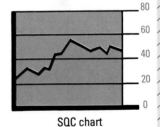

SQC chart

Progress and Performance using various control reports

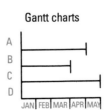

Gantt charts

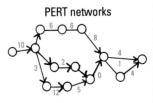

PERT networks

# APPLYING "FUTURE" PRODUCTION METHODS NOW

*General Electric Co.'s factory of the future is already 7 years old. It isn't all robots and automation either. Located in Louisville, Kentucky, this GE facility is the largest—and most productive—dishwasher plant in the world. The reason for the amazing efficiency of this plant lies in its use of advanced manufacturing methods, both high-tech and human. In an age of automation, this plant was conceived as much with people in mind as with machinery. As the plant manager says, "A human assembly-line worker can twist a slightly out-of-specification part into place; a robot rejects it." On the other hand, workers who used to be called upon to check control panels got so bored with pushing buttons all day long that they often missed signs of malfunction. Engineers then designed a device that has a robot pushing the buttons and a television camera and computer reading the display; virtually no defects get past that point. The human who used to do the testing now runs the testing machine.*

*The plant also uses "point-of-use" manufacturing stations that make parts right where they will be used on the assembly line. The old-fashioned way was to make the parts in large quantities on heavy presses elsewhere in the plant and store the parts for later use. Now, small presses right on the factory floor make parts only as they are needed. It saves space and inventory costs and provides greater flexibility.*

*Another nonautomatic device reverses typical assembly-line thinking. Since Henry Ford's day, the "right" way to run an assembly line was to have the conveyor belt keep pulling the product past the workers. Unfortunately pulling would continue, whether or not the product was defective. In this GE plant, however, each part stops in front of the human being performing a step in the production process. Not until the worker is satisfied that the job is properly done does he or she pull the green handle that sends the part moving farther down the line. To stop and go like this may seem inefficient, but for every part that "escapes" down the line, it costs $45 to fix it under warranty in the field. Parts that are caught in the plant can be fixed for an average of $3.50 each.*

*By running its factory of the future today with ideas that fit not only advanced technology but also the humans who are essential to the process, General Electric has captured 40 percent of the dishwasher market.*

SOURCES: Mark Potts, "GE's Future Factory," *The Washington Post*, December 18, 1983, p. F1–2; Howard Gold, "And Then There Were. . . ?" *Forbes*, April 8, 1985, p. 50.

# 1 KINDS OF BUSINESS PROCESSES
*Processes fall into two broad classes*

Many of the decisions about how a business is run depend on the nature of the process to be performed. All business processes may be divided into the broad categories of industrial, or manufacturing, and nonindustrial, or nonmanufacturing. All processes that create goods or services may be called production. The term **production,** however, is commonly used only for processes where the physical form of materials is changed. Thus manufacturing processes are production processes. Other business processes that do not create physical goods are called **operations.**

The management of business processes that create physical goods is called **production management.** Management of processes that mainly create services may be called **operations management.** Both production and operations management are concerned with layout of processes, location of facilities, planning of operations, purchase of materials and merchandise, and control of production, inventories, and quality. Many of the concerns of nonmanufacturing operations, such as retail stores, are similar to those of manufacturers. McDonald's fast-food chain is a good example. It establishes a number of measurable standards for the quality of its hamburgers, carefully details every processing method in their preparation, and judges its success by how efficiently it converts its raw materials into a finished product.

## INDUSTRIAL AND MANUFACTURING PROCESSES
*These produce goods*

Industrial and manufacturing processes are distinguished from other processes in that manufacturing, mining, or construction changes the physical form of materials. It adds value to starting materials by reshaping, combining, or transforming them. This value is called utility of form. The different industrial processes may be described as extractive, analytical, fabrication, synthetic, and assembly.

**Extractive processes** take physical resources from the earth, sea, or air for use in further manufacturing or for use directly by consumers. Pumping crude oil from the ground, digging out copper ore, growing and harvesting vegetables, fishing, and chopping timber are all examples of extraction. While extraction usually provides starting materials for further manufacturing processes, some extracted products, such as vegetables and shellfish, may be sold directly to consumers.

*Analytical processes* break materials down into new and more useful forms. An analytical process separates iron ore into iron and waste rock. Copper and other ores must be treated in the same way. Raw petroleum is separated into useful components such as gasoline, heating oil, asphalt, and polymers. Threshing wheat separates the useful grain from the worthless chaff.

*Fabrication processes* change the size or shape of materials and may join them together in various ways to create new products. Fabricating may involve cutting parts from sheet metal and stamping them into shape, cutting fabric and making it into clothes, cutting and shaping wood into pieces and gluing them together to make furniture. The construction industry fabricates when putting up bridges and buildings. Fabrication may produce finished products for sale to final buyers, or it may create component parts to be used in further manufacturing.

*Synthetic processes* create new materials by chemically or physically combining and changing other materials. The original materials are no longer distinguishable. Plastics, for example, are synthetics made from binders such as cellulose or synthetic resin and other materials. Many fibers for cloth are made in a similar way. Steel is created from iron and other substances.

*Assembly processes* create products by joining together component parts without changing their shape or composition. A bicycle can be made by screwing and bolting together the proper frame, hubs, spokes, brake parts, and so forth. A new product has been created, but all of the component parts have retained their original physical form. They have merely been attached to one another. The final manufacturing process for many goods, from automobiles to pocketknives, is assembly. The component parts have been produced by previous manufacturing processes from extraction through subassembly.

## NONINDUSTRIAL AND SERVICE PROCESSES
### *These perform services*

Nonmanufacturing processes perform operations other than changing the physical form of materials. Some of the important processes are warehousing, wholesaling, and retailing, transportation and communications, and a variety of direct service operations.

*Warehousing* includes a number of activities in addition to the simple storing of goods. Grading, sorting, packing, and contracting for shipping contribute to making goods more valuable by making them available when and where they are needed. These activities contribute utility of time and place.

*Wholesaling* and *retailing* also add utility of time and place to goods. The process includes buying goods for which there is an anticipated demand, keeping them on hand until buyers want them, and then reselling these goods at a profit. Food service and provision of hotel or motel accommodations are important forms of retailing that also resemble manufacturing in that they convert materials into useful products—prepared meals and comfortable resting places.

*Transportation services* add utility of place. By moving goods from their place of origin to where they will actually be used, the goods become more valuable. Although this process usually includes only loading, moving, and unloading, the management decisions can be complex. Scheduling equipment use and maintenance of aircraft, for example, is critical to airline operations. Communications—such as telephone, radio, and television—is also a form of transportation, in that sounds or images are transported from one place to another. The products in these instances are information and entertainment; the service provided involves their creation (or manufacture) and distribution.

*Direct service operations* cover a multitude of activities. Typically, however, these services provide labor, skill, methods, or facilities to aid individuals or organizations. Various kinds of utility may be created indirectly as a result. A bank is one example. Its operations deal with recording, storing, and distributing information as it processes deposits, withdrawals, and checks. The bank may also earn money by lending it to others and pay interest to those who have placed money in the bank's keeping. The bank itself contributes the equipment, methods, and personnel to handle these processes.

There are also a great many other direct service operations, such as dry cleaning of clothing, repairing of automobiles and appliances, issuing insurance protection, caring for hair, painting and papering homes, lawn mowing, removing trash, providing security, fixing teeth, and burying the dead.

Increasingly, the processing of paperwork for insurance, purchase and sale of stocks and bonds, and financial transactions of every kind has created massive operating problems. The handling of this process is known in many circles as "back-office operations," and represents a challenge to those who provide these and other similar direct services.

## PROCESS TERMINOLOGY
*Key to production planning*

All processes may be continuous or intermittent. *Continuous processes* run for long periods of time with few pauses or changes. Chemical plants, steel mills, and auto assembly lines usually operate around the clock for months with no essential changes in their production activities. *Intermittent processes* operate for shorter periods, in batches and often only for an hour or two, and are easier to change. Commercial printers, for instance, often use a different setup for every job.

Continuous processes produce *standard products.* A great quantity of the output is produced to the same specifications. Standard products are usually made in advance of sale to unknown customers. Toothpaste, for example, is made in huge quantities without the producer knowing specifically who will buy it or when. Similarly, certain services are available continuously, like telephone service and television entertainment. Intermittent processes are suited to *custom products* or services. Custom goods, for example, are not made until an order is placed; the customer usually has some latitude in determining the specifications of the products. A custom-made suit, for instance, will be cut to the buyer's measurements and made of material that the buyer selects.

Processes differ in the amounts of labor and capital they require. *Capital-intensive processes* use expensive equipment or materials and are less dependent on the activities of workers. Petroleum refining and electrical power generation are capital-intensive processes. They use expensive plants and relatively few workers, compared with the quantity and value of output. In *labor-intensive processes,* workers make a significant contribution to the value of the output. The production of hand-carved furniture is an example. The relatively inexpensive starting materials are converted into high-priced products through the skill of workers. Many repair services—like automobile repair, television repair, or plumbing—are labor-intensive also.

## EQUIPMENT TRENDS
### Toward automation and robotics

Mechanization replaces the labor of humans with work done by machines. At one time, garden shovels were made using the methods of the blacksmith: they were hammered out by hand. Today, machinery powered by steam or electricity can stamp out millions of shovel blades with little hand labor involved. Mechanization has greatly reduced the number of workers needed to produce a given amount of goods. At the same time, it has greatly increased the amount of capital needed for equipment.

One result of mechanization has been the increasing standardization of goods. A worker making products by hand can make each one to different specifications. For most machines to be efficient, they must make a large number of identical products. Frequent retooling of manufacturing machinery to new specifications is simply too expensive.

A modern extension of mechanization is automation. **Automation** is a collection of methods for controlling machinery and production processes by automatic means, usually with electronic equipment. Automation requires a device that is capable of two-way communication with the machinery it is controlling. The control device must be able to send messages to the machine instructing it to perform certain operations. The machine returns **feedback** to the controller communicating the results of the operations.

An increasingly popular form of automation is **robotics.** This is the use of mechanical devices that duplicate the motion of the human hand. They are especially good for dirty, dull, repetitive, and precise work. In 1987, there were more than 10,000 robots employed in the United States (far fewer than in Japan), and the prediction is that there will be 120,000 in place by 1995.

Another important trend is the use of computers to direct, assist, and/or control manufacturing and other processes. **Computer-assisted design (CAD)** and **computer-assisted manufacturing (CAM)** have added a form of automation to the work of designers and drafters and to engineers who design manufacturing and production machinery.

## 2  PHYSICAL LAYOUT OF PROCESSING
### Work flow determines efficiency

The efficiency of business processes depends partly on how well the physical components are arranged. Designers of production facilities, stores, and offices strive to create a physical setting that will allow work to be done with minimum congestion, backtracking, and interference of one activity with another. For any kind of process, a simple arrangement or layout is usually best. Designs that result in the least amount of paperwork and handling of materials usually result in less wasted effort.

---

### Action Brief

**COMPUTERIZED LAYOUT FOR RETAIL STORES**

*CAD is old hat for designers and drafters who create and delineate new product designs. It's a brand new idea, however, for planning retail store layouts. Planmark, an architectural unit of Super Valu Stores, used a program obtained from IBM to design 40 supermarkets and a number of warehouses. The program automatically spots locations for shelving, display gondolas, checkout stations, and parking. Similar CAD systems were used to design K mart's Payless Drug Stores layouts. The computer not only does the design work but also calculates store traffic flow and storage capacities for alternative arrangements.*

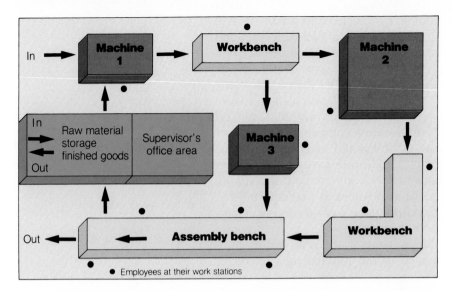

Figure 11-1 Layout for a manufacturing operation.

Layouts also attempt to make maximum use of the space available. Office, store, and plant floor space is expensive, and wasted space reduces profits. Most layouts for production processes arrange workers and equipment in relatively fixed workstations and then move the material to be converted from station to station selectively, according to what product is being made and what operations must be performed on it. This is called a ***process layout,*** since it allows for a variety of products to be handled in a number of different sequences. In its illustration in Figure 11-1, product A might be routed according to a path that brought it from machine 1 to machine 2 and then to the assembly bench. Another product B might skip machine 1 and start on the first workbench, and then proceed to machines 2 and 3 before reaching the assembly bench. Process layouts are very adaptable, as shown in Figure 11-2, where one is used

Figure 11-2 Office layout in high-rise building.

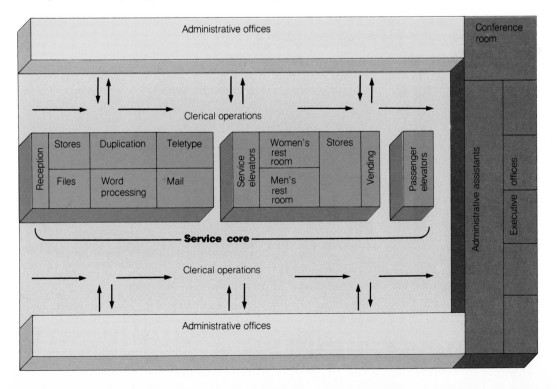

to lay out an office in a high-rise building. Employees and paperwork will move or be moved to the various processes (such as files, teletype, and word processing) selectively, according to the needs of a particular situation or processing requirement.

A process layout is not always the most suitable for the process being performed. A *product layout*, like that shown for the car wash in Figure 11-3, has a distinct advantage if all products are relatively the same and must follow the same sequence. Manufacturing companies use product layout on long assembly lines of automobiles and electric appliances.

In retail stores, layouts often follow a *customer layout*, as shown in Figure 11-4. The store manager wants to have a smooth flow of customer traffic while displaying as many goods as possible to potential buyers.

A fourth type of layout is the *fixed-position layout* used in assembling heavy, fragile products like space shuttles, large engines, ships, and bridges. With this layout, the product remains where it is, and machinery, materials, and workers are moved to the product to work on it.

# 3 LOCATION OF FACILITIES
## *Locations must optimize several factors*

Modern transportation and communication systems have broadened the range of potential business sites. At one time, it was nearly impossible to produce iron at any distance from ore deposits and charcoal sources because means of moving materials in any quantity did not exist. Today, many such barriers can be overcome if there is sufficient reason to do so. In selecting a location for facilities now, managers must balance a number of sometimes conflicting needs. The major considerations are the availability of markets, resources, utilities, and reasonably priced building sites, and an encouraging social and political setting.

## MARKETS
### *Vital for retailers*

Nearness to markets has long had an important influence on the location of facilities. Areas with high concentrations of people—such as

Figure 11-3 Product layout.

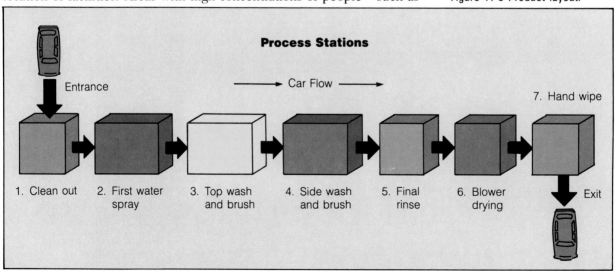

**Process Stations**

Entrance → Car Flow →

7. Hand wipe

1. Clean out  2. First water spray  3. Top wash and brush  4. Side wash and brush  5. Final rinse  6. Blower drying  Exit

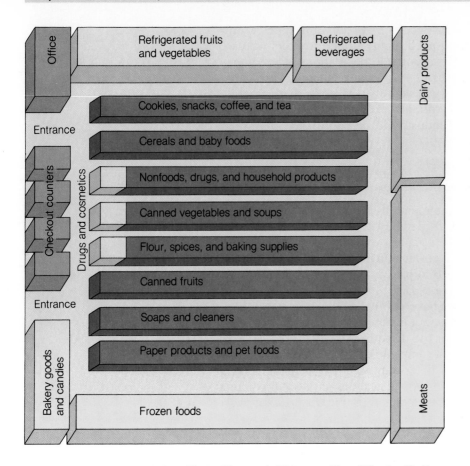

Figure 11-4 Typical layout for a small supermarket. The layout of merchandise in a retail shop is often critical to its success. Layouts are designed to direct customer flow past high profit and impulse products and make the customer work harder to find low profit staple items. Here, frequently purchased perishables are placed at the sides and rear to divert customers from the center aisles where staples are located. Nonfood items, such as drugs and cosmetics are displayed near checkout counters to promote impulse buying.

the corridor between New York City and Chicago, Fort Worth, Dallas, and Houston, Texas, and the areas around San Francisco and Los Angeles—continue to attract many companies. This is because of the many buyers who can be reached with low shipping costs. The southern and southwestern regions of the United States have seen striking business growth in recent years due to the increased size of their markets, which resulted in part from population growth.

Moving close to markets is particularly important for manufacturers of products that are difficult and expensive to ship. Goods that require a significant amount of service, like computers, must be produced close to markets or a separate facility must be maintained to provide the service. Businesses that provide services almost always select locations mainly on the basis of nearness to markets.

# RESOURCES

## Labor and materials

The availability of the resources a business uses often affects the choice of the facilities' locations. Being close to the sources of raw materials is important for many industries. Those that use bulky and heavy materials or perishable farm produce are especially affected. Some industries use huge amounts of water and must establish their operations in areas where it is available. Companies that use partially processed materials—such as lumber, sheet metal, or component parts—in their operations may benefit by locating near these sources.

Labor is another resource that affects the location of facilities. Companies that provide services often need highly skilled workers who are hard to find except in areas with concentrated populations. The same is true of many manufacturing processes that require laborers with highly developed skills. Companies that use workers with skills that are easily taught are often attracted to areas with low average pay scales. This was another reason for the growth of industry in the South and Southwest.

## UTILITIES
*Increasingly important*

Most industries today rely on tremendous amounts of power for their operations. If coal or oil is used, it may be beneficial for companies to locate near their sources. Prices are usually lower there because transportation costs are minimal. Electric power purchased from utility companies also varies in price from place to place.

Some companies need unusual capacities for the disposal of solid or liquid wastes. Some communities have public facilities capable of handling these problems. In other cases, a natural resource, such as a large body of water, may be needed for the disposal of treated liquid waste. Transportation is important to most companies. The availability of major highways, waterways, airstrips, or other transportation facilities plays a role in business location. Communications facilities are also important, but they are becoming so widespread that their impact on location is diminishing.

## COMMUNITY INFLUENCES
*Attitudes and amenities*

The overall attitude of a community influences whether businesses locate there. Many towns and cities give temporary preferential tax rates or other incentives to new businesses. Local ordinances on land use and other aspects of development often affect companies' decisions. Some companies are attracted to communities with no zoning restrictions, while others believe that communities with strong zoning restrictions are preferable. Zoning is the practice of restricting the use of certain areas for specific purposes, such as residential, commercial, agricultural, and industrial uses.

A community's attitude toward education and other public services influences company location decisions as well. A good educational system produces people who are generally more capable workers. Adequate fire and police protection and other local services, such as hospitals, make some places more desirable for workers to live in than others. And since workers are an important resource, communities that attract the best potential employees are the most attractive to business.

## SITE AVAILABILITY
*Room to grow at the right price*

The final requirement of a good location is the availability and suitability of an appropriate building or site. A good site must be large enough for the proposed operations. Room for parking and future expansion must be considered. The land itself should be suitable for building—neither so soft as to require deep pilings for support nor so rocky as to require blasting. The property must be zoned to permit the kind of operations intended. Finally, the price must be affordable.

## TYPE OF BUSINESS
### Sensitivity varies

The relative importance of different influences on facilities location will vary with the types of operations a company engages in. Manufacturing companies often must give nearly equal weight to all factors. However, some manufacturers of goods that are easily shipped find it less important to be near markets. Warehousing operations may give first consideration to the availability of transportation facilities. Distributors may need a location that has access to several different means of transport. Nearness to markets is usually more important to their operations than it is to manufacturers. The prime consideration for a retail business is easy access to its markets. Retailers must try to locate in a market area that is sufficiently large and will generate demand for the products they sell. Expensive furs will not sell well in a low-income neighborhood, for instance. Companies that provide services—banks and restaurants, for example—usually emphasize easy access to markets in their location decisions. Table 11-1 lists the variety of factors that different types of businesses might consider in locating their facilities.

## 4 PRODUCTION AND OPERATIONS PLANNING
### Provides plans for conversion of materials and other resources into products and services

The role of production and operations planning is to decide how the production (or operations) capacity is to be used to fill orders. We will mainly use the term "production" here, but the process applies equally to operations that provide services. Production managers control the quantities of products actually turned out by the machinery and people assigned. Production planning determines when production of a particular item (or "lot" of items) begins and ends. It prescribes the sequence in which products are fabricated and assembled. Planning tries to balance the capacity of the production facilities with existing or projected customer orders. The result of this effort should be detailed production plans and schedules showing how workers, machines, and materials are to be used on a day-to-day basis.

The goals of production planning are to use operating facilities as efficiently as possible in order to produce goods of prescribed quality in time to fill customer orders, present and future. There are four important steps that lead to these goals: planning, routing, scheduling, and dispatching.

**STEP 1: PLANNING** The first concern of production planning is to decide what to make and how much to make. Some companies make only one product. If a firm produces glass jars in only one size, no decision on what to make will be necessary. Many companies, however, even

**TABLE 11-1**
**HOW DIFFERENT BUSINESSES ARE INFLUENCED BY SITE LOCATION FACTORS**

| Location Factor | Kinds of Businesses Most Concerned |
| --- | --- |
| Markets and customers | Producers of perishable products, such as bakeries; producers of products that are expensive to transport, such as road surfacing tars, asphalt, and concrete; or businesses that depend upon consumer traffic, such as banks and retail stores. |
| Transportation | Producers of goods that are relatively heavy in weight and low in price, such as bricks and roofing shingles; or costly to ship in relation to their value, such as beer cans and soft drink bottles. |
| Labor supply | Businesses that require a highly educated and/or skilled work force, such as computer and electronic design systems manufacturers and research and development laboratories. |
| Raw materials | Businesses that depend largely upon raw materials that are costly to ship, like cement and steel plants; or whose raw materials are perishable, like food-packing plants. |
| Taxes | Businesses that have great investments in facilities and other fixed assets such as chemical plants and real estate developments. |
| Community attitudes | Businesses operating processes that are likely to pollute, like chemical and bleaching plants; whose products are dangerous, like insecticides and explosives; or whose products have an odor, like rayon, paper, and rubber. |
| Land | Businesses that need large acreages of land for cultivation, such as growers of large crops of tomatoes, lettuce, onions, and so on; for paper and forest products; or for processing operations, like steel mills and petroleum plants. |
| Climate | Businesses that require optimum conditions of temperature, humidity, and rainfall, such as farming or aircraft manufacturing. |
| Utilities | Businesses that require large amounts of power or water, like aluminum and paper plants. |

small ones, produce a range of products. A manufacturer of bicycle chains may make five different sizes in each of two different materials. The production manager must decide how many of each of these ten products to manufacture. These decisions will be based partly on known customer orders and partly on overall company plans and objectives. In recent years, marketing managers have been helpful in making production decisions because of the increasing accuracy of market projections.

**STEP 2: ROUTING** Once the decision has been made about what to make and how much, the next concern is "where?" **Routing** answers this question by prescribing the exact path materials must follow through the production facilities and workstations for a particular production order, lot, or "run." Routing decides which machines are to be used and in what order. It sets job assignments for workers and determines how they will use tools and machines to perform the specific steps of a production process.

**STEP 3: SCHEDULING** The next decision in production planning solves the question of "when?" **Scheduling** answers this question by performing two related tasks. Its first function is to fit entire production runs into a span of time when facilities are available. This function might decide that a 6-week run of 18-inch aluminum lamp bases would be turned on the lathes beginning April 1 and that another 4-week run of 24-inch bases could be placed on the lathes on May 15. This kind of scheduling views jobs as blocks of work and fits them together in a way that will make the best use of the facilities.

The second scheduling function deals with the details of job steps within a single production run. Just as routing sets the sequence in which operations will be performed, scheduling sets the amount of time allowed for individual tasks and decides when each begins and ends. For processes with many different steps, each taking different amounts of time and resources, this detailed scheduling can be a complex undertaking. A number of scheduling techniques have been worked out to help. One particularly useful, yet simple, aid is the Gantt chart.

In 1917, Henry Gantt devised a method for planning and controlling production schedules of shells for World War I. It is still widely used for scheduling manufacturing processes, marketing campaigns, and many other service-oriented business activities. A **Gantt chart** plots on the horizontal axis the time a specific work step takes. The machines, workers, or departments involved in performing the work are indicated on the vertical axis. The vertical axis may also be used for different jobs, customer orders, or production runs if the technique is used for overall scheduling rather than for scheduling the work steps of a single job.

Figure 11-5 shows how a Gantt chart was used to schedule orders in a machine shop so as to load each machine most productively. Gantt chart B shows how the production planner has juggled the orders. Order number 105 starts on machine B, while number 102 begins on machine C, and number 101 begins on machine A. By overlapping the jobs, all five orders that were logged in can be finished by Friday. If they had merely been run in sequence as they arrived, as in chart A, even order number 103 would not have been completed by then. Furthermore, Gantt chart B used, through Wednesday, 75 percent of machine A's time, 92 percent of machine B's time, and 100 percent of machine C's available time.

Gantt charts can handle relatively simple, straight-line, step-by-step scheduling. Even with the help of computers, which handle many of the more difficult computations involved, Gantt-type planning is limited to production scheduling and rather simple controls of progress in marketing and other service departments. Another, far more complicated, technique has been developed to handle complex projects. **PERT** networks can manipulate a great variety of tasks required to complete large and lengthy plans. This makes it especially useful for one-of-a-kind projects

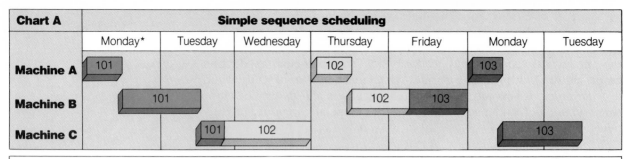

| Chart A | Simple sequence scheduling | | | | | | |
|---|---|---|---|---|---|---|---|
| | Monday* | Tuesday | Wednesday | Thursday | Friday | Monday | Tuesday |
| Machine A | 101 | | | 102 | | 103 | |
| Machine B | 101 | | | 102 | 103 | | |
| Machine C | | 101 | 102 | | | | 103 |

| Log of orders for Charts A and B | | | | | | | | | | | | | | | |
|---|---|---|---|---|---|---|---|---|---|---|---|---|---|---|
| Order number | 101 (mask) | | | 102 (knob) | | | 103 (optic) | | | 104 (pan) | | | 105 (quoit) | | |
| Operation sequence | 1 | 2 | 3 | 1 | 2 | 3 | 1 | 2 | 3 | 1 | 2 | 3 | 1 | 2 | 3 |
| Machine number | A | B | C | C | A | B | B | A | C | A | C | B | B | C | A |
| Machine time (hours) | 4 | 8 | 2 | 10 | 4 | 6 | 6 | 4 | 8 | 4 | 10 | 12 | 4 | 2 | 6 |

| Chart B | Gantt chart | | | | | | |
|---|---|---|---|---|---|---|---|
| | Monday* | Tuesday | Wednesday | Thursday | Friday | Monday | Tuesday |
| Machine A | 101   104 | 102   105 | | 103 | | | |
| Machine B | 105   101 | | 102   103   104 | | | | |
| Machine C | 102 | 105 101   104 | | | 103 | | |

*Each day represents eight hours.

such as the construction of a bridge or the building of a ship. It is also good for simpler, shorter projects, like building a house or planning for all the activities of an advertising campaign. PERT was first developed in the late 1950s by the Special Projects Office of the U.S. Navy to launch the Polaris missile. The initials stand for program evaluation and review technique. Its purpose is to schedule activities and allocate resources in a way that will help complete complex projects in a minimum amount of time.

The PERT network for building a house shown in Figure 11-6 demonstrates features of this technique. PERT deals with the relationships between events and activities. *Events* refer to the times at which activities begin or end. *Activities* refer to segments of work that make up the total process. In building a house, installing the floor is an activity that is bounded by two events: a beginning and an end. The most important consideration in this network is whether one activity has to follow another or whether two or more can be done at the same time. In Figure 11-6, activities leading up to events 1, 2, 3, and 4 must be done sequentially. The floor deck cannot be built until the foundation is complete, for example. Activities leading up to events 5, 6, 7, and 8 can all be done at once.

An important use of a PERT network (or chart) is to find out which activities set the lower limit on the time needed to complete the whole project. This is accomplished by finding the longest-time path of activities that must be performed sequentially. This **critical path** identifies the activities that have to be managed most carefully. If any of the tasks

Figure 11-5 Development of a Gantt chart from a series of production orders. Chart A shows jobs lined up in sequence as they were received. Chart B shows jobs rearranged (overlapped for maximum machine loading, with the prescribed sequence of operations for each job maintained).

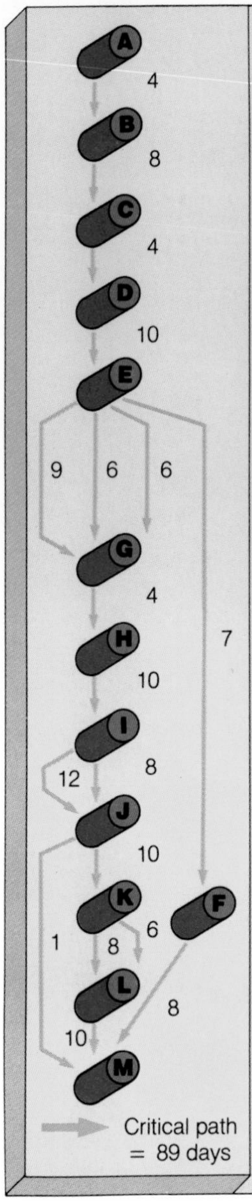

| | Activities or tasks to be performed | Estimated time needed (in days) |
|---|---|---|
| **A** | Foundation crew arrives | 0 |
| **A–B** | Rough grade and excavate | 4 |
| **B–C** | Build foundation | 8 |
| **C–D** | Build floor deck | 4 |
| **D–E** | Erect wall and roof framing | 10 |
| **E–F** | Install exterior siding | 7 |
| **E–G** | Install roofing | 6 |
| | Install rough wiring | 6 |
| | Install rough plumbing | 9 |
| **G–H** | Install wall insulation | 4 |
| **H–I** | Finish inside walls | 10 |
| **I–J** | Do final wiring and heaters | 8 |
| | Do final plumbing | 12 |
| **J–K** | Lay finished flooring | 10 |
| **K–L** | Install appliances | 6 |
| | Finish trim, install floors and cabinets | 8 |
| **F–M** | Paint exterior | 8 |
| **L–M** | Paint interior | 10 |
| **J–M** | Turn on water and electricity | 1 |
| **M** | Occupy house | 0 |

The activities are indicated by arrows. The numbers over the arrows show the estimated time in days needed to complete the activities. Each circled letter indicates an event. The longest time from A to M is the *critical path*. The activities along the critical path need the most careful scheduling. The total time to complete a project can be shortened only if the times needed to complete them can be shortened by putting more workers on the job, using faster machinery, using different materials, and so on.

Critical path = 89 days

Figure 11-6 PERT chart for planning a house construction project.

on the critical path actually take longer than expected, the total project cannot be completed on time. Activities on other paths are not so critical; they have slack time. Delays in some of these activities can be accepted without affecting the projected completion date.

**STEP 4: DISPATCHING** The next step of the planning process puts the plan, and its resources, into action. **Dispatching** involves issuing orders for production operations to begin. A dispatcher issues work orders that actually bring together information and instructions for all the planned activities. Orders will be sent to move materials from storage areas and to place them where they will be used. Orders may be needed to set up equipment or to gather the tools needed for the particular production run. Other orders will tell workers what their particular job assignments will be in the scheduled production or operations process.

# 5 INDUSTRIAL PURCHASING
## *Buying for conversion, not resale*

Most companies make extensive purchases of goods and services from outside suppliers. Manufacturing companies have to buy raw materials and semifinished goods, supplies, machinery, equipment, and services. This buying for use in manufacturing is called *industrial purchasing*. It is different from the buying done by a wholesaler or retailer. Those commercial companies buy goods for resale without further processing. That kind of purchasing is called *mercantile buying*.

## THE PURCHASING PROCESS
### *Requisitions, orders, and receipts*

The main function of industrial purchasing is to decide how much to buy, at what price, from whom, and when. These decisions are part of a purchasing process that uses a flow of information among the company departments that will use the goods bought, the purchasing department, and outside suppliers.

**INITIATING PURCHASES** The decision to buy goods and services usually originates within the department that is to use them. One of the tasks of production planning is to determine what starting materials must be bought. Other departments determine their need for supplies, equipment, and services in their own planning processes. The initiating department will also decide on the most desirable specifications of the goods or services to be bought. The required specifications are formally communicated to the purchasing department on a *purchase requisition*. This is a written request to obtain the goods or services described.

In practice, the exact specifications of purchases are often negotiable. Similar goods not exactly meeting the requesting department's specifications may serve the intended purpose as well or better. If these can be found at a lower price or from a more reliable supplier, exceptions may be made to the specifications.

**PURCHASING ACTIVITY** When a requisition has been received, actual purchasing activity begins. The main steps are to locate potential suppliers, determine prices, and issue a purchase order. For goods that are bought routinely and frequently, there may be no question about who the supplier will be or even about the price. For many purchases, however, an extensive search may have to be made to find suppliers capable of meeting required specifications. Purchasing agents rely heavily on experience and personal contacts to maintain a current stock of knowledge about the capabilities and reputations of suppliers. Prices may be accepted after a simple quotation, or they may require lengthy negotiation or multiple bids from different suppliers. Prices of some commodities—like vegetable oil, cocoa, or soybeans—change sharply from day to day. Purchasers who buy products like these must stay in constant contact with the trading places when prices are set.

When the supplier and price have been set, the purchasing agent issues a *purchase order.* This is a formal request for an outside supplier to provide goods or services. It is, in effect, a legal document setting forth the terms of the purchase: specifications, price, quantities, shipping instructions, delivery date, and any other specifications agreed on between the purchaser and supplier.

## MAKE-OR-BUY DECISION
*Compares total costs*

A manufacturing company usually has the option of buying semifinished goods for some of its processes or of making the goods itself. This **make-or-buy decision** is usually made by top management as part of overall planning for company operations. Cost is a frequent determining factor. Managers compare the quoted cost of buying from outside suppliers with the estimated cost of making the goods in-house. Full costs, including such items as training employees and buying and maintaining equipment, must be considered. In some cases, materials or parts may not even be available for purchase and must be made by the user. Many companies have secret product designs that give them a competitive advantage. To avoid the risk of exposing their secret design to others, these companies do not order materials or subassemblies from outside suppliers.

## VALUE ANALYSIS
*Focuses on function*

The importance of good communications between the purchasing department and operating departments of a company is clearly demonstrated in a procedure called **value analysis.** Its purpose is to reduce production costs—mainly of materials—for products while maintaining or increasing the quality of the products. The analysis focuses on a product's function. Engineers and purchasing agents work together to examine every part of the product to see if less expensive substitutes can be used without impairing function. If even very small cost reductions can be achieved, the effect will be substantial over a long production run.

## 6  PRODUCTION AND OPERATIONS CONTROLS
### Monitor inventories, quality, and progress

Production processing is an essentially economic activity. Conversion of materials and other resources into finished goods or useful services requires that materials be assembled and consumed prudently, that the quality of outputs measure up to specified character and performance, and that progress toward goals and completion proceed according to planned schedules. Managers accomplish these ends through procedures of inventory, quality, and progress control.

## INVENTORY CONTROL
*Juggles material costs and availability*

Managers responsible for inventory control are faced with the problem of having enough, but not too much, of everything. This applies to materials used in production and to goods that result from production, as symbolized in Figure 11-7.

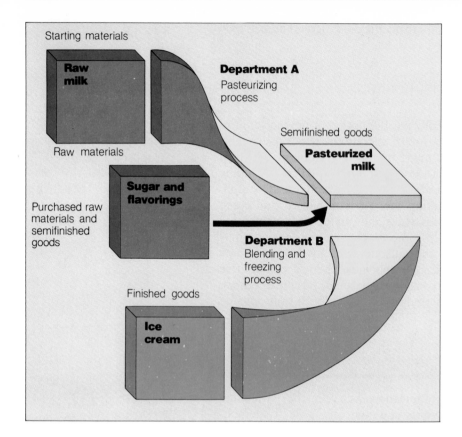

Figure 11-7 Materials that must be managed in converting raw milk into ice cream.

The **materials inventory** includes all of the starting materials and supplies used in a manufacturing process. If the stock is not sufficient to keep up with production, operations will be disrupted. If too much is kept in storage, money that could be used more profitably in other ways will be tied up in materials.

The **finished products inventory** is a list of the stock of finished goods awaiting sale. An adequate stock must be maintained so that customer orders can be filled with minimum delay. However, the stock must still be small enough to minimize investment and storage costs.

A similar inventory problem faces managers and buyers in retailing and wholesaling establishments. The **merchandise inventory** is the stock of goods that a wholesaler or retailer has purchased for resale. Managers of these companies must constantly balance the need to meet customer orders quickly with the high cost of keeping a large stock of goods. Thus they seek the highest turnover of inventory. **Inventory turnover** measures the average number of times a year that stock must be replaced. Whether for production or retailing, the better the management, the higher the turnover.

Purchasing, production, and inventory control must be coordinated to have any chance of achieving the balances needed. Inventory levels for both materials and finished goods constantly fluctuate as materials are purchased and goods are produced, and as materials are used and goods are sold. These changes in inventory levels make up the **inventory cycle.**

**CONTROLLING INVENTORY LEVELS** For any kind of inventory, managers try to control the minimum and maximum levels as the stock on hand fluctuates with receipts, use, production, or sales. Figure 11-8 shows the inventory cycle for a material used in a manufacturing process. Every week 500 pounds of the material is used. The manufacturer wishes to keep a 2-week supply, or *safety stock,* on hand in case regular deliveries of the material are delayed. During the normal cycle, 500 pounds of the material is received and used in a week's time. This allows normal inventory to fluctuate between 1,000 and 1,500 pounds. In the fourth week, normal supply does not arrive and part of the safety stock is used. The delayed shipment and the normal shipment for the fifth week are received at the same time, and inventory returns to its maximum of 1,500 pounds.

This kind of inventory cycle determines how purchases are made. Purchasing managers must take into account the desired safety stock, the daily or weekly use of material, and the *lead time,* the length of time between the placement of an order and the receipt of the goods. Only by considering all three factors can purchasing managers be reasonably assured that a constant supply of materials will arrive in time to continue uninterrupted production.

*ECONOMIC ORDER QUANTITIES* Mathematicians have developed a useful method for determining how much of a material to order at one time. It is called the *economic order quantity (EOQ).* The EOQ is based upon finding the best economic balance between the cost of maintaining inventory levels and the cost of ordering again and again. This concept stems from very practical considerations.

When deciding how much stock to order at a time and how often to order it, purchasing agents must be guided by a number of considerations. Placing very large orders infrequently might allow goods to be bought at a lower unit cost. The danger of running out of stock on materials or goods also makes buyers favor large orders. If the sources of supply are not reliable, large orders may be necessary to ensure the availability of goods when they are needed. Even the cost of negotiating prices and placing orders is considerable and would lead purchasers to try to make orders as infrequently as possible.

At the same time, however, the practice of placing large, infrequent orders ties up capital, uses expensive storage space, and may cause loss or

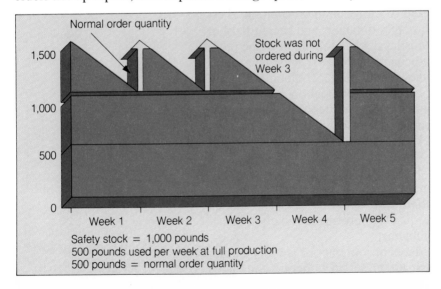

Figure 11-8 Example of an inventory cycle.

damage to goods in storage. Managers try to determine exactly the costs associated with different-sized orders and pick an order size and frequency that result in the greatest advantages at the least cost. EOQ formulas developed as an aid in this decision are widely used.

**PERPETUAL INVENTORY CONTROL** Most companies periodically take an exact count or measure of the amount of all the inventory on hand. In this way, inventory may be checked annually or more often. Between these exact assessments of inventory, or **periodic inventories,** managers must have some way of knowing on a continuous basis how much stock is on hand. A **perpetual inventory** provides this information. This is a frequent, often daily, tabulation of how much has entered inventory and how much has left. If an accurate beginning count is used, it is possible to figure an approximate daily or weekly inventory balance by adding to the starting amount all receipts and subtracting all quantities used. The figure is only approximate because there is usually some unrecorded damage or loss of goods in inventory. The development of barcoding techniques and computerized record keeping from data generated at workstations, warehouse shipping and receiving docks, and retail checkout counters has greatly advanced the practice of perpetual inventory control.

In recent years, inventory control and planning managers have adopted a technique made popular in Japan called **Kanban,** or simply **"just-in-time" (JIT)** inventory systems. The idea is to schedule work progress so precisely and order materials and component parts so prudently that they arrive at each factory and workstation at the exact time that they are needed. This method requires extreme coordination between production, purchasing, and inventory control managers and suppliers of materials and parts. When carried out successfully, Kanban conserves on storage space and saves on inventory costs.

## INSPECTION AND QUALITY CONTROL
*The consumer's ultimate protection* ━━━━━━━━━━━━━

The main goal of inspection and quality control is to ensure that products going out to consumers meet specifications. With physical goods, **quality control** tries to make sure that products conform to established standards for size, shape, weight, durability and strength, color, texture, taste, or any other characteristics that are important to the product's function. As an aid to operators and inspectors, some companies provide a *trouble code list*, like that shown in Table 11-2. Mounted at each workstation, a trouble code alerts workers to potential trouble spots and also provides them with a simple, uniform way for describing and reporting quality defects as they occur. Similar quality controls for service operations focus on effectiveness, timeliness, errors, and other indications of acceptable performance.

Data gathered from trouble code lists and other inspection measurements leads to analysis of errors and deviation by statistical techniques. Many companies rely upon **statistical quality control** which, through analysis of data, points out where quality problems are likely to occur and, often, the source of these problems.

Although quality control procedures first attempt to identify and reject substandard products, they must also be set up to identify the source

**TABLE 11-2**
**TROUBLE CODE LIST FOR A MOTOR-DRIVEN PUMP***

| Code No. | Trouble or Defect | Code No. | Trouble or Defect |
|---|---|---|---|
| 01 | Shaft improperly aligned | 20 | Shorted or grounded |
| 02 | Gears stick or bind | 30 | Loose or leaking |
| 03 | Housing not secure | 40 | Bent or warped |
| 04 | Packing leaks | 50 | Broken or damaged |
| 05 | Mounting holes not threaded | 60 | Dirty or corroded |
| 06 | Rusty interior chamber | 70 | Incorrect or missing |
| 07 | Exterior finish scratched | 80 | Alignment wrong |
| 08 | Lubrication fitting missing | 90 | Needs adjustment |
| 09 | Motor insulation damaged | | |
| 10 | Shipping plugs missing | | |

*Code nos. 01 to 10 represent specific troubles most likely to be found with a particular part or expected function. Code nos. 20 to 90 represent general types of troubles or defects that might be found with any kind of part or function.

and cause of inferior quality. The comparison of output with standards in most cases is only an indication that some corrective action must be taken. The adjustment or repair of faulty machinery, the improvement of work methods, or the substitution of better materials may be needed to keep production up to standards.

Quality control is based on the inspection of materials and products. Inspection, which can occur at numerous points in the production process, may involve something as simple as visual observation. It may also require measurements of size, weight, and other characteristics or various kinds of tests to check the product's performance.

In recent years, many companies have come to believe that improvement in quality depends greatly upon the attitudes and training of employees. This has led to two different quality control approaches, each of which has been very effective. *Zero defects* is a concept popularized when the United States was trying to put a person on the moon. It emphasizes a commitment by everyone in the organization, from top executive to least-skilled worker, not to make errors. *Quality circles* is a concept that has been perfected by the Japanese. It emphasizes the mutual dependence of everyone in an organization and the belief that workers themselves will identify and remove obstacles to good quality if they are given the opportunity to present their ideas to management.

One of the unexpected benefits from the new thinking about quality control, and quality circles, is that as quality improves so does productivity. Traditionally, management has viewed quality and production efficiencies as a trade-off. That is, management felt that the more it got of one, the less it obtained of the other. It is now apparent that improved quality saves on both material and labor inputs in the long run without a resultant sacrifice in output. That equates to higher productivity.

Quality concerns extend to services too. It is important to minimize errors in word processing and order entries, to have motel rooms cleaned and prepared according to specification, to have airline registrations entered correctly, and the like. As service occupations begin to dominate the United States economy, quality control in service operations is becoming just as important as in production functions.

## PROGRESS CONTROL
### *Compares performance with plans*

Planning is inevitably linked to control. Progress toward goals requires continual surveillance. Production control compares actual results with plans. If there are deficiencies, these must be corrected. In spite of good planning, routing, scheduling, and dispatching, many things can go wrong in the production or operation processing. Needed materials are sometimes unexpectedly found to be unusable. Machines break down without warning. Workers are absent. The Gantt charts and PERT charts used in planning are often invaluable in tracking progress and alerting management to the need for corrective action. Two other controls are also useful.

*Schedule performance reports* are used to determine how well production activities are kept within their established time limits. Any problem in keeping on schedule must be explained and made up for. This is accomplished either by allocating more workers or equipment or by delaying later production. *Scrap reports,* for example, show how many items in process have had to be discarded because of defects. This allows corrections to be made if faulty work or equipment can be identified These reports also may be a signal to extend the production run to make more goods to replace the faulty ones. They also call to the attention of management the fact that some starting materials are not being converted into end products as planned. Additional materials may need to be obtained.

# *Key Concepts*

1. Business processes may be divided into two broad categories: production processes, where the physical form of materials is changed, and operations, which do not create physical goods. Industrial processes are classified further as extractive, analytical, fabrication, synthetic, and assembly. Nonindustrial and service processes include warehousing, wholesaling, retailing, transportation, communications, and direct service operations such as banking.

Products are viewed by production planners as either standard or custom-made, and processes are viewed as either capital- or labor-intensive.

Modern conversion processes depend greatly upon the application of automation (where feedback of information plays a large role), computer-aided manufacturing direction and controls, and robotics.

2. The physical layout of processing facilities must be designed to promote orderly flow of materials and activities. The principal layout

patterns are based on process, product, customer, or a fixed-position orientation.

3. The location of business facilities should seek to find the most advantageous balance, for that particular process, of nearness to markets; availability of process resources, utilities, and services; favorable civic and legal conditions; and room to grow.

4. Production and operations planning establishes an orderly sequence of planning and scheduling, and determines how and when process capacity will be used to fill customer orders. It follows a sequence of planning, routing, scheduling, and dispatching. Gantt charts are useful in planning manufacturing and service operations. PERT charts are networks especially useful in planning large one-of-a-kind projects.

5. Industrial purchasing provides the activities that ensure a flow of appropriate raw materials, component parts, and operating supplies for use in the production processes. An important deci-

sion is whether to make a particular component part or purchase it. Value analysis directs management's attention to the ultimate function a material or component part is intended to serve and seeks ways to reduce the cost of these parts through simplified design or use of substitute materials.

**6.** Production and operation controls are directed toward the assurance that planned outputs really do occur and at minimum costs. Inventory control tries to maintain an optimum balance of materials so that production is not interrupted by shortages, while keeping inventory levels as low as possible. Of special use in managing inventories are such factors as inventory turnover, the inventory cycle, purchasing lead time, economic order quantities (EOQ), and perpetual inventory record keeping.

The goal of inspection and quality control is to ensure that products and services meet specifications that have been promised to buyers. Statistical quality control is useful in alerting managers to the possibility of defects and analyzing their causes. Increasingly, quality control efforts invite employee involvement in programs like zero defects and quality circles.

Progress control is maintained by a number of information systems and reporting techniques such as Gantt and PERT charts and other reports that track (1) progress toward completion of schedules and (2) factors such as waste that contribute to missed deadlines.

# *Review Questions*

1. Define, explain, or identify each of the following key terms or phrases, found on the pages indicated.

*analytical processes (p. 240)*
*assembly processes (p. 240)*
*automation (p. 242)*
*capital-intensive processes (p. 241)*
*computer-assisted design (CAD) (p. 242)*
*computer-assisted manufacturing (CAM) (p. 242)*
*continuous processes (p. 241)*
*critical path (p. 250)*
*customer layout (p. 244)*
*direct service operations (p. 241)*
*dispatching (p. 251)*
*economic order quantity (EOQ) (p. 255)*
*extractive processes (p. 239)*
*fabrication processes (p. 240)*
*feedback (p. 242)*
*finished products inventory (p. 254)*
*fixed-position layout (p. 244)*
*Gantt chart (p. 249)*
*industrial purchasing (p. 252)*
*intermittent processes (p. 241)*
*inventory cycle (p. 254)*
*inventory turnover (p. 254)*
*just-in-time (JIT) inventory control (p. 256)*
*Kanban (p. 256)*

*labor-intensive processes (p. 241)*
*lead time (p. 255)*
*make-or-buy decision (p. 253)*
*materials inventory (p. 254)*
*mercantile buying (p. 252)*
*merchandise inventory (p. 254)*
*operations (p. 239)*
*operations management (p. 239)*
*periodic inventories (p. 256)*
*perpetual inventory (p. 256)*
*PERT (p. 249)*
*process layout (p. 243)*
*product layout (p. 244)*
*production (p. 239)*
*production management (p. 239)*
*purchase order (p. 252)*
*purchase requisition (p. 252)*
*quality control (p. 256)*
*quality circle (p. 257)*
*robotics (p. 242)*
*routing (p. 249)*
*safety stock (p. 255)*
*scheduling (p. 249)*
*standard products (p. 241)*
*statistical quality control (p. 256)*
*synthetic processes (p. 240)*
*value analysis (p. 253)*
*zero defects (p. 257)*

2. Name the five industrial processes and give an example of each.

3. What are two main differences between standard products and custom-made products?

4. Would a plant that produced canned corn, lima beans, and tomatoes be more likely to locate near its sources of supply or near its markets? What about a bread manufacturer? Why?

5. What is the chief goal when designing the physical layout of production or operation facilities?

6. How do Gantt charts and PERT charts differ? What is each type of chart most suitable for?

7. What is the difference between industrial purchasing and mercantile buying?

8. How does lead time affect the inventory cycle?

9. What is the principle behind Kanban and just-in-time inventory control? What are the main benefits from using this technique?

10. Is it true that quality improvements can be made only at the sacrifice of extra production time and/or costs? Why?

# Case Critique 11-1
## What? No robots? No Kanban?

Japanese production processes have been so successful in the use of robots and Kanban inventory planning that many American manufacturers were beginning to think that without them, their factories were doomed. That isn't so, says William G. Stoddard, a manufacturing consultant with Arthur Andersen & Co. Strict attention to plant—or office—layout may produce just as many efficiencies. His belief is that American engineers were overly impressed with long production runs of days or more. If you can set up a new production run quickly, Stoddard reasons, then it may be more efficient to make fewer products at a time. That way, the plant paces its output to its customers' demands, not the sometimes-false economies of long production runs. How are machine or assembly-line setups (or changeovers) speeded up? By better use of special loading and unloading devices and by designing the product to make the handling process simpler.

Stoddard's next idea is to rethink production layouts. A typical layout might be like the one shown for a valve plant in Figure 11-9A. The product being produced—valves made in lots of about three each—would be routed along a sequence from machine to machine; each product or lot might follow a different sequence. A typical valve lot traveled a half mile back and forth between two departments and took as long as 2 months from the time it hit the first machine until it was discharged from the

last one. Now the plant has regrouped its machines into machine "families," as shown in Figure 11-9B. The machines are arranged in semicircles so that valve lots flow through a single family from start to finish. One machine feeds the work to another. Parts don't sit waiting to be worked on, and forklift trucks don't have to travel great distances to move parts and materials. Using these U-shaped layouts, valve lots travel only a few hundred feet at most and are produced in 2 to 3 days rather than 2 months as before.

1. What kind of layout was the valve company originally using? What were its drawbacks?

2. By using the new families layout, what advantages has the company gained? What kind of layout does this new one most resemble?

3. In order to make the new layout work as well as it is designed to, what sort of scheduling method might be most appropriate? Why?

4. Can you think of how office machines might be rearranged into family groups to improve flow and efficiency?

*SOURCE:* James Cook, "Kanban, American-Style," *Forbes*, October 8, 1984, pp. 66–67, 70.

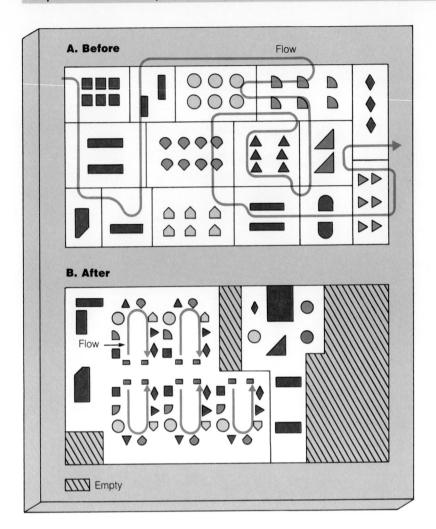

**A. Before**

Flow

**B. After**

Flow →

▨ Empty

Figure 11-9 Kanban, American-style. Source: James Cook, "Kanban, American-style," *Forbes,* October 8, 1984. Copyright © Forbes Inc., 1984.

# Case Critique 11-2
## The Out-of-Stock Tape-Reel Labels

"We're out of tape-reel labels again!" exclaimed Bill Becket, administrative assistant at the Miracle Data Processing Center. "I checked on them a couple of weeks ago, and we had more than 5,000. Someone must be pilfering them for labeling packages at home."

"I don't think that 5,000 labels is an awful lot, the way that we use them," observed Mary Jo McGuire, the center's processing supervisor. "My guess is that we use more than 500 a day. What with spoilage and the like, we probably used up that batch of 5,000 in the last 10 days."

"Well," said Bill, "I'm going to set up some sort of inventory control system so that this doesn't happen again." Then Mary Jo asked what system he would use.

"It's going to be very simple. I'm going to mark my calendar for the last day of each month. Then, on those days, I'm going to make a count to see how many labels are on hand. Whenever I see fewer than 5,000 labels, I'll place a purchase requisition to build up our inventory again."

**1.** What do you think of Bill's inventory control system? What is such a system usually called? What are some of the possible flaws in it?

**2.** What better kind of inventory control system could you suggest?

## CHAPTER 12

# Information and

# Computer Systems

## Learning Objectives

*The purpose of this chapter is to define information and management information systems and explain the functions of data processing. This chapter will also describe the elements of a computer system and the function of computer programs, and identify major computer applications and some of their drawbacks.*

*As evidence of general comprehension after reading this chapter, you should be able to:*

1. *Define information, its sources, and its classifications.*

2. *Explain the purpose of a management information system.*

3. *Describe the major functions performed by a data processing system.*

4. *Describe the major elements of computer hardware and their functions.*

5. *Explain the purpose of computer software and how a computer program is designed.*

6. *List a number of business applications for computers, and discuss the advantages and disadvantages of computers and their impact on society.*

*If your class is using* SSweetco: Business Model and Activity File, *see Chapter 12 in that book after you complete this chapter. There you will find exercises and activities to help you apply your learning to typical business situations.*

## 1 INFORMATION IS KNOWLEDGE

gathered for business from

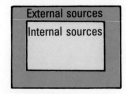

External sources
Internal sources

and is classified as

Primary     or     Secondary

## 2 MANAGEMENT INFORMATION SYSTEMS (MIS)

make information useful for

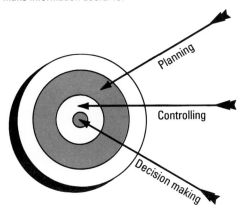

Planning

Controlling

Decision making

## 3 DATA PROCESSING ADDS VALUE

to information.

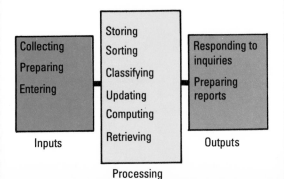

| Inputs | Processing | Outputs |
| --- | --- | --- |
| Collecting | Storing | Responding to |
| Preparing | Sorting | inquiries |
| Entering | Classifying | Preparing |
| | Updating | reports |
| | Computing | |
| | Retrieving | |

## 4 COMPUTERS ADD SPEED AND ACCURACY

to data processing.

 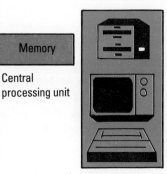

Memory

Central
processing unit

Input units                  Output units

## 5 SOFTWARE PROVIDES INSTRUCTIONS

for computers.

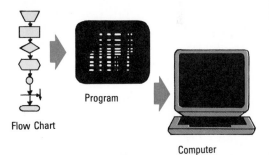

Program

Flow Chart

Computer

## 6 COMPUTER APPLICATIONS

are almost limitless.

Word processing   Decision-support   Factory-type
Office automation   systems           automation

But there are social concerns.

PRIVACY

CLOSED

Invasion of privacy        Threat to employment

# COMPUTERS: REVOLUTIONIZING INDUSTRY

*Computers are the industrial revolution of the twentieth century. They have pushed their way into just about every production or operation process of business. Here are just a few examples.*

*A small home builder in Ohio uses a computer to estimate the costs of construction, watch over accounts payable, and monitor the progress of sales.*

*At a company that makes saw blades in Massachusetts, computers find the cost of raw materials, gather data from the scales that weigh ingredients that go into the saws, maintain a statistical check of quality, and regulate inventory levels.*

*Managers at a giant truck-parts company in Iowa ask their computers to make all the calculations that affect borrowing, cash flow, and financial planning.*

*A woman in Connecticut who acts as an independent franchiser of vitamins and food supplements uses a computer to keep the names of all her customers and to automatically select a list for mailings to customers who have shown interest in a particular product.*

*Offices that have postage meters no longer have to take them to the post office for refills and certification! A tiny built-in computer does it all automatically via a telephone line.*

*Maintenance workers who troubleshoot malfunctions in electrical systems of diesel locomotives use a computer that diagnoses causes and generates repair instructions. Mechanics at a major airline get maintenance information the same way.*

*A chain of supermarkets uses a computer to evaluate possible store locations and identify the ones with the greatest profit potential.*

*At a factory where the world's tiniest electronic chips are made, a computer makes them because people inevitably bring dust and other contaminants into the processing room.*

*A department store buyer of women's fashions in Atlanta asks her computer to remind her when it is time to reorder and to calculate the amount of the order, based upon cost of holding the merchandise and profits of selling at the regular price.*

*At a can factory in Denver a tiny mill for casting beer cans from recycled aluminum cans is run by a computer.*

*A small bookstore in San Francisco uses a computer to control inventories, record daily sales, trigger its reorder system, and assist in checking bills of lading from incoming shipments.*

*In a large office building in Chicago, "intelligent" building management systems are run by computers that control heating and air-conditioning, alert owners to fire and smoke, and interconnect with the telecommunications and office automation systems of the tenants.*

*Computers do all the obvious things too. They enter sales orders, handle billing and payments, prepare payrolls, type letters, and do almost everything a modern office wants them to.*

# 1 INFORMATION FOR BUSINESS
## *Provides the substance for decisions*

Can computers do everything? No! But they can handle an incredible variety of work often better, always faster, than human beings can. They can do so because they have a miraculous ability to manipulate vast quantities of information at the speed of light. It is these characteristics that make computers so valuable to businesses. Information is what computers feed on. Information is what they juggle so fantastically. Information is what they give back to the business. The process goes something like this. Businesses feed information into computers. Managers ask the computers to process this information in a predetermined way. The computer delivers the processed information, either automatically or on command, to the employees and managers who operate the many functions of the business *and* the machinery and equipment involved in the business's processes. Managers and others use this information to respond to customers and other employees, to solve problems, to make decisions, and to create new ideas.

It is clear also that managers have a great many information needs. Indeed, the operation of a business requires great inflow of information—about sales and markets, production and quality, inventories and purchases, cash levels and costs, and much more. To restate an old adage, "Information is knowledge." For business managers, the knowledge of what to do now, or next, comes from information found in a business's environment and within the business itself.

## INFORMATION AND DATA
### *All the facts and circumstances*

**Information,** in the business world, is defined as the knowledge of facts or circumstances. "Data," though often implying numerical information, is interchangeable with "information." Information has different levels of usefulness. The manager of a large retail store could be presented with thousands of individual sales slips at the end of a day. The slips, however, are only raw data. Analyzing and summarizing them can make them far more informative. A brief report showing total sales, sales by departments, sales by product type, and sales by cash or credit payments would be far more effective in helping with most decisions than the individual sales slips.

# COLLECTION OF DATA
*Selectivity is required*

The precise information needed for planning and decision making depends on the careful, consistent collection of data. Managers need knowledge of what is going on within their own organizations. This information about internal affairs is used to monitor and control current operations and is used for planning. Information about developments external to the organization is also important. Government action, impending price changes by competitors or suppliers, shifts in population, and scores of other issues may affect management decisions.

*INTERNAL SOURCES* Tallies of the amount of goods or services produced, the number of working hours spent on each unit of production, the time spent on maintenance, the amount of materials used, the amount of materials wasted, the number of products rejected by inspectors, and the amount of utilities used are only a few kinds of data resulting directly from the production process. The accounting system yields data about the sales of various products, the costs of financing and operating, changes in personnel costs, the profits and losses of particular divisions or product lines, and so on. The purchasing department, the shipping department, and the warehouses all have information about inventory levels and changes. Data on absenteeism, injuries and accidents, and employee turnover is available from the personnel department.

*EXTERNAL SOURCES* Companies also need information from external sources to anticipate important changes in the business environment. Among the most important sources of data are government agencies. The federal government publishes a huge quantity of data, analyses, and regulations that may be of interest to business managers, covering such areas as population, housing, business, agriculture, labor and the work force, manufacturing minerals, and government organizations. State and local governments often maintain and publish similar information for their own jurisdictions.

Information useful for business management is also available from many private sources. One of the main functions of trade and professional associations is the collection and publication of statistics, new technical developments, new product information, new legislation, and other information. Many private companies are in the business of providing information. Scores of commercial newsletters and journals meet special needs. Some companies carry out sophisticated surveys of retail sales, buying power, building construction, and other important fields. They then sell the results to subscribers.

# CLASSES OF DATA
*Recycled information or brand new*

Data that is collected and published by others is called **secondary data.** It was not compiled specifically to help solve a specific problem of an individual company. **Primary data** is gathered to meet particular needs and has not been published before in a usable form. Some companies have sufficient need and resources to collect primary data for their own use. They may survey customers to find out their product preferences or their response to a new credit plan. They may observe buyers' behavior in stores to get information on the effects of a certain package design or point-of-purchase display. They may use highway traffic counts to help pick a location for a new store. Gathering primary data on business problems can be quite expensive. In many large projects, however, it is unavoidable because other relevant and reliable information is unavailable.

# DATA BASES
## *Electronic libraries of information*

The current trend in information collection is to assemble interrelated data into computer files for easy access, retrieval, and updating. Such a file, or system of files, is called a *data base*. It is, in effect, an electronic library. A data base may be developed and maintained by a company for its own internal use. The customer data base shown in Figure 12-1 is used by a single company to keep track of its customers, the products each buys, and the date of billing. Management can retrieve from this data base such things as a report showing which customers bought what kind of product or a report showing how many times a particular product was purchased by all customers and in what quantities.

A data base may also be developed jointly by companies with a mutual interest (such as a hotel trade association), and from it all parties may draw information. Many data bases are put together by independent firms that offer access to the files to any organization that pays a fee for review or retrieval.

Increasingly, the terms "data base" and "data bank" are being used interchangeably.

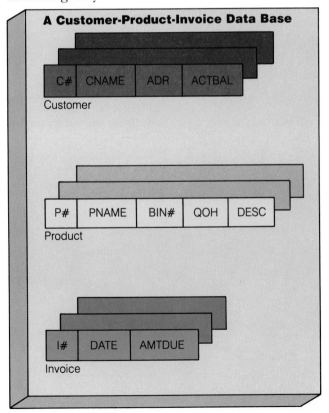

A Customer-Product-Invoice Data Base

| C# | CNAME | ADR | ACTBAL |

Customer

| P# | PNAME | BIN# | QOH | DESC |

Product

| I# | DATE | AMTDUE |

Invoice

Figure 12-1 A customer-product-invoice data base.

# 2 MANAGEMENT INFORMATION SYSTEM (MIS)

*Provides the basis for planning and control*

The sheer volume of information generated by a business is enormous. Even in a small business, it can flow like a deluge from dozens of sales slips, bills received from suppliers, invoices returned from customers, new products to consider making or purchasing, time sheets for employees, and on and on. In larger businesses, the amount and complexity of information that must be interpreted and acted upon often exceed the mind's grasp. To sort out and help make sense of this welter of potentially valuable information, businesses increasingly rely upon management information systems. A ***management information system (MIS)*** is an organized set of processes that provides information to managers to help them operate the business effectively. MIS procedures include collecting, analyzing, and reporting past, present, and projected information from within and outside of the company, as illustrated in Figure 12-2. The information is arranged so that it is directly usable (often in the form of computer "printouts") for decision making, planning, and controlling.

***SYSTEM GUIDELINES*** In devising a management information system, the users constantly focus on clarifying and meeting organization objectives. In deciding what information their system will provide, they must judge the usefulness, timeliness, and affordability of every proposed kind of information:

■ The *usefulness* of output is a prime criterion of the effectiveness of MIS. A production manager wishing to reduce costs must know where the total costs originate, how much comes from worker wages, how much from waste materials, how much from utility charges, and so forth. The manager needs that information presented in a clear and simple report, free of all extraneous and useless data.

■ To be of real help in making decisions, information must be *timely*. Reports must be produced quickly or the information they contain will not help with current decisions.

■ An effective MIS must be *affordable*. Large data collection and proc-

Figure 12-2 Components of a management information system.

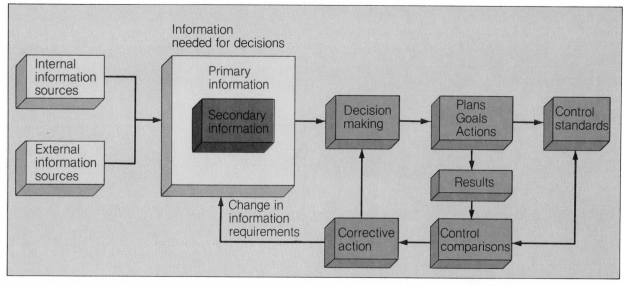

essing systems often cost hundreds of thousands or even millions of dollars a year to operate. The system must be designed so that the information gathered is worth its cost. Systems must be scaled to match the size and needs of the company that uses them.

## 3  INFORMATION PROCESSING

*Converts raw input data into specified output information*

Information processing is to paperwork what manufacturing processes are to materials and products. The daily transactions of a business, along with its historical records and other background information, must somehow be collected, stored, analyzed, and made available to those who operate the business. Until the introduction of the computer, this process was first done manually, and then mechanically with the familiar IBM (punched) card. With the advent of the electronically driven computer, the process of collecting, organizing, and analyzing information was designated as *electronic data processing (EDP)*, and then simply *data processing*.

### DATA PROCESSING FUNCTIONS

*Gathers inputs, processes them, and provides outputs*

Data processing encompasses a number of functions. Sometimes it is hard to distinguish one from the other or to determine where one begins and another ends, since there is inevitably a great deal of overlapping. Figure 12-3 provides a simple way of thinking about data processing functions. It classifies these functions in three basic ways.

**INPUT FUNCTIONS** The information processing system must first *collect* the data from sales slips, production tallies, time sheets, and other operation sources. Next, it *prepares* this data for entry—sometimes by hand, mostly by machine—by putting the data in a format that can be

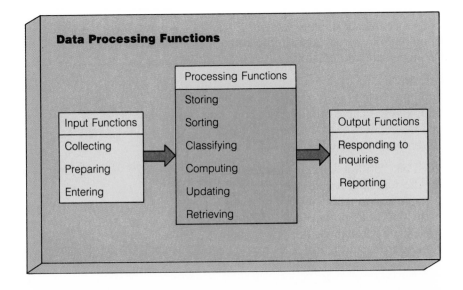

Figure 12-3 Data processing functions.

accepted by a computer. For example, a written figure like "twelve" is prepared for entry by changing it to numerical characters "12." Finally, the input to the processing system is *entered*—by keypunch, tape, credit card reader, optical scanning wand, or whatever means is most appropriate to the system.

**PROCESSING FUNCTIONS** Once the data has been put into the system, a number of different things can happen to it, according to what the business desires. Data can be *stored;* today this is done electronically, but it is not much different conceptually from placing it in steel file cabinets. It can be *sorted* or arranged—alphabetically, numerically, according to dates, according to geography, or by any determinant specified. Similarly, the data can be *classified*, or grouped, according to classes such as unpaid invoices that are from 10 to 30 days past due, 31 to 45 days, 45 to 60 days, and more than 60 days. Data in the system can also be *updated*: to add new information about a customer's purchases, for example, or to change an address or delete an inactive customer from the file. A fifth major function of processing is *computation*. This is the capability of the process to add, subtract, multiply, and divide. Finally, the process must be able to *retrieve* the data that was stored, either in its original entry form or as sorted, classified, and updated information.

**OUTPUT FUNCTIONS** Generally speaking, data processing systems provide two kinds of outputs. Direct *response to inquiries* occurs when, for example, a salesperson in a retail store calls a data bank (by voice or electronically) to determine the credit status of a customer wishing to make a purchase using a charge card. *Reports*, long or brief, may be generated by the processing system on a regular, periodic basis, or they can be prepared to reflect a current transaction in response to a specific inquiry.

Figure 12-4 shows how a centralized data processing system can convert inputs from various internal operational sources into outputs for management use in planning, controlling, and decision making.

## DATA PROCESSING MODES
*From periodic to instant processing*

The **mode** of processing refers to the timing of the updating and response processing with respect to the occurrence of a transaction. Data from a sale or collection or a production run may be collected at the end of the day, or it can be collected and processed immediately.

**BATCH PROCESSING** This is probably the most common mode. Data is accumulated before it is put into, processed, or retrieved from the system. Credit card holders, for example, can charge purchases daily, but they are billed (in batches) at the end of the month. In this case, the data may be entered immediately but sorted and retrieved only periodically.

**TRANSACTIONAL PROCESSING** This "on-line" mode implies that the data is entered and processed as the transaction takes place. Instead of collecting data from sales slips and then keypunching it into the system at a later time, the salesclerk enters the data at a "point-of-sale" terminal at the cash register. The clerk may key in such data as the price, quantity, stock number, department, clerk identification, and sales tax. The data processing system takes over automatically for further processing.

---

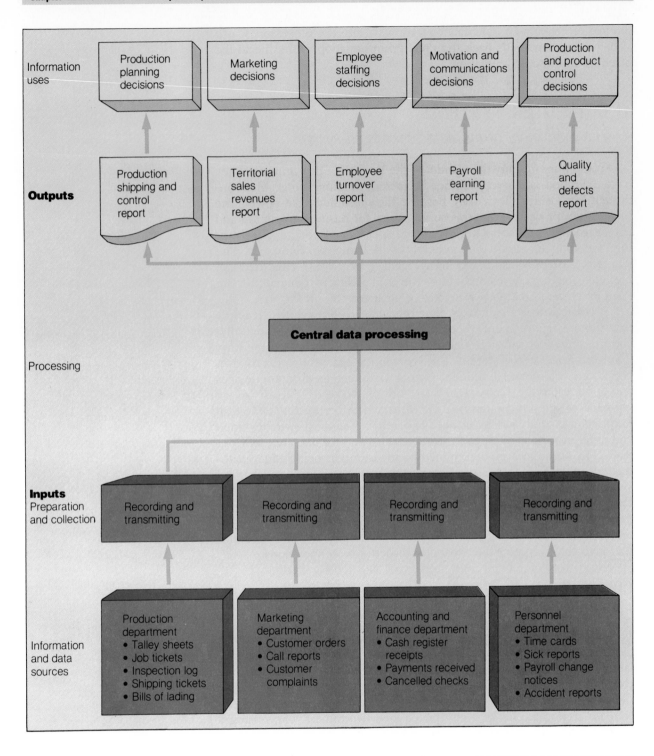

Production planning decisions

Marketing decisions

Employee staffing decisions

Motivation and communications decisions

Production and product control decisions

**Outputs**

Production shipping and control report

Territorial sales revenues report

Employee turnover report

Payroll earning report

Quality and defects report

Central data processing

Processing

**Inputs**
Preparation and collection

Recording and transmitting

Recording and transmitting

Recording and transmitting

Recording and transmitting

Information and data sources

Production department
• Talley sheets
• Job tickets
• Inspection log
• Shipping tickets
• Bills of lading

Marketing department
• Customer orders
• Call reports
• Customer complaints

Accounting and finance department
• Cash register receipts
• Payments received
• Cancelled checks

Personnel department
• Time cards
• Sick reports
• Payroll change notices
• Accident reports

**REAL-TIME PROCESSING** This mode enables the processing itself to affect the transaction while it is taking place. For example, when a ticket request is made of an airline reservation system, the master file for that flight is checked for seat availability. If a seat is available, it is held as "booked" temporarily while the reservation is sold to the traveler. Once the seat sale is confirmed, the file is updated by the transaction. Real-time processing is also very useful in the control of machinery. In effect, a

Figure 12-4 How a data processing system links up input source with output users in a management information system.

production machine enters data continuously into the processor, which also continuously feeds back the updated information in the file to the machine to direct its operation.

# 4  COMPUTER SYSTEMS
## The machinery of the data processing system

Computers are truly the wonder of the last half of this century. They have extended human capabilities by incredible dimensions. Most important for business, they have become the machinery that powers the information processing systems so necessary for business operation and management. Computers have reshaped methods of obtaining, recording, and applying information in nearly every company of any size. The increasing use of statistics and formal management control and decision methods has largely resulted from the availability of general-purpose computers. Such methods were nearly inconceivable in the past.

A **computer** is a system of electromechanical devices that receives data from its environment, processes the data arithmetically or logically, and transmits the converted data back to the environment in some way. The data read by the system usually includes instructions for its own operations. This broad definition covers a wide range of different devices and applications.

Most business computers use the **binary number system**, where all numbers are combinations of ones and zeros. Electrical switches open and close in various sequences, to represent "on" for one and "off" for zero. The sequences are determined by the numbers being added, subtracted, multiplied, and so on. The original computers used mechanical switches, later ones vacuum tubes. All of today's computers use some form of transistors that act as on-off switches capable of performing at incredible speeds. The operation of these switches is dictated by a system that combines the appropriate computer equipment and instructions that give the computer the capability to perform its operations.

## COMPUTER HARDWARE
### Receives, manipulates, and transmits data

The most visible components of a computer system are the various devices that function in combination to receive data, process or manipulate it, and transmit the processed data on to whoever will be using it at the next step. In many instances, this will be the same person who put the data into the computer in the first place. This occurs when a salesperson, for example, checks a customer's creditworthiness when using a charge card. The salesperson inserts the card into a device that reads, or receives, that data and relays it into a computer. The computer processes the data to find out if the customer's credit balance has not been exceeded. Then the computer transmits this information back to a screen that the salesperson can read. The card reader, the computer, the readout screen, and even the electric wires that connect them are all part of the hardware.

Computer **hardware** is the term applied to the physical devices that send and receive data and perform operations on it, as shown symbolically in Figure 12-5.

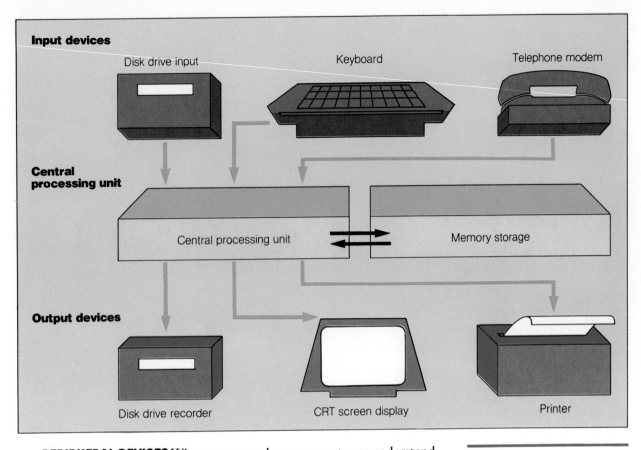

**Input devices**

Disk drive input          Keyboard          Telephone modem

**Central processing unit**

Central processing unit          Memory storage

**Output devices**

Disk drive recorder          CRT screen display          Printer

Figure 12-5 Hardware components of a small computer.

**PERIPHERAL DEVICES** What most people see, operate, or understand best about computers are the peripheral devices. These are the variety of means (shown in the pictures of Figure 12-6) by which information is fed into or received from a computer. Every computer, large or small, must have one or more pieces of equipment capable of reading data in the form of numbers, symbols, letters, or even sounds and converting it into electrical codes that can be used by an electronic processing unit. This data is called input. The most common **input units** are keyboards (similar to those of a traditional typewriter), magnetic tape (similar to that used for sound recording), and magnetic disks (much like those used for "instant replays" on television). An optical scanning device (something like an electronic wand that is moved over printed figures, symbols, or letters) is also an important source of input. It is seen at grocery checkout counters and in schools for grading test questionnaires. Another device increasingly in use, especially for smaller computers, is the "floppy disk drive." It is the receptacle and transmitter into which the magnetic tape or disk is inserted. It operates in somewhat the same way as the device into which the cassette is placed in a home video game.

Computers must also have devices for sending output, or processed information, back to users. These **output units** record information on a media similar to that used for transmitting input. Output is commonly seen on a video display tube (also called a cathode ray tube, or CRT) or simply in printed form. When output is printed, this is popularly known as hard copy.

A **modem**—a device that enables a telephone to transmit data to and from peripheral devices, data bases, and computers—greatly extends the range and convenience of computers.

**PROCESSING DEVICES** The computer, itself, consists of two major components.

A *central processing unit (CPU)* operates between the input device and the output device. The CPU is the heart of the computer because it actually operates on the input, changing it in some way to create useful output. Most CPUs are able to perform only very simple operations, such as adding, subtracting, or comparing one number with another to determine which is larger. However, when performed in the right sequence on the numbers and letters read by the input devices, these operations can create very complex, highly structured, and useful output.

An essential component of the central processing unit is its **memory unit.** These memories are capable of storing vast amounts of information for further use and/or examination. The memory may be an integral part of a computer or a separate unit connected to it electrically.

Other terms for particular units of hardware are often encountered. Very large computers, with which smaller computers may interact, are called "mainframe computers." The proliferation of much smaller computers that are seen almost everywhere, in small businesses and in homes, are variously called "minicomputers," "microcomputers," or "personal computers." In 1975, only a few thousand small computers were made. By 1985, there were about 4 million. The forecast is for over 10 million computers of all sizes to be in place by 1990.

Figure 12-6 Some input devices— optical scanning devices.

## COMPUTER SERVICES
*From time-sharing to networking*

Originally, computers were so expensive to own and operate that a special kind of company was formed to provide computer services for small companies. Even today, these computer centers sell $20 billion of data processing services, computer systems analysis, and software programs. Many user companies purchase not only computer time—time-sharing—but also access to "banks" of certain kinds of information held by the service company. A newer development establishes networks of cooperating computer owners who have common information needs. Members of the network, through remote access devices, may add to or manipulate data in the network's bank. Several industry associations have created computer networks for their member companies. Some states operate such networks for farmers.

## COMPUTER NETWORKS
*Interconnect computers, users, and data bases*

As computer usage in business has grown, so has the need for data processing to be able to handle information from many sources, often widely separated physically. Such distributed data processing (DDP) enables a clerk in a purchasing office, for instance, to exchange processed data directly with a vendor or with another clerk in the inventory control department. This interchange of data, often tapping the same data bases (or data banks), is now commonplace between company headquarters and salespeople in the field, between commercial banks and their branches, between warehouses and retail stores, and more. When DDP occurs within a building or limited geographic area, the system is called a *local area network (LAN).* When a company operates a system using its own telephone lines, the system is called a *private automated branch exchange (PABX).*

## 5  COMPUTER SOFTWARE
*Provides instructions for the computer*

Computers would not function without instructions. As a consequence, an array of instructional information is an inseparable part of a computer system. This array is called *software.* In the restricted sense, software is simply a collection of instructions read by the computer to tell it where to find the input, what specific processing functions to perform on the data once it has been captured, and where (and in what form) to deliver the resulting output. In the data processing field, the term "software" may be used more broadly to include all of the procedures used to gather and verify data, prepare it for input, locate and correct errors, and check and distribute output. Regardless of strict definition, computer software and hardware must work together to produce a specified output.

---

*Action Brief*

### SOFTWARE FOR ROCKY ROADS

*When trucking companies leave the choice of the routes to travel up to the drivers, the companies win some and lose some. DuPont's Air Products & Chemicals division, for example, has to schedule deliveries to serve 3,500 customers scattered over 50 different routes. Trucks hauling perishable chemicals for the division travel 22 million miles a year. Joanne Weldin, distribution manager, had the main responsibility for picking the most economic routes. A variety of factors had to be juggled mentally, like warehouse locations, total weight to certain destinations, weight limitations per truck, quality of roads, maximum speeds, and delivery time guarantees. With advice from truck drivers she and her staff did a pretty good job of scheduling. But it wasn't nearly so good as when a couple of computer experts created a computer program to weight all these factors mathematically. Using this program, DuPont saves $1.7 million, or about 7 percent, a year on trucking costs. One big problem in developing the program was that truckers often know something the computer doesn't. A customer may say it wants delivery by noon; a trucker may know that this means any time before 2 p.m.*

# PROGRAMMING
*The art of preparing computer instructions*

Software used for instructing computer processing is composed of one or more programs. A **program** is a list of extremely detailed, rigorously specific instructions telling the computer what to do in step-by-step sequence. A program is created by first defining what the inputs will consist of and what the outputs are expected to be. Thereafter, the programmer, using symbols of the trade, constructs a flowchart. The **flowchart** is a graphic description of the principal steps the computer must accomplish in carrying out the process prescribed by the program. Figure 12-7 shows a very simple program flowchart for billing a single customer. The flowchart serves only as a guideline for preparing the exact instructions in a code that computers can understand.

# COMPUTER LANGUAGE
*Converts English into numbers*

Computer programmers not only write the instructions for a computer but also must find a way to communicate this information to the

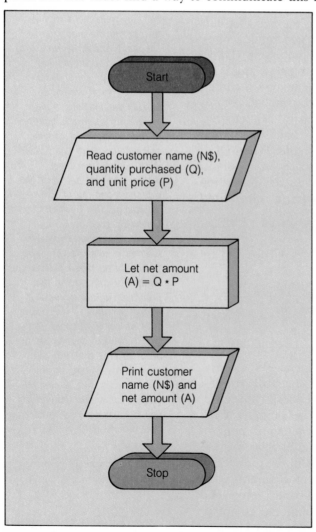

Figure 12-7 Flowchart diagramming a program for billing a single customer. Source: Donald H. Sanders, *Computers Today.* Copyright © by McGraw-Hill, Inc., 1983. Used with permission.

computer. They accomplish this with special languages that convert English and algebra into the binary number system the computer can understand. Three computer languages are commonly used by programmers.

**COBOL** (COmmon Business-Oriented Language) is designed especially for business applications. It employs English words and sentences almost exclusively.

**FORTRAN** (FORmula TRANslation) may be used for business, but its principal application is for scientific work where mathematical equations are solved.

**BASIC** (Beginners All-purpose Symbolic Instruction Code) is especially adaptable for input and output users, which is making its application common in business. Figure 12-8 lists the BASIC program for the customer billing flowchart in Figure 12-7.

In addition, there have been a number of "user-friendly" programs developed for people who have no training in any of the formal computer languages. These conversational programs allow a clerk or a manager to use the computer by following the computer's instructions. For example, here's how an inexperienced person might proceed.

*You* turn on the terminal.
*Terminal:* Hello. What do you want?

Figure 12-8

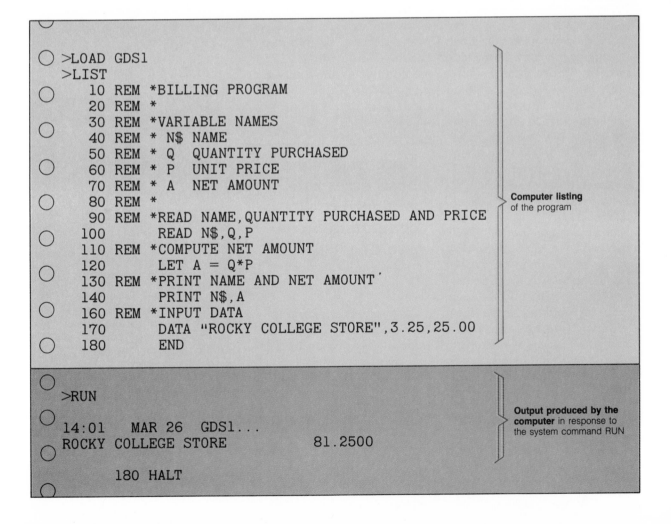

```
>LOAD GDS1
>LIST
   10 REM *BILLING PROGRAM
   20 REM *
   30 REM *VARIABLE NAMES
   40 REM * N$  NAME
   50 REM * Q   QUANTITY PURCHASED
   60 REM * P   UNIT PRICE
   70 REM * A   NET AMOUNT
   80 REM *
   90 REM *READ NAME,QUANTITY PURCHASED AND PRICE
  100      READ N$,Q,P
  110 REM *COMPUTE NET AMOUNT
  120      LET A = Q*P
  130 REM *PRINT NAME AND NET AMOUNT
  140      PRINT N$,A
  160 REM *INPUT DATA
  170      DATA "ROCKY COLLEGE STORE",3.25,25.00
  180      END
```

Computer listing of the program

```
>RUN

14:01   MAR 26  GDS1...
ROCKY COLLEGE STORE             81.2500

      180 HALT
```

Output produced by the **computer** in response to the system command RUN

# B·I·L·L·B·O·A·R·D

## HAVE COMPUTERS LIVED UP TO THEIR PROMISE?

Everyone knows by now how incredibly fast and accurate computers can be. But this still doesn't answer questions like, If they are so good, why do they make so many mistakes? Or, are they really necessary in every place they are used? Or, don't they shift much of the burden of doing things from the company that should be providing the service to the consumer?

Many critics say that the computer increasingly forces consumers to shift for themselves. We dial our own long-distance numbers without personal assistance. We withdraw cash from the bank without seeing the teller. We are told by a computer to wait for service when we call a business to make an inquiry.

It's not just consumers who are making these complaints. More and more businesses are wondering whether computers have been oversold. At Imperial Oil Ltd., for example, an Exxon affili-ate, a "hold" was put on computer purchases after seeing four straight years of 18 percent spending increases for them. Not only that, employment in Imperial's data processing department grew by leaps and bounds to 500 people. Further computer purchases, the company said, would have to show that they advanced Imperial's strategic plans.

*More and more businesses are wondering whether computers have been oversold.*

Even Steve Wozniak, fabled cofounder of Apple Computer, Inc., wondered whether the sale of computers had reached an unjustifiable level. "In the home market-place, at least," Wozniak observed at the pit of the computer recession of 1985, "computers are sort of modern-day playthings, like sophisticated railroad sets." Maybe computers have gone too far in business also.

### QUERIES

What's your feeling about business's use of computers? Is it time to call a moratorium until we know what their long-term value really is? Or should we continue to move ahead with computers as vigorously as in the past? ∎

*SOURCES:* Bill Javetski, "Making Sure Computers Earn Their Keep," *Business Week*, June 24, 1985, p. 78; Francesca Lunzer, "A Complete Fiasco," *Forbes*, June 17, 1985, p. 178; Jane Ferrell, "The Wiz Takes Aim at the Overselling of Computers," *Ad Week*, April 1985, p. 4.

# PROFILE

**R**AINER PAUL oversees the planning and implementation of office automation at Avon Products, Inc. His title, however, indicates the greater breadth of his responsibilities. He is vice president of information systems for the company. As such, he has the responsibility of managing the output of 2,000 employees at Avon's New York City headquarters. These employees provide a variety of office services such as typing, copying, reading documents, and the like. The managers they serve devote considerable time to telephone conversations and attending meetings. Under Paul's direction Avon installed an integrated office automation system, along with a network of personal computers and word processors for managerial use. This system is predicted to raise secretarial and clerical productivity 31 percent and managerial productivity 19 percent. When the system was first proposed, however, the response was negative. Says Paul, "It's hard to perceive how a personal computer will help someone do a better job if that person has never used one before." To gain acceptance of the plan, it was implemented first in selected departments. And Paul assigned departmental coordinators on a full-time basis for 3 months to field the inevitable problems and to gather the necessary documentation to verify that the time and cost savings predicted actually occurred. ∎

**RAINER PAUL**

SOURCE: Rick Minicucci, "Avon's OA Make-Over: Crafted With Care," *Today's Office*, November 1985, pp. 22–26.

*You:* I want to find a customer's account balance.
*Terminal:* Do you need instructions?
*You:* Yes.
*Terminal:* Type in customer's account number.
*You:* 312 5719
*Terminal:* Balance is $258.57 on January 15, 1984.
*You:* Thank you.
*Terminal:* Do you want anything else?
*You:* No.
*Terminal:* Turn me off. Bye.

The trick, of course, is that the computer has been programmed to recognize and respond only to the exact words that the operator has been told to use when conversing with the computer. If the operator were to say, in answer to the first query, "I want a customer's account balance," the computer would reply, "I don't understand you. Will you check your instructions and ask me again?"

# 6  COMPUTER APPLICATIONS AND SOCIAL IMPACT

*Seemingly endless uses, but some social concerns*

As can be seen from the opening paragraph of this chapter and from the dozens of new and different applications cited in the Careers of the Future features at the end of each unit, the uses for computers are seemingly endless. Computers can perform almost every human task that is repetitive, and the computer can do it with infinitely greater accuracy and speed. Everywhere that paperwork is handled, computer systems can be found. In every simple, routine factory operation, there is a good chance that a computer-driven and computer-controlled device will replace human hands. Computers fly the major airlines, except for brief moments at takeoff and landing. Computers operate the telephone system and the public power systems. It no longer is a question of whether or not a computer will enter a particular business operation or occupation. The questions that remain are "when?" and "to what extent?"

Three areas of computer application warrant special attention, however. They are word processing and its all-embracing extension into office automation, personal workstations, and the automation of traditional mechanical equipment.

## WORD PROCESSING

*Leading the way to automation of the entire office* ━━━━━

Computers have had their biggest impact upon clerical operations that involve the processing of numbers: accounting, inventory, and payroll systems, in particular. Increasingly, however, computers have been combining with other devices to make major changes in the traditional office activities of stenography and secretarial work. This kind of automation has had its most dramatic effect in the introduction of word process-

## Action Brief

### HOW DO YOU SPELL RELIEF?

*One research study of 500 secretaries and typists concluded that for tension relief, word processing was the best medicine. When the extensive array of electronic equipment entered offices during the last decade, one worry was that secretaries and typists would rebel. Instead, an overwhelming number (83 percent) said they "loved" the new equipment. "Why?" asked the researchers. The new electronic gear reduces stress, said the respondents, and 80 percent said that stress was one of the biggest problems on their jobs. About half of those surveyed said that word processing skills improved their relationships with their bosses. More than three-quarters indicated that electronic office equipment allowed them to spend less time typing and more time doing work that involved decision making. More than 80 percent said that the office automation opened up more avenues for advancement.*

ing. **Word processing** is the production of written communications through the combined use of systems management procedures, automated technology (primarily computer-related), and skilled personnel. The least sophisticated word processing equipment is the automatic typewriter. The most complex are literally small computer systems (like the schematic one shown in Figure 12-9) with an ability to set type and compose charts and other illustrations for printing into hard-copy records or other publications.

Word processing appears now to be only the beginning of full-scale office automation. **Office automation** encompasses any aspect of traditional clerical work and administration that is assisted by a computer. At its ultimate, office automation links (integrates) all the clerical activities in an office. Few installations reach this extreme, although more than 40,000 integrated office systems are forecast by 1990. In addition to word processing, office automation will be put together, probably step by step, with such computer-oriented devices and systems as electronic mail, voice message systems, electronic filing, advanced telephone systems, and personal workstations. Estimates are that by 1990, three out of four clerical jobs will be affected in some way by these developments. Office automation will not necessarily do away with jobs, but it will change many of them radically. Some jobs will become more interesting and challenging, even more difficult; others may become more boring.

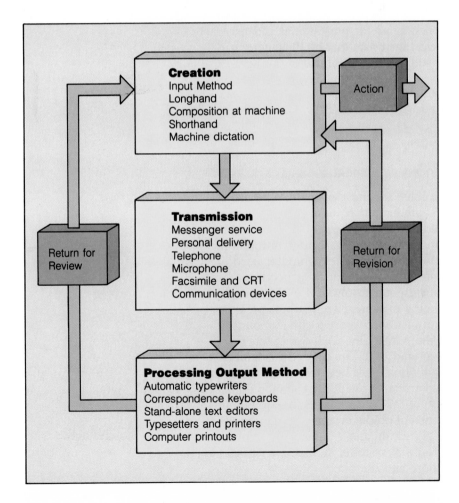

Figure 12-9 Simplified word processing system.

# PERSONAL WORKSTATIONS
*Greater control over one's work*⸺⸺⸺⸺⸺⸺⸺⸺⸺⸺⸺

The first strong move toward computerizing employees' work areas, or stations, on a personal basis began, predictably, at the top. Since the advent of personal computers, thousands of executives have been equipped with computerized workstations that enable them to retrieve, review, and manipulate data from a company's main computer and/or data bases. One of the most valuable services to executives has been the computer's ability to provide answers to "what if?" questions, such as "what would happen if we raised our prices by 5 percent?" or "what if we increased our advertising budget on product X?" etc. The computer can be programmed to furnish such what-if information in spreadsheet format. A *spreadsheet* shows the distribution of data (usually numbers) in checkerboard fashion for a range of variables when certain main variables are changed. If, for example, the price of product X were raised 5 percent, the spread sheet might show what happens to an entire range of costs (such as production, inventory, distribution, sales commissions) and revenues (such as unit and dollar sales in several territories for product X and other products in the company's line). Computerized management information systems that provide such data are called *decision-support systems.*

What is probably just as important as the growth in personal workstations and decision-support systems for executives is the even greater growth in the use of personal workstations for professional and other nonmanagerial employees. Reliable estimates are that by 1990 more than half of all personal computers sold will be bought for use in business. A significant portion of these will be for personal workstations.

# SHOP-FLOOR COMPUTER SYSTEMS
*A growing frontier for computerized equipment*⸺⸺⸺⸺⸺⸺⸺⸺

Computerized office systems receive the most visibility. The use of computers to operate and regulate production equipment is an established practice, but it receives less attention from the general public. One reason is that the computers used for such purposes are often different in concept and operation from the binary-coded digital computer used in offices. *Analog computers* operate on information that need not be represented numerically. They can respond to physical changes in dimension (such as when a part is being machined on a lathe), pressure (from a steam gauge), temperature (of a food process), the amount of light falling on a surface, and the like. Originally, such computers were restricted to "numerical" machining and other specialized machinery. Today, there are few limits to their application. They, too, can be linked into networks, either with similar computers or with the common digital computers. Needless to say, the use of analog computers for equipment control extends beyond the production of products to any kind of equipment operation and control, such as heating and ventilation control for large hotels and office buildings, railway systems in airport terminals, postal service sorting and distribution, and the like.

# COMPUTERS IN BUSINESS: PRO AND CON
*From an operations point of view, a mixed blessing* ━━━━━

To a great extent, the introduction of computer methods to business operations has been a positive step. However, like nearly all technological innovations, computer use has its advantages and disadvantages.

***ADVANTAGES*** The principle advantages of computers are as follows:

■ They are extremely fast, sometimes performing millions of simple operations every second.
■ Computers can store and rapidly locate and organize tremendous amounts of information.
■ They are very accurate. With well-written and thoroughly tested software, computers are virtually error-free.
■ Computers can relieve employees of some of the routine clerical and mechanical work that accompanies all production activity.
■ Because of their speed, memory, and ability to handle so much data, computers have made possible the use of complex statistical and analytical methods that could never be used with manual processing.

***DISADVANTAGES*** The chief drawbacks to the use of computers in business are as follows:

■ Mainframe computers are very expensive to own and operate. Many larger mainframe models cost several hundred thousand dollars a month to rent, plus the cost of highly trained analysts, programmers, and operators.
■ All computer systems require accuracy and detail in their operating software. To create an effective application is a demanding and expensive undertaking. Extensive program testing is needed.
■ Software preparation or modification is still a major problem for computer users. While there is a multitude of proprietary programs that can be purchased from software companies and service centers, a great many of these programs must be modified at considerable cost to accommodate the characteristics of the user's computer system.
■ Computers are only tools. The real requirement for success is an outstanding human organization surrounding the computer to decide on its use, accurately prepare input, and usefully interpret output.
■ Increasingly, computer systems are vulnerable to damage, such as careless erasures and willful sabotage. Facilities where computers operate and/or where vital data bases are stored require sophisticated protection and security.
■ There is also the real problem of unauthorized access to and/or theft of a data base's private information. Here again, sophisticated password and user identification systems are needed to protect against casual invasions. Deliberate theft (so-called computer crimes), perpetrated by persons inside or outside a company, still remains a considerable threat.

# SOCIAL IMPACT OF COMPUTERS
*Their good works exceed their drawbacks, but doubts linger* ━━━

Aside from the contributions that business receives from computers, there are other benefits that extend to consumers and the general public as a result of their use in business. Here are just a few of these benefits:

■   Computers enable employees to use their higher-level skills rather than expend their energy on boring, repetitive, nonchallenging activities. Computers tend to enhance human creativity, judgment, and intuition rather than replace these qualities.

■   Computers tend to increase the productivity of businesses; often these benefits are passed on to consumers in terms of greater service and lower prices.

■   Computers relieve humans from working in unsafe or intolerable atmospheres. Computers can function in corrosive solutions, noxious fumes, high temperatures and pressures, and radioactive conditions.

■   Computers enable handicapped people to find useful employment by performing or assisting with tasks beyond the person's physical limitations.

■   Computers extend the range of services, such as banking and telephone, to individuals who might otherwise not be reached.

There is another, darker, side to the computer picture, of course. Consider just these two problem areas:

■   Computer systems tend to invade personal privacy. Data about us has been gathered, not only by the federal and state governments but also by our employers, vendors, utility service companies, and dozens, if not hundreds, of other organizations. A Senate Subcommittee on Constitutional Rights a few years ago found that there were 858 data banks in 54 federal agencies containing more than 1.25 billion records and dossiers on individuals. In addition, there are hundreds of private organizations, such as insurance companies and credit bureaus, that maintain files on most of us. Even if this information were to be used legally and legitimately, there is always the danger of improper and illegal usage by others who find ways to gain access to this information.

■   There is a legitimate concern that increased usage of computer systems in offices and in factories (along with automation and robotics) will lead to a serious rise in unemployment. When an economy or a particular industry is growing, computer usage tends to accelerate that growth. Employees displaced by the computer in one area of a company's operations are probably transferred to jobs elsewhere in that company. When the opposite is true of an economy or an industry, the search by businesses for improved productivity through computer usage often leads to a reduction in employment. The great unanswered question is, What will computer usage hold in terms of employment opportunities over the long run? There were similar fears when mechanization and electric power were introduced into manufacturing industries. These fears proved, mainly, to be groundless. The first wave of automation in the United States during the period from 1940 to 1960 saw more jobs created than destroyed. It is still too soon to make an accurate projection for the new wave of automation that is powered by computers.

# Key Concepts

1. Business management depends greatly on a regular, relevant, and reliable flow of information. Information, or data, is knowledge gathered from internal sources of a business (such as its daily sales and accounting transactions) and external sources (such as the federal government). Data is classified as primary if it is new and original and collected for a company's specific use, and secondary if it is gathered from previously compiled, often public, sources. Data of a related nature that has been collected and maintained in computer files is called a data base or data bank.

2. A management information system (MIS) is a set of processes designed to collect, store, and process data that is especially relevant to a company's interests and to make it available to a company's managers in a form that is directly usable for planning, controlling, and decision making. The effectiveness of an MIS is judged by its usefulness, timeliness, and affordability.

3. Data processing adds value to information by performing a variety of functions including (1) the *input* functions of collecting, preparing, and entering data; (2) the *processing* functions of storing, sorting, classifying, updating, computing, and retrieving; and (3) the *output* functions of responding to inquiries and preparing specified reports, either periodically or on demand.

   Data processing may be performed in batches, as transactions occur, or in a real-time mode so that processing itself affects the transaction.

4. Computers are systems of electromechanical devices that greatly enlarge human capabilities with their incredible accuracy and speed in processing numbers and related information. Computer hardware consists of a central processing unit and a memory; peripheral devices provide inputs to the computer and receive its outputs. The trend in computer usage is to interconnect computers and input and output units in networks that share common data bases.

5. Computer software represents the instructions that tell computers what to do and how to do it. Software appears in the form of essentially numerical programs that are written in various symbolic computer languages such as COBOL, FORTRAN, and BASIC.

6. Computers are usefully applied today in almost every aspect of the business functions of production, operations, marketing, personnel, accounting, and finance. Computers are especially efficient in handling paperwork; hence they are increasingly used for word processing and office automation. There is also a trend toward personal workstations, for executives in particular to use in connection with decision-support systems. A special analog form of computer broadens the application of automation and robotics in manufacturing.

   Computers have various drawbacks as well as their obvious advantages of speed and accuracy. There is a growing concern for the security of computer systems, their potential for invading personal privacy, and their long-term threat to employment.

# Review Questions

1. Define, identify, or explain each of the following key terms or phrases, found on the pages indicated.

*analog computer (p. 282)*
*BASIC (p. 277)*
*batch processing (p. 270)*
*binary number system (p. 272)*
*central processing unit (CPU) (p. 274)*

*COBOL (p. 277)*
*computer (p. 272)*
*data (see information) (p. 265)*
*data base (p. 267)*
*data processing (p. 269)*
*decision-support system (p. 282)*
*electronic data processing (EDP) (p. 269)*
*flowchart (p. 276)*
*FORTRAN (p. 277)*

*hardware (p. 272)*
*information (p. 265)*
*input unit (p. 273)*
*local area network (LAN) (p. 275)*
*management information system (MIS) (p. 268)*
*memory unit (p. 274)*
*mode (p. 270)*
*modem (p. 273)*
*office automation (p. 281)*
*output unit (p. 273)*
*primary data (p. 266)*
*private automated branch exchange (PABX)*
*(p. 275)*
*program (p. 276)*
*real-time processing (p. 271)*
*secondary data (p. 266)*
*software (p. 275)*
*spreadsheet (p. 282)*
*transactional processing (p. 270)*
*word processing (p. 281)*

2. Differentiate between primary and second-ary data. Which type is more costly to gather?

3. What sort of information might be collected in a data base?

4. Describe the main functions of a management information system. What criteria are used to judge its effectiveness?

5. When a computer in a remote location informs a retail salesclerk that a customer's credit rating is all right, what phase of data processing is involved?

6. Distinguish between batch processing and transactional processing. Give an example of each.

7. What sorts of devices make up the hardware associated with a computer system?

8. Explain the purpose of a flowchart in creating a computer program.

9. What does a computer program consist of?

10. List some of the advantages and disadvantages of computers and identify those that have a significant social impact.

# Case Critique 12-1
# 60,000 photographs. Instantly!

When advertising agencies and publishers need a photograph of a special subject, they don't send a photographer out to take a picture. Instead, they call up a stock photo house and describe the picture they are looking for. A typical photo house will then search its files of up to 3 million existing photographs and send the picture over to the agency for approval. The process is full of misfires. It is expensive and time-consuming. A couple of years ago, however, Image Bank, an enterprising photo house in New York City, decided to break the technology barrier. It placed an assortment of 60,000 of its prime photos on a videodisc that could be searched with a computer program to locate desired categories of the photos almost instantly. If a client wanted a particular photo, now the buyer used computer software to search a series of menus for the photo. A keyboard command flashed pictures from the videodisc onto a monitor. If the client decided to buy the photo, he or she called up Image Bank using the videodisc catalog number and the slide or photo was sent over.

It sounded like a great idea, but there turned out to be a few problem spots. Many potential clients weren't ready for modern times; they'd rather have the stock photo house search for the right picture the old-fashioned way. In addition, the client had to equip itself with an industrial-grade high-resolution videodisc player at the cost of $10,000 or more. Some potential clients figured that they might have to buy $25,000 of photos a year to make the videodisc system economically feasible, despite its convenience. Few customers were large enough to buy that many photos. Furthermore, each time the Image Bank wanted to add a picture, it had to make a new disc, at about $5,000 each (duplicates were rented at a nominal price to clients). Then some pessimists got into the act. They wondered whether technology might soon advance beyond the videodisc to sending the pictures over telephone wires. Clients could then search the company's files directly without the need for a videodisc player.

1. What are the principal drawbacks of the videodisc system?
2. What do you think of the potential for the videodisc technique? Will it succeed or won't it?
3. Should Image Bank have waited until the new technology for sending pictures by telephone is perfected? Why?

---

*SOURCE:* Nancy Madlin, "Putting Photos on Videodiscs," *Venture*, July 1985, pp. 112–114.

---

# Case Critique 12-2
## Do-It-Yourself Bosses

Two companies, in particular, make extensive use of executive workstations. Zale Corp., Irving, Texas, is the world's largest jeweler, with 800 retail outlets. Its top executives use workstation computers arrayed in a decision-support network to shape the plans of the company. At first, only Zale's technical and market research specialists used the system for making forecasts and for allocating sales quotas, for example, to various geographic territories. Then, some of the division and district managers at headquarters asked for their own computers so that they could make their own analyses and decisions directly. Eventually, the company installed some 300 computer terminals with access to the system; about 20 of them were used by do-it-yourself men and women in the executive suites.

At Mead Corp. in Dayton, Ohio, an "executive information system" is used directly by the top managers at the home office of this large paper maker. From the company's president, chairperson, and senior vice presidents on down to most staff department heads, Mead says that these executives are all "hands-on users." The decision-support system at Mead offers several programs—including a 5-year forecast, flash-earnings report, corporate planning, and a human resources data base. Executives who have access to the system can call up data, analyze it, and ask "what-if" questions; or they can program their personal computers to furnish them "exception" reports when something is not going according to plan. Which executives make the most, and best, use of the plan? Says Mead, "Use of technology is still limited to those with computer knowledge. The leading edge executive, who is a closet computer hobbyist at home, is most likely to use the system."

1. Who do you think should get personal computers first at work: technicians like market research people, office employees, or executives? Why?
2. From what you can gather in the case, how does the information provided by the decision-support system differ from the information provided in routine retail and office situations?
3. What similarities do you see between the attitude toward computers and use of them expressed by some executives at Mead and the attitude of the average person when first confronted with a computer? What would you do to improve such attitudes and increase computer usage?

---

*SOURCE:* Ellis Booker, "Decision Support Systems: Computers Help You Win the Game," *Computer Decisions*, September 15, 1984, pp. 15–28.

# Accounting for Managerial and Financial Control

## Learning Objectives

*The purpose of this chapter is to describe the accounting process and its uses; explain standard accounting principles and practices; describe the role of public accountants, audits, and accounting standards; and explain, illustrate, and interpret the basic financial statements of a business.*

*As evidence of general comprehension, after studying Chapter 13, you should be able to:*

1. *Describe the accounting system and distinguish between managerial and financial accounting.*

2. *Recognize the basic language and procedures of the accounting process and identify and apply the accounting equation.*

3. *Describe the roles of public accountants, audits, and accounting standards and explain the concepts of inventory and inflation accounting.*

4. *Understand the purpose and explain the distinctive features of a balance sheet.*

5. *Understand the purpose and explain the distinctive features of a statement of income and retained earnings.*

6. *Explain the purpose of the statement of changes in financial position.*

7. *Read and interpret selected data from financial statements.*

*If your class is using SSweetco: Business Model and Activity File, see Chapter 13 in that book after you complete this chapter. There you will find exercises and activities to help you apply your learning to typical business situations.*

# 1 ACCOUNTING

is a <u>numerical information system</u> that records, classifies, summarizes, and interprets a company's transactions

and it is used two ways:
<u>internally</u> by a company's managers and <u>externally</u> by investors, bankers, creditors, and the government.

Managerial accounting        Financial accounting

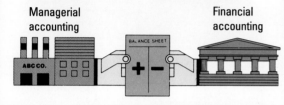

# 2 THE ACCOUNTING EQUATION

is the basis for all recordkeeping

| ASSETS $ | = | LIABILITIES $ | + | EQUITY $ |
|---|---|---|---|---|

carried out by the <u>Double-Entry Method</u>

| BALANCE ||
|---|---|
| DEBIT | CREDIT |
| 720 00 | 720 00 |

# 3 ACCOUNTING PRACTICES

must conform to standards set by the government and professional associations

SEC    GAAP    ICPA    FASB

and are audited by CPAs.

| BALANCE ||
|---|---|
| DEBIT | CREDIT |
| 720 00 | 720 00 |
| | OK |

# 4 A BALANCE SHEET

summarizes a firm's financial position on a particular date.

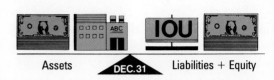

Assets    DEC.31    Liabilities + Equity

# 5 AN INCOME STATEMENT

summarizes what has happened financially to a firm over a period of time.

Income    Expenses    Profit or Loss

# 6 A STATEMENT OF CHANGES IN FINANCIAL POSITION

explains changes in working capital that take place from one year to another.

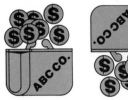

Start                  Finish

# 7 THE INTERPRETATION OF FINANCIAL STATEMENTS

is essential in assessing a company's financial position, its liquidity and profitability, and the quality of its management.

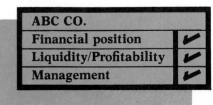

| ABC CO. ||
|---|---|
| Financial position | ✔ |
| Liquidity/Profitability | ✔ |
| Management | ✔ |

# ACCOUNTING: THE LIFEBLOOD OF INFORMATION SYSTEMS

When the recession of 1980–1982 struck, businesses all over the United States struggled to keep their heads above water. Many failed. Those that succeeded often owed a large debt to their accountants. The image of accountants as little old people in alpaca jackets, stiff white collars, and green eye shades was dispelled forever. Instead, the accountants became the white knights of business. They did so by shining the light of their records on corporate weak spots, like too many fixed assets and costs of sales that were out of line. To reduce fixed assets, a firm's accountants turned steely eyes on such frivolities as company planes and luxurious offices. "Did the business really need them?" they asked. To cut the cost of sales, accountants sorted out figures that showed that in many areas, companies were overstaffed with fat-cat assistants and extra secretaries for executives. "Could these be justified?" the accountants asked. "Or were they just a drain on profits?"

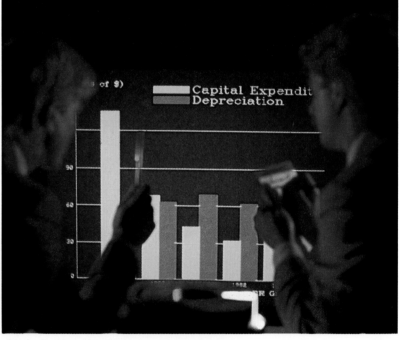

Accountants focused their attention on the health of two important documents: a firm's balance sheet and income statement. When either statement gets sick, it shows that the firm is about to get sick also. A major indicator of a sick balance sheet is one that shows that a company owes too much money in relation to its ability to pay it back. It was even happening to such corporate giants as DuPont, Caterpillar Tractor, and Allied Corporation. The medicine prescribed by the accountants to executives in the ailing companies was, "Get your debt down to a figure where payments won't bleed you dry." Another symptom of financial statement illness is a buildup in inventories. This sometimes happens so slowly that it isn't noticed until a company's warehouses are bulging with unsold, and often unsalable, out-of-date merchandise. An ever-vigilant accounting profession makes inventories a prime target of its reporting system. Especially with computerized inventory control, accountants in companies that survived the recession were able to alert corporate executives to buildups before they drained profits away.

Accounting sometimes appears to be routine and unexciting. Those who are employed in the work of accounting don't think so. The companies that benefit from accountants' vigilance during recessions and hard times know that the accountants are the life blood of their information systems. Without *the timely reports that accountants provide of a firm's financial health, many companies might not still be alive.*

SOURCE: Clark E. Chastain, "How Management Accountants Coped With the Recession," Management Accounting, *January 1985, pp. 34–38.*

## 1 THE ACCOUNTING PROCESS AND USES
### A numerical information system

Of all the information that is transmitted within a business and between a business and its environment, none is ultimately more important than information about money. Businesses are established for the purpose of making profits. After all the costs are added up and subtracted from income, the resulting profit or loss—the "bottom line" on an income statement—will be the final measure of whether a business succeeds or fails.

The accounting system provides this information about money. It is absolutely fundamental to management because every function and activity of the business depends on adequate funds. Accounting tracks the flow of funds into and out of a business. For that reason, many consider it the most vital of all business information systems.

Like so many other business functions, accounting incorporates various methods for meeting goals. **Accounting** may be defined as a numerical information system designed to record, classify, summarize, and interpret an organization's day-to-day business transactions. Accounting monitors the flow of cash and the continuing changes in financial obligations. The accounting system's function of supplying financial information is entirely interdependent with a company's other activities and resources. Personnel, equipment, material, and everything else a business uses or produces are reflected in its accounting information.

The sources and nature of accounting information make it necessary to include two kinds of activities in an accounting system: recordkeeping and true accounting. **Recordkeeping** records and classifies raw data that is used in the accounting function. A recordkeeping system keeps track of all transactions in which money changes hands, whether in the form of cash, credit, or some other kind of financial obligation. The main responsibility of recordkeeping is to make sure that there is an accurate written record of every transaction. The records may be classified or summarized in many different ways, as required by the accounting system.

**True accounting** focuses on the analytical requirements of keeping and using financial records. Accountants work out the methods used by recordkeepers. They determine the classifications in which records must be placed. They summarize the data to make it usable for decision making. They interpret the information to clarify its true meaning for the current and future operations of the business.

In a small retail store, for instance, the distinction between accounting and recordkeeping is clear. The recordkeeper actually writes records of business transactions: sales, rent payments, payroll, inventory purchases, and so forth. An accountant decides how the records are to be organized and how they are to be grouped together and interpreted. The accountant puts the data into useful form for deciding what price to set on new merchandise, when to undertake business expansion or reduction, and how to pay for new display racks. All of the information will be extracted so that any necessary reports may be made, and income taxes and payroll taxes may be filed.

The accounting process actually encompasses six phases (as shown in Figure 13-1). Each financial transaction—sales, purchase, payment, and so on—is first recorded in a sort of business diary, called a journal. Periodically, the journal entries are sorted out and transferred, or posted, to a record book, or ledger, according to various kinds of accounts. At the end of a month, the total of all income accounts is matched against the total of all outgo accounts to be sure that no moneys have been lost or are unaccounted for. In Step 4 (work sheet analyses), the various accounts are broken down or combined to analyze and explain where the money has gone during the month. From this analysis, accounts are arranged to subtract the costs of doing business from a company's sales receipts; the difference represents what accountants call "income," commonly called either profit or loss. In the final step, accounts are sorted and analyzed to show what is owned by the company (assets), what is owed by the company (liabilities), and what might remain for the owners (equity) of the assets if the liabilities were paid off. These figures appear on the balance sheet. An analysis of what appears on the income statement and the balance sheet provides data for the preparation of the statement of changes in financial position now required by the Securities and Exchange Commission (SEC) for all firms listed on organized stock

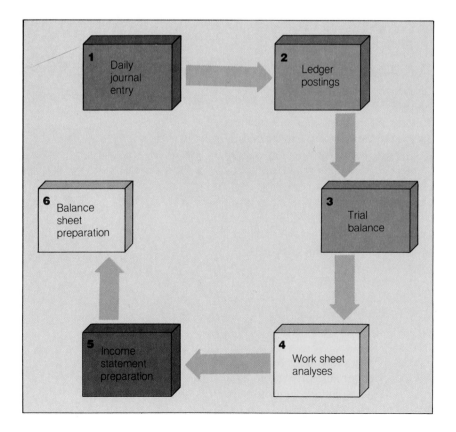

Figure 13-1 The accounting process.

exchanges. (The statement of changes in financial position is also required for all companies audited by public accounting firms.)

## USES OF ACCOUNTING INFORMATION
*Managerial and financial* ━━━━━━━━━━━━━━━

The information produced by the accounting system must meet internal and external needs:

■ Accounting must provide information for managers to use for running their company. This function is usually called **managerial accounting.** It provides information on costs and revenues that managers use for controlling operations and in their efforts to make a profit. Accounting information on sales income, production results, personnel, cost of equipment and materials, size and value of inventory, and other data is used for planning, budgeting, and controlling.

■ Financial information must also be gathered for reporting to and dealing with the world outside the organization. This external **financial accounting** reports financial conditions to stockholders, investors, banks and other financial institutions, and the government, when required. External reporting is especially important to corporations that must send financial statements to owners, potential investors, brokers, stock exchanges, regulatory agencies, and others. All companies need accurate and complete accounting information to pay income taxes and payroll taxes, such as social security, and to deal with creditors, banks, and government agencies.

## 2 ACCOUNTING PRINCIPLES
### A standardized language and procedure

Accounting methods used today are often complex and sophisticated. The goal of accounting remains fairly simple, however: to maintain a complete and accurate record of every transaction and to organize and summarize the records so that they are useful to management. Accounting is so important to every aspect of operations that it has become a standard means for expressing business results.

## THE ACCOUNTING EQUATION
*Assets equal liabilities plus equity* ━━━━━━━━━━━━━━━

Accounting methods are based on an understanding of the general financial makeup of an organization. Every company has control of certain things of value: land, equipment, cash, accounts receivable, and others. These are the company's assets. Assets may be acquired in two ways. They may be acquired through **equity,** or money invested by owners. They may also be borrowed or bought on credit. In either case, when money is owed by the company, it has a **liability.**

Since liabilities and equity are the only two sources of assets, together they must equal assets. This is the **accounting equation:**

$$\text{Assets} = \text{Liabilities} + \text{Equity}$$

This equation is basic not only to modern accounting methods but also to understanding the reports accountants use to reflect the financial conditions of businesses. Regardless of the size of assets, they must *always* be balanced by the sum of liabilities and equity, as shown in Figure 13-2.

## RECORDING TRANSACTIONS
*Two balancing entries every time*

To help ensure that accounting records are correct, record keepers and accountants use a **double-entry method** of record keeping. This is a technique for entering every transaction twice in such a way that the sum of all of the first entries will equal the sum of all the second entries if the records are complete and accurate. This provides a built-in check.

An accountant will develop categories of sources for a business's funds and for the uses of these funds. The most basic categories are assets, liabilities, and equity. Each of these is broken down further into specific accounts to maintain more detailed records. Assets might include separate accounts for real estate, equipment, and checking and savings accounts. Liabilities might include notes payable and accounts payable. Equity includes the actual values owned by investors. For a proprietorship, equity would usually be in the form of a single account belonging to one owner. A larger corporation might keep a number of different accounts for different types and classes of stock.

For further controls, separate accounts are maintained for specific **expenses** and **revenues.** Expense accounts will include payroll costs, purchase of supplies, rents paid, and other similar operations expenditures. Revenue accounts will include income from sales, interest received, rents received, and so forth.

**AN EXAMPLE** An acounting system, even for a small business, may be quite complex. A greatly simplified example illustrates the general principle of double-entry accounting. Someone who has recently become a licensed accountant might begin a business to provide computerized record-keeping and accounting services for small retail stores. Figure 13-3

Figure 13-2 The accounting equation:
Assets = Liabilities + Owner's equity

shows four accounts that might be established for such a business and demonstrates how transactions are recorded in these accounts.

Each account (sometimes called a T account because of the T shape formed by the rulings) has space for two columns of entries below the account title. The left-hand column is always called **debits** and the right-hand column **credits.** Some general rules for entries are:

- For expense and asset accounts, enter a transaction on the *left* if it *increases* the account and on the *right* if it *decreases* the account.
- For revenue, liability, or equity accounts, enter a transaction on the *right* if it *increases* the account and on the *left* if it *decreases* the account.

These rules are necessary to make the built-in checking mechanism work. It is always possible to check for accuracy by comparing the sum of the left-hand entries with the sum of the right-hand entries. It is also easy to check that assets really do equal liabilities plus equity.

***HOW IT IS DONE*** In the first transaction in Figure 13-3, the proprietor takes $12,500 and deposits it in the business checking account (A). This increases the account (an asset) and is entered in the left column of "cash in bank." It also increases equity, since it is the owner's investment and is entered in the right column of "owner's equity." The owner then writes a check for $370 to buy a new desk. This decreases "cash in bank" and is placed in the right column. It increases "office equipment," also an asset, and is placed on the left (B). Note that this purchase makes no change to liabilities or equity. Assets have not been increased but have only changed in form from cash to a desk.

The proprietor then borrows $15,000 from a bank to buy a small office computer. The loan increases liabilities (it is a note payable) and increases "cash in bank" (C). The owner writes a $15,000 check for the computer, decreases "cash in bank," and increases "office equipment" (D). In a real accounting system, complications such as depreciation and interest payable would have to be considered.

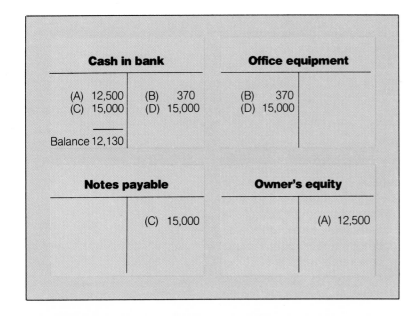

Figure 13-3 Example of double entry account records.

The "cash in bank" account has been increased by $27,500 and decreased by $15,370. Its present balance is $12,130. The "office equipment" account—the only other asset shown—has been increased by $15,370. Total assets are the sum of the asset accounts: $12,130 + $15,370 = $27,500. This equals the total liabilities ("notes payable") plus equity ("owner's equity"): $15,000 + $12,500 = $27,500. In an actual system with many accounts and entries, numerous other checks are also possible.

**THREE FUNCTIONS** Double-entry accounting serves three especially important functions when appropriate accounts are set up:

- It keeps track of assets and liabilities, showing what form they are in.
- It keeps accurate records of revenue and expenses.
- It allows the financial condition of a company to be determined by adding up all account balances for assets, liabilities, and equity.

# 3  ACCOUNTING PRACTICES AND STANDARDS
## An increasing conformance to prescribed standards

To be successful, an accounting system must include a large number of standardized procedures. It is essential that a company's accounting methods record every transaction without error or omission. Accounts must be established to accurately reflect the financial activities and condition of the business. Standard practices must be developed specifying how, and how often, records will be balanced and summarized. The length of time between the preparation of summaries of income, expenses, and profit or loss is called the *accounting period.* Accounting periods may be monthly, quarterly, yearly, or over any other length of time desired by management.

For a number of reasons—including the requirement to pay income taxes and for corporations to report to stockholders—nearly all companies prepare an annual summary of accounting information in addition to any other summaries they prepare. These annual accounting periods may coincide with the calendar year and end on December 31. They may also end on any other day that is convenient for the organization. A year set up for accounting purposes is called a *fiscal year.* The most common fiscal year—other than the calendar year—begins on July 1. The federal government begins its fiscal year on October 1.

## PUBLIC ACCOUNTANTS
### They certify accounting accuracy

Many companies—especially corporations—must make statements of their financial condition to the public, to organizations such as stock exchanges, and to the government. Such statements must usually be examined for accuracy by independent accountants. These public accountants are licensed by the state after meeting rigorous requirements. An accountant who is licensed to express an opinion on the completeness and accuracy of a company's financial reports is a *certified public accountant (CPA).* Most states require a college degree in accounting, passing scores on a series of accounting tests, and a minimum period of accounting experience before granting certification.

## AUDITS
*A means of verifying accuracy*

An *audit* is a careful examination of accounting methods and of financial records and reports to ensure that the financial activities and condition of a company are being truly and completely reported. When they are required for presentation to the public, to the government, or to lending institutions, audits are most commonly performed by independent CPAs. Companies also often have internal auditors for their own assurance of accuracy. The government may also perform audits, especially when tax disputes exist.

## ACCOUNTING STANDARDS
*For consistency and credibility*

Accountants adhere to what are known as *generally accepted accounting principles (GAAP).* Since 1973, however, the *Financial Accounting Standards Board (FASB)* has been designated by the SEC and the Institute of Certified Public Accountants to establish rules governing the preparation of financial reports. The intention of GAAP and of FASB is to establish methods of reporting that are consistent and comparable between companies and that reflect honestly the financial transactions and conditions of a business, especially one that is publicly owned.

## INVENTORY AND INFLATION ACCOUNTING
*Adjusts for the impact of rising prices*

Two areas of accounting practices have, in recent years, gotten considerable attention. These involve the valuation of inventories and the adjustment for the effects of inflation.

Inventory accounting offers a choice of two methods: FIFO or LIFO. *FIFO* means first in, first out. Under this system, the accountant assumes that the cost at which an inventory was accumulated will be charged to the finished goods made from them when sold. As a result, in times of rising prices, this system makes profits look better than they may really be. *LIFO,* on the other hand, means last in, first out. Under this system, the accountant charges the latest costs of accumulating inventories against the cost of goods sold. In times of rising prices, this system makes profits look worse than they may really be. There are arguments for either method, but many major firms have chosen the LIFO system because they feel that this approach is more realistic and offers tax benefits. Table 13–1 shows the effect of LIFO on one hypothetical company's earnings.

Rising prices affect much more than inventories. Most important, price inflation also affects the cost of replacing other assets such as land, building, and equipment. Accordingly, many firms add a note to their financial statements (they are encouraged to do so by the SEC) showing a comparison between present values and what they might have been if inflation had not taken place.

**TABLE 13-1**
**HOW LIFO ACCOUNTING CHANGES THE VALUATION OF INVENTORIES***

| Inventory Accounts | 1987 | 1986 | 1985 |
|---|---|---|---|
| Finished goods | $18,750,128 | $14,260,256 | $13,783,625 |
| Goods in process | 9,179,649 | 9,553,797 | 9,879,875 |
| Raw materials and manufacturing supplies | 18,928,563 | 17,825,964 | 20,107,876 |
| Total | $46,858,340 | $41,640,017 | $43,771,376 |
| LIFO adjustment | 4,429,179 | 1,547,347 | —0— |
| Total | $42,429,161 | $40,092,670 | $43,771,376 |

*XYZ Furniture Industries, Inc., changed from FIFO to LIFO method of pricing its inventories on December 31, 1985. This had the effect of lowering the value of the inventories shown on its balance sheet while adding to its cost of goods sold and reducing its net income.

# 4  BALANCE SHEET

*Balances the accounting equation
on a particular date*

The information that is collected and organized in the accounting system is presented and used in many ways. Three summary reports show the financial position and performance of a company: the balance sheet, the income statement, and the statement of changes in financial position.

The **balance sheet** is the main report of overall financial condition. It shows the assets, liabilities, and equity of a company at a particular time, usually on the last day of a fiscal year. The balance sheet shows what a company owns or controls and what the sources of the assets are.

Figure 13-4 shows the balance sheet for Abaco Industries (a hypothetical company) on December 31, 198X. The statement is arranged according to the accounting equation. Assets are entered in the top section, liabilities in the center, and equity at the bottom. It can be seen that the total assets are equal to, or in balance with, the combined liabilities and equity.

## THE ASSETS SECTION

*Tells what a business owns or controls*

The assets section of a balance sheet records those items of value that a business owns, or has control of, at the time of the statement. A company may, for example, own the truck it operates, but have a long-term mortgage on the building it occupies, and owe the bank some money on the merchandise displayed on its shelves. It owns the truck outright. It "controls" the occupancy of the building and the goods on its shelves, even though it still owes money on both. For accounting purposes, these assets are divided into current and fixed assets.

**CURRENT ASSETS** Current assets are those that can ordinarily be turned into cash within a year. The merchandise on the shelves would be current assets. Like other companies, the current assets of Abaco Indus-

# ABACO INDUSTRIES INC.

**Consolidated Balance Sheet**
December 31, 198X

## ASSETS

**Current Assets**

| | | |
|---|---:|---:|
| Cash, certificates of deposit, and marketable securities | $68,000 | |
| Accounts receivable | 44,000 | |
| Inventories | 40,000 | |
| Prepaid expenses | 2,000 | |
| Total current assets | | $154,000 |

**Property, Plant, and Equipment**

| | | | |
|---|---:|---:|---:|
| Buildings | $40,000 | | |
| Machinery and equipment | 68,000 | | |
| | 108,000 | | |
| Less accumulated depreciation | 60,000 | 48,000 | |
| Land | | 14,000 | |
| Goodwill | | 2,000 | 64,000 |
| Total assets | | | $218,000 |

## LIABILITIES AND STOCKHOLDERS' EQUITY

**Current Liabilities**

| | | |
|---|---:|---:|
| Accounts payable | $16,000 | |
| Accrued liabilities | 6,000 | |
| Current maturities of long-term debt | 1,000 | |
| Accrued income taxes payable | 5,000 | |
| Total current liabilities | | 28,000 |
| **Long-Term Debt** | | 4,000 |
| Total liabilities | | $32,000 |

**Stockholders' Equity**

| | | |
|---|---:|---:|
| Common stock: 10,000 shares outstanding | 38,000 | |
| Retained earnings | 148,000 | 186,000 |
| Total liabilities and stockholders' equity | | $218,000 |

Figure 13-4 Example of a balance sheet.

tries include (1) *cash* and temporary investments (such as CDs) that can easily be turned into cash, (2) *accounts receivables* (payments due from customers), (3) *inventories*, including finished products, work in process, materials, and supplies, and (4) *prepaid items*, like leases and insurance policies that have been paid for and have not expired.

*FIXED ASSETS* Fixed, or long-term, assets are those that a business expects to hold onto for a year or more. These typically include land, buildings, and equipment, owned or leased by the business. These fixed assets, especially those of buildings and equipment, are usually listed at the price that was paid for them, minus their accumulated depreciation. As a delivery truck grows older, for example, its value decreases—or depreciates—due to wear and tear. Federal tax laws allow a company to charge a depreciation expense each year against the original cost of the truck. If it cost $36,000, the company might be allowed to charge one-third of the cost (or $12,000) each year as depreciation. The balance sheet after the second year would show for the truck $36,000 less accumulated depreciation of $24,000 for a net asset of $12,000.

When one company buys another and pays more money than the concrete assets of the purchased company, **goodwill** may be included as an asset. The excess payment is in return for the good reputation, customer relations, work methods, and other intangible assets of the purchased company. Those intangibles are called goodwill.

## LIABILITIES AND EQUITY SECTION
*Tells what the business owes to others and to its owners*

The second half of a balance sheet records everything that a company owes to others and to its owners or stockholders. These debts are divided into liabilities and equity. It bears repeating that the sum of these two must exactly equal the total of all the assets on the first section of the balance sheet.

**LIABILITIES** The Abaco Industries balance sheet also divided liabilities into current and long-term. *Current liabilities* include short-term debts, long-term debts due for repayment during the current year, and accounts payable to suppliers and other creditors. Accrued liabilities are obligations that have built up but that are not yet due for payment. Examples are interest owed on debts or money owed to employees for their work during the current pay period. Income tax is another accrued expense. The amount owed increases every day income is earned, but the taxes only have to be paid quarterly or annually.

*Long-term liabilities* consist mainly of bonds, notes, and mortgages that do not have to be repaid during the year. Abaco Industries has a relatively small long-term debt of $4,000. It is the unpaid portion of the mortgage on its building. Large corporations frequently have several entries under long-term liabilities, such as mortgages, bonds of various types, and long-term notes.

**EQUITY** The remaining section of the balance sheet shows the monetary value of owners' equity. Earnings the company has generated but not paid out to investors still belong to, and are owed to, the owners. These are listed in the equity section under "Retained Earnings."

The point of a balance sheet is to show the financial condition of a company. Abaco Industries, on the date of the statement, had $218,000 worth of assets. The balance sheet shows what form the assets were in, how much money the company owes, and where the capital that produced the assets came from.

## 5  INCOME STATEMENT
*Reports profit or loss over a period of time*

An **income statement**—technically a "statement of earnings and retained earnings"—is an accounting report that shows the revenue received and expenses paid during a certain period of operations. One of its main purposes is to show the profit or loss resulting from operations. The income statement is often called a "profit and loss statement," or an "operating statement." It shows income and its sources, and expenses and their sources. It reports the financial results of a period of operations, usually a month, a quarter, a half-year, or a year. The income statement for Abaco Industries, for the 52 weeks ending December 31, 198X, is shown in Figure 13-5.

**REVENUES** Abaco Industries' revenues of $310,000 come from two sources. *Net sales* equal the total income from the sale of goods and services after refunds, discounts, and other similar adjustments have been deducted. *Other income* includes interest earned on investments, savings accounts, and loans and rental from properties.

**EXPENSES** Expenses are divided into four major categories, plus depreciation. *Cost of sales* (also called "cost of goods or products sold") includes all expenses that were necessary for producing the goods and services sold. Production materials and labor, direct supervision of production, utilities for production facilities, equipment maintenance, and other similar costs are placed in this category. Depreciation of production facilities is also included here. *Depreciation* is an expense resulting

Figure 13-5 Example of income statement (statement of earnings and retained earnings).

## ABACO INDUSTRIES INC.

**Statement of Consolidated Income and Retained Earnings**
For the 52 weeks ended December 31, 198X

**Revenues**

| | | |
|---|---|---|
| Net sales | $300,000 | |
| Other income | 10,000 | |
| Total revenues | | $310,000 |

**Costs and expenses**

| | | |
|---|---|---|
| Cost of products sold | $230,000 | |
| Marketing, administrative, and general expenses | 29,000 | |
| Interest expense | 1,000 | |
| Total costs and expenses | | 260,000 |
| **Earnings before income taxes** | | 50,000 |
| Less income taxes | | 20,000 |
| **Net income** | | $30,000 |

**Retained earnings**

| | | |
|---|---|---|
| At beginning of the year (from last year's balance sheet) | | 118,000 |
| Retained earnings before dividends | | $148,000 |
| Deduct cash dividends declared | | 10,000 |
| Retained earnings at end of year | | $138,000 |
| **Net income (or earnings) per share** | | $3.00 |
| **Dividends per share** | | $1.00 |

from the loss in value of equipment, buildings, or other fairly permanent assets caused by normal wear and tear and age.

The overhead costs of marketing, selling, and distributing products and of generally administering operations are shown as a second separate expense category. A third expense category is interest paid on borrowed money used in the business. Subtracting the total of these three kinds of expense from total revenues shows the company's earnings before income taxes. A fourth major expense, income taxes, is then deducted.

**INCOME** Subtracting income taxes paid produces the final earnings—or profit—for the year. Abaco Industries paid $20,000 in federal and state income taxes, leaving a net profit of $30,000.

**RETAINED EARNINGS** The income statement also gives additional information on retained earnings. Companies usually keep part of their earnings in the business and use them to expand, to improve or buy new facilities, or in other ways. Abaco Industries, up to the beginning of the period shown in the income statement, had reinvested $118,000 this way. Of the latest year's earnings, $10,000 was paid to the stockholders as dividends and $20,000 was retained. This left a new balance of $138,000 for retained earnings. Earnings per share is calculated by dividing the $30,000 profit by the 10,000 shares of stock outstanding listed in Figure 13-4, which is equal to $3.00 per share. Dividends per share is smaller than this. It is found by dividing the $10,000 declared in dividends by the number of shares, or $1.00 per share.

# 6  STATEMENT OF CHANGES IN FINANCIAL POSITION

*Reveals where the money came from and how it was used*

The last of the major accounting reports is the **statement of changes in financial position,** also called a "funds statement." This statement explains the overall changes in the balance sheet from one year to the next. It shows the sources of funds the business used during the accounting period and the uses to which the funds were put. It shows how ongoing operations are financed and gives an idea of a company's ability to finance future operations.

Sources of funds include earnings from operations, depreciation, revenue from selling property, and money gained from debt financing.

Funds are used for adding capital assets, such as buildings and machinery, paying dividends, paying off part of a loss on a discontinued operation, and repaying borrowed money. If the funds received are greater than the funds used, the difference can be added to working capital. Working capital is important in financial analysis because it shows a company's capabilities for meeting upcoming financial obligations and for financing operations.

# 7 INTERPRETATION OF FINANCIAL STATEMENTS

*Analyzes a firm's financial position and the quality of its management*

Financial statements reveal a great deal of information about the assets, liabilities, ownership, and operating success of companies. More information can be derived from the statements by analyzing and interpreting them. This is also the job of accountants, and it is one of their greatest contributions to successful business operation.

## RATIO ANALYSIS

*Selected comparisons of financial-report data* ━━━━━━

Accountants and managers use a technique called **ratio analysis** to help interpret financial statements. This technique compares certain categories of assets, earnings, expenses, liabilities, and equity to make statements more informative. By computing ratios, the performance and condition of one company can be compared with that of other companies and with standards of performance established by analysts. Data on financial ratios in companies and industries is available from Dun & Bradstreet, Inc., from other business publishers, from trade associations, and, in some cases, from government publications. Individual analysts often use information provided by corporations in their annual or quarterly reports. All figures used below are extracted from either the balance sheet or the statement of earnings and retained earnings for Abaco Industries, using data from Figures 13-4 and 13-5.

## LIQUIDITY INDICATORS

*Measure the ability of a firm to pay its debts* ━━━━━━

Several of the most important ratios indicate the extent to which a firm has sufficient liquid assets to meet its financial obligations. These are called measures of **liquidity.** Other closely related indicators show how effectively current funds are being used to create income for the company.

■ The **current ratio** is a measure of a company's ability to pay current debts and other financial obligations. The current ratio equals current assets divided by current liabilities. Although factors specific to the condition of an individual company should be considered, many analysts believe that the current ratio should be two or higher. A company with twice as much in current assets as current liabilities should have no difficulty making payments as they are due. A company with a current ratio of one is likely to have recurring problems of coming up with cash in time to pay bills. A current ratio of less than one is a clear indication that more funds will have to be located to keep the company operating.

$$\text{Current ratio} = \frac{\text{current assets}}{\text{current liabilities}} = \frac{\$154,000}{\$\ 28,000} = 5.5$$

# B·I·L·L·B·O·A·R·D

## WHO IS GOING TO AUDIT THE COMPUTER?

**H**ave you ever been settled in your assigned seat on an airline, only to have another passenger say that you're sitting in her seat? You both pull out your computer-generated seat confirmation number and, to your surprise, they are identical. The excuse quickly proffered by the steward is, "The computer made an error." Some people think that this excuse is like blaming a broken window on a "hammer error." Computer errors are not usually the fault of the computer's innards. More likely they are the result of a lack of controls in the first place. In the airplane example, the computer was not programmed to check for duplicate seat assignments.

This example raises a more basic question. How can we be sure that someone is maintaining proper surveillance over the design of computer programs and the entry of data into them? Have programs been changed, or can they be changed, without authorization? What controls are in place to make sure that no one tampers with the master files? Even more important,

> *"How can consumers know that the computer is actually functioning as it is supposed to?"*

how can consumers know that the computer is actually functioning as it is supposed to or as a service company's representatives say it is? When you get a notice of failure to pay a past due account, for example, and you've already paid it, who is at fault? Who is making sure that the computer isn't the culprit? Shouldn't the accounting system be made to defend itself?

### QUERIES

**1.** How often have you felt victimized by an accounting error attributed to a malfunctioning computer? What sort of redress should you have to be certain that the fault isn't yours?
**2.** To what extent should computer-generated notices be verified by a third party?
**3.** How satisfied are you with verbal explanations and excuses rather than replies in writing—from a person rather than a computer? ∎

SOURCE: Alfred M. King, "Computers and Accounting: Who'll Audit the Computer System?" *Management Accounting*, June 1985, p. 16.

# PROFILE

IRMA WYMAN didn't come into computers the easy way. She began with an old-fashioned hand calculator into which she cranked 11-digit numbers all day long. But she soon became a leading figure in the development of the new-fangled "machines" that were to become so commonplace as "computers." When the computer revolution took off, says Wyman, it was "like trying to hang onto the end of a Roman candle as it went up."

Today, Irma Wyman is vice president of Corporate Information Management for Honeywell Inc., a major manufacturer of controls and factory automation systems. In her position, Wyman supervises a staff of 450 people that coordinates all of the company's in-house information services throughout its worldwide offices.

As for useful application of computers, Wyman foresees room for vast improvement. "There are still thousands of things that we know how to do technically," she says, "but we can't figure out how to make sense of, either from the business point of view or the personal point of view." She observes that "there are few user-friendly capabilities. Almost all computers require the person to compensate for the technical capability." Nevertheless, Wyman expects to see everyone who needs a computer eventually having one on his or her desk. "Anyone who thinks that typing more than three lines is demeaning," she says, "will have to change her—or his—mind."

**IRMA WYMAN**

SOURCE: Karen Cook, "Technology at the Top," *Working Woman*, May 1986, p. 36.

■ The **quick ratio,** or **acid-test ratio,** is a more sensitive indicator of the ability to meet current obligations. It includes as current assets only those assets that can very quickly be used to pay bills: cash, marketable securities, and accounts receivable. These are called quick assets. Other current assets, like inventory or prepaid expenses, may sometimes be difficult or impossible to convert to cash and are eliminated from this ratio.

The acid-test ratio equals quick assets divided by current liabilities. An acid-test ratio of one is usually considered a comfortable minimum.

$$\frac{\text{Quick}}{\text{ratio}} = \frac{\text{current assets} - \text{inventory}}{\text{current liabilities}} = \frac{\$154,000 - \$40,000}{\$28,000} = 4.1$$

■ **Inventory turnover** measures the number of times the average inventory of merchandise is sold, or turned over, during a year. It is computed by dividing the cost of goods sold by the average inventory. The average inventory is usually approximated by adding the inventory level at the beginning of the year with the level at the end of the year and dividing by 2. A similar figure can be compared by using net sales and retail value of inventories, which is illustrated below. The meaning of inventory turnover can only be determined by comparing similar companies with one another, because it varies considerably. In general, however, a higher inventory turnover will indicate higher sales and a greater potential for creating profit.

$$\text{Inventory turnover} = \frac{\text{net sales}}{\text{inventories}} = \frac{\$300,000}{\$\ 40,000} = 7.5 \text{ times}$$

■ Receivables turnover and collection period are also of value since they show how diligent a company is in collecting its bills. **Receivables turnover** is found by dividing net sales by accounts receivable.

$$\text{Receivables turnover} = \frac{\text{net sales}}{\text{accounts receivable}} = \frac{\$300,000}{\$\ 44,000} = 6.8 \text{ times}$$

**Collection period** simply converts the number of times that receivables are turned over into a figure that shows, on average, how long it took the company to collect its bills—the average number of days a bill is left unpaid.

$$\text{Collection period} = \frac{365 \text{ days}}{\text{receivables turnover}} = \frac{365 \text{ days}}{6.8} = 53.7 \text{ days}$$

Both the receivables turnover and collection period figures must be compared with industry norms to judge whether they are favorable or not.

## PROFITABILITY INDICATORS
*Measure how good the firm is at making money*————

A number of other measures and ratios indicate how profitable a business is, how well it is using its funds, and what kinds of funds are contributing to profits:

■ **Return on sales,** one of the most common ratios, is also called "ratio of net income to sales," or the "net profit margin." It is calculated by dividing net income (or "net earnings") by net sales. When used as a means of comparing different companies, it is a clear indication of a company's ability to derive profits from sales. For most businesses, this figure is surprisingly low. For supermarkets, for example, this ratio is likely to be less than 3 percent.

$$\text{Return of sales} = \frac{\text{net income}}{\text{net sales}} = \frac{\$\ 30,000}{\$300,000} = 10.0 \text{ percent}$$

■ **Return on investment** is a measure of how much income was produced from the capital invested in the business by owners. To many analysts, this is the true test of a business's success, since the whole purpose of investing capital in a business is to earn profits. Return on investment can be determined a number of ways. The most commonly used formulas are shown here.

$$\text{Return on assets} = \frac{\text{net income}}{\text{total assets}} = \frac{\$\ 30,000}{\$218,000} = 13.8 \text{ percent}$$

$$\text{Return on equity} = \frac{\text{net income}}{\text{stockholders' equity}} = \frac{\$\ 30,000}{\$186,000} = 16.1 \text{ percent}$$

■ **Capitalization ratios** show the proportions of funds used by a business that come from certain sources. They indicate the extent to which a company is relying on borrowed funds or permanent owners' investment to carry on operations. The debt-to-equity ratio is calculated by dividing total liabilities by stockholders' equity. This ratio will be less than one for a company with more equity than debt financing, more than one when debt financing exceeds equity, and equal to one when the two sources of funds are equal. A similar measure, known as debt-to-assets ratio, is derived by dividing total liabilities by total assets. This index shows the proportion of the assets that were obtained by borrowing.

$$\text{Debt-to-equity ratio} = \frac{\text{total liabilities}}{\text{stockholders' equity}} = \frac{\$\ 32,000}{\$186,000} = 17.2 \text{ percent}$$

A similar measure is derived by dividing stockholders' equity by total assets.

$$\text{Debt-to-assets ratio} = \frac{\text{total liabilities}}{\text{total assets}} = \frac{\$32,000}{\$218,000} = 14.7 \text{ percent}$$

## TRENDS AND COMPARISONS
*Tell more than the ratios themselves* ━━━━━━━━

Once the ratios have been calculated, they make more sense when they can be used to track a trend or to make comparisons with some sort of standard.

**TREND ANALYSIS** It may be nice for a business to know that its return on sales is 7 percent. That doesn't really tell whether 7 percent is good or bad. One of the first ways to judge how good this ratio is, is to compare it with past values of that ratio. If it was 4 percent 3 years ago, 5 percent 2 years ago, and 6 percent last year, then 7 percent this year indicates that the company is steadily improving its profitability. And that's good. In **annual reports** that companies make to their owners and stockholders and to the federal government, they provide not only the three basic financial statements for the year but also data for past years so that trends can be seen. Figure 13-6 shows how some trends in financial measures and ratios are shown in an annual report for one company.

**COMPARISONS** A second very important way to judge the meaning of a financial ratio, or how good or bad it is, is to compare it with the average for that ratio of other similar-sized companies in the same business or industry. As indicated earlier, a number of private companies, trade associations, and government agencies publish such average ratios. A sample taken from a Dun & Bradstreet report is shown in Figure 13-7.

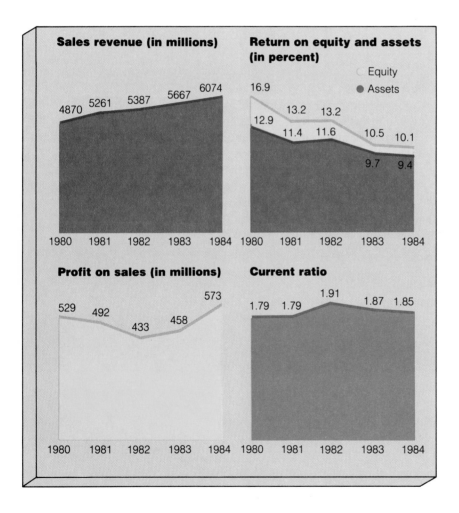

Figure 13-6 Trends in financial measures and ratios as shown in an annual report.

# Key Concepts

1. Accounting is a numerical information system designed to record, classify, summarize, and interpret business transactions. Accounting provides information (1) for internal use (managerial accounting) in planning, budgeting, cost estimating, and controlling activities and (2) for external use (financial accounting) in paying taxes and reporting business results to interested outside parties.

2. The accounting equation (assets equal liabilities plus owner's equity) is the basis for all accounting procedures. Accountants set up double-entry record-keeping systems in which every transaction is entered twice so that records can easily be checked for accuracy and completeness. The records are organized into debits and credits to conform to the accounting equation.

3. Accounting practices are standardized by rulings of federal agencies and professional associations so that reporting by different businesses will be comparable. Certified public accountants provide accounting and auditing services to ensure conformance to these practices and standards. Accounting practices encourage the adjustment of reported inventory figures (with LIFO and FIFO methods) and the adjustment of asset figures (using "current dollars" methods) to reflect the impact of inflation.

4. A balance sheet is a statement of financial condition on a particular date. It shows the amount and type of the firm's assets, amounts and types of liabilities, and owner's equity.

5. An income statement is a summary of revenues and expenses over a period of operation. It shows profit or loss for the period.

6. A statement of changes in financial position shows the amounts and sources of funds acquired during an operating period and how the funds were used.

7. Accountants use comparisons between different categories of assets, revenues, expenses, liabilities, and equity to help interpret financial statements. The comparisons are often expressed as ratios, which are useful to compare similar companies and trends within the same company.

# Review Questions

1. Define, explain, or identify each of the following key terms or phrases, found on the pages indicated.

accounting (p. 291)
accounting equation (p. 293)
accounting period (p. 296)
annual report (p. 308)
audit (p. 297)
balance sheet (p. 298)
capitalization ratios (p. 307)
certified public accountant (CPA) (p. 296)
collection period (p. 306)
cost of sales (p. 301)
credits (p. 295)
current ratio (p. 303)
debits (p. 295)
depreciation (p. 301)
double-entry method (p. 294)

equity (p. 293)
expenses (p. 294)
FIFO (p. 297)
financial accounting (p. 293)
Financial Accounting Standards Board (FASB) (p. 297)
fiscal year (p. 296)
generally accepted accounting principles (GAAP) (p. 297)
goodwill (p. 300)
income statement (p. 300)
inventory turnover (p. 306)
liability (p. 293)
LIFO (p. 297)
liquidity (p. 303)
managerial accounting (p. 293)
quick ratio (acid-test ratio) (p. 306)
ratio analysis (p. 303)

*receivables turnover (p. 306)*
*record keeping (p. 291)*
*return on investment (p. 307)*
*return on sales (p. 306)*
*revenues (p. 294)*
*statement of changes in financial position*
*(p. 302)*
*true accounting (p. 291)*

2. Describe the four basic activities that must be performed by an accounting system.

3. What is the difference between record keeping and true accounting?

4. How does managerial accounting differ from financial accounting?

5. What is the accounting equation? Why must both sides of the equation be equal?

6. Why is double-entry record keeping in ac-

counting so widely used?

7. In what important ways does a balance sheet differ from an income statement? Which one shows profit for the year?

8. Into what two main parts is a balance sheet divided? What entry causes the figure for the value of a building, for example, to differ from the original price paid for it?

9. What must be deducted from revenues on the income statement to find the earnings before income taxes? What four classes of expenses appear on the income statement?

10. Why are both business operators and the creditors of a business so interested in the current ratio of a firm? How does the quick ratio differ from the current ratio? What is significant about this difference?

# Case Critique 13-1
## Mike's Bike Shop

Mike Malone operates a bicycle sales and repair shop just off the college campus. The business has grown impressively. So have the profits, up to a point. They have been steady for the past 3 years. Mike has heard that you know something about accounting practices and financial statements, so he asks you to give him some help. Will you look at the figures he has extracted from his income statements and his balance sheets (see below)? Mike has income

| MIKE'S BIKE SHOP | | | |
|---|---|---|---|
| **Income Statement Figures** | **1985** | **1986** | **1987** |
| Net sales revenues | 500,000 | 600,000 | 750,000 |
| Cost of sales | 300,000 | 350,000 | 450,000 |
| General & administrative expenses | 115,000 | 165,000 | 215,000 |
| Interest expense | 10,000 | 10,000 | 10,000 |
| Income taxes | 25,000 | 25,000 | 25,000 |
| Net earnings | — | — | — |
| **Balance Sheet Figures** | | | |
| Current assets | | | |
|   Cash | 100,000 | | |
|   Accounts receivable | 40,000 | | |
|   Inventory of bikes and parts | 50,000 | | |
|   Prepaid insurance | 10,000 | | |
| Total of current and fixed assets | 550,000 | | |
| Current liabilities | 100,000 | | |
| Long-term liabilities | 150,000 | | |
| Owner's equity and retained earnings | 250,000 | | |

data for the last 3 years and his balance sheet for the first of these years. Here's what he wants you to do:

1. Calculate the net earnings for each of the 3 years.
2. Use figures from the appropriate financial statements, calculate the following ratios for 1985.

    a. Current ratio           \_\_\_\_\_
    b. Quick ratio            \_\_\_\_\_
    c. Inventory turnover     \_\_\_\_\_
    d. Accounts receivables turnover   \_\_\_\_\_
    e. Collection period       \_\_\_\_\_

    f. Return on sales (profit on sales percent)     \_\_\_\_\_
    g. Debt to equity     \_\_\_\_\_

3. Mike has been told that in his business, the average figure for a current ratio is 2.1 and for a quick ratio 1.2. For 1985, are Mike's ratios better or worse than the average for his industry?
4. Calculate the return on sales percent (7) for 1986 and 1987. What is the trend (upward or downward) for this ratio since 1985? What is the trend for net sales revenues during the same period? How can you explain the difference in trends? What should Mike do to have the trend in return on sales match the trend in sales revenues?

---

# Case Critique 13-2
## It's OK Only If the Financial Shoe Fits

The chances are pretty good that at one time or another you have bought a pair of shoes from Melville Corporation. It operates 1,261 Thom McAn outlet stores. Melville isn't too happy about its shoe business, since it doesn't really make money very fast. Melville is more enthusiastic about its Marshall men's clothing stores, its Mack Drugs chain, and its Kay-Bee's toys and hobbies shops. When Melville gets unhappy with the results of one of its businesses, it closes it down or sells it. In recent years, the company got rid of Clothes Bin, a network of off-price women's apparel shops, and Metro, a men's pants manufacturer. What kinds of results does it take for a particular business to make Melville happy? It's simple, says the company's president: "Just give us a 20 percent return on equity and a 5 percent return on sales." On average, the company does far better than that.

1. Which kind of financial indicator, in general, and financial ratios, in particular, appear to be most important to Melville Corporation?
2. Why might Melville wish to get rid of businesses that do not come up to the ratio levels the company prescribes?
3. According to the information in the case, would Melville be likely to acquire a business that made a profit of $100,000 on an equity investment of $1,000,000 and sales of $2,000,000? Why?
4. If Melville were only concerned with the two ratios mentioned in the case, overlooking what other key indicators might lead to financial trouble? Why?

*SOURCE:* Howard Rudnitsky, "Fancy Footwork," *Forbes,* March 29, 1982, p. 74.

# Business Forecasts and Budgets

## Learning Objectives

*The purpose of this chapter is to explain the uses of business forecasts and describe some of the techniques for making them, describe and illustrate various kinds of budgets, and explain a flexible budget and show how it is used for managerial control.*

*As evidence of general comprehension, after studying Chapter 14, you should be able to:*

1. *Distinguish between background forecasts and business forecasts and identify the sources of data for each.*

2. *Identify the three basic forecasting techniques.*

3. *Define a budget and explain its purpose.*

4. *Explain the purposes and uses of the sales, expense, cash, and capital expenditure budgets.*

5. *Distinguish between a fixed budget and a flexible budget and explain how the latter may be used for managerial control purposes.*

6. *Describe a typical variance report and justify its importance as an instrument for budgetary control.*

*If your class is using SSweetco: Business Model and Activity File, see Chapter 14 in that book after you complete this chapter. There you will find exercises and activities to help you apply your learning to typical business situations.*

## 1 BUSINESS FORECASTS

are projections of future business conditions.

Background forecasts

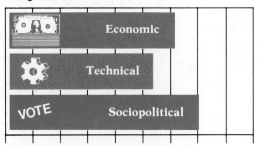

Economic

Technical

VOTE Sociopolitical

Business forecasts

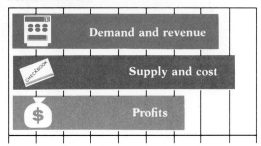

Demand and revenue

Supply and cost

Profits

## 2 FORECASTING TECHNIQUES

include

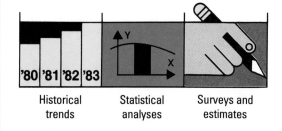

| '80 '81 '82 '83 | Y / X | Surveys and |
| Historical trends | Statistical analyses | Surveys and estimates |

## 3 BUDGETS SERVE AS GUIDES FOR PLANNING AND CONTROL

They are specific financial plans that anticipate overall company income and outlay and establish controls for departmental expenditures.

IN
DEPT. A

IN
DEPT. B

IN
DEPT. C

## 4 THE MAJOR KINDS OF BUDGETS

are

Sales

Cash

Expense

Capital expenditures

BUDGET

## 5 BUDGETS MAY BE EITHER FIXED OR FLEXIBLE

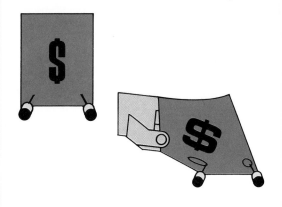

## 6 THE VARIANCE REPORT

is the principal form of budgetary control.

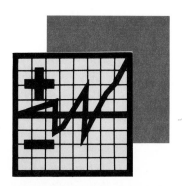

# BATTLE OF THE BUDGET

*About the time each fall that sports fans think of baseball's World Series and the start of the football season, there is another, perhaps more important, contest about to begin. It is played in very well run businesses. It is called the battle of the budget. The players are the top executives of the company, including its key department heads. The goal for the company is to come up with a sales target for the next year that will secure or advance its position in its field.*

*The goal for each executive is to get as much money for his or her department as is needed to get the job done, while still contributing to the overall company goal. The challenge is that there is never enough money to allow each department to do everything it might want to do.*

*Let's take a look at how the budgeting game is played in the executive suite of the Yankee Hinge & Hardware Co. in Vermont. It manufactures a complete line of hinges, door locks, drawer pulls, and fixtures used by home builders. The same parts are also sold in retail hardware stores throughout the country. Yankee's president, Rose Boots, has called her staff together to start the budgeting process for next year. Boots turns first to the company's controller and planning director, Jill Jenks. "What's the economic outlook like for next year?" "It looks good," says Jenks. "Most cheerful of all is the number of housing starts predicted. They should be up 15 percent over last year. Our business is closely tied to them, and if they pick up, our business is sure to pick up soon after. The general economy appears favorable too. Disposable income has been rising 3 to 5 percent and should continue that way." Bill Martin, the marketing director, chimes in, "The latest estimates from our trade group, the National Builders' Hardware Association, are not quite that optimistic, but they do predict an upturn. And not only that, at a meeting of the National Retail Hardware Association last month in Chicago, most of the dealers I spoke to were promising to increase their orders for next year."*

*"That's all very good," said Boots, "but what terms should we be thinking of for our business next year?" Jenks paused to riffle through a sheaf of computer printouts, and then said, "The trend in our business has been showing a slight rise each year for the past 5 years. It isn't as steep as those in the rest of our industry, but I think we can plan for a target growth in sales of at least 10 percent next year."*

*"Let's settle on 10 percent increase for the time being," said the president. "We can use that as a basis for budgeting. We will do $10 million in sales this year; let's shoot for $11 million next year."*

*The meeting was about to break up, but Mark Mapes, the production manager, asked, "What will that mean to our production schedules? If you expect us to produce 10 percent more, you'll have to increase my budget to take care of that. I'll need more money for labor costs and materials and new equipment." Bill Martin interrupted, "Don't give all the increased money available to production. If we're going to deliver more sales to the company, our sales commissions are going to go up, too, and travel expenses. So be sure to take care of those in our budget."*

*"Wait a minute," said the president. "Increased sales ought to mean increased profits. A 10 percent increase in sales won't be very good if it's all swallowed up by increased expense budgets."*

*"That won't happen," said Jenks, "not while I'm around. We will make 8 percent net profit on sales this year, and we're going to try to do better next year. I'll give production and marketing their fair shares of the additional revenues, but we'll have to reserve enough to ensure our profits." On that note, the president concluded the meeting. "Let's hope the forecasts turn out to be true. We'll go ahead for now on that basis. But if things turn sour, I want us to be able to tighten our budgets before expenses get out of hand."*

## 1  BUSINESS FORECASTS
### *Numerical expressions of business plans*

Most decisions are made with the future in mind. The decision to buy new production machinery may have been made to avoid the anticipated failure of present equipment or to increase production to meet expected demand. Some of the information needed for this kind of decision comes from forecasts.

A *forecast* is a projection of future business conditions both within a particular company and in the social, political, and economic environment in which the company operates. Forecasts contribute to setting organization objectives. A description of what a company is trying to achieve can have no reliability without some idea of what the future holds. For instance, a goal of increasing sales by 15 percent a year for 5 years is useless to management unless there is some reason to believe that customer demand will be adequate. Forecasts are also of help in making plans to meet objectives. Having estimates of future costs, for instance, will help managers decide whether to plan for certain activities.

Good forecasts result from well-planned and well-operated management information systems (MIS) and accounting information systems. The entire collection of organized facts and summaries in these systems may be useful for forecasting future events and conditions. Many forecasts, especially projected sales and costs, will be routinely produced by an accounting system. In other cases, the MIS and accounting information will provide a basis for special studies used in forecasting. Projecting the effects on the profitability of a proposed change in production methods is an example of an analysis of this type.

In general, forecasts may fall into two classes. Some provide a preview of the conditions in the environment outside the company. These are called **background forecasts.** Others forecast the future operations of the company itself. These are called **business forecasts.**

# BACKGROUND FORECASTS
## Readings of the environment

Plans are the specific guides managers use to control operations. All plans are based on assumptions or beliefs about what the future may hold. If, for example, a company plans to expand its production facilities within the next 3 years, many factors external to the company will affect the success of that plan. Will the financial markets be in a position to lend money at an affordable rate? Will adequate raw materials be available to support the new production? What will the price of the raw materials be? Will workers be available in sufficient numbers? Will consumers have enough money to buy the goods? Will the government impose any regulations that would make the production more difficult or less profitable?

Obviously, none of these questions can be answered with certainty. Risk is involved in any business decision. The purpose of background forecasting, however, is to gather as much information as possible about projected conditions in the company's environment to reduce uncertainty. The sources of data used in background forecasting are generally the ones used in management information systems: government statistical publications, private abstracts and periodicals, trade associations, government censuses, annual reports, and so forth.

Background forecasts usually try to predict changes in economic and financial conditions, in technological resources, and in the social and political environment.

Economic conditions affect nearly every aspect of a business. Managers and analysts use measures of economic activity called **economic indicators** to try to judge the direction in which the economy is moving. Many indicators may be used: employment statistics, measures of worker productivity, consumer spending, capital investments by businesses, the money supply, interest rates, prices on major stock exchanges, the inflation rate, measures of imports and exports, the gross national product, and many others. As well as giving the general outlook for the economy, many of these measures directly affect the operations of an individual business. Figure 14-1 shows graphs of several commonly used economic indicators.

Forecasts of expected technological changes can have an important effect on the success or failure of a business. Managers must always consider technology for possible application in the company. An equally important consideration is the anticipation of technological changes employed by competitors. Technology makes new products possible. A clearly superior or more desirable product can make an existing product obsolete in months. Technological changes can also increase profitability or allow companies to reduce prices and improve their competitive position. Manufacturing methods, storage and transportation systems, and the use of new materials can all help to reduce production costs.

Social and political changes are often the most difficult to forecast. Changing tastes and expectations among consumers can create important changes in the demand for specific products. Even the public's attitudes toward manufacturers can affect success. Government regulations can increase costs by requiring expenditures to improve product safety or to reduce pollution. Some products or business activities may be restricted or prohibited. The best defense against such environmental changes is to be well informed and to attempt to devise plans that are flexible enough to be adapted to changing conditions.

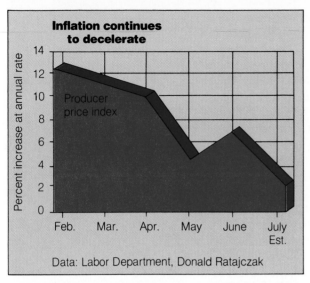

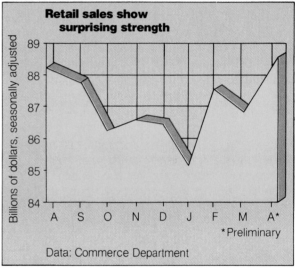

Figure 14-1 Economic indicators.
*Source:* Adopted from "Economic Diary," edited by Gene Koertz, *Business Week,* with permission of the copyright holder, McGraw-Hill Publications Company, 1981–1982.

# BUSINESS FORECASTS

## *Specific expectations*

Much of the information used in managing and planning business operations results from activities within the company itself. Although it is somewhat easier to forecast these internal developments than it is to predict changes in the business environment, uncertainty still remains. The three most common classifications of forecasts used by individual businesses are demand and revenue, supply and costs, and profits.

■ ***Demand and revenue forecasts*** of customer demand for products and of sales are used primarily to predict the amount of revenue a company will have to work with in the future. Although sales forecasts are one kind of internal prediction, they depend heavily on background forecasts for their accuracy. General economic conditions, consumer spending, interest rates, and inflation have a strong effect on sales in almost any industry.

Sales forecasts are useful for more than predicting revenues. Many expenses—including direct selling, advertising, and promotion costs—will depend to a great extent on anticipated sales. Expected sales also control plans for production quantities and help to determine a company's break-even point as discussed in Chapter 10.

■ *Supply and cost forecasts* aim first at getting an accurate idea of what it will cost to operate the company at some future time. This estimate is obviously useful in financial and general management. Forecasts of this kind are also useful for highly detailed planning and management. Projections of the labor supply and of the cost of hiring workers may result in efforts to help workers to be more productive or in more efficient production methods. Forecasts of the availability and costs of starting materials may force managers to use alternative materials or to make other adjustments to reduce waste. Similarly, a retailer's plans will be affected by forecasts of price changes of merchandise.

■ *Profit forecasts* are arrived at through the other projections of revenues and costs. Profit estimates are important because they provide a standard with which to evaluate income and costs. Profit forecasts show whether the company will be able to realize its goals and expectations.

In projecting profits, managers want to be able to use some of the same analyses that are applied to income statements for past operating periods. They want to know the projected profits in dollars, sometimes adjusted to offset the effects of inflation. They also use the ratios of profits to sales and profits to investment. Other standard ratios, such as the various capitalization ratios, can be used on projected financial information to estimate the financial condition of the company at some future time. Since growth is one of the most common objectives of businesses, these kinds of projections can be especially important. By assessing the prospects for future resources and obligations, managers are better able to stimulate growth in a controlled setting.

# 2  FORECASTING TECHNIQUES
*More than a crystal ball is needed*

Many forecasting techniques in common use today are highly sophisticated and require specialized technical knowledge. The main overall approaches, however, are usually the same, even for complex mathematical analyses. The most common forecasting methods include projecting trends from historical data, analyzing relationships, and using surveys and other specific data-gathering techniques.

## HISTORICAL TRENDS
*The past predicts the future* ━━━━━━━━━━━━━━━━━━━━━

*Historical trend forecasts* reveal the consistent patterns that have occurred in the past and assume that these will continue in the future. Figure 14-2 shows a historical trend forecast plotted on a graph. If, for example, a company's sales have increased by about $1 million a year for each of the last 5 years, a forecast would project that sales of a particular

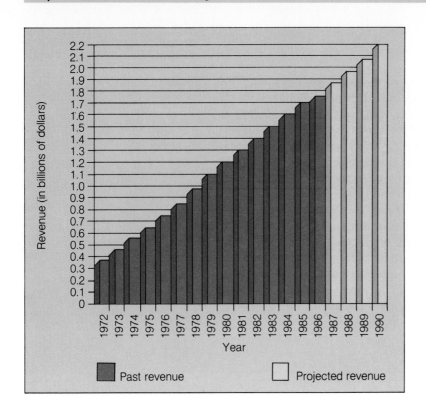

Figure 14-2 Example of a historical trend. Red bars show past revenue. Yellow bars project revenue will continue.

product will continue to increase by $1 million a year. A similar analysis of trends could be based on the historical relationship between two or more variables. A large home-building company might find that in the past, sales have increased by 5 percent every time mortgage interest rates have decreased by 0.05 percent. This relationship might be assumed to continue in the future.

Sometimes, forecasts based on the continuation of past trends can be dangerously inaccurate. They usually do not take fully into account what *causes* the changes. As general economic and social changes occur, the relationships may become unreliable for predicting the future without the forecasters' realizing it.

## STATISTICAL ANALYSIS OF RELATIONSHIPS
*Cause relates to effect*

Forecasts may be based on assumptions or theories about what really causes changes in the economy, business, costs, sales, or profits. ***Statistical relationship forecasts*** bring together many different kinds of data on factors believed to affect sales volume, for example. Analysts may decide that the advertising budget, the number of sales calls made, the money supply in the economy, the consumer credit interest rates, the sales volume of competitors, and many other factors actually control a company's sales volume. They will assign numerical values to each factor identified and describe mathematically the effect those factors taken together have on sales. The method allows sales projections to be successfully updated as the predictive factors change.

## SURVEYS AND ESTIMATES

*Put an ear to the ground*

A number of specific data-gathering methods are used to make forecasts of future conditions. One method uses the opinions and estimates of people within the organization. This is especially common in cost and sales volume forecasting. **Survey and estimate forecasts** may use the opinions of a group of informed executives. Sales predictions, in particular, may be based on estimates made by the people who actually do the selling. This grass-roots approach has often been successful. Salespeople maintain constant contact with customers and get to know their likes and dislikes, their plans, and their current moods and expectations.

More formal methods are used to determine the buying behavior of consumers. Direct surveys may be made of customer buying plans and expectations for the future. When new products are introduced, test marketings are commonly used to estimate future demand. A trial introduction of the product is made in a limited geographic area. The results are then applied to the entire final sales area to get a rough idea of the sales volume when the product is fully introduced.

## 3  BUDGETS

*Financial guides for planning and control*

A **budget** is a specific type of plan in which data is presented in numerical form, often in dollars, for a specified period of time, usually a year or less. Budgets are derived from goals and forecasts, as illustrated in Figure 14-3. For most businesses, the sales budget (stated in dollars and numbers of units to be produced and sold) becomes the fountainhead for all other budgets. Typically, the budgeted revenues are apportioned into two major classes of expense budgets. One class covers expenses that vary with the amount of sales or production volume. The other class covers expenses that are relatively constant, or fixed overhead, with re-

Figure 14-3 How budgets are derived from forecasts.

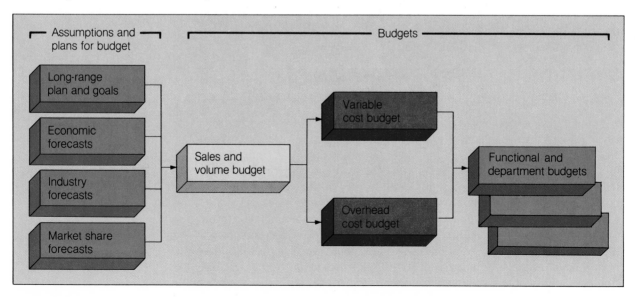

spect to sales or volume. Out of these two classes of expenses, dozens or more budgets are prepared for various functions, departments, and activities of a business.

Budgets allow managers to be specific in anticipating revenues and uses of funds. This is indispensable for good financial planning. When managers do not look ahead and determine in detail how much money will be needed and where it will come from, they must continually react to unexpected needs that will arise. Budgets also help in evaluating the usefulness of various activities carried on within the organization.

Budgets also set limits on how much will be spent on each business activity and provide a means of controlling those expenditures. A shipping department, for instance, may be given a maximum amount of money to use for wages, materials, repairs, freight and postage, and other controllable costs of operation. If the costs are exceeded, managers have a basis for evaluating the sources and causes of the excess and for making future improvements if needed.

Actual dollar values or other units are used in stating expected costs, income, production quantities, and other forecasts. Stating these objectives precisely makes them easier to achieve.

Finally, budgets provide a convenient time frame within which operations can be controlled and evaluated. Budgets are usually annual, often with quarterly or monthly reviews. They provide short-range goals within consistent time periods that are useful for comparative analysis.

# 4 TYPES OF BUDGETS
## One for every purpose

In practice, a company usually has a group of budgets that are designed to work together. If properly planned and coordinated, the different budgets will function collectively to meet the company's goal of guiding and controlling operations and expenditures. Most companies have sales, expense, cash, and capital expenditure budgets.

## SALES BUDGETS
### Fountainhead for expenses

The sales or revenue budget is usually the first one to be prepared. The amount of revenue expected to be received sets the upper limit for the total of the expense budgets. If income from all sources is expected to be $1 million, a company cannot plan to spend $2 million without running into debt or into trouble. *Sales budgets* are forecasts of income anticipated from sales in an upcoming budget period. They are prepared by one or more of the methods mentioned in the "Business Forecasts" section in this chapter. Often, the opinions of executives and of the sales force will be used to modify a projection made by a statistical technique. A *revenue budget* usually shows total income from all sources that will be available during the budget period. It starts with sales revenue and adds income from interest on savings accounts, dividends, or from other sources not related to sales.

# EXPENSE BUDGETS
*Limits on spending*

Managers usually prepare an overall ***expense budget*** showing the total amounts that are planned to be spent for specified purposes during a budget period. This general expense budget may show, for instance, total amounts for direct production expenses, administrative costs, distribution costs, and other general categories. There are several ways of breaking down overall costs into more detailed operating budgets.

Production expenses usually show specific dollar amounts for materials, wages, equipment maintenance, and other costs directly related to creating products for sale. Depending on how the budget is to be used, overhead costs may or may not be allocated to operating activities at this point. Administrative cost budgets include management salaries, part or all of the general overhead costs, and other expenses such as employee training, legal fees, and accounting charges. Distribution expenses include costs such as advertising, maintaining a sales force, shipping, storing, and promoting products. Expenses shown in this manner give one a good idea of the detailed purposes for which money will be spent in the budget period. Such expense budgets, however, are often not arranged in a way to give good operations control.

For administrative control of day-to-day operations, additional, more detailed budgets are often required. There may be any number of separate departments that will have some production expenses and will use different amounts and types of materials, labor, supplies, and equipment. The same is true of administrative and distribution expenses. For effective control, each of these operating departments usually has its own budget with specific cost categories related to the work it does.

# CASH BUDGET
*Watches the bank balance*

It is not only essential that a business have more money coming in each year than going out but also important that the flow of cash coming in be timed so that it is available to make purchases and pay bills as they come due. Many businesses use a cash budget to ensure that this will happen. A ***cash budget*** shows the expected receipts of incoming cash from every source, including bank loans, and the expected payments to be made each month for a given period of time, typically a year. (See Figure 14-4.) It shows when there will be an excess of cash, which might be moved from a checking account to a savings certificate or a money market fund for greater interest earnings. It also shows when there will be a deficiency of cash (a negative cash flow), which will usually require borrowing to pay bills. Even the largest and wealthiest of companies, like IBM and DuPont, must constantly juggle their cash flow and use a cash budget to guide them in doing so.

# CAPITAL EXPENDITURE BUDGET
*Provides for equipment purchases*

The buildings, machinery, offices, and other fixed assets are an indispensable resource. But these assets are not truly fixed. They wear out

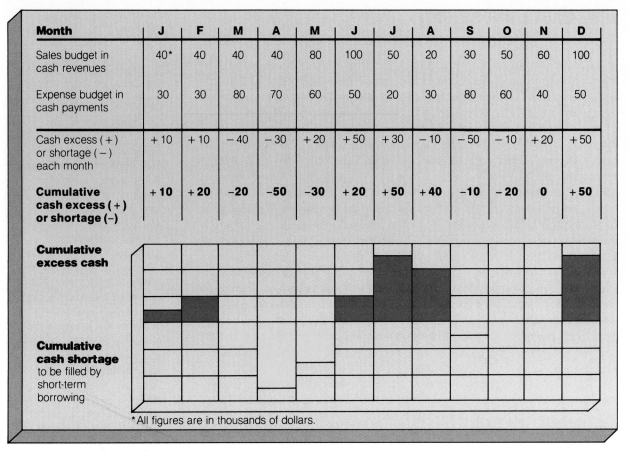

| Month | J | F | M | A | M | J | J | A | S | O | N | D |
|---|---|---|---|---|---|---|---|---|---|---|---|---|
| Sales budget in cash revenues | 40* | 40 | 40 | 40 | 80 | 100 | 50 | 20 | 30 | 50 | 60 | 100 |
| Expense budget in cash payments | 30 | 30 | 80 | 70 | 60 | 50 | 20 | 30 | 80 | 60 | 40 | 50 |
| Cash excess (+) or shortage (−) each month | + 10 | + 10 | − 40 | − 30 | + 20 | + 50 | + 30 | − 10 | − 50 | − 10 | + 20 | + 50 |
| **Cumulative cash excess (+) or shortage (–)** | **+ 10** | **+ 20** | **−20** | **−50** | **−30** | **+ 20** | **+ 50** | **+ 40** | **−10** | **− 20** | **0** | **+ 50** |

**Cumulative excess cash**

**Cumulative cash shortage** to be filled by short-term borrowing

*All figures are in thousands of dollars.

and must be replaced. They must be expanded as a company grows. Spending money on these fixed, or long-term, assets is a capital expenditure. Companies must carefully control capital expenditures. Companies must make sure they always have adequate facilities without dangerously straining their financial resources. **Capital expenditure budgets** help to accomplish this.

These budgets are based on analyses of future needs for the replacement or expansion of facilities. Since costs for machinery, factories, and office buildings are very high, it is especially important to plan for them in advance. A capital expenditure budget shows what kind of capital expenditures will be made, when they will be made, and where the funds will come from. Decisions to make capital expenditures are often based upon whether or not the earnings from a proposed investment will meet a company's criteria for a capitalization ratio. For example, if a plastics factory wanted to purchase an extruding machine for $10,000 and the machine was calculated to save money at the rate of $1,000, or 10 percent, a year, it would not be placed on the capital expenditures budget if the company's requirement was that it wanted a 15 percent return on assets.

The time value of money (as will be discussed in Chapter 18) also plays an important role in deciding on the capital budget. Since capital expenditures are long-term investments, they involve long-term assets and often long-term liabilities as well. Accordingly, when interest rates are high and forecast to remain that way, a projected return on assets must also be high to allow for higher interest payments.

Figure 14-4 Example of a cash budget showing cumulative monthly excess or shortage.

## ZERO-BASED BUDGETING

*Starts each year from scratch*

Another approach to budgeting challenges the traditional approach, which is often based upon historical trends. The traditional budget assumes that if a function or activity had a budget last year, it should be given budget moneys this year. The main decision is usually how much money. ***Zero-based budgeting*** requires, instead, that every year each manager justify his or her entire budget from scratch. Each budget request is then treated as a separate "decision package" for higher-level management to examine. This is done by examining each package in terms of its costs and its measurable results in the form of benefits or profit contributions. Each package is assigned a numerical value as a consequence of this costs-versus-profits analysis. All packages are then ranked in order of value for each department or activity, as shown in Figure 14-5. Since zero-based budgeting starts from the bottom and works its way upward, in Figure 14-5 packages A-1 in purchasing, B-1 in stores, and C-1 in maintenance are ranked as most valuable. These are then stacked in the right-hand column, and the budget is built, package by package, until it reaches the cutoff line. This is the point at which the total of all packages reaches the total amount of money approved by the company. The packages above that point lose out and get no budget money.

Zero-based budgeting is widely used in government, but it is also used by many large companies, most notably Texas Instruments Corp., and for the budgeting of industrial research programs.

## 5 FIXED OR FLEXIBLE BUDGETS

*Room for adjustments*

At the beginning of a fiscal year, the manager of a billing department, for instance, may receive a budget showing how much he or she will be

### Action Brief

**BUDGETING BECAUSE EXPENSES ARE TOO HIGH**

***In mid-1985, American Broadcasting Companies (ABC) laid off 350 employees. When queried about the cause of this action, ABC replied that sales revenues were on target for the year, but that expenses were higher than it had budgeted. "We are trying to maintain our profit goals," said ABC's president. The variable costs of producing network programs were rising 5 to 7 percent a year, which was in line with expectations. It was overhead costs that were over budget. The reduction in force was aimed mainly at corporate staff jobs, especially in the personnel areas. "These savings," said the president, "will show up rather quickly in our quarterly financial statements."***

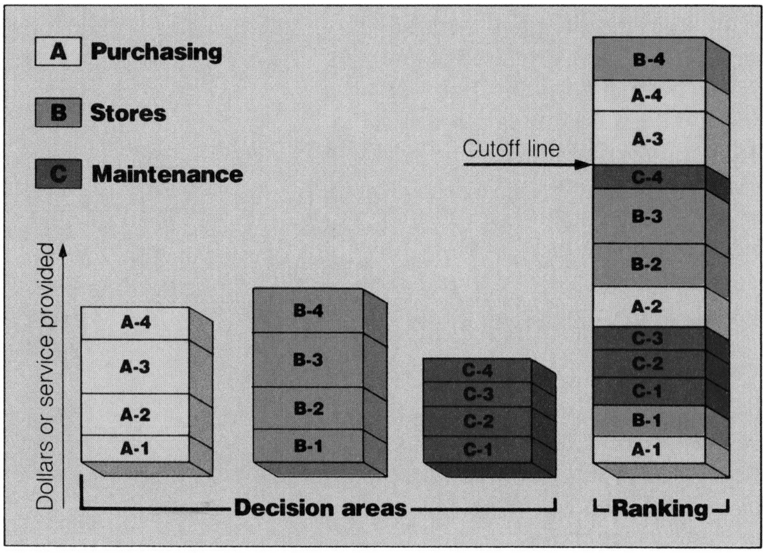


Figure 14-5 How budget packages are ranked in a zero-based budgeting system.

allowed to spend for certain things during the year. There may be amounts allotted for payroll, supplies, equipment rental and maintenance, and part of the company's overhead cost appropriated to the department. The budget shows anticipated maximum amounts, and the manager is expected to spend no more. This is a *fixed budget.*

But what happens if sales unexpectedly double during the year? The existing staff will not be able to handle the volume of billing, certainly not without a lot of overtime. More equipment or office space may be needed. In instances like this, *flexible budgets* provide adequate control even when conditions change. A number of techniques permit this flexibility to be built into the budgeting process.

Several budgets may be prepared for a single department, each based on a different level of output. A production department may have four budgets, one for 3,500 tons produced, one for 4,000, one for 4,500, and one for 5,000. A budget of this type is shown in Table 14-1. The actual

## TABLE 14-1
## EXAMPLE OF A FLEXIBLE BUDGET

| ACCOUNT TITLE | Monthly Allowances Based Upon Four Operating Levels in Terms of Tons Produced | | | |
| --- | --- | --- | --- | --- |
| | 3,500 TONS | 4,000 TONS | 4,500 TONS | 5,000 TONS |
| Direct labor | $ 7,000 | $ 8,000 | $ 9,000 | $10,000 |
| Indirect labor | | | | |
| Material handling | 600 | 600 | 900 | 1,200 |
| Shop clerical | 500 | 500 | 500 | 500 |
| Supervision | 1,200 | 1,200 | 1,200 | 1,200 |
| Overtime premium | 0 | 0 | 450 | 450 |
| Shift premiums (2d and 3d) | 0 | 0 | 0 | 100 |
| Operating supplies | 350 | 400 | 450 | 500 |
| Maintenance and repairs | 1,200 | 1,400 | 2,000 | 2,800 |
| Gas, water, steam, compressed air | 1,500 | 1,800 | 2,100 | 2,400 |
| Electrical power | 700 | 800 | 900 | 1,000 |
| Total controllable costs | $13,050 | $14,700 | $17,500 | $20,150 |
| Insurance | $ 120 | $ 120 | $ 120 | $ 120 |
| Taxes | 80 | 80 | 80 | 80 |
| Depreciation of equipment | 400 | 400 | 400 | 400 |
| Building occupancy | 800 | 850 | 900 | 950 |
| Total allocated costs | $ 1,400 | $ 1,450 | $ 1,500 | $ 1,550 |
| Total allowable costs | $14,450 | $16,150 | $19,000 | $21,700 |

budget to be used is selected according to the amount of output actually required.

A company may also reduce the budgeting period to take into account changing conditions. For example, a new budget may be prepared every month. Then, as sales or production increases or decreases, expense budgets can be adjusted to match. The same kind of adjusting may be done at the end of a budget period. Budgets are recalculated to show what costs should have been for the output levels actually achieved. These methods provide flexible budgets that can respond to changing conditions while still fulfilling their purpose.

# 6  BUDGET VARIANCE REPORT
## An investigative and control tool

The control function of a budget is directly provided by a **budget variance,** or **cost variance, report.** This is a listing, similar to that shown in Figure 14-6, of all proposed expenditures compared with actual costs that were incurred for each item. Its primary purpose is to identify which expenses were higher than planned so that efforts can be made in

```
O  MFG DIVISION      600     600                          PAGE 1
O  PERIOD 13 19--
```

| | Period expense | | | Year-to-date expense | | |
|---|---|---|---|---|---|---|
| | Planned | Actual | -Over* Under | Planned | Actual | -Over* Under |
| DIRECT LABOR | 59,758 | 51,502 | 8,256 | 693,389 | 622,754 | 70,635 |
| 01 INDIRECT LABOR | 42,224 | 30,844 | 11,380 | 497,953 | 468,998 | 28,955 |
| 07 SUPERVISION | 14,622 | 15,804 | -1,182 | 186,842 | 184,942 | 1,900 |
| 09 CLERICAL SALARIES | 11,771 | 9,083 | 2,688 | 141,646 | 134,530 | 7,116 |
| PAYROLL WORK DONE | 128,375 | 107,233 | 21,142 | 1,519,830 | 1,411,224 | 108,606 |
| 06 ALLOWED TIME | 1,136 | 577 | 559 | 13,868 | 15,321 | -1,453 |
| 12 VACATIONS | --- | 3,024 | -3,024 | 78,543 | 77,339 | 1,204 |
| 13 HOLIDAYS | 6,882 | 13,588 | -6,706 | 62,402 | 57,861 | 4,541 |
| 33 TAXABLE SICK ACCDE | 1,494 | 846 | 648 | 18,239 | 17,534 | 705 |
| 34 NONTAXABLE SICK AC | 1,513 | 2,283 | -770 | 18,435 | 34,691 | -16,256 |
| PAYROLL BENEFITS | 11,025 | 20,318 | -9,293 | 191,487 | 202,746 | -11,259 |
| TOTAL PAYROLL COST | 139,400 | 127,551 | 11,849 | 1,711,317 | 1,613,970 | 97,347 |
| 14 IND LAB POT | 1,699 | 5 | 1,694 | 12,222 | 1,645 | 10,577 |
| 16 DIRECT LAB POT | 1,855 | 6 | 1,849 | 12,731 | 2,125 | 10,606 |
| 18 PAYROLL TAXES | 7,490 | 9,316 | -1,826 | 99,482 | 94,090 | 5,392 |
| 19 INS WK MENS COMPEN | 1,045 | 9,921 | -8,876 | 13,736 | 22,857 | -9,121 |
| 46 INSURANCE ALL OTHE | 522 | 3,009 | -2,487 | 6,786 | 9,273 | -2,487 |
| 47 TAX PROPERTY MISCE | 4,257 | 2,489 | 1,768 | 55,341 | 45,371 | 9,970 |
| 52 TRANSPORTATION | 2,768 | 3,303 | -535 | 32,358 | 35,960 | -3,602 |
| 53 SUPPLIES | 3,678 | 5,803 | -2,125 | 44,545 | 41,137 | 3,408 |
| 54 HEAT | 1,281 | 2,069 | -788 | 19,400 | 19,367 | 33 |
| 55 WATER | 600 | --- | 600 | 7,936 | 5,353 | 2,583 |
| 56 POWER LIGHT | 3,026 | 2,783 | 243 | 32,585 | 35,896 | -3,311 |
| 57 PERISHABLE TOOLS | 119 | --- | 119 | 1,175 | 86 | 1,089 |
| 62 MACHINE RENTAL | 10,769 | 376 | 10,393 | 140,357 | 64,376 | 75,981 |
| 64 TRAVEL | 189 | 38 | 151 | 1,904 | 744 | 1,160 |
| 65 REPAIR MAINT | 1,375 | 2,105 | -730 | 14,833 | 13,591 | 1,242 |
| 67 DEPRECIATION | 16,722 | 14,894 | 1,828 | 217,386 | 215,570 | 1,816 |
| 68 MISCELLANEOUS | 198 | 204 | -6 | 1,834 | 942 | 892 |
| 70 PATTERNS OUTSIDE | 1,848 | 2,358 | -510 | 23,708 | 16,478 | 7,230 |
| 71 SEVERANCE PAY | --- | --- | --- | --- | 2,103 | -2,103 |
| 80 PERISHABLE TOOLS M | 5,437 | 5,653 | -216 | 63,478 | 47,449 | 16,029 |
| 81 REPLACEMENT GAGES | 412 | 186 | 226 | 4,306 | 2,106 | 2,200 |
| 82 TEMP AGENCY EMPLOY | --- | --- | --- | --- | --- | --- |
| 84 OUTSIDE DP SER | 174 | 1,023 | -849 | 1,953 | 1,921 | 32 |
| 85 RENT EXPENSE | 5,505 | 5,506 | -1 | 71,565 | 71,566 | -1 |
| 86 REPLACE TIP TOOLS | 197 | 197 | --- | 1,958 | 2,253 | -295 |
| 87 SERVICE CONTRACTS | 26 | --- | 26 | 730 | 661 | 69 |
| 89 EXPENDABLE EQUIPME | 323 | 561 | -238 | 1,890 | 891 | 999 |
| 90 MACH SHOP OIL | 895 | 618 | 277 | 10,283 | 8,192 | 2,091 |
| 95 MACH SHOP SUPPLIES | 235 | 75 | 160 | 2,347 | 3,099 | -752 |
| 99 OVT BILLED | --- | --- | --- | --- | 10,510 | 10,510 |
| TOTAL OTHER EXPENS | 72,645 | 72,498 | 147 | 896,829 | 754,592 | 142,237 |
| GRAND TOTAL | 212,045 | 200,049 | 11,996 | 2,608,146 | 2,368,562 | 239,584 |

*Accounting practice here identifies expenses that exceed plans (over budget) with a minus (−) sign, since these figures deduct from planned profit. Figures without minus signs indicate that actual expenses are under budget.

Figure 14-6 Example of a computer printout of a budget variance report.

the future to bring excessive costs back in line. This exactly fits the definition of the control function: comparing actual performance with a standard for the purpose of identifying areas where improvements can be made.

When properly used, the cost variance report is an investigative tool. Its purpose is to locate the specific sources of excessive costs so that corrective action can be taken. Many times, unexpectedly high costs may be unavoidable. Moving up a production deadline may require extra overtime. Increased production and sales will raise expenses and will not be reflected in a fixed budget. In any case, the variance report should be useful in identifying the sources of costs and should point the way to improvements.

# Key Concepts

1. Forecasts are projections of future business conditions. They are used for developing and carrying out business plans in order to meet organization objectives. There are two types of forecasts: (1) background projections of conditions in the environment of a company, such as economic, technological, social, and political influences; and (2) business forecasts specific to an individual company, including estimates of future demand and revenue, supply and costs, and profits.

2. The most common forecasting techniques are (1) assuming that significant trends in past performance will continue in the future, (2) statistically analyzing the interrelationships among the causes of business changes, and (3) using surveys, collected opinions and estimates, and other data-gathering methods.

3. Budgets are specific forecasts or plans expressed in numbers. Financial budgets are most common. They (1) help to anticipate company revenues and expenditures, (2) help to control the use of company funds by departments and activities, (3) force plans to be specific by requiring the use of dollar values or other units, and (4) provide a convenient time frame—the budget period—for the evaluation and control of operations.

4. Most companies use a group of coordinated budgets. Common types are sales and revenues, expense, cash, and capital expenditure budgets.

5. Budgets may be fixed or flexible. Flexible budgets are capable of responding to changing conditions while still guiding and controlling operations.

6. The budget variance report is the direct means by which budgets are used for controlling. The report compares actual expenses with budgeted amounts to locate sources of excess costs and to allow corrective action to be taken if needed.

# Review Questions

1. Define, identify, or explain each of the following key terms or phrases, found on the pages indicated.

*background forecast (p. 315)*
*budget (p. 320)*

*budget variance (cost variance) report (p. 326)*
*business forecast (p. 315)*
*capital expenditure budget (p. 323)*
*cash budget (p. 322)*
*demand and revenue forecast (p. 317)*

2. Why do businesses make forecasts?
3. What are the two general classes of forecasts? Give some examples of the kinds of questions each of the two might try to answer.
4. What are some techniques a company might use to forecast sales volume for the coming year?
5. What makes the sales budget so important to the budgeting process?
6. Why must forecasts based on the projection of historical trends be used with caution?
7. Name four important ways in which budgets contribute to better management.
8. Explain the purpose of a cash budget.
9. Upon what key variable does a flexible budget depend?
10. Describe a budget variance report, and tell what it is used for.

# Case Critique 14-1
## The Uncertain Aerobics Class

Helen Clark was a top-notch baton twirler in her high school marching band. She had been a whiz at gymnastics too. When everybody started getting into aerobics, Helen entered local and then regional competitions, and came home with a number of prizes. She soon was employed by the local health spa as an aerobics instructor. Her pay was good, and she developed a large personal following. Helen had her own thoughts, however, about how aerobic classes should be run. It was inevitable that she'd break away from the spa and organize her own classes. They were an immediate success. By the end of her first year in business for herself, Helen had more classes than she could handle without help. She hired an assistant on a per-class basis and rented a studio in the local shopping mall on the same basis. Everything seemed to be going well, except that when the end of the year came, Helen didn't seem to know whether or not she had really made any money.

Helen mentioned her problem to the manager of her local bank branch. The manager advised Helen that she should develop a budget for the next year. Only with that, she said, would Helen know how much business to take on, how much to set aside for expenses, and how much money she would really retain in addition to her own salary.

Helen sat down with her paper and pencil and made a list of expenses. She knew, for example, that rent at the studio was $30 an hour. She hired only first-rate assistants, those who had great athletic skills and good personalities. She paid them $50 a class. For each student, Helen found it cost her about 50 cents a class for miscellaneous supplies like name tags, balloons, and other accessories. These were her *variable expenses* per class. When Helen examined her *fixed expense,* she came to the conclusion that first of all, come what may, she wanted to draw $400 a week for her own pay. Insurance was surprisingly high. It came to $20 a week. Operation of her auto averaged $30 a week, as did the cost of mail and telephone.

"I know my expenses, variable and fixed," said Helen, "but how can I predict what my income will be?" Her policy was to cut off her classes when she had an enrollment of 30 people. She charged $5 a class per student. The real problem, Helen observed, was predicting how many classes she could fill in a week for 50 weeks a year. She thought that her present business justified 10 classes a week. If business were to pick up a little, she could handle as many as 12 classes. If business fell off, the number of classes she could fill might drop to 8. (All these figures are restated in Table 14-2.)

"What sorts of things might affect your enrollments?" asked her friend at the bank. Helen thought about it. Right now, there were no competitors near her except the health spa. The chamber of commerce told her that population forecasts for her community showed a steady increase. Besides, the chamber said that economic measures showed disposable income in the area rising significantly. The interest in personal health conditioning had been keen for a few years now. Helen wondered whether this interest would continue. That night, as Helen was watching television, she was surprised to see an advertisement for an aerobics class starting in a religious center on the other side of town. She was a little discouraged, too, when later on the news commentator mentioned that

economists expected a slight downturn in the economy next year.

When Helen again discussed her problem with the bank manager, the manager suggested that Helen draw up a flexible budget for next year with three forecasts: 10 classes a week as the base, 8 a week if things slow down, and 12 a week if they continue to grow the way they have been.

1. Your assignment is to complete the flexible budget for the three ranges of forecasts using the data in Table 14-2.

2. Which level of business do you think is most likely to occur for Helen next year? Why? Which environmental conditions would tend to make it improve? Which might tend to make it fall off?

3. If enrollments fall to 8 classes next year, will Helen make any money above the salary she pays herself? If not, what might she do to tighten her budget?

**TABLE 14-2**
**FLEXIBLE BUDGET FOR HELEN'S AEROBICS CLASSES**

| ACCOUNT TITLE | Monthly Allowances Based Upon Three Operating Levels in Terms of Numbers of Classes Per Week | | |
|---|---|---|---|
| | 8 CLASSES | 10 CLASSES | 12 CLASSES |
| Sales revenue—$5 a student × 30 a class | _____ | 1,500 | _____ |
| Variable expenses | | | |
|   Aerobic assistant instructor—$50 a class | _____ | 500 | _____ |
|   Studio rental—$30 a class | _____ | 300 | _____ |
|   Supplies—50 cents a student per class | _____ | 150 | _____ |
| Fixed expenses | | | |
|   Helen's salary—$400 a month | _____ | 400 | _____ |
|   Insurance—$20 a month | _____ | 20 | _____ |
|   Postal and telephone—$30 a month | _____ | 30 | _____ |
|   Automobile—$30 a month | _____ | 30 | _____ |
| Total of variable and fixed expenses | _____ | 1,430 | _____ |
| Net profit of sales over total expenses | _____ | 70 | _____ |

# Case Critique 14-2
## Gunslinger's Lament

On Winchester Avenue in New Haven, Connecticut, there is a life-sized bronze statue of John Wayne waving a Winchester Model 94 lever-action carbine. The gun was made by the U.S. Repeating Arms Company and is marketed to deer hunters as "the gun that won the West." John Wayne's statue stands just outside the gun plant, where employment declined from 1,300 a few years ago to under 1,000 today. Rifle production in the United States peaked in 1975; handguns in 1982. Since then, production and sales of all firearms have been on a downhill slide. Gun sales rose during the recession of the late 1970s; they fell off during the recovery of the mid-1980s. Says Repeating Arm's president, "Our buyer is not the high-tech worker. It's the smokestack employee and the farmer. These two sectors were hardest hit during the recession, and they're still reeling." Furthermore, the president said that many people have decided to bar hunters from their land. This makes hunting more difficult and more expensive.

Handgun dealers verify this decline in sales. Says one dealer in New York City, "We believe that the youth of today aren't really gun-oriented." Said another dealer, "In the high schools, the antigun propaganda has been damaging. We used to service five high schools with target-range pistols for shooting teams; now we're down to just a couple."

A spokesperson for the National Rifle Association attributes declining gun sales to a declining crime rate. "When crime is high, citizens go out and buy a gun. When crime starts dropping, people don't feel as threatened."

On the other hand, stricter gun-control laws have deterred gun ownership, observes a spokesperson for Handgun Control, Inc., who estimates that there are now about 20,000 state and local laws restricting gun ownership.

Meanwhile, the manufacturers also lament the long life of a well-made gun. They last about 50 years. Said one gun dealer, "Everyone who has wanted a gun has one now. Whatever sales there are now take place between individuals."

1. What factors in the economy, the environment, and the market have caused gun sales to decline?
2. How have these factors affected gun purchases in the past, and today?
3. If you were advising the managers of the Repeating Arms Co. about sales for next year, would your forecast be for an increase or decrease? Why? How would your forecast affect their production budget and marketing budget?

SOURCE: James Brooke, "Sales Decline Jolts Connecticut Gun Makers," *New York Times*, July 9, 1985, p. B1.

## Foiling computer piracy

Those who steal data from computer data bases, or the software itself, fall into three classes: (1) the casual person (a teacher, student, employee) who thinks there's really nothing wrong with obtaining privileged information for future use or a copy "for free"; (2) the computer "hacker," who sees computer security as a challenging game to play; and (3) the professional thief who captures data for resale to a competitor or a program for copying and sale to the public. There have been all sorts of electronic approaches to "lock out" would-be pirates, such as providing an "electronic key" with the floppy disk that contains the program. This plug-in device is inserted into a computer, and the program will not run unless its identification number matches that of the key. Mostly, however, protection systems are either too complicated or expensive or both. As one authority said, "If you leave your computer turned on 24 hours a day and you have a modem capable of automatic answering, then your system is accessible on a remote basis to anyone who can supply the telephone number and the entry code. If someone really wants to wiretap the system, an electronic password doesn't help. All the thief needs is a pair of alligator clips and a cassette recorder." The fact remains that the biggest problem isn't from the hacker or the professional thief; it's from the company employees, who, intentionally or not, can mix up the data beyond recall.

SOURCES: Gerald L. Pressman, "The Issue of Stealing," *Modern Office Technology,* February 1985, pp. 97–106; Kellyn S. Betts, "Foiling Data Thieves," *Modern Office Technology,* April 1985, pp. 114–118.

## Needed: Computer repair technicians

The hot job in computers a decade ago was keypunch operator. As more computer inputs went real-time, however, the demand for these skills declined. Then came the boom in programmers. Demand for their skill, along with that of systems analysts, continues to grow. The forecast indicates there will be 60 to 80 percent more of them by 1990. The surprise, though, is the increasing need for computer service technicians. These are the people who install, test, and maintain the equipment. There were 83,000 of these jobs in 1980; there will be more than double that number in 1990. Even companies that do not make computers have an increasing interest in technically trained people, especially those who have "computer literacy."

SOURCE: *Occupation Handbook of the United States,* 1985, U.S. Government Printing Office.

# UNIT 5

# *The Contribution of Human Resources*

Unit 5 sets forth some of the factors to be considered in obtaining maximum productivity from human resources in a business and in establishing a nurturing environment for human effort.

## CHAPTER 15

Human bodies and minds are needed by businesses to carry out their plans. The labor force in the United States provides a reservoir of human resources, people with high expectations who, when employed, must be motivated in such a way as to make their work productive and meaningful.

## CHAPTER 16

It is the function of human resources management to plan for and assemble a work force that is suitable for obtaining a company's objectives. This work force requires effective personnel programs for its recruitment, selection, training, development, maintenance, and compensation.

## CHAPTER 17

The interests of many workers are represented by trade unions, with whom businesses must bargain. When conflict arises between management and labor, individually or collectively, a body of laws helps to ensure fair treatment of employees.

# Human Relations
# and Productivity

## Learning Objectives

*The purpose of this chapter is to demonstrate the increasingly important role of human resources in business and, specifically, to identify some of the major forces that influence the motivation of employees and work groups toward greater productivity.*

*As evidence of general comprehension, after studying this chapter you should be able to:*

*1. Explain how factors in the environment have encouraged better human relations in business.*

*2. Describe the process of motivation and recognize each of the levels in Maslow's hierarchy of human needs.*

*3. Identify the way in which informal roles and group norms affect individual behavior and the productivity of work groups.*

*4. Compare the relationships between a number of generally accepted theories of motivation and the influence of financial reward systems.*

*5. Describe the importance of the design of work itself on human performance and recognize instances of job enlargement and job enrichment.*

*If your class is using SSweetco: Business Model and Activity File, see Chapter 15 in that book after you complete this chapter. There you will find exercises and activities to help you apply your learning to typical business situations.*

## 1 BUSINESS RESPONDS

to human forces
in the environment

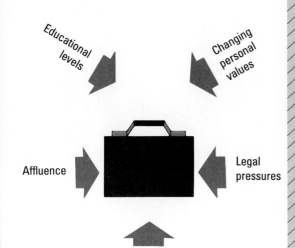

Educational levels

Changing personal values

Affluence

Legal pressures

Labor unions

while seeking to improve
employee productivity.

## 2 THE MOTIVATION PROCESS

serves to satisfy
individual needs.

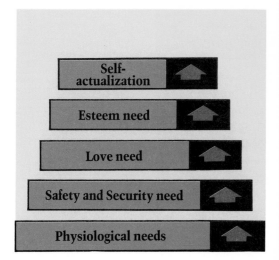

Self-actualization

Esteem need

Love need

Safety and Security need

Physiological needs

## 3 WORK GROUPS

establish informal roles

and exert pressure to conform to its norms:

## 4 MOTIVATIONAL THEORIES

anticipate varied employee responses.

| Theory Y | | Motivation |
| Theory X | | Maintenance |

McGregor          Maslow          Herzberg

## 5 DESIGN OF THE WORK ITSELF

influences employee production.

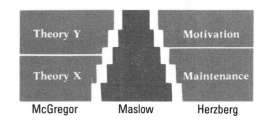

Job enlargement

Job enrichment

Output

# PUTTING HUMAN RELATIONS IN THE SPOTLIGHT

Business has always been puzzled by its principal resource—human beings. Management laments that employees are often unpredictable and unproductive. "Why can't people be more like machines?" has been an underlying concern of business since its inception.

Frederick W. Taylor had that question in mind when, in those gaslight days at the Midvale Steel plant in Philadelphia, he worked with a pig-iron handler named Schmidt. Taylor told Schmidt that if he did exactly as he was told, he would be able to move 47 1/2 tons a day instead of 12 1/4. Taylor would give him a special shovel, just made for handling pig iron, and would insist that Schmidt rest periodically, up to 43 percent of his 12-hour day. Schmidt followed directions to the letter and found that he could more than triple his capacity, without being any more tired than before. As a reward for his efforts, Taylor raised Schmidt's wages from $1.15 a day to $1.85. Taylor believed that the human body could be made into an efficient machine. And he was also convinced that the most compelling reward for effort was money.

Taylor's views were held without question until a funny thing happened at Western Electric's Hawthorne plant near Chicago in the middle of the Great Depression. Management was, as usual, complaining that employees weren't as productive as they ought to be. The Hawthorne works followed Taylor's reward plan to the letter, but the results weren't what were hoped for. The company thought it was time to find another approach to improving productivity. It brought in two psychologists from Harvard to study the problem. The professors set out to find a relationship between physical working conditions and work productivity. First the professors raised the lighting levels in the plant; and worker productivity increased. Then they lowered the lighting levels. Incredibly, worker productivity increased again. Next the researchers altered other environmental factors such as rest periods, the length of the work day, and noise. To the professors' astonishment, it made little difference whether conditions were improved or made worse. Productivity always increased! "What is happening?" the researchers asked. They observed that other, less obvious, things than physical working conditions were of vital importance to employees. The professors discovered that the workers involved in the project took their participation as a sign of status and recognition of *their value by management. As a consequence, they worked hard to do better, whatever the conditions. The Harvard professors finally concluded that workers are deeply affected by psychological and social conditions. They can and do react to such things as individual recognition, group pressures, and an opportunity to become involved in decisions that affect their work.*

*The Hawthorne study marked the beginning of an awareness on management's part that humans are far more complex than machines. Financial rewards might be important. So are working conditions. But the productivity of employees is also greatly influenced by the quality of the relationships each worker has with his or her boss and with coworkers.*

# 1 HUMANIZING FORCES IN THE ENVIRONMENT
*Change keeps blowing in the wind*

Many factors have caused business management to have an increasing concern for its most valuable resource, the human one. Among the most important factors are the forces of labor and legislation, the significant rise in the number of women in the workplace, and the general change in the expectations and life-styles of the American public.

## LABOR UNIONS AND LEGAL PRESSURES
*An enforced awareness*

The development of organized labor has forced managers to focus on working conditions, training, fair treatment of employees, and the many factors that affect employee morale. Union efforts, especially in the last 10 to 15 years, have reflected workers' growing expectations of what work should provide. Workers desire more respect, varied and interesting jobs, and nonmonetary rewards. Some labor unions have begun to present these attitudes to management in an assertive way, while a few unions, particularly in the troubled automobile and steel industries, recently have made concessions to management—through so-called givebacks—on matters concerning monetary and other types of rewards.

Certain legal regulations have also obliged businesses to increase their awareness of how their human resources are handled. The Occupational Safety and Health Act, to cite one example, has required managers to become deeply involved in efforts to create and maintain a safe workplace. The Equal Employment Opportunity Act has led many companies to begin thorough "open enrollment" employee training and development programs. Frequently, when forced by law to have wider contact with minorities and women, managers and workers have in fact reduced their prejudices and preconceptions.

The latest, and perhaps most important, legal pressure arises from a growing belief that management can no longer fire employees without just and documented reasons. At the turn of the last century it was very different. The doctrine prevailed that a boss had the absolute right to fire subordinates at will. In fact, one court ruled that management had the right to discharge employees "for good cause, for no cause, or even for cause morally wrong." In the most recent decade of this century, federal courts have made it increasingly clear that every employee, whether represented by a labor union or not, is entitled to **due process** before any discipline, including discharge, can take place. This means that an employee is entitled to a fair hearing of his or her case. Discipline or discharge that does not follow this process is judged as "wrongful." Many notable employers—like American Airlines, AT&T, IBM, and McGraw-Hill—have been forced to retract or face sizable settlements in such cases.

## CHANGES IN HUMAN OUTLOOK AND BEHAVIOR
### Greater affluence, but less materialism

The expectations and goals of American workers have changed a great deal over the years. Compulsory education, together with an increasingly democratic attitude about which individuals ought to receive higher educations, has created a highly trained work force in the United States. The sophistication that gives workers the capability to handle today's technical jobs also leads them to expect greater rewards. Higher wages have also allowed individual workers to build up their own financial resources. This protection from financial disaster and the overall affluence of our society have caused workers to demand fair treatment and more rewarding jobs.

Just as individual workers have partially changed their focus from wages to a desire for broader fulfillment on the job, so business managers are also changing their values. Many managers feel a real sense of social responsibility and concern for the welfare of the people within and outside of their organization. This has helped to make positive human relations a desirable end in itself, rather than just a tool for increasing human productivity.

To make sure that they understand the changes that are taking place in our society, managers have turned to the work of psychologists, sociologists, anthropologists, and others who study human behavior. Many of the approaches and goals of human resources management have developed from the scientific study of social interactions, group behavior, motivation, leadership, communication, and other aspects of human relations.

## MORE DEMANDING LIFE-STYLES
### Require flexibility at the workplace

Three changes in American life-style have greatly affected the routine operation of a business: (1) the greater participation of women in the work force, (2) the rapid growth of numbers of married couples with both partners working, and (3) the value placed by individuals upon their leisure, or nonworking, hours. These changes have had a most dramatic impact upon the traditional 8-hour workday.

Consider these changes reflecting the participation of women in the United States work force:

■  In the early 1960s, about half the women in the United States were keeping house full-time while 37 percent were in the labor force. By 1982, these proportions were reversed: 53 percent were working or looking for work while 35 percent were keeping house. Predictions are that this trend will persist until 1990 or longer.

■ In 1985 more than 4 out of every 10 workers were women. Families where both husband and wife worked outside the home accounted for 52 percent of all married-couple families. Nearly 55 percent of all children had working mothers.

The net effect of these two trends is increased pressure for greater work-hour flexibility so that parents can stagger their sharing of child care, manipulate their commuting arrangements to save time and expense, and find ways to share their leisure time together. The existence of dual-income families, in itself, often makes leisure-time activities more affordable, which adds to the demand for work-hour flexibility.

Employers' response to this demand has been the creation of flexible work hours, or *flexitime.* By 1980, the U.S. Labor Department reported that 7.5 million full-time workers were on flexitime. Another 1.8 million full-time workers were on schedules of 4.5 days or less. Under a typical flexitime arrangement (see Figure 15-1), employees must be on the job during a certain core period, say 9:30 a.m. to 3:00 p.m. They then work the balance of their 40 hours before or after that core period. Flexitime schedules cause problems where there is a need for one employee to communicate with another working a different schedule. In some instances, however, this is offset by having scarce space or equipment better utilized by this extension of the overall workday.

Another aspect of mothers—and fathers—working is the increasing need for day-care centers. For a person whose take-home pay is little more than $100 a week, paid day care is often a painful necessity of employment. On the one hand, labor unions press for day-care allowances for their members when bargaining with management. On the other hand, some 2,000 companies offer some sort of child care assistance. It is another example of the belief that human resources need, at the very least, the same kind of attention and maintenance given to machines.

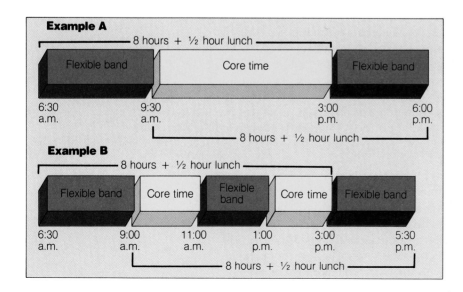

Figure 15-1 Two ways of designing flexitime schedules.
*Source:* Barbara L. Fiss, *Flexitime—A Guide,* U.S. Civil Service Commission, May 15, 1974.

# 2 NEEDS AND MOTIVATION
## A complex, often conflicting, individuality

To be successful in human relations, a manager ought to have some conception of why people behave the way they do when they become members of an organization. Managers must consider what causes, or motivates, people to work effectively. They must understand something about how people interact in groups. They must also be sensitive to what it is that leads employees to feel satisfied or dissatisfied with their work.

## THE PROCESS OF MOTIVATION
### Behavior that satisfies needs

From the point of view of a business manager, an individual is "motivated" if he or she "works hard," "keeps at it," and "does what helps us to make a profit." In behavioral terms, motivation would be described as involving effort, persistence, and goals. The bottom-line question is, What causes people to work hard, be persistent, and strive to reach important goals? Management's wish is that they follow a process of motivation that matches management's idea of how they should act. Unfortunately, the motivation process, which every person follows in order to exist, doesn't always guarantee the behavior management expects. The *motivation process* involves a three-part chain reaction: (1) an individual feels a need for something; (2) the individual behaves in a way that he or she hopes will help attain a goal that will satisfy that need; and (3) when the goal is reached, the need is satisfied. Managers who want to motivate employees must always consider the three elements of the chain: an unsatisfied need, behavior that employees believe will lead to satisfaction of that need, and a reward for that behavior (in the form of need satisfaction) when that behavior persists. Said another way, if the need satisfaction isn't assured or doesn't take place, there will be no persistent effort in the behavior desired by management.

## A PRIORITY OF NEEDS
### Needs vary in their importance to different individuals

Although many theories exist about what causes people to work effectively, the *hierarchy of human needs* proposed by Abraham H. Maslow has been especially popular among business managers. The theory is important because it predicts that rewards such as wages, bonuses, and salary increases are not the only considerations that motivate workers. Threat of punishment, such as demotion or dismissal, may also be ineffective. Employees will work best when their jobs satisfy their personal needs. These needs may be more complex than was widely believed before Maslow's time.

Maslow's hierarchy summarizes human needs that must be satisfied in order to achieve fulfillment. The five needs he identified are described in Figure 15-2. Maslow arranges human needs in a hierarchy because he believes that they operate on a priority system. A person's lower-level needs almost always have priority over higher-level needs. Only when a person has adequate food, water, and shelter, for example, is he or she free to be concerned with higher needs like love or esteem.

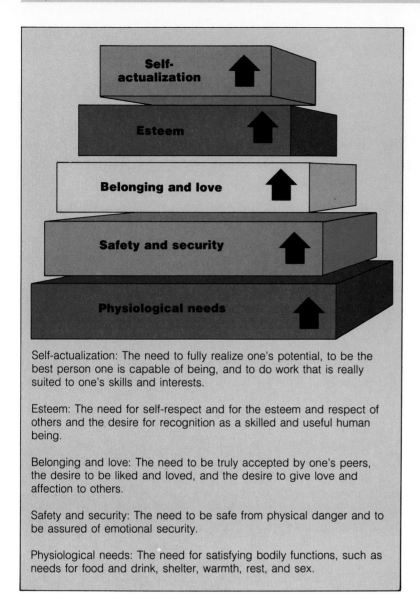

Figure 15-2 The hierarchy of human needs proposed by Abraham Maslow. Lower level needs normally receive priority over higher level needs.

Self-actualization: The need to fully realize one's potential, to be the best person one is capable of being, and to do work that is really suited to one's skills and interests.

Esteem: The need for self-respect and for the esteem and respect of others and the desire for recognition as a skilled and useful human being.

Belonging and love: The need to be truly accepted by one's peers, the desire to be liked and loved, and the desire to give love and affection to others.

Safety and security: The need to be safe from physical danger and to be assured of emotional security.

Physiological needs: The need for satisfying bodily functions, such as needs for food and drink, shelter, warmth, rest, and sex.

Maslow's priority system has an important practical consequence. Once a person's need is satisfied, it no longer motivates. This means that with today's high wages, insurance, and other benefits, an individual's desire to satisfy higher-level needs—such as esteem, respect, praise, or self-actualization—becomes more important. Most gainfully employed people already will have achieved considerable satisfaction of their low-level needs.

## CONFLICTING MOTIVATIONS
*Psychological influences offer explanations* ━━━━━━

Another authority on motivation interprets Maslow's hierarchy of needs, especially the upper-level ones, from a psychological viewpoint. David C. McClelland believes that many of the things people do are in response to their needs for affiliation, achievement, and/or power.

People with a high degree of *affiliation*, says McClelland, will be motivated by work in organizations where people are friendly and supportive.

People for whom *achievement* is a strong need will be motivated by organizations where they can demonstrate their competency. They like to show that they can get a job done well, often better than their associates, and they want to be recognized for these achievements.

People to whom *power* is important find motivation in organizations that grant them authority and in companies where lines of authority and responsibility are clearly defined. These people view power as a necessity for security and achievement.

The interplay of these psychological needs within an individual is sometimes in conflict. A person who wants to be considered one of the team, for example, may want to achieve without embarrassing his or her peers. Other persons may not wish to become enmeshed in power struggles in order to get their work done. Still others will seize power anywhere they can get it in order to achieve.

## MODIFICATIONS AND EXPECTATIONS

*Behavior is learned; people can't be fooled for long*

Everybody has heard about the carrot and the stick. The twentieth-century version of this old concept has two different twists. First, the carrot doesn't have to be money; it can be what money can buy, or almost any sort of recognition and esteem that an employee holds dear. The second angle is that if you want to induce productive behavior, the carrot is always the motivator, never the stick. Productive **behavior modification** can be made to take place in an individual if the desired behavior is reinforced by praise and encouragement; undesired behavior is not praised, and is thus considered unrewarding enough by the individual to desist. Desirable behavior is designated as **goal-oriented behavior** since it is engaged in by an individual in order to satisfy a need. The challenge to management is to make clear to an employee that the desired behavior not only is reasonable but also will lead to gratification.

Another important behavioral contribution is the concept of **expectancy.** This is also a four-part chain reaction by which (1) an employee believes that if he or she tries to do the job the way it is prescribed, (2) he or she will, in fact, be able to do the job that way; and (3) once the performance is achieved, it will be rewarded (by praise, promotion, job security, a raise, etc.). This system breaks down, however, if (4) the employee does not value the outcome (or reward) enough to make the effort in the first place. Said another way, employees must *expect* that hard work leads to suitable performance, *expect* that this performance will lead to a reward, and *expect* that the reward will be worth the effort. If a salesclerk, for example, is told to be polite to every customer because this will lead to increased sales, the salesclerk must believe that this will really happen. If fellow clerks say otherwise, however, management will have a difficult time trying to keep the salesclerk polite to all customers. And even if the salesclerk believes these things, the clerk may want to know what the payoff will be. For some clerks, an assurance of job security will be enough of a motivation. For others, this will not be satisfying; only a raise in pay will be deemed a satisfactory reward.

# 3 BEHAVIOR IN WORK GROUPS
## Determined by roles and norms

Individuals satisfy their needs through interactions with others at home and at work. Inevitably, informal groups form at work to help individuals satisfy these work-related needs. Work groups are formed on the basis of physical proximity or closeness, common tasks to perform, a similarity in interests or needs, and mutual goals. Groups within the same company are often different in behavior, one from the other. Some groups work together with minimum internal friction. Others develop factions that interfere with individual and group actions. Most groups change in character over time.

**POSITIVE AND NEGATIVE BEHAVIOR** Groups are made up of individuals who interact with one another. The members of a group talk, help one another, use gestures, stand and/or sit together, and express feelings, ideas, beliefs, and desires. All of the interactions among the members are embraced by the term *group dynamics.* The dynamics of a particular group at a particular time may be positive or negative. If positive, they bind the group together to make it cohesive. If negative, they may cause the group to dissolve and may interfere with effective cooperation. Negative dynamics may be caused by excessive competitiveness, by personality conflicts, by lack of direction, by unequal treatment of group members by those outside the group, such as supervisors, or by scores of other factors operating together.

**GROUP STRUCTURE** As work groups form and mature in a company, certain structures emerge. These rarely coincide with the formal organizational structure established by management. Formal job assignments, responsibilities, and authority relationships may continue on the surface, but within the group, a pattern evolves. "Leaders" and "followers" develop. These informal *roles* are prescribed by the group's interactions so that each member gradually learns the part, or role, he or she will play in the group's power structure. Some leadership roles will have to do with determining how the group's task is to be approached, either favorably or negatively. Other leadership roles will focus on social relationships, on helping members to feel good about being in the group, and on resolving interpersonal conflicts.

As the group matures and roles and structure crystallize, work groups take on certain fixed patterns of thought and behavior. These patterns, or *norms,* are group-defined rules of conduct. They provide a consensus as to acceptable behavior and attitudes within the group. A degree of variance from these norms is tolerated so long as the individualistic behavior doesn't threaten the group's security or goals. During the famous Hawthorne experiments it was observed that if any worker exceeded a production level that the group had established as its norm, an "enforcer" was designated by a "leader" to "bing" the person who was speeding up the job. A person was binged with a snapped finger against the back of the neck as the enforcer passed behind the deviant on the way to the rest room.

When an individual is a member of a group, his or her behavior will be partially controlled by the group. The amount of influence a group has on a person's behavior depends on (1) how cohesive the group is, (2) how forceful the members' individual personalities are, and (3) how different the group's goals, motivations, and behaviors are from those of the individual members. Some people are more likely to be strongly influenced by groups because their needs for love, esteem, and acceptance are strong. They are often willing to give up the satisfaction of other desires in order to gain acceptance.

**GROUP GOALS** The goals of individuals often come into conflict with the goals of the group. This places the individual in a paradoxical position. A worker, for example, may want and need the group's support. At the same time, however, the worker may wish to do things differently from the group's norms in order to reach his or her own levels of achievement. If the group puts pressure on the worker to conform to the group's norms, this begs the question of what management should do to protect the individual's rights. The answer is not always clear. More often it depends upon an assessment of the individual's goals and behavior and the group's goals and norms—and their conformance to the behavior and goals prescribed by management.

Some understanding of group behavior is important to managers because it points to some practical steps that make groups work better. Cooperation within work groups and the adjustment of individuals to groups are almost always better when the group's manager (1) helps establish clear goals, (2) treats group members fairly and consistently, (3) encourages communication, and (4) does not treat individuals so poorly that they seek all of their rewards solely from the group rather than from both their work and the people they work with.

**MORALE AND SATISFACTION** Individual and group *morale* is usually thought of as a satisfaction with and enthusiasm for work. Morale cannot be easily evaluated because it is largely emotional. Morale, however, does show itself in a number of ways. Workers with high morale will usually be cooperative, committed to their work and to mutual goals, loyal to the organization, confident, and self-motivated. Low morale will, sooner or later, cause a change in these behaviors.

A number of studies of morale among American workers have conflicting conclusions. In general, however, it seems that morale is fairly high. About two-thirds of the work force expresses considerable job satisfaction. One interesting point that some of the studies bring to light is that the causes of low morale are not usually related to low wages or salaries. Problems with the work itself—the lack of responsibility, the lack of opportunity to use initiative, and the lack of fulfillment in the type of work done—are cited as frequent causes of dissatisfaction.

# 4 MANAGERS AND MOTIVATION
*The toughest managerial task of all*

Managers make conscious efforts to motivate their employees to do their best work. They motivate indirectly by trying to create the kind of physical and emotional environment that encourages workers. They motivate directly through authority, discipline, and rewards. A number of different approaches to this task are popular today.

# McGREGOR'S THEORY X AND THEORY Y
## *An insight into managerial beliefs*

How managers try to motivate others is determined partly by their attitudes toward people. Douglas McGregor has described two common views, calling them theory X and theory Y. Some managers hold the view that the average human being has an inherent dislike for work, must be pushed into it, prefers to be directed by others, and wishes to avoid responsibility. This is **theory X.** Managers who uphold **theory Y** believe that mental and physical work is as natural as play or rest, that employees commit themselves to goals that satisfy their need for self-respect and personal fulfillment, and that they readily accept responsibility for such work, disciplining themselves as they strive to achieve these goals.

Managers who hold one or the other view use different methods to motivate employees. Theory X managers usually stress material rewards and job security: wages, salary increases, and employee benefits. When these fail as motivators, they may rely on strict discipline, threats of job loss, suspensions, demotions, and other punishments. Theory Y managers usually try to create work conditions that will bring more fulfillment to workers. They will often be more democratic and encourage workers to participate more in planning and management.

# HERZBERG'S TWO-FACTOR THEORY
## *Maintenance or motivation?*

Frederick Herzberg has devised a useful system for organizing motivating forces. According to Herzberg, two general factors influence motivation: (1) the need for survival, physical well-being, and comfort, and (2) the need for self-development, responsibility, and expression.

He calls the first group **maintenance,** or **hygiene, factors** because they relate to the maintenance of life and health. These probably have little effect on American workers today because the needs are adequately satisfied for a majority of them. These hygiene factors can only cause dissatisfaction when they are not present. When they are satisfied, they are ignored.

The second group consists of positive **motivating,** or **satisfying, factors.** Their presence brings actual satisfaction and fulfillment to humans. The positive motivators Herzberg lists include:

- Opportunities to achieve something important: reaching a difficult goal
- Recognition for achievement: honest praise for goals attained
- The nature of the work itself: how interesting and challenging the work is
- The extent of responsibility an individual has

# LIKERT'S SYSTEM 4
## *Stresses employee participation*

Rensis Likert, in his extensive studies of managers and management styles, has identified an approach to management that ought to provide employees with positive motivators. He calls it **system 4,** or participative management, contrasting it with three other systems: exploitive-authoritative, benevolent-authoritative, and consultive. System 4 stresses the active participation of employees in the management process. This gives workers greater opportunities in achievement, recognition, interesting work assignments, and responsibility. Likert's studies indicate that these factors really are motivating. He found greater group loyalty and more cooperation—along with higher outputs, better quality work, and lower costs—under system 4 management

# RELATIONSHIPS AMONG THE THEORIES
## An underlying consistency

Although these different approaches to management and motivation were arrived at independently, they all have a common base as Figure 15-3 illustrates. The needs and rewards of the lower levels of Maslow's hierarchy are generally the same as Herzberg's hygiene factors. These are the kinds of rewards theory X managers usually offer as motivators. The higher-level needs in Maslow's hierarchy generally correspond to the factors Herzberg identifies as genuine motivators. These motivators are employed by theory Y managers and by those who follow Likert's system 4 management style. In recent years, *participative management* has become a very popular, and often effective, approach to motivation. This managerial approach invites employees to take part in the problem-solving and decision-making process. It encourages individual initiative and self-direction. It depends upon the use of positive motivators by providing opportunities to satisfy the need for recognition and achievement. Quality Circles and other employee involvement programs are manifestations of participative management.

Figure 15-3 Common base of management/motivation approaches.

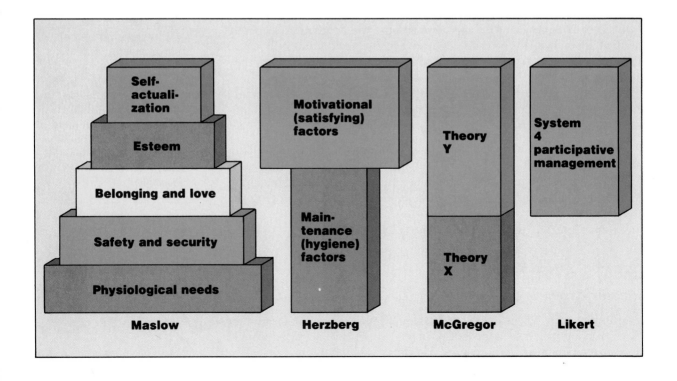

# REWARD SYSTEMS
*Combine financial and psychological incentives* ▬▬▬▬▬▬

Motivating with money is the most visible, the most common, and perhaps the most effective means for a business to provide individuals with the wherewithal to satisfy physiological needs. Money—in the form of wages, salaries, bonuses, and commissions—is readily translatable into food, clothing, housing, transportation, entertainment, status symbols, and fulfilling hobbies. Figure 15-4 illustrates how financial rewards can enable a person to satisfy needs at any level of Maslow's hierarchy.

As Herzberg has demonstrated so well, nonfinancial rewards have an important place in a compensation and motivation system. At the lower levels of needs, job security and good people to work with are important. At the higher levels, status (in the form of a reserved place in the company parking lot, for example) and other perquisites (like special dining rooms and career counseling) take on importance. Most vital of all at the higher need-levels are challenging work and opportunities to demonstrate one's true capabilities.

Regardless of the form that the rewards and compensation system take, employees are very sensitive to equity. *Equity* implies that employees believe that their rewards are fair (1) in terms of the effort and skill they put into their work and (2) in comparison with what others doing the same kind of work receive as rewards. Employees may be less bothered by low pay generally than by a situation where the pay differs among employees doing the same work in the same group.

Figure 15-4 How financial rewards satisfy psychological needs as well as physiological needs.

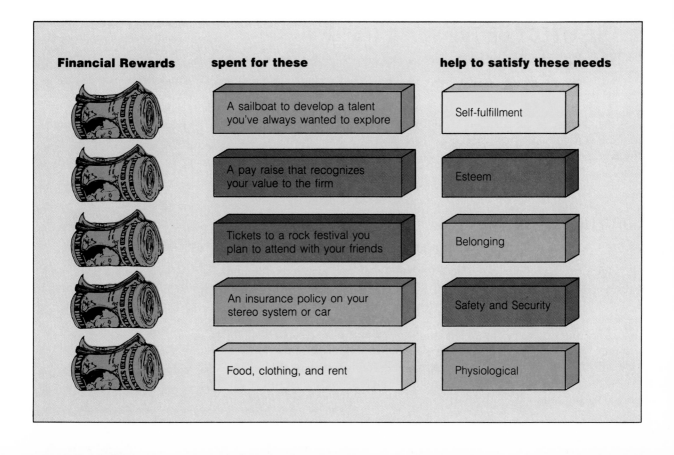

| Financial Rewards | spent for these | help to satisfy these needs |
|---|---|---|
| | A sailboat to develop a talent you've always wanted to explore | Self-fulfillment |
| | A pay raise that recognizes your value to the firm | Esteem |
| | Tickets to a rock festival you plan to attend with your friends | Belonging |
| | An insurance policy on your stereo system or car | Safety and Security |
| | Food, clothing, and rent | Physiological |

# MANAGEMENT BY OBJECTIVES
*Emphasis on self-direction* ━━━━━━━━━━━━━━━━━━━━━

Many companies rely upon an employee's knowledge of what is expected from him or her to furnish the necessary motivation. In essence, the objectives set for the individual provide the leadership. Generally speaking, this technique, called *management by objectives (MBO)*, is used only with higher-level employees, usually middle- and upper-level managers.

When MBO is used, a company's ongoing activities are planned and evaluated at periodic intervals, typically on a yearly basis. At the beginning of each period, a manager sits down with a subordinate and together they work out the subordinate's objectives for the coming period. They also mutually agree upon what measures will be used to tell whether and how well the subordinate has achieved these objectives. Performance is judged by the results that are attained rather than by what the subordinate does to achieve them. Management by objectives helps employees to concentrate on what is really important: what must be accomplished. It improves motivation because clear objectives are easier to work toward than fuzzy ones, and because subordinates are consulted about goals and allowed greater freedom in choosing the methods they will use to reach them. A weakness of MBO is that a manager may depend entirely upon the program to provide the leadership, when in fact subordinates will still need and expect direction and encouragement.

# 5  THE EFFECT OF THE WORK ITSELF
*Shaping jobs for people*

Despite management efforts, many jobs remain boring and uninspiring. The simplest solution to the low morale that may result from these jobs may be to make changes in the jobs themselves. While continuing to require certain basic activities, jobs can often be redesigned to make them more satisfying and challenging.

# JOB ENLARGEMENT
*Stretching jobs heightens interest* ━━━━━━━━━━━━━━━

One way to make a job more interesting is to increase its scope and variety. Increasing the number and kinds of activities performed by a single worker is called *job enlargement.* It can give employees more personal responsibility, more opportunity for achievement and recognition, and more of a feeling of making a real contribution. At IBM, for instance, managers redesigned jobs so that machine operators do their own setup work and actually deliver finished goods to the next workstation. Some machinist jobs are extended to include preparing specifications, sharpening tools, and doing some machine maintenance. American

Telephone & Telegraph Co. enlarged jobs for their keypunch operators by assigning full responsibility for complete batches of work. Each operator would punch, verify, record error rates, and take responsibility for the quality of a whole job, rather than being assigned a small, arbitrary job step.

## JOB ENRICHMENT
*Involvement makes work meaningful* ━━━━━━━━━━━━

*Job enrichment* makes work more satisfying by increasing the depth of employee involvement. Taking the time to show how an individual job contributes to the entire production process is important. Allowing workers a choice of methods or encouraging employees to make improvements in work methods also humanizes work. Texas Instruments Inc., for instance, trains employees in the principles of work simplification and then encourages them to make changes to improve their own jobs. Managers there also meet regularly with employees to ask directly for their help in solving department and company problems. Jobs can include activities that provide recognition for employees. General Motors' Rochester Products Division, for example, uses hourly workers to train other hourly workers and includes the training assignment as a recognized part of the job. Acknowledging that a worker has the ability to train someone else is clearly a form of praise.

## QUALITY OF WORK LIFE
*Upgrading the psychological environment* ━━━━━━━━━━

As the 1980s began, it was increasingly evident that Americans were caught on the horns of a dilemma. Productivity in the United States was slipping behind that of other major nations, while at the same time American workers were becoming disenchanted with the demands of the traditional work environment. Their complaints were not about the physical aspects so much but about work that was endlessly repetitive, boring, and seemingly without meaning. Technical approaches for improving productivity were taken for granted. Those approaches, however, tended to make work even more meaningless and demeaning to some people, and were often resisted. A search by management to improve the quality of work life while at the same time improving the productivity of the work force led to a number of innovative approaches. Most of these were characterized by greater involvement by employees in the problem-solving and decision-making processes of business. As with job enlargement and job enrichment, these approaches included a large measure of participatory management. Some of these participatory approaches are now widely used in business to meet the dual objectives of improving the quality of work life and improving productivity. Table 15-1 explains a number of these.

**TABLE 15-1**
**EXAMPLES OF PARTICIPATORY APPROACHES USED TO IMPROVE QUALITY OF WORK LIFE AND PRODUCTIVITY**

*Joint Labor-Management Committees*

This is the core of many quality of work life efforts. Both union and management representatives form a committee to talk over mutual problems. They may launch problem-solving activities to give workers more control over some aspects of local work areas.

*"Semiautonomous" or "Self-Managed" Work Teams*

A team of workers is given responsibility for turning out the whole product or task and can make its own decisions about division of labor. Members police themselves, and may elect their own team leader; in some situations, they may hire and fire.

*"Quality Circles"*

Modeled after the Japanese system, this mechanism gives workers responsibility for taking their own steps to monitor quality and improve productivity, based on group meetings and other forms of cooperation. Theoretically, it is strictly voluntary.

*Problem-Solving Task Forces or Committees*

This creates involvement of a group in making recommendations and sometimes decisions. They may be investigatory, fact-finding, or advisory. They may set their own agenda, but usually the agenda is defined. Temporary and ad hoc, they may be broadly representative, but more often members are drawn from management ranks.

*Communication Councils*

These are diagonal slices through the organization that represent clusters of employees and serve as a forum for communication. They may be elected but are more often appointed. Membership may rotate, and there is usually no decision-making authority.

*"Team Building"*

This is a highly variable, local, sporadic, occasional process. It may involve a work unit in airing concerns, discussing goals, clarifying roles and responsibilities, recommending changes. More often than not, it is focused too heavily on feelings and relationships and not enough on tasks and content.

*Source:* Rosabeth Moss Kantor, "Dilemmas of Participation," *National Forum: Phi Kappa Phi Journal,* Spring 1982, p. 17.

# Key Concepts

1. Important social, economic, and political developments in the United States have led managers to try to increase the effectiveness and satisfaction of the work force. This trend has resulted from the influences of legal pressures and the growth of labor unions, as well as from changes in human attitudes and behavior.

2. The process of motivation involves the desire of each person to satisfy a felt need. These needs tend to be arranged in a hierarchy, with physiological ones at the lower levels and psychological ones at the higher levels. Motivation also varies according to each person's need for affiliation, achievement, and power. Individual behavior is an expression of a person's desire to satisfy a need. This behavior can be modified by a positive reward system, and the rewards must be related to each individual's expectancy of a valued outcome.

3. Behavior in work groups may be either positive or negative according to the roles and norms that develop within the group and the goals that it sets. A work group exerts pressure upon its members to conform to its norms. Overall, the morale of both individuals and work groups is surprisingly high, with over two-thirds of the United States work force expressing considerable satisfaction with their jobs.

4. A number of theories that help interpret employees' responses to supervision have evolved to guide management in its efforts to increase worker productivity and job satisfaction. Principal among these theories are McGregor's theory X and theory Y, Herzberg's two-factor theory, and Likert's system 4. All point to the value of praise, respect, recognition, and opportunities for responsibility and self-fulfillment as positive motivators. Financial as well as nonfinancial rewards continue to play an important part in motivation, with the doctrine of equity, or fairness, an essential element.

5. Making changes in the work itself—through job enlargement and enrichment—is one way to increase worker productivity and job satisfaction. These changes increase the variety and scope of work and provide more opportunities for personal responsibility, recognition, and involvement in decision making. Participatory approaches such as quality circles can also improve work.

# Review Questions

1. Define, explain, or identify each of the following key terms or phrases, found on the pages indicated.

*behavior modification (p. 342)*
*due process (p. 338)*
*equity (p. 347)*
*expectancy (p. 342)*
*flexitime (p. 339)*
*goal-oriented behavior (p. 342)*
*group dynamics (p. 343)*
*hierarchy of human needs (p. 340)*
*job enlargement (p. 348)*
*job enrichment (p. 349)*
*maintenance (hygiene) factors (p. 345)*
*management by objectives (p. 348)*
*morale (p. 344)*
*motivating (satisfying) factors (p. 345)*

*motivation process (p. 340)*
*norms (p. 343)*
*participative management (p. 346)*
*roles (p. 343)*
*system 4 (p. 345)*
*theory X (p. 345)*
*theory Y (p. 345)*

2. How has the affluence of society forced business managers to stress human resources management?

3. What important predictions about human motivation derived from Maslow's theory have significant applications to business management and reward systems?

4. What similarities can you find between Maslow's hierarchy of human needs and Herzberg's two-factor theory?

5. What are some factors that partially control the amount of influence a group will have on an individual's behavior?

6. Describe some of the beliefs about work and workers held by theory X managers and theory Y managers.

7. What kind of management is used in Likert's system 4? What kinds of motivators does it provide employees?

8. Can you find a relationship between expectancy theory and the concept of equity in the reward system?

9. What are some of the ways in which jobs can be redesigned to make them more satisfying?

10. Why is the growing interest in the quality of work life deeply related to participatory management?

# Case Critique 15-1
## The Apathetic Insurance Clerks

Sam Spates, manager of the records department in a major insurance company, was puzzled by the apathy of his work force. When the firm had moved to its rural location a couple of decades ago, employees had appeared to be careful, energetic, and compliant. Gradually, however, their attitudes and work behavior had changed. Or so it seemed to Sam. Whereas in the past a simple order to move an employee from one workstation to another was never questioned, it now seemed to induce endless arguments. The pay scale, which was once regarded by local people as unbelievably high, was now the subject of bitter complaints. Then there was the matter of misfilings. Ten years ago, more than 1 percent of misfiled records was considered intolerable. Now, no matter how hard Sam stayed on the back of his clerical crew, their apparent carelessness and indifference resulted in a misfiling rate of more than 3 percent.

Sam reviewed the situation this way: "These employees have better than average working conditions. Their pay, if not exceptional, is more than adequate. The employment record here at the company shows them that they have secure jobs. What more could they possibly want?" Finally, at clock-out time after a particularly discouraging day, Sam came to this conclusion. "This situation has gotten out of hand. If ever I'm going to correct it, I'll have to really crack down on this bunch of malcontents. Tomorrow, I'll begin putting it to them."

1. What do you think of Sam's conclusion about what he should do?
2. What are some of the influences outside the company that may have caused the changes in employee attitude and behavior?
3. If you were Sam, how would you approach this problem?

# Case Critique 15-2
## Red Light for Quality

By the time Casey Powell was 37 years old, he was a general manager of one of the world's largest computer companies. His operation was centered in Portland, Oregon, where his home was. Then, in 1982, Powell's employer asked him to move to its San Francisco headquarters

to take over the rejuvenation of one of its divisions. Powell told the company executives he could get the job done without moving from his home in Portland. This did not set well with the company. When Powell made his presentation to headquarters executives describing how he would handle the new assignment, he found himself being grilled in an unfriendly, "depersonalizing" way. Powell was taken aback. He had been a loyal, hardworking employee who had done very well by the company. He had moved twice in the past 3 years, and he wasn't about to move again. And here he was being treated like a little boy, being forced to answer "Yes, sir" and "No, sir" in a public grilling in front of his associates. Something inside Powell snapped, and spelled the end of his employment with the big company.

Within a year, Powell had formed a small computer company of his own in Portland. He was determined, he said, to provide himself with an opportunity to satisfy professional goals without sacrificing his family. Furthermore, he was just as determined to create a working environment that motivates people "without beating up on them." Since then his company, Sequent Computer Systems, not only has prospered but has gained a reputation as a company that treats its employees differently. After Powell's new company had hired its first 18 people, he held a public meeting, first to pick a name for the company, and then to draft a set of corporate objectives. The name chosen was originally "Sequel," after a popular local rock band. (Later, for copyright purposes, the name was modified to Sequent.) Among the corporate objectives were these two key phrases: "A culture that rewards our employees for their contributions," and "an organization that provides individuals with the means to accept maximum responsibility for the overall success of the company."

Periodically, Sequent asks its human resources director, Barbara Gaffney, to hold workshops in which about 20 employees spend the day talking about whether the company is living up to its values. To promote closeness and easy communications, there are no walls between departments. The vice president for finance, for instance, has his desk right out on the factory floor. To make the families of employees feel closer to and supportive of those who often work very long hours, Sequent installed, at a cost of $2,500, a computer terminal in every employee's house. The company encourages family members to talk to one another all day, and to go home for dinner, if working late, and tuck their children into bed.

Since quality is the most competitive feature of the computer business, employees devised a unique "red light" system. A red light is turned on whenever anyone finds a quality problem on the production line. The entire line shuts down, with the red light burning night and day until the problem is solved. When the company found itself falling behind its first critical deadline, it devised a "red and green button" system. A few key people were issued a red "priority" button to wear. Anything they needed to get a product moving along the critical path to the deadline was to be given to them by all other employees, who wore a green "How can I help?" button. The system respected no other authority lines. Everyone pitched in and the company met its deadline. As Barbara Slaighter, vice president for marketing, says about Sequent, "It's how we work together, not our technology, that will make or break us."

1. What kind of a manager is Casey Powell, theory X or theory Y? Why? Which of Herzberg's two-factor theory factors does his company emphasize?
2. How does Sequent's approach to management compare with that of the company where Powell previously worked?
3. Where in Maslow's hierarchy and in Herzberg's two-factor theory would you classify Sequent's putting computer terminals in employees' homes? Why?
4. How strong a pressure does the work group at Sequent place on individuals to conform to group norms? Do you think these norms represent positive or negative forces, so far as Sequent's goals are concerned? Why?

*SOURCE:* Susan Benner, "Culture Shock," *INC.*, August 1985, pp. 73–82.

## CHAPTER 16

# Human Resources
# Management

## Learning Objectives

*The purpose of this chapter is to show how the varied activities associated with personnel administration are essential to sound human resources management.*

*As evidence of general comprehension, after studying this chapter you should be able to:*

1. *Explain the objectives of human resources management and the role human resource managers play in it.*

2. *Describe the process of human resources planning and work force estimating.*

3. *Outline the sequence of the employment process and explain the role of recruitment, selection, and orientation.*

4. *Identify the principal methods used in employee training and management development.*

5. *Understand the purpose of personnel records and distinguish among transfers, promotions, and separations; and describe management's approach to accident prevention and health protection.*

6. *Explain how pay rates are determined and differentiate between the basic compensation plans.*

7. *Outline some of the more common employee benefit plans and evaluate their cost to and impact on business in general.*

*If your class is using SSweetco: Business Model and Activity File, see Chapter 16 in that book after you complete this chapter. There you will find exercises and activities to help you apply your learning to typical business situations.*

# 1 HUMAN RESOURCES MANAGEMENT

is concerned with

obtaining

and

maintaining

the most effective work force

# 2 HUMAN RESOURCES PLANNING

makes plans for future employee requirements in terms of

Size

Quality

# 3 THE EMPLOYMENT PROCESS

establishes procedures for

Recruitment

Selection

Orientation

# 4 EMPLOYEE DEVELOPMENT

focuses on

Training

Development

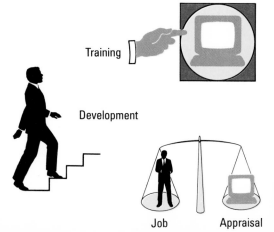

Job          Appraisal

# 5 PERSONNEL ADMINISTRATION

maintains personnel records

Job changes

| S | M | T | W | T | F | S |
|---|---|---|---|---|---|---|
|   | X |   | X | X |   |   |
|   |   | X | X | X | X |   |
|   |   |   |   |   |   |   |
|   |   |   |   |   |   |   |

Attendance

monitors safety and health programs

OSHA OK

# 6 COMPENSATION PROGRAMS

provide financial rewards.

A.B.C. COMPANY PAYROLL

Job evaluation

Job pricing

Compensation systems

Legal compliance (wages, hours, EEO)

# 7 EMPLOYEE BENEFITS

add significantly to compensation.

Group life
and health insurance
Pensions
and profit sharing
Nonfinancial
benefits and services

# BALANCING PART-TIME AND FULL-TIME EMPLOYMENT

*At tiny LyphoMed Inc. in Chicago, human resources director Edward Khamis tries to avoid layoffs of the company's permanent employees. To do so, he hires 35 or more temporary workers to handle the surges in the company's production requirements. When business for this pharmaceutical manufacturer slackens off, Khamis can let the part-time workers go with little regret. At large-sized Packard Electric Division of General Motors Corp. in Warren, Ohio, the company promises its 8,900 full-time employees jobs for life. When production schedules go up, GM fills the open positions with part-time employees, up to a limit of 10 percent of the total permanent work force. After that, if production requires it, the company fills the jobs with permanent employees. Why do companies handle employment this way? It's a reflection of their concern for human resources management. Full-time employees represent a long-term, and often expensive, commitment on a company's part. As a consequence, it makes economic sense to hold down the level of permanent employees. In return, most companies will extend great care in recruiting, selecting, and training these employees. A company will also be prepared to pay better wages and provide more side benefits for these employees than for those who are hired mainly to fill temporary gaps during production peaks or vacation periods.*

*While the practice of making a distinction between permanent and part-time or temporary help is not new, the use of this technique in human resources planning and management has been growing. Roughly 20 percent of the United States work force, or 12 million employees, are affected by it. Many workers, of course, seek part-time or temporary employment as a convenience or to accommodate their choice of life-style. Many others are part-time employees not by their own choice. Involuntary part-timers made up 4.1 percent of the workforce in 1976; today their numbers are up to 5.5 percent. It is evident that businesses increasingly make a conscious decision about this phase of human resources management. They are concerned with not only the surface economies involved but also the long-term effect such employment practices have on their total work force, permanent and temporary. Will, for example, full-time employees relax because their jobs are assured? Are part-time employees likely to be less motivated and more careless about their work because*

*the company has made no long-term commitment to them? How should pay scales and benefit programs be proportioned between the two kinds of employees? These and many other questions must be resolved in deciding upon such a personnel policy.*

*The emerging profession of human resources management plays a prominent role in such decisions. Human resources, as indicated in earlier chapters, account for a significant portion of the cost of doing business. This figure is pegged at anywhere from 20 to 80 percent of all expenses, according to the nature of a business's operation. Furthermore, the quality of a firm's human resources, not just its quantity or cost, is a pivotal element in a company's strategy. A first-rate work force can contribute unique competitive advantages. On the other hand, if flawed or poorly managed, a company's work force can become a fatal weakness.*

---

SOURCE: *Deborah C. Wise and Alice Z. Cuneo, "Part-Time Workers: Rising Numbers, Rising Discord,"* Business Week, *April 1985, pp. 62–63.*

---

# 1 HUMAN RESOURCES MANAGEMENT
## *Making the most effective use of people*

As seen in Chapter 6, the way in which a business organizes internally greatly affects the jobs that people are required to do and how well they do them. As the awareness of the value of the human contribution to profits has intensified, so too has the need grown for managing these human resources wisely.

**Human resources management** is the function that is concerned with obtaining and maintaining an employee work force that is most appropriate in size and quality for a business's internal organization structure. Every manager, regardless of his or her particular specialty, is concerned with this responsibility. Nevertheless, this task is so pervasive and vital to an organization that a special type of manager has evolved to coordinate human resources management. This manager may actually be called a **human resources manager** (or a personnel administrator or personnel director).

## RELATIONSHIP TO LINE MANAGEMENT
### *Service, advice, and control* ━━━━━━━━━━━━━━━

Robert Townsend, the former president of Avis Rent-A-Car Company, once recommended that executives should "fire the whole personnel department." He was emphasizing the point that the responsibility for people management belongs to every manager, not just to those who specialize in human resources management. This is true, but it fails to recognize that every manager also needs help in this area. There are innumerable details to take care of (like placing advertisements in newspapers for help) and records to keep (about promotions and pay, sicknesses and accidents, for example). There is also the need for expertise in finding new ways to motivate, train, and counsel employees. Human resources managers are the experts in these matters. Accordingly, their role in relation to other managers in a business is threefold:

■ *They provide specialized services to assist other managers as they engage in human resources management.* Personnel managers take care of recruiting and screening new employees and placing them on the payroll. They may provide training and development for these employees. The personnel department will certainly maintain the legal records of attendance, illness, accidents, compensation, and the like. Other managers may intervene in this process, such as making final decisions about whom to hire and whom to promote, but they will expect the specialist to provide assistance and prepare the paperwork.

■ *They offer informed advice in their specialized function.* Because they devote their entire efforts toward a concern for the effectiveness of people, human resources managers are especially helpful in advising other managers about motivational or disciplinary problems. They provide objectivity when personality problems arise. They can do so because they may know what is happening broadly throughout an entire company rather than focusing on the operation of a single department, as so many other managers are required to do.

■ *They exercise control over certain activities in order to ensure consistency in a company's human resources management.* A personnel department must make certain that all managers conform to legal requirements of hiring, promoting, training, compensating, and the like. It must also establish companywide procedures so that there is genuine equity in dealing with employee concerns and compensation matters. Line managers often feel that these controls are restrictive. This leads to the attitude characterized by Robert Townsend when he advises firing the personnel department. Without such controls, however, most companies would not be able to live up to their legal obligations or obtain optimum performance from their human resources.

## FUNCTIONS OF PERSONNEL DEPARTMENTS
*Numerous and varied* ━━━━━━━━━━━━━━━━━━━━━━━━━━

Over the years, the functions performed by personnel departments have grown in number and variety, as illustrated in Figure 16-1. Not every personnel department performs them all. Sometimes, the responsibilities are split between departments. In general, however, human resources managers will have responsibility for the following functions:

■ Work force planning, which is concerned with the number of employees and their performance capabilities and potential
■ The employment process, including recruitment, selection, and placement of new employees
■ Training and development of all employees, incumbents as well as new ones, blue-collar and white-collar, nonmanagerial and managerial
■ Appraisal of employee and managerial performance in relation to training and development, pay, promotion, and discipline when necessary
■ Administration and control of personnel movement, including the coordination of and record keeping of job changes, illnesses, accidents, and compliance with job safety and health requirements

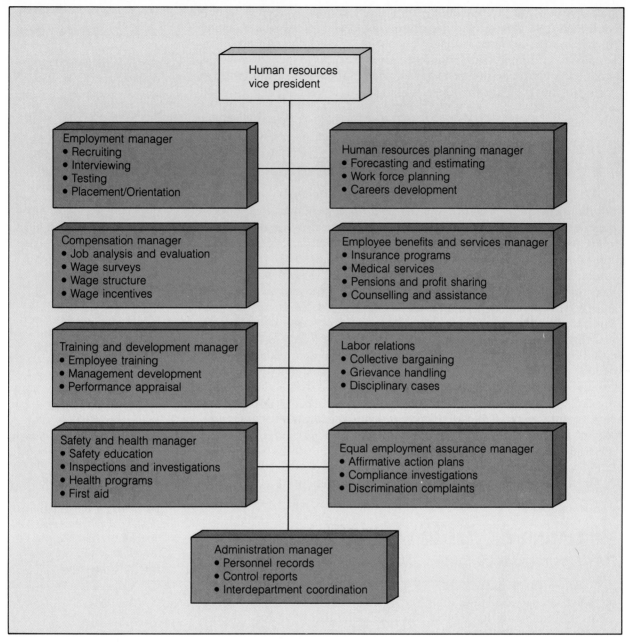

- Design and supervision of the financial reward systems, including compensation and employee benefit programs
- Relationships with labor unions, as discussed in Chapter 17

Figure 16-1 Typical jobs and functions in a human resources department.

## 2 HUMAN RESOURCES PLANNING
*Establishes size and nature of the work force*

A basic responsibility of human resources management is to estimate a company's personnel needs. The two most important features of this estimate are the number of employees needed and their characteristics or performance requirements. When a company divides its tasks and re-

sponsibilities, it establishes the qualifications and skills needed to perform each task. Based upon this division of labor (described in Chapter
6), the human resource manager can make a projection of how many
people will be required to perform each of these tasks to meet established
production and operation schedules. The combination of the two features provides the basis for hiring, training, and developing of personnel.

## QUALITIES NEEDED IN EMPLOYEES
### *Job analysis, job description, and job specification*

The rough division of labor used to design a company's internal organization structure is used as a starting point in determining the personal
qualities and skills needed to perform the jobs that must be filled. Each
job requires a different combination of physical, mental, creative, social,
and personal knowledge and skills. The determination of the specific
combination required for each job is accomplished through a systematic
study of the job's characteristics and activities. Such a study is called ***job
analysis.*** It is usually performed by a specialist who observes the job as
it is being performed and who also interviews the person doing the job
and that person's supervisor. The objective of the study is to find out
exactly what a person in a given job does and what qualifications are
needed to do that job. This information is summarized in a ***job description,*** which spells out the activities and responsibilities of each job and
the skills and other characteristics needed to do the job. A ***job specification*** is often used when actual hiring is done. It generally lists measurable information—years of schooling, length and type of experience,
physical characteristics, and others—that would most likely describe an
employee who would be suitable for a given job. Table 16-1 shows a
typical job description and job specification combined.

## ESTIMATING THE SIZE OF WORK FORCE
### *Planning around uncertainties*

Companywide plans usually include specific targets for the quantity
of goods and services to be produced. These can be used to make estimates of future work force needs. In a company that has been in operation for some time, it is possible to estimate fairly accurately how much
production can be expected from one person. With this information, the
number of staff members needed to meet production goals can be projected.

A number of complicating factors make these projections more difficult in practice. Employee illnesses and absences may vary from time to
time. The number of employees who leave work permanently and must
be replaced (called ***employee turnover***) should be considered. Promotions, dismissals, deaths, or retirements can all create openings and are
often difficult to plan for. Sometimes changes in procedures, equipment,
or products that are on the drawing board create uncertainty about personnel needs. Normal growth will usually be reflected in production
plans, but changing business conditions and unknown market factors can
make actual growth considerably different.

---

## *Action Brief*

### EQUAL OPPORTUNITY REPORT

*Affirmative action programs encouraged by the Equal Employment Opportunity Commission (EEOC) ask that a company put its good intentions into practice. Sears—the nationwide retailer, banker, and insurance company—felt that it was particularly vulnerable. After establishing a good record in employing minorities, however, it wanted to tell its story, not only to the EEOC but also to its stockholders and its public. Accordingly, Sears published figures showing that during the early 1980s, it had reduced its work force by over 80,000 persons, or 20 percent. At the same time, the proportion of minorities in its work force rose from 19.9 to 23.5 percent. During the same period, it reduced the number of its officials and managers by 19,311 persons. In spite of this reduction, the proportion of women and minorities in this category rose to 42 percent.*

## TABLE 16-1
## SAMPLE JOB DESCRIPTION

*Position:* Shipping Clerk     *Department:* Shipping and Receiving     *Location:* "C" Building Warehouse

### JOB SUMMARY

Under general supervision of warehouse manager, processes shipments to customers in accordance with shipment authorization forms forwarded by the sales department. Together with other clerks and packers, removes goods from shelves by hand or by powered equipment and packs them in containers for shipment by truck, rail, air, or parcel post. Prepares and processes appropriate paperwork and maintains related files.

### EDUCATION

High school graduate.

### EXPERIENCE

None required.

### DUTIES PERFORMED

1. The following represent 70 percent of working time:
   a. Removing stock from shelves and racks and packing into proper shipping containers
   b. Weighing and labeling cartons for shipment by carrier designated on the shipping order.
   c. Assisting in loading carriers.
2. The following represent 15 percent of working time:
   a. Preparing and/or processing authorization forms (e.g., packing lists, shipping orders, and bills of lading).
   b. Maintaining shipment records by tally sheets or keypunch.
   c. Doing miscellaneous typing of forms and labels.
   d. Maintaining appropriate files.
3. The following represent the balance of working time:
   a. Driving company truck to post office or for an occasional local delivery.
   b. Assisting in taking inventory.
   c. Acting as checker for other shipping or receiving clerks.
   d. Keeping workplace clean and orderly.

### SUPERVISION RECEIVED

Except for general instructions and special problems, works mostly on his or her own.

### RELATIONSHIPS

Works in close contact with packers, material handlers, and other clerks. Has contact with truck drivers when loading. Has occasional contact with order department personnel.

### EQUIPMENT

Operates mechanized stockpicker, powered conveyor belts, carton sealing machinery, keypunch recorder, and typewriter.

### WORKING CONDITIONS

Clean, well-lit, and heated. Requires normal standing, walking, climbing, and lifting. Subject to drafts when shipping doors are open.

For an example of how an electronics firm forecasts its human resources needs, see Table 16-2. It begins with (column A) a list of existing position categories and the present number of staff incumbents. It adds to that list (column B) all the new jobs that will be created to fulfill growth plans as well as anticipated cutbacks to provide a picture (column C) of the future staff. An estimate is then made of how many of the present job

**TABLE 16-2**
**HUMAN RESOURCES PLANNING**

| Components Division | A | B | C | Forecast Period Jan.–Dec. | | | G |
|---|---|---|---|---|---|---|---|
| | | | | D | E | F | |
| POSITION CATEGORIES | PRESENT STAFF JAN. | PLANNED CHANGES, GROWTH AND CUTBACKS | FUTURE STAFF DEC. | ATTRITION* | | | NET OPENINGS |
| Managers | | | | | | | |
|   Operations | 30 | +10 | 40 | +3 | +1 | +2 | +16 |
|   Sales | 10 | 0 | 10 | +1 | 0 | +1 | +2 |
|   Other | 20 | +5 | 25 | +1 | +1 | +2 | +9 |
| Engineers | 20 | −5 | 15 | 0 | +3 | +2 | 0 |
| Technicians | 40 | +10 | 50 | 0 | +2 | +2 | +14 |
| Clerical | 80 | −10 | 70 | +5 | +5 | +3 | +3 |
| Hourly, skilled | 300 | +50 | 350 | +20 | +13 | +13 | +96 |
| Hourly, other | 500 | +90 | 590 | +20 | +40 | +25 | +175 |
| Total | 1,000 | +150 | 1,150 | +50 | +65 | +50 | +315 |

*Attrition = **Column D** (promotions and transfers) + **Column E** (unplanned outs) + **Column F** (planned retirements).
**Columns A + B = C** Future staff size in December.
**Columns B + D + E + F = G** Net openings to be filled between January and December.

incumbents will leave for one reason or another, including (column D) promotions and transfers from that location, plus (column E) unplanned quits and discharges, plus (column F) planned retirements. The total number of open positions predicted for the future (column G) will simply be the sum of those needed for growth plus those needed to replace employees who leave.

Work force estimating is made more difficult by the trend toward using part-time employees, as described in the opening section of this chapter. A U.S. Department of Labor study, for instance, showed that temporary workers are engaged in productive work 90 percent of the time, while permanent employees only 65 to 80 percent of the time. Part of this difference is caused by peaks and valleys in the work load of a business. Permanent employees report for work even in slack time; temporary employees are hired only during busy periods of the year. Another related factor involves flexitime schedules (described in Chapter 15) and the desire of many creative and professionally qualified people to vary their hours from a traditional fixed workweek.

## LEGAL INFLUENCES ON WORK FORCE PLANNING
*Equal employment opportunity is a major factor*

Numerous laws and federal executive orders may affect a business's work force planning. Most federal laws to eliminate discrimination are administered by the Equal Employment Opportunity Commission (EEOC). In general, the regulations bar employers from failing to hire or promote because of sex, age, race, religious beliefs, or other similar reasons. Job specifications regarding age, sex, and other characteristics, as well as questions asked during recruiting interviews, are restricted to those that can be demonstrated to be undeniably relevant to job performance. This legal requirement is called a **bona fide occupational qualification (BFOQ).**

Differences in salaries paid for equal work are also against the law. The regulations normally apply to companies with 15 or more employees, to most public institutions, such as local governments, to most labor unions, and to organizations with federal grants or contracts. Some organizations may be required to have **affirmative action plans** that not only rule out discrimination but also spell out positive steps to increase the hiring and promotion of minorities and other groups.

In an attempt to offset years of discrimination in employment that affected minorities, especially blacks and women, the EEOC occasionally seeks to have employers agree to **employment quotas.** These are usually based upon population makeup in the surrounding community. If, for example, 25 percent of the community is black, the quota target might be for a company to employ 25 percent blacks. Another aspect of the quota concept is that minorities should also be proportionately distributed throughout the range of jobs within a company. If, for example, 75 of the positions are at the management level and one-third of all employees are women, then the company is asked to try to see that 25 of the management jobs are filled by women. As companies try to conform to this concept, they often are subject to charges of "reverse discrimination." That is, white candidates may feel that they are being excluded in favor of blacks. Or men believe that they are unfairly passed over for promotions in order to place women in jobs where their representation is not proportional.

# 3 MANAGING THE EMPLOYMENT PROCESS
## Creating an effective work force

Businesses need systematic procedures for recruiting, selecting, hiring, and orienting new employees if personnel plans are to be met.

## RECRUITING
### Searching for the best candidates

When jobs are open, most organizations look first to their current employees to find possible candidates. Promoting someone from within to fill a vacancy has important advantages. A present employee will already be familiar with company operations and will usually need less orientation and training. The work habits, interests, and abilities of a current employee will also be well known to management. Promoting from within improves morale: workers will see that it is possible to progress in their work and will often remain more loyal to their employers. Moving a current employee into an opening also saves the time and expense of recruiting from outside the company.

---

## Action Brief

### RECRUITING BIRDS FROM THE SAME FLOCK

*"Birds of a feather flock together" is a time-tested and ornithologically accurate adage. Many employers believe that the same principle should be applied when recruiting new employees. "Before placing a want ad or calling an employment agency," says human resources consultant Andrew Sherwood, "encourage your own employees to recruit for you." Employee referrals result in better candidates, he says. Good employees will generally know and refer well-qualified applicants, and employees usually have a better feel for the skills requirements of open positions than employment people. Such word-of-mouth recruiting is a time-tested technique. Its major drawback is that it tends to build a bias in favor of present employees and makes it difficult for true outsiders to enter a company and feel comfortable.*

In many cases, however, no current employee is really suitable for a position that is open. Organizations then are compelled to go outside to find candidates with the combination of skills, training, and experience the position requires. A variety of recruitment practices are commonly used:

■ Private or state employment agencies maintain records of many people who are seeking work. These agencies can do preliminary screening and refer candidates to the hiring company. Private agencies charge a fee to be paid by the employer or the employee. State agencies normally do not charge for their services.

■ Recruiting at colleges, universities, vocational schools, or trade schools has been successful for many companies. It is often possible to pick a candidate with exactly the training desired.

■ Most employers at some time must advertise in newspapers or in trade or professional association publications. These advertisements often draw a number of well-qualified candidates.

■ Many labor unions keep registers of members seeking work. In some fields, such as the construction trades, this is a major recruiting method.

■ Present managers or other employees will often be able to suggest friends or acquaintances for unfilled positions.

■ Most companies receive numerous unsolicited applications for employment. Some of these candidates may also be qualified for an opening.

Recruitment to fill managerial and certain professional vacancies may get special treatment. ***Executive recruiters*** (sometimes called "head-hunters") actively search for qualified individuals who are already employed successfully in similar positions elsewhere. This costly practice, however, is used only when the positions are critical to a company's success and the qualified candidates are scarce.

## SELECTION
*Picking the most suitable people* ━━━━━━━━━━━━━━━━━━

*Selection* is the process of picking the one candidate thought to best match the job specification and thought to be the most likely to succeed in the job. A thorough selection procedure will typically include application, testing, interviews, investigation, and physical examination:

■ A written *application* form is an effective selection tool. By asking all candidates to describe their job interests, training, work history, and other experience and to provide business or personal references, employers can eliminate applicants who are clearly unsuited for a particular opening.

■ *Testing* has a clear role in the selection process, but its use must be carefully controlled to avoid unfairness. Some employment tests are clearly relevant to a candidate's ability to perform on the job. Asking an applicant for an office clerk job to type a sample report or an auto mechanic to rebuild a carburetor is an example. Personality, motivation, or intelligence tests may also be useful to companies that have had wide experience with them. They have been particularly effective in selecting salespeople and managers. A frequent problem with these tests, however, is that they generally reflect the values and interests of white middle-class Americans and may unfairly penalize minorities who do not share that cultural background. For this reason, there is active pressure from many sources, including the EEOC, to validate the usefulness of tests before using them for selection purposes.

■ The face-to-face job *interview* remains a central part of the selection process for most employers. Careful interviewers can learn important information about a candidate's attitudes, experience, interests, and aspirations. A disadvantage of interviews is that irrelevant facts, such as a style of dress or personal bias, may interfere with objective evaluation. The potential for bias in a job interview (or in an application blank, for that matter) is so great that the EEOC either prevents or inhibits the asking of certain questions that might bring prejudice to bear on the applicant. Table 16-3 lists some of the questions that generally are avoided in order to ensure equal employment opportunities for all candidates.

---

**TABLE 16-3**
**WHAT ONE COMPANY TELLS ITS INTERVIEWERS**
**NOT TO ASK OF JOB APPLICANTS**

■ *Race or color.* Don't ask. Don't comment.
■ *Religion.* Don't ask. Don't say, "This is a (Catholic, Protestant, Jewish, or other) organization."
■ *National origin.* Don't ask. Don't comment.
■ *Sex.* Don't ask. Don't comment. Don't indicate prejudgment about physical capabilities.
■ *Age.* Don't ask age. Don't ask for a birth date. You *may* ask if the applicant is between the ages of 18 and 65.
■ *Marital status.* Don't ask for this, or for ages of children, or if (or where) a spouse works.
■ *Disability.* You may ask if the person has a present disability that will interfere with the job to be performed, but not about past disabilities or illnesses.
■ *Address.* You may ask for this and how long the person has lived there. You may ask if the applicant is an American citizen and, if not, whether the person has the legal right to remain permanently in the United States. It is generally unlawful to press for answers beyond this point.
■ *Criminal record.* You may ask if the person has ever been convicted of a crime and when and where it took place. You may *not* ask if the person has ever been arrested, nor can you deny employment on this basis unless it can be proved that this would damage the employer's business.
■ *Physical capabilities.* Don't ask how tall or strong an applicant is. This may imply a sexist prejudice. You may explain physical aspects of the job—such as lifting, pulling, and so forth—and show how it must be performed. You may also require a physical examination. The intent is that if the applicant has a clear opportunity to estimate the job's physical requirements, the application will be withdrawn if the job appears too demanding or beyond the person's capabilities. Legally, however, you may not make that decision during an interview.

Questions about *education* and *experience* are generally unrestricted. It is vitally important, however, that all questions asked bear an undeniable relevance to the job for which the applicant is a candidate.

■ Most companies carry out at least a brief *investigation* of the information given by the applicant. The investigator may contact past employers, former teachers, or other people who know the candidate. One goal of the investigation is to check the accuracy of the information given on the application and to uncover any facts that might point to future problems with the applicant, such as a poor attendance record or dishonesty. Great care is needed by investigators to treat the applicant fairly.

■ Many companies require a *physical examination* before hiring. One purpose of this is to eliminate candidates who may be disabled in the near future because of an existing health problem.

Selection of candidates for supervisory positions at the entry level of management is sometimes aided by an **assessment center** process. This method exposes a group of candidates to a number of exercises that enable them to demonstrate their skills (or lack of them) in getting along with others, communications, problem solving, and supervision. As the candidates engage in these activities, they are observed by other managers and behavioral scientists who make judgments about how the candidates approach their assignments. Applicants are rated according to ten or more characteristics of good supervision, and the selection is based on this rating.

## PLACEMENT AND ORIENTATION
*A supportive induction to the job*

The final step in the employment process is the assignment of the individual to an appropriate job and making sure that he or she starts off on the right foot. The personnel department must process the paperwork that puts the new employee on the payroll and introduce the newcomer to his or her supervisor and the employment procedures unique to the company. This is the time when rules and regulations must be made clear. The work required by the specific assignment must be detailed as well as the employee's limits of authority. An explanation of the procedures for reporting to work, calling in sick, eating lunch, getting paid, and other related matters helps to make the new employee more comfortable and feel more supported on the first day of the new job.

## 4  TRAINING AND DEVELOPING PERSONNEL
*Improvement of knowledge, skills, and attitudes*

One result of management's intensified interest in improving the effectiveness of employees is the emphasis on training. Many companies and other organizations, large and small, have formal programs to teach new employees specific job skills or to retrain present workers to use new technology. Oftentimes, managers are also aware of the skills needed in their own jobs and have established development programs to produce better managers, now and in the future.

## JOB TRAINING FOR EMPLOYEES
*From simulated to actual experience*

A number of approaches are used to teach specific job skills such as those used by production workers. Many kinds of work, such as machine operation and computer operation, can be effectively taught by the *vestibule method.* This training technique sets up a simulation of the work environment and allows trainees to perform the actual job activities in a classroom. To train a computer operator, for example, the actual console and equipment could be used for training. The student would receive simulated jobs to process and would be taught to use the equipment in the proper way. This method is useful when a large number of employees must be taught specific skills.

Actual *on-the-job training* is by far the most commonly used method for training employees in routine job competencies. This approach, widely used during World War II, was known as job instruction training (JIT). Hundreds of thousands of shop and office supervisors were shown how to use this method. They were given, as a reminder, a little card upon which the following four-step training procedure was listed (although with slightly different wording):

- Step 1: Prepare the worker to learn.
- Step 2: Demonstrate how the job should be done.
- Step 3: Try the worker out by letting him or her do the job.
- Step 4: Put the worker on his or her own gradually, and check back.

On-the-job training today follows much the same procedure. It takes advantage, of course, of modern technology such as audiocassette and videotape demonstrations. It still depends mainly, however, on the close attention of the employee's supervisor rather than on a professional trainer or instructor.

*Apprenticeship training* normally combines on-the-job training with classroom work, which covers the theoretical aspects of the job being taught. It is a very effective training method if adequate time and resources are committed to it. Straight classroom lecture and discussion training is useful when verbal information has considerable use on the job. All of these methods have been used successfully for retraining present employees as well as for training new workers.

**GOVERNMENT ASSISTANCE** Two areas of job training receive considerable attention from the federal and state governments. The first is the problem of providing job skills training for economically and/or culturally disadvantaged minorities. The second problem concerns the retraining of people whose jobs have been removed from their local communities or whose skills have become obsolete in the face of new technology. Many states provide skills training for both groups or make funds available to these individuals while undergoing training from private companies. The federal government makes funds available under the Job Training Partnership Act (JTPA). This program is administered by the Department of Labor and replaces the previous Comprehensive Employment and Training Act (CETA). Cooperating firms work with JTPA through private industry councils (PICs) in various states and local communities.

## SUPERVISOR AND MANAGEMENT DEVELOPMENT
*Insights and maturity are emphasized*

Many organizations have formal development programs that help managers perform their duties more effectively. *Management development* programs use a variety of techniques:

---

## Action Brief

### McTRAINING TO MAKE McMONEY

*The world's largest restaurant chain, McDonald's, also runs the world's largest chain of colleges. It operates 30 Hamburger Colleges around the United States, where thousands of eager candidates learn to become assistant managers at the local outlets. Emphasis is on company-specific training. "Just take care of that one hamburger," advises an instructor, for example, "and the rest will take care of itself." Or, consider pumpkin pie: it is cooked for 7 minutes, while cherry and apple pies require only 6 minutes. And how do you recognize that the fat in the fryer is going bad? It darkens in color, smokes excessively, and has slow, lazy bubbles. McDonald's makes no claim for the intellectual challenge of its Hamburger College courses. It does, however, say that its graduates will all know exactly where their next paychecks are coming from.*

■  Formal classroom training is often used, either at workshops or training sessions given by the company or at colleges and universities. These courses usually aim at teaching specific information and management techniques.

■  New methods requiring managers to act out various management roles in a training situation are widely used. This role playing helps managers develop greater sensitivity to human expectations and interactions in organizations.

■  Coaching in actual work situations is still the most common management development technique. Managers with more experience and responsibility usually make a conscious effort to advise, guide, and train younger managers.

■  Many companies give managers special assignments that will broaden their experience and skill. Some companies use job rotation, placing a manager trainee in a number of different jobs in succession to widen his or her experience. This can give the employee a broad perspective on company operations and, at the same time, teach many different management skills.

No matter which techniques are used, the goals of development programs are usually similar. They attempt to give managers the insight and maturity they need. They teach specific techniques of administration and organization. They try to provide thorough technical skills and knowledge in a manager's particular area of concern.

## PERFORMANCE APPRAISALS
*In transition from subjective to objective judgments* ━━━━━━━

An important managerial and supervisory function is judging the quality of the work of others in order to maintain general productivity at as high a level as possible. ***Performance appraisals*** of subordinates are used in decisions about salary increases, training, promotions, assignment changes, and dismissals.

Most performance appraisals are guided by a form that lists several criteria against which the employee's performance will be judged. These criteria lend themselves to either objective or subjective judgments.

Objective judgments are those that can be readily counted or measured, like quantity of work output, work quality in terms of the number of errors made, and attendance in days absent or late. These judgments stress the results of an employee's efforts. When properly established, objective criteria also relate clearly to the company's goals and the extent to which an employee contributes toward their attainment.

Subjective criteria—no matter how important they may be—are difficult to describe and to measure. They suffer from distortions in human perceptions and from prejudice. As a consequence, the trend in business is toward appraisal criteria that are increasingly objective.

There are many variations of appraisal forms. Many of them include some sort of scoring system to simplify the summary of an employee's overall performance rating. Many such scoring systems also employ a *forced choice technique*. That is, the form lists a number of alternative gradings (such as unsatisfactory, acceptable, good, excellent, or superior). The appraiser is forced to choose the term or phrase that best describes the employee's performance in that category. Table 16-4 illustrates a

**TABLE 16-4**
**EXAMPLE OF A FORCED CHOICE PERFORMANCE APPRAISAL FORM**

Describe the employee's personal characteristics. Which is most (**M**) and least (**L**) characteristic of the employee?

| *Group 1 Statements* | | |
|---|---|---|
| a. Always criticizes, never praises. | M | L |
| b. Carries out orders by passing the buck. | M | L |
| c. Knows the job and performs it well. | M | L |
| d. Plays no favorites. | M | L |
| *Group 2 Statements* | | |
| a. Commands respect by his or her actions. | M | L |
| b. Cool-headed. | M | L |
| c. Indifferent. | M | L |
| d. Overbearing. | M | L |

forced choice technique for rating aspects of an employee's personality. This particular form forces the appraiser to choose not only the most descriptive but also the least descriptive phrase.

Still another appraisal technique is the use of **critical incidents.** This approach was devised to encourage superiors to identify and record incidents in an employee's performance that represent either exceptionally good or poor examples of behavior. It has the advantage of citing specific examples in support of an appraisal judgment rather than a general impression. It has the weakness, so common to most appraisals, of depending mainly upon the memory, impressions, and judgments of the superior.

The performance appraisal, in one form or another, is widely used in business and thought by many authorities to be an effective tool of personnel management. There are many critics of performance appraisals, however, who do not believe that the techniques can be used without bias or in a nonthreatening manner. For this reason, perhaps, the way in which performance appraisals are designed and conducted by a business is subject to challenge by the EEOC.

# 5 ADMINISTRATIVE AND CONTROL PROCEDURES

*From record keeping to accident prevention*

The task of record keeping in personnel departments is enormous. In small companies as well as large, there is a continual movement of employees onto or off of the payroll and within the organization structure. Changes normally result from transfers and promotions within the company or from those who leave for a variety of reasons. Additionally, the human resources function must regularly examine actual practices within the company to make certain that established personnel policies and practices are adhered to. Many of these concerns have to do with attendance and compensation. A particular concern is shown for health and safety.

## RECORDING JOB CHANGES
### Lateral, upward, or outward moves

The three most common forms of job changes for people already on the payroll involve transfers, promotions, or separations.

A *transfer* is a lateral move from one job to another within the organization without a significant change in salary or in the amount of responsibility or authority. Transfers often result from changing company needs or to take better advantage of an employee's abilities or interests.

A change to a job at a higher level in an organization is a **promotion.** The employee who is promoted is given more responsibility and authority and usually receives a higher salary. Progressive companies try to tie promotions in closely with their performance appraisal system. Provision is often made in the appraisals to evaluate an employee's suitability for promotion. Evaluations based on merit are sometimes combined with, or replaced by, evaluations based on length of service with the firm or in a particular position. This basis for promotion or for salary increases is called **seniority.**

A **separation** occurs when a worker leaves a company. **Layoffs** are temporary separations. These occur when a certain number of employees are told not to report to work because the company wishes to reduce production because of declining demand. When sales increase, workers who have been laid off are given priority for rehiring.

*Terminations* are permanent separations from a firm. Voluntary termination has many causes. Workers may decide to leave a job expecting higher salaries, faster advancement, or greater benefits elsewhere. They may have lost interest in their present job or may have decided to change careers altogether. Each year, thousands of workers resign voluntarily. Involuntary terminations also have various causes. Workers may have to be permanently let go if part of a business fails or if new procedures or products eliminate certain jobs. Poor attendance, dishonesty, or poor work performance may cause workers to be dismissed.

## MONITORING ATTENDANCE AND APPRAISALS
### Indicators of performance and possible discipline

It is traditional that blue-collar employees punch time clocks when they report to work to record their attendance. The attendance of white-collar employees is often simply noted by their supervisors, or is maintained by the employee on a personal attendance sheet. These time cards and personal records become the basis for their pay. In addition, many personnel departments maintain copies of these records as a continuing indicator of an employee's absences and tardiness. When these exceed certain minimums, the personnel department alerts the employee's supervisor. The supervisor then discusses this problem with the employee and often issues a warning of the consequences if unsatisfactory attendance persists.

---

## Action Brief

### WHO WORKS OVERTIME?

When employees work overtime, it reduces the total number of people needed to get the work done. Employees who are paid for working overtime sometimes look forward to it. Others, who do not receive additional pay for overtime, don't particularly like it. What kinds of workers put in the most overtime, that is, over 40 hours a week? Salespeople top the list: 46 percent work more than 40 hours. Many of them do not get paid extra. Professionals and managers come next with 41 percent working overtime. They usually don't get paid extra either. Some 33 percent of craft workers and group leaders work overtime, and most of them get paid for this. Only 17 percent of all clerical workers work more than 40 hours a week, but most of them get paid extra when they do.

Many companies also maintain in each employee's personal file a record of the employee's performance appraisal. These appraisal records may be used, if necessary, to support terminations as well as promotions. In the case of termination, the performance appraisal is one of several documents needed to substantiate legally the decision of the company to exercise the disciplinary action.

# ENSURING SAFETY AND HEALTH
## *For economic as well as legal reasons* ━━━━━━━━━━━━

The provision of safe working conditions and the protection of employees' health are prime concerns of human resources management. These are important legal considerations, but their value goes far beyond compliance with the law. Careful safety and health management also helps to reduce insurance costs, protect against liability losses, and attract better workers. Reducing injuries and damage to health usually requires a formal management effort. Collecting information and devising solutions cost money. The expenditure is justified by a genuine regard for the welfare of workers. Profits can actually increase by avoiding the interruption of work and reducing insurance costs and liability claims.

**ACCIDENT PREVENTION** At the beginning of this century, work accidents took a tremendous toll in American industry. Today, work-related accidents are relatively infrequent. This is a direct consequence of enlightened business action taken to (1) design safer machinery and workplaces and (2) provide safety education programs for managers and employees. Human resources management plays a major role in these actions.

Before accidents can be prevented, their causes and the causes of the resulting injuries must be determined. A careful, long-term record of accidents and their causes is essential to creating a safe working environment. Similar records for other companies and for whole industries can usually be obtained from the government or from industry trade associations. This information, combined with a thorough analysis of operations, will suggest changes for safer workplaces. Many companies institute safety training programs for their employees, redesign machines, place guards over dangerous machine parts, require hard hats in areas where tools or materials may fall from above, start new traffic patterns, or change the whole layout of their operations to make them safer.

**HEALTH PROTECTION** For over a century, businesses took little responsibility for health hazards caused by exposure to dangerous contaminants in the work atmosphere or in the materials of manufacture. Today, the law has clearly shifted this responsibility to the business and its managers. The most notorious recent case involved the Johns Manville Corporation, where for nearly 50 years employees were exposed to the crippling and often killing effects of asbestos. Employee lawsuits against that company eventually forced it to resort to bankruptcy to protect itself. Many industrial environments present less obvious, more subtle hazards to employees' health. Dust, dirt, unsanitary washrooms, biological compounds, chemical fumes—and even noise—endanger health. Management must now apply the same prevention techniques it uses with accidents. It must locate the sources of potential health hazards and find ways to eliminate them or protect employees against them.

**OSHA STANDARDS** Since 1970, employers have been required by law to provide safe and sanitary working conditions. The *Occupational Safety and Health Administration (OSHA)* administers a complex set of safety and health standards. OSHA regulations apply to all workers except government employees and those covered by other safety laws. They are especially aimed at industries with high injury rates, such as roofing, metalworking, construction, mining, and manufacturing of wood products. Portable toilets seen at construction sites and the plastic bag placed in public wastebaskets are examples of OSHA requirements. So, too, are the warnings placed on stepladders, power lawn mowers, and portable gasoline cans.

OSHA requires businesses to avoid many specified work hazards and to take positive steps to create a safe workplace. Failure to comply can result in fines. Many businesses, especially small ones, have objected, stating that compliance is expensive and complex. As experience with the regulations increases, however, companies are finding affordable ways to meet the intent of the law: to protect the health and lives of their workers.

# 6  COMPENSATION PROGRAMS
*Wages and salaries form the basis of employee motivation*

Although for many people the rewards of working go beyond monetary values, salary and wages are extremely significant to most employees. They are especially important as a means of attracting and holding good workers. Only on this basis can other efforts to stimulate morale and motivate good performance be effective. Great care is therefore necessary in setting up and administering compensation programs. *Compensation* includes everything of monetary value that employees receive in return for work. It includes salary, wages, bonuses, and many other benefits.

## JOB EVALUATION
*Measures difficulty and importance* ▬▬▬▬▬▬▬▬▬▬▬▬

The basis of a rational compensation policy is often a formal *job evaluation.* By using existing job descriptions, personnel specialists are able to analyze every job to determine its responsibilities and its requirements for skills and training. These analyses are then used to rank jobs in order of their difficulty and their contribution to the objectives of the organization. The job levels thus established are then assigned a monetary pay range. Table 16-5 illustrates one approach to evaluating jobs using a scale of points for various job factors.

Like many human resources management techniques, job evaluation has its flaws, both technical and human. Because of the proliferation in some industries of jobs that were in the past evaluated as "men's" or "women's" or "black" or "white," job evaluation plan design and implementation are open to scrutiny by the EEOC.

An issue that continues to crop up regarding job evaluation and, ultimately, job pricing is the concept of *comparable worth.* This con-

## TABLE 16-5
## POINTS ASSIGNED TO FACTORS IN A JOB EVALUATION PLAN*

| Factor | First Degree | Second Degree | Third Degree | Fourth Degree | Fifth Degree |
|---|---|---|---|---|---|
| **Skill** | | | | | |
| Education | 14 | 28 | 42 | 56 | 70 |
| Experience | 22 | 44 | 66 | 88 | 110 |
| Initiative and ingenuity | 14 | 28 | 42 | 56 | 70 |
| **Effort** | | | | | |
| Physical demand | 10 | 20 | 30 | 40 | 50 |
| Mental or visual demand | 5 | 10 | 15 | 20 | 25 |
| **Responsibility** | | | | | |
| Equipment or process | 5 | 10 | 15 | 20 | 25 |
| Material or product | 5 | 10 | 15 | 20 | 25 |
| Safety of others | 5 | 10 | 15 | 20 | 25 |
| Work of others | 5 | . . . | 15 | . . . | 25 |
| **Job conditions** | | | | | |
| Working conditions | 10 | 20 | 30 | 40 | 50 |
| Unavoidable hazards | 5 | 10 | 15 | 20 | 25 |

*Points vary for each factor according to the degree of job demand for that factor. For example, if the physical effort required on a job is low, it may rate only 10 points (first degree), but if it is a very physically demanding job, it may rate 50 points (fifth degree).

cept tries to find a way of equating the worth to a company of, say, a truck driver and a secretary. Or it may try to compare the value of the work performed by a cafeteria employee with the value of the work performed by a garbage handler. Underlying the issue is that many jobs (like the secretary and the cafeteria worker) have been held traditionally by women, while other higher-paying jobs have traditionally been held by men. Advocates of comparable worth believe that this approach would eliminate discrimination in pay. Women, collectively, earn only 60 cents for every dollar earned by men. Those who oppose comparable worth insist that the concept would try to "compare oranges with potatoes" and that it is the marketplace that determines pay rates rather than any intent to discriminate.

## JOB PRICING
### Determines how much a job is worth ════════════

Setting the pay scale for each level and type of job is called *job pricing.* A number of factors combine to influence job pricing decisions. The general prices of goods and services have a double effect. A company that receives high prices for its goods and services is financially able to pay higher wages as long as sales remain good. High prices for consumer goods also cause workers to demand higher pay in order to maintain their standard of living.

Surveys of prevailing pay rates within an industry are almost always a strong influence on the salaries and wages paid by individual companies.

Variable production costs also affect a company's ability to pay wages. General economic conditions have the same kind of effect. Supply and demand in the labor market are important considerations. A skill that is in short supply will usually justify higher pay than one that is common among large numbers of workers. The existence of labor unions in a particular industry or company will influence pay rates. Collective bargaining by labor unions with management sets wage levels through negotiation. The effect of collective bargaining, in a particular company or in an entire industry, is thus a major consideration in setting pay scales.

# METHODS OF COMPENSATION
*From straight salary to incentives*

Compensation for work done by employees can be paid in one or more different ways:

■ A straight **salary** pays a set amount at regular intervals. Salaried workers are usually paid weekly, semimonthly, or monthly. Their pay is not based directly on the number of hours worked or on the amount produced. Management, white-collar, and professional employees are usually paid salaries.

■ Time **wages** are directly based on the amount of time worked within a pay period. Each wage position has a pay rate that is multiplied by the number of hours worked to calculate the amount to be paid. Time wages are usually paid blue-collar workers for production work and for direct labor jobs as in construction or mining.

■ **Piece rates** base pay on the number of units produced by an employee without regard to the number of hours worked. Piece rates are common in certain skilled and semiskilled manufacturing jobs, such as garment making. They are also commonly paid in conjunction with, or as a supplement to, wages. When this method is used, piece rates are called **wage incentives.**

■ **Bonuses** are often paid in addition to a regular wage or salary as compensation for outstanding performance or unusually high production. These extra payments are usually thought of as incentives for better performance.

■ **Commissions** are paid to certain kinds of workers, especially sales personnel, as a variation on piecework rates. Salespeople often receive a percentage of their gross sales as their pay. Pay is thus based directly on productivity. As an incentive, commissions are sometimes paid in addition to a regular salary.

**TWO-TIER SYSTEMS** Triggered by the recession years of the late 1970s, many firms established **two-tier compensation systems.** These systems generally specify that employees hired after a certain date will be paid less for the same kind of work than those already on the payroll. In 1984, more than 10 percent of all labor union contracts had such a provision. On average, the pay scales for new employees are 15 percent below those for incumbents. Typically, starting wages are considerably lower but catch up with existing pay scales eventually. Proponents claim that the two-tier system is realistic and enables many companies to remain profitable and to create more employment. Critics of the system say that it is, at best, only a stopgap measure and that it alienates workers.

# LEGAL REGULATION OF COMPENSATION
*Wages and Hours Law sets standards*

As with most other areas of management, legal restraints affect compensation programs. The most important is the requirement that no employee be paid less than a minimum wage established by state or federal law. The Federal Wages and Hours Law (Fair Labor Standards Act) requires most companies to adhere to established policies concerning overtime pay. According to this law, a higher wage rate (1 1/2 times the base hourly wage) must be paid for any hours over 40 worked in 1 week. The Walsh-Healy Public Contracts Act requires companies on government contracts to pay overtime for all work over 8 hours a day.

Additionally, the Equal Employment Opportunity Commission (EEOC) also watches over pay practices to ensure that they do not discriminate on the basis of age, sex, race, religion, or national origin. The Commission's board, when asked to rule on the issue of comparable worth in 1985, refused to accept this concept as a remedy for wage discrimination, however.

# 7 EMPLOYEE BENEFITS
*Add up to major employment costs*

Hard cash is usually only a portion of the financial reward that employees receive for their work. **Employee benefits** (sometimes called "fringe benefits") make up the balance of this reward. These benefits are things of value given to employees in addition to their pay. Benefits are often not paid in money, but may have some present or future monetary value. Employee benefits are an important form of payment for workers and an important source of expense for employers. Benefits often cost 30 to 40 percent or more of the amount paid for basic compensation.

# LIFE AND HEALTH INSURANCE
*Group insurance is an American way*

Among the most common benefits are life and health insurance. They are valuable because they protect workers from possible future losses. Employers normally are able to buy group policies and can provide high-quality insurance at a lower cost than is available to individual purchasers. Health insurance has the added benefit of encouraging employees to seek medical care early when they suspect illness. Without insurance, employees might put off checkups or treatment because of lack of money. This widespread practice contributes to better medical care for employees who are covered and may possibly result in a generally healthier population in the United States.

# PENSIONS AND PROFIT SHARING
*Supplement social security*

A **pension** is a payment made at regular intervals to a retired employee or, in some cases, to his or her family after the worker's death.

Payments are made from pension funds built up from regular contributions while the employee is working. Sometimes, the employer makes the entire contribution; sometimes it is shared by the employee.

*Profit sharing* is an increasingly popular benefit which distributes part of a company's profits to employees even when they do not share ownership in the company. Profit sharing is thought of as an incentive. If workers increase productivity, profits will usually rise and more will be available for sharing.

## OTHER BENEFITS
*From holidays to family picnics*

Supplementary unemployment benefits (SUBs) are important, especially in industries where layoffs are common. They pay a compensation in addition to unemployment insurance to help employees maintain their standard of living during a layoff.

A guaranteed annual wage (GAWs) is offered by some companies and is a popular union demand in contract negotiations. This offers almost complete protection for workers from layoffs as it provides a minimum salary or wage to be paid should a layoff occur.

Many other benefits are available in different combinations. These include sick-leave pay, recreation programs, company-paid doctors and nurses, credit unions, holidays, vacations, paid rest periods, severance pay, free meals, educational assistance to workers and their families, workers' compensation and unemployment insurance, parties and picnics, stock and bond purchase plans, discounts on purchases, and others.

Because the number of potential benefits seems inexhaustible, and their cost is so high, some companies offer a *cafeteria benefit plan.* Under such a system, the company establishes a maximum dollar figure for each employee. The employee can then choose from a number of available benefits until their cost matches the maximum.

# *Key Concepts*

1. Human resources are the most unique resource of most businesses. Accordingly, management must seek to obtain and maintain a workforce that is most appropriate to the firm's objectives. Human resources management is the concern of all managers, but it receives special attention from human resources managers who provide related services, advice, and controls in this area.

2. Human resources planning requires estimates of the number and kinds of employees that will be needed by a company in the future. Based on these estimates, plans are made for hiring and developing workers to meet those projected needs.

3. Managing the employment process requires procedures for recruiting and selecting employees and orienting them to their new work. A thorough selection process includes a written application, testing, one or more interviews, investigation, and a physical examination.

4. A variety of methods are used to train and develop workers and managers. Job instruction, on-the-job, and apprenticeship training are commonly used for rank-and-file employees. Most management development programs teach specific administration and organization techniques. Performance appraisals serve as guides for training and work improvement.

5. Personnel management provides record

keeping services and coordination procedures for:

(a) job changes, including transfers, promotions, and separations,

(b) attendance, and

(c) performance appraisals.

It also monitors safety and health programs in conformance to federal law. This is an important social concern, but it also lowers insurance rates, reduces work interruptions, and helps to avoid liability claims.

6. Compensation programs form the basis of employee motivation. Administrators evaluate jobs in order to rank them, assign monetary ranges, and decide on compensation methods for each type and level of job.

7. Employee benefits—including life and health insurance, pensions and profit sharing, vacations, educational assistance to workers, and many others—are an important source of reward to employees and a significant expense to business.

# *Review Questions*

1. Define, explain, or identify each of the following key terms and phrases, found on the pages indicated:

*affirmative action plans (p. 363)*
*apprenticeship training (p. 367)*
*assessment center (p. 366)*
*bona fide occupational qualifications (BFOQ) (p. 363)*
*bonus (p. 374)*
*cafeteria benefits plan (p. 376)*
*commission (p. 374)*
*comparable worth (p. 372)*
*compensation (p. 372)*
*critical incidents (p. 369)*
*employee benefits (p. 375)*
*employee turnover (p. 360)*
*employment quotas (p. 363)*
*executive recruiters (p. 364)*
*human resources management (p. 357)*
*human resources manager (p. 357)*
*job analysis (p. 360)*
*job description (p. 360)*
*job evaluation (p. 372)*
*job pricing (p. 373)*
*job specification (p. 360)*
*layoffs (p. 370)*
*management development (p. 367)*
*Occupational Safety and Health Administration (OSHA) (p. 372)*
*on-the-job training (p. 367)*
*pension (p. 375)*

*performance appraisals (p. 368)*
*piece rates (p. 374)*
*profit sharing (p. 376)*
*promotion (p. 370)*
*salary (p. 374)*
*seniority (p. 370)*
*separation (p. 370)*
*termination (p. 370)*
*transfer (p. 370)*
*two-tier compensation system (p. 374)*
*vestibule method (p. 367)*
*wages (p. 374)*
*wage incentive (p. 374)*

2. Explain the role of human resources managers in relation to other managers.

3. Describe the basic steps in estimating future work force needs.

4. What are some of the resources for recruiting new employees when openings exist?

5. How might employment quotas affect a company's selection decisions?

6. Distinguish between objective and subjective criteria for performance appraisal.

7. Define the three major kinds of job changes personnel departments must record.

8. Differentiate between job evaluation and job pricing.

9. In what ways would a two-tier compensation system affect wages paid by a company?

10. Name some of the benefits that workers may receive in addition to their wages or salaries.

# Case Critique 16-1
## ETP to the Job Rescue

ETP—not extraterrestrial, but Employment Training Panel of the State of California—succeeds where other government-supported training programs often fail. ETP focuses not on training of the hard-core unemployed but on retraining experienced workers for jobs in companies where they are already employed. Kim Trau is a good example. She had worked as an assembler on a low-skill job at Noel J. Brown Manufacturing, Inc. Then, a technological change in the way the company manufactures its electronic gear threatened Trau and other assemblers with a possibly permanent layoff. ETP granted the company $216,000 to train Trau and 39 other incumbent employees and 20 new ones in the higher-level skills now needed on the job. Trau upgraded her job level to electromechanical technician, where she now does drafting-board work and more advanced assembly than simple bench work. Not only has she retained her job, but her new skills also give her more occupational security in the West Coast high-tech area where she lives.

Bank of America automated many of its operations, and in the process closed down 130 branch offices. Ordinarily, this might have meant the end of jobs with B of A for 2,000 of its least-skilled workers. Instead, ETP came to the rescue by funding a $5 million training program to fit these employees with skills the bank still needed in its other branches. Similarly, displaced auto workers at Ford Motor Co. were retrained as microwave technicians and other electronic specialists and given jobs at Ford's nearby Aerospace & Communications Corp. The ETP program has also been used to upgrade the jobs of 1,400 salesclerks at Carter-Hawley Hale Stores, Inc. to help keep the stores competitive to prevent their closing down. The ETP program has even been used to train people who work in seasonal occupations, like agriculture and construction, for off-season employment elsewhere.

The ETP approach differs from other government retraining in that it targets exclusively on experienced workers who either are unemployed now or will soon be displaced. The program has a novel feature that assures retrained workers of a job at least temporarily. The company that hires and retrains the worker is reimbursed for training employees only after the job has lasted 90 days. Another obvious, but often ignored, aspect in the program is the choice of the type of training to be provided. Instead of retraining workers as welders, for example, simply because a vocational school happens to have a welding machine, the training chosen is specified by the company that gets the training grant. Employers can choose (1) the workers to be trained, (2) the kinds of skills to be trained for, and (3) the training site—either in-house or at a vocational school or community college.

1. How are the skills chosen for retraining? In what way does this differ from typical hard-core-unemployed training programs?
2. Even if Kim Trau's job with her present employer should disappear for some unexpected reason, how has the retraining helped improve her occupational security?
3. From the trainee's point of view, what are some major drawbacks in the ETP program?
4. How might this program be extended to include all kinds of people who need training or retraining?

SOURCE: Joan M. O'Connell and John Hoerr, "There Really Are Jobs After Retraining," *Business Week*, January 28, 1985, pp. 76–77.

# Case Critique 16-2
## The Appraisal Disagreement

Jack O'Connor was glaring at his boss, Mr. Plum. The two were in the midst of a semi-annual performance appraisal session. Jack, the assistant manager of a fast-food chain outlet, felt that his hard work was not sufficiently recognized. Mr. Plum was just as sure that Jack's work was anything but satisfactory.

"First of all," said Mr. Plum, "your job is to make sure that the deep-fry tanks are cleaned each night. You agree to that. But I've spot-checked them a half dozen times in the last 6 months and found that this is not being done with any degree of regularity."

"That's possible," said Jack, "but if you were to see how tired the fry crew is at the end of the shift, you'd not want to push them too hard on something that can be postponed occasionally."

"Second," said Mr. Plum, "the records clearly show that the so-called spoilage on the cherry pies has been running at 5 percent as compared with the specified 2 percent. You're responsible for seeing that these pies are not damaged or eaten by the staff."

"I can't keep track of everything," said Jack. "I'm working a 10-hour day, 6 days a week. I doubt if any of the assistant managers, here or in the other outlets, put in the time that I do."

"Hard work is commendable," said Mr. Plum, "and I give you a good rating for your efforts and dedication, but in the long run it is results that count. On 6 out of the 10 performance criteria set for your job, I can see something, touch something, or measure something that is below par. On the other 4 criteria, it's a matter of judgment as to how good you are. And even on these, you and I don't agree."

1. Upon what kinds of judgments of Jack's performance does Mr. Plum's appraisal depend?
2. Upon what kinds of criteria would Jack prefer to be appraised?
3. If you were Jack, what might you try to do to get more recognition from Mr. Plum for outstanding performance in the areas you think are important?

## CHAPTER 17

# Labor and Management Relations

## Learning Objectives

*The purpose of this chapter is to describe the role of labor-management relations and collective bargaining, and specifically to illustrate the occupational makeup of the labor force, describe briefly the history of organized labor and the different types of unions, explain the collective bargaining process, and discuss the principal legislative guidelines for labor-management relations.*

*As evidence of general comprehension, after studying this chapter, you should be able to:*

1. *Analyze occupational trends in the United States labor force.*

2. *Identify the main factors leading to the development of trade unionism in the United States.*

3. *Distinguish between the various types of labor unions.*

4. *Identify issues that are negotiable between management and labor and explain the collective bargaining process.*

5. *Recognize the principal bargaining tactics of labor and management and distinguish between mediation and arbitration.*

6. *Explain the main points of legislation affecting labor unions and employee rights.*

*If your class is using SSweetco: Business Model and Activity File, see Chapter 17 in that book after you complete this chapter. There you will find exercises and activities to help you apply your learning to typical business situations.*

## 1 MAKEUP OF THE LABOR FORCE

changes as business needs change:

More service and clerical workers
More skilled and professional workers
Fewer industrial and farm workers

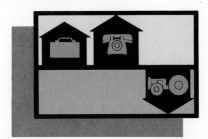

## 2 THE LABOR MOVEMENT

throughout its history, has attempted to satisfy employee needs:

Improved working conditions

Better wages

Job security

NO LAYOFFS

## 3 LABOR UNIONS

are classified according to type and structure:

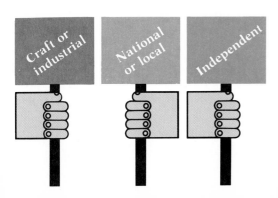

Craft or industrial

National or local

Independent

## 4 COLLECTIVE BARGAINING

addresses itself to these issues:

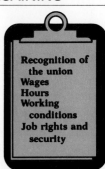

Recognition of the union
Wages
Hours
Working conditions
Job rights and security

## 5 LABOR DISPUTES

typically involve these tactics:

By union:
  Strike
  Slowdown
  Picket
  Boycott

By Management:
  Lockout
  Strike-breaking
  Injunction
  Lobbying

By Both:
  Grievance procedures
  Mediation
  Arbitration
  Government action

## 6 LANDMARKS OF LABOR-MANAGEMENT LEGISLATION

include these laws:

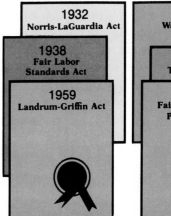

1932
Norris-LaGuardia Act

1935
Wagner Act

1938
Fair Labor Standards Act

1947
Taft-Hartley Act

1959
Landrum-Griffin Act

1968
Fair Employment Practices Act

# THE EBB AND FLOW OF UNION POWER

*The tide of affairs between organized labor on the one hand and management of businesses on the other ebbs and flows. During the early years of this century, labor unions were all but submerged by the powers granted to business. Then, just before World War II, an irresistible surge of public support swept the forces of labor into the dominant position. Beginning with the recessions of the late 1970s and early 1980s, the tide flowed back the other way.*

*Management gained the upper hand in negotiations. There is evidence now, however, that the powers of organized labor are beginning to well up once again. The unanswered question is not how strong the concerted forces of working men and women will be, but toward what objectives will these forces be directed?*

*In 1981*, U.S. News and World Report *featured an article entitled "Givebacks: Latest Twist in Union Bargaining." It cited the case of the United Auto Workers, which had just agreed to give back to the automakers pay hikes and other benefits that had been obtained through hard-won negotiations over a period of years. Said UAW president Douglas Fraser, "It's an enormous sacrifice, but when you're talking about the maintenance of thousands of jobs, what can you do? . . ."*

*It was obvious in the early 1980s that job security was a more important issue to union bargainers than wages and related benefits. Management spokespeople, like economist Audrey Freedman of the Conference Board, a business research corporation, were pleased. Freedman commented, "What we're seeing is a wonderful new responsiveness on the part of unions to the economic conditions around them." A more objective observer, Wayne Horvitz of the Federal Mediation and Conciliation Service, wasn't as convinced. He cautioned employers not to take union cooperation for granted. "Unions will not lie down and play dead," he said. And a spokesperson on the labor side, Curtis Brown of the United Rubber Workers, warned, "There's a fine line between being statesmanlike in negotiations and being namby-pamby."*

*Organized labor did not lie down and play dead nor was it namby-pamby for long, even though it was shaken by hard times in the heavy industries. By the spring of 1985, with the economy swinging upward, the top leaders of the largest labor organization, the AFL-CIO, met in Bal Harbor, Florida, to prepare for battle. "We want to start reclaiming what was ours," said William Wynn, president of the United Food and Commercial Workers. The new president of the United Auto Workers, Owen Bieber, echoed this warning. Speaking of the unions' plans to get back the "givebacks," he said, "We won't be deterred."*

*What accounts for the recent swings seen in the bargaining power of organized labor and management? The shift from a manufacturing-centered economy toward a service and information economy, which has so profoundly affected the makeup of the labor force, is a major contributing factor.*

---

SOURCES: *"Givebacks: Latest Twist in Union Bargaining,"* U.S. News and World Report, *October 26, 1981, pp. 73–74; Marilyn Adams, "Labor: Now It's Firms' Time to Give,"* USA Today, *February 22, 1985, p. B1.*

---

# 1  MAKEUP OF THE LABOR FORCE
## *More skilled, service, and white-collar workers*

Human labor is the most powerful resource that businesses possess. Like other resources, it has been exploited from time to time. The rise of the trade union movement, coupled with laws that protect labor's rights, has served to make today's management more enlightened in its treatment of this valued resource. At the same time, the makeup of the labor force changes constantly. Some occupations (like farm laborers) diminish in number and value while other new ones (like data processing, machine mechanics) are created and are in short supply. These changes in makeup of the labor force affect the role of labor unions and the way in which management and unions quarrel over their respective roles in dealing with employees.

Figure 17-1 illustrates four major changes that are taking place in the United States labor force today:

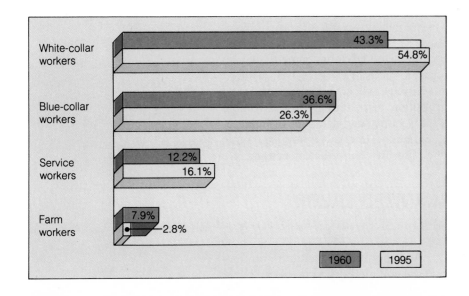

Figure 17-1 Occupational forecast by major kinds of employment.

■ The number of white-collar jobs has increased substantially in proportion to other jobs. These are generally more attractive, cleaner, and higher-paying jobs with more status. This group includes professional and technical workers (about 17 percent of all men and women), managers (15.4 percent of the men and 7.7 percent of the women), salespeople (about 6 percent of both men and women), and a great mass of clerical workers (16.3 percent of the men and 35.2 percent of the women).

■ The number of blue-collar jobs continues to decrease in proportion to other jobs. These are the traditional factory and industrial jobs represented by trade unions. So-called craft workers make up, for men, 21.2 percent of the labor force and for women, only 1.8 percent. The less-skilled operative jobs are populated by 16.5 percent of the men and 10.3 percent of the women. Blue-collar jobs also include a grouping of non-farm laborers, or 6.0 percent of men and 1.1 percent of women.

■ Service workers continue to increase in numbers and in their proportion to other workers. This reflects the growth of airlines (although this is moderating), fast-food establishments, office personnel, and computer-related service industries. The increase, at least up until 1980, is also partly due to the growth of government employment.

■ Farmers and farm workers have decreased in numbers to such an extent that agricultural production work is no longer an important source of employment. Farm work, as a percent of all employment, was at 7.9 percent in 1960, but it is forecast to drop to only 1.8 percent in 1990.

In general, more workers are employed in higher-level, more rewarding jobs than ever before. More and more of the undesirable, repetitive, and dangerous production jobs are now being performed by machines.

Projections of the makeup of the labor force in the near future show that this trend is likely to continue. The U.S. Department of Labor expects that workers will be needed most in industrial research and technology, educational and health services, and office "paperwork" jobs—all of which can be classified as skilled or white-collar positions.

Unemployment, however, remains a severe threat to job security for everyone. Some economists believe that because of basic changes in the economy, society must accept a higher level of unemployment than has been the case in the past. Unemployment continues to be especially severe for minorities and for young people. Despite government intervention in business cycles, layoffs and cutbacks are still a reality in many industries and promise to continue.

Against this economic backdrop, organized labor has come to play an important role in business. The economic status of workers in the United States today is the standard for most industrialized nations. Organized labor has made an important contribution to fostering these favorable conditions. Still, threats remain to the security and standard of living of workers. Unemployment, layoffs, inflation, and sweeping economic changes cause uncertainty and the desire for even greater security.

## 2  HISTORY OF U.S. ORGANIZED LABOR
### A struggle for recognition

When artisans during the Middle Ages performed the entire production process, from buying raw materials to selling finished products, there was virtually no distinction between labor and management. The establishment of the factory system during the Industrial Revolution changed all this. It created a clear separation between the people who owned the factories and the people who worked in them. At the same time, working conditions—which had been poor all along—grew even more unpleasant and dangerous. Workers had no security and received poor wages. Most owners regarded workers as simply another production expense, like iron or coal, and had no reservations about exploiting their employees.

These conditions led to the labor union movement. Long ago it was recognized that an individual worker could achieve very little by complaining about unfair conditions. If many workers banded together, however, they would have a strong voice. By withholding their labor, they could take away a basic necessity of production, forcing the factories to close and keeping the owners from making their profits.

The influence of labor unions has increased since the eighteenth century. Local craft unions flourished in the United States in the nineteenth century. The Knights of Labor, however, was the first national labor organization and had its greatest impact in the 1880s. The Knights of Labor was later succeeded in national importance by the American Federation of Labor (AFL), which was founded in 1881. The AFL continued to organize only skilled workers. The increase of mechanized production, however, created tens of thousands of unskilled jobs, most of them with no union representation. The Congress of Industrial Organizations (CIO) was created in the mid-1930s largely to organize these unskilled workers. The AFL and CIO continued their side-by-side growth until 1955. In that year, the two organizations merged to create a very strong union force. Independent national and local unions not associated with the AFL-CIO have also developed in many fields.

All union organizations have had the same aim: to increase the power, influence, and rewards of workers. They have pushed for higher wages, better hours and working conditions, job security, and protection from discrimination.

## UNION MEMBERSHIP
### A diminishing appeal

Labor unions do for their members collectively what they cannot accomplish separately. The power that an individual can bring to bear in an organization to assert his or her rights or to protect against discrimination is limited. Collectively, and given the legal status granted by an employer's recognition of the union, union members can approach management as equals. Membership in a union also offers social benefits, a sense of belonging to a respected organization. It provides an opportunity to fraternize with people who have similar interests and aggravations.

Despite some obvious advantages of joining a labor union, fewer than one out of five American workers belong. In fact, this percentage has been declining since its peak in the late 1950s. In 1970, 30.8 percent of all nonfarm workers belonged to unions; by 1980 this figure had dropped to 25.2 percent, and by 1985 it had dropped to about 20 percent. (See Figure 17-2.) There are several reasons for this decline. The most important may have been the steady decline of employment in the traditional blue-collar, goods-producing industries. This was the major stronghold of trade unionism. The growth of employment in the services industry did

## Action Brief
### BLACK LABOR

*In the beginning, blacks were either denied union membership or relegated to segregated units. Today, blacks make up about 15 percent of trade union membership, . . . Blacks, however, have not always been happy about the . . . quality of the advocacy provided by their unions. Perhaps for that reason, there are a dozen or more black employee associations (not labor unions) active today. Their emphasis is not on bargaining but on providing information and career guidance for members and opening up a direct dialogue with management. The Black Professional Organization (BPO), for example, is active at United Air Lines, where BPO's president says it gets support from the upper reaches of the company's hierarchy. At Bell Labs there are 14 chapters of ABLE (Association of Black Lab Employees). . . . Similar organizations are active at Equitable Life, CBS, and Xerox.*

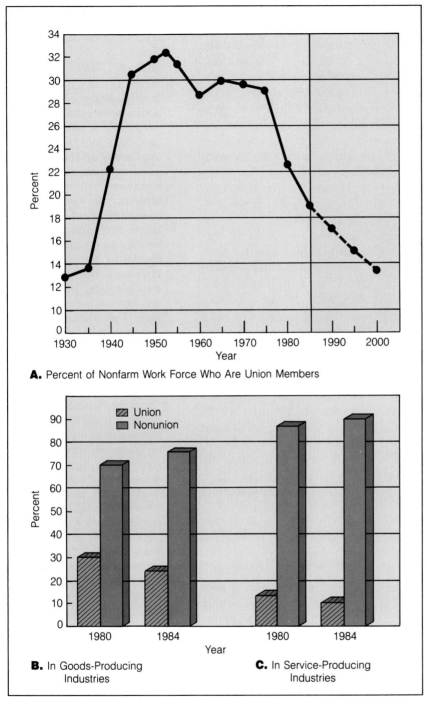

Figure 17-2 Trends in union membership.

**A.** Percent of Nonfarm Work Force Who Are Union Members

**B.** In Goods-Producing Industries

**C.** In Service-Producing Industries

not replace union losses elsewhere. (See parts B and C of Figure 17-2.) White-collar workers still tend to be largely unorganized. Other reasons for the decline in unionism cluster around the general improvement in wages and working conditions, a more enlightened management approach to dealing with employees and with union organizers, and the increase in protection provided individual workers by federal and state laws.

This is not to say that labor union membership has not grown in certain fields. It has. Between 1977 and 1980, for example, the number of white-collar union members grew from 7.3 to 8.5 million. The United States Bureau of Labor Statistics expects this figure to reach 9.5 million members by 1990. This growth has been in spite of the fact that white-collar workers tend to identify more closely with management than do blue-collar workers. Nearly 6 million public employees are union members. Some 65 percent of all supermarket chain employees are unionized as are 33 percent of grocery wholesaler warehouse personnel.

Union membership figures do not accurately represent the influence of organized labor. Many workers in unionized companies and industries receive the benefits of higher wages and better working conditions negotiated by labor unions, without being union members. Even in nonunionized companies and industries, management usually provides benefits that would probably not be offered were it not for organized labor. Knowledge of union gains elsewhere, or the threat of unionization of their own companies, induces management to more liberal practices.

# 3 TYPES OF LABOR UNIONS
## Size and extent predominate

The historical development of labor unions is still reflected in their organization today. Unions vary (1) as to whether they are organized by crafts or by industries, (2) in the extent and level of representation, and (3) as to whether they are independent or affiliated with the AFL-CIO.

## CRAFT AND INDUSTRIAL UNIONS
### Specialization versus conglomeration

Skilled workers were the first to organize. Many of their unions remain influential today. Unions like the United Brotherhood of Carpenters and Joiners of America are *craft unions.* They are organized according to the craft or skill performed by member workers, regardless of the kind of company or industry for which the work is done.

*Industrial unions* are organized around a particular industry, such as automobile manufacturing, steelworking, or coal production. In theory, all workers in the industry—skilled and unskilled and workers in every craft and trade—belong to the same union when it is organized this way. A few of the largest and best known are the United Steelworkers of America; the Transport Workers Union of America; the United Mine Workers; and the International Union of United Automobile, Aerospace and Agricultural Implement Workers of America (UAW).

## NATIONAL AND LOCAL UNIONS
### Power stems from the grass roots

*Local unions* are the foundation of organized labor. They are made up of craft workers in a restricted geographic area or of the industrial workers of one or more local plants. Some locals are independent and have as their only goal the representation of local workers. They have the complete authority and responsibility for negotiating local contracts. Other locals are parts of national or international unions.

*National unions* represent the interests of members all over the United States and even the world. They may be craft or industrial unions. The national organization gains its financing and authority from local unions. Some national unions are the primary bargaining agents for all member workers. They negotiate contracts for entire industries. Locals may then further negotiate local conditions. Other nationals operate mainly to assist locals, which retain the primary bargaining role. For example, the nationals may assist locals in their organizing efforts or in handling grievances.

## INDEPENDENT UNIONS
### They avoid the AFL-CIO

About three-quarters of the unions in the country are members of the AFL-CIO. Those that are not members are said to be *independent unions.* Some of the largest independents are the International Brotherhood of Teamsters, the United Auto Workers, the National Association of Government Employees, the United Electrical, Radio, and Machine Workers of America, and the United Mine Workers of America. The largest of these are the Teamsters and the Auto Workers, together representing about 3.25 million workers.

## 4   THE COLLECTIVE BARGAINING PROCESS
### Give-and-take between management and unions

Labor unions often provide many services to their members: job placement, training, day-care for children, and many others. Despite the importance of these, the essential role of the union is to carry on collective bargaining with management. *Collective bargaining* is a process of negotiation. It is "collective" because union negotiators represent all the member workers as a group. The issues that are negotiated revolve around the rights and responsibilities of labor and management.

## ISSUES FOR NEGOTIATION
### Recognition comes first, then wages, hours, working conditions, and job security

The first bargaining issue must always be the recognition of a union as an agent of the workers in a company or industry. Management, in general, does not encourage the organization of workers. Managers often delay and attempt to avoid recognizing unions. Initial goals sought by unions are the right to represent workers, the right to collect dues, the right to exchange information about union activities, and others. Once recognition is achieved, negotiations are aimed at four basic issues:

■   *Wages and wage policies*—Virtually every aspect of compensation is fair game for negotiation: pay rates for types and levels of jobs, determination of pay increases and promotions, payment of trainees and apprentices, benefits, pensions, and insurance. The two-tier compensation system, described in Chapter 16, represents the result of intensive bargaining over this fundamental issue.

---

## *Action Brief*
### SPREAD THE WORK!

That was the cry of union members at Bethlehem Steel Company's Sparrows Point plant in Maryland. They advised fellow workers not to accept overtime opportunities so long as other employees remained laid off. Observed one worker, "As long as people are on the street, it just isn't right." Said another laid-off worker, "It's cheaper for the company to pay overtime than hire someone back and pay Blue Cross and all the other benefits." The union-local official estimated that by working overtime, the company prevented the rehire of 500 employees. The company justified the practice by saying, "We don't want to break up crews that are working very efficiently on what are short-term projects, rather than long-range increases in production schedules."

- *Hours of work*—Shorter workweeks for the same pay are of obvious benefit to workers. In times of high unemployment, such changes may also put more people to work. With each worker putting in fewer hours, the work can be spread out over more employees.
- *Working conditions*—These include safety measures, plant temperatures, operating procedures, rest breaks, work rules, job assignments, and many other factors.
- *Job security and related rights*—Many union contracts (1) prohibit dismissal without good cause, (2) include controls over layoffs and rehiring, (3) specify how promotions will be decided, (4) spell out disciplinary procedures that may be used against workers, and (5) define a grievance procedure for workers who have been unfairly treated.

## ESTABLISHING THE BARGAINING PROCESS
*Union recognition is the most difficult step*

Historically, the most difficult and dangerous step in establishing the bargaining process has been gaining management's recognition of a union as a bargaining agent. In the past, the use of violence was common when union leaders were determined to represent workers, and company owners and managers were equally determined to keep the unions out. Armed battles actually erupted at Carnegie Steel's Homestead plant, at the Toledo Auto-Lite plant, and elsewhere.

Among the first important actions taken to prevent such hostility and violence were the government's recognition of the legality of unions and the establishment of the National Labor Relations Board (NLRB) in 1935. The NLRB supervises elections in which workers decide whether they wish to be represented by a union and, if so, by which one. If a majority of the workers vote for union representation, management is obliged to begin negotiations. The NLRB helps to establish the initial collective bargaining procedure.

## DEGREES OF UNION RECOGNITION
*Open, union, and agency shops*

One issue that arises early in negotiations is the extent to which the union is protected and its authority to impose membership on employees. Companies and industries vary in their degree of unionization:

- An **open shop** has no officially recognized union, although individual workers may belong to unions of their choice. In a true open shop, managers make no formal efforts to avoid unionization. Workers are free to make their own choices.
- A **union shop** requires all employees to join a recognized union by a specified time after they have been hired. They need not be members before being hired. A union shop gives considerable strength and security to union representation. A **closed shop** is an even stronger agreement—now outlawed—which forbids companies to hire employees who are not union members.
- An **agency shop** allows employees to belong to the recognized union if they choose, but they are not required to do so. However, all workers must pay union dues.

# B·I·L·L·B·O·A·R·D

## COOPERATION OR AVOIDANCE?

Leaders from all segments of American society, including many corporate executives, call for more employee cooperation at the workplace. They ask union leaders to support cooperative efforts and to moderate their wage demands. At the same time, however, businesses continue to try to avoid unionization. Even in firms with well-established labor unions, there is a shift in facilities investments away from union sites to nonunion locations. The government appears to take little action to prevent such avoidance. Why then, ask union leaders, should we cooperate?

As the threat of unionization lessens, many firms feel less motivated, or pressured, to make improvements and innovations in their relationships with employees. In the newer entrepreneurial firms, the potential for growth and advancement is so great at the start that employees do not look toward unions for support. But as firms grow older and competition in their industries intensifies, there is a need to hold labor costs down. Unless companies are innovative in this regard (finding ways to make employees more productive rather than holding wages down to keep labor costs down), employees have typically been hurt in their paychecks. It is then that union organizing campaigns have their greatest appeal.

### Why then, ask union leaders, should we cooperate?

In the meantime, there is a continuing erosion of unionized employment and membership. Under these circumstances, it is difficult to see how unions can continue to act cooperatively in an environment where their basic security is being threatened and undermined. In the face of the continuing trend on the part of management to avoid unionization, it seems only logical that union leaders will withhold their support for cooperation and innovation at the workplace. If that proves to be the case, there will be a return to the bitter confrontations that have characterized labor-management relations in the past.

### QUERIES

1. Should cooperation and innovation on the part of management and employees replace unionization in America?
2. Should the government prevent union avoidance on the part of business, imposing penalties on companies that shift their operations from union to nonunion locations?
3. Are adversarial relations between unions and management best for the nation in the long run? ∎

SOURCE: T. A. Kochan, R. B. McKersie, and H. C. Katz, "U.S. Industrial Relations in Transition," *Monthly Labor Review*, May 1985, pp. 28–29.

# PROFILE

**K**AREN NUSSBAUM is a new breed of union leader. She's founder and executive director of 9 to 5, the National Association of Working Women, an organization of more than 12,000 office workers, mostly women. She is also president of District 925, a national union affiliated with the Service Employees International Union (SEIU). Her local won bargaining rights for 50-plus workers after a stormy campaign which included a boycott. Nussbaum says, "This was a group of workers who organized primarily because of problems exacerbated by automation." She says that her union doesn't necessarily oppose office automation. Instead, "we quarrel with the way it is implemented." Her union contends that the trend in office automation is to deskill workers, increase the work load, and pay small wages. That may be typical union talk, but Nussbaum's 9 to 5 has led the "campaign for VDT safety." It lobbies vigorously for legislation to correct such problems as visual fatigue, muscle strain, and stress caused by visual display terminals (VDTs). "We see almost no movement on the part of management towards providing safety measures," says Nussbaum, "so

**KAREN NUSSBAUM**

we've chosen to go the legislative route. Management needs to be told what will be considered minimum standards." ∎

SOURCES: David L. Farkas, "White Collars With Union Labels," *Modern Office Technology*, May 1985, pp. 118–122; D. Pauly, A. Hughey, D. L. Gonzalez, and B. Cohn, "2001: A Union Odyssey," *Newsweek*, August 5, 1985, pp. 40–42.

# CONTRACT NEGOTIATION

*A labor contract is the outcome*

Once the extent of union representation has been established, collective bargaining focuses on negotiating and administering periodic **labor contracts.** These are written agreements between the union and company management specifying wages, worker and union rights, work conditions, management rights, and other provisions. A labor contract usually is in force for a period of 1, 2, or 3 years. At the end of the period, it may be renewed or renegotiated.

There are a number of steps in routine contract negotiations:

■ Union and management representatives gather information relevant to the issues likely to be discussed. This may include data on the general economy and surveys of other plants and working conditions.

■ Representatives meet to establish the rules that will govern the negotiation process.

■ Union negotiators usually present their demands for contract changes first.

■ Management studies labor's proposals and makes counterproposals. Table 17-1 illustrates some of the bargaining tactics used by management during negotiations.

■ In ensuing meetings, both sides argue in favor of their positions and negotiate a compromise agreement acceptable to both the union representatives and to management.

■ Union members then vote on the agreement. If they accept it, it is ratified and becomes effective. If they reject it, the negotiation process must begin again to try to draft a contract that they will approve.

# ADMINISTERING THE LABOR CONTRACT

*Grievance procedures provide relief*

Arriving at an acceptable labor contract is only the first step. For collective bargaining to be truly effective, the contract must be administered in a way that is fair to workers and to the company. In practice, this administration must result from a cooperative effort by the company's personnel and line managers (especially supervisors) and union officials and shop stewards.

The company supervisors who have direct contact with unionized employees are especially important. They must often make the final detailed interpretation of work rules and other matters in the actual work situation. **Work rules** refer generally to contract clauses that affect working conditions. Work rules involve procedures and precedents such as how many machines an operator may tend at one time or who among a list of employees will get the first choice of overtime.

The union shop steward has a similar role as an on-site union official. He or she must make the first moves in protecting workers' day-to-day interests. Cooperation between stewards and supervisors can often prevent disputes from breaking out.

When a dispute does occur, especially over unfair treatment of workers, a grievance procedure is set up. Most contracts spell out an orderly manner in which claims of ill-treatment can be appealed through various levels of union and company management until they are settled. This

## Action Brief

### TRAITORS TO THEIR CLASS?

*That's what liberal writer Jack London once called strikebreakers. Today, crossing a picket line no longer seems to hold that stigma. At least when Greyhound, Continental Airlines, Phelps Dodge, and Danly Machine Corp. employees were on strike, management found an abundance of jobless people or workers who wanted a better job and were willing to cross picket lines. The law permits a permanent replacement of strikers. Unions complain that this isn't consistent, since the law won't let a company fire an employee for striking but will allow a replacement. Union supporters believe that a better legal solution would be to permit a temporary replacement, who would only become permanent if the strike extended beyond a certain time limit.*

**TABLE 17-1**
**BARGAINING TIPS FROM A MANAGEMENT POINT OF VIEW**

1. Never give a false signal.

2. Never indicate you will consider a demand on which you do not intend to move.

3. Spend plenty of time listening.

4. Be sincere about your motives—do not attempt to conceal the fact that you are in business to make money.

5. Do not indicate you cannot afford their demand or cannot compete if a demand is given in to; unless you are willing to show your books or are sure they will not be demanded.

6. Do not index economic items on a percentage base; negotiate on fixed cost so that you can negotiate on the item in the future, and both company and union gain credit for improvements.

7. Do not indicate you will not negotiate on a subject unless you are sure that you have no legal duty to negotiate on it.

8. Let the union drop its demands gracefully.

9. Do not lose self-control or attack any member of the union committee personally.

10. Do not take or give abuse; adjourn the meeting until tempers have cooled.

11. Work from the company's language.

12. Make sessions last as long as is necessary to obtain satisfactory understanding.

*Source:* Paul W. Bockley, "Labor-Management Relations," in *Handbook for Professional Managers,* McGraw-Hill, New York, 1985, p. 461.

*grievance procedure* is meant to make sure that all complaints will receive a fair and full hearing. It is probably the single most important guarantee that collective bargaining will actually result in fair treatment of individual workers. Complaints and grievances are usually handled first at the shop steward–supervisor level. They then move up by designated steps to higher levels if their resolution continues to be unsatisfactory to the aggrieved party. Figure 17-3 illustrates the grievance procedure in a large corporation.

# 5 LABOR DISPUTES AND THEIR SETTLEMENT
*Both parties employ power tactics*

Labor disputes do occur, despite procedures and efforts to avoid them. The most likely time for unresolved disagreements to develop is

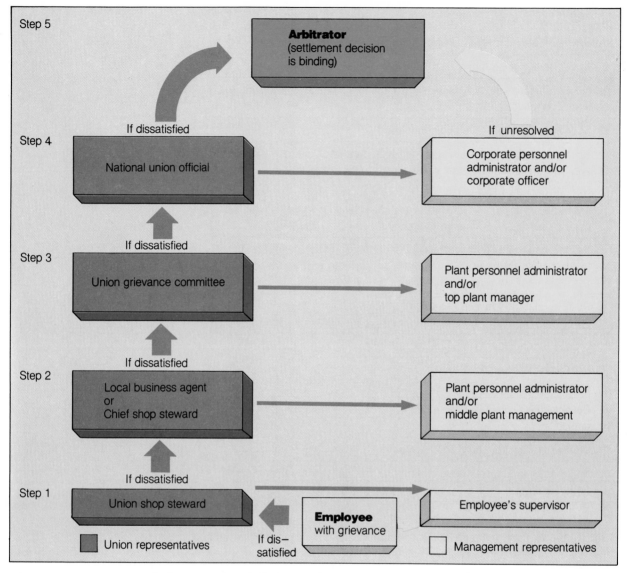

Figure 17-3 How the settlement level moves upward in a typical grievance procedure.

when new contracts are being negotiated. Labor and management are often unwilling or unable to reach compromises acceptable to both. Negotiations can be emotional and may lead to severe disputes. The day-to-day administration of contracts also can cause disputes that are not settled by organized, rational means. Unions and managers use a variety of tactics and strategies for furthering their own cause when disputes arise.

## UNION TACTICS

### *The strike is a union's ultimate weapon*

The methods most often used by unions to help achieve their goals are strikes, slowdowns, picketing, boycotts, and lobbying.

A **strike** attempts to force management to give in to union demands. Workers refuse to work and thus damage the company financially by shutting down production and cutting off income. Strikes are most effective when sales are highest and inventories lowest. Strikes may result from efforts to gain union recognition, from on-the-job grievances, from the breakdown of contract negotiations, from sympathy with other unions engaged in disputes, and from other causes. Recent historical data seems to indicate that unions are increasingly hesitant to resort to the strike weapon.

A work *slowdown* is another union method for exerting force on companies. Slowdowns have the same effects as strikes, except that production is reduced rather than completely stopped. Also, workers continue to be paid during a slowdown, unless employers take some action, such as a lockout, to stop wages.

*Picketing* is the practice of advertising a union's complaints against management by walking around with signs near the entrances of a company's facilities. Picketing usually accompanies strikes and may be used when major grievances remain unresolved. Picketing is effective because it helps publicize the union's position and because it may cut off services and supplies that the company needs or prevent it from shipping goods from its inventory.

A *boycott* is an organized refusal to buy the products of a company or industry. A large union with many members can sometimes significantly reduce a company's sales with a boycott.

Unions use lobbying in local, state, and national governments to protect their long-term interests. *Lobbying* is any effort by a group to influence legislators and government administrators to pass laws and interpret them to the advantage of that group. The use of Political Action Committee (PAC) funds has become an important source of lobbying strength for unions and management.

## MANAGEMENT TACTICS
*They depend upon a business's financial strength* ━━━━━━━

The chief methods management uses to combat union demands and to strengthen its position are lockouts, strikebreaking, injunctions, industry associations, and lobbying.

In a *lockout,* management refuses to allow workers into the plant to work. The company forces economic hardship on workers by cutting off wages. Lockouts can work only when the company is in a strong financial position and can endure a period of reduced or lost production. Lockouts have grown less common as a management tactic in recent years.

*Strikebreaking* is the practice of hiring replacement workers to continue production while union workers are on strike. This has been the cause of much violence in the past. As the Action Brief "Traitors to Their Class?" suggests, strikebreaking tactics seem on the rise.

*Court injunctions* can sometimes be obtained against strikes in industries that are critical to the national defense or welfare. These injunctions forbid workers to strike while negotiations continue.

*Industry associations* may help strengthen management's position by providing bargaining information, appealing to public opinion, and increasing companies' solidarity to offset that of the union.

Companies and industries also use lobbying to influence legislators to pass laws favorable to business and management. Lobbying has proved to be management's most effective tactic in the long run, as management is usually better able to subsidize lobbying efforts than unions. PAC funds, available to either side, seem to have equalized the power of this tactic.

### Action Brief

## BARGAINING WITH ABSENTEE OWNERS

*Union leaders who try to bargain with conglomerated hotel owners increasingly find it difficult to find the real decision makers. Instead, the negotiators sit down with local hotel managers who don't have authority to say yes or no. "We're dealing with corporate bookkeepers," said Domenic M. Bozzotto, president of Local 26 of the Hotel, Restaurant, Institutional Employees and Bartenders Union of the AFL-CIO. "Home office bookkeepers," says Bozzotto, "think 'if we cut back on a busboy, we can have the waiter do the busboy's work.' But then the waiter doesn't get back to the customer to suggest an appetizer or a dessert." Like many other union leaders in today's corporate world, Bozzotto claims that the union gets a runaround during negotiations. "The management company says, 'You have to talk with the owners,' and the owners say, 'You have to talk with the management company.'"*

# RECONCILIATION OF LABOR-MANAGEMENT DISPUTES
## *Outside parties intervene*

Often no compromise agreement can be reached because of the interplay of pressure tactics used by labor and management. Grievance procedures at the management level may be exhausted without an acceptable settlement. Contract negotiations may drag on for months without effective compromises. In these situations, two procedures are available to help bring about settlements: mediation and arbitration.

*Mediation* is a process in which a third party not directly involved in a dispute attempts to facilitate a settlement by clarifying issues, bringing in new information, and generally influencing the negotiators to compromise. Compliance with a mediator's suggestions is entirely voluntary.

*Arbitration* is similar, except that negotiating parties agree to be bound by the decisions of an arbitrator. Arbitrators may attempt to achieve a voluntary settlement but are empowered to impose a settlement. Many labor contracts specify that when an agreement cannot be reached in other ways, a dispute should be subject to arbitration.

In general, any person or agency acceptable to both sides may serve as a mediator or arbitrator. Some industries have industrial relations organizations to help in negotiations. Many state and city governments use effective mediation and arbitration boards. The Federal Mediation and Conciliation Service provides assistance with negotiating and can also provide mediators or arbitrators. The National Labor Relations Board also provides information and aid in the resolution of labor disputes, particularly when union representation is first being sought.

Labor unions also have disagreements among themselves. In such *jurisdictional disputes* they may differ as to which union has the right to represent a particular group of employees or which union's employees have the right to certain kinds of work. When jurisdictional disputes occur, labor unions have the same options as management in seeking relief or in using bargaining tactics. Often, however, management, employees, and the public are caught in between the adversary unions.

# 6 LANDMARKS OF LABOR-MANAGEMENT LEGISLATION
## *The law tries to equalize the distribution of power*

The important labor legislation enacted in the twentieth century evolved as a result of centuries of struggle. Up until the 1930s, court cases in labor-management disputes were regularly decided in favor of management. Since then, stronger feelings nationwide in favor of unions have resulted in legislation that has diverted the pro-management trend.

## MILESTONE LEGISLATION OF THE 1930s
### *Includes labor's "Magna Carta"*

The Norris-La Guardia Act, passed in 1932, sharply reduced the ease with which companies could get court injunctions to stop union activity. Up until that time, courts had been unfailingly cooperative in stopping strikes, picketing, and membership drives. This law gave considerable legal legitimacy to these activities.

The National Labor Relations Act of 1935 was hailed as labor's "Magna Carta," since it provided the legal foundation for the rights of unions and workers. This act, which is commonly called the Wagner Act after its main sponsor, (1) guaranteed the right to collective bargaining and union membership, (2) outlawed employer interference in labor organization and administration, (3) outlawed company discrimination against union members, (4) required companies to bargain with legally elected unions, and (5) created the National Labor Relations Board to administer the act. The Wagner Act was followed by the Fair Labor Standards Act of 1938, which deals in a general way with the rights of workers. It established the minimum wage, prohibited hiring children in certain occupations and circumstances, and required companies engaged in interstate commerce to pay higher wages for overtime work.

# LAWS LIMITING UNION POWER
*Prevent abuses by unions*

Many businesses and other interest groups believed that the legislation of the 1930s gave unions too much power. By the end of World War II, union membership had greatly increased. There were numerous strikes once the wartime restraints on wages were ended, and there were some unions that actually did abuse their freedom and power. Public sentiment moved somewhat away from unions and influenced the passage of two bills limiting the unions' freedom.

The Taft-Hartley Act (the Labor-Management Relations Act of 1947) amended the Wagner Act. Most of the restrictions on management interference in union activities were retained, and new restrictions were placed on unions. Unions were prohibited from coercing members or prospective members, from discriminating against workers who were not union members, and from refusing to take part in collective bargaining. The Taft-Hartley Act also gave the states the option of passing *right-to-work laws.* These laws, which prohibit compulsory union membership in order to hold a job, have been passed in 20 states, mainly in the South and Great Plains.

The Landrum-Griffin Act (the Labor-Management Reporting and Disclosure Act), passed in 1959, protects union members from possible misuse of power by their own union's leadership. It enforces the use of democratic procedures in union efforts to expand membership and requires fuller disclosure of unions' financial affairs.

# LEGALIZATION OF EMPLOYEE RIGHTS
*Replacing a dependence upon unions*

Rather than enact new laws to strengthen unions, recent legislatures have been concerned with protecting the rights of individual workers. The most momentous of such laws was the Civil Rights Act of 1968, which contained a group of provisions referred to as the Fair Employment Practices Act. These provisions prohibit employers from discriminating against job applicants and job holders because of race, color, religion, national origin, or sex. Subsequent laws added this protection for veterans, older people, and the handicapped. Other court rulings and laws, some of them limited to a particular state, keep extending such protection for individual workers (see Table 17-2). The most important aspect of this trend toward individual protectionism is the growing public

**TABLE 17-2**
**THE GROWING WEB OF LAWS AND COURT RULINGS**
**PROTECTING THE RIGHTS OF INDIVIDUAL EMPLOYEES**

*Employee rights are being expanded at the state and local level by:*

- Right-to-know laws requiring companies to divulge information on hazardous substances used in the workplace (25 states)
- Laws protecting corporate and government whistle-blowers (21 states)
- Court decisions eroding employment-at-will doctrine (30 states)
- Laws prohibiting any mandatory retirement age (19 states)
- Laws requiring notice of plant shutdowns and severance pay for affected workers (3 states)

*Employee privacy is protected by:*

- Limits on data about individuals that the government can disclose to employers (10 states, plus Federal Privacy Act of 1974)
- Laws limiting use of polygraph tests for job applicants (20 states); laws giving employees access to their personnel files (9 states); laws restricting the use of arrest records in the hiring process (12 states)

*Standards for a safe and healthful workplace are established by:*

- Occupational Safety & Health Act of 1970; 24 state laws
- Federal Mine Safety & Health Act of 1977

*Basic protection against discrimination in hiring, promoting, and discharging is granted by:*

- Civil Rights Act of 1964
- Age Discrimination in Employment Act of 1967; 1978 amendment disallowing mandatory retirement before age 70
- State and local laws, some of which add protection for marital status and sexual orientation

*Sex discrimination in pay is prohibited by:*

- Equal Pay Act of 1963
- Some federal court decisions requiring equal pay for comparable work

*Funding, vesting, and other standards for pensions and other benefit plans are set by:*

- Employee Retirement Income Security Act of 1974; state laws

*National minimum wage, 40-hour workweek for regular pay, and other working conditions are set by:*

- Fair Labor Standards Act of 1938; state wage and hour laws (all states)

*Company ability to discharge and discipline employees for union activity is limited by:*

- National Labor Relations Act of 1935; Railway Labor Act of 1926 belief that a person should not be discharged from his or her job without just cause. Until recently, the courts were guided by the so-called doctrine of employment at will. This meant, in effect, that without a contract, an employer could hire and fire for any reason whatsoever. Within the past few years landmark rulings by courts in several states have tended to make this doctrine obsolete.

## EMPLOYEES AS OWNERS
### ESOPs: a form of industrial democracy ———

Still another movement is affecting the role of trade unions in the United States. It is the trend toward **employee stock ownership plans (ESOPs).** Today, more than 10 million workers participate in such plans in 7,000 companies. This ideal of having workers control their own destinies is as old as the Knights of Labor, but it was given fresh impetus by special federal legislation in 1978. ESOPs are not quite the same as profit sharing, since there is great potential for *loss* sharing when one is an owner. Furthermore, only in about 100 of all such plans do employees completely own the business. Where employees do, in fact, own the business, their record for success has been spotty. Rath Meatpacking Company in Waterloo, Iowa, for example, failed soon after employees took over. Eastern Airlines' 25 percent employee ownership did not forestall its merger with another airline company. The problem, however, is not necessarily inexperience or incompetency in management; many such plans were offered only after a company was on the verge of bankruptcy. Nevertheless, some very well known companies are succeeding because of their ESOPs. Weirton Steel (100 percent) and W. L. Gore & Associates (Goretex fabrics) are among them. At first, many unions opposed the formation of ESOPs, but that, too, has changed. The future of ESOPs is unclear. Since many ESOPs were begun in the recession years with firms that were in trouble, it is difficult to predict just how far the concept of employee ownership will go in America.

# *Key Concepts*

1. Changes in the United States labor force today include an increase in the number of professional, technical, clerical, and service workers but a decrease in the number of farm workers. Unemployment and layoffs remain a threat to workers' job security.

2. The main goals of the organized labor movement in the United States have been fairer wages, better hours and working conditions, more job security, and protection from discrimination.

3. Labor unions may be organized according to the skills performed by members or by the industries in which members work. Unions may

be local, national, independent, or affiliated with the AFL-CIO.

4. Collective bargaining is a process of negotiating work-related issues. Workers are represented collectively by negotiators who are chosen by election. Issues negotiated include union recognition, wages and wage policy, work hours, working conditions, job rights, job security, and others.

5. Labor and management both use tactics to further their positions and to try to force the other to give in or compromise. Union tactics include strikes, slowdowns, picketing, boycotts, and lobbying. Management tactics in-

clude lockouts, strikebreaking, injunctions, industry associations, and lobbying. When pressure and negotiation do not produce a settlement, mediation or arbitration of disputes may be used.

6. Government legislation has partially directed the growth of organized labor. In the 1930s, several bills gave labor union activities legal protection and gave unions great freedom. Later laws have restricted their freedom somewhat in an effort to reestablish the power balance between unions and management. Increasingly, court decisions and legislation have been directed toward the protection of individual employee rights.

# Review Questions

1. Define, explain, or identify the following key terms and phrases, found on the pages indicated.

agency shop (p. 389)
arbitration (p. 396)
boycott (p. 395)
closed shop (p. 389)
collective bargaining (p. 388)
court injunction (p. 395)
craft union (p. 387)
employee stock ownership plan (ESOP) (p. 399)
grievance procedure (p. 393)
independent union (p. 388)
industrial union (p. 387)
industry associations (p. 395)
jurisdictional disputes (p. 396)
labor contract (p. 392)
lobbying (p. 395)
local union (p. 387)
lockout (p. 395)
mediation (p. 396)
national union (p. 388)
open shop (p. 389)
picketing (p. 395)
right-to-work laws (p. 397)
slowdown (p. 395)
strike (p. 394)
strikebreaking (p. 395)
union shop (p. 389)
work rules (p. 392)

2. What changes have already occurred and will continue to occur in the makeup of the United States labor force?

3. What have been the main goals of organized labor in the United States?

4. Do membership figures for labor unions truly represent the influence of organized labor? Why, or why not?

5. What is the difference between a craft union and an industrial union? Give some examples of each.

6. What are the most common issues that are subject to collective bargaining?

7. Describe the process of routine labor contract negotiation.

8. Why is the establishment of a grievance procedure important to the unions?

9. Explain the difference between a strike and a lockout.

10. What was the aim of the Taft-Hartley Act?

# Case Critique 17-1
## Hardball Bargaining

When it comes to Westinghouse Electric Corp. and labor union bargaining agreements, it used to be certain that they would follow General Electric's lead. Over the years, this has caused a serious problem for Westinghouse. By and large, GE not only is much larger but also is more profitable. So, while GE could be generous in seeking settlements with the International Union of Electronic Workers (IUE) in 1982, Westinghouse found it costly to follow suit. The GE contract raised the average wage at GE by 17 percent to $10.75 an hour. GE also guaranteed $1,800 in retraining money for any employee who lost his or her job due to a plant closing.

Then, a couple of new factors entered the bargaining picture. The IUE bargainers insisted that in the future the union wanted more job protection from GE. The union wanted guarantees for workers who were laid off not only for plant closing but also because of production cutbacks. The union also asked that GE set up a companywide hiring policy that would give laid-off employees first crack at work in other plants. (Both GE and Westinghouse sometimes lay off workers in one city while they are hiring in others.)

While GE and the IUE were facing off for a new round of bargaining talks in 1985, Westinghouse announced that it would no longer follow the me-too policy patterned after GE's bargaining agreements. Westinghouse claimed that it had reorganized the company around distinct business units. Each unit functions autonomously, the company said, and some are profitable while others are not. Accordingly, declared Westinghouse, it would bargain unit by unit rather than on a national scale.

The IUE didn't like the Westinghouse proposal. And it wasn't pleased with what was happening to union jobs at either Westinghouse or GE. Total IUE membership at GE had shrunk during the past few years by 10,000 to a total of

185,000. In the 1960s, the IUE's GE membership had been over 300,000. At Westinghouse, IUE membership had declined by 17 percent in 2 years, and union employment there was falling faster than nonunion employment. Furthermore, both GE and Westinghouse were having a profitable year. The union president was realistic. He said, "Our philosophy is that it makes no sense to win a huge wage increase if our members aren't going to have a job in six months." Accordingly, he was determined to press GE for job security. As for Westinghouse's plan to bargain unit by unit and not follow the GE settlement, the union president stated flatly, "If they insist on doing this, we'll strike."

1. What are the key issues that must be resolved during the union-management negotiations?
2. If you were the IUE president, which issue would you put up the strongest fight for: job security at GE or national bargaining at Westinghouse? Why?
3. If you were a worker at a General Electric plant, which would you prefer the union to fight for: job security for the future or higher wages now? Why?
4. What difference does it make to an employee at Westinghouse whether or not the union bargains separately for his or her plant unit or on a national basis?

---

*SOURCE:* Aaron Bernstein, "Hardball at GE and Westinghouse," *Business Week,* July 8, 1985, pp. 30–31.

---

# Case Critique 17-2
## Caught in the Middle

Just when the automobile industry was getting back on its feet, trouble struck. More than 20,000 members of the International Brotherhood of Teamsters refused to climb into the cabs of trucks that haul new cars from manufacturing plants to dealers and railroad delivery points. The basic pay rates offered by the two

dozen hauling companies that employ them seemed to be acceptable, but other contract provisions were not. Of particular concern on the part of the union was a wage policy that would pay new employee drivers less than drivers with more seniority, at least for the first 2 years of employment. In addition, the hauling companies were asking that drivers be paid a lower mileage rate than before on return trips when their trucks are empty. This would make the cost of shipping by truck more competitive with the railroads and might produce more business for the trucking companies.

As the strike continued, some 19,500 independent auto dealers saw their showrooms emptying out, with fewer and fewer models to sell. Customers who had already ordered cars "were going crazy," said one Toyota dealer.

The automobile manufacturers were disturbed too. New cars waiting for shipment were taking up all available space in the plants' shipping lots. Even those that were shipped to delivery points by rail were running into the same bottleneck. Furthermore, it was late summer and the automakers were eager to start their changeover to next year's models, and the strike was delaying their schedules.

A few dealers weren't *too* unhappy about the situation. They had a lot of slow-moving, unpopular cars on their lots, and these were starting to sell. Used car dealers also reported a pickup in sales.

What was particularly upsetting was that the union negotiators and representatives of the hauling companies had reached a tentative agreement earlier. When the proposal was presented to the union membership for ratifica-

tion, however, it was overwhelmingly voted down. The auto haulers' spokesperson said that the proposal was "a very fair one." An official of the Teamsters, on the other hand, disagreed. The drivers had given contract concessions to the employers 3 years earlier, the union official said. "This proposal really aggravated them now."

1. What is the term that is usually applied to the kind of wage arrangement paying new drivers less than those with seniority, as was offered the drivers by the auto haulers?

2. What are the issues involved in this strike? Which are most important to union members?

3. Why do the auto hauling companies want to reduce the mileage rate for drivers on empty return trips?

4. While the strike continues, what parties are affected by it? In what ways?

5. Which of the affected parties listed in your answer to question No. 4 are most likely to put the most pressure on the union and hauling-company management to settle the strike? Why?

---

SOURCE: Laurent Belsie, "Haulers' Strike Leaves New Autos Stranded," *Christian Science Monitor*, August 1, 1985, p. 3.

## Technology IN THE WORKPLACE

### Workplace video

The video revolution has overtaken the workplace, both from a management and a labor union point of view. Video training cassettes have long been popular. They are relatively easy to make and can be tailored to company-specific jobs. They can be purchased, too, with professional performers who put the kind of life into safety lectures that most plant supervisors cannot. At one General Motors plant, video monitors in time-clock alleys, rest areas, and lunchrooms provide a special kind of "Today" show for employees. The morning report, for example, consists of a word roll of employee birthdays and updates on news events and the weather. The afternoon show features a spokesperson from the personnel department who reports a variety of information, from scores in the bowling league to the latest sales figures for GM cars. Once a month, the video show does a profile on a plant employee with an unusual hobby or record of accomplishment.

Labor unions have found that a portable "movie in a briefcase" is helpful in membership drives and organizing campaigns. Union headquarters also put together "video newsletters" and send them to local officials for updating developments. The messages in the videos, says one union official, emphasize classic union philosophy: "Education, motivation, and agitation."

*SOURCE:* Cynthia Piechowiak and Don Hopey, "Movie Memos," *The Pittsburgh Press,* April 9, 1985, pp. C1–C8.

### Human resources data base

Many large companies, like Consolidated Edison Company of New York, place selected career-oriented information about each of their employees into a computerized data storage system. Information about each individual at Consolidated Edison is gathered from two sources: (1) the ongoing personnel files for basic company employment, wage, promotion, training, and performance appraisal details and (2) a questionnaire about career capabilities and expectations that is completed voluntarily by employees. The final data file on each employee contains such information as educational background; off-job interests such as activities in union, fraternal, civic, political, or professional organizations; and particular outside skills and hobbies that employees feel may be relevant to career advancement. With this inventory of its human resources in the data base, the company can search for potential candidates to fill job openings, matching an individual's education, experience, and present and potential knowledge and skills with the job specifications.

*SOURCE:* John S. Jenness, "Human Resources Planning," in *Handbook for Professional Managers,* McGraw-Hill, 1985, pp. 390–394.

# UNIT 6

# *Financial Aspects of Business*

Unit 6 analyzes the financial needs of business and describes where and how funds are obtained. It also examines the money and banking system in the United States and explores the ways in which businesses can reduce their financial risks, especially through insurance.

## CHAPTER 18

One of the essentials of business is to obtain financing for such permanent assets as buildings and machinery and for current needs such as payrolls and purchases. These financing needs, which include both long-term and short-term funds, can be met either by selling a share in the ownership or by borrowing or using trade credit.

## CHAPTER 19

The banking systems, as regulated by the Federal Reserve System, are a prime source of money for business. Other financing is provided by private and institutional investors, who participate in business through the securities markets and exchanges.

## CHAPTER 20

The operation of a business entails many risks. Exposure to risk may be reduced by watchful management, and the cost of damage can be minimized by insurance protection. Prudence in extending credit also helps to minimize financial risks.

| AL | (3) LOAN ORIGINAL AMOUNT | (4) APPRAISED VALUE | (5) LOAN TO VALUE | (6) TER OF LOA |
|---|---|---|---|---|
| 2.63 | 75000 | 12?00 | 63 |
| 3.36 | 57600 |  | 63 |
| 6.27 | 85300 | 118000 | 72 |
| 2.57 | 75000 | 166000 | 45 |
| 2.47 | 93700 | 190?0 | 79 |
| 4.67 | 35000 | 6500? | 54 |
| 7.81 | 53800 | 1240? | 43 |
| 5.61 | ?6000 | 4200? | 38 |
| 4.75 | 74?00 | 125000 | 59 |
| 7.00 | 75000 | 156000 | 48 |
| 5.92 | 64700 | 130000 | 50 |
| 7.72 | 96500 | 135000 | 71 |
| 2.95 | 60200 | 100000 | 60 |
| 3.37 | 73200 | 91500 | 80 |
| 6.15 | 53300 | 118000 | 45 |
| 9.25 | 74000 | 95500 | 77 |
| 0.43 | 70000 | 88000 | 80 |
| 0.67 | 49800 | 98000 | 51 |
| 9.44 | 92800 | 116000 | 80 |
| 7.32 | 98500 | 230000 | 43 |
| 2.89 | 49500 | 88000 | 56 |
| 4.13 | 50900 | 125000 | 41 |
| 9.67 | 79700 | 232500 | 34 |
| 9.40 | 95600 | 173000 | 55 |

# CHAPTER 18

# Financial Management and Sources of Funds

## Learning Objectives

*The purpose of this chapter is to describe the functions of financial management in business, explain the factors that affect financial planning, identify the sources of funds for a business, distinguish between equity and debt financing, and illustrate their application for either short- or long-term needs.*

*As evidence of general comprehension, after studying this chapter you should be able to:*

1. *Distinguish between current and fixed assets, and show how financial management plans for the acquisition and use of funds out of current and fixed assets.*

2. *Explain why the source and method of financing depend on how long capital is needed.*

3. *Differentiate between equity financing and debt financing.*

4. *Identify the standard methods of short-term debt financing.*

5. *Identify the standard methods of long-term debt financing.*

6. *Recognize and explain the common methods of long-term equity financing.*

*If your class is using SSweetco: Business Model and Activity File, see Chapter 18 in that book after you finish this chapter. There you will find exercises and activities that will help you apply your learning to typical business situations.*

## 1 FINANCIAL PLANNING

decides how much money a firm needs for how long and how the firm will use that money.

Acquiring a new plant
Hiring workers
Buying additional
   equipment

## 2 SOURCES OF FUNDS

are determined by the duration of a firm's needs.

## 3 EQUITY FINANCING

for business shares ownership and the possibility of profit or loss.

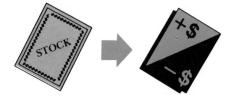

## DEBIT FINANCING

commits the borrower to payment.

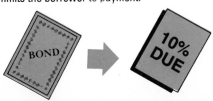

## 4 SHORT-TERM DEBT FINANCING

comes from:

| Trade credit | ✔ |
|---|---|
| Bank loans | ✔ |
| Factors | ✔ |
| Commercial paper | ✔ |

## 5 LONG-TERM DEBT FINANCING

comes from:

Mortgages

Corporate bonds

Government

## 6 LONG-TERM EQUITY FINANCING

comes from the sale of preferred or common stock.

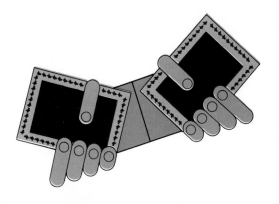

# FINANCIAL PLANNING: THE BAREST NECESSITY

*Nancy and Timothy Atkins launched Bear Necessities, a chain of specialty shops featuring teddy bear novelties, from a pushcart. Their only source of capital was $8,000 worth of trade credit from manufacturers and wholesale distributors of the products they sold. Bear Necessities grew within 8 years to sales of nearly $2 million annually. Unfortunately, during most of that time the company spent more money than it took in, sometimes more than $60,000 each year. Said Tom Atkins, "The cash register rings and you see the money come in, but you're not thinking about how the cash goes out at the other end." To keep the company's head above these troubled financial waters, the Atkinses borrowed a lot of money from the bank. They paid a lot of interest on that money, too, up to $70,000 one year. When things got so bad that the company couldn't borrow money any longer, the Atkinses sold shares of their business, more than 50 percent of their ownership, in fact, to investors. That way, they raised another $750,000. They used this money to pay off debts, to rebuild their inventories, and to promote the sale of their specialties through direct mail catalogs.*

*Bear Necessities used a catch-as-catch-can approach to financial funding. This approach inevitably led them into trouble. Most successful businesses approach their financial funding according to a systematic plan. This minimizes the chances that they won't be able to pay their bills as they come due. And it strengthens the financial foundation of the company so that it can draw upon many sources for its funding. Wyle Laboratories, a major supplier of high-technology electronic components and systems to the aerospace and energy system industries, for example, added more than $43 million to its working capital in 1984. It did so according to a plan that drew funds from a number of sources. For example, profit alone contributed nearly $10 million. Sale of shares of ownership (in the form of common stock) accounted for $22.7 million. It tapped its accounts receivables for nearly $2 million, sold property and equipment it owned to generate another $1.4 million, and issued a form of long-term bond for over $500,000. At the same time, Wyle made arrangements with its various banks to borrow up to $30 million if it needed to do so.*

*The cases of Bear Necessities and Wyle show that it is money that makes business go 'round. These cases illustrate, quite dramatically, that the acquisition, disbursement, and control of a company's funds are critical for its survival and success, whether a company is small or large.*

---

*SOURCES: Jennifer Lin, "Unbearable Trouble in Pooh Land," Venture, August 1985, p. 12;* Annual Report of Wyle Laboratories for 1984.

---

# 1  FINANCIAL PLANNING FOR BUSINESSES
## *Establishes plans for the acquisition and use of funds*

---

Financial planning must cover all aspects of how money is acquired and used in a business. ***Financial management*** encompasses the managerial activities of planning what funds will be needed for a business and when, where these funds will come from, and for what purpose they will be used. Money for operating businesses is acquired from the personal assets of the owner or owners, by issuing and selling stocks, or by borrowing from other people or institutions that own capital. Money is used to pay for the resources needed to operate the business.

## WHY BUSINESSES NEED MONEY
*Capital is needed to pay for resources* ▬▬▬▬▬▬▬▬▬▬▬▬▬

Although land, labor, technology, and capital are all needed to keep businesses running, in practice, capital is the most fundamental resource. Capital is used to obtain the other three resources. The physical labor, skill, and knowledge of the women and men who work for businesses are purchased with wages, salaries, and other kinds of payment. The materials used in production processes—whether they be starting materials, supplies, or power sources—must be bought. Businesses buy (or rent) their facilities—buildings, equipment, and machines. When businesses borrow money, they must make payments—in the form of interest. ***Interest*** is a charge made by lenders for the use of their money.

## CURRENT AND FIXED ASSETS
*For short-term or long-term needs* ▬▬▬▬▬▬▬▬▬▬▬▬▬

All of the valuable resources that a business has gathered together for its use are called ***assets.*** Assets may be of two types: current assets and fixed assets.

Assets used to support the day-to-day operations of a company are ***current assets,*** or ***working capital.*** These assets normally can be converted into cash within a short time, usually a year or less. Current assets are used to meet the short-term obligations of a company: paying employees' wages, paying bills, shipping goods to meet customer orders, and allowing credit purchases by customers. Current assets consist of cash or securities that can readily be converted to cash, inventories, and accounts receivable. Inventories are current assets because the company expects to sell them soon and recover the cash for other uses. *Accounts receivable* are the amounts owed to the company for goods or services provided to customers but not yet paid for. They are current assets because they represent the cash expected in a short time.

*Fixed assets* are relatively permanent goods or resources owned by a company. Most companies do not expect to turn their fixed assets into cash on a regular basis. Examples include land, factories, office buildings, durable equipment, and other long-lasting facilities of a business. The fixed assets of a company provide the long-term setting in which operations take place.

## MOVEMENT OF FUNDS IN BUSINESS OPERATIONS
*More money must flow in than out*

For operations to continue, there must be a flow of money into and out of a business. Figure 18-1 shows some of the specific forms the flow of funds may take.

The top drawing in the figure shows the sources of a business's financial input. Cash is received when customers pay for goods or services (**A**). This is called income or revenue. A sizable portion of the money that flows into a business, however, does not come from sales revenue. Companies need money to buy their production facilities when they start operations and to replace and expand them later. Also, the original working capital has to come from somewhere. No current assets can be generated from sales until some goods or services are first produced. Companies need funds for this. This money can come either from borrowing or from investments by owners. Money that is borrowed by the business is called *debt financing* (**B**). Money that enters a business from its owners is called *equity financing* (**C**).

At the same time that money flows into a business, it is also expended in the form of cash to be paid out (**D**) to cover bills for materials, wages, rent, and so forth. The surplus, if there is any, is the profit (**E**) a business makes.

Some outflow of money results from a business's use of equity or debt financing. Owners who invest money will usually wish at some point to withdraw part of the profits. Companies that are publicly owned (corporations) ordinarily pay out part of the profits in the form of dividends (**F**) to shareholders. Companies with debt financing must also make some provision to pay off, or retire, the debts (**G**). Although many companies maintain a long-term indebtedness, part of the debt must be retired periodically, even if new debts are incurred. Interest (**H**) must also be paid to the lender in return for the use of the borrowed money.

Cash flow is also affected by the ability of a business to supervise the credit it extends to its customers and its effectiveness in collecting payments. Though interest (**I**) is accrued by the company on charge accounts, the inflow of money is usually restricted to some extent by the slow payments (**J**) of customers. Some customers will never pay. This money is lost to *bad debts* (**K**)—money not paid to the business even though goods or services have been provided.

Financial management must plan for and control all of these incoming and outgoing funds by trying to balance income from sales with the costs of operating. Equity and debt financing for facilities and working capital must be arranged. All money paid out to investors or lenders must be accounted for, all money owed to the company collected, and bad debts limited.

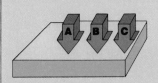

While a portion of a company's financial input is derived from **A** sales income, additional funds are acquired by the financial manager through **B** debt financing or **C** equity financing.

Figure 18-1 How the flow of funds into and out of a business affects the responsibilities of financial management.

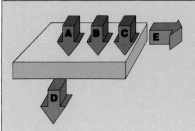

Money flows out of a firm's reserves in the form of **D** payment of bills. It is the responsibility of financial management to balance its input and its payments while trying to create **E** profits.

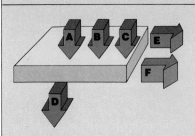

Financial management must see to it that a certain amount of the profits are paid out as **F** dividends to equity shareholders.

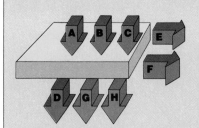

Financial management must plan for debt retirement. When the firm borrows money, it must be prepared to make **G** repayments and **H** interest payments.

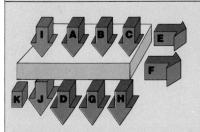

Additional income is accrued from **I** interest on charge accounts. However, input is reduced as a result of **J** slow payments and **K** bad debts when income from sales comes from charge accounts and debtors are reluctant to pay. Financial management, thus, involves supervising credit and collections.

# 2 SOURCES OF FUNDS FOR BUSINESS
## Duration of need dictates the source

Businesses need funds for different purposes. The specific use to which money will be put partly determines the best source for the money. Different uses for funds tie up money for different lengths of time. Money used for current assets is expected to be converted into cash within a year. Funds for fixed assets may be tied up for decades or even for centuries in some companies.

Financial needs for current assets vary. Many companies have significant changes in the levels of their current assets at different times of the year. Retail stores usually increase their merchandise inventory before Christmas, for example. A cannery might need large amounts of cash during the summer and fall to meet increased payroll and to buy fruits and vegetables. The money borrowed is expected to be recovered from sales within a short time. These are some examples of short-term requirements for funds.

There is a certain minimum level of current assets that must be maintained at all times, however. The retail store must have some merchandise inventory, and the cannery will have some inventory and accounts receivable throughout the year. These minimum current assets require funds for long periods. They may be financed differently from short-term current assets.

Long-term financing is needed for nearly every kind of fixed asset. Buildings, equipment, land, and other kinds of facilities tie up money for long periods. They must be bought with funds that are appropriate for this long-term use. Figure 18-2 illustrates the three types of funds needed for a retail store with a large increase of inventory for the Christmas season: short-term for current assets, long-term for current assets, and long-term for fixed assets.

Each business has its unique set of financial requirements, and these tend to dictate the extent to which the company can use a particular source of funding. If vendors are accustomed to shipping goods on credit, then trade credit may be a prime source of funds. If the business requires seasonal inventories, banks may be ready and willing to make loans based

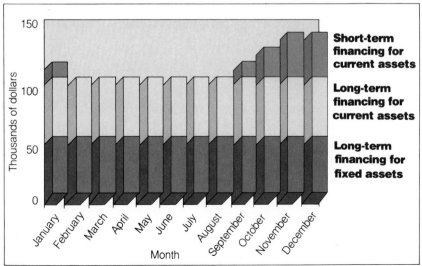

Figure 18-2 Analysis of financing needs for a store. The store builds merchandise inventories for the Christmas selling season and uses short-term debt sources to finance this temporary need.

upon them. If a business needs a great deal of heavy equipment, it may be able to rely on long-term borrowing. If the proprietor has an unusual product or service to offer and a good reputation as a manager, then he or she may be able to attract investors to share in the ownership by providing funds. In almost all cases, however, a firm must build a financial structure that relies on a number of sources, rather than a single source.

# 3 EQUITY VERSUS DEBT FINANCING
## *Methods of obtaining outside funding*

Most companies try to finance expansions at least in part by reinvesting—or plowing back—profits from ongoing operations. This use of *retained earnings* is a sound, stable method of growth for established companies. All businesses, however, must have financing from outside sources when they first begin operation, and most businesses need additional financing at certain points in their growth. These outside funds may come from equity financing or from debt financing. Financial management must decide what contribution each type will make to the total funds available to the business. See Figure 18-6 for an example of how three major companies use different sources of funds to sustain their businesses.

## EQUITY FINANCING
### *Equity shares ownership, risk, and profits*

In equity financing, funds are raised by selling a portion of ownership, or equity, in the business, as by selling stock to shareholders. With this type of financing, the original owners of the business agree to share the ownership, risks, and profits of the firm with new owners or investors.

The major advantages of equity financing are:

■ No interest charges must be paid. This is a particular advantage in an economic slump when sales and revenues may be reduced.
■ Businesses with a high proportion of equity financing are generally more stable. Their solvency is less likely to be threatened by an inability to meet obligations to lenders.
■ Profits produced by a business financed by owners rather than lenders belong to the owners and are not reduced by loan payments.

The major disadvantages of equity financing are:

■ Capital needs of businesses vary over time. If requirements decrease, invested money may remain idle and not produce income.
■ A greater total investment by owners is required to maintain a given scope of operations when little or no borrowed money is used.

Equity financing has the major drawback of diluting ownership; in effect, the original owners sacrifice a portion of their control and profits.

Suppose, for example, the owners of a restaurant sold 25 percent of their ownership to an investor for $50,000. The company could use these new funds to acquire current assets (like an inventory of frozen foods and cases of wine) or fixed assets (such as a renovated kitchen). Any profits generated by the business in the future, however, must now be split so that the investor gets 25 percent of these while the original owners receive only 75 percent.

## DEBT FINANCING
*Debt commits the borrower to payment* ━━━━━━━━━━━━━━

Debt financing is accomplished by borrowing funds. The borrowing may, for example, take the form of a loan from a bank or the sale of bonds. Some advantages of borrowing money for a business are:

■ Interest paid for the use of borrowed money is not taxed. This effectively reduces the cost of using the money.

■ Borrowing is convenient for short-term needs. It makes it unnecessary to keep large amounts of cash for peak needs.

■ Borrowed money provides additional capital without giving up any ownership or control of the business.

■ Owners who are able to borrow money and make profits on it can enjoy the increased profits without increasing their investment. The ability to create profits from the total capital, part of it owned and the rest borrowed, is called **leverage.** (See Figure 18-3.)

The leverage of a company increases as its financing increases its dependency on borrowing. The use of some leverage is usually considered good business, since you are using "other people's money" for your own purposes to make a profit. Too much leverage, however, is considered dangerous, since the firm is saddled with interest payments and may have to repay borrowed money at a time when it is inconvenient, such as when business is slow.

Debt financing also has disadvantages:

■ Borrowed money is sometimes unavailable or can only be obtained at high interest rates. Companies that have come to rely on debt financing may encounter severe difficulties in this situation.

■ Companies that use borrowed money must meet interest payments regularly. This can be a burden—or even an impossibility—when revenues are down or the company is facing other financial difficulties.

Most companies today try to strike a balance between equity and debt financing. The ratio of borrowed assets to owned assets, or *debt ratio*, is another meaning of leverage. If a company's debt is $100,000 and its equity is $50,000, its debt ratio is 2:1, or 200 percent. Companies with high leverage are often believed to have a good profit potential—especially when interest rates are low. However, they are also believed to be more susceptible to failure in an economic slump.

## 4  SHORT-TERM DEBT FINANCING
*This is the staple of finance*

Companies that wish to use borrowed money for short-term needs have a variety of sources. Some of the terminology used in discussing these sources applies to almost all kinds of financing. An **instrument** is a document that represents the terms of a financial transaction. A dollar bill is an instrument, as is an IOU, a stock certificate, or a government

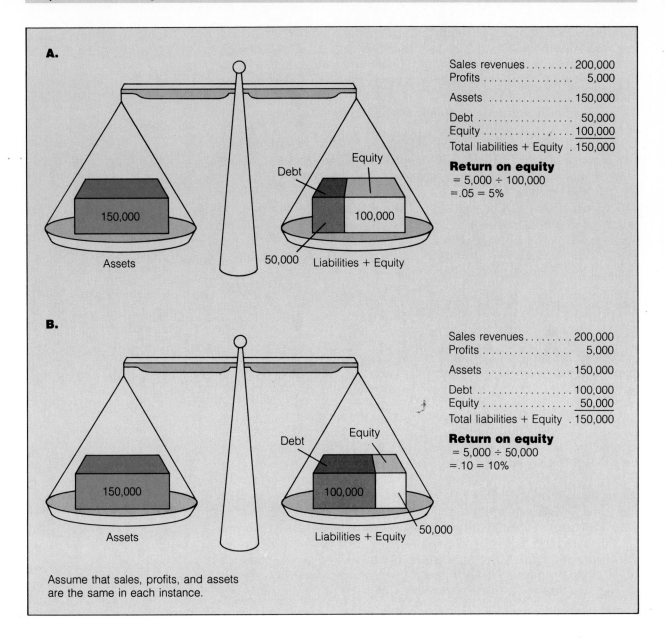

**A.**

Sales revenues . . . . . . . . 200,000
Profits . . . . . . . . . . . . . . . 5,000
Assets . . . . . . . . . . . . . . 150,000
Debt . . . . . . . . . . . . . . . 50,000
Equity . . . . . . . . . . . . . , . . . 100,000
Total liabilities + Equity . 150,000

**Return on equity**
  = 5,000 ÷ 100,000
  =.05 = 5%

150,000 — Assets

Debt — Equity

50,000 — 100,000 — Liabilities + Equity

**B.**

Sales revenues . . . . . . . . 200,000
Profits . . . . . . . . . . . . . . . 5,000
Assets . . . . . . . . . . . . . . 150,000
Debt . . . . . . . . . . . . . . . 100,000
Equity . . . . . . . . . . . . . . . 50,000
Total liabilities + Equity . 150,000

**Return on equity**
  = 5,000 ÷ 50,000
  =.10 = 10%

150,000 — Assets

Debt — Equity

100,000 — 50,000 — Liabilities + Equity

Assume that sales, profits, and assets
are the same in each instance.

bond. **Collateral** is anything of value that a borrower promises to give the lender if the borrower is unable to repay a loan. When a bank lends money to an automobile buyer, the bank normally keeps the title to the car until the loan is paid off. The car is collateral and can be taken and sold by the bank if the borrower does not repay the loan. A loan for which collateral is held is **secured;** one with no collateral is **unsecured.**

The main types of short-term debt financing are trade credit, unsecured or secured direct loans, factoring, and commercial paper.

Figure 18-3 How leverage is increased by debt financing.

## TRADE CREDIT
### Suppliers furnish this free

The most common source of short-term borrowed funds is **trade credit,** or purchases made on credit from suppliers. Suppose that a company buys $10,000 worth of component parts from a supplier and is not required to pay for them until 30 days after they are received. This way, the purchaser is, in effect, borrowing $10,000 from the supplier for 30 days. The buyer enjoys the use of the goods for a month without having paid for them.

Vendors try to reduce the amount of credit they extend to customers because giving large amounts of credit requires a large investment in current assets. Many firms allow a small discount if bills are paid quickly. Invoices may show terms such as 2/10, net/30. This means that 2 percent may be subtracted from the invoice amount if it is paid within 10 days, but that in any event the total (net) amount is due in 30 days. A bill for $800, for example, may be paid with $784 if this is done within 10 days; otherwise, the full amount must be paid. Increasingly, firms that extend trade credit apply an interest charge (typically of 1.5 percent a month) on the unpaid balance. This practice is similar to that used on consumer charge cards, such as VISA or MasterCard.

# DIRECT SHORT-TERM LOANS
*Banks are the primary source*

Banks and other financial institutions lend money to businesses for short-term use. Numerous different instruments and borrowing methods are used. The loans may or may not require collateral.

**UNSECURED LOANS** Unsecured loans for business use may be obtained from banks and other lending institutions, individuals, or other companies. The most common forms are promissory notes and lines of credit. A **promissory note** is one way of formalizing a direct loan. (See Figure 18-4.) It states that the borrower, who signs the note, will pay to the lender the money borrowed plus a certain interest rate at a specified future date. Most promissory notes specify periods of less than 6 months. These loans are generally used by businesses for short-term purposes such as harvesting crops or building inventory for a heavy sales season.

A **line of credit** is an agreement between a lender and a borrower that loans up to a specified maximum will be extended if needed. A retail business might establish a line of credit for $50,000 with a commercial

Figure 18-4 Example of a promissory note.

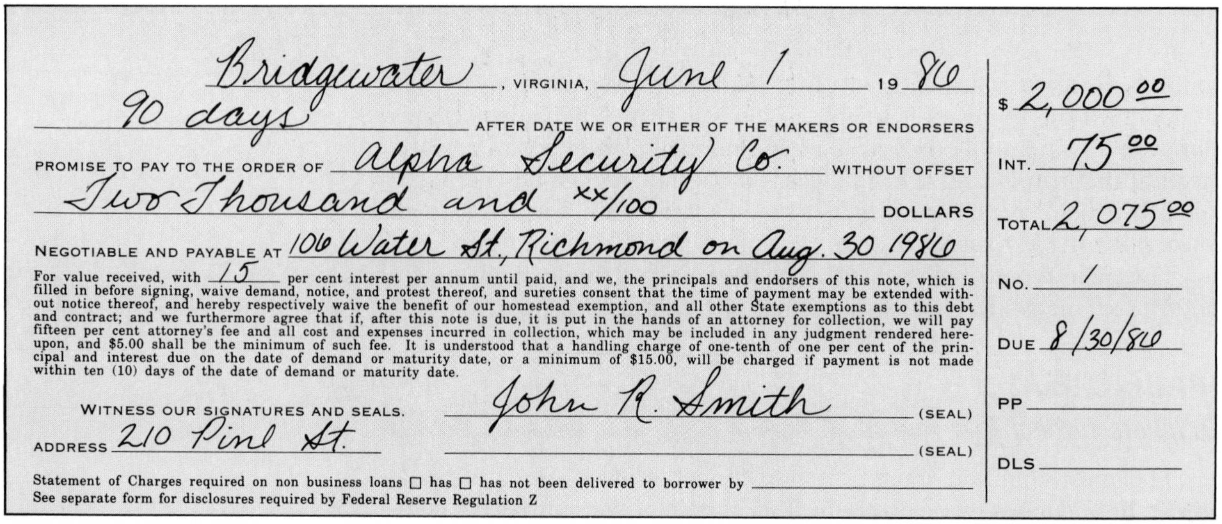

bank. The bank agrees to lend the store any amount up to the maximum during a specified period of time. Early in the summer, the store may not use any borrowed money. It may borrow $15,000 for the back-to-school season, repay $5,000 in October, and borrow $40,000 more in November for Christmas inventory. A line of credit is convenient for both lender and borrower because a number of loans can be made without separate credit investigations for each.

**SECURED SHORT-TERM LOANS** The amount of money that can be borrowed without collateral is limited, except for the largest companies. Small or recently formed companies may not be able to get unsecured loans at all. A wide variety of valuable property may be used to secure a loan. Equipment or other movable goods such as trucks and automobiles are commonly used as collateral. Other business facilities, such as buildings, may be used, although this is less usual for short-term loans. Inventories, whether of starting materials or of finished goods, are common collateral.

Accounts receivable—the money owed to a firm by its customers—may be pledged as collateral in some cases. The borrower may select a number of outstanding accounts and promise to pay the lender the proceeds from these accounts in return for a loan of 75 to 80 percent of their total value. The borrower retains responsibility for collecting money owed on the accounts and must make up the difference if any of the accounts cannot be collected. Lending money secured by proceeds of accounts receivable is called **discounting.** The term is used because the lender is paying out a smaller amount than is expected to be received from the collateral. The difference serves as interest on the borrowed money. For example, the ABC Manufacturing Company may obtain a loan of $8,000 on accounts receivables that are worth $10,000. When collected, the lender will receive the entire $10,000. The $2,000 difference represents the discounting of 20 percent of the value of the receivables.

## FACTORS AND SALES FINANCE COMPANIES
### They lend for accounts receivables ━━━━━━━━

Factors and sales finance companies are businesses that provide money in return for accounts receivable. Factors may simply discount, or lend only a portion of the face value of, receivables and consider the accounts as collateral on a loan. **Factoring,** however, often involves buying the accounts outright. The factor pays whatever it thinks the accounts are worth and takes over responsibility for collecting them. Many companies that deal with customers who are not expected to make repeat purchases sell accounts receivable to factors. Factoring is common in the sale of lots in vacation housing developments, for instance.

A **sales finance company** is similar to a factor in that it buys accounts receivables or lends money with receivables as collateral. Sales finance companies usually specialize in accounts for installment plan purchases. Expensive consumer goods, like home appliances and cars, are often sold with an agreement that the buyer will make monthly payments for a period of 1 to 3 years. These installment sales tie up significant amounts of money for long periods. The seller is often glad to sell the accounts receivable to a finance company, even at a relatively heavy discount. The purchaser who is delinquent in payments may be surprised to find that it is the finance company that sends dunning collection letters rather than the store where the purchase was made.

## COMMERCIAL PAPER
*A source for large corporations*

Some large companies have such an unquestionably high credit standing that they are able to borrow large sums of money simply by offering short-term promissory notes without any security. When a large company issues such notes, they are called **commercial paper.** They usually specify a repayment period of from 3 to 6 months. Companies with reputations good enough to have their commercial papers accepted by lenders prefer this method of short-term financing. Businesses often can borrow at a lower interest rate than that offered by a commercial bank for an ordinary loan. This preferred interest rate is called the prime rate and is described more fully in Chapter 19.

# 5  LONG-TERM DEBT FINANCING
*May be used for both current and fixed assets*

Most companies have important long-term money needs. Fixed assets tie up money for long periods. Good financial management usually calls for a substantial portion of the current assets to be paid for with long-term financing also. Two sources for these funds are loans and bonds. Almost any successful company will qualify for some kinds of long-term direct loans. Bonds can usually be issued only by organizations like corporations and governments. Investors are willing to buy bonds from these enterprises because their continued operation is more certain than is the continued operation of proprietorships or partnerships.

## LONG-TERM LOANS
*A secured mortgage is the most common*

When funds are available, banks frequently make loans for periods of 1 to 5 years—and sometimes longer. These are called **bank term loans.** They often carry certain restrictions for the borrower, such as the requirement to get the lender's permission before assuming more debts. Other direct loans are available from insurance companies, savings and loan associations, trust companies, and the government.

The most common long-term loan is a **mortgage.** This is a loan secured by some kind of valuable property. Tangible property such as buildings, land, and equipment may be used as collateral, as may stocks and bonds, insurance policies, and other financial instruments. In recent years, such loans have come to be known as "equity loans" because it is "borrowing against equity." The term is most commonly used when obtaining "second" mortgages.

# CORPORATE BONDS

*A mortgagelike pledge*

A **bond** is a written pledge to lenders stating the borrower's intention to repay a loan. (See Figure 18-5.) A bond specifies (1) the amount of money that has been borrowed, or the **principal,** (2) the date the principal will be repaid, or the **maturity date,** and (3) the rate of interest that will be paid periodically over the life of the bond. If a company wishes to borrow a million dollars, for example, it might issue a thousand bonds worth $1,000 each. An individual investor who buys one of the bonds gives the company $1,000 (usually through an agent). In return, the

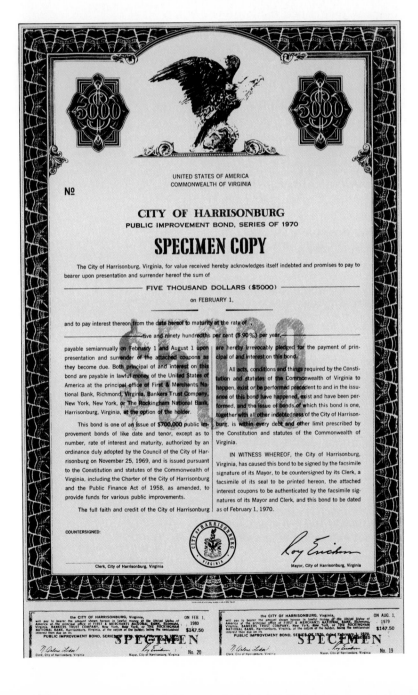

Figure 18-5 This is a tax-free, municipal coupon (or bearer) bond. It has the same promissory elements as a corporate bond: face (or cash) value of $5000; interest rate of 5.90 percent; issue date of February 1, 1970; and the due date of 1980. Coupons are attached to the bond: they are redeemable on February 1 and August 1 of each year for $147.50 each. Bonds issued from July 1, 1983 on do not require the coupon feature. All new issues from that date on must be sold in registered (not bearer) form, so named because the issuer must keep a record of ownership. Knowing the identity of bondholders means that interest can be mailed directly to investors without their clipping coupons.

investor receives a bond certificate that may promise to pay the bond-holder $1,000 in the year 2000 plus 12 percent interest every year up to maturity. Most individual bonds have a value of at least $1,000; some may run as high as $50,000. Maturity dates may extend to as much as 100 years and are rarely less than 10 years from date of issue.

When bonds are issued, the total amount borrowed may be very large, and individual bonds may be sold to many different investors. For these reasons, a *trustee* is appointed to deal with and protect the interests of bondholders. Trustees are usually banks or trust companies. Their job is to enforce all of the specific terms of the bond issue. These terms are spelled out in a written agreement called an *indenture.* Trustees may hold collateral, if any is called for. They oversee the payment of interest and the repayment of principal. If the company that issued the bond is unable to meet its required payments, the trustee must take action—including forcing the sale of collateral, if necessary—to protect the financial interests of bondholders.

**REGISTERED AND BEARER BONDS** Issuers of bonds, or their trustees, may keep a record of all the people and organizations that buy individual bonds and send interest payments to them when due. Such bonds are *registered.* They are convenient and safe for bondholders but expensive to administer for the issuing company. Other bonds pay interest to whoever physically possesses them when interest is due. No record is kept of individual owners. These are called *coupon,* or *bearer*, *bonds.* When such bonds are printed, a series of coupons is made part of the certificate. To collect interest, bondholders must cut off a coupon and present it to the issuing company or its agent. Beginning in 1983, the federal government forbade the issuance of bearer bonds, although millions of these bonds will continue to exist until they mature.

**TYPES OF CORPORATE BONDS** Although many variations are in common use, three types of bonds are seen most frequently.

■ *Mortgage bonds* are secured by property owned by the issuer. Mortgage bonds are relatively safe investments because the collateral can be sold to satisfy the indebtedness if the issuing company is unable to make payments. A real estate mortgage bond is secured by property. A chattel mortgage bond is secured by movable goods like aircraft. Collateral trust bonds are secured by other stocks and bonds owned by the issuing company.

■ *Debenture bonds* are unsecured, except by the credit standing of the issuer. For this reason, their use is restricted to large, stable companies with long records of consistent earnings.

■ *Convertible bonds* can be exchanged for common stock at a rate specified in the indenture. This provision makes bonds more attractive to many investors. If a $1,000 bond can be converted to 100 shares of stock, the value of the bond increases substantially if the value of a share of stock rises above $10.

There are many other variations on these three basic types of bonds, as can be seen in Table 18-1.

**BOND RETIREMENT METHODS** Companies use a variety of methods to retire bonds. Retirement means paying back the principal that was originally borrowed. Some companies issue *serial bonds.* Under this

## TABLE 18-1
## VARIATION IN BOND OFFERINGS

### Bond funds

These are offered by investment companies and include a number of different bonds (a portfolio) from many sources pooled together (into a mutual fund) so that a buyer can buy a share in the ownership of the portfolio. These funds can be "open-ended," meaning that the firm that assembles the bonds may sell some and replace some with new bonds continually. Other funds are "closed-end" unit-investment trusts (UITs); these are fixed packages of bonds that share the interest and/or proceeds with owners of shares in the package until the bonds have all been redeemed.

### Zero Coupon Bonds

These have no coupon or any way of paying the usual semiannual interest rate until the bond is due. Typically, the bond is purchased at a discount from its face value at maturity. A bond with a face value of $1,000 due in the year 2000 might have been purchased in 1980 for $104. This means that the interest rate is approximately 12 percent; the $104 "compounded" at 12 percent for 20 years will equal $1,000 at that time, although the owner of the bond will not have had the use of the interest during the 20-year period.

### CATS, TIGRS, AND STRIPS

CATS (Certificate of Accrued Treasury Securities), TIGRS (Treasury Investment Growth Receipts), and STRIPS (Separate Trading of Registered Interest and Principal Securities) are all zero coupon bonds issued by (or composed of bonds issued by) the U.S. Treasury.

### LOCs

LOCs are bonds secured by a Letter of Credit from a bank.

### FLOATERs

FLOATERs are long-term bonds with interest rates adjusted periodically; sometimes they are called adjustable-rate bonds. (See Action Brief "Innovative Financing" on page 417.)

### PUTs

PUTs are bonds that permit the bondholder the option of redeeming his or her bonds at par value to maturity, a privilege usually retained exclusively by the issuing company.

plan, a portion of the "issue" matures each year. The company continues interest payments on all outstanding bonds and repays the principal on part of the issue each year. These bonds carry serial numbers that are used to identify the year of maturity.

Companies may establish a **sinking fund** to accumulate the money to retire bonds. The company sets aside a given amount each year so that by the maturity date of the bond issue, the fund contains enough money to retire, or sink, the issue.

Indentures sometimes specify that bonds are **callable,** or **redeemable.** This allows the issuing company to retire the bonds before their maturity date, at the company's option. Management might wish to retire bonds early to reduce a corporation's leverage or in order to borrow money elsewhere at a lower interest rate.

## NONCORPORATE BONDS

### For governments and nonprofit organizations

Governments and nonprofit organizations also raise debt financing by issuing bonds. Local, state, and national governments use bonds for funds to build schools, libraries, and sewer and water treatment plants, for example. The interest received from many bonds issued by local and state governments is not subject to federal income tax. Some are also free from state and local taxes as well. This feature makes **tax-exempt municipal bonds** popular with investors who have high incomes and heavy tax burdens. (See Figure 18-5.)

The federal government issues a range of bonds to finance its operations. The most familiar are United States Savings Bonds. The U.S. Treasury also directly issues large bond offerings, and a variety of other notes, bills, and certificates are used to promise repayment of money borrowed by the government.

## GOVERNMENT SOURCES OF BUSINESS FUNDS

### Primarily for small businesses

The federal government has programs designed to make it easier for businesses to get long-term financing. Small businesses have especially benefited from these programs. The Small Business Administration makes direct loans or guarantees loans made by private lending institutions. These loans are available only to companies that cannot get financing at a reasonable rate from ordinary private sources. The Veterans Administration guarantees certain types of business loans for veterans, especially for purchasing business facilities. The Federal Housing Administration also provides some loans for buying business facilities.

## 6  LONG-TERM EQUITY FINANCING

### This is a source of funds for corporations only

Proprietorships or partnerships raise no question about ownership; all of their equity financing comes from the assets of the proprietor or partners. A corporation, however, is owned by a group. Equity financing is gained by selling shares of ownership to investors. The shares are represented by a financial instrument called **stock.**

## CORPORATE STOCK

### A way of sharing ownership

The people and organizations that own corporate stock actually own shares of the assets of the corporation. This contrasts with bondholders who have only lent money to the company. Bondholders do not participate in ownership.

**PAR VALUE** Many stocks have a price assigned to them when they are issued. This price is called *par value,* but it has little relation to the actual value or selling price of the stock. If, however, investors buy a stock below par value, they may, in some cases, be charged an additional amount to bring the stock up to par value. This can happen only if the corporation becomes insolvent and needs the money to pay off creditors. Many companies issue *no-par-value stock.* No arbitrary value is shown on the certificate. The choice between par- or no-par-value stocks is usually based on the rules of incorporation in specific states.

**DIVIDENDS** An important reason to acquire part ownership in a company is to share in its profits. Corporations divide surplus profits among stockholders by paying *dividends* on shares of stock. Rules about the distribution of profits make an important distinction between the two major types of stock: preferred and common.

# PREFERRED STOCK
## *It shares in the profits first* ━━━━━━━━━━━━━━━━

*Preferred stock* receives preference over common stock in the payment of dividends, in receiving the proceeds of assets if the corporation fails, and in other ways. The specific ways in which a particular issue of stock receives preference are described on the stock certificate. Many variations are possible.

**PREFERRED STOCK DIVIDENDS** Owners of preferred stock almost always receive the first portion when profits are distributed. It often happens that, except when profits are unusually high, owners of preferred stock receive dividends and owners of common stock do not. Preferred stock certificates state a rate at which dividends will be paid, such as $8 per $100 face value. The stated dividend will only be paid, however, when the company has adequate profits to cover it. Interest on bonds and all other payments due creditors must be paid before a profit is computed. When a dividend is not paid because of inadequate profits, it is said to be *passed.*

Some stocks are made even more preferred by being cumulative. *Cumulative preferred stocks* require that any passed dividends must be made up before any profits can be distributed to owners of common stock. A company might, for example, pass the preferred dividend for the last quarter of one year because of low profits. If, in the next quarter, profits are high, the company must pay cumulative preferred stockholders the passed dividend and the new dividend before paying anything to holders of common stock. Noncumulative preferred stock does not have this provision. If a dividend is passed, it need not be made up.

**PARTICIPATING AND NONPARTICIPATING STOCKS** Preferred stocks also vary in the extent to which they benefit from large profits. *Nonparticipating preferred stocks* are never paid a dividend larger than the rate shown on the certificate. *Participating preferred stocks* do receive a share of profits in addition to the stated dividend rate when such profits are available.

*VOTING AND NONVOTING STOCKS* Many preferred stocks do not carry the privilege of voting on company matters. Even though they represent ownership, these stocks do not give the stockholders active control of the corporation. Some preferred stockholders are given voting rights limited to matters that might affect the stocks' preferred status, such as issuance of a large bond offering or merger with another company.

*CALLABLE OR REDEEMABLE STOCKS* Preferred stocks may sometimes be made **callable** in the same way bonds are. The issuing corporation retains the right to buy back callable stocks at a stated price.

*CONVERTIBLE STOCKS* Preferred stocks may share another feature with bonds: they may be **convertible.** Some stock issues state that a given number of shares of preferred stock may be exchanged for a given number of shares of common stock at the option of the stockholder. The purpose of this provision is the same as that of bonds. The preferred stock is made more attractive to investors because they can make a profit by converting it if the value of common stock increases.

Many companies do not issue preferred stock, as can be seen in Figure 18-6. This reflects the variety of sources a firm can use to build its financial structure.

## COMMON STOCK
*Greater risk, greater chance of gain*

The shareholders of a corporation's common stock participate fully as owners of the corporation. The sale of **common stock** provides the day-to-day risk capital with which the company will try to make a profit. All corporations have common stock, though they may or may not have preferred stock or bonds. Preferred stock also represents ownership of a company, but it has safeguards and special protections which decrease the risk for investors. Owners of common stock participate fully in the risk of the business operation. They may also participate fully in the profits if the company is successful.

Common stock has no stated rate of return. The corporation is not bound to pay any dividends on common stock at all. When large profits are made, however, large distributions are sometimes made. Because holders of common stock share the ownership of a corporation, they are allowed to vote on important issues related to the company's management. Common stockholders, for example, elect the board of directors that is responsible for the operation of the company. It is possible to establish a class of common stockholders without voting rights, but this is far less usual than allowing all common stockholders to vote.

Since owners of common stock actually own the corporation, they receive any proceeds that are left over from the sale of assets if the company dissolves. As owners, however, they are responsible for paying off all of the company's obligations. For this reason, all agreements must be met with creditors, bondholders, and owners of preferred stock before any assets can be distributed to holders of common stock. If a corporation fails, however, and owes more than it owns, no stockholders—of either common or preferred stock—must make up the difference. Their liability, unlike that of a sole proprietorship or partnership, is limited to the price they paid for their shares of stock.

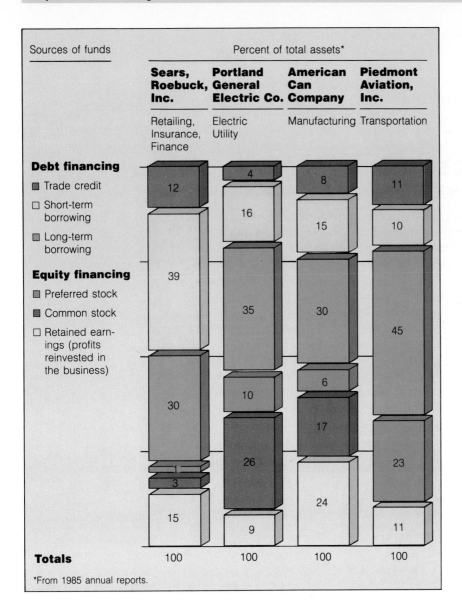

| Sources of funds | Percent of total assets* | | | |
| --- | --- | --- | --- | --- |
| | **Sears, Roebuck, Inc.** | **Portland General Electric Co.** | **American Can Company** | **Piedmont Aviation, Inc.** |
| | Retailing, Insurance, Finance | Electric Utility | Manufacturing | Transportation |
| **Debt financing** | | | | |
| ■ Trade credit | 12 | 4 | 8 | 11 |
| □ Short-term borrowing | | 16 | 15 | 10 |
| ■ Long-term borrowing | 39 | 35 | 30 | |
| **Equity financing** | | | | 45 |
| ■ Preferred stock | 30 | 10 | 6 | |
| ■ Common stock | 1 | 26 | 17 | 23 |
| □ Retained earnings (profits reinvested in the business) | 3 | | 24 | |
| | 15 | 9 | | 11 |
| **Totals** | 100 | 100 | 100 | 100 |

*From 1985 annual reports.

Figure 18-6 How sources of funds differ among four major companies.

# STOCK DIVIDENDS AND STOCK SPLITS
*Mainly paper transactions*

A corporation may wish to pay a dividend to stockholders. At the same time, however, it may wish to retain substantial portions of its profits for reinvestment. In this situation, corporations may issue a **stock dividend.** Some or all of the dividend will be paid in the form of new shares of stock rather than cash. The shares may be converted to cash if the stockholder chooses to sell them on the market, or the shares may be retained as a continuing investment.

One feature of common stocks that makes them attractive to investors is that they increase in value when a company is successful. A stock that is bought for $10 today may be worth $50 a number of years from now. This increase in value may eventually make individual shares too expensive to attract small investors. Corporations may then declare a **stock split** to reduce the price of single shares. This procedure divides each share of existing stock into two or more new shares. Since the new shares represent smaller portions of ownership, they will be proportionately lower priced. If shares of common stock were selling for $210, the corporation might declare a three-for-one stock split. This would create three times the existing number of shares, with each share having an initial value of $70. The lower price per share might make the stock salable to a larger number of investors.

## ISSUING AND TRADING STOCK
*Intermediaries—bankers and brokers—prevail*

A corporation originally issues stock to raise capital needed to begin and to carry on operations. It sells stock to individual investors or to other companies or financial institutions in return for cash to use in its operations. The first time the stock is sold is the only time the issuing company receives money from the stock.

Initial issues of stock are often sold in very large blocks to only a few buyers. Often a single investment bank may buy a whole issue. These original buyers may then resell shares in smaller lots to other investors. Even though a single share of stock may be sold and resold hundreds of times during the life of a corporation, the issuing company does not normally take part in these transactions. Stock shares are bought and sold through stockbrokers, who simply inform the issuing corporation of the transaction and of the present owner. This is covered in greater detail in Chapter 19.

# *Key Concepts*

1. Financial management plans and controls the acquisition and use of funds needed for business operations. Funds may be acquired either from investments or by borrowing. They are used to buy the facilities, materials, and other resources needed by a business.

2. The length of time for which funds will be needed affects the source from which they will be obtained. Some sources are best for short-term needs and some are best for long-term needs.

3. Business funds may be obtained from equity financing or from debt financing. Equity financing uses money invested by owners; debt financing uses borrowed money.

4. Some sources of short-term debt financing are trade credit, direct unsecured or secured loans, discounting, factoring, and commercial paper.

5. The most common sources of long-term debt financing are bank term loans, mortgages, and bonds. Bonds are secured or unsecured promises issued by an organization to repay principal and interest in return for borrowed money.

6. Long-term equity financing results from the investments of proprietors or partners or from the sale of stock by corporations. Common stock represents basic shares of ownership in a corporation. Preferred stock also represents shares of ownership but receives priority in the payment of dividends and in other ways.

# Review Questions

1. Define, explain, or identify each of the following key terms or phrases, found on the pages indicated.

assets (p. 409)
bad debts (p. 410)
bank term loans (p. 418)
bond (p. 419)
callable, or redeemable, bond (p. 422)
callable, or redeemable, preferred stock (p. 424)
collateral (p. 415)
commercial paper (p. 418)
common stock (p. 424)
convertible bonds (p. 420)
convertible stock (p. 424)
coupon, or bearer, bonds (p. 420)
cumulative preferred stock (p. 423)
current assets (p. 409)
debenture bonds (p. 420)
debt financing (p. 410)
discounting (p. 417)
dividend (p. 423)
equity financing (p. 410)
factoring (p. 417)
financial management (p. 409)
fixed assets (p. 410)
indenture (p. 420)
instrument (p. 414)
interest (p. 409)
leverage (p. 414)
line of credit (p. 416)
maturity date (p. 419)
mortgage (p. 418)
mortgage bonds (p. 420)
nonparticipating preferred stock (p. 423)
no-par-value stock (p. 423)
participating preferred stock (p. 423)
par value (p. 423)
passed dividend (p. 423)
preferred stock (p. 423)

principal (p. 419)
promissory note (p. 416)
registered bonds (p. 420)
sales finance company (p. 417)
secured loan (p. 415)
serial bonds (p. 420)
sinking fund (p. 421)
stock (p. 422)
stock dividend (p. 425)
stock split (p. 425)
tax-exempt municipal bonds (p. 422)
trade credit (p. 415)
trustee (p. 420)
unsecured loan (p. 415)
working capital (p. 409)

2. What are current assets? What three things of value usually make up current assets? Why might a firm use long-term debt to finance current assets?

3. What are some of the advantages of using borrowed money to finance business operations?

4. Why is trade credit considered debt financing?

5. What are two ways accounts receivable may be used to raise short-term financing?

6. As a firm increases its financial leverage, which rises fastest: its debt or its equity? What is the danger in using too much leverage?

7. Why are bonds usually issued by organizations like corporations and governments?

8. What is the main difference between bonds and preferred stocks?

9. How do common stocks differ from preferred stocks?

10. What is meant by the statement that "a company that issues stock receives payment for that stock only one time, no matter how many times it is resold thereafter"?

# Case Critique 18-1
## Hatching the Nest Egg

Barbara O'Brien had an idea for making money. The idea was to make curtains for dollhouses. O'Brien had a nest egg, although it was pretty small, only $1,000. Nevertheless, from this nest egg, she was able to hatch a fledgling business. The business inched along satisfactorily. As orders were received, O'Brien farmed them out to contract workers, operating in their own homes, and delivering the finished curtains to O'Brien at so many dollars a curtain. The time came, however, when O'Brien wanted to expand her business so that it would provide her with more than "side money" as profit. She began bringing her samples to the New York trade shows attended by toy and department store buyers. She was able to write a significant number of orders this way. The buyers, however, weren't happy about the delay in shipments while they waited for O'Brien to farm out the orders to her suppliers. The process involved her writing up manufacturing specifications before her subcontractors could get busy. It would be much better, reasoned O'Brien, to keep her suppliers busy blocking and sewing during the off-season so that she would have a finished inventory of curtains on hand to ship immediately after the trade shows. To do this, she figured she needed $5,000.

O'Brien considered borrowing this sum from family or friends, but felt that she would prefer a more businesslike arrangement. Accordingly, she went to her local bank and arranged to borrow up to $5,000. She found that she didn't have to borrow it all at once. She could borrow all or a portion of it for 90 days. She would then use the proceeds of each loan to pay off her suppliers and ship the curtains to her buyers. As soon as her buyers paid for these orders, she could pay back the outstanding loan and borrow again as needed. Using borrowed money, O'Brien's business grew quickly, enabling her to accept twice as many orders after each show as she had previously. Her profits went up proportionately.

1. What kind of funding did O'Brien use to start her business? To expand her business? What kinds of assets did she acquire with her expansion funds?
2. What is the term applied to O'Brien's arrangement for loans from the bank? If she borrowed $3,000 and repaid it, what was the limit on how much she could borrow the next time?
3. If O'Brien were to ask her suppliers to join with her in the ownership of her business, by buying shares of common stock in it, what kind of funding would that be? If O'Brien were to continue to operate the business out of her home and subcontract her orders, and her business grew to say $10 million a year, would it be likely that she could obtain funds through the sale of mortgage bonds? Why or why not?

---

SOURCE: Debra Ann Hatten, "Where to Look for Nest Eggs to Hatch Your Enterprise Soundly," *Christian Science Monitor*, June 11, 1985, p. 27.

# Case Critique 18-2
## Family, Faith, and Finances

The Rambusch Co. has been flourishing in New York's Greenwich Village for nearly 90 years. It makes two products: stained-glass windows and custom-made lighting fixtures. Its president attributes the firm's survival through thick and thin to three factors: a founder who left a succession of sons to carry on the business, the Roman Catholic Church, which has been its most loyal customer, and tight financial controls.

The company's revenues approach $10 million annually, and it employs 74 artists, designers, craft workers, engineers, and mechanics. The business has been described by architects who buy Rambusch's products as "half art, half engineering." Its first customer was a local Roman Catholic Church, which bought a stained-glass window in 1898. Since then, Rambusch has completed more than 18,000 projects. These include the Art Deco-style Macy's New York department store and the largest leaded-glass window in the United States—13,000 square feet—at Lover's Lane United Methodist Church in Dallas. The company also produced the lighting fixtures for The Kennedy Center for the Performing Arts and for the East Wing of the National Gallery of Art in Washington, D.C. In between, it executed works in more than 30 state capitol buildings and more than 100 cathedrals.

*Interiors* magazine attributed the firm's survival to "family vitality—since the founder's sons took over from him, and their sons from them in an unbroken line, which seems to include talent and scholarship, as well as financial responsibility for the enterprise." Interestingly, grandson-president Viggo Rambusch says, "This business is not run strictly for profit or to exploit the marketplace. We feel a great desire to do exceptional work and to be responsible for creating an environment. You should never do anything that you're not proud of." Nevertheless, says Rambusch, art cannot be sustained without sound financial management of the business. "We have good financial control."

For example, all of Rambusch's stained-glass customers (who make up 40 percent of the company's business) are required under contract to pay 85 percent of the final invoice prior to delivery or completion of the contract. Customers of the lighting division, who make up the remaining 60 percent of the volume, are billed under the standard practice of requiring payment within 30 days after delivery. Viggo Rambusch adds, "We try not to borrow money, and we have as little long-term debt as possible. Our only long-term debt now is a $250,000 bank mortgage on our headquarters building. If we had been loaded with short-term debt during the recessions of 1973 and 1982, we might have gone out of business."

1. To what financial practice does Rambusch's president attribute the company's ability to weather the recent recessions? Is that necessarily a good practice for a firm to follow?
2. Would you say that Rambusch is an easy company to obtain trade credit from? Why?
3. Rambusch limits its use of long-term borrowing to a mortgage on its headquarters building. How might this policy of limited long-term financing restrict the company's growth? What other methods of financing might the company pursue if it wished to double or triple its size in the next 5 years?

*SOURCE:* William F. Doescher, "Three Generations of Craftsmanship," *D&B Reports,* September–October 1984, p. 1214.

# Money Supply, Financial Institutions, and Securities Markets

## Learning Objectives

*The purpose of this chapter is to define money and its function, show how financial institutions and securities markets operate, and describe the process of buying and selling stocks and bonds.*

*As evidence of general comprehension, after you study this chapter you should be able to:*

1. *Explain the function of money and how its supply and demand affect business conditions.*

2. *Explain the objectives and basic functions of the Federal Reserve System. Distinguish among the services offered by commercial banks and other lending institutions.*

3. *Identify the securities markets and securities exchanges.*

4. *Differentiate between investors and speculators; define the role of stockbrokers, and describe a typical stock transaction.*

5. *Read and interpret stock and bond reports.*

6. *Outline the purpose of government regulation of the securities and investment markets.*

*If your class is using SSweetco: Business Model and Activity File, see Chapter 19 in that book after you complete this chapter. There you will find exercises and activities to help you apply your learning to typical business situations.*

## 1 MONEY

provides a medium of exchange.

Currency

Checking

Plastic

## 2 THE BANKING SYSTEM

provides a place to

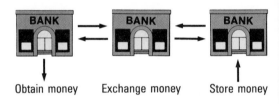

Obtain money     Exchange money     Store money

and it is regulated
by the

Federal Reserve System.

## 3 SECURITIES MARKETS

provide

Stocks     Bonds

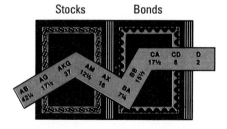

Exchanges for buying and selling long-term
securities.

## 4 SECURITIES TRADING

involves

Individuals

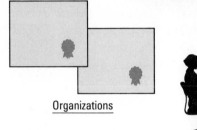

Organizations

Stockbrokers

## 5 FINANCIAL NEWS REPORTS

list daily prices of securities and average price
indexes.

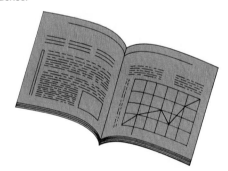

## 6 REGULATION OF STOCK AND BOND SALES

is carried out principally
by the Securities and
Exchange Commission
(SEC). Its goal is to
protect investors and
financial markets.

# A TYPICAL DAY IN THE FINANCIAL MARKETS

*It was a typical day in late summer of 1985. It was like almost any day, any year from 1980 to 1990. There was more than $500 billion of ready money circulating in the economy. Credit was easy: millions of United States citizens owed nearly $500 billion in installment loans. The prime interest rates that banks were charging their most substantial customers had dropped below 10 percent. The Federal Deposit Insurance Company closed a small bank in Illinois that had extended itself too far with loans to farmers. The Federal Reserve System was contemplating raising the interest rate it charged to banks for loans: the Fed was worried about too much ready money and the ease of obtaining installment loans.*

*More than 81 million shares of stock were traded on the New York Stock Exchange. The index of average stock prices fell a few points for the day. The prices of 659 stocks went up, 895 went down, and 432 remained unchanged. Millions of investors made purchases in the nearly 300 major money market mutual funds and over 850 other mutual investment funds. The Aluminum Company of America issued $150 million in debenture bonds due in the year 2015, and the Southland Corporation (parent of 7-Eleven stores) issued $3 million of preferred stock. . . .*

*The famed Revere Copper and Brass Corporation filed a formal notice under Chapter 11 of the bankruptcy laws of its intention to reorganize in an attempt to settle its debts to creditors and its obligations to its equity securities holders.*

*On the commodities exchange the price of a future pound of orange juice fell from its peak of $1.80 a year ago to the year's low of $1.39. A school teacher in Texas discovered that the majority of her $35,000 investments of her life savings were worthless; and informed people warned investors and speculators once again that it is safer to invest in financial institutions regulated by the Federal Reserve Board and/or insured by a Federal Deposit Insurance agency or in securities regulated by the Securities and Exchange Commission. It had been a typical day in the money and securities markets of the United States.*

---

*SOURCE: The Wall Street Journal,* August 12, 1985, various news reports.

---

# 1 MONEY: THE BASIC MEANS OF EXCHANGE
## Money makes the world go round

Most people are more likely to think of a market as the place where they shop for groceries rather than for money. If they give the subject a moment's thought, however, they will quickly see that they often shop for money too. Individuals shop for personal loans to tide them over a barren patch when their bankbooks are bare. Or they shop for installment loans to buy an auto or a major appliance. They also go to the money market when they want a mortgage to buy a home or a loan to finance a college education.

Businesses, like individuals, need money. It is needed to start and expand operations. It is the grease that keeps the wheels of business moving. Certain characteristics of money make it an especially good medium of exchange for business.

The use of money as a means of exchange developed early in most societies. It has many advantages over the **barter system** that it replaced, where specific kinds of goods or services are directly exchanged for other goods or services, as illustrated in Table 19-1. Because money can be exchanged for any kinds of goods or services, it is valuable to everyone. This universal acceptability makes trade much easier. Money is also divisible. An ax might be worth ten sacks of flour, but suppose the owner of the ax needs only one sack. While there is no way to divide an ax into ten parts, money can be divided into units as small as needed. These "units of account" enable money to measure the relative value of things.

Money makes commerce easier because it serves as a standard of value. The value of many different kinds of products can be expressed in a single standard: 20 yards of cloth may cost $50 and a box of nails $5. This is far more convenient than the barter system, where the cloth may be worth a single boot, a thousand buttons, or a tenth of a horse. Money also provides a convenient means of storing value. A person's or a company's income does not always match current needs for buying goods and services. A farmer may produce nearly all of the year's income at harvest season; the farm produce can be sold and thus converted to cash, which is kept for use throughout the year. Surplus income from a number of years can be accumulated for later use or for investment in enterprises requiring large amounts of capital. Such accumulation is difficult in a barter system.

### Action Brief

## BACK TO BARTERING?

*As a tax dodge, it's illegal; but many corporations, to say nothing of individuals, are finding that bartering saves money. For example, Pan American World Airlines traded "sponsorship" seats to officials of the United States Football League in order to have that designation. Hotels routinely trade "free" conference rooms and meals to firms that hold meetings there. Or company A gets insurance and trucking services from company B (valued at $40,000) and gives 3,000 square feet of carpet (also valued at $40,000) to company B, which trades the carpets to company C for four cars and three copying machines, while company C trades 32,000 pounds of coffee (valued at $75,000) to an airline in return for $75,000 worth of tickets.*

**TABLE 19-1**
**DESIRABLE CHARACTERISTICS OF MONEY**

- *Means of exchange* simpler and more flexible than the barter system

- *Universal acceptability* as a *standard of value*

- *Divisibility* that creates convenient *units of account,* such as pennies and dollars, enabling the relative value of things to be measured and the exchange of goods and services to be simplified

- *Means of storing value* for the future so that surplus income can be accumulated for later use

- *Durability* in handling and *difficulty in counterfeiting*

# MONEY SUPPLY AND DEMAND
*The Federal Reserve System controls the supply* ━━━━━━━━

The chances are that when you think of money, you consider only the coins and paper money you can put in your pocket. These are called **currency,** but the basic money supply also includes **demand deposits,** which is money kept in checking accounts. **Checks** are considered to be money because they can be used like cash and exchanged immediately for goods and services.

Deposits in savings accounts, if they are called **time deposits,** cannot be used directly in exchange for goods or services. Time deposits are considered investments and are not usually counted as part of the basic money supply. They are, however, considered when economists and the federal government take a broader look at money supply.

Money is supplied to the economy mainly by the Federal Reserve System (FRS, or sometimes the "Fed"). It issues new currency and gives credit to banks. Some commercial banks also supply money under the supervision of the Fed. The FRS also keeps track of the total supply of money according to four different classifications, as shown in Table 19-2. The **basic money supply** (M1 in Table 19-2) consists of currency in circulation and a great variety of demand deposits, including those held in money market mutual funds, and NOW and Super NOW accounts. In early 1987, M1 was $720 billion, of which about 2 percent was in coins, 24 percent in paper money, and 74 percent in demand deposits. The grand total of all money counted by the FRS (M1 + M2 + M3 + L in Table 19-2) was over $4,000 billion.

| TABLE 19-2 THE FEDERAL RESERVE SYSTEM'S FOUR CLASSIFICATIONS OF MONEY | |
| --- | --- |
| **M1** | Currency in circulation, traveler's checks, and demand deposits, including regular savings accounts from which withdrawals can be made without advance notice; plus certain other checking accounts, such as negotiable orders of withdrawal (NOW and Super NOW) accounts, which allow depositors to write checks on interest-bearing accounts; automatic transfer accounts (ATS); and "share drafts," which approximate checking accounts for credit unions. |
| **M2** | All of the above; *plus* savings and small-denomination time deposits; shares in money market mutual funds; money market fund accounts offered by savings institutions; and certain overnight commercial deposits. |
| **M3** | All of the above; *plus* large-denomination time deposits and long-term business borrowing arrangements; and balances of institutions-only money market mutual funds. |
| **L** | All of the above; *plus* other liquid assets such as certain moneys (Eurodollars) held in foreign banks but owned by United States residents; commercial paper; and notes, bills, and other securities issued by the U.S. Treasury Department, including U.S. Savings Bonds. |

***MONEY SUBSTITUTES*** Bank checks are still the most commonly used substitute for currency. There is good reason to believe, however, that by the end of the century, checks will be a thing of the past. The first invader has been ***plastic money,*** the ubiquitous charge (or credit) card carried by almost every adult American. VISA, MasterCard, Diners Club, and American Express cards are so commonly used that the distinction between what is money and what is credit has become hard to make. Many consumers use their credit cards as a ready substitute for currency or checks, although ultimately their payments must be made in real money.

The use of some form of ***electronic funds transfer (EFT)*** system, however, is almost certain to revolutionize the exchange of both money and credit. EFT is used by banks, or by other service organizations, to transfer money from one person's or company's account to another in payment for goods or services. This is seen most often today in electronic banking (see page 441). EFT is also becoming a fairly common practice in POS (point-of-sale) transactions. For example, in Florida a participating gas station operator can arrange to have the receipts of sales paid by a credit card instantly transferred to the operator's bank. Still another variation of EFT is to have payroll and pension payments transferred directly to the recipient's bank account. The final step in EFT may be the use of home banking, by which a special computer-connected device allows an individual to switch money between accounts and to command his or her bank to pay bills directly.

# INFLATION AND DEFLATION
*Related to money supply*

The demand for money is created by individuals and organizations who want to use money as a means of exchange and for its storing and investing value. The effects on the economy of money supply and this demand for it are complex and not entirely understood. There are, however, two general effects that are widely accepted:

■  If the demand for money remains constant and the supply of money increases, the prices of goods and services increase. One interpretation of this effect is that an increase in the money supply leads to more buying. This increases the demand for goods and services and thus increases their prices. This increase in price is called ***inflation.***

■  If the supply of money remains constant and demand for money increases, economic production decreases. Limits on the supply of money reduce purchasing power and limit the total amount of goods and services that can be sold and produced. If this brings about a drop in prices, it is called ***deflation.***

# INTEREST
*The cost of borrowing money*

The supply of and demand for money also affect and are affected by interest rates charged for borrowed money. ***Interest rates*** are usually expressed as a percentage to be applied as a charge over a specified period of time to the sum of money (principal) borrowed. For example, an interest rate of 12 percent a year on a loan of $1,000 means that the charge for the use of the borrowed money for 1 year would be $120. The borrower would be obliged, of course, to return the principal ($1,000) as well as the interest.

Among many complex interactions between interest rates, money supply, and demand for money, two are particularly noteworthy:

■   As interest rates rise, the demand for money decreases or at least lowers its rate of increase. High interest rates tend to encourage savings and discourage installment purchases of autos and homes.

■   When the demand for money remains constant and the supply increases, short-term interest rates usually decrease. Low interest rates tend to discourage savings and encourage purchases.

## THE TIME VALUE OF MONEY
*One dollar in hand is worth two in the future*

Although money itself does not produce any income, it can be invested in ways that will produce income. This makes the value of money vary with the time when it is received. Money received next year is less valuable than money received today because today's money can be earning interest during the coming year.

For example, if a dollar can earn 5 percent interest in a savings account, the dollar is actually worth $1.05 if its owner is free to leave it in the account for a year. If the dollar is free to be invested for 15 years, it is worth about $2. Accumulated interest at 5 percent will about double the value of an account in that period.

The time value of money is especially important when managers or others wish to evaluate the true cost or return from an investment. Suppose, for example, a company was considering whether or not to purchase a labor-saving machine. The machine costs $100,000 and is expected to last 15 years. It would help the company to decide on this purchase if it also knew the true—or accumulated cost—of the machine over the full 15 years. The time value of the money to be invested ($100,000) becomes increasingly important as the interest rate rises. If, for example, at the time of purchase interest rates were 10 percent and were forecast to continue at that rate through the life of the machine, a calculation can be made to show what the $100,000 might have earned if it were in a bank drawing 10 percent interest all that time.

The true cost would be something like $417,700! It is computed by the principle of **compound interest.** This is done by applying the interest rate of 10 percent to the principal of $100,000 to find the value of the sum after 1 year: $110,000 ($100,000 + $100,000 × .10). The computation is repeated in that form for 14 more years, always applying the interest rate to the latest sum. For example, in the second year, the computation would be $110,000 + $110,000 × .10 = $110,000 + $11,000 = $121,000. In effect, the company must weigh the cost of investing $100,000 in the new machine against the possibility of putting the $100,000 in a compound-interest savings investment, which would accumulate another $317,700 over the 15-year period. This principle is illustrated graphically in Figure 19-1.

Ordinary citizens were made especially aware of the time value of money during 1981 when the federal government was urging them to invest in Individual Retirement Accounts (IRAs). The interest rates at

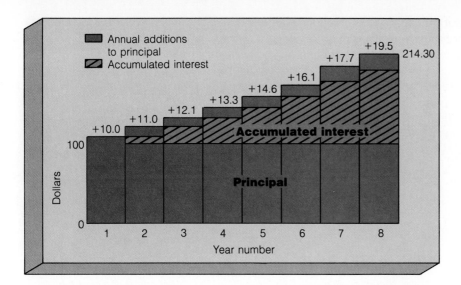

Figure 19-1 The accumulative effect of compound interest.

that time were about 12 percent. The individual limit for investment in an IRA was $2,000. Banks were speculating that if a 30-year-old individual put $2,000 per year in a compounding IRA, and if the interest rates were to continue at 12 percent, the cash value of the IRA at age 65 would be $1,216,000!

The danger in estimating the future value of money is that it is directly dependent upon the interest rate that prevails each year. The lower the interest rate, the lower will be the future value of the money. Conversely, of course, the higher the interest rate, the higher the future value of the money. Predicting future interest rates is extremely difficult and uncertain, however. The most skilled economic forecasters are often wrong about future interest rates, even when the future is only a month or two away.

# 2  THE AMERICAN BANKING SYSTEM
## The mainspring of the business system

Once money is used as a medium of exchange, a well-run banking system becomes a necessity. Banks provide a safe place for people to keep their money and facilitate its exchange through checking accounts, letters of credit, and other instruments. Banks also make loans to individuals, businesses, governments, and other organizations, and provide a method (savings accounts) for accumulating capital. In the United States, the banking system consists of the Federal Reserve System, commercial banks, and other kinds of financial institutions.

## THE FEDERAL RESERVE SYSTEM
### Its goals: stability and productivity

The Federal Reserve Act of 1913 created a partly governmental, partly private organization to improve the overall operation of the United States banking system. The organization, called the **Federal Reserve System,** consists of a seven-member board of governors, twelve Federal

Reserve Banks, and thousands of privately owned banks throughout the country. Two top-level advisory groups are also part of this system. Each of the Federal Reserve Banks is responsible for certain banking activities within its region.

The goal of the Federal Reserve System is to regulate the supply of money and credit in order to promote a stable and productive economy. The board of governors maintains orderly economic growth by using information it has about the demand for money and credit and by using its ability to affect interest rates and to expand and contract the money supply.

The Federal Reserve System also (1) helps establish general banking procedures, (2) carries out transactions between banks, especially checking account transactions, (3) serves as a warehouse for cash belonging to banks, and (4) examines the records of member banks.

## INFLUENCE ON MONEY SUPPLY AND CREDIT

*The Federal Reserve System applies three techniques* ━━━━━

The Federal Reserve has three main tools for performing its job of regulating the money and credit supply. It can (1) set the amount of cash reserves banks must keep, (2) buy and sell government securities to affect the money supply, and (3) affect interest rates by changing the amount it charges for loans to banks.

**CONTROL OF BANK RESERVES** Banks receive money from deposits to checking and savings accounts and lend part of the money to borrowers. A bank's profits depend on earning more interest on loans than is paid out to savings account depositors. For safe operations, a bank must keep on hand some of the money that is taken in. These **reserves** are used to cover day-to-day withdrawals and can never be lent out. The Federal Reserve specifies what proportion of deposits member banks must keep in reserves. If the reserve requirement is raised, banks will have less money to lend, and the total supply of money available to business and consumers is reduced. If the reserve requirement is lowered, more money is available for borrowing, and the money supply is increased.

**OPEN MARKET TRANSACTIONS** The Federal Reserve significantly affects the money supply by buying and selling government securities on the open market. **Securities** include all types of stocks and bonds and certain other financial instruments. When the Federal Reserve buys government bonds, it issues new money to pay for them. This increases the money supply. The money filters into the economy through government spending for goods and services. Also, when the Federal Reserve—rather than private investors—buys government bonds, private capital is still available for investment in other ways.

When the Federal Reserve sells bonds and keeps the proceeds, the money supply is reduced. The money received from the sale of bonds is actually taken out of circulation.

**CONTROL OF THE DISCOUNT RATE** Commercial banks lend large amounts of money, especially for business uses. They are able to lend more money than they take in through deposits because they are themselves able to borrow from the Federal Reserve. The Federal Reserve charges interest on the loans it makes to banks. The rate is called the *discount rate* because the transaction is similar to discounting accounts receivable or other accounts. When the Federal Reserve charges a high interest rate to banks, the banks must pass on the cost to their borrowers. This raises the general interest rate and makes borrowing less attractive. Changes in private interest rates are usually measured by the *prime rate,* or the interest charged by major banks for short-term loans to large commercial customers with the best credit standings.

## COMMERCIAL BANKS
*Privately owned, publicly regulated*

*Commercial banks* in the United States are privately owned businesses that provide a variety of financial services to customers. They must obtain a government charter before they can begin operations. National banks are chartered by the federal government; state banks are chartered by individual states.

Commercial banks maintain savings accounts and pay interest on them. With the help of the Federal Reserve, they also handle checking accounts. Figure 19-2 shows how the system works when a check is sent from one city to another. Federal Reserve banks provide the communication between the local banks that maintain the accounts of the buyer and seller. No actual cash changes hands in the transaction. It involves only an addition to the balance of one bank's account and a subtraction from the balance of the others.

**MAJOR SOURCES OF SHORT-TERM BORROWING** Most of the profits of commercial banks come from interest earned by making loans to businesses and individuals. Much of the short-term and long-term debt financing for business described in Chapter 18 comes from commercial banks. Such financing includes promissory notes, secured and unsecured bank term loans, mortgages, discounting, lines of credit, and others. A number of these loans are also available to individuals as personal installment loans for automobiles, home repairs, travel, and education. Banks also make short-term personal loans through certain credit cards that they manage.

**FINANCIAL SUPERMARKETS** Commercial banks also offer a broad range of other financial services. They act as a depository for the stocks and bonds owned by their customers and give investment advice. They also give advice on taxes, estate planning, pension funds, and business investments. Many of the large banks hire specialists in the various business fields who can give business clients expert advice. Commercial banks have also taken full advantage of computers and now can perform such time-saving services as paying bills and preparing payrolls.

Commercial and other banks and thrift organizations (see below) have progressively begun to see themselves as "retail" bankers. Instead of assuming that depositors and borrowers must come to them, bankers now try to attract customers like other retail merchants. In the face of increasing competition among banks, they have become marketing-oriented and typically offer their customers a wide variety of investing and borrowing options.

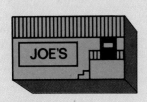

Joe, who runs a diner in Bixby, Nevada, buys a gas range made in Atlanta and sends his $1,250 check to the manufacturer.

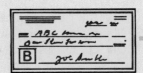

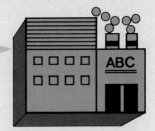

ABC Mfg. Co. deposits the check in the Mobile Bank.

Joe receives the canceled check at the end of the month from the Bixby Bank.

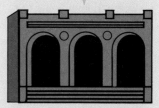

The Mobile Bank deposits the check for credit in its account at the Federal Reserve Bank of Atlanta.

The Federal Reserve Bank of San Francisco forwards the check to the Bixby Bank, which deducts $1,250 from Joe's account.

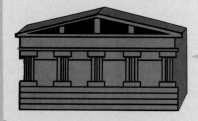

The Federal Reserve Bank of Atlanta sends the check to the Federal Reserve Bank of San Francisco for collection.

The Bixby Bank authorizes the San Francisco Federal Reserve Bank to deduct $1,250 from its deposit account with the reserve bank.

Funds are shifted from the San Francisco Reserve Bank to the Federal Reserve Bank of Atlanta. It credits the Mobile Bank's account, which, in turn, adds $1,250 to the account of the ABC Mfg. Co.

## OTHER BANKS AND THRIFT INSTITUTIONS

*A wide variety of services*

Figure 19-2 How a check travels through the Federal Reserve System.

There are other kinds of financial organizations that perform some of the services of commercial banks or play other roles in transacting financial business.

*Investment banks* act as financial agents for businesses, governments, or other organizations wishing to raise money by selling stocks, bonds, or other securities. When a corporation, for example, wants to sell 1,000 bonds worth $1,000 each, it does not ordinarily go directly to individual investors. It arranges to sell the entire issue to one or more investment banks. The investment banks resell the issue to private investors and receive a commission from the issuing corporation.

*Mutual savings banks* maintain savings accounts for depositors and use part of the deposits for making mortgage loans and other investments. A unique feature of mutual savings banks is that they operate like a cooperative: all earnings are distributed to depositors as interest or are retained within the bank as reserves.

*Savings and loan associations* provide many of the same services as savings banks. Depositors maintain savings accounts on which regular dividends or interest is paid. A portion of the deposits is then lent out at interest for mortgages or other kinds of loans. In most states, the banking laws have been changed to allow mutual savings banks and savings and loan associations to handle demand deposits and offer other investment opportunities such as insured money market funds, thus making them more competitive with commercial banks.

*Credit unions* are associations of members (usually employees of a private company or a government agency) who buy shares of ownership and make savings deposits in the union. Part of the money is then used to make loans to credit union members. Loans are usually small, although some of the larger organizations make real estate mortgage loans.

Other important sources of loans are insurance companies and pension funds, which can accumulate sizable assets. *Pension funds* are moneys set aside by firms, insurance companies, labor unions, and other organizations to provide an income for retired employees. While neither insurance companies nor pension funds are classified as banks, both are important factors in the money and securities markets.

# BANKING OF THE FUTURE
## *Electronics, bells, and whistles*

The impact of electronic banking is just beginning to be felt. This extends well beyond electronic funds transfer, although EFT is the heart of the technology. It includes widespread use of computers, telephones, and a variety of electronic devices. Eventually, EFT will draw many nonbanking institutions into retail, as well as commercial, banking. Most visible to the people who make deposits or withdraw funds from a bank is the *automated teller machine (ATM)*. In its simplest form, a customer obtains cash from an ATM by inserting a proprietary "debit card" issued by the bank for its own machines. In 1987 there were already more than 260 regional ATM computer networks linking together debit cards from competing, but participating, banks. These served more than 55 million cardholders. The Dallas-based Southland Corp., for example, put thousands of ATMs in its 7-Eleven stores.

As a consequence of electronics and deregulation (see next section), the nature and variety of bank services have changed measurably in the past decade. The predictions are that banks will undergo change in both their location and appearance. The large lobbies lined with tellers' cages are being replaced with automated teller machines inside as well as outside. These are complemented with computer terminals that can read payroll checks and answer credit and investment inquiries. Banks are shifting their branches closer to consumer shopping patterns and into all manner of retail locations. Sears Roebuck, already officially in the banking business, has installed banking and other financial services in hundreds of its stores. K mart has followed suit.

The trend toward banks targeted at unique population segments has not been so successful, however. Many banks founded to serve women and blacks, for example, have found that deregulation opened them to heavy competition from broad-based institutions. Accordingly, many minority banks have either failed or widened their market scope to attract depositors and borrowers. On the other hand, marketing innovations continue. The Bank of San Francisco, for example, in 1985 announced that it would try to segment an upscale market. Its target customer list is for people making $75,000 or more a year and with a net worth exceeding $500,000. It specializes in personal loans from $50,000 to $1 million.

Another trend toward nontraditional banking is the proliferation of **money market mutual funds.** Technically, these are speculative investments in securities that are not under the supervision of the Federal Reserve System. Technicalities aside, many investors view these funds as a banking service. Investors buy shares in a money market mutual fund whose business is exclusively that of buying and selling commercial paper from very large borrowers (directly or from banks that have issued the paper), U.S. Treasury bills, and other borrowing instruments of the federal government. Most money market funds require a minimum initial deposit (for example, $1,000 or more) and offer only limited checking services (such as requiring a check minimum of $500). The growth of these funds was nothing short of spectacular, as can be seen from Figure 19-3. With declining interest rates, however, the trend in money market funds has reversed itself. Banking institutions view the operators of money market funds as competitors, since a significant portion of the money invested in the funds represents transfers from commercial and savings banks. Not surprisingly, under a trend toward increasing deregulation, banks now offer services that combine the security of a banking deposit with the higher-paying interests of money market funds.

# REGULATION OF BANKING AND THRIFT INSTITUTIONS
*New problems after deregulation*

The **Banking Act of 1980** was designed to deregulate many existing banking practices and to promote competition between many kinds of thrift institutions. A major feature of the act enables all deposit institutions to offer checking accounts. Other features permit savings and loans and mutual savings banks to make business and personal loans, issue credit cards, and set up remote "branches." Credit unions are now officially allowed to make mortgage loans. Ceilings on interest rates paid to depositors, once imposed by law, are being removed. Another significant change is the extension of the Fed's regulatory authority over nonmember deposit institutions. All institutions that accept deposits must maintain reserves against checking accounts, including the various types of interest-paying (NOW, Super NOW) accounts.

**BANK FAILURES AND DEPOSIT INSURANCE** Before 1934, depositors had little or no protection against the loss of their life savings if a bank failed. Losses were often enormous as more than half of the 30,000 banks in the country failed between 1920 and 1933. In response to these failures, the **Federal Deposit Insurance Corporation (FDIC)** was created on January 1, 1934. It insures savings up to a maximum balance of $100,000 per account in most national and state banks and also sets re-

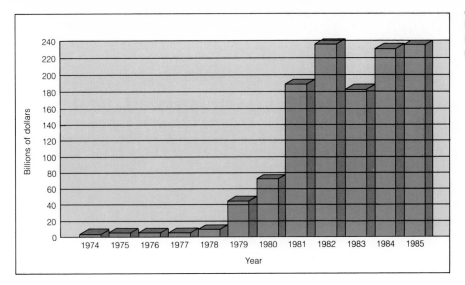

Figure 19-3 Growth of investments in money market mutual funds.

quirements for prudent banking practices. This has made investors willing to keep larger sums of money in savings accounts. Since money that banks lend comes partly from invested savings, the FDIC has indirectly increased the amount of funds available for borrowing. The **Federal Savings and Loan Insurance Corporation (FSLIC)** plays a similar role for savings and loan associations. The National Credit Union Administration insures deposits in federally chartered credit unions. This leaves relatively few eligible thrift institutions still without such protection.

When the FDIC entered the picture in 1934, it also initiated regular supervision over the banking practices of its member institutions. It did this so well that whereas 4,000 banks failed in 1934, only 4 failed in 1979. The basic method that the FDIC uses is to make an unannounced inspection of each member bank at least once a year. A *bank examiner* is a qualified specialist who conducts a detailed and rigorous inspection of the financial records and management practices of the bank. In addition, examiners from the U.S. Comptroller of the Currency, Federal Reserve System, and state regulatory commissions also inspect commercial banks.

Despite these precautions, banks do occasionally fail. In fact, since deregulation, the number of bank failures has increased again dramatically. (See Figure 19-4.) When an FDIC-insured bank fails, the agency follows two options: (1) It seeks to find another bank that will, for a fee paid by the FDIC, take over the failing bank and operate it without interruption of services or default to its depositors; or (2) it moves in quickly to close down the bank and pay off all accounts under $100,000 in full, usually within a few days.

# 3  THE SECURITIES MARKETS
*Principal source of equity funds*

When a business wishes to sell shares of its ownership to raise equity funds, it usually enters the securities markets. These markets exist at two levels. A business that is raising equity funds deals in the *primary securities*

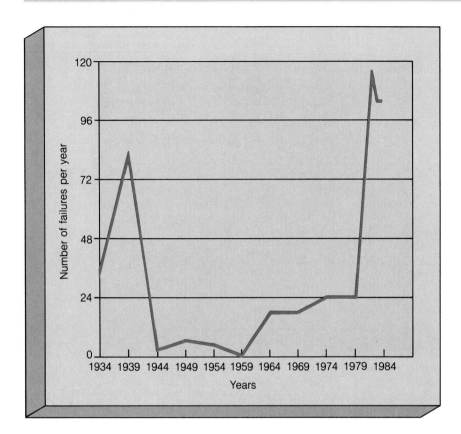

Figure 19-4 Failures of banks and savings & loans.

*market.* This market provides a means for corporations that are issuing shares of their stock (or selling bonds) to make contact with buyers. The general public is usually unaware of this market, which is handled mainly by financial intermediaries. (This will be discussed at greater length in Chapter 21 as "initial public offerings.") The *secondary securities market* consists of those markets where individuals or organizations that own shares of stock or bonds and wish to sell them make contact with other individuals or organizations that may wish to buy them. The secondary markets are those that are most visible to the general public and are the ones in which most people buy and sell securities. The relationship between the primary and secondary securities markets is shown in Figure 19-5.

## SECURITIES EXCHANGES
*Where the stocks and bonds are exchanged*

Stocks and bonds are bought and sold in the same manner as other valuable possessions. For example, a person who owns 50 shares of one company's stock may wish to sell them and buy 100 shares of stock in another company. Or the owner of bonds issued by one company may wish to sell them now, rather than wait until their maturity. The secondary marketplaces where this can be accomplished in a systematic, regulated manner are called *securities exchanges.* Not only do these exchanges provide a convenient way for buyers and sellers to contact one

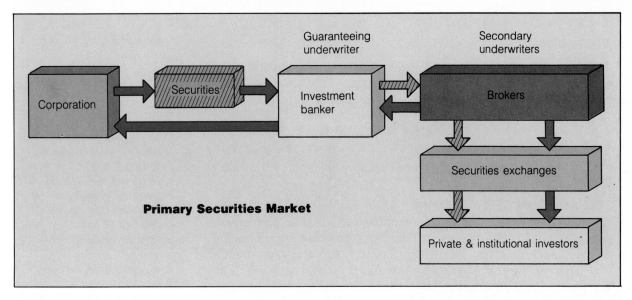

**Primary Securities Market**

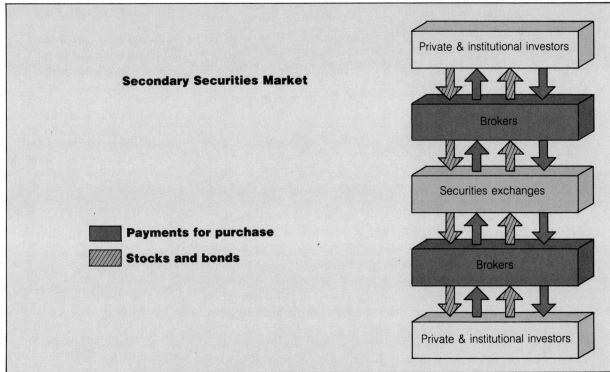

**Secondary Securities Market**

**Payments for purchase**

**Stocks and bonds**

another but they also provide traders with up-to-date information about current prices of securities. The existence of securities exchanges makes the securities traded there more valuable. Bringing together a large number of buyers and sellers makes the securities more liquid. *Liquidity* is the ease with which a possession can be sold, or turned into cash. The major exchanges make stocks a liquid investment because a buyer for them can always be found.

The securities exchanges also have a regulatory function. They establish rules of trading that make the exchange of securities safer for investors and more orderly for both buyers and sellers.

Figure 19-5 Relationships between primary and secondary security markets.

# THE PRINCIPAL EXCHANGES
*Regional, national, and worldwide*

Of the approximately 15 formal stock exchanges in the country, the New York Stock Exchange is by far the largest. The American Stock Exchange is second in size, and a number of regional markets follow, varying in size and importance. Many stocks are not traded at a specific location but are exchanged through a network of brokers in different cities. These stocks and bonds are called over-the-counter securities. Exchanges in foreign countries also trade the securities of United States companies.

**THE NEW YORK STOCK EXCHANGE** The New York Stock Exchange (NYSE) serves as the major national securities market. The exchange is an association of brokers who have come together to establish a trading place. Members must buy "seats" on the exchange and must be approved by the governing board. Membership is limited to 1,366. The NYSE and other exchanges carry on the trading of stocks and bonds only for organizations listed with the exchange. This exchange currently lists about 1,600 stocks and 2,700 bonds. For a company to be listed on the NYSE, it must apply and be accepted by the board of governors. Listed companies must have (1) annual pretax earnings of at least $2.5 million, (2) 1 million shares publicly held, (3) 2,000 or more investors holding a minimum of 100 shares each, (4) a value of at least $8 million for outstanding shares of common stock, and (5) tangible assets of at least $16 million.

**THE AMERICAN STOCK EXCHANGE** The American Stock Exchange (Amex) is also located in New York City and is also primarily a national exchange. Its listed companies are often, but not always, smaller than those on the NYSE. The American Stock Exchange lists about 1,000 companies.

**REGIONAL AND FOREIGN EXCHANGES** A number of regional exchanges outside of New York are growing in importance. Examples are the Midwest Exchange in Chicago, the Pacific Exchange in Los Angeles and San Francisco, the Philadelphia-Baltimore-Washington Exchange, and the Boston and Cincinnati city exchanges, as well as those in a number of other cities. These regional and local markets normally trade securities from local corporations and from some of the national companies listed on the NYSE or Amex.

Stock trading was carried on in foreign countries before the United States was founded. Important exchanges are located in London, Amsterdam, Paris, Tokyo, Zurich, Frankfurt, and a number of other cities. Some important American companies trade on these exchanges. Some foreign companies trade in the United States.

**OVER-THE-COUNTER TRADING** Many companies are not listed with a specific exchange. Their stocks and bonds are traded by a network of brokers who participate in **over-the-counter (OTC) trading.** The trading is similar to that on a city exchange except that no central location is established for the exchange. Brokers buy from and sell to other brokers across the country, making transactions by telephone or teletype. They deal in the securities of industrial firms and utility and insurance compa-

## Action Brief
### SOCIAL INVESTMENTS

The Pax World mutual fund is different from most other investment funds. It has not only a profit motive but also a social objective. It does not want to make money for its investors from sources it believes to be bad for society. It rejects investments, for example, involving defense contractors. It invests, instead, in corporations serving health care, pollution control, and housing. A similar fund, Dreyfus Third Century Fund, screens companies on the basis of protection of the environment, occupational health and safety, consumer protection and product purity, and equal employment opportunities. Despite their "do good" orientation, both funds have very profitable track records.

nies, in federal government bonds, and in municipal bonds. Some securities are listed with an exchange and also traded over the counter. Far more are traded exclusively over the counter. However, the greatest volume of trading, both in number of shares and in dollar value, is done by the large central exchanges. An independent group of brokers (National Association of Securities Dealers) provides a self-regulating body for OTC markets.

**THE OPTIONS MARKET** A form of investment that is highly speculative involves not the actual purchase of a share of stock but the *option*, or privilege, of buying it at a reduced price. The risk is that the purchaser of an option must predict either a specific *call* (rise) or *put* (fall) in the market price of a stock. Additionally, this change must take place within a stipulated period of time, usually 3 months. If the market price does not rise or fall as predicted, the investor loses his or her entire investment. If the *exercise price* (or price prediction) does come true, the purchaser wins the bet. Odds, as high as ten times the purchase price, are paid at that time. The payment is provided by investors who, in effect, buy the option from the original holder so as to complete the actual stock purchase (or sale) at the price advantage provided by the option.

Options may be bought and sold on a number of exchanges, including the Chicago Board Options Exchange (CBOE), the American Stock Exchange, the Philadelphia Exchange, and the Pacific Exchange.

**MUTUAL FUND MARKET** A *mutual fund* is an investment company in which individual investors, mainly small ones, pool their money to buy stocks, bonds, and other securities. Shares in these funds may be purchased directly from the company itself or through stockbrokers. Shares may be sold directly or through brokers. The advantage to the investor is that the company provides professional management of the purchase and sales of the securities it owns, something few individual investors are able to do effectively. Prices and sales charges are listed daily in financial papers such as *The Wall Street Journal* and are provided by the National Association of Securities Dealers.

**COMMODITY EXCHANGES** Many processing and manufacturing firms, and other investors, regularly trade a variety of commonly used raw materials. These include grains like corn and wheat; livestock and meat; foods and fibers like coffee, cotton, and sugar; lumber; copper and gold; and currencies of various nations. A number of commodity exchanges exist for the purpose of such trading. Notable among these are the Chicago Board of Trade, the New York Mercantile Exchange, American Board of Trade, and the Kansas City Board of Trade. Trading may be done for immediate delivery—spot or cash trading—or for delivery at some future date—futures trading.

# 4 BUYING AND SELLING SECURITIES
*Investors, brokers, and transactions*

Over 100 million shares of stock change hands every day the securities exchanges are open. The great majority of these transactions do not involve the corporation that originally issued the stock. The transactions take place among individual and institutional investors.

Investors can be classified according to their objectives. Those who buy securities and expect to hold them for a long time, for whatever reasons, are usually called *investors.* They tend to identify themselves as genuine owners of the company and look forward to sharing the company's fortunes as it grows. In contrast, there are many other people, called *speculators,* who buy and sell securities hoping to make profits from short-range swings in their prices. *Institutional investors* are organizations—trust fund administrators, foundations, investment funds, pension funds, insurance companies, banks, and others—that invest large amounts of money. They may buy or sell for "investment" purposes, or they may speculate on short-term price movements. Whatever their purpose, their buying and selling activities have a strong influence on the price of securities.

Investors are typically concerned with more than the price of a stock. They look for growth and yield. Growth occurs when a stock that is bought at one price, such as $25 a share, increases as a result of market demand to, say, $40 a share. Investors are also interested in the yield of a stock. *Yield* is a measure of the income that a stock generates for its owner in relation to the price the purchaser pays for it. Yield is calculated by dividing the dollar amount of dividends paid in a year by the price of the stock. If, for example, a share of oil stock is purchased for $50 and it pays an annual dividend of $5, then its yield is 10 percent.

Investors and speculators are often characterized by their attitude toward the securities market at a particular time. *Bulls* are people who think stock prices will rise soon. *Bears* expect the market prices to fall.

## STOCKBROKERS
*The intermediaries of exchange*

Millions of people and thousands of organizations in the United States own stocks and bonds. If all of these investors tried to deal directly with securities exchanges, the trading system would completely break down. A kind of intermediary—the stockbroker—channels the trading of securities into manageable trade routes. A *stockbroker* is a person or company that represents investors in the buying and selling of securities. If an investor wishes to buy 100 shares of stock, he or she will instruct a broker to make the purchase. In return for their services, brokers receive a commission based on the size of the order.

## STOCK TRANSACTIONS
*Take place in minutes*

Stocks are sold in standard quantities of 100 shares, called a *round lot.* Any number of shares less than 100 is called an *odd lot.* Odd-lot transactions are more complicated to handle than round-lot transactions. Brokers must group together odd-lot orders from different investors to make up round lots. For this reason, they charge extra for trading odd lots. Current stock prices, or *quotations,* are available to brokers through several automatic telephone services or on a ticker tape, an electronic service that projects quotations for many important stocks on a lighted board. Many brokerage houses have a ticker tape in a public area for investors' use. Increasingly, quotations can be "called up" by a broker at a video screen on his or her desk or by individual investors at a terminal in their homes.

***AN NYSE TRANSACTION*** If someone in Texas wishes to buy 100 shares of IBM stock, a complex chain of communication must take place before the certificates are actually delivered. The buyer calls or visits a broker at a local office, who places the order. The local office transmits the order to its firm's New York office by teletype. The New York office passes the order to its floor broker, who operates in the trading room of the NYSE where IBM stock is listed. The floor broker goes to a specific trading post where IBM stock is handled and bargains with other brokers there who have orders from their clients to sell IBM stock. If the Texas client placed a *market order*, the floor broker tries to get the best price possible immediately. If the client placed a *limit order*, the broker does not buy unless the stock can be gotten for the price specified in the order. Once the transaction is made on the trading floor, the New York broker-age office transmits details of the purchase, including price, to its Texas office and the broker there informs the client that the purchase has been made.

***OVER-THE-COUNTER TRANSACTIONS*** Over-the-counter transactions are similar. Brokers negotiate prices by offering a certain price—the *bid price*—when they wish to buy, or asking a certain price—the *ask price*—when they want to sell. The ask price is normally higher than the bid price. The price of the final sale is usually a compromise between the ask price and the bid price. Many over-the-counter dealers keep their own inventory of stocks and make a profit by selling them at a higher price than they paid.

***BOND TRANSACTIONS*** Bonds are also traded on exchanges, and their values change just as the values of stocks do. If a bond is issued with an 8 percent interest rate, the bond becomes more desirable to investors whenever interest rates for other investments fall below 8 percent. Investors would then be willing to pay a **premium;** they might pay $1,050 for a bond with a $1,000 face value. If general interest rates (paid by banks, for example) rise above the rate paid by a particular bond, however, that bond will be less valuable to investors. In that case, the bonds are sold at a **discount;** for instance, a $1,000 bond might be sold for only $950.

# SPECULATION STRATEGIES
*Gambling on the market's movement*

*Speculators* often buy large quantities of stocks with the expectation that prices of their stocks will rise rapidly so that they will be able to resell them at a profit. They may buy a block of stock and resell it within a few weeks, or even within the same day. A number of buying and selling strategies are especially used by speculators. It is possible to buy stock partly with borrowed money. The part of the purchase price that is paid in cash is called the **margin.** This practice allows buyers to take advantage of leverage. They can take all of the profits if the stock increases in value without having put up the full purchase price of the stock. If the stock goes down in price, however, they can lose both the money they invested and the money they borrowed. Even when a stock's price falls, a profit can be made. Speculators who **sell short** borrow shares of stock from their broker and sell them at the current market price. If the price of the stock then goes down significantly, they can buy shares at the new lower price to replace the borrowed shares. The difference between the price at which they sold and that at which they were bought is left as a profit.

## MUTUAL INVESTMENT FUNDS
### Managed by professional investors

It should begin to be apparent that investing in securities requires expert and current knowledge of the securities themselves and of the markets in which they are traded. Stockbrokers not only buy and sell an investor's securities but also offer professional advice. Many investors, however, prefer to purchase shares of a mutual fund, rather than shares of a particular security. These may be purchased through a broker or directly from the fund itself. A *mutual fund* is a financial intermediary that pools the funds it receives from individual investors and uses these funds to invest in a "portfolio" of stocks, bonds, and other securities. If, for example, an individual has only $500 to invest, he or she would be able to buy only a round lot of one stock whose market price was less than $5 or an odd lot of one that was more expensive. By investing the $500 in shares of a mutual fund, the individual can own shares in many stocks and bonds. There are often more than 100 different stocks and bonds in a fund pool. This diversity tends to make the value of the fund's shares less susceptible to rapid swings in market prices. And, since the funds are managed by full-time professional investors, the choices of securities to place in the fund are likely to be better than those an inexperienced investor would make. Mutual funds can try to strike a balance of stocks that reflect the market. Or they can focus on one segment of the securities market, such as "income" stocks and bonds or "growth" stocks or "high-technology" securities or "tax-free" bonds. In recent years, the number of mutual funds offering shares in the pooling of financial investments has risen into the hundreds, perhaps thousands, of options.

## 5 FINANCIAL NEWS REPORTS
### Information about where the action is

Most business managers and individual investors pay careful attention to financial news in magazines and newspapers. Many people in business invest in stocks and bonds and use financial news to guide investments and to follow current values of their holdings. Many facts and trends needed for management—such as the costs of borrowing money—are reported in financial news sections. Activities of the securities markets and related financial institutions reflect the general condition of the economy and help in decision making.

## STOCK AVERAGES AND INDEXES
### Barometers of the financial market

Investors follow trends in stock prices by noting the changes in certain well-known averages of prices. The Dow-Jones Industrial Average is

## Action Brief
### PLENTY OF COOKS

Stockholders sometimes wonder why they have so little say in running the companies of which they hold shares of ownership. A look at the number of different owners who hold stock in major companies may supply the answer. In 1985, for example, the numbers of different people holding shares of stock in leading companies were as follows: AT&T—2,927,000; General Motors—1,990,000; Exxon Corporation—785,000; IBM—798,000; General Electric—490,000; Texaco—288,000; Eastman Kodak—184,000; and DuPont—241,000. That's probably why so many stockholders consider their ownership from the point of view of an investment rather than as having much, if anything, to do with operating a particular company.

the most publicized. It is computed from 30 large, stable industrial corporations, such as Procter & Gamble, AT&T, General Electric Co., Texaco, Inc., and DuPont Co. Dow-Jones also publishes averages for 15 utility companies, averages for 20 transportation companies, and a composite average that combines all 65 of the industrial, utilities, and transportation companies. Standard & Poor's calculates a similar index based on 500 companies, mainly industrials but also a number of railroads and utilities.

The New York Stock Exchange and the American Stock Exchange both compute a stock value index, as do OTC (National Association of Securities Dealers Automated Quotation, the so-called Nasdaq index) and many other exchanges. The NYSE index is a good example of this type. It is based on all of the stocks traded, rather than on a small sample. It shows, among other figures, the increase or decrease in price of an average share of stock.

## DAILY STOCK AND BOND REPORTS

### *The records of buying and selling, prices, and interest rates*

Most newspapers give extensive coverage to daily trading activity on the major exchanges. Reports are printed of trading activity for the securities listed on the NYSE and Amex, and often regional and over-the-counter trading activity is reported as well. Figure 19-6 shows a typical listing of these daily individual trading reports.

Figure 19-6 How to read stock quotations reported in a newspaper.

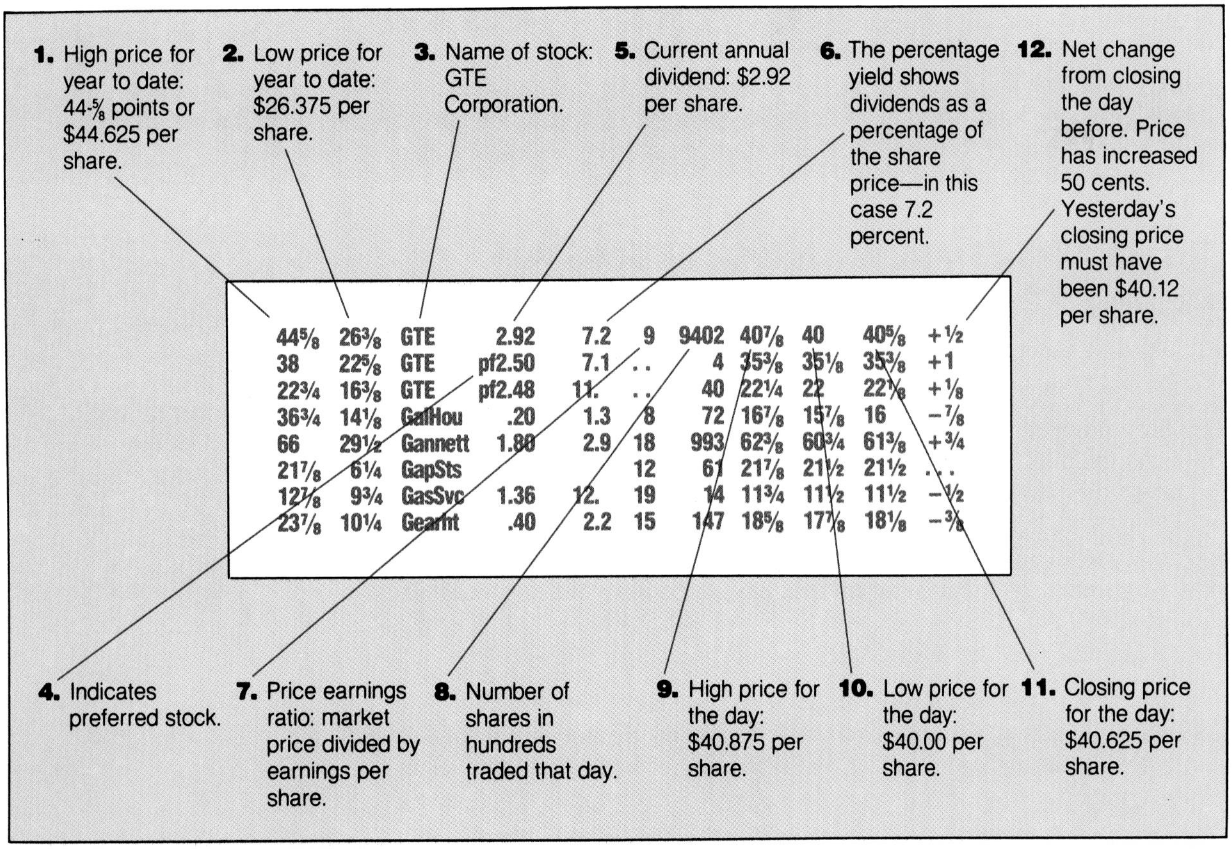
1. High price for year to date: 44-⅝ points or $44.625 per share.
2. Low price for year to date: $26.375 per share.
3. Name of stock: GTE Corporation.
5. Current annual dividend: $2.92 per share.
6. The percentage yield shows dividends as a percentage of the share price—in this case 7.2 percent.
12. Net change from closing the day before. Price has increased 50 cents. Yesterday's closing price must have been $40.12 per share.
4. Indicates preferred stock.
7. Price earnings ratio: market price divided by earnings per share.
8. Number of shares in hundreds traded that day.
9. High price for the day: $40.875 per share.
10. Low price for the day: $40.00 per share.
11. Closing price for the day: $40.625 per share.

| | | | | | | | | | | |
|---|---|---|---|---|---|---|---|---|---|---|
| 44⅝ | 26⅜ | GTE | 2.92 | 7.2 | 9 | 9402 | 40⅞ | 40 | 40⅝ | +½ |
| 38 | 22⅝ | GTE | pf2.50 | 7.1 | .. | 4 | 35⅜ | 35⅛ | 35⅜ | +1 |
| 22¾ | 16⅜ | GTE | pf2.48 | 11. | .. | 40 | 22¼ | 22 | 22⅞ | +⅛ |
| 36¾ | 14⅛ | GalHou | .20 | 1.3 | 8 | 72 | 16⅞ | 15⅞ | 16 | −⅞ |
| 66 | 29½ | Gannett | 1.80 | 2.9 | 18 | 993 | 62⅜ | 60¾ | 61⅜ | +¾ |
| 21⅞ | 6¼ | GapSts | | | 12 | 61 | 21⅞ | 21½ | 21½ | ... |
| 12⅞ | 9¾ | GasSvc | 1.36 | 12. | 19 | 14 | 11¾ | 11½ | 11½ | −½ |
| 23⅞ | 10¼ | Gearht | .40 | 2.2 | 15 | 147 | 18⅝ | 17⅞ | 18⅛ | −⅜ |

A number of bond averages are also watched carefully by investors and managers. The Dow-Jones bond averages are popular indexes. They show the average price for ten bonds issued for industrial companies, ten bonds for utility companies, and a composite. The averages show the price per $100 of bond face value. An average of 92.57 means that a typical $1,000 bond would cost $925.70 to buy. At that price, bonds are being sold with a discount. That is, they are selling for $74.30 below their face value. Daily bond transactions are also shown in many newspapers. A typical listing is explained in Figure 19-7.

# 6  REGULATION OF STOCK AND BOND SALES
*Its goal: protection of investors and financial markets*

Extensive government regulation controls and influences the selling and trading of stock and bonds. The objective of this regulation is to (1) ensure that investors are protected from fraud, (2) maintain order in the financial markets, and (3) limit risk to the financial system by controlling the proportion of borrowed money that may be used in speculative investment. The Securities Act of 1933 and Securities Exchange Act of 1934 require that a corporation provide detailed information to investors before stock or bonds are first offered for sale. A summary of information is contained in a **prospectus** showing financial, legal, management, and operations data on the issuing corporation. The purpose of the prospectus is to inform potential buyers of facts about the company and the issues that affect its value. The **Securities and Exchange Commission (SEC)** establishes general policies and regulations for trading stocks and bonds. The Federal Reserve System, by raising or lowering margin requirements, regulates the practice of borrowing money to use for speculating in the stock market.

## THE SECURITIES AND EXCHANGE COMMISSION
*Watchdog of the investment markets*

The SEC acts as the watchdog of the investment markets, exercising extensive regulatory powers. The most important of these are:

■  Requiring registration of new securities and disclosure of important information about stocks and bonds and about the issuing company pursuant to the various federal securities exchange laws

■  Requiring that companies listed with exchanges register and disclose information even when they are not issuing new securities

■  Registering and regulating investment trusts, investment companies, and investment advisers

■  Regulating public utility holding companies

Exercising its authority in these areas, the SEC has done much to reduce incidents of securities fraud. It has made the securities markets safer places for investment. The SEC cannot, however, protect investors from their own poor investment decisions. In that sense, the investors always assume some degree of risk whenever they invest in securities.

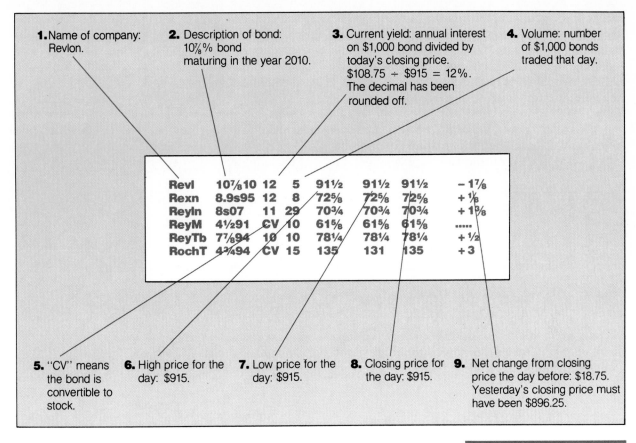

Figure 19-7 How to read bond quotations reported in a newspaper.

# *Key Concepts*

1. Money serves society and business as a means of exchange, as a standard of value, and as a medium for storing value. The supply of and demand for money have complex and important effects on prices and interest rates. The time value of money affects the way businesses look at borrowing and investments. Increasingly, the use of credit and debit cards, money market mutual funds, and electronic transfer of funds play a major role in the money markets.

2. The United States banking system consists of the Federal Reserve System and thousands of private commercial banks. Together they provide (1) safe places to store money, (2) methods for making financial transactions, (3) sources of borrowed funds, and (4) means of accumulating capital. The Federal Reserve System influences the supply of money to pro-

mote economic stability and growth. In addition, there are a number of other thrift institutions. Deregulation of banking has led to a wide variety of financial services including many from nontraditional sources, such as the money market mutual funds.

3. The securities markets are the principal sources of equity capital and long-term funding for a business. The various securities exchanges—such as the NYSE, Amex, and OTC—provide an easy, safe, and systematic way for buyers and sellers to trade their stocks and bonds.

4. Investors are concerned with the growth, income, and safety of their securities. Speculators are mainly concerned with short-term price changes. Institutional investors buy and sell for financial and other organizations. Stockbrokers

act as intermediaries for investors and speculators who trade on a security exchange. Transactions on an exchange are accomplished in minutes and reflect the strategies of the buyer or seller. Mutual financial funds provide a convenient method for an investor to share in a pooled investment in many securities.

5. Financial news reports provide market prices and other related information about securities being traded on the various exchanges to business managers and individual investors.

6. The federal government regulates the securities and bond markets with the object of protecting investors from fraud, maintaining order in financial markets, and limiting risk to the financial system caused by speculative practices. The Securities and Exchange Commission (SEC) is the principal federal governmental agency involved in regulating the offering, trading, and selling of securities.

# Review Questions

1. Define, explain, or identify each of the following key terms or phrases, found on the pages indicated.

*automated teller machine (ATM) (p. 441)*
*Banking Act of 1980 (p. 442)*
*barter system (p. 433)*
*basic money supply (p. 434)*
*checks (p. 434)*
*commercial bank (p. 439)*
*compound interest (p. 436)*
*credit union (p. 441)*
*currency (p. 434)*
*deflation (p. 435)*
*demand deposits (p. 434)*
*discount (p. 449)*
*discount rate (p. 439)*
*electronic funds transfer (EFT) (p. 435)*
*Federal Deposit Insurance Corporation (FDIC) (p. 442)*
*Federal Reserve System (p. 437)*
*Federal Savings and Loan Insurance Corporation (FSLIC) (p. 443)*
*inflation (p. 435)*
*institutional investors (p. 448)*
*interest rates (p. 435)*
*investment bank (p. 440)*
*investors (p. 448)*
*liquidity (p. 445)*
*margin (p. 449)*
*money market mutual fund (p. 442)*
*mutual fund (p. 447)*
*mutual savings bank (p. 441)*
*odd lot (p. 448)*

*over-the-counter (OTC) trading (p. 446)*
*pension funds (p. 441)*
*plastic money (p. 435)*
*premium (p. 449)*
*prime rate (p. 439)*
*prospectus (p. 452)*
*reserves (p. 438)*
*round lot (p. 448)*
*savings and loan associations (p. 441)*
*securities (p. 438)*
*Securities and Exchange Commission (SEC) (p. 452)*
*securities exchange (p. 444)*
*selling short (p. 449)*
*speculators (p. 448)*
*stockbroker (p. 448)*
*time deposit (p. 434)*

2. What are the three main ways that money is used in our economy? Name the two most commonly accepted components of the money supply.

3. Describe four important functions served by the banking system.

4. Describe the purpose and functions of the Federal Reserve System.

5. Distinguish between the primary and secondary securities markets.

6. What is the difference between an investor and a speculator? Which one is more likely to buy stocks on margin? Which one is more likely to be concerned with the yield offered by a stock?

7. What is the function of stockbrokers? How are stockbrokers paid?

8. Why might a small investor choose to invest in a mutual financial fund?

9. On what information is the Dow-Jones In-dustrial Average (or index) based?

10. Why does the federal government regulate the selling and trading of stocks and bonds? What are four important powers of the Securities and Exchange Commission (SEC)?

# Case Critique 19-1
## Happy Ending

One Friday, in 1985, 21 people from various locations in the United States moved into a small motel 100 miles southwest of Chicago. They registered as employees of a firm called "TV Associates." By 7 p.m. this team had engineered the closing of the Taylor State Bank 14 miles away in Emington, Illinois. TV Associates was, in fact, a task force from the Federal Deposit Insurance Corporation. On the previous Thursday, the team's leader had met with presidents of 20 banks in the area and asked them to bid for the ownership—and debts—of a bank whose name was still unknown to them. On Friday, John Gardner, president of the First National Bank of Dwight (nearby in Illinois), was notified that his bank had been selected to take over the Emington Bank.

The Taylor State Bank was first officially closed by the Illinois commissioner of banks and trust companies, and the FDIC was named receiver. The commissioner issued a statement to the public saying that "the bank's capital was impaired as a result of its inability to generate sufficient income to offset continuing loan losses, coupled by the inability of the bank's board of directors to infuse new capital." What this meant was that the bank had loaned out so much money to borrowers who could not make their payments that the bank now owed its depositors more money than it could readily pay back if they asked for it. The FDIC stepped in because it thought conditions at Taylor would get worse instead of better. And it wanted to make sure that the depositors did not lose their savings.

The FDIC worked out the following arrangement with the Dwight bank. Dwight would now operate the Taylor bank as the Emington branch of the First National Bank of Dwight. Dwight would take over full responsibility for the $4.5 million owed to Taylor's 1,200 depositors. The Dwight bank would pay the FDIC a purchase premium of $185,000. It would also purchase the failed bank's installment loans, real estate loans, and certain other assets for $2.1 million. The FDIC retained the other assets of the Emington bank, which had a value of $2.7 million on the books. In return, the FDIC advanced $2.3 million to Dwight to keep the deposit accounts liquid until the Emington branch was back on its feet. The FDIC took over the commercial loans, although it extended an option to Dwight to buy these loans within 30 days and sell the installment loans within 60 days, if Dwight wished to do so.

The Emington bank continued to operate without interruption. All three of the bank's former employees took jobs with Dwight. A month after the takeover, officials of the FDIC and the state banking commission held a town meeting in Emington to explain what had taken place and how the depositors' accounts would not be affected by the change in ownership. A few members of the FDIC team stayed in the area for 90 days until all operating details were resolved.

The owners of the Taylor Bank were not villains. In fact, they were popular in town. The bank had been chartered in 1917 mainly to make agricultural loans, but it had been poorly managed lately. As it turned out, the bank owners were far too lenient in making personal and commercial loans. A number of people and business firms in neighboring communities had made it a practice of coming to Taylor after having been turned down at other banks. Many borrowers had poor credit records to begin with. Taylor's owners had a hard time saying no. As a consequence, the "quality" of Taylor's loan portfolio was judged to be substandard. The number of "nonperforming" loans (those for which the bank could collect neither interest nor principal) kept increasing. Meanwhile, interest from performing loans did not increase fast enough to cover the bank's indebtedness to its depositors. Nor were the owners able to raise money from other sources to increase its capital. Bank experts cited this as an all-too-familiar pattern of events that leads to bank failures.

1. What led to the failure of the Taylor State Bank?

2. The Illinois state banking commissioner said that one problem was the bank's inability to "infuse new capital." Where might that capital have been generated?

3. How might the Taylor bank have improved the quality of its loan portfolio?

4. From the depositors' and the community's points of view, what do you think of the method by which the FDIC arranged for the bank's closing and eventual takeover by Dwight?

---

SOURCE: Richard B. Miller, "A Bank Fails in Emington," *Bankers Monthly Magazine*, June 15, 1985, pp. 5–20.

---

# Case Critique 19-2
## The Overambitious Investor

Don had a good job. He was making nearly $20,000 a year and had prospects for advancement. Of course, after income and social security taxes, and insurance deductions, the take-home pay was only about $15,000. His rent, telephone, and utilities, however, took over $7,000 a year. Meals and routine entertainment ate up another $3,000. Don had to have a car—a sports car at that—which cost him $2,500 a year in finance charges and $1,000 to operate. You can see that Don had only about $1,500 left each year for vacations and big weekends, when he dearly loved to swing. He had no savings account.

One day, when Don was broke and feeling blue, dreaming of his next big vacation fling—skiing in Colorado—a good friend made a suggestion. "Why don't you take a flyer on the stock market? I know of a number of nickel stocks where you can make a big killing for an investment of only a few hundred dollars."

"Nickel stocks!" said Don. "What kind of stocks can they be?"

"They are not really nickel stocks, but they do sell for less than $5 a share. You can buy 100 shares right now of one I know about that sells for $3 a share. This company has invented the most dynamic television game that can be imagined. Its stock is so hot that when people catch on, it will go to $30 or more a share. For $300 now, you can probably make a cool $3,000 in 2 or 3 months."

Don thought this was a great idea. He took every last penny he could lay his hands on and bought 100 shares at $3. For a week, or two, he called his broker daily and was elated to find the stock climbing up to $4 and then $5. On the strength of his good fortune, Don put a down payment on a $1,500 stereo that he had been admiring. Then, something began to go wrong with the stock. Its price dropped back to the $3 that Don had paid for it. Then it continued to drop—as low as 25 cents—and there it stayed. If he were to sell it, he'd get less than $25.

About that time, Don was hit with an unexpected repair bill of $250 for his car. And the payment for his stereo came through. Don looked at his checkbook. It was about to be overdrawn. And he didn't have enough money to pay the rent. Payday was still a week away. Don then set out to sell his sports car and his stereo for the amount still owed on them. He put an ad in the newspaper but got no response that week on the car and only what he considered a ridiculously low offer on the stereo.

1. When Don bought his stock, was he acting like an investor or a speculator?
2. Which of Don's purchases—the stock, the stereo, or the sports car—has the greatest liquidity?
3. If Don had wanted to be sure to make a profit from his $300, would it have been better for him to put his money into an ordinary checking account or a savings account?
4. Was Don in a financial position that was sound enough for stock purchasing? Why?

## CHAPTER 20

# Risk, Insurance, and Credit Management

## Learning Objectives

*The purpose of this chapter is to relate the role and importance of risk, insurance, and credit management in the financial operations and financial planning of a business.*

*As evidence of general comprehension, after studying this chapter, you should be able to:*

1. *Distinguish between speculative risk and insurable risk and describe the process by which a firm enters bankruptcy.*

2. *Outline and explain the four ways that a firm may cope with risks.*

3. *Explain the importance of the law of large numbers and differentiate between public and private insurers and between stock and mutual insurance companies.*

4. *Identify and explain the principal kinds of property and casualty insurance.*

5. *Identify and describe the three main forms of life insurance coverage.*

6. *Explain the importance of credit management to a business and list the "four Cs," of credit.*

*If your class is using SSweetco: Business Model and Activity File, see Chapter 20 in that book after you complete this chapter. There you will find exercises and activities to help you apply your learning to typical business situations.*

## 1 RISK

is the possibility of loss or failure. There are two basic kinds of business risk:

Speculative (unavoidable) risk, which is inherent in the nature of the private enterprise system

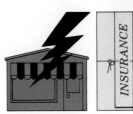

Insurable (pure) risk, for which losses may be anticipated and shared

## 2 RISK MANAGEMENT

attempts to avoid or reduce the possibility of loss and lessen its impact when it occurs. A business can cope with risk through:

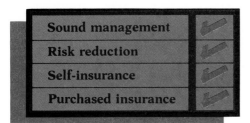

Sound management
Risk reduction
Self-insurance
Purchased insurance

## 3 INSURANCE

is a method of sharing risk protection

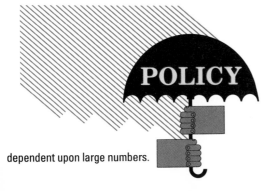

dependent upon large numbers.

## 4 PROPERTY/CASUALTY INSURANCE COVERAGE

includes

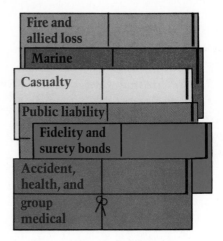

Fire and allied loss
Marine
Casualty
Public liability
Fidelity and surety bonds
Accident, health, and group medical

## 5 LIFE INSURANCE COVERAGE

is available in many forms.

Whole life

STOP
After 10 yrs.

Term

Endowment

## 6 CREDIT MANAGEMENT

evaluates

Character
Capacity
Capital
Conditions

ABC CO.

OK

# BUSINESS INSURANCE: COSTLIER THAN EVER

*Mary Branner opens a dress shop. She puts all her money into the venture. After 9 months, the business fails. Can Mary get her money back? No way! That's the risk she took when she got into the business game of chance, where there is always the likelihood that you lose rather than win.*

*Richard Hedblom spent a lifetime as an auto mechanic specializing in the repair of brake drums. At age 81, he developed a hacking cough. He hadn't smoked for 30 years, but his condition was diagnosed as lung cancer. Its source? Dust from brake pads made with asbestos. He sued eight companies that made these pads and received $169,750 as payment for the risk he took when he worked with asbestos. Most people thought this was little enough for such an illness. James Vermuelen developed a lung disease while working with asbestos as a Manville Corp. employee. It cut his breathing capacity by 40 percent and caused him to run up medical bills of $11,000. Vermuelen processed his claims for redress through workers' compensation, a state insurance program. It took him 4 years to get compensation of $8,932, the amount designated for such an injury by the laws of his state. He did not feel that he was fairly compensated for the risk he took. Meanwhile, Manville Corp. sought protection from thousands of possible suits regarding asbestos exposure by entering into Chapter 11 bankruptcy.*

*In a related area, Aemet Corp., a company that specializes in removing asbestos from ceilings in public places, such as schoolrooms, suddenly found that it could no longer purchase insurance coverage for its employees. Aemet could get general coverage, said the insurance carrier, but only if it got out of the asbestos business, which represented half of its $50 million a year revenues. Aemet agreed to the deal and bowed out of the asbestos removal business.*

*A supermarket chain was paying $8,000 in 1984 for insurance protection for each of its stores. Suddenly rates jumped to an average of $40,000 a store. Florida Power & Light, a public utility, was being insured for $400 million. Then, between 1984 and 1985, the insurance carrier cut the coverage to $200 million but doubled the cost of coverage!*

*At the same time, insurance companies were reporting that in four major areas of commercial coverage they paid out anywhere from $135 to $160 in claims for every dollar in premiums collected. The insurance companies, however, were not making these payments easy to obtain. In 1984, an estimated 16.6 million Americans (1 of every 15) went to court to recover damages. The* *litigants weren't particularly interested in who paid—businesses, individuals, or the insurance companies—but the insurance companies were the major target.*

*What's the message behind these examples? Protection against risk is expensive; often it cannot be obtained at any price. Without such protection, however, a business may find itself financially injured by costly accidents, damages caused by nature, and a variety of other hazardous and unpredictable outcomes.*

*SOURCES:* T. Gest, R. Taylor, M. Galligan, and R. Scherer, "Product-Liability Suits: Why Nobody Is Satisfied," *U.S. News & World Report,* August 19, 1985, pp. 49–50; J. Andresky, M. Kuntz, and B. Kallen, "A World Without Insurance," *Forbes,* July 15, 1985, pp. 40–43.

# 1  RISK
## *The possibility of loss or damage*

For a business, **risk** is the possibility of the loss of invested money or the loss of or damage to other valuable possessions. Accordingly, there are two main classes of business risks: speculative and insurable.

## SPECULATIVE RISK
### *The uninsurable chance of failure*

Owners who invest money in a business are speculating on the outcome of the business operation. They hope that their investments will increase in value as the business grows and makes profits. They always face the possibility, however, that they may lose some or all of their investments if the business fails. **Speculative risks** are basic to the private enterprise system.

Managers must always use care in trying to reduce speculative risk. They must try to manage product development and quality, prices, distribution, and the availability and costs of materials to produce a sound and profitable business. They must juggle the constantly changing influences of market demand, interest rates, and government regulation. No matter how carefully managed, businesses cannot be immune to speculative risk as long as private capital is invested with the expectation of making a profit. There is always the possibility that a point may be reached where income is not sufficient to meet expenses and the business becomes *insolvent.* If that occurs, the firm may be declared—or declare itself—bankrupt. **Bankruptcy** is the legal condition where liabilities exceed assets with no hope of reversing this condition. When this happens, the courts will appoint a *receiver* to *liquidate* the firm, that is, to sell off its assets so as to pay a firm's creditors.

**COMMERCIAL BANKRUPTCY** In the last decade there have been spectacular business bankruptcies such as those that saw W. T. Grant (discount chain), Revere Copper Co., and Braniff International (airlines) go under to the tune of several hundred million dollars. Big or small, however, the reason is the same: debt that is far larger than the company's assets and growing faster than it can possibly be paid off. Bankruptcy not only destroys the individual firm but also does damage to its employees and suppliers in the form of unpaid wages and bills. It is not unusual for a sinking company to drag its suppliers down with it—those who risked their own business safety by continuing to extend trade credit when it was no longer prudent.

There is a sort of halfway house for firms on their way to complete bankruptcy. It is called **Chapter 11 bankruptcy** because Chapter 11 of the Federal Bankruptcy Law allows the receiver to try to reach an agreement with the firm's creditors short of liquidation, so that the firm may reform its financial structure and recover. One way or another, however, the number of firms being compelled by their creditors to declare bankruptcy or who do so on their own initiative has risen dramatically in recent years, as shown in Figure 20-1.

**PERSONAL BANKRUPTCY** Individuals may also go to federal court to declare themselves bankrupt. An increasing number of people do so: 440,024 in 1983 compared with 172,423 in 1978. They do so for the same reason that businesses do—because they owe far more than they can ever expect to pay back. Under a **Chapter 7 bankruptcy** as mandated by federal law, individuals who are declared bankrupt must allow the courts to sell their assets to pay their creditors as much as possible from the proceeds and cancel whatever debt is remaining. The law does permit debtors to keep certain assets for survival purposes. This includes up to $7,500 equity in a house and up to $1,200 equity in a car, and a certain exemption for personal jewelry up to $500. Landlords, finance companies, department stores, and other creditors are understandably upset when individuals to whom they have loaned money or extended credit are forced to declare bankruptcy. This is a major reason why businesses

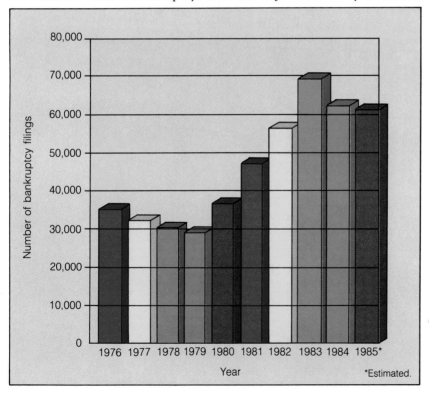

Figure 20-1 Business bankruptcy filings.

and financial institutions are often so careful about extending consumer credit.

As a less drastic option, individuals are able to seek **Chapter 13 bankruptcy.** This provides for the debtor to pay all or part of his or her debts over a period of 3 years under a plan approved by the courts. Its impact is somewhat like that of a nonprofit *Consumer Credit Counseling Service (CCCS)* sponsored by banks, loan companies, retailers, and other companies that extend credit. The CCCS has 200 offices throughout the country and handles about 110,000 cases each year. Its method is to ask the insolvent debtor to give up all credit cards and to promise not to do any further borrowing without the permission of the CCCS. Then it works out a survival budget that enables the debtor to pay back part of the debt every month. At the same time CCCS gets the creditors to agree to wait for their money and also assumes responsibility for equitably dividing up whatever repayments there are.

## INSURABLE RISK
*The pure chance of accident or loss* ━━━━━━━━━

Some risk is called *pure risk* because it can result only in loss and never in gain. This kind of risk consists of the chance hazards of nature such as fire, illness or injury, and many other kinds of damage to property or life. Speculative risk is different from pure risk because speculative risk carries the possibility of gain as well as loss and is accepted voluntarily by investors.

*Insurance* can be bought as protection against pure risk. Insurance companies make contracts with businesses, agreeing to pay the businesses for losses resulting from pure risk. The insured business makes regular payments, called *premiums,* into a pool maintained by the insurance company. The insurance company can afford to pay for losses suffered by their client companies because many companies pay into the pool, but relatively few have to be paid for losses at any one time.

Insurable risks, therefore, must meet several criteria:

■ The risk must be pure. It must be an accidental hazard and not a fundamental risk of doing business.
■ The extent of the potential loss from the risk must be measurable in some fairly accurate way.
■ The likelihood of any individual business suffering an immediate loss from a given risk must be slight.
■ There must be a very large number of companies subject to the risk. Many companies must contribute to the pool to provide enough money to pay for losses.

Accidental destruction of business property by fire is a good example of an insurable risk. It is a pure risk because it is not a basic risk of business investment. The value of the property can be determined accurately. An individual business is not likely to be destroyed by fire if precautions are observed. There is, however, enough risk to all business that large numbers are willing to pay premiums for protection.

## 2 RISK MANAGEMENT
*Managers can and must guard against risk*

Business managers can respond to risk in a number of ways. They can respond with sound management, risk reduction, self-insurance, and purchased insurance.

## SOUND MANAGEMENT
*Prudent finances and trained personnel*

Sound management is clearly the best way to reduce speculative risk. Careful control of financing, product development and production, marketing and distribution, and other management concerns help ensure that the result of speculative risk will be profits rather than loss and failure. Good credit management will reduce losses from bad debts and delayed payments. Good human relations management can reduce losses from strikes or other labor problems. Good general management policies also reduce pure risk. Well-trained personnel with good morale using modern equipment that is properly maintained are unlikely to have many accidents.

## RISK REDUCTION
*Precautions must be taken*

Good managers take prudent steps to reduce insurable risks. Many companies specifically train employees in safe working procedures. Buildings may be built with fireproof materials. Sprinkler systems, adequate exits, and sources of water reduce losses if fire does occur. Plant and office security systems reduce theft and danger to employees. Machine designs and building layouts can also be made safer.

## SELF-INSURANCE
*Reserves cushion the losses*

One sound way to deal with insurable risk is to remain financially prepared to accept a loss without damaging a business's strength. Small losses must be accepted as daily occurrences. Some materials and inventory will be damaged or lost. Machinery will break down. Windows will be broken. Roofs will leak. For most companies, these small losses are normal business expenses.

Some businesses also establish reserve funds to be used if a major loss occurs. This practice is called *self-insurance.* The advantage of self-insurance is that the money in the reserve can be earning interest for the company. Self-insurance, however, is usually practical only for large companies and for a limited range of risks. It is very difficult to keep a reserve large enough to cover all possible risks without tying up so much money that it harms normal business operations. Large corporations with numerous stores or plants in different locations, however, may be able to self-insure against fire since it is unlikely that more than one facility will burn at a time. DuPont Corporation is an example.

### Action Brief

**FIRE IN THE COMPUTER ROOM!**

*Studies by IBM show that half of all major data processing disasters are caused by fire. The simple precaution of duplicating operational software is a key element in minimizing the ensuing losses. Many companies, however, expose themselves to this risk because of the high cost of duplication and off-premises storage. The problem is that traditional fire detection devices are geared to paper records, which don't ignite until the heat is more than 400 degrees. Deterioration in a computer's magnetic disks starts taking place at 150 degrees, and computer hardware begins to act strangely at 120 degrees. Prudent data processors install a particularly sensitive computer-based detection system, which triggers a suppressant gas (Halon) that human beings can tolerate.*

# PURCHASED INSURANCE
*Backstops all other measures* ━━━━━━━━━━━━━━━

Nearly every company relies on purchased insurance to protect itself against pure risk. Despite good management, risk reduction efforts, and the ability to accept some losses, there will always be risks that threaten the company's strength. These risks include fire and other natural hazards, damage to buildings and property, injury to employees and customers, interruption of business, and losses due to theft and vandalism, among others. Insurance is usually the answer.

# 3 INSURANCE
## *A means of sharing risk protection*

Providing insurance is a process whereby many people or organizations contribute regular payments to a fund. The fund is then used to reimburse a contributor who suffers a loss of a type specified in a contract, or **policy,** with the insurer. The effect of this arrangement is to share risk protection among a large group. In this way, each individual contributor to the fund is protected from major loss.

An insurance fund is based on the likelihood of specific losses occurring. For example, an established insurance company might decide to begin offering a new kind of coverage: protection for storefront plate-glass windows. In researching the policy, they might find that, on the average, 170 of every 100,000 windows of the type they cover are broken each year. They may also find that the average loss from a single break is $1,000. They then compute their average payout a year to be about $170,000 (170 breakages × $1,000 a breakage) per 100,000 policyholders. They will establish premium rates to provide a fund of that size each year, plus an additional amount to cover the expenses of administering the fund and handling claims. The portion of the fund waiting to be paid out is also available for investment by the insurance company.

# LAW OF LARGE NUMBERS
*Protection based upon averages* ━━━━━━━━━━━━━━━

As indicated above, it is the pooling of the risks encountered by many companies engaged in a particular activity that makes insurance possible. The insurer can examine the historical records of a great many companies, or people, and find the average number of occurrences of accident or fire, for example. Such figures are often referred to as the "law of averages"; statistically, this averaging out of a great many occurrences is called the **law of large numbers.** It is illustrated by "mortality tables," which record the actual number of years that men and women have lived over the past century. These figures are then treated statistically to provide life-expectancy figures for the purpose of issuing life insurance policies. Current mortality tables, for example, show that a woman who is 19 years old today has a life expectancy of 58 years or, on average, will live to be 77. A man of that age, however, is expected to live for only another 53 years on average, or until he is 72.

# PUBLIC INSURERS
*From bank deposits to social security* ━━━━━━━━━━━━━━━

Different kinds of organizations provide insurance. These sources of insurance can be classified as either public or private. **Public insurers** include the federal and state governments, whose services are prescribed by legislation. They may charge for providing insurance coverage either directly or through a tax levied by an employer on an individual. Unemployment insurance (provided through state governments) and social security (provided by the federal government) are two examples. Premiums in the form of taxes are withheld at the source. Both employer and employee pay them in most states; employers' contributions match employees' contributions in the case of social security. Federal programs provide a wide range of insurance covering bank deposits, home mortgages, life insurance for veterans, Medicare for people over 65, flood damage, and many other things. State governments provide against losses to individuals resulting from unemployment and also offer various other insurance plans to their employees.

Nearly all commercial insurance in the United States, however, is provided by insuring organizations that are either stock companies or mutual companies. These are called **private insurers.**

# INSURANCE COMPANIES
*Profit-seeking or policyholder cooperatives* ━━━━━━━━━━━

There are about 4,900 private insurance companies in the United States. Some of these sell almost any kind of insurance. Others specialize in property and liability insurance or life insurance. An insurance company organized as a **stock company** is a normal profit-seeking business corporation. Stockholders invest money in the corporation with the hope of earning dividends. The corporation manages its operations in an attempt to make a profit. Except for life insurance, most private insurance is provided by 4,500 or more stock companies.

**Mutual insurance companies** are owned exclusively by policyholders and not by stockholders. Their operation is similar to that of a cooperative. They are nonprofit and do not pay regular dividends. If a surplus accumulates, it is sometimes distributed to policyholders as a rebate.

Most mutuals collect full advance premiums. This means that they collect in advance the full premium needed to create a fund large enough to meet all likely payments for losses. Some smaller mutuals use an assessment system. They charge a lower premium and assess policyholders for an additional amount if and when it is needed to cover losses that are paid for.

Of the nearly 2,000 life insurance companies, only 132 are mutual companies, although these companies provide nearly half of all life insurance coverage. The Prudential and Metropolitan are mutual companies, while Allstate is a stock company. Differences in operations are slight between the two types of insurers. One strives for profits; the other distributes its surpluses to its policyholders in the form of discounts.

# CHARACTERISTICS OF INSURANCE POLICIES
## Legal language predominates

The insurance policy is a legal contract. It sets down in writing a statement of the basic conditions under which it operates and then adds, according to the type of policy, a number of additional clauses that supplement or extend the basic coverage. In similar fashion, the contract also states what conditions are exempt from the policy and will not be covered.

Much of the language of insurance policies appears old-fashioned and hard to understand by consumers. One reason for this is that the real meaning of a policy, as with any contract, depends upon the way it is interpreted in court cases arising from it. When a particular clause or policy has had many legal decisions made about it, its meaning is clearly fixed. For that reason, insurers do not like to change to new language that might be interpreted in a different way by the courts. An historic example of such precise language that has lasted for over 200 years is part of the ocean marine policy of Lloyds of London. It was written in 1780 and still appears in today's policies:

> *Touching The Adventures and Perils which we the Assurers are contented to bear and to take upon us in this Voyage, they are, of the Seas, Men-of-War, Fire, Enemies, Pirates, Rovers, Thieves, Jetisons, Letters of Mart and Countermart, Surprisals, Taking at Sea, Arrests, Restraints and Detainments of all Kings, Princes and People, of what Nation, Condition, or Quality soever, Barratry of the Master and Mariners, and of all other like Perils, Losses and Misfortunes that have or shall come to the Hurt, Detriment, or Damage of the said Goods and Merchandise and Ship, etc., or any Part thereof.*

In recent years, there has been consumer pressure for insurance companies to present their conditions in clearer language. Some insurers have responded by rewriting the principal clauses of policies or by providing the consumer with descriptive material about the policy that is written in nontechnical language.

# 4  PROPERTY AND CASUALTY INSURANCE
## Pay your money and take your choice

Insurance coverage is generally classified into two types: property-casualty and life insurance. The former holds great importance for business operations, although many individuals purchase fire insurance for their homes and property and casualty insurance for their automobiles. The kinds of insurance a small business might carry are fire and burglary, public liability, workers' compensation and social security, business interruption, and perhaps automobile insurance and fidelity and surety insurance. Large corporations usually hold a greater variety of policies.

# FIRE AND ALLIED LOSS INSURANCE
## Offers basic property protection

Loss resulting from destruction of property by fire, wind, water, and smoke damage and other hazards is covered by *fire and allied loss insurance.* Normally, coverage is purchased both for real property—such as factories, office buildings, and warehouses—and for personal property, which includes inventory, furniture, machines and equipment, and other supplies. Premium rates for fire protection vary considerably. Much lower rates are charged for fire-resistant buildings located in areas with good fire protection than for frame buildings in an area with a poor water supply and limited fire-fighting capability.

Basic fire, wind, and water protection is **direct coverage.** It pays only part or all of the direct costs of replacing the damaged property. Many policies also cover specified **consequential losses** resulting indirectly from the damage. A business that is damaged by fire will often lose at least part of its income as a result and will have the added expenses of trying to operate while the damage is being repaired. Certain policies will pay some of these costs, such as rent on temporary business quarters. See Table 20-1 for the differences between direct and indirect damages.

A **business interruption policy** is an extension of this concept. This covers temporary loss of income from a variety of insurable causes. Interruption of operations by fire is the most common example, but coverage can also be obtained for power or fuel loss or other occurrences that cause loss of business income.

Most fire policies include a **coinsurance provision.** This states that if property is insured for less than its total value and suffers only partial damage, the insurance company will pay for only a specified portion of the loss. The owner of the property must pay for the remainder as coinsurer. This clause is included because it has been a common practice for business managers to insure property for less than full value since losses from fire are usually not total. Carrying less insurance reduces the premium. Without the coinsurance provision, insurance companies would often be accepting lower premiums but would still be paying the entire cost of a partial loss.

Coinsurance works this way. Suppose an industrial distributor has a warehouse building assessed at $100,000. The insurance company establishes a coinsurance clause stating that the building must be insured for 80 percent of its assessed, or market, value. Suppose, then, that the industrial distributor decides to insure the warehouse for only $40,000, and subsequently the building is completely destroyed in a fire. The insurance company will pay only $20,000 or 50 percent of the insurance coverage on $40,000, because the industrial distributor insured the building for only half of the required amount. If the industrial distributor had taken out $60,000 in coverage, it would have received only $45,000 (since $60,000 is three-quarters of the $80,000 coinsurance requirement). To get reimbursed for the full amount of coverage, the industrial distributor would have had to insure for $80,000.

## MARINE INSURANCE
### Covers ocean or land shipping

Marine insurance originated for protection against the risk of shipping goods at sea. It has now been extended to cover other kinds of shipping. The two major types are ocean and inland shipping.

**Ocean marine insurance** protects goods and ships while they are at sea and temporarily while they are in port. Although specific variations are possible, policies usually cover capsizing, sinking, fire and water

---

## Action Brief

### EARTHQUAKES OK, LIQUOR A NO-NO

*California law requires insurance companies to offer earthquake coverage to those home owners who want to buy it. Most standard policies specifically exclude earthquake damage. Premiums for earthquake coverage are high, and required deductibles are set at 10 percent of the assessed value of the home. For most businesses in the United States, the law does not require that insurers provide coverage for risks they believe are too high. The most difficult kinds of coverage to obtain are in the following areas (in order): pollution, liquor liability (as in what happens to people who consume too much on your premises), day-care centers, medical malpractice, asbestos removal, and commercial fishing-boat operations.*

**TABLE 20-1**
**INSURING AGAINST DIRECT AND INDIRECT DAMAGE**
**TO COMMERCIAL PROPERTY**

*Direct Damage*

1. Damage resulting directly from fire, lightning, floods, high winds, vandalism, etc.

2. Leakage from sprinkler systems

3. Water damage from fire fighting

4. Damage done by demolition in connection with hazards removal

5. Replacement cost of buildings and facilities

6. Replacement cost of machinery, equipment, and furnishings

7. Replacement cost of inventories

8. Injury to employees and occupants

*Indirect Damage*

1. Loss due to interruption of business

2. Extra expenses during rehabilitation

3. Loss of rents

4. Rental of temporary operating space

5. Loss of profits or commissions

6. Loss of markup value of inventories

damage, and vandalism, as well as other kinds of damage. Rates are based on estimates of the likelihood of loss.

The oldest ocean marine insurer is Lloyds of London, founded in 1779. This is a group of over 18,000 individuals who form syndicates under Lloyds' supervision to underwrite (or insure) just about every kind of high-risk venture, at sea or elsewhere. A ship's bell hangs in its chambers, and whenever an insured ship is lost at sea, the bell is rung.

*Inland marine insurance* covers the risks of shipping goods on inland waterways. It also covers other more widely used means of transportation—railroad lines, trucks, and airlines. Goods in transit are normally protected for loss or damage resulting from accidents such as train collisions, derailment, and road accidents. Coverage also usually includes damage from fire, wind, earthquakes, and other natural forces. Damage caused by people, such as theft or vandalism, may or may not be covered in a specific policy.

## CASUALTY INSURANCE
*Includes automobile, accident, and theft coverage* ━━━━━

A number of different types of insurance are traditionally grouped under the heading **casualty insurance.** Casualty generally refers to death or injury in an accident, but for insurers it may apply to automobile;

public liability; burglary, robbery, and theft; and workers' compensation insurance.

**AUTOMOBILE INSURANCE** Automobile insurance is important for business vehicles as well as for drivers' personal cars. Using an automobile is a considerable risk. Not only may the car itself be damaged or destroyed, but there is a danger of injuring other people or damaging their property. Causing injury to others can result in large losses from lawsuits. Basic automobile insurance coverage includes collision, fire, theft, and liability–bodily injury.

■ *Collision insurance* pays for damage to or destruction of the insured's car. Collision policies have a deductible clause. A *deductible provision* in any insurance policy means that the insured must pay a stated amount for the loss before the insurance company pays anything. If a collision policy has a $100 deductible, the insured must pay for all accidents causing less than $100 damage and must pay for the first $100 for more serious accidents.

■ *Fire and theft coverage* pays for losses resulting from these causes. Other risks—such as windstorm, vandalism, and water—can also be included. The protection is then called *comprehensive coverage.*

■ *Liability–bodily injury coverage* pays for losses resulting from damage done by an automobile to other people or their property. Personal injury or property damage can result in expensive lawsuits. The person at fault may be asked to pay hundreds of thousands of dollars. Liability insurance, including both property damage and bodily injury done to others, could protect a small company from failure if a business vehicle is involved in a serious accident.

■ *No-fault insurance* is mandated in many states. This requires an insurance company to make payments for medical and hospital expenses to accident victims, up to a certain limit, without having to decide in advance who was at fault. Most of these states place some restrictions on the right to sue. Some states provide payment from the state's own insurance company if the parties are not insured. The purpose of no-fault insurance is to minimize litigation and to make recovery from auto accidents simple and speedy. Originally, it was presumed that no-fault laws would have the effect of lowering insurance premiums, but this has not always happened.

**PUBLIC LIABILITY INSURANCE** Damage or injury to others is not caused only by automobiles. A restaurant customer may become ill from eating spoiled food. A box in a warehouse may fall on a visitor. A dangerous stairway may cause a customer to fall and be injured. Damage may be caused to nearby buildings by construction work. A doctor or pharmacist may make an error that causes illness or death. All of these occurrences, and countless others, may result in a company's having to pay settlements to injured parties. *Public liability insurance* protects the insured from such losses up to a maximum value stated in the policy.

In addition to covering losses, insurance companies that sell liability policies provide many services that help protect the insured. The insurance company will thoroughly investigate the legal claims of the injured person or company. It will provide legal representation for the insured in court cases. It will usually advise the insured of ways to improve property or of procedures to avoid claims.

**BURGLARY, ROBBERY, AND THEFT INSURANCE** Various policies are available to protect businesses from theft losses. *Burglary, robbery, and theft insurance* may cover payrolls, inventory, securities, contents of safes, or any other things of value. As with other types of insurance, rates vary according to the probability of loss, based on past experience with theft around the location of the protected property.

**FEDERAL CRIME INSURANCE** Federal Crime Insurance is low-cost insurance that the federal government makes available to businesses in high crime areas where private insurance is normally not available. Often, business owners are unaware that they can obtain this.

## REGULATION OF CLAIMS
*Some states place ceilings*

Because of the rapidly accelerating number and size of jury-awarded settlements of claims against large companies and insurance firms, 32 states have recently passed laws placing ceilings on lawsuit damages or lawyers' fees. For example, Kansas put a $1 million limit on damages stemming from medical malpractice cases. Wisconsin set a 33 percent cap on lawyers' fees earned on a contingency basis. Indiana established penalties for persons filing "frivolous" lawsuits deemed by judges to be without merit. Consumers rights groups, however, contend that the laws are unjustified and will not result in lower insurance premiums.

## FIDELITY AND SURETY BONDS
*Pay for employee dishonesty*

Businesses are subject to risk resulting from the possible dishonesty of their employees, especially those who have access to money. Insurance, in the form of a *fidelity bond,* can be purchased to make up for losses resulting from embezzlement, forgery, or outright theft by employees. Such bonds may be bought to cover specified employees, such as retail clerks, treasurers, salespeople, or others who handle money.

A company, government organization, or other organization may seek protection from losses that could result from a breach of contract. This guards against loss should a company with which a contract has been made fail to carry out the terms of the contract. That company may be required to purchase a *surety bond* in advance. If, for instance, a school board hires a building contractor to build a school, the board may require a surety bond. Should the contractor fail to build the school adequately and in an acceptable time, the amount of the bond must be paid by the insurer to the school board.

Other bonds are available as protection from losses caused by contested title to real property. They are called *title insurance.* If a piece of land becomes less valuable because of unknown claims against it or if possession is lost because of a defective title, the insurer pays the amount specified in the policy. Bonds are also available to cover unexpected bad debts. These credit bonds pay a specified amount if a customer with a normally good credit rating fails to pay an obligation to the insured.

# BILLBOARD

## CHEATING THE INSURERS

**W**hy is it that basically honest people are tempted to cheat when it comes to making insurance claims? Insurance premiums continue to rise, not only due to companies' operating costs or inefficiencies but because so many people expect protection or redress for the most minor incidents of damage or loss. Still other injured parties inflate their claims far beyond the true loss. There was the man, for instance, who slipped on a half-eaten tuna sandwich in New York's City Hall and sued the city for $1 million in damages. You might ask, "Who was at fault—the city, the person who dropped the sandwich, or the man who slipped on it?" Some people, of course, are just plain dishonest, like the husband and wife who collected three times from three different insurers for a "theft" of jewelry that didn't even happen once. Still others are pushed into litigation that is costly for the in-

---

*Injured parties often inflate their claims far beyond the true loss.*

---

surer by lawyers who hope to get a fee for their efforts.

Down deep, however, many people pad their claims because they feel that getting something extra from a rich, greedy insurance company isn't stealing at all. But the net effect is to make insurance protection more expensive for others.

### QUERIES

1. What do you think should be done—if anything—to reduce dishonest or unreasonable claims?
2. If you were sitting in judgment during a trial for damages, who would you favor—the insurance company or the person seeking damages? Would it make any difference to you if the person who was being sued had no insurance protection? Why? ∎

---

SOURCE: Carol J. Loomis, "A Non-Boring Look at Insurance," *Fortune*, March 8, 1982, p. 105.

# PROFILE

**B**ERNICE GISCOMBE has worked her way to near the top in a difficult, demanding profession. She is vice president and senior credit officer for one of the world's largest banks, Citibank, in New York City. She began her career 19 years ago as a teller. Today, because of her outstanding performance, she holds an important executive position, overseeing the extension of credit to the bank's large and small clients. "People may doubt your ability," she advises, "so you must know your specialty area better than anyone else." In addition, Giscombe observes that to occupy a position in mahogany row, an individual needs a high energy level. She also comments that a minority person may not always be made to feel comfortable in the corporate social scene. For everyone, however, Giscombe says that life in upper management can be "a very lonely experience." Accordingly, Giscombe suggests that young people on their way up in their careers

**BERNICE GISCOMBE**

should develop a "supportive network you can rely upon" to help overcome the rough spots professionally and socially. ■

SOURCE: Charles Whitaker, "How to Make It in the White Corporate World," *Ebony*, March 1986, pp. 102–107.

# ACCIDENT AND HEALTH INSURANCE
## Blue Cross/Blue Shield leads the way

*Accident and health insurance* policies usually provide one or more of three types of coverage: (1) it may pay some or all of the expenses of hospitalization, surgery, and other medical care resulting from accidents or illness, (2) it may pay the insured some or all of the income lost when illness or injury prevents working, or (3) it may make lump sum payments for loss of sight or limbs or for death resulting from an accident. Policies combine these benefits in different ways. Rapidly rising costs for medical care have made premium rates for high-quality health insurance increase proportionately.

Another response to increasing health care costs has been the growing popularity of major medical insurance. These policies provide payment for the treatment of serious injuries resulting from accidents or major illnesses such as cancer and heart disease. Medical care for many conditions can run to tens of thousands of dollars. Consequently, major medical plans set a high maximum payment, often $50,000 or higher. They also usually have a high deductible—$1,000 is a common figure.

Some businesses provide health insurance for their employees. As an added benefit, many companies maintain a ***group insurance*** policy that provides payments to employees if they become sick or injured. The plans usually cover occurrences that are not covered by workers' compensation. Some companies pay the entire cost of the coverage. Others share the cost with employees. The total cost of the protection is usually lower than for an individual policy because it is less expensive for an insurance company to administer one policy for many people than many single policies.

### HEALTH MAINTENANCE ORGANIZATIONS (HMOs)
As an alternative to the traditional Blue Cross/Blue Shield insurance, Kaiser Permanente of California began offering its employees a prepaid medical expense plan that enabled them to make unlimited use of a health care facility. This concept has grown into a number of HMOs offered by employers and by private insurers for a monthly prepaid premium. The ***HMO*** provides doctors, nurses, and other medical assistance and places great emphasis on prevention. Participants have no choice of their doctor, however, and sometimes complain of impersonal or cost-oriented treatment.

Two other approaches to health care insurance are growing in popularity. *Preferred Provider Organizations (PPO)* involve a pricing agreement between an insurance company and medical care providers. It may be based upon simple discounts resulting from group services, or it may rely heavily upon rigorous screening of patients before hospital admission. A somewhat similar approach involves *hospital utilization reviews (HURs)* before a person enters a hospital for nonemergency treatment. Testing and consultation are done beforehand, and entry is often based upon a review by an independent third party. These two approaches are aimed at reducing medical, and hence insurance, costs for the policyholder as well as for the insurance company. Here again, employee participants may feel that the quality and extent of services received are lowered under these plans.

### WORKERS' COMPENSATION INSURANCE
All 50 states require businesses to carry insurance to compensate employees for losses caused by

physical injury suffered on the job. **Workers' compensation insurance** usually pays for medical expenses and for a portion of workers' salaries while they are unable to work. Workers' compensation (also called workmen's compensation in some states) also usually makes a payment to a worker's family if death results from a job-related accident.

# 5  LIFE INSURANCE
## *Emphasizes income for survivors*

In return for premiums, **life insurance** pays a sum to survivors if the insured dies while the policy is in effect. Many policies include provision for the accumulation of savings and other special features. Its basic purpose, however, is to repay survivors for some of the financial losses that result when a person dies. Medical and funeral expenses must be paid. Outstanding debts may be a burden. Loss of income formerly provided by the insured may greatly lower the standard of living of survivors.

**PREMIUMS** Life insurance differs in an important way from other kinds of insurance. Premiums for fire insurance, for instance, are based on an estimation of the likelihood that a fire will occur. In contrast, death is certain. The only unknown factors are the time and the cause. Insurance companies, therefore, use mortality tables that show the probability of death occurring at different ages in determining premium rates. If, for example, an insurance company has policies on 100,000 people 35 years of age, the tables show that 209 of these policyholders will be expected to die during the year. By combining these expectancies for all ages, the total amount likely to be paid out is estimated. Premiums can then be set to provide an adequate fund, considering variables such as the length of time policies will be in force, the type of policy, and others.

**TYPES OF LIFE INSURANCE** Life policies can generally be categorized as whole-life, endowment, or term.

**Whole-life insurance** may be considered the standard life insurance policy. The insured makes equal payments periodically from the purchase date until death. When the insured dies, the face value of the policy is paid to the survivors or to other specified people or organizations. This type of insurance automatically includes a savings plan. As premiums are paid, over the years, the policy attains a **cash surrender value.** The policy may be traded at any time for its accumulated cash value, or the cash value may be used as collateral for a loan.

On some policies, the insured person is required to pay premiums only for a certain period, for 20 or 30 years, for instance. Protection continues, however, for the rest of the insured's life. In this plan, premiums must be set higher. A recent development has been the payment of a single, up-front premium that provides lifetime coverage.

**Endowment life insurance** policies stress the savings possibilities more than does whole-life. Higher premiums are charged so that the cash surrender value increases rapidly. Premiums are set so that in a specified number of years, the cash value will have added up to the total value of the policy. Thus, the insured will have built up a savings fund equal to the face value of the policy and will have been insured during the period of saving.

*Term life insurance* provides payment if the insured dies within a certain number of years stated in the policy. A 10-year term policy, for example, requires the regular payment of premiums for 10 years and pays the face value of the policy if the insured dies within that period. Term policies normally do not build up a cash surrender value. If the insured does not die during the specified term, all premiums remain the property of the insurer. Group life insurance coverage that companies offer employees is typically written as a term policy.

Each kind of life insurance policy has advantages and disadvantages and is best suited to particular situations. Term policies provide inexpensive protection for temporary periods. Their lack of cash value and increasing costs as the purchaser's age increases are limitations. Term policies are difficult and expensive for older people to buy. Whole-life insurance is a compromise between term and endowment policies. It provides good protection at a reasonable cost. It is more expensive than term and does not have the extensive savings capabilities that endowment policies have. Endowment policies stress savings more than protection. Their premiums are the highest of the three types. The savings features of endowment policies can only be judged in comparison with other types of investment.

**SPECIALIZED LIFE INSURANCE** Other kinds of life insurance policies are available for particular needs. Partnerships often maintain policies on each partner with the other partners named as beneficiaries. If one partner dies, the remaining partners can be sure of having adequate funds to buy the ownership share of the insured or to cope with other losses caused by the death. This, in effect, helps to insure the continued life of the partnership. A similar plan is sometimes used by corporations. They may buy "key employee" insurance to help cover losses caused by the death of an important manager or decision maker.

People who are making a large installment purchase or are seeking a mortgage loan on real estate often buy credit life insurance. These policies pay off the remaining part of the loan if the insured dies.

Life insurance is often provided by firms for their employees in the same way group health insurance is. The employer maintains a single policy covering some or all employees. Many such policies are renewable 1-year term insurance. They provide a low-cost but valuable benefit that companies can offer, free or partially paid, to their employees.

# 6  CREDIT MANAGEMENT
*Minimizes risk on credit sales*

A potential source of loss that can be minimized by good management is bad debts resulting from credit sales. Nearly every business of any size sells a large portion of its goods or services on credit. When wholesalers buy from manufacturers, they almost always have at least 30 days to pay. Producers selling materials and equipment to each other offer credit terms. A substantial part of retail sales are made with some kind of deferred or extended (installment) payment plan. Deciding when to allow credit purchases and in what amounts is the basic job of credit management. Its goal for most companies is to allow credit to as many buyers as possible in order to increase sales while prohibiting credit purchases by bad credit risks to minimize losses from bad debts.

## THE FOUR Cs OF CREDIT
*Character, capacity, capital, and condition*

The majority of commercial sales are made on credit, allowing payment to be delayed at least 30 days. Managers concerned with commercial credit must decide which firms will be allowed to buy on credit and what maximum amount of credit purchases will be allowed each customer. They attempt to determine the credit worthiness of each customer, often using the "four Cs" of credit:

■ "Character" refers mainly to the buyer's reputation for meeting obligations in good faith. To many managers, customers' honesty and desire to pay are the fundamental requirements for credit.

■ "Capacity" is the basic financial ability of a customer to pay. Earning power can often be evaluated by considering the general business practices of a customer.

■ "Capital" is a measure of a customer's assets. If a credit customer's earning power fails, assets can be sold to pay off debts.

■ "Conditions" of the individual credit customer (how well the business is doing at a given time) and of the economy in general have an important effect on credit worthiness. Even a well-managed firm may have difficulty paying its debts on time when business conditions are very bad.

Generally speaking, there is no insurance protection against bad debts other than prudent management, although risk in lending or extending credit is often lowered by having the creditor obtain a cosigner, or guarantor, who "underwrites" or shares the responsibility.

**CREDIT INVESTIGATION** Credit management is so important to the financial condition of companies that a number of services have been developed to help rate customers for credit worthiness. Dun & Bradstreet, Inc., is probably the best known of those that specialize in commercial accounts. A number of trade organizations also maintain credit data. They often publish references giving credit ratings and prepare reports describing in detail the financial status of firms.

In deciding whether or not to extend credit, companies sometimes conduct their own investigations. They may seek information from other companies that have extended credit to a particular company or individual in the past. In so doing, however, they must be especially careful to obey the laws involving the extension of consumer credit and the furnishing of related information about individuals. This is covered in greater detail in Chapter 23.

# Key Concepts

1. Every business is subject to two kinds of risks. Speculative risk results from investing money in a business with the hope of making a profit. Pure risk results from hazards that are not willingly undertaken by a business: fire, theft, and so forth. Businesses can protect themselves against pure risk with insurance. Companies that fail because of either speculative or pure risk often enter bankruptcy.

2. Business managers cope with risk through good management, risk reduction, self-insurance, and purchased insurance.

3. Insurance is a process by which many people or organizations that are subject to similar types of risks contribute premiums to a central organization. These premiums are placed in a fund from which losses are reimbursed when damage occurs to a contributor. Businesses and individuals may obtain insurance coverage from public insurers and from private stock companies and mutual insurance companies.

4. Property and casualty insurance provides coverage for fire; inland and ocean marine; auto collision and liability; public liability; burglary, robbery, and theft; workers' compensation; fidelity and surety bonds; and accident and health. No-fault auto insurance and health maintenance organizations represent recent trends toward controlling the escalating costs of providing insurance.

5. Life insurance coverage may be obtained in many forms, including whole-life, term life, and endowment life insurance. Each differs as to premium payments and features.

6. Good credit management contributes to a company's solvency by helping to maintain adequate available working capital. Credit managers try to extend credit to customers to increase sales and avoid giving credit to customers who are unwilling or unable to pay. In doing so, the four Cs of credit are applied to customers: character, capacity, capital, and conditions.

# Review Questions

1. Define, explain, or identify each of the following key terms and phrases, found on the pages indicated.

*bankruptcy (p. 461)*
*business interruption policy (p. 468)*
*cash surrender value (p. 475)*
*casualty insurance (p. 469)*
*Chapter 7 bankruptcy (p. 462)*
*Chapter 11 bankruptcy (p. 462)*
*Chapter 13 bankruptcy (p. 463)*
*coinsurance provision (p. 468)*
*collision insurance (p. 470)*
*comprehensive coverage (p. 470)*
*consequential loss (p. 468)*
*deductible provision (p. 470)*
*direct coverage (p. 468)*
*endowment life insurance (p. 475)*
*fidelity bond (p. 471)*
*fire and allied loss insurance (p. 467)*
*fire and theft coverage (p. 470)*
*group insurance (p. 474)*

*health maintenance organization (HMO)*
*(p. 474)*
*inland marine insurance (p. 469)*
*insurance (p. 463)*
*law of large numbers (p. 465)*
*liability–bodily injury coverage (p. 470)*
*life insurance (p. 475)*
*mutual insurance company (p. 466)*
*no-fault insurance (p. 470)*
*ocean marine insurance (p. 468)*
*policy (p. 465)*
*premium (p. 463)*
*private insurer (p. 466)*
*public insurer (p. 466)*
*pure risk (p. 463)*
*risk (p. 461)*
*self-insurance (p. 464)*
*speculative risk (p. 461)*
*stock company (p. 466)*
*surety bond (p. 471)*
*term life insurance (p. 476)*

*title insurance (p. 471)*
*whole-life insurance (p. 475)*
*workers' compensation insurance (p. 475)*

2. In what ways do Chapter 11 and Chapter 13 types of bankruptcy proceedings resemble each other?

3. What is the difference between speculative risk and pure risk? Can both risks be handled by management in the same way?

4. What are the four principal ways for a business to cope with risk?

5. What is the basic method by which an in-surance company can provide repayment for losses suffered by its policyholders?

6. What is business interruption insurance? What kind of health insurance is it like?

7. What are some of the advantages and disad-vantages of no-fault insurance?

8. In general, how does a health maintenance organization operate?

9. What is the most important use of each of the three types of life insurance policies?

10. Describe each of the "four C's" of credit worthiness.

# Case Critique 20-1
## The Big Chance

Tom and Aretha, husband and wife, ran the best little coffee shop in Montana. Their red shack stood near the main highway and was frequented by tourists as well as "locals." They weren't getting rich, but, as Aretha said, "We're having a lot of fun." That was before a flash fire in the kitchen duct work this summer put them out of business.

As Tom and Aretha looked back, they had some misgivings. Their fire insurance agent had visited the coffee shop in the spring of the year. Records showed, he said, that there was a terrible tendency for fires to start in kitchen ducts in which grease had built up. Tom and Aretha, he advised, could do two things. They could increase the amount of their fire insur-ance coverage to make sure that fire damage would be fully compensated. That would mean a much higher premium. Or, he said, they could install a sprinkling system in the duct work. This would involve an initial cost on their part, but it would serve to add protection as well as reduce the insurance premium.

Tom's reaction was, "We don't need it. We run a very clean kitchen. Aretha scrubs up that duct work regularly, and we keep a close eye on the grease filter to make sure it is clean."

"You two are the operators here," said the agent, "but, the way your coverage is right now, if your place burns down, your insurance would cover only about half of the restaurant's replacement cost. Do you have enough money set aside so that if you do have a fire, your sav-ings will make up the difference between your coverage from us and what it might cost to re-build?"

"We don't have that much money set aside," said Tom and Aretha. "We'll have to rely on the precautions we take to prevent a fire. For the time being, we'll just have to take our chances."

After the fire struck, Tom and Aretha found that they didn't have the money needed to re-build. Like nearly half of all business establish-ments that are severely damaged by fire, the best little coffee shop in Montana never did reopen.

1. What risk management technique was im-plied both by the suggestion to install a sprin-kler system and by Aretha's regular cleaning of the duct work? What are some limitations on the effectiveness of this technique?

2. When Tom and Aretha decided to "take their chances," they were engaging in what other kind of risk management technique? What was its drawback?

3. What was the third kind of risk manage-ment technique that Tom and Aretha em-ployed? What were its advantages and draw-backs?

# Case Critique 20-2
## A Little Beauty of a Sports Car

John Ordano is single. He makes a fair income as a salesperson for a high-fidelity components store. Much of his income is dependent upon commissions. If he has a good week, he may take home $500. A slow week may see his take-home earnings dip to $300. When John's little imported sports car broke down on the way to work for the third time in 2 weeks, John decided that enough was enough. He had to get a new car. John's first stop in his search for a new car that would reflect his personality was at the showroom for a leading import. He saw just the sports car he wanted, with all the options that would make driving a pleasure: a super hi-fi tape-deck stereo system with all sorts of digital accessories. Once he had settled on his choice, John made that familiar trip to one of those little paneled offices next to the showroom. Then he heard what this little beauty of a car would cost in the way of monthly payments above his $5,000 down payment. It came to about $300 a month for 48 months for a loan of $8,000. That was a pretty good deal, he was assured. John felt that by cutting corners in his life-style, he could make the payments. "OK," said John, and he reached for the papers to sign. The salesperson then shoved a couple of other papers toward him.

"What are these for?" asked John.

"You're going to be borrowing money to purchase this car," said the salesperson. "That means that there will be a lien on it by the lending company until the loan is paid. The company won't lend you the money unless you carry collision insurance. That comes to $180 a year or $15 a month."

"I guess that since I've got to have it, I can manage another $15 a month," said John. "But what's the other document you want me to sign?"

"This is optional," said the salesperson, "but it's something you ought to consider. It's called 'credit insurance.' Take this policy, and if anything happens to you, the insurance company will guarantee that the loan will be paid off."

"What do you mean by 'if anything happens to me'?" asked John.

"That means that if you die before the loan is fully paid, the balance will be paid to the lending company by the insurance company," said the salesperson.

"Then this is a life insurance policy," John said.

"That's right."

"How much is the policy worth after the 48 months that it takes me to pay off the loan?"

"Nothing. Your monthly payments just go to pay for the insurance on the unpaid balance of the loan. You don't acquire any equity or savings with this policy."

"How much does this policy cost?" asked John.

The salesperson consulted a little black book. "Let's see. The book says that your insurance will cost 50 cents a year for each dollar of the unpaid balance. That comes to only about $185 over the 48 months of the loan, or about $3.85 a month."

"Why should I worry about whether or not the car is paid for if I die?" asked John. "I'm single, and I can't see my mother driving a sports car."

"Perhaps you might want someone else to have the car," said the salesperson.

1. Should John take out the credit life insurance policy? Why or why not?
2. John was pressed to buy two kinds of insurance coverage for his purchase. What important type of auto owner protection would these still leave uncovered? Why didn't the salesperson press John to buy that protection?
3. What is the general name of the kind of life insurance offered John for insuring his loan?
4. If John were married with a wife and two small children, how might this affect John's attitude toward insurance coverage—full auto coverage as well as life insurance?
5. Why might an auto salesperson be interested in selling John insurance other than that which the lending institution required in the first place? Do you think that the salesperson was ethical in doing so?

## Intercom for bank operations

In one of the nation's ten largest banks, 1,000 managers and staffers are automatically linked by "dedicated" intercom units at their workplaces. This enables employees at Bankers Trust Company in New York City to talk hands-free to one another while manipulating data that can also be transmitted via the system's display terminals. Departments served include auditing, purchasing, data center operations, management services, and foreign exchange.

The intercom is quicker and more convenient than telephone dialing. Support staff keep their stations in the "open mode," allowing calls to come through automatically, not unlike the system used in interconnected taxicab communications.

*SOURCE:* Gary Katen, "Bank Reaps Impressive Return on Intercom Investment," *Today's Office,* June 1985, pp. 73–74.

## Electronic collating for insurance policies

One big reason that there will be fewer people working in mind-deadening clerical jobs in the back offices of insurance companies is the development of electronic forms preparation. The computer was quick to catch on to the mathematics of calculating premiums. But it was very slow in helping out with the nitty-gritty task of assembling, stapling, and distributing the actual policies. There is still an incredible amount of handwork in attaching the appropriate documents and forms to the policy file and in collating the documents to be mailed to the policyholder. Now, electronic computerized forms publication has come to the rescue. Instead of a multitude of forms that must be filled in and manipulated by hand, forms can be created and electronically stored for on-demand printing in a matter of hours or days. Previously, this took weeks for typesetting and printing. At the Hartford Insurance Group, for example, the computer takes care of the policy assembly process. It creates a total document, customized to the end recipient, without the need to attach forms manually. Jobs that were once spread out all over the system are now centralized. This makes the insurance clerk's job more challenging, too, since much of the repetitiveness of manual manipulation has been eliminated.

*SOURCE:* Mary E. Laufer, "Electronic Publishing for Policy Issuance," *Best's Review,* August 1985, pp. 76–78.

# UNIT 7

# *The Wider Horizons of American Business*

Unit 7 explores growth of American business, especially that of corporations, and the participation of American companies in international trade. It also shows how the American public guides and controls business activity through a system of laws and regulations. It examines the ethical standards of business and the exercise of social and economic power by consumers, employees, and citizens.

## CHAPTER 21

In the United States, the economy is presently dominated by large corporations. They offer many economic and noneconomic advantages, but also exhibit certain flaws that disturb the public, the government, and the shareholders.

## CHAPTER 22

For many companies, participation in the international market represents an attractive opportunity for growth. Some multinational companies have so much power that they are not welcome in other countries. However, most nations cooperate in business matters.

## CHAPTER 23

The American legal system strives to ensure competition and to protect property rights, consumer interests, and the general welfare of the public.

## CHAPTER 24

Some businesses seek to make a profit in almost any way they can to stay alive. In so doing, they may damage human lives and spoil the environment. Some people believe that business as a whole will improve ethically only when under pressure from power groups or by order of law. There is growing evidence, however, of more responsible behavior on the part of business.

# Big Business

# and Corporations

## Learning Objectives

*The purpose of this chapter is to explore more fully the implications corporations have with respect to management and to the public, explain the way in which a corporation is formed and makes its stock available to the public, assess the role of the stockholder, and examine the advantages and disadvantages of corporate size.*

*As evidence of general comprehension, after studying Chapter 21, you should be able to:*

1. *Understand the importance of corporations to the United States economy and explain the formation process and structure of a corporation.*

2. *Distinguish between open and close corporations, describe the process of "going public," and explain the purpose of a prospectus.*

3. *Discuss stockholders' rights and the relationship between stockholders and corporate management.*

4. *Explain the economies of scale of large corporations and their methods of growth through diversification, combination, acquisition, and merger.*

5. *Identify the principal shortcomings of large corporations and of their management.*

6. *Debate future directions of corporations—either greater government intervention or greater social responsibility.*

*If your class is using SSweetco: Business Model and Activity File, see Chapter 21 in that book after you complete this chapter. There you will find exercises and activities to help you apply your learning to typical business situations.*

## 1 CORPORATIONS DOMINATE

the business scene,

are chartered by law,

ARTICLES OF
INCORPORATION
NAME
PURPOSE
CAPITAL STOCK

BYLAWS
OFFICERS
BOARD OF
DIRECTORS
STOCKHOLDERS

and are guided by corporate bylaws.

## 2 CORPORATIONS GO PUBLIC

by offering stock
to the general public

STOCK
CERTIFICATE

FOR
SALE

PROSPECTUS

through a prospectus.

## 3 STOCKHOLDERS ARE OWNERS

of corporations,

ABC

MANAGEMENT

STOCK  STOCK  STOCK

but their control
is limited.

## 4 CORPORATIONS GROW AND DIVERSIFY

Internally
by plowing
back
profits

Externally
by combining
with other
companies

## 5 BIGNESS HAS DRAWBACKS

Inefficiency

WASTE

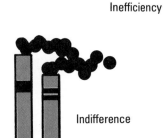

Indifference

Conformity

## 6 FUTURE CORPORATIONS

will have

either greater
regulation

STOP    STOP

FTC     SEC

or greater social
responsibility.

# CORPORATIONS: DOMINATING THE BUSINESS LANDSCAPE

*During the 1980s, big business got bigger, much bigger. Small businesses came on strong, too, and created new jobs faster than the larger companies. But there was no denying that a phenomenon, called "merger mania" by some, had struck American corporations. Nowhere else was it so visible as in the petroleum and food industries. Gigantic Texaco became even more gigantic by swallowing Getty Oil Corporation for $10.1 billion. Not to be outdone, Mobil gobbled up Superior Oil for $7 billion. Then Chevron topped them both by acquiring Gulf Oil for $13.2 billion. It was in the food business, perhaps, where bigness became most evident to American consumers. R. J. Reynolds Industries (once noted mainly for its Lucky Strike cigarettes) merged with Nabisco Inc. to put Oreos into its product line. Nestlé S. A., a Swiss firm, acquired Carnation Co. And Ralston Purina Co. added Continental Baking's Wonderbread to its dog food, cat food, and commercial feeds.*

*The growth of large corporations by merger with, or acquisition of, other large companies has become a corporate way of life. It presumes that big means better—or more profitable. This isn't always true. Regardless of purpose, the corporate form of business has, for many years, been the dominant form of business in the United States. With no exception, very large corporations generate the most sales, draw down the largest profits, and provide the most jobs in every major industry. The statistics are overwhelming. Corporations that employ 100 or more employees represent less than 3 percent of all business establishments. Yet they account for over 80 percent of all business sales and profits. These corporations employ only 45 percent of the labor force; the other 55 percent is scattered among nearly 2 million much, much smaller establishments. . . .*

*Many of the people who work for large corporations perform their work on a very large scale too. Their titles may not reflect the size of their jobs. Unlike the thousands of "presidents and chief executive officers" of firms employing only a handful of people, corporate job titles are likely to be less impressive. They may be far more important than they sound, however, when judged by the scope of their influence. Doug Davis, for example, works for Texaco. He carries the title of "supervisor of purchasing," but he buys $200 million of iron pipe each year for the corporation's refineries. He is only one of 91 employees in Texaco's purchasing operations, where the department's purchases amount to about $1 billion each year. Based upon the power of such* *large-scale buying, Texaco estimates that it saves a minimum of 10 percent on its purchases.*

# 1 CORPORATE FORM AND STRUCTURE
## A unique power in American business

A corporation was defined in Chapter 3 as an association of individuals, created under the authority of the law, that exists and has powers and liabilities independent of its members. The corporate form of ownership is appropriate for most large profit-making enterprises because, among other reasons, corporations (1) are able to raise large amounts of capital from their many stockholders, (2) can attract numerous investors because owners are protected from personal liability, (3) can have a continuous existence independent of any individual employees or owners, (4) are easy to invest in and to withdraw investment from, and (5) can attract managers who are specialists in the varied duties involved in running a large company.

These factors are attested to by thousands of examples. Over 300,000 individual stockholders have invested over $13 billion of their own money in Texaco, for instance. The DuPont Co., one of the world's largest corporations, has existed profitably for over 200 years, due mainly to its ability to pass the reins of leadership down through a long succession of professional managers. The actual ownership of these corporations is constantly changing, however, as investors and speculators buy and sell their shares of common stock on the open market. Of course, corporations dominate the American economy not only because of their size but also because of the products and services they offer, the work force they employ, and the profits they earn. Some of our corporations have grown so large that their annual sales are now greater than the gross national products (GNPs) of many nations.

## FORMATION OF CORPORATIONS
### A routine legality open to any group

A corporation is an artificial "proprietor" created by law. It has the right to carry on business in its own name, to own property, and to incur debts. These rights are usually granted to corporations by state governments, but sometimes by the federal government. Forming a corporation requires a **charter,** or **articles of incorporation.** This is a state-issued document legally recognizing the existence of a new corporation. It is based on information provided by the people who establish the company.

Charters include the legal name and present address of the corporation. They describe the purpose for which the corporation has been formed. The type of business and its purpose are usually defined in terms as general as possible to avoid severely limiting the future activities the company may undertake. Detailed information on the maximum amounts and types of stock the corporation is authorized to issue is usually included in the charter. Provisions for the length of time the corporation is allowed to exist, the adoption of bylaws, and other administrative matters may also be included.

A corporation that carries on business in the state in which it is chartered is called a **domestic corporation.** A corporation that does business in a state other than the state of its incorporation is a **foreign corpo-**

*ration.* A corporation doing business in Iowa, for instance, but chartered in Delaware is known as a foreign corporation in Iowa. Many states have extensive licensing and taxation measures for foreign corporations like Nestlé S. A. It is increasingly common for corporations formed in other countries to trade in the United States. These are called *alien corporations.*

## STRUCTURE OF CORPORATIONS
### *Operations are delegated to management*

Corporations are owned by stockholders. In theory, at least, the stockholders retain final control over how the corporation will be operated. However, except in corporations with very few owners, it is not practical for stockholders to perform day-to-day management tasks. When a corporation is formed, the owners decide on rules, stated in the corporate *bylaws,* describing how stockholders should go about delegating management control to achieve effective organization and operation.

The delegation of management authority usually is a two-step process. Stockholders first elect a board of directors. The board then appoints corporate officers who directly run the company. The board of directors usually elects from among its members a chairperson, a vice chairperson, a secretary, and a treasurer. All board members are obliged to remain informed about company operations and to represent the interests of stockholders. The boards of different companies vary in the extent to which they make actual operating decisions. Boards often establish committees to do detailed studies and provide guidance in certain areas, such as finance or corporate development. Figure 21-1 shows an example of the corporate structure.

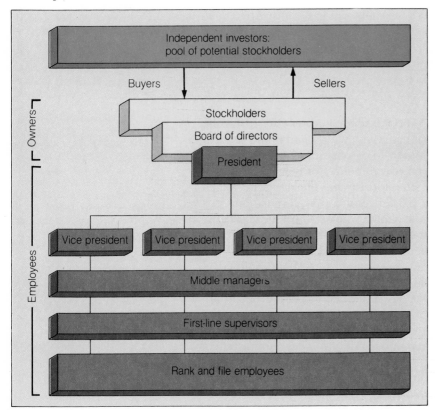

Figure 21-1 Relationship among stockholders, managers, and employees in a typical corporate structure.

One important function of all corporate boards is to select the officers who will actually run the corporation. Most corporations have a president and one or more vice presidents. Final operating responsibility does not always rest with the president, however. In many large companies, the person who chairs the board of directors may be a full-time operating executive and may act as chief executive officer. Other board members may also assume direct operating control of certain functions, such as when the corporate treasurer acts as the highest financial officer and directly manages financial affairs.

Boards of directors meet periodically—usually monthly or quarterly— to review company operations and to make the decisions required of them. Corporations with numerous stockholders have, in addition, a special annual meeting at which stockholders with voting privileges select members of the board. Annual stockholders' meetings in the past have been largely routine affairs, where a slate of board members proposed by existing directors or managers was rubber-stamped by the stockholders. Today, however, more and more annual meetings are marked by lively discussions of operating issues, especially those related to social concerns and stockholders' influence on operations. The treatment of unions, consumer issues, pollution, bribery, and illegal contributions are beginning to take their place along with profitability as subjects of concern for some stockholders. Stockholders' concerns may even extend to the morality of doing business in countries where alleged violations of human rights exist. For example, stockholders at some firms have heatedly debated the ethics of carrying on business in South Africa because of its policy of apartheid, or racial separatism, with respect to blacks.

## 2  GOING PUBLIC
### Sale of stock to the general public

Many corporations, especially small ones, do not offer their stock for sale to the general public. These are called **close corporations** because ownership is closely held and not generally traded. Such companies often have a limited number of owners, sometimes as few as three. The owners are usually directly involved in the management and operation of the business. The reason for creating a close corporation is not to obtain large amounts of capital but to gain other advantages such as limited liability.

**Open corporations** are also called "public" corporations because they offer their stock for sale to the general public. Anyone who has the money may buy shares of ownership from present stockholders or from company issues of stock. Nearly all large corporations are open. They use the sale of stock to the public to acquire the capital assets needed for major enterprises.

## OFFERING AND SALE OF STOCK
### A task for the underwriters

Corporations may sell their stock directly to investors. A company wishing to sell 100,000 shares of its stock can contact private investors and others known to buy stock, negotiate a sales price, and directly sell its own offering. This method of selling stock is the exception, however.

Most stock offerings are sold through an intermediary, often called an **underwriter,** who buys all or a large portion of an issue and resells it to actual investors, thereby guaranteeing its sale. Underwriters receive a commission for their services. Investment bankers commonly act as underwriters for corporations.

Although underwriters handle stock offerings even for the best-known and most stable large corporations, they are especially important when a new corporation sells stock to the public for the first time. For new or unknown companies, the reputation of the underwriter is often very important in making stock salable to investors. The act of making the first public offering of stock is called *going public.* A close corporation may go public and become an open corporation in order to raise expansion capital. A proprietorship or partnership may incorporate and go public for the same reason.

## REGISTRATION AND PROSPECTUS
*A closely regulated procedure* ━━━━━━━━━━━━━━━━━━━━━━

When issuing stock, corporations must comply with the legal regulations mentioned in Chapters 18 and 19. All public offerings must be registered with the Securities and Exchange Commission (SEC). The SEC must compile and make available extensive information on the company's financial position, operations, and management. The SEC must summarize this information in a **prospectus** (a written statement) given to every potential investor before an attempt can be made to sell shares.

# 3  STOCKHOLDERS AND THE CORPORATION
## *Owners but not managers*

Anyone who has excess money to invest may buy stocks. All kinds of people hold stocks as investments. These figures from the New York Stock Exchange indicate that stockholders have diverse occupations, lifestyles, and income levels. Stock is also bought by large institutional investors such as banks, insurance companies, investment funds, and similar institutions with large amounts of capital to invest. In the United States about 35 percent of the stock in public hands is owned by institutions and 65 percent by individuals.

## THE RIGHTS OF STOCKHOLDERS
*Their influence is limited* ━━━━━━━━━━━━━━━━━━━━━━

Stockholders' rights stem from their ownership. They may receive shares of profits. They can claim a share of assets if the corporation dissolves. They are entitled to annual reports on the financial status of the company. They may inspect company records. They may receive preference for buying future stock or bond issues. At the same time, stockholders cannot individually seize their share of the assets unless the company dissolves and there are assets left after all liabilities are paid. Nor can a stockholder individually direct the corporation as to how to use his or her share of the assets. Decisions on the use of resources are made by the corporate management with authority delegated by all stockholders collectively through elections.

Owners of common stock and of some kinds of preferred stocks have voting privileges. They elect members of the board of directors. They may amend the bylaws or request changes in the articles of incorporation. They may vote directly on company policies. Such voting takes place at the annual meeting. Since many stockholders cannot attend these meetings, there is a way for them legally to allow another person to vote in their place. This is called voting by **proxy.** Since current officers or directors of the company are usually chosen as the ones to cast the proxy votes, the system usually has the effect of concentrating more company control with the management.

Direct control of a company by stockholders clearly has definite limits. At times it has been difficult for stockholders to exert any control at all over management. When present managers and directors have extensive proxy rights, they may perpetuate their own positions and make decisions with little influence from stockholders. One or two stockholders who own a large portion of the company's shares may be able to elect all the board members, even against the desires and best interests of other stockholders. A related problem occurs when representation is not granted to minority interests, even when ownership is equal and widespread.

One procedure that helps achieve fairer representation of minority ownership and more democratic elections of directors is **cumulative voting.** Each stockholder may cast all of his or her votes for a single director, if desired. If a company were electing 11 directors, for example, and a stockholder owned 100 shares of stock, the stockholder could cast 1,100 votes for a single candidate, 550 for each of two candidates, or any other combination desired. Under **noncumulative voting,** the stockholder would only be allowed to cast 100 votes for each position open. Cumulative voting enhances representation of small groups of stockholders.

# 4  GROWTH OF LARGE CORPORATIONS
## *The benefits of bigness provide justification*

It isn't that there are more large companies than in previous decades. Instead, the change is that large corporations are getting bigger than ever before. In some ways, the value of the corporate form of business to society has been undeniable. Most Americans associate their standard of living with products and services provided by such giant firms as General Electric, Ford Motor Company, Sears Roebuck & Co., IBM, DuPont, McDonald's, Burlington Industries, Coca-Cola, and hundreds of others. Many Americans believe in the axiom that big should mean better, despite occasional backsliding on the part of remote corporate monoliths. A great many citizens, however, are concerned about the rapidity of recent corporate growth. They wonder what it will mean to their freedom of choice as consumers and to their opportunities for stable, purposeful employment.

# ECONOMIES OF SCALE
## *In production, purchasing, and marketing*

The most commonly voiced justification of large corporations is their ability to take advantages of economies of scale. A large company can usually produce, purchase, and distribute more efficiently than smaller ones. One large assembly line is able to produce 100,000 washing machines faster and more cheaply than if ten different companies were producing them on separate assembly lines. As noted above, companies that buy in large quantities get better discounts, and pay lower prices, than those who buy a little bit now and then. Larger companies inspire confidence in suppliers because they usually are deemed to be more stable and have better credit standings than many smaller companies do.

Corporate advertisers, too, enjoy economies of scale. General Motors, for instance, can earmark half as many dollars per automobile that it sells as American Motors Corp., and still spend ten times as much money. As a consequence, the sheer volume of GM's sales enables it to communicate with millions more potential buyers than AMC and on a much more frequent basis. Not only that, most buyers tend to select well-known brands from large companies, even when given the alternative of buying a similar but lesser-known brand, regardless of price.

The availability of resources is also related to size. Larger companies have the resources needed for research, for the development and introduction of new products, and for entering new geographic markets. In many industries—like automobiles, steel, aluminum, oil, and large construction projects—only a large corporation could assemble the financial resources and facilities required to start up and sustain operations.

In the eyes of the public, such economies of scale—when they, in fact, are obtained—are of value only if their benefits are passed on to consumers. Where competition is strong, this is likely to occur, either in the form of lower prices, better service, or higher quality. Where a few large corporations dominate an industry, however, this likelihood is not so certain.

# HOW COMPANIES GROW
## *Diversification and combinations*

Large companies in cyclical businesses often find stability and growth through diversification. Diversification is the extension of a business's products, services, or markets beyond a dependence upon a single one. Economic cycles can be hard on companies with only one or two products. A large company with many products and services is partially protected from business slumps. If sales are off in their retail stores, income from insurance sales or grain exporting, for example, may offset the retail losses. Diversification helps to provide income stability. This is one important reason why so many companies have merged or formed business ties with other companies.

Companies also grow to a great size by successfully producing profits and reinvesting them in expansion to produce even greater profits. Another way to grow is by joining a number of smaller companies together into one large company. Many United States businesses have expanded through this latter method.

There are three main types of business combinations: vertical, horizontal, and conglomerate.

***Vertical combinations*** bring together some or all of the processes that contribute to producing and selling a single product. Gasoline is a well-known example of a vertical combination. A company that combines oil exploration, drilling, refining, shipping, and retailing companies is one example. Vertical combinations are created by joining different levels of the same general production process. These companies either advance their operations toward the customer (forward integration) or bring their operations backward toward the supplier (backward integration).

***Horizontal combinations*** join more than one company operating at the same level of production or distribution of the same kinds of goods or services. If one hardware store buys out another hardware store in town, a horizontal combination will be formed. When Warner-Lambert merged with Parke, Davis & Company, this was a horizontal combination. Both firms manufactured pharmaceutical supplies and were formerly direct competitors in many of their service areas. Horizontal combinations typically eliminate a competitor producing the same goods or services.

***Conglomerate combinations*** join together companies that produce different, generally unrelated, goods and services. If, for example, a wool manufacturer buys a copper mine, a conglomerate combination is the result. Conglomeration is one of the main sources of diversification in this country. Notable conglomerates include ITT, Textron/Greyhound Corp., Gulf & Western Industries, W. R. Grace, and Walter Kidde.

## MERGERS AND ACQUISITIONS
*Instant growth through pooling of assets*

When two or more companies join together so that only one company remains, they are said to undergo a ***merger.*** Mergers may occur in two general ways: (1) firms may decide to pool their resources and assets and create a new, larger company, or (2) one firm may buy another by paying its present owners (stockholders, partners, or proprietor) for the value of the assets acquired. This is called an ***acquisition.***

The organization of merged companies may also vary. Often, a completely new organization is created so that the original companies are no longer recognizable as separate units. Sometimes, an acquired company may be continued as a recognizably different company with its own management. Such a company, whose assets are mainly or entirely owned by another company, is called a ***subsidiary.*** Though subsidiaries retain corporate identity and run their own operations, they report their financial conditions with the parent company. Some companies buy most or all of the stock of other companies without taking a direct role in their management. The buying company operates as a holding company in these instances. A ***holding company*** receives income in the form of dividends on the stock it owns. Sometimes, companies will join for a short-term purpose, such as underwriting a large stock offering of a corporation. These combinations are called ***syndicates*** and exist only for as long as needed to accomplish their single, specific purpose. Another kind of temporary combination, called a ***joint venture*** (see Chapter 3), is very similar to a syndicate but is usually longer-lasting. For example, two real estate companies may wish to pool their resources and technical skills to subdivide and resell a piece of land for residential building lots. They could undertake a joint venture that would be dissolved when the lots are sold.

# MERGER MANIA
*Growth out of control* ━━━━━━━━━━━━━━━━━━━

In recent years, the trend toward mergers and acquisitions has accelerated at an ascending rate. Many observers are concerned that such growth is not sound economically. They contend that this growth is not stimulated by new ideas or by increased market demand, but simply as a profitable convenience for the companies involved. The objective of such mergers is often a consolidation of facilities, with a resulting reduction of employment. In many instances, consumers suffer from a shrinkage in available services and from fewer opportunities to choose where they will shop or what products they will buy.

Some mergers occur when two companies see a mutual advantage in their combination, as when Nabisco Brands Inc. and R. J. Reynolds Industries Inc. joined. Some acquisitions take place when one company becomes disenchanted with a particular line of business and sells it to get its money back, as when RCA Corp. sold Hertz Corp. to United Airlines. Shortly thereafter, RCA allowed itself to be acquired by General Electric Company.

Some mergers are described as "hostile takeovers," as when Ted Turner (owner of the Atlanta Braves baseball team and Turner Broadcasting) tried to acquire CBS by buying up a large portion of its stock on the open market. The CBS board and executives did not like the idea and marshaled enough stockholder support to discourage Turner, who sold his shares of stock back to the company.

Many mergers simply do not work out as planned. The parties involved, or the businesses themselves, do not fit well together. Mobil Oil's acquisition of Montgomery Ward & Co. has become a notable failure. So, too, was Exxon's acquisition of Reliance Electric Co. and General Electric's purchase of Utah International, Inc., a minerals company, which it sold after 6 years of unsatisfactory performance. In fact, so many mergers have been unsuccessful that beginning in 1985, there was a wave of demerging, or of selling off, of acquired companies by their conglomerate owners. Such selling off of company businesses by a parent company is called *divestiture.* Gulf & Western, for example, dumped more than 50 businesses between 1983 and 1985, while superconglomerate ITT Corp. sold 19 subsidiaries in 6 months, bringing its total divestitures to 85 within the decade.

# EMPLOYMENT IN LARGE CORPORATIONS
*For most people, advantages outweigh the drawbacks* ━━━━━━━━━

The question that job seekers ask about large corporations has less to do with mergers, acquisitions, and growth than with employment and career opportunities.

Some people are attracted to employment in small businesses, but the great majority of people not only work for large corporations but also find it more desirable. They do so for a number of reasons. Large companies usually pay better wages and salaries. They offer more benefits in the way of health care and life insurance and pension plans. Working conditions are generally better too. Since large companies are so visible to the law and to the public, there is greater pressure put upon them to create and maintain clean, safe work environments. The law also pays greater attention to the way in which large firms comply with legislation that affects employment. In enforcing the Equal Employment Opportunity laws, for example, the federal government chose to initiate its investigations against the largest corporations first, even those, like AT&T, whose reputation for fairness was exemplary at the time.

Large corporations usually offer more opportunities for training and advancement. The cost of developmental programs, which might represent an unbearable overhead to small businesses, is considered routine in larger companies, where these costs can be spread over thousands of people. The sheer size of employment in large companies also creates larger numbers of opportunities for individuals to move from one occupation to another and to be promoted to positions of increasing responsibility.

The major drawbacks of working for large corporations are probably the pressures to conform to prescribed behavior and procedures and the tendency for many jobs to be narrowly specialized, routinized, and—as a consequence—boring.

# 5  BIG BUSINESS SHORTCOMINGS
## Inefficiency, indifference, and conformity

Huge corporations are difficult to manage. Errors of judgment are magnified when output is measured in millions of units. A company with hundreds of thousands of employees and thousands of managers is especially subject to loss of control, lack of accurate communications, and disorganization. Large companies have struggled for years with the question of decentralizing versus centralizing. In theory, a centralized organization gives top management more direct control over operations. Often, however, it creates a huge and expensive bureaucracy that is unresponsive to changing conditions and opportunities. Decentralized management gives more control to local, regional, or division managers. It allows greater flexibility, but may result in poor communications and conflicting policies and actions.

## INEFFICIENT AND SLUGGISH
### Tripping over its own big feet

One thing seems certain. Bigness, alone, does not ensure corporate efficiency or survival. The bellwether industries of the United States have not had a good record in adapting to changing market and competitive environments. The steel and auto companies, in particular, have been slow to accommodate change. In both industries, the major corporations failed to modernize their production facilities as rapidly as overseas

# B·I·L·L·B·O·A·R·D

## SHOULD MERGERS BE ABOLISHED?

In 1969 there were over 6,000 mergers or acquisitions among United States corporations. Since then, the number has declined steadily to the point where there are about 2,000 each year. Because there are nearly 3 million corporations of all sizes, many people feel that the number of mergers is slight by comparison. On the other hand, the dollar value of these mergers is staggering. And it continues to increase. In 1969, the numbers of dollars involved in all merger transactions amounted to about $50 billion. For several years the total value of all mergers declined to less than $20 billion a year. Beginning in 1976, however, the size of mergers has been increasing until, in 1984, the total value of all mergers was $125 billion. Chevron acquired Gulf Oil for $13.3 billion. Texaco bought out Getty Oil for $10.1 billion. Beatrice acquired Esmark for $2.5 billion. Nestlé sucked up Carnation for $2.9 billion. Champion International Paper (itself the result of a merger between two paper-making giants) bought out St. Regis for $1.8 billion. IBM bought Rohm for $1.3 billion. General Electric acquired Employees Reinsurance Corp. from Texaco for $1.1 billion. There were many more mergers like these.

The record of successful mergers is anything but impressive. Mergers fail more often than they succeed. They disrupt jobs. They make huge profits for some investors and speculators. They are often so arranged that the executives involved are provided with

## Mergers fail more often than they succeed.

special job or income protection. Pension funds are often endangered or misused as a consequence of mergers. The larger the companies involved in a merger, the larger the cost of failure when it occurs. More and more mergers are financed through risky borrowing techniques using "junk" bonds. Tax deductions on the ensuing interest rates make the federal government an unwitting partner in some merger transactions. Consoli-

dation of companies in the same field reduces competition. Unpopular products can be cut out of the line, even though many consumers would like to continue buying them. The larger the company resulting from a merger, the less likely it is to be interested in the welfare of the communities in which its facilities are located. In summary, mergers lead to bigness; bigness doesn't necessarily lead to better products, better service, or better pricing.

### QUERIES

1. How can mergers be good for the economy if they have the potential of reducing the number of jobs and the number of active competitors?
2. Should mergers and acquisitions be restricted? By the dollar value of the transaction? By the number of employees involved? By the number of transactions a company can make in 5 years? Or should the system continue as it is, allowing natural forces in the open financial market to take care of problems that may emerge? ∎

# PROFILE

**J.** W. MARRIOTT Jr., is perhaps the kind of corporate executive that most Americans admire. He has been described as "an executive whose leadership, integrity, and management skills have profoundly, visibly, and favorably influenced the outstanding performance of a key element of American industry." The company that Marriott heads operates more than 1,400 restaurants, 90 air flight kitchens, over 290 food service management facilities, and airport terminal shops in more than 40 domestic airports. The Marriott Corporation owns and operates more than 142 hotels, employs more than 120,000 people, and has about 28,000 shareholders. J. W. Marriott serves on dozens of trade, professional, and charitable boards. He is a zealous advocate of the free enterprise system. In that regard, he says, "Corporations must work constantly to change and improve their products. We must continually search for new and more effective ways to serve our customers. As we look to the future, we must operate differently. We will have more information to process and to deal with than ever before. There will be more and tougher competition. . . . In this country we have the greatest environment for free enterprise of any country in the world. We know it works; we have seen it work. We know that if the government will just leave business alone and let us compete, grow, and prosper by competition, the future will be fantastic." ∎

**J. W. MARRIOTT JR.**

*SOURCE:* "J. W. Marriott, Jr.: American Manager of the Year," *Manage,* Second Quarter, 1985, pp. 18–20.

competitors did. The auto companies were slow to react to consumer demands for smaller, more reliable cars. Not only did foreign carmakers capture a large share of the American and international market, but United States automakers set records for operating losses during the early 1980s. Only with the threat of failure staring them in the face did the United States car builders adopt modern styling and convert their plants to modern technology. Their resources had been enormous; their operations were sluggish and inefficient. Similar shortcomings of operation and responsiveness plagued the tire makers and the machine tool builders. Even IBM, with its tremendous resources, lagged behind in its field when change was imminent. It was the newer, smaller companies like Apple—not IBM—that triggered the development and proliferation of mini-, micro-, and personal computers.

Even Kodak, once so powerful that it dictated what would happen in its markets, flounders. Polaroid beat it to the punch with the instant camera and Xerox, with the automatic copier. The Japanese took over the fine 35-mm camera market. When Kodak did retaliate with a first-rate instant camera and a copier even better than Xerox's, it was so tentative in its marketing efforts that it could not gain a market edge. Since 1978, Kodak's profit picture has been irregular.

**WHEN SMALLER IS BETTER** In case after case, companies that did not prosper under the umbrella of a large corporation have succeeded after they were turned free. A study of 15 businesses that were divested by large corporations between 1970 and 1982, for example, showed that all but one of them did better on their own. Under smaller, less bureaucratic management, fat was trimmed from corporate staffs, inventories and accounts receivables were better managed, and marketing became more aggressive. One such example is Talon Inc. It was once America's zipper king, but it stagnated after being acquired by the Textron conglomerate. Japan's YKK invaded the United States and seized most of the prime zipper market. Meanwhile, Textron changed Talon's president five times in 10 years. Textron finally sold the company in 1981 after 4 years of successive losses. The new owner promptly turned the company around and produced a profit within 11 months. Talon is now expanding aggressively and is a major factor in the zipper market once again.

**INERTIA ON THE BOARDS** Another inefficiency arises from the fact that corporate boards are often given important responsibilities without having the information or direct involvement needed to fulfill them. In large corporations, maintaining even a casual contact with actual operations requires many long hours of study and familiarity with thousands of pages of data. Many board members are unable to keep this contact. Furthermore, a great many boards of major corporations are made up of members who do not truly represent the interests of the public.

# INDIFFERENT AND ARROGANT

*A failure to assume a responsibility to the public* _____

In their pursuit of profit—the bottom line—all too many corporate executives fail to give adequate consideration to the impact of their decisions upon the public. As a consequence, damage to, or waste of, natural resources has been common. Prevention of air and water pollution has

---

## Action Brief

### BREAK UP THE BIG GUYS!

*That's a common outcry from consumers. But when the FTC ordered AT&T to split up into several separate, smaller corporations, public response wasn't all that enthusiastic. Not only did service suffer but confusion about telephone ownership and maintenance reigned. Phone charges shot up too. Basic monthly telephone charges rose from a national average of about $11 in 1983 to $16 in 1985. Residential installation rates varied widely according to company, from $23 to $65. Furthermore, local telephone users were tapped $1 a month in 1985 and $2 a month in 1986 for access to long-distance lines, whether or not they used them. "Who needs this?" asked many consumers, "when what we really need is Ma Bell."*

required the intervention of the federal government. In many other instances, big-company management has displayed an indifference to public opinion by shirking corporate tax responsibilities and by placing its own interests above those of the public or even those of the stockholders by whom it is employed.

***MONOPOLISTIC PRACTICES*** Many large corporations have achieved true dominance over their markets. Often, competing goods or services are simply not widely available. This has, in many cases, significantly reduced the variety of products. In the long run, higher prices and lower quality may result from the reduced competition as well. Even where competition exists, rival corporations show a tendency to set the same prices to share the market.

***ENVIRONMENTAL DAMAGE*** Large corporations have frequently shown irresponsibility by causing severe pollution, using unsafe work methods, producing low-quality or dangerous products, and engaging in political corruption and accepting bribes. It may be true that corporations are no more guilty of these practices than other organizations or individuals. The size and power of major corporations, however, make the effects of their irresponsibility much more severe.

***LEGALIZED TAX EVASION*** One of the most persistent criticisms of big business has to do with a seeming lack of proportion in its payment of federal taxes. (See Figure 21-2.) Much of this "tax dodging" is attributable to legal loopholes in the tax laws themselves. For example, General Electric Co. (under the accelerated cost recovery system, ACR) paid no federal income taxes whatsoever on $6.5 billion in profits between 1981 and 1983. In fact, GE received $283 million in tax refunds. Boeing Company, during the same period, paid no taxes on $1.5 billion in profits and also received a tax refund of $267 million. These were not exceptional cases. The Citizens for Tax Justice, a coalition of citizens' groups and labor unions, studied 250 large profitable corporations. It found that more than half paid no federal taxes during the period 1981 to 1983, or actually

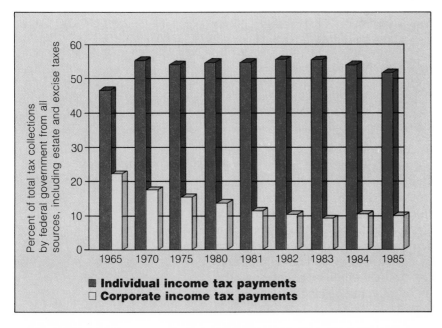

■ **Individual income tax payments**
□ **Corporate income tax payments**

Figure 21-2 Declining income tax contributions of corporations.

received rebates. The federal income tax for large corporations is 34 percent, and many pay the full amount, of course. In the years prior to 1987, tax loopholes were regularly introduced into the system for various reasons, often with the view that they stimulate business growth and economic prosperity. Large corporations do, of course, pay huge taxes at the local and state level and to the federal government for programs such as social security.

**SELF-SERVING EXECUTIVES** Another source of criticism is the arrogance with which many executives treat the power associated with their high-level positions. Many executives see that they are paid enormous salaries without an apparent relationship to their contribution to corporate success. For example, An Wang, chairperson of Wang Laboratories, paid himself $5,356,000 in 1984 and granted himself a potential for even greater gains in stock options even though his company's finances were sliding downhill. Richard L. Gelb, of Bristol-Myers, received $5,063,000, while his company was barely profitable. And T. Boone Pickens, Jr. was rewarded with $23,773,000 as his company, Mesa Petroleum, stayed just about even with the market.

Even more criticism is directed at corporate executives who, in the face of their company's acquisition by another, vote themselves long-term high-paying contracts. These "golden parachutes," say many critics, place the interests of the executives far above those of stockholders and employees as merger negotiations take place.

**DISREGARD FOR LOCAL INTEREST** Because corporate business activities may be far removed from top management, corporations often show a disregard for local interests. If an oil company wishes to tear down a local historical landmark to build a gas station, executives in New York or Chicago or Houston cannot see it from their office windows. They may not even know anything about it. Locally based companies are more subject to local pressures, needs, and interests. Some companies, however, have begun to respond positively to these failings of social responsibility by appointing ombudsmen, whose duty it is to discover and solve problems resulting from the company's products. These efforts, along with those of consumer departments and committees, have begun to exert an influence on corporations.

# A STIFLING CONFORMITY
*Unique corporate cultures*

In every organization, large or small, a unique organizational culture ultimately evolves. People tend to dress the same way, talk about the same things, frequent the same restaurants, and, most important, hold the same value systems. Large organizations, especially, stress conformity among their members. The conformity results partly from a competitive urge to get ahead in the organization by imitating those who are in the upper levels of the hierarchy. Conformity is also often encouraged by management as one means of achieving consistency and of keeping control over large numbers of employees. Many authorities believe that this atmosphere seriously interferes with the inventive and innovative creativity required for progress.

# 6 FUTURE DIRECTIONS

## A choice between more restrictions or greater responsibility

The extreme power of large corporations in the United States has been a continuing topic of political debate, especially in the last decade. The financial and management capabilities of the giant companies make them competitors even of national governments. Federal antitrust laws are designed to prevent business combinations that cause an unfair reduction of competition. These laws generally have had little effect on recent business combinations, especially conglomerates. Creating a monopoly—by joining all steel manufacturers, for example—can be prevented by the antitrust laws. However, a large and effective company that wishes to gain dominance of a market is not prevented from doing so, nor is a huge conglomerate prevented from acquiring great financial power. Both of these situations can be damaging to the economy and to customers. Lawmakers and the public will be challenged in the future to find effective ways of eliminating the negative effects of corporations without also destroying the advantages offered to society.

The future direction of corporate business is uncertain. Some see a phase ahead where corporations will be subjected to increasing regulation by government. Others see a phase developing in which corporations will exercise more self-discipline and demonstrate more initiative and creativity.

Stock market and other business scandals in recent times have led some to call for increased government regulation of certain business activities. For example, it has been suggested that the Securities and Exchange Commission tighten its rules affecting corporate mergers and acquisitions. Looming always in the background is the threat of public ownership of basic industries such as steel, autos, and utilities. Despite popular criticism of government management, there always remains the thought of government ownership as a solution to mismanaged and inefficient industries. However, most Americans probably still believe that corporate business practices should be improved not by government regulation or ownership, but by self-discipline and initiative generated within the traditional corporate framework.

## CONCERN FOR ETHICS

### Voluntary codes and education

In the past two decades, many attempts to improve the self-discipline of corporate management have been introduced. These voluntary efforts include such things as "codes of ethics," consumer departments, grievance boards, **ombudsmen** (individuals appointed to receive and investigate complaints from employees, consumers, and the public), and the seating of consumer and minority representatives on the board of directors. In the view of many observers, these techniques, combined with various legally required actions and programs, have had a measurable impact. Some, however, question whether these steps are enough. They argue for specific educational and training programs now and in the future to indoctrinate corporate managers regarding ethically acceptable business behavior. Already many community colleges, private schools of

*Action Brief*

## "APPLES" WILL NOT RIPEN HERE

In the face of mounting public reaction to South Africa's policy of apartheid, Apple Computer Inc. became the first United States firm to cut off sales to that nation for purely social and political reasons. Other companies, like Pan American World Airways and Chase Manhattan, for example, had withdrawn from the African nation earlier, but their reasons were economic. An Apple spokesperson said that Apple's sales in that country had been on the rise, but that the company could no longer accept a relationship there, no matter how profitable: "Like many other institutions, we are abhorred by apartheid." Overall, Apple's fortunes were on the decline at that time, but the decision was in line with the corporations' policy of accepting social responsibility for its actions.

More recently, other large corporations, such as IBM, General Motors, Honeywell, and McGraw-Hill have pulled out of South Africa. They did so in opposition to the system of apartheid and because the climate for doing business in South Africa had deteriorated.

business, and universities routinely offer a number of programs relating to the wisdom and productivity of responsible, equitable behavior in dealing with employees and consumers.

## ENCOURAGING CREATIVITY
*Entrepreneurship and intrapreneurship* ━━━━━━━━━

Ethics aside, some observers see conformity as a major factor preventing corporations from doing more to improve the economy and society. Conformity, they argue, is the enemy of both creativity and initiative. Many informed corporate executives now recognize this. Accordingly, there has been a salutory trend toward encouraging entrepreneurship and initiative within large corporations. For example, many companies have established formal programs to encourage intrapreneurship. **Intrapreneurship** is entrepreneurship within, and with the support of, the formal corporate structure. When IBM, for example, developed its PC, the corporation provided the needed flexibility by isolating a team of researchers in a "skunk works," an airplane hangar far away from corporate headquarters. PacTel (a West Coast telephone utility) created a separate "property management" subsidiary run by an individual given the mandate to take risks, set up a separate office, and get the company into a new business. It worked. The subsidiary built up a $500 million asset base in real estate within 5 years. At the Merrill Dow Pharmaceutical Company in Cincinnati, a "wellness concepts" marketing arm was created by an individual who was given seed money, a small staff, and an office. He launched into a related business that did not depend, however, on the sale of its commercial chemicals and drugs.

Corporations like IBM, PacTel and Merrill Dow that believe in the value of creativity and meaningful nonconformance modify their rigid control structures to encourage employee initiative. They permit well-intended actions that result in failure, and reward initiative that gets results outside of routine channels. Some observers believe that these efforts are necessary to invigorate corporate America, maintain faith in the business system, and meet the challenge of an increasingly competitive business environment at home and abroad.

# *Key Concepts*

1. The corporation is the dominant form of business ownership in the United States in terms of size, assets, number of employees, amount of goods and services produced, and profits generated. Corporations are formed when a charter is issued by the state or federal government. The charter states the corpora-

tion's name, purpose, stock authorization, and other information. Corporations are managed by officers appointed by a board of directors elected by stockholders according to procedures in the corporation bylaws.

2. Corporations may be "close" if they do not offer stock for sale to the public or "open" if

they do. Open corporations raise equity financing by preparing a prospectus and selling issues of stock to investors, using investment bankers or other underwriters as sales agents.

3. Stockholders have the right to obtain information about the corporation and usually the right to elect board members. Other than that, stockholders can exert very little control over a corporation's direction and operations. The actual supervision of a large corporation is undertaken by paid professional managers.

4. Large-sized corporations have a number of advantages: economy of scale, the confidence of suppliers and consumers, and a stable income resulting from diversification. Many corporations have grown to large size through internal expansion financed from profits. Many companies have also grown through acquisition of, or merger with, other companies. Business combinations may be horizontal, vertical, or conglomerate and may be carried out in various ways. Large corporations are a significant source of employment and make major contributions to the economy.

5. On the negative side, large companies are difficult and expensive to manage. They are often inefficient, wasteful, and slow to react to changing conditions. Many large corporations are indifferent to public responsibilities. They tend toward monopolistic practices and endanger the physical environment. Large companies typically take advantage of tax loopholes, and their managers are self-serving. Large companies also tend to foster conformity and stifle initiative among their employees.

6. The future of large corporations will depend upon which public and private viewpoints prevail—toward either (1) greater government regulation or (2) greater acceptance of social responsibility on the part of corporate management—and upon increased self-discipline and creativity by corporations to meet the challenge of a more competitive environment.

# Review Questions

1. Define, identify, or explain each of the following key terms and phrases, found on the pages indicated.

    *acquisition (p. 493)*
    *alien corporation (p. 488)*
    *bylaws (p. 488)*
    *charter (articles of incorporation) (p. 487)*
    *close corporation (p. 489)*
    *conglomerate combination (p. 493)*
    *cumulative voting (p. 491)*
    *divestiture (p. 494)*
    *domestic corporation (p. 487)*
    *foreign corporation (p. 487)*
    *going public (p. 490)*
    *holding company (p. 493)*
    *horizontal combination (p. 493)*
    *intrapreneurship (p. 501)*
    *joint venture (p. 493)*
    *merger (p. 493)*
    *noncumulative voting (p. 491)*
    *ombudsman (p. 501)*
    *open corporation (p. 489)*
    *prospectus (p. 490)*
    *proxy (p. 491)*
    *subsidiary (p. 493)*
    *syndicate (p. 493)*

    *underwriter (p. 490)*
    *vertical combination (p. 493)*

2. What five factors have allowed corporations to achieve their present size and dominance?

3. What is the difference between a close corporation and an open one? In which category do large corporations like General Motors fall?

4. What role do stockholders play in managing a large open corporation? To what extent are stockholders able to control the assets of the corporation in which they share ownership? What does their ownership mean?

5. How can diversification benefit a corporation?

6. Distinguish between internal methods of diversification and those used by combining with other companies.

7. Compare the advantages and disadvantages of working in a large corporation with those of working in a small company.

8. Why might corporate boards of directors be ineffective?

9. Briefly describe some of the problems that great size can present a large corporation.

10. Distinguish between intrapreneurship and entrepreneurship.

# Case Critique 21-1
## Otis Doesn't Live Here Anymore

A master mechanic by the name of Elijah G. Otis invented the elevator in Yonkers, New York, in 1853. His company eventually became the world's biggest manufacturer of elevators. It made most of them right there in Yonkers. As the 1970s began, however, Otis Elevator Corporation, like many other companies, found the nature of its business changing. Furthermore, it had allowed its eight plants in Yonkers to become run down and their equipment to become obsolete. Otis felt that the best thing it could do was to close down these old buildings and build a new plant elsewhere. The city of Yonkers was upset by this idea. Otis was the largest employer in this suburb of New York City. Yonkers' officials proposed that under an urban renewal program, Yonkers and the federal government would make land for a new facility available at a bargain price. Otis agreed to the plan. Yonkers accepted $14 million from the federal government to move 30 small businesses and 350 families and to demolish the buildings they had occupied. In turn, the city sold the cleared building site to Otis for $1.3 billion. Otis added $10 million to build a new, modern facility. As a result, company employment there grew from 1,300 to nearly 2,000 workers. That was 1975.

Since then, several unanticipated things took place. First, Otis was acquired by the international conglomerate United Technologies, Inc., with its headquarters in Hartford, Connecticut. Next, the demand for elevators plunged as the construction of high-rise buildings slumped during the late 1970s. Probably most important, elevator technology changed. The devices manufactured in Yonkers and assembled onto Otis elevators elsewhere became obsolete. These devices were a "controller" and a "selector" that old Mr. Otis had invented to tell elevators where to stop and which floor to move to next. These mechanical devices were no longer used in modern elevators. Instead, they were replaced by small computerlike miniprocessors installed in each elevator.

Faced with the once-new facility which was growing old by 1983, high union wages in Yonkers, and a decaying market, United Technologies announced that it would close the Yonkers facility, forever.

Citizens and public officials in Yonkers were dumbstruck. They became angry, however, when it became apparent that Otis would continue to make 20,000 elevators in 26 other plants around the world. The mayor of Yonkers threatened to sue United Technologies to make the company stay. A local Otis official said that the company's original intentions were sincere. "We wouldn't have spent the $10 million if we hadn't intended to stay," said the plant manager. A United Technologies spokesperson said, however, that Otis never promised to remain open indefinitely when it accepted the grant: "It was a business decision. We signed a contract and fulfilled our obligations. I don't think it is a moral question." When asked to comment upon the issue, a community planning official of the Department of Housing and Urban Development (HUD) said, "It's a local dispute. The city did benefit from the period of time the company was operating."

1. By what sort of diversification or combination was Otis Elevator Corporation joined with United Technologies Corp.?
2. Should Otis have accepted the urban renewal grant proposal in the first place? Why?
3. Why might it have been easier for United Technologies to make the decision to move than for the original Otis Corporation owners? Would the decision have been different, regardless of who the present owner was?
4. Should the federal government have entered this dispute to prevent the company from leaving town? Why?

SOURCE: Howard Kurtz, "Unusual Question in Yonkers Touches Off Acrimonious Debate," *The Washington Post*, May 15, p. A5.

# Case Critique 21-2
## One Giant Where Two Once Stood

Mergers and acquisitions may seem like rather abstract concepts when people read about them. They are often thought of as "something that happens to other people." That's the way employees of Gulf Oil Corporation felt for years. After all, Gulf was one of the largest, and most profitable, oil companies in the world. Its headquarters was in a 44-story skyscraper in Pittsburgh. The company and its executives were regarded as pillars of the community. The Gulf chairperson typically served as voluntary chairperson of such public-minded activities as the Pittsburgh Symphony, the United Way, and U.S. Savings Bond drives. Some 1,300 employees worked in the Gulf building, and the company pumped more than $75 million yearly into the city's economy. More than 50 Pittsburgh organizations looked for the over $2 million in contributions that could be expected each year from Gulf. Then, suddenly in 1985, everything changed. In the largest corporate merger ever, Chevron, a California-based petroleum company, acquired Gulf Oil for $13.3 billion. Life would never again be the same for Gulf employees.

One of Chevron's first decisions was to close down Gulf's headquarters in Pittsburgh and sell the building to a real estate company. Next, it gave termination notices to a large portion of Gulf's headquarters employees. The rest were offered jobs in Chevron's San Francisco headquarters. Only 35 percent accepted. Many who turned down the offer to move cited family ties in Pittsburgh and the high cost of housing on the West Coast. The rest of Gulf's Pittsburgh employees were left looking for work. Similar terminations were taking place at Gulf's Houston operations, which employed 9,000 workers.

Not all Gulf employees suffered from the deal. Many high-level personnel received generous separation benefits. For example, Chevron was reported to have paid $52 million to Gulf's top-echelon executives to match what might have been their profits from stock options they held.

There were dozens of cases of upsetting circumstances in family life. One manager had just moved his family from Houston to Pittsburgh when the ax fell. "Our boxes weren't even unpacked," he said. He was offered a job in San Francisco but opted to return to Houston and look for employment in his home state. Other employees, who left Gulf after years of loyal employment, were troubled even after receiving substantial termination allowances. Said one employee, "It's traumatic leaving the company after 16 years of service. It's more than a job, it's my way of life."

Those who remain with the new owner have their problems too. Some complain that they feel like second-class citizens under the new regime. Others describe themselves as pawns in the game of corporate warfare. "We're almost like POWs," said one who transferred to San Francisco. "We lost, so they treated us like they were the conquerors."

1. Why would some Gulf employees lose their jobs because of the merger? Why would some be offered jobs with Chevron?
2. What is the term often given to the special benefits received by Gulf's high-echelon executives? How do you feel about that practice?
3. How difficult would you find it if you were asked to move from your present home to a city 1,500 miles away in order to hold your job? Which of the following incentives would be most important in persuading you to make the move? A 10 percent salary increase? Sale of your old home and purchase of a new one at no extra cost to you? Guaranteed employment for a minimum of 5 years? A promotion to the next higher-level job? None of these?
4. If you were managing the merger for Chevron, what different approach might you suggest to make the consolidation less painful to the people involved?

SOURCE: Kenneth R. Sheets, "People Pay the Highest Price in a Takeover," *U.S. News & World Report*, July 22, 1985, p. 51.

# International
# Business Operations

## Learning Objectives

*The purpose of this chapter is to provide insight into the factors that help or hinder a nation's ability to trade and conduct international business operations, describe how companies do business on an international basis and what obstacles they must overcome, discuss the impact of multinational companies on world affairs, and explain some of the ways in which international trade is encouraged.*

*As evidence of general comprehension, after studying Chapter 22 you should be able to:*

1. *Define international trade and operations.*

2. *Evaluate the various influences on a nation's ability to trade, and distinguish between absolute advantage and comparative advantage.*

3. *Explain various methods of international trade participation and business operations and their relationship to direct and indirect distribution.*

4. *Outline some of the principal obstacles to international business.*

5. *Evaluate the impact of multinational operations on international and domestic affairs.*

6. *Identify the various vehicles of international cooperation in trade.*

*If your class is using SSweetco: Business Model and Activity File, see Chapter 22 in that book after you complete this chapter. There you will find exercises and activities to help you apply your learning to typical business situations.*

## 1 IMPORT AND EXPORT TRADE AND OPERATIONS

make business an international activity.

## 2 A NATION'S NATURAL, HUMAN, AND ECONOMIC RESOURCES INFLUENCE ITS ABILITY TO TRADE

Some countries have more to offer than others.

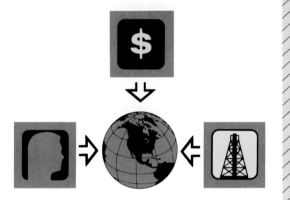

## 3 UNITED STATES COMPANIES

do business abroad directly without a broker or indirectly through a broker.

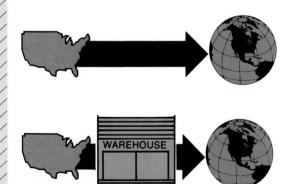

## 4 THERE ARE MANY OBSTACLES TO CARRYING OUT INTERNATIONAL BUSINESS

Cultural        Financial

Trade        Operational

## 5 MULTINATIONAL CORPORATIONS

may own, produce, or market in many nations.

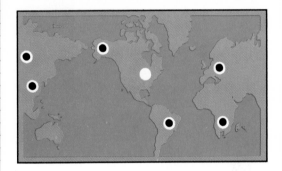

## 6 BUSINESSES ARE AIDED BY INTERNATIONAL COORPORATION

in the form of:

 Multinational economic communities (Common Market)

 International laws and treaties

 International banks

 International trade associations

# INTERNATIONAL BUSINESS: A TWO-WAY STREET

*Undeniably, the playing field for the game of United States business has now encircled the globe. As a result, the game has taken a number of odd, and often unhappy, turns. The National Association of Manufacturers' chief economist, for example, cried, "Imports are killing us." The Brown Shoe Company of St. Louis closed 8 of its 30 domestic plants, and then got into the international action itself by purchasing an importer of Italian shoes. DuPont, the huge chemical company, saw a greater advantage for its operations overseas and raised its investment in assets abroad from 17 percent of its holdings to 26 percent. Record imports in copper have caused Asarco, Inc., a major United States mining company, to close down more than half of its domestic capacity. The chairperson of a Vermont tool company said when it acquired a West German tool company, "If we can't be competitive with foreign manufacturers, then we'll become foreign manufacturers ourselves."*

*The internationalization of auto manufacturing has been a revolution in our time. Of the 10 million or more cars sold each year in the United States, over 40 percent are imported. Nearly 2 million of them are Japanese. Informed people around the world say that the United States shouldn't complain. United States products—like wheat, chemicals, and farm equipment—have been major factors in world markets for years. Even American fast-food outlets such as McDonald's are becoming internationalized, causing some to dub the franchiser "McWorld." Nevertheless, the invasion of American markets by foreign companies, either on land or by sea, keeps on coming. A German company, for example, now owns A&P supermarkets. British Petroleum (BP) now operates Sohio. Hair-styling mousse came to America by way of France. Toothpaste in a pump, now dominating 30 percent of domestic toothpaste sales, was a West German invention. A French line of beauty products is now distributed through Clairol, Inc. Those narrow green storefronts of Benetton, the Italian knitwear producer, are becoming almost as American as McDonald's golden arches; there are now 400 of them in the United States.*

*Estimates are that foreign imports have had the effect of taking more than 2 million jobs away from American workers. The other side of the coin is that the more than $300 billion derived from United States exports—of merchandise, military equipment, and other aid programs—and from investments abroad accounts for more than 3 million American jobs. According to the* *rules of the international trading game, countries that export, unfortunately, must also be ready to import. As the lines of the song go, "You can't have one without the other."*

*SOURCES:* Madlyn Resener, "Europe's Invasion," *Newsweek*, August 13, 1985, p. 55; Wayne Beissert, "The Shift in Imports," *USA Today*, February 21, 1985, p. 1A.; Monroe W. Karmin and Robert F. Black, "Where Surge of Imports Is Hitting Hardest," *U.S. News & World Report*, May 6, 1985, pp. 45–46.

## 1  WHAT MAKES BUSINESS INTERNATIONAL?
### *When they buy from, sell to, or operate in foreign lands*

Trade between nations is as old as the Bible. Since the middle of the twentieth century, it has become the way of business life for more countries, and more United States companies, than ever before in history. An American automobile, for example, may contain material and parts directly or indirectly contributed by hundreds of nations. And, paradoxically, as United States auto builders ship or manufacture millions of cars

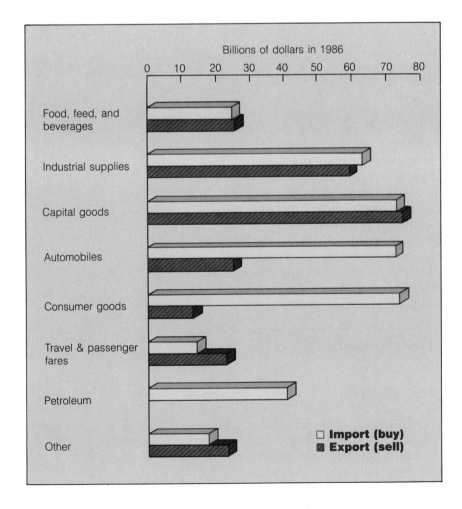

Figure 22-1 What the U.S. buys from and sells to other nations.

overseas, millions of autos and trucks built overseas or built by foreign companies flood the domestic markets in America.

International business makes available a range of materials and processes that could not conceivably exist in one restricted area. (See Figure 22-1 for an illustration of the extent to which the United States depends upon the products of other nations and they depend upon us.) It would be practically impossible to make a fruit salad in any area of the world which included locally grown apples and bananas. The two fruits do not normally flourish in the same climate. The same situation exists with metals, oil, timber, and many other products.

Companies may be involved in international business in two main ways:

■ They may buy from or sell to companies or governments in other countries. This *importing* and *exporting* activity is called *international trade.*

■ They may directly engage in *international operations,* that is, marketing or producing goods and services in another country.

Many large corporations carry on both kinds of international business with and in many different countries. Although any particular international business may result from a variety of particular needs, there is a general need that stimulates trade between nations. The resources of every region or country are limited to some extent. Every country needs materials or products that are only available in other countries. The United States is unusually rich in resources. Still, we import all our tin, industrial diamonds, natural rubber, coffee, tea, cobalt, platinum, tungsten, manganese, nickel, antimony, bauxite, chrome, and many other goods and materials.

Even when a country may be able to produce certain kinds of goods, those goods can often be produced more inexpensively and more efficiently elsewhere. Countries specialize in making the goods for which their resources are best suited. When free trade exists, the effect of this specialization is greater efficiency and lower prices for everyone.

International business makes a huge contribution to the economy of nearly every country. In the United States, exporting accounts for about 8 percent of the gross national product. We import slightly less than that amount. Many American-based companies depend on overseas sales and operations for significant parts of their revenues and profits. Table 22-1 shows a few of these companies. Our entire economy is becoming more and more intertwined with those of other countries. Manufactured goods of all kinds—chemicals, steel, sulfur, cotton, wheat, corn, and hundreds of other products—flow out to buyers in other countries. Zinc, tin, copper, silk, tea, bananas, and other materials and goods flow in.

## 2  INFLUENCES ON A NATION'S ABILITY TO TRADE

*Many have more to offer than others*

Since international trade arises partly because of the unequal distribution of specific resources, countries and regions differ in the extent and nature of their involvement in world trade. The conditions and resources in any country control how much it imports and exports and determine the kinds of products traded.

## TABLE 22-1
## CORPORATE INVOLVEMENT IN INTERNATIONAL BUSINESS

| *Corporation* | *Extent of Participation in Foreign Markets in 1985* |
|---|---|

### R. J. Reynolds Industries
To conduct business in its more than 400 subsidiaries and branches overseas, the company utilizes 33 different currencies. Its profit before taxes outside the United States was $439 million, or about one-quarter of the company's total. Among its exotic international brands are Ardilla Pastas and Cannelloni, Minizza Snack Crackers, Petit Coeurs Sweet Biscuits in Europe, Del Monte Banana Ketchup in the Far East, and Powdered Milk in Latin America.

### Xerox Corporation
The company operates in Europe as Rank Xerox and in Japan as Fuji Xerox. Sales from international operations came to $3.926 billion as compared with United States sales of $5.962 billion. Profits from international business amounted to 40 percent of the company's total, although these profits were substantially affected by devaluation of the Mexican peso and a strong United States dollar in Europe that year.

### Grolier Incorporated
This worldwide publisher of encyclopedias and textbooks markets internationally solely through independent distributors in 57 countries— from Aruba to Egypt and from Jamaica to Japan, Sri Lanka, and West Germany. About 28 percent of its sales came from outside the United States, as did its profits. As might be expected, the company took a $4.9 million loss in foreign currency exchange, especially since 40 percent of its international sales came from Mexico, where the peso was dramatically devaluated that year.

### Tandy Corporation
This company, known for its domestic Radio Shack stores, garnered 13.5 percent of its sales from outside the United States. Interestingly, the company made net gains of 3.5 percent in European sales based upon local currencies, but due to the strength of the United States dollar, this converted to a sales decrease of 8.7 percent in United States currency. Tandy has manufacturing and purchasing operations in several Asian countries. Its Asian subsidiary purchases some 40 percent of the products that appear in the Radio Shack catalog.

### Sears Roebuck and Co.
While Sears gathered the bulk of its gigantic revenues of $40.7 billion from its domestic operations, it also operated an international trading company. Sears World Trade, Inc., participated in overseas transactions valued at $592 million, from which it netted a loss of $12 million.

### The Goodyear Tire and Rubber Company
This multinational company divides its operations into six segments: United States, Europe, Mediterranean-Africa, Latin America, Asia-Pacific, and Canada. Of its assets of $6.9 billion, nearly $1.3 billion are located outside the United States. Of the $155 million in income taxes it paid in 1985, over two-thirds of this payment went to foreign governments.

*Source:* 1985 Annual Reports of the companies described above.

## NATURAL RESOURCES
*Unevenly distributed advantages*

Natural resources are a vital part of every country's economy. They determine, among other things, what a country can sell to other countries and what it must buy. For example, a country with great wealth in the form of mineral deposits is in a very favorable position. If it has the skilled labor, facilities, technology, and capital to do so, it may manufacture and export finished metal products, or it may use the minerals directly for export. Oil is probably the best example of a pure natural resource dominating international trade. Nations that export oil have reaped tremendous profits. Importing nations have been so strained by the need to pay for oil that, in some cases, their economies have suffered.

As for agricultural products, the kinds and amounts that a country can export or must import depend on the country's climate, terrain, and soil, as well as on its technology. The United States is so favored on all these counts that in recent years, over 18 percent of our exports have been agricultural products.

## HUMAN RESOURCES
*Skilled or specialized labor*

In the modern world, skilled labor is usually a necessity of production. Fewer jobs than ever before require only brute strength or thoughtless repetition. Any country with a trained, capable work force will have an advantage in producing goods for trade. Unlike climate and other natural resources, an outstanding work force can be created through good education systems and company training and incentive programs.

Some developing countries view the low wages paid to their workers as a resource giving their nation a competitive advantage. Some goods can be effectively produced at a lower total cost where wages are low. However, the advantage can only be temporary. If the competitive strategy is successful, the country will gain in international trade. Its standard of living will rise, and workers may no longer be willing to accept low wages.

It was, for nearly 100 years, the proud claim of the United States that its workers were the most skilled and productive in the world. Since World War II, this claim has been seriously challenged by several nations. Japan, in particular, with few natural resources except the human one, has put United States workers on the defensive, as illustrated in Figure 22-2. For example, since 1974 Japanese productivity has grown by more than 110 percent compared with 33 percent in the United States.

## CAPITAL, TECHNOLOGY, AND TRANSPORTATION
*Money and modern methods*

Trying to assemble capital resources can be one of the most frustrating aspects of producing goods for international trade. Even abundant natural resources cannot be adequately exploited without production facilities. Production facilities are difficult or impossible to build without the revenue from the natural resources. However, that revenue is unavailable without the facilities. A country with a large stock of production

**Who's Better?**

U.S. News & World Report *asked 10 leading scholars who have studied both Japanese and American workers to rate them on a variety of qualities. Although the experts disagreed on some issues, the comments are representative of their remarks.*

**U.S.**                 **Concern for Quality**        **Japan**

★ Japanese workers possess an almost religious desire to do jobs well. They pay great attention to detail. Many Americans just want to finish the job. ●

**Initiative**

★ On an individual level, Americans are willing to take the lead. They are concerned with who gets credit for exceptional work. ☐

**Hard Work**

☐ The work ethic is strong in both countries, but the experts give the Japanese a slight edge because they routinely put in extra hours. Their company is the central focus of their lives. ●

**Honesty**

☐ Because of strong identification with their company, Japanese are less likely to steal office supplies or cheat on time cards and expense accounts. ●

**Ambition**

★ America's individualistic culture encourages workers to strive to get ahead. Japanese, though ambitious, try not to stand out, especially early in their careers. ☐

**Loyalty**

☐ The average Japanese worker expects to spend an entire career at one firm. Companies, in turn, take a paternalistic interest in employees. ●

**Basic Skills**

☐ Japan's schools produce graduates with good basic skills. Japanese learn discipline and good work habits that they transfer to the job. ●

**Advanced Skills**

★ A close call. Workers in both nations are highly educated, but the U.S. has more college graduates and white-collar professionals. ☐

**Reliability**

☐ Japanese are reluctant to show up late or call in sick, largely because they don't want to let down their bosses and coworkers. Many skip parts of their vacations. ●

**Cooperativeness**

☐ Japanese subordinate individual concerns to group needs. This fosters a spirit of togetherness that is especially effective on the assembly line. ●

Figure 22-2 Comparative qualities in U.S. and Japanese workers. Copyright © 1985, U.S. News & World Report. Reprinted from issue of Sept. 2, 1985.

plants and equipment in operation is at a tremendous advantage, even if the facilities are outmoded.

The same problem must be faced with technology. Profitable finished products cannot be created without it, but it is difficult to develop technology without sufficient revenue. A lack of high-level technology is likely to prevent a country from participating in world trade. Even countries that exploit pure natural resources, such as oil or nitrogen fertilizers, need access to modern methods of extraction in order to remain competitive.

Countries also need a modern system of transportation to get their goods to market. Minerals that lie deep in a jungle are inaccessible until a railroad or a good system of roads is built. This is one of the factors that puts developing countries at a disadvantage in world trade. However, even under the best of circumstances, transportation is expensive. Modern transportation methods have made the world one big marketplace, but this situation can continue only if importers are willing to pay higher prices for the goods.

## TRADE ADVANTAGES
*These determine specialization* ═══════════════════

A country has an ***absolute advantage*** in the production of a product when it (1) is the only country that makes the product, or (2) can make the product at a lower cost than another country. A country with a much needed mineral product found nowhere else in the world would obviously devote its effort to producing and exporting that mineral. The country would profit from its monopoly position. A country that can make a particular product at a lower cost than another country also has an absolute advantage. In some cases, however, a country may do well to import that product and concentrate on producing some other product. Such a decision will be based on comparative advantage.

The theory of ***comparative advantage*** embraces two related concepts: (1) a country with absolute advantages in a number of different products should concentrate on the products which bring the greatest advantage, and (2) a country with no absolute advantages should concentrate on products which bring the least disadvantage.

The production and trade of agricultural products is a simple example of how trade advantages operate. Country X has an absolute advantage in wheat and corn production. Country Y is at a disadvantage in growing both products but has a much greater disadvantage with corn than with wheat. According to the theory of comparative advantage, it would benefit country X to specialize in growing corn and import wheat from country Y. Similarly, country Y should concentrate on growing wheat and should import corn.

This principle is illustrated by the striking rise in imports of food products by the United States. In recent years, the United States imported almost half as much food as it exported. The great bulk of American exports were in foods, like wheat and corn, that could be planted, cultivated, and harvested mechanically. The foods we imported were ones like coffee, fresh produce like broccoli, and even processed foods like tuna fish. It is not that many of these agricultural products cannot be grown in the United States; it is the high cost of stoop labor here, as compared with lower labor costs in countries like Mexico, Brazil, Colombia, Spain, Costa Rica, and Chile. This lower stoop-labor cost provides these food exporters with a comparative advantage. Even in such an unlikely product as processed apple juice, imports now account for more than half of all consumed in the United States. The apples are picked and the juice processed before shipment to the United States, where our mechanized packing plants have a comparative advantage.

---

## *Action Brief*

### AT A COMPARATIVE DISADVANTAGE

*When the 101-year-old shipyard in Quincy, Massachusetts, closed its gates, the reason was clear, but unpleasant. Commercial shipbuilding in the United States was suffering from old, inefficient facilities and high labor costs. As a consequence, shipbuilders were being lured to locate in Western Europe or Asia. It takes twice as long and costs twice as much to build a ship in the United States as it does in South Korea or Japan, for example. Other nations offer lower interest rates and better loan terms. Other governments often subsidize this industry. The United States used to do the same, but it ended its 44-year program of direct construction subsidies in 1981.*

# 3  HOW COMPANIES TRADE AND OPERATE INTERNATIONALLY
## *Degree of participation varies broadly*

Just about any company can enter international trade. It can do so in many ways. Some methods of entry are more risky than others. Despite the fact that risk can be held to a minimum, less than 10 percent of United States firms make an attempt to sell their products overseas. Only a very small minority of companies actually operate overseas. This reluctance stems from a feeling of uncertainty about international trade and from a difficulty in obtaining specific and reliable information about opportunities and operating methods for any given type of business.

Companies may engage in international business in any of six principal ways:

■ *Casual* exporting occurs when goods are produced and sold locally but also exported or resold overseas by the local buyer. Many companies engage in this kind of international trade without even being aware of it.

■ Many companies produce goods with the specific intention of exporting them. *Active* participation in export trade may be achieved through distribution channels different from the domestic ones. A manufacturer may sell and ship directly to an import firm abroad. The import firm may sell to a domestic export firm, which in turn resells to a foreign importer. In many cases, as with the sale of component parts, for instance, companies sell directly to a user firm abroad.

■ *Foreign licensing* is a transitional stage between exporting and international operations. Under this procedure, a domestic manufacturer of a particular product grants a company in a foreign country a license to make the product there. In return for the production rights, the foreign firm pays the domestic manufacturer a fee or a portion of its revenues. This arrangement allows the domestic company to take at least partial advantage of the foreign market. It saves transportation costs and may avoid high tariffs or other trade barriers. At the same time, it is far simpler than creating a new overseas operation to produce and sell the product.

■ *Marketing abroad* is the first way in which most companies become involved with overseas operations. Production facilities remain in the company's home country. By maintaining a marketing subsidiary or affiliate abroad, a company gains far greater control of sales operations and can aggressively and creatively promote its products to foreign markets.

■ A company strongly committed to international business will often *manufacture and sell* its own goods abroad, sometimes in several countries. This makes selling easier. It saves transportation costs, eliminates unnecessary intermediaries, and avoids trade restrictions and tariffs. Normally, this option is available only to relatively large companies capable of decentralizing their organizations to some extent.

■ *Joint ownership* of an enterprise with a company or government in the foreign country sometimes has unique advantages. The foreign co-owner's specialized knowledge of local conditions often contributes to success. Such an arrangement has a preferred legal status in some countries. For large ventures, more capital may be available and the risk is shared.

■ *Offshore* or *contract manufacturing* has become increasingly popular as firms in the United States subcontract the production of parts and assemblies to overseas firms. These parts are made in countries that specialize in certain skills or processes or are made in countries where labor costs are relatively low compared with those in the United States. When auto, television, and other workers complain that their jobs have been "shipped overseas," they usually mean that their company is engaged in offshore manufacturing.

## DIRECT AND INDIRECT DISTRIBUTION
*Resembles marketing channels*

Many of the methods of engaging in international business correspond to direct and indirect distribution in domestic trade. Companies with international operations—marketing, manufacturing, or both—use a direct channel. They may establish a branch or subsidiary abroad to handle the marketing or manufacturing activities. Often, the foreign operation is established by acquiring an existing foreign company. A domestic company with its own export company to sell directly to foreign customers is also using a direct channel.

Indirect channels involve intermediaries. Much of the import-export trade of any country is handled by import or export merchants, agents, brokers, or buyers.

## 4 OBSTACLES TO INTERNATIONAL BUSINESS
*The hurdles are many, but they are not insurmountable*

Engaging in international business is a very sophisticated activity. It requires great personal and business skill, experience, and knowledge. Even the best international business manager will encounter political, legal, social, and financial obstacles that may be difficult to overcome.

## CULTURAL BARRIERS
*Language, attitudes, and customs*

Dealing with a country that uses a different language creates many problems. It is often difficult to find top managers who speak more than one language fluently. Advertising written in one language often cannot be translated into another and retain its meaning and force. Even product names can be troublesome. Chevrolet's Nova automobile would seem oddly named to the world's 200 million Spanish-speaking people for whom "no va" means "doesn't go."

Language difficulties can often be solved. On the other hand, deep cultural differences—social expectations, manners, and methods of doing business—can be persistent problems to a salesperson or manager doing business in a foreign country. Countries differ in their preferred meeting times, the formality or informality of discussion, the length and styles of negotiation, and in scores of other subtle approaches to business.

Consumers also differ in their preferences from country to country. Color, shape, packaging, and advertising may have different effects in different nations. Marketers in Japan, for example, have found all of these cultural barriers. Western instructional manuals seem cold and impersonal to Japanese buyers accustomed to the cordial, personal, explanatory tone of their own manuals. Japanese buyers expect to find their goods packed in containers that are clean, unmarked, and unbent. Western marketers sometimes have to double-pack goods being sent to Japan, with an attractive display box packed inside another box for shipping. Men's toiletries cannot be displayed near women's cosmetics in Japan, because the men usually will not approach the women's counter. Cultural differences like these can make marketing a challenging undertaking in a foreign country.

American children eat candy as a treat between meals. Italian children are likely to put a bar of chocolate between two slices of bread for a snack. French cooks routinely use bar chocolate in their cooking.

People in France and West Germany eat more packaged spaghetti than Italians do. The catch is that Italians buy theirs loose. German and Dutch businesspeople take their spouses with them on business trips. This is less likely to occur with the British and is almost unheard of in Asia.

## FINANCIAL TRANSACTIONS
*Much can be lost in conversion*

Trading between sovereign nations creates financial complications because currencies are not of equal value and the rates of exchange between currencies are not fixed. An **exchange rate** is the amount of one currency that exactly equals a given amount of another currency at a given time. On one day in 1987, for example, one United States dollar equaled 1.82 West German marks. A United States company in Germany could exchange 1,820,000 marks for $1 million (minus the exchange fee). However, if the exchange rate rose to 2.0 marks to the dollar, the company's dollars would be worth 2 million marks. The shifting rates complicate transactions and can cause a significant loss of value to a company's currency assets.

## TRADE BARRIERS
*Protection for domestic industries*

Countries often limit international trade by legal means. The most common methods are tariffs and quotas. A **tariff** is a tax collected on imported goods. Many tariffs, called **revenue tariffs,** are levied only to raise money for the government. Others are **protective tariffs,** established to discourage importation of certain products or to raise their price so as to reduce competition with domestic goods of the same type. A **quota** is a legal limit on the quantity of specific goods that may be imported. An **embargo** is a final extreme quota. It actually prohibits trade in certain goods or with certain countries. The United States has prohibited trade with certain communist countries, partly in an effort to weaken their economies. Most Arab nations have a trade embargo on Israeli shipments, resulting from their political and religious differences.

*Action Brief*

### GUERNSEY OR JAMAICA?

*American manufacturers are bombarded by offers from foreign nations to relocate their offshore operations. For example, the tiny island of Guernsey, located between England and France, pitches these advantages to American high-tech companies: political stability, skilled workers, straight 20 percent tax rate, 40 banks, free trade in the European Economic Community (EEC), excellent labor relations, and a temperate climate with beautiful surroundings. Jamaica, the home of calypso in the Caribbean, is just as aggressive in soliciting manufacturers from the United States. Its investment promotion cites manufacturing at low cost, high productivity, 12 years of duty-free, quota-free access to United States markets, and preferential access to the markets of the EEC.*

The underlying reason for imposing protective tariffs and quotas is to encourage the growth of domestic industries and to protect them from price competition from foreign companies. This is considered to be especially important for those industries that are essential for the national defense.

By the middle 1980s, so many industries in the United States felt threatened by imports that, increasingly, they were asking the federal government to establish trade barriers or to set quotas for their protection. Notable among these industries were steel, textiles, and footwear. Three-quarters of all nonrubber shoes bought by Americans today are imported, for example. Figure 22-3 shows the extent to which many other products consumed in the United States are imported.

## IMBALANCES IN TRADE
*A critical economic problem for the United States*

Tariffs are also used to maintain a favorable balance of payments. A nation's **balance of trade** may be defined as the total value of its exports minus the total value of its imports. The balance of trade closely affects another figure, the **balance of payments,** which is the total of all payments made to foreign countries minus total receipts from abroad. This figure includes trade plus other factors, like international loans and spending by tourists. The balance of trade is said to be favorable, or positive, when exports exceed imports. It is unfavorable when imports exceed exports, because the country is not receiving adequate revenue from selling exports to pay for needed imports. For that reason, governments may impose tariffs or quotas to limit imports, thereby making the balance of payments more favorable.

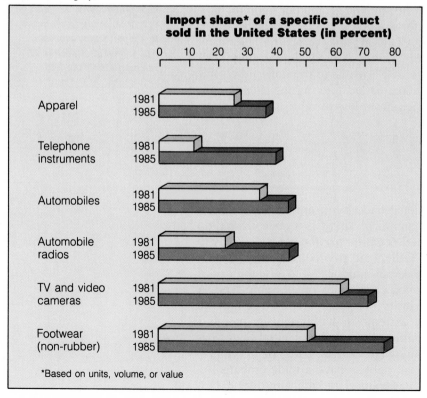

Import share* of a specific product sold in the United States (in percent)

| Product | Year |
|---|---|
| Apparel | 1981 / 1985 |
| Telephone instruments | 1981 / 1985 |
| Automobiles | 1981 / 1985 |
| Automobile radios | 1981 / 1985 |
| TV and video cameras | 1981 / 1985 |
| Footwear (non-rubber) | 1981 / 1985 |

*Based on units, volume, or value

Figure 22-3 The growing American appetite for imported consumer products.

Since 1975, the United States has suffered from a serious trade imbalance. Imports of merchandise far exceed United States exports. Much of the problem stemmed from the fact that the United States dollar was worth so much more than currency in other nations that they couldn't afford to buy much from us, while Americans could buy foreign products at bargain prices. Japan, in particular, was singled out as causing an unfavorable balance of payments, as illustrated in Figure 22-4.

A persistent imbalance in trade often leads to charges by one country that firms in another country are *dumping* products on it. This term implies that selected products are being exported for sale in the United States, for example, at prices below their true cost. Furthermore, it is inferred that the government of the exporting firm is underwriting a portion of the cost in order to subsidize industries that are important to that nation's economy.

## OPERATIONAL PROBLEMS
*Delays and uncertainty*

Complex problems arise in international business. Transportation between countries is more difficult than domestic transportation because goods must pass through customs each time they cross a national border. A great deal of paperwork is usually needed to get import and export

Figure 22-4 What a trade imbalance looks like.

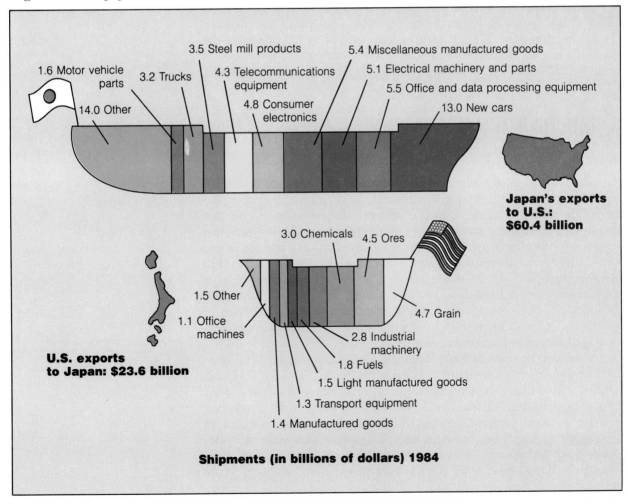

1.6 Motor vehicle parts
3.2 Trucks
3.5 Steel mill products
4.3 Telecommunications equipment
4.8 Consumer electronics
5.4 Miscellaneous manufactured goods
5.1 Electrical machinery and parts
5.5 Office and data processing equipment
14.0 Other
13.0 New cars

**Japan's exports to U.S.: $60.4 billion**

3.0 Chemicals
4.5 Ores
1.5 Other
1.1 Office machines
4.7 Grain
2.8 Industrial machinery
1.8 Fuels
1.5 Light manufactured goods
1.3 Transport equipment
1.4 Manufactured goods

**U.S. exports to Japan: $23.6 billion**

**Shipments (in billions of dollars) 1984**

licenses. Delay and outright harassment are not unusual. Transportation is also more expensive in international trade when distances are great.

Foreign political climates are often unpredictable. Production facilities have been expropriated by unfriendly governments. Terrorism and kidnapping have been directed against United States companies operating abroad. Foreign tax structures may be unfavorable in some cases.

Foreign business climates and methods may create ethical problems. In some parts of the world, bribery is more widely accepted than in the United States, although it is practiced (illegally) here too. In major sales efforts abroad, many United States firms have offered and paid large "commissions" to government officials, company officers, and others in return for sales orders or for help in getting orders. This is illegal in the United States but has been commonly practiced by United States companies trading in other countries.

Standardization represents another operational problem. The metric system of measurements, for example, is used widely around the world. The United States, generally, uses feet and inches, quarts and pints, pounds and ounces as its standards.

Many nations, especially the lesser-developed "third-world" countries, have a policy of buying only from their own nationals. This requires that, at the least, an American firm would have to enter into a joint venture in a third-world country so that its products could be sold there.

Some nations, like Japan, engage in long-range planning for their political and economic futures. The Japanese Ministry of International Trade and Industry (MITI), for example, guides and coordinates the country's pivotal industries. Other countries, seeking to do business with or in Japan, recognize MITI as a potent force in international trade.

# 5  MULTINATIONAL COMPANIES
## *The ultimate international involvement*

The expansion of international business, particularly since the end of World War II, has resulted in the creation of a unique structure: the multinational corporation. A ***multinational corporation*** is one that carries on operations in a number of different countries. Its international operations contribute significantly to overall revenues and size. In recent years, differences among countries have decreased. Markets in the Philippines, Hungary, Zaire, Indonesia, and in every other country have grown in similarity. Demands exist nearly everywhere for the same general kinds of consumer goods. This, combined with the advantages of producing goods in the country where they will be sold, has greatly encouraged the growth of multinationals.

Many people think of Avon Products, Inc., the cosmetics firm, as an exclusively American company. Yet Avon has more than 700,000 ladies "calling" outside of the United States. Avon representatives sell in 35 countries including Nigeria, Peru, Portugal, and Taiwan. The company operates a major printing operation in London, one that produces 93 million promotional brochures in eight languages each year. All told, Avon generated 36 percent of its sales revenues, or $888 million, from international markets in 1985. Avon is truly multinational in that about 36 percent of its assets are overseas.

IBM, General Motors Corporation, General Electric Co., Exxon, Texaco, Deere, International Telephone and Telegraph Co., and scores of other giant companies are true multinationals. Table 22-1 (on page 511) lists several multinational corporations and shows the extent of their involvement in foreign trade.

A company usually evolves into a multinational over a period of time. First, it places more and more emphasis on exporting goods produced by its home factories. Then, it opens one or more foreign offices to allow for more aggressive marketing efforts. The offices may expand to include the production of goods. The company often buys foreign companies already in business producing the same or different kinds of products. Soon, full-fledged multinational operations are under way.

The countries in which multinationals operate often are not enthusiastic about their presence there. The citizens of those countries tend to regard the companies as basically foreign rather than multinational. This view is justified to the extent that the company's profits from international operations are returned to its home country for distribution to owners. The multinationals are becoming more truly international, however, and it is likely that this feeling will fade. Big corporations are now concentrating on hiring natives of the countries in which they operate. Multinationals are also encouraging their other employees to learn more about foreign cultures and languages. Management is becoming more decentralized, and actual ownership of many companies is becoming more and more international.

## A TWO-WAY STRETCH
### The "foreigners" are coming

Multinational operations are by no means an exclusively American activity. The names of foreign (to the United States) multinationals extending their operations to America are already familiar. Shell Oil, Datsun, Matsushita, Electrolux, Nestlé, Beechum Groups' Aquafresh and Sucrets, Lyon's Baskin-Robbins, and Bayer are just a few. Foreign investments in United States business total more than $150 billion. United States affiliates of foreign companies account for over $500 billion in sales and employment of nearly 2.5 million people. Foreign acquisition of American businesses has centered in manufacturing, real estate, retail trade, and insurance.

## IMPACT ON WORLD AFFAIRS
### Companies bigger than countries

The great size and true international character of multinational corporations are bound to give them intentional and unintentional influence in the political and economic affairs of the countries in which they operate. The most famous example concerned International Telephone and Telegraph Co. (ITT) in Chile. The traditional business of ITT had been constructing and operating telephone and telegraph companies in foreign countries, but it has diversified into many other lines, from cosmetics to hams. In one of a succession of scandals concerning the company, it was alleged that ITT had made serious efforts in the early 1970s to block the election of presidential candidate Salvador Allende and later to encourage his overthrow.

---

## Action Brief

### A GLOBAL SALES PITCH

*For companies that sell their products worldwide, the cost of tailoring their advertising to dozens of different countries is expensive. Accordingly, most try to find a single pitch that has universal appeal. This isn't easy. Camel cigarettes, for example, believed that the macho image of the ruggedly handsome 25- to 35-year-old "Camel man" would need no translation. That is, until the ads got to Brazil, where the median age of males is 17. Since the Brazilian culture is at a stage where peer-group support is particularly important, the Camel man is still waiting for teenage Brazilians to grow up. Coffee makers, too, have a problem finding a universal appeal. Coffee is so expensive that in many countries it is associated with only a certain class of people. Says one advertiser, "It is much easier to make coffee appeal to a doctor in Germany and a doctor in Italy than it is to find a common appeal for a doctor in Germany and a factory worker in Germany."*

Regardless of the legality of ITT's efforts, it is clear that the large multinationals are capable of exerting decisive power in the countries in which they operate. Chile's entire GNP in 1972, the year of Allende's election, was only $7.7 billion. For that year, ITT's sales were $8.6 billion. Effective and fair means of controlling this kind of influence have not been developed. The corporate executives of the top multinationals can wield as much power internationally as most heads of state.

A form of business combination, illegal in the United States, is actively encouraged by many foreign countries. This combination is called a **cartel** and usually represents a loosely structured, but powerful, marketing agreement between companies active in the same industrial field. There have been steel, mineral, and chemical cartels, but the most notable one of all is the Organization of Petroleum Exporting Countries. OPEC, through control of production supplies and resultant oil prices, did much to influence the economies of most industrial nations, particularly the United States, during the 1970s and early 1980s.

# 6  INTERNATIONAL COOPERATION IN TRADE
## An easing of restraints

Nations erect trade barriers. The political decisions of individual countries often complicate and interfere with international business. Still, there are many instances of multination cooperation, making trade easier, fairer, and more beneficial for all involved.

## MULTINATIONAL ECONOMIC COMMUNITIES
### Success in the common market

Countries with close mutual interests often join to create trade communities. The best known and most successful is the European Economic Community, often called the **Common Market.** The Common Market currently includes nine European nations. Its most notable contribution has been to completely eliminate tariffs among member nations and to establish a uniform tariff for all goods shipped to the Common Market nations from nonmember nations. The cooperative effort appears to be enjoying considerable success in encouraging the free movement of labor, capital, technology, goods, and services among members. In addition, the Common Market's share of world trade has increased substantially.

Economic agreements elsewhere have been less successful, but progress is being made. Honduras, El Salvador, Nicaragua, Guatemala, and Costa Rica, despite recent political differences among these nations, have formed the Central American Common Market. Its purpose is to promote the economic integration of member nations, including the elimination of tariffs among members and the establishment of a uniform currency. The Latin American Free Trade Association is working toward creating a cooperative economic community similar to the European Common Market. Its members are ten South American countries and Mexico. Progress has been slow, but some members have succeeded in reducing trade barriers. A number of trade associations in other parts of the world exist but are generally not so close-knit as the Common Market

---

## Action Brief
### MULTINATIONALS MOVING OUT

*International operations aren't always that sweet. Parker Pen Co., for example, abruptly ended its unified global marketing campaign after finding its efforts falling flat. Three-quarters of Parker's sales are in overseas markets, but differences in consumer preferences vary widely from country to country. For the time being, Parker has decided to try its marketing one country at a time, especially since Parker couldn't get its prices up high enough abroad to cover the manufacturing costs at home. In the end, Parker sold its pen business to a European manufacturer.*

*Levi Strauss & Co. closed eight overseas plants in the space of a couple of years during the middle of the 1980s. The company cited a 15 percent drop in demand for basic jeans in Europe. The closings eliminated nearly 1,000 jobs in England and France. The company, however, lost $25 million on its European sales of $91 million during the same period.*

and the other economic communities mentioned. However, they also encourage communication and cooperation in business matters.

## INTERNATIONAL TREATIES
*Toward fewer trade barriers*

The General Agreement on Tariffs and Trade (GATT) is a treaty pledging that all subscribing nations will work for freer trade with fewer barriers. The agreement has the practical effect of bringing nations together periodically to discuss their trade differences. Some progress has been made in reducing trade barriers. Individual nations may also establish treaties spelling out terms of trade. The United States, for instance, gives preferred status to certain favored trading partners.

## INTERNATIONAL BANKING INSTITUTIONS
*Sponsored by the United Nations*

An institution called the World Bank has been established to provide financial assistance for international development and trade. In recent years it has been engaged in a major effort to help debt-ridden countries—such as Mexico, Brazil, and Argentina—avoid default on their international loan obligations. The World Bank includes three subsidiary institutions, all associated with the United Nations:

■ The International Bank for Reconstruction and Development was formed after World War II to borrow money to relend to countries needing financial assistance to recover from the effects of war.
■ The International Finance Corporation makes loans to help finance projects that will contribute to economic development.
■ The International Development Association makes long-term low-interest loans, mainly to developing nations. The association provides these nations with funds so that they can build or acquire production facilities that will enable them to participate in world trade.

The United States maintains its own federally operated Export-Import Bank. Backed by the U.S. Treasury, this bank makes loans for United States international trade ventures when private sources of funds are unavailable.

## THE UNITED STATES DEPARTMENT OF COMMERCE
*Numerous assistance programs*

For companies engaging in or planning to engage in international business, the United States Department of Commerce has numerous assistance programs. The Bureau of International Commerce, in particular, is a source of information and aid useful for the planning and management of exporting, importing, and overseas operation. The Department of Commerce also compiles information on the United States balance of payments and other overall indicators of world trade performance.

Businesses seeking preliminary assistance in developing international projects receive help from the United States government's Overseas Private Investment Corporation (OPIC). Further information is provided by the United States Department of Commerce, which publishes

"Country Market Surveys" (CMS), "Global Market Surveys" (GMS), and "International Market Research Surveys" (IMRS). These furnish data on a single industry in a single country, summarize the industry for many countries (in GMS), or provide in-depth detail of a market (IMRS) for a given product in a given country. Two other United States agencies also target their efforts overseas. They are the Trade Development Program (TDP) of the United States International Development Corporation Agency and the Foreign Agricultural Service of the United States Department of Agriculture.

## Key Concepts

**1.** International business includes (1) international trade—importing and exporting of goods among nations—and (2) international operations—carrying on marketing and production in foreign countries.

**2.** Resources control a nation's ability to engage in international business. Countries specialize in producing certain products for international trade based on their absolute advantages or comparative advantages over other countries.

**3.** Companies engaging in international business may undertake casual or active exporting, foreign licensing, overseas marketing and production, or joint ownership of foreign production facilities. They may also engage directly or indirectly in international distribution channels.

**4.** There are many obstacles to easy, free trade among nations. Among these are different languages and customs, varied currencies with shifting exchange rates, tariffs, quotas, embargoes and other trade barriers, and operational problems such as transportation costs and unfavorable tax policies. Increasingly, the United States has suffered from an imbalance of trade with other countries.

**5.** Multinational corporations do business in a number of different countries and view their international operations as an essential part of their business. Some multinationals are so large and powerful that they exert an uncontrolled influence on some of the nations in which they operate. The United States continues to encourage international trade and operations among its nationals.

**6.** Common markets, trade agreements, treaties, and international banks and lending institutions are methods countries use to encourage and regulate international business.

## Review Questions

**1.** Define, identify, or explain each of the following key terms or phrases, found on the pages indicated.

*absolute advantage (p. 514)*
*balance of payments (p. 518)*
*balance of trade (p. 518)*
*cartel (p. 522)*
*Common Market (p. 522)*
*comparative advantage (p. 514)*
*dumping (p. 519)*

*embargo (p. 517)*
*exchange rate (p. 517)*
*exporting (p. 510)*
*importing (p. 510)*
*international operations (p. 510)*
*international trade (p. 510)*
*multinational corporation (p. 520)*
*protective tariff (p. 517)*
*quota (p. 517)*
*revenue tariff (p. 517)*
*tariff (p. 517)*

2. International business includes two different kinds of activities. Name and define them.

3. Why is it difficult for a developing nation to acquire the capital resources needed to successfully take part in world trade?

4. The concepts of absolute advantage and comparative advantage include three ways a country may decide on which goods to specialize in for foreign trade. Describe them.

5. Define casual exporting and active exporting. How do they differ?

6. Distinguish between direct and indirect distribution methods in international trade.

7. Why are fluctuating exchange rates an obstacle to international business?

8. What is the underlying reason for imposing protective tariffs and quotas?

9. What distinguishes a multinational company from others that do business overseas?

10. What is the European Economic Community? How has it affected international trade?

# Case Critique 22-1
## Turning the Tables

What's the best-selling razor blade in Japan? Guess again. It's the American-made Schick injector blade! It accounts for about 70 percent of the $150 to $200 million in blades sold annually in Japan. The Schick injector is available in 120,000 shops and supermarkets in Japan and has driven the once-dominant Japanese brand into obscurity. The secret of Schick's success? Smart marketing, perseverance, and just a little luck. Schick proved that an American company could do in Japan what many Japanese companies were doing in the United States.

After World War II, Feather, a Japanese razor, held 80 percent of the national market. Its double-edged razor was the norm. Instead of introducing a similar blade, Schick, in 1956, brought its injector-style blade to Japan. It made an instant hit with Japan's gadget-loving male population. Schick's blade immediately grasped 5 percent of the market. When American manufacturers conceived of the twin-blade injector, Schick quickly packed them into special packages and airmailed large quantities to Japan before Schick's American archrival, Gillette, could move in effectively in Japan. This new product made an even greater impression on Japanese buyers, and Schick's share of the market leaped ahead to 25 percent. Since then, Schick's market share has risen steadily to near the three-quarters level. All blades are made by Schick outside of Japan and imported into that country. Japan, meanwhile, ships to United

States razor manufacturers, including Schick, the special stainless steel used in contemporary blades.

Schick did get a break because Japan exercises only a small import tariff on the blades, and the industry has never received strong government protection, as many other local industries have. Schick, a subsidiary of America's Warner-Lambert Corp., leaves the Japanese distribution problem up to locals. Japanese businessmen like to deal with a stable company, and Warner-Lambert can add to the Schick product the reputation of a 75-year-old company. Schick began by signing up an import agent, Hattori Seiko, the producer of Seiko watches. Hattori sells to a sales agent, who sells to large-scale wholesalers, who in turn sell to retailers.

One big advantage that Schick enjoys is that while Japanese men prefer locally made television sets and autos, they are eager to purchase foreign-made clothing and toiletries because these products give them a cosmopolitan flair.

Gillette, which dominates the United States razor market, has been able to gain only about one-tenth of the Japanese market. Observers say that when Gillette came to Japan, it tried to short-circuit the complex Japanese distribution network. It established its own subsidiary, Gillette (Japan), and began dealing directly with the 150 local wholesalers. Later on, Gillette (Japan) cut back the number of its wholesalers to 15. There have also been several changes in Gillette's local management.

Said one Japanese wholesaler, "Gillette saw Japan as a colony. It wanted to sell its products by force, which did not fit the Japanese system. Our philosophy is that everyone in the distribution chain, from top to bottom, should coexist." Gillette's general manager, a Japanese national, replies, "Gillette's basic policy all over the world is to do it themselves."

Meanwhile, Schick uses innovative American marketing methods. It sponsors a Tokyo-Osaka football match. It passed out 100,000 sample shaving kits to Japanese college freshmen. Its ads appear regularly on national television and on the back covers of Japanese magazines. Schick even labels its product "Schick—Born in the USA" and sticks tiny American flags on its display stands.

As for Feather blades, many young Japanese men have never heard of the brand.

1. What special cultural appeal did Schick's product have as compared with the Japanese brand?
2. Besides its product popularity, what other factors helped Schick's razors to succeed in Japan?
3. Compare Gillette's approach to the Japanese market with that of Schick.
4. How do you explain the effectiveness of Schick's American-style promotion and advertising in Japan?

*SOURCE:* John Burgess, "Schick Mixes Perseverance, Luck, Product Appeal to Succeed in Japan," *The Washington Post*, May 12, 1985, p. F3.

# Case Critique 22-2
## We Do It Differently Here

"We invite and welcome an American company like yours to start up a manufacturing operation here in our lovely country," said the minister of international development of the small developing country of Z. He was speaking to the owner of an American toy manufacturer (A) that distributed nationally in the United States. As a consequence of this invitation, the American firm invested $150,000 in a plant in Z for the hand fabrication and assembly of small paper and wooden parts for its toys. The low cost of labor in Z and the workers' reputation for being able to manipulate tiny pieces quickly were looked upon by the company as offering a unique advantage compared with manufacturing the parts in the United States.

After deciding to manufacture in Z, the firm encountered a number of problems. First of all, the American company wanted to ship its own specially designed assembly benches to Z. The company was politely, but firmly, informed that wooden products of any kind could not be imported. They would have to be purchased locally. It took the company a month or

more to find a local carpenter shop to build the benches to A's specifications.

Finding the right kind of labor, too, turned out to be more difficult than anticipated. After A's manager on the spot hired a head man to run the assembly room, it became clear that the head man would insist on taking care of all further hiring. A's manager was assured by Z's minister of international development that this would be the best way. "A local person knows much more about the kinds of employees who will serve you best," the minister said. The trouble was that, among many good employees, there were many others hired whose main qualification was that they were relatives or village neighbors of the head man. Some of these employees were indifferent about the amount and quality of their work. Their attendance was poor. When A's manager pressed to have them dismissed, the head man always had a reason why that should not be done.

When company A's business in the United States started peaking for the Christmas season, the message came to the local manager in Z that production must be increased. "That's easy," thought the manager. Accordingly, a notice was posted announcing that the plant would work overtime and Saturdays until further notice. There would be extra pay in accordance with the extra hours. Surprisingly, few employees stayed to work overtime. "Why is that?" asked A's manager of the head man. "Many of these people value time with their families more than the material things they can acquire by working additional hours," said the head man. "For them, sociable ways are more important than possessions."

Since overtime couldn't be used to solve the production problem, A's manager directed the head man to add another ten workers "just for the peak period." When the Christmas rush ended, however, there was great reluctance on the part of the head man to let the ten new employees go. "I have a responsibility to them for having taken them away from their other occupations," he said. "They expected that when you employed them you would honor this obligation and keep them year-round."

In frustration, A's manager went to Z's minister of international development. He recited the various problems encountered and got little satisfaction. Finally, A's manager said, "Company A's venture in Z has not been nearly as productive or profitable as you implied. If things don't improve, we will sell our business here to someone else and take our money and go home."

"I'm sorry that you feel that way," said the minister. "You should reconsider your thought of selling your operation, however, since our laws will not permit you to do so without full agreement of our legislature. Furthermore, if the sale is approved, it will probably take many months for our department to determine how much of your investment you will be allowed to 'repatriate.'"

"That's unfair. It would not be tolerated where I come from," said A's manager.

"I regret that any of our laws might cause you an inconvenience," said the minister, "but you should know that we do things differently here."

1. What sort of national policy did company A encounter in not being able to ship its own shop benches?
2. The difficulties with hiring, firing, and managing the work force represent what sort of barriers to international trade? Should A's manager insist on controlling the hiring process himself? Why?
3. How might company A have minimized the problems it encountered in country Z? Where might it have gotten helpful information beforehand?
4. What do you think company A should do now? Should it find a way to accommodate local practices or take its losses and move out?

## CHAPTER 23

# Legal and
# Tax Environment
# of Business

## Learning Objectives

*The purpose of this chapter is to explain federal government regulation of business, to outline and interpret certain business laws, and to describe the reasons and methods of taxation related to business firms.*

*As evidence of general comprehension, after studying this chapter you should be able to:*

1. *Explain the purpose of law and the role of litigation, and distinguish between statutory, common, and administrative laws.*

2. *Identify the basic rules concerning law of contracts, sales, agency, and negotiable instruments; and describe how the Uniform Commercial Code is related to these laws.*

3. *Explain the difference between express and implied warranties; describe the purpose of bankruptcy; and identify trademarks, copyrights, and patents.*

4. *Explain the underlying reasons for and aims of government regulation of business, and identify certain regulatory agencies.*

5. *Recognize the two basic reasons for taxation and identify various revenue and regulatory taxes.*

*If your class is using SSweetco: Business Model and Activity File, see Chapter 23 in that book after you complete this chapter. There you will find exercises and activities to help you apply your learning to typical business situations.*

## 1 LAWS ARE FORMAL RULES AND REGULATIONS

enforceable by government:

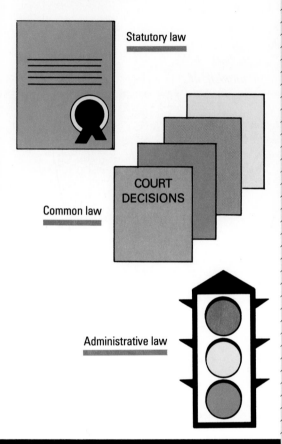

Statutory law

Common law

COURT
DECISIONS

Administrative law

## 2 CERTAIN LAWS APPLY PARTICULARLY TO BUSINESS

These laws may be enforced on a federal, state, or local level.

UNIFORM
COMMERCIAL
CODE

Contract law
Sales and property law
Agency law
Negotiable instruments

## 3 OTHER BUSINESS LAWS

apply to

Warranties

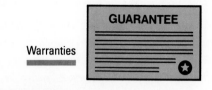

GUARANTEE

Bankruptcy

BANKRUPT

Trademarks, copyrights, and patents

MY OWN

## 4 GOVERNMENT PROTECTS BOTH BUSINESSES AND CONSUMERS

It insures competition, protects property rights and human rights, licenses certain businesses, and regulates utilities.

FTC    EEOC    ICC    FPC

## 5 BUSINESSES IN THE UNITED STATES ARE TAXED

so that the government can collect operating revenue and regulate or restrict certain business practices.

TAX

Revenue taxes

TAX

CIGARETTES

Restrictive laws

# BUSINESS LAW: GUARDIAN OF FAIRNESS, NOT PROFIT

At one time or another, some 13,000 people joined the Fun & Fitness Exercise and Aquatic Center, a close corporation in Arlington, Virginia. Members paid fees, which for many ran as high as $1,300 for a 7-year membership. Memberships were sealed by a legal contract, which both the member and a center representative signed. All went well for a number of years until interest in this kind of exer-

cise leveled off, competition increased, and operating costs of the center escalated. Inevitably, the center failed and closed its doors. Legally, the center entered bankruptcy. This left hundreds of its current members holding the bag. It also left the owner of the property on which the center was located high and dry. Not only was the center not able to operate for its members but it couldn't pay its rent of $350,000 a year. Furthermore, the company that had leased Fun & Fitness the gym and exercise equipment had it hauled away. What was left at the center was a swimming pool. Irate members wanted to know how valid their contracts were. Local attorneys told them that the contracts were good only so long as the center remained legally in business. Once it entered bankruptcy proceedings, members would have to get in line . . . and would have to wait and see how much money, if any, would be available to distribute among creditors. Many members wanted to sue the center for their money back. "You can sue," said the lawyers, "but you won't get much blood out of a stone."

Too late, the Virginia legislature enacted a statute requiring health spas selling memberships of longer than 3 months to post bonds or letters of credit from $25,000 to $50,000. The only redress for the center's members now was to file their names with the consumer office of Arlington and hope that some money might be found. . . .

Because of instances like this one, the United States government tries to make contracts as watertight as possible and tries to regulate commercial activities to offer consumers and businesses the maximum amount of protection with the least restraints on their activities. In general, the legal environment for doing business, while very complex, is fair to all parties. The law, however, cannot provide guarantees of . . . profitable outcomes.

---

SOURCE: Barbara Carton, "Clients Trying to Revive Spa," *The Washington Post*, May 7, 1985, p. C-12.

# 1 LEGAL ENVIRONMENT OF BUSINESS
*A network of restrictions and prescribed conduct*

The American Law Institute defines law as "the body of principles, standards, and rules which the courts . . . apply to the decision of controversies brought before them." Ex-Supreme Court Justice Stone advised further that "law . . . is made up of those rules of human conduct which are made mandatory by the state upon all its citizens and, without which, social order and well-being could not exist." These views can be summarized in a succinct definition: **law** is a collection of formal rules and regulations enforced by the power of government.

The supreme law of the United States is its Constitution. All other laws, written and unwritten, must be in harmony with it. Laws can be found in some sort of legislation, established either at the federal, state, or local level. Law may be written or unwritten. For the purpose of simplification, most laws can be placed into three general classifications: statutory, common, and administrative.

## STATUTORY LAW
*Stems from legislation*

Legislation enacted by Congress or by a state legislature is usually referred to as a **statute.** Statutes regulate major business activities, such as how a corporation can issue stock. Or, at the local level, a statute, called an *ordinance*, may prohibit the establishment of a business in a residential neighborhood. When various statutes are compiled in a systematic way, they are called *codes*. Your hometown, for example, may have a local traffic code, governing speed limits and the like. Various statutes affecting business have been compiled to form the Uniform Commercial Code. The statutes of the United States government are known as the United States Code.

## COMMON LAW
*Based upon precedents*

Much of the law that governs business is not found in the written statutes. Instead, this **common law** is derived from decisions handed down in settlement of cases tried in the various courts. These decisions, taken either one at a time or in concert, establish precedents. A **precedent** is an example, or rule, that guides a future decision regarding an act of a similar nature. Thus, it is the history of court decisions that makes up common law. Courts give great weight to precedents and are hesitant to change the common law that has been established.

Common law is less specific than statutory law, but this makes it more flexible. Each case examined may have slight variations that make it different from previous cases. This often causes problems for businesses. Contract law, for example, evolved from court cases to form a common law. As a consequence, many court cases today involve suits by individuals or businesses who disagree about the interpretation or application of common contract law.

# ADMINISTRATIVE LAW
## *Enforces government regulations*

Over the years, as civilized life has become more complex, the public has sought government protection from a very broad range of contemporary problems. These include such areas of potential harm as product and workplace safety, employment discrimination, food adulteration, misleading advertising, and the purchase of securities. In response to these concerns, the federal government has established more than 150 regulatory agencies, bureaus, and commissions to develop appropriate laws and to administer them when passed by the legislature. The legal impact of these rules and regulations on business is immense. In fact, administrative agencies, like those listed in Table 23-1, create and enforce the majority of the laws that make up the legal environment of business. These administrative laws range widely from the establishment of an enforceable standard for how many parts of sulfur per million parts of air may be permitted to escape from a smokestack to the requirement that

**TABLE 23-1**
**IMPORTANT FEDERAL AGENCIES WITH REGULATORY POWERS**

| *Name* | *Regulatory Functions* |
|---|---|
| Consumer Product Safety Commission (CPSC) | Protects the public against unreasonable risks of injury associated with consumer products |
| Environmental Protection Agency (EPA) | Administers all laws relating to the environment, including laws on water pollution, air pollution, solid wastes, pesticides, toxic substances, etc. |
| Federal Communications Commission (FCC) | Regulates interstate and foreign communications by means of radio, television, wire, cable, and satellite |
| Federal Reserve Board (FRB) | The nation's central bank, which regulates the availability of and the cost of money and credit |
| Federal Trade Commission (FTC) | A law enforcement agency to protect the public from anticompetitive behavior and unfair or deceptive business practices |
| Food and Drug Administration (FDA) | Administers laws to prohibit distribution of adulterated, mislabeled, or unsafe food and drugs |
| Equal Employment Opportunity Commission (EEOC) | Seeks to prevent discrimination in employment based on race, color, religion, sex, or national origin and other unlawful employment practices |
| National Labor Relations Board (NLRB) | Conducts union certification elections and holds hearing on unfair labor practice complaints |
| Nuclear Regulatory Commission (NRC) | Licenses and regulates the nuclear energy industry |
| Occupational Safety and Health Administration (OSHA) | Ensures all workers a work environment as safe and healthy as possible |
| Securities and Exchange Commission (SEC) | Enforces the federal securities laws which regulate sale of securities to the investing public |

every trash receptacle in a public place must be lined with a disposable plastic bag.

Taxes, too, are a form of administrative regulation, with special influence on business operations, as seen later in this chapter.

## ENFORCEMENT, PROSECUTION, AND LITIGATION
### Variations of the legal process

The federal and, in particular, the states' court systems provide a fair and open way for enforcing the various statutes, for prosecuting wrongdoers, and for providing a systematic way of settling legal disputes. Small-claims courts, in particular, are especially important to businesses. They may be used by businesses as a means for collecting accounts or by individuals for seeking redress from damages caused by defective merchandise or services improperly rendered.

Administrative agencies of the various governments also play a major role in law enforcement. They interpret broad legislative statutes and develop the hundreds of procedural details necessary for their practical application. The Congress and the states, in effect, delegate to these agencies the power to enforce these procedures and settle disputes that arise from them. The court system would find it impossible, for example, to handle the tens of thousands of tax cases or industrial accident cases that occur annually. Accordingly, the Internal Revenue Service or a state's workers' compensation commission handles these cases. Agencies may make rules, conduct investigations, issue orders, pass judgments, and, if necessary, prosecute.

Increasingly, individuals and businesses turn to the courts for settlement of their disputes. Accordingly, they enter into *litigation,* which is the process of carrying on a dispute within the legal framework of the established judicial (or court) system. In the Commonwealth of Virginia in 1985, for example, there were about 50 suits pursued for every 1,000 residents. Interestingly, in 1639, the rate was 240 cases per 1,000! While either of these figures may seem high, there is another important side to this matter. Experts point out that the overwhelming proportion of business disputes are settled by mutual agreement without resort to litigation. Furthermore, it is estimated that more than 90 percent of all lawsuits filed are settled without a court decision.

## 2 COMMERCIAL LAW
### Contracts, sales, agency, and negotiable instruments

Businesses and business employees are subject to general laws as are all other individuals. Specifically, criminal law and law of torts must regulate their actions in addition to laws concerned directly with the conduct of business. *Criminal law* is a group of laws enforced by the government for the good of the general public. Forgery, embezzlement, the use of violence, and many other actions are subject to punishment under criminal law. It is the government itself that seeks relief in the case of a criminal offense. In the case of a *tort,* which is a civil offense that does not arise out of a contract, it is the person who has been injured who seeks redress. A few examples of torts common in business operations are trespassing, fraud, and copyright and patent infringements.

The body of law that applies specifically to the conduct of business activities is called **business** (or **commercial**) **law.** These laws mainly deal with agents, warranties, bankruptcy, the making and enforcing of contracts, and the ownership and sale of property.

## CONTRACTS
### *Make agreements binding*

Contracts among individuals and companies are basic to conducting business. A **contract** is a voluntary agreement in which two or more parties (people or corporations) bind themselves to act or not to act in a certain way. A sales agreement is a typical example. A seller might agree to provide a certain quantity of goods by a specified date. The buyer might agree to pay an established price upon receipt of the merchandise.

For a contract to be valid, it must meet certain requirements:

- There must be an offer by one party and an acceptance by another.
- The contract must be voluntary. An agreement resulting from force or fraud is not normally enforceable.
- The parties to the contract must be competent. They must be legally sane and of legal age, although minors can also enter into contracts that have special rules.
- The parties must exchange a **consideration,** something of value such as money, property, and a promise to perform work.
- The specified considerations and actions must be legal. A price-fixing contract or one for the sale of illegal drugs would not be legally enforceable because the contracted service is illegal.

If these requirements are met, most contracts are valid and binding (as shown in Figure 23-1), even if they are not written down. An oral contract can be just as enforceable as a written one if the parties involved can later prove the pertinent facts. The law requires, however, that some contracts be written: those lasting longer than a year, for example, and transfers of ownership of real property.

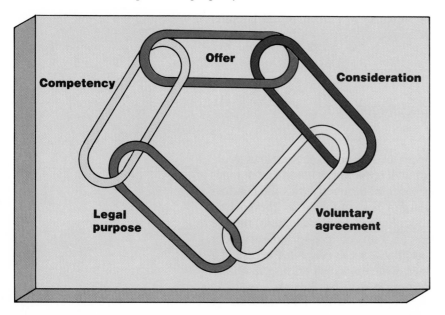

Figure 23-1 Elements needed to make a contract legal and binding.

Many contracts include promises of some future actions that will or will not be carried out. Contract performance is the process of actually doing what was promised. For example, a contract to work for a company for one year is not satisfied until the year's work is done. Some contracts have such complex specifications that special legal analysis and interpretation may be needed to determine whether parties have performed adequately. If one or more parties fail to carry out the terms agreed to, the contract is broken. In some situations—such as bankruptcy, death, or serious illness—the nonperforming party may be excused from the contract with no penalty. In other cases, nonperformance may be handled in one of three ways;

- All the provisions of the contract may be disregarded. If one party does not perform, the other party does not have to perform either. The obligations are said to be "discharged."
- A court order, backed up by a fine or jail sentence, can be obtained to force the other party to perform.
- A court may be requested to force a nonperformer to pay damages for the monetary loss that resulted from the nonperformance.

# LAW OF SALES
*Governs the transfer of property*

Governments in the United States protect private property. Property may be **real property**—land or possessions with a long-term attachment to land, such as buildings or uncut timber—or **personal property,** such as automobiles, machinery, and furniture. An important aspect of protecting property ownership is defining the terms and procedures by which control passes from one owner to another. Real property may be transferred by deed or lease. A **deed** actually transfers ownership to a new owner. A **lease** gives temporary, partial control of real property. Extensive and complex legal guidelines and traditions surround the writing and interpretation of these legal documents.

Ownership of personal property is transferred by sale. Even such a seemingly simple transaction requires considerable legal definition and regulation. Laws control who is capable of entering into sales agreements, at which exact point the sale has taken place (which is important in deciding who loses if damage occurs), what action can be taken when deceptive practices have been used, and many other issues.

# AGENCY LAW
*When others act on the company's behalf*

An **agent** is a person or company authorized to carry out business and enter into agreements on behalf of another person or company, called the **principal.** This relationship exists when employees of a company—executives, purchasing agents, sales representatives, and others—act on behalf of the company. An agent may also be an outside third party especially skilled at handling certain kinds of business. Lawyers often act as agents, particularly in real estate trading. Actors, writers, professional sports figures, and others use agents to negotiate contracts. The law has quite clearly defined the responsibilities of both principal and agent in these relationships. The agent is obliged to work for the benefit of the principal and to follow his or her instructions, while the principal is required to compensate the agent for his or her performance.

## NEGOTIABLE INSTRUMENTS
### Checks and promissory notes

Important legal controls exist on the use of **negotiable instruments,** which are written documents that stand for currency in business transactions. The best known negotiable instruments are checks and promissory notes. The law specifies the characteristics a negotiable instrument must have in order to be transferable to a new owner, that is, to circulate much like cash. It must, for example, be written and properly signed. It must contain an unconditional promise to pay, either on demand or at a definite future date. Other requirements must be met in certain situations.

The law also specifies the circumstances in which a person does or does not actually own a negotiable instrument. It must not, for instance, be past due or show any sign of tampering. Transfer from one person to another is controlled. Endorsing a check by signing it on the back, for example, is one way of transferring a negotiable instrument. Specific methods of endorsement such as "for deposit only," "payable to," or "accepted in full settlement of" and their contractual obligations are all defined by law, as illustrated in Figure 23-2.

## UNIFORM COMMERCIAL CODE
### A guideline for consistency in state laws

Many laws that affect the conduct of business, especially in interstate commerce, are federal. Individual states, however, have the authority to pass laws controlling business practices and transactions within their own boundaries. In addition, state courts interpret existing laws. Interpretations, however, may vary considerably from state to state. Many of the most important legal controls of day-to-day business transactions fall

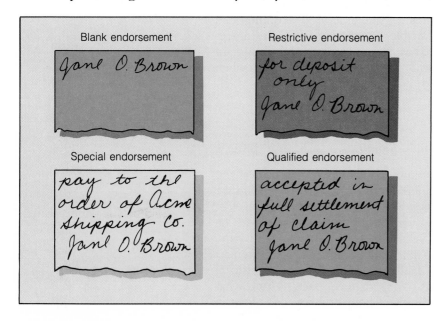

Figure 23-2 Various forms of endorsement on a negotiable instrument.

under state laws. When every state had different rules for contracts, sales, agencies, and other significant aspects of business law, great confusion resulted. Regional and national operations were complex and difficult.

To help solve this problem, a commission of legal experts wrote a large body of laws called the *Uniform Commercial Code.* The code itself, first published in 1957, has no legal force. State legislatures, however, have adopted it as a guideline and have made most parts of the code enforceable law. Many provisions of the code have been adopted by nearly every state and are truly uniform nationwide.

The code is a large body of commercial law that includes statutes on sales, negotiable instruments, banking practices, shipping and warehousing, securities, and general business transactions and contracts. Every major area of business law that falls under state jurisdiction is covered. The wide adoption of the Uniform Commercial Code has facilitated regional and national business. In general, what is legal in one state is also legal in others.

The partial standardization of state business laws by the Uniform Commercial Code has made business's job of dealing with its legal environment somewhat simpler than it was 25 years ago. However, the growth during the same period of federal, state, and local regulation has largely offset the gain. State and federal laws, regulation by as many as five separate governments, and regulation by countless agencies at a single business location are not uncommon. Sometimes, there are scores of different taxes to pay. Such regulation makes dealings between business and government an extremely complex management responsibility.

## 3 RELATED COMMERCIAL LAW
### Warranties, bankruptcy, trademarks, and patents

Related to the basic commercial laws are a number of other legal considerations. Among the more important are those affecting legal assurances (such as warranties), the escape from creditors provided by bankruptcy, and the protection offered by trademarks, copyrights, and patents.

## WARRANTIES AND PRODUCT LIABILITY
### Legal assurance of performance

A *warranty* is a legal assurance that goods or services being sold have certain characteristics. An *express warranty* is a statement, often written, made by the seller that the property being sold is of a specified quality and type. Express warranties often state that the seller will repair any defects or replace the merchandise if defects are found. An *implied warranty* accompanies most sales as a standard part of law, even when the seller does not actually express it. The main provisions of an implied warranty are that (1) the buyer is receiving ownership of the property and that the seller is authorized to sell it, and (2) the goods are what they were represented to be and can be used for their intended purpose.

Closely related to the law regarding warranties is the law of *product liability.* Under the impetus of the Consumer Product Safety Act, the federal government places a legal responsibility on the manufacturer or seller of a product to compensate a buyer who suffers injury when using that product. Over 1 million product-liability claims seeking damages in excess of $50 billion were filed in one recent year. The owners of businesses, especially small enterprises, often complain that the high costs of purchasing product-liability insurance make it extremely difficult to continue with their operations.

# BANKRUPTCY
## *Procedure for handling insolvency*

Bankruptcy laws are intended to protect as fully as possible both a company or person with not enough assets to pay debts and the creditors to whom the debts are owed. ***Bankruptcy*** is a legal procedure by which a court divides up the remaining assets of an insolvent person or company among the people and organizations to whom money is owed. Bankruptcy is a way for someone who is in severe financial distress because of debt to get a new start.

When bankruptcy is declared, nearly all of the assets of the debtor are eventually sold for cash. The proceeds are used to pay court costs and other costs, unpaid employee wages up to a maximum limit for each worker, taxes, and secured loans. If any money is left after these charges, it is divided among general creditors according to the percent of total debt each is owed. The creditors then have no further claims. Bankruptcy is handled under federal law in federal courts. Other bankruptcy laws provide businesses with temporary protection from creditors' suits while the company tries to reorganize and make enough money to pay its creditors in full. (For more about bankruptcy, see the section entitled "Commercial Bankruptcy" in Chapter 20.)

# TRADEMARKS, COPYRIGHTS, AND PATENTS
## *Provide identification, protection, and ownership*

As consumers, all of us are exposed to trademarks daily. They are on practically every product we use. Even when we turn on television, we may hear the NBC chimes of the *Today* show, a registered trademark. So are *Today* and "NBC," as are "CBS" and its "eye" design. So is the name of your daily newspaper; almost every advertisement features at least one trade or "service" mark. The Patent and Trademark Office of the United States estimates that the average American is exposed to 1,500 trademarks every day.

By its legal definition, a ***trademark*** distinguishes goods supplied by a particular manufacturer or merchant from similar goods manufactured or sold by others. It helps consumers to choose between different products or services. For this reason, the entire law of trademarks depends upon how consumers perceive them. Questions as to whether or not a mark can be registered or protected focus upon what might go on in the buyer's mind.

When a trademark owner sues an infringer, two things are accomplished. First, the monetary interests of the trademark owner are protected from a form of unfair competition. Second, the public is also protected from being deceived or misled. It is in this view that trademarks are not considered a form of monopoly, since they protect the public as well as the proprietor.

*Copyrights* are somewhat similar to trademarks in that they provide a legal means of protecting one's ownership. In the case of copyright it involves property created by the mind. The most commonly eligible copyright properties are literary, musical, and dramatic works; pictorial, graphic, sculptural, and choreographic works; motion pictures; and sound recordings. Generally ineligible are ideas, methods, systems, principles, and concepts (although some of these might qualify for a patent). Also usually ineligible are names, titles, and slogans in which the creative content is slight (although these may qualify for trademark protection). The United States Copyright Act has been simplified so that an individual's copyright belongs to him or her immediately upon creation of the work. Registration, for which there is a small fee, is a legal formality and not a condition of copyright protection.

*Patents,* unlike trademarks, are considered a limited form of monopoly. They give the owners exclusive rights to make and sell a patented product or to use a patented process. To be patentable, a product must consist of an idea or process not known before. It must be a discovery as distinguished from mere mechanical skill or knowledge. In the United States, this privilege lasts for 17 years after a patent is issued. When other persons or companies use the patented product or process without permission, they are trespassing and may be sued for damages.

# 4  GOVERNMENT REGULATION OF BUSINESS
## Protects business as well as consumer interests

As protector of the rights of individuals and organizations against harm caused by others, government has assumed an active role in regulating many business practices. This is accomplished through a variety of agencies. The most important of these are shown in Table 23-1. Basically, the goals of the federal government have centered on protecting fair competition; promoting property rights, consumer interests, and the general welfare; and overseeing certain essential industries. State governments also engage in regulation of certain business and professional activities.

## PROTECTING COMPETITION
### Curtails monopoly and price fixing

Chapters 1 and 2 point out that even though free enterprise is partly based on the operation of free competition, actual conditions in the marketplace and the activities of certain companies often limit competition. During the nineteenth century particularly, it became clear to some business owners and managers that competition in the marketplace was limiting the prices they could charge for their goods and was thus lowering profits. The period was one of *laissez-faire* business management, a French phrase meaning nearly complete freedom of operation. Given this freedom, many businesses set out to systematically destroy the competition that was reducing profits. Frequently, the goal was to create a business organization that was the sole source of a needed commodity. With such a monopoly position, prices—and profits—could be raised almost as high as desired, causing great hardship to consumers.

Businesses that reached a monopoly position combined two approaches: (1) driving competitors out of business, or (2) buying up or merging with them. The most common method for driving competitors out of business was for a large company to charge unreasonably low prices in one area while supporting its losses with income from other products or from other parts of the country. A small local competitor could not match the artificially low prices and would be forced to sell out or close down.

Many former competitors simply merged, to their mutual benefit. Many large companies bought out their competitors, often having first beaten them down in a price war. Combinations other than formal mergers were also common. Standard Oil Company devised a scheme whereby they gave dividend-paying trust certificates in return for voting control of the stock of other companies. This method of controlling competitors without actually owning them was called a *trust.* That term soon came to be used for any business combination that limited or eliminated competition. Another scheme was *interlocking directorates.* Under this plan, different companies had the same, or some of the same, people on their boards of directors. Thus companies that were supposed to be competitors were actually run by the same people.

The end results of these efforts were manipulated markets that caused high prices and loss of choice for buyers. Trusts ended forever the laissez-faire business climate. The federal government stepped in to protect the public from trusts, and regulation has been the rule ever since. A number of important acts have been passed specifically to combat monopoly and encourage competition. See Table 23-2 for a list of these acts and the specific activities which they outlaw.

The general effect of all these laws has been to promote competition and retard the development of monopolies. Another more general goal of providing consumers with a wide range of goods at prices determined by the market has been met to a lesser degree. Unwritten pricing agreements among competitors still interfere with the operation of the market in some industries. Outright price fixing has been uncovered from time to time and prosecuted.

Competition is also lessened in many cases by the high technology common today. It is so expensive and difficult to enter many industries that potential new competitors are discouraged from the start. Entrenched producers may then sometimes enjoy relative freedom from effective competition. On the other hand, the burgeoning of electronic technology, which often requires more creative inputs than capital, has stimulated competition. The proliferation of computer hardware, software, and peripheral equipment manufacturers is testimony to this. Still, in one of the most significant antitrust cases of all times, American Telephone & Telegraph Company agreed to voluntarily break up its vast network of interlocking telephone companies. The government's argument was that AT&T, with its enormous resources in technology, would simply overwhelm competing information companies if it were allowed to retain all the advantages of its size.

## PROTECTION OF RIGHTS AND WELFARE
*Safeguards the public interest*

Another major area of government regulation concerns the protection of property rights and human rights and the promotion of the general

**TABLE 23-2**
**FEDERAL ANTITRUST LAWS**

| Act | Activities Prohibited | Significance |
|---|---|---|
| Sherman Antitrust Act of 1890 | Outlaws contracts, combinations, and conspiracies in restraint of trade. | First statute to combat monopolies and trusts. Labor unions included in definition of combinations in restraint of trade. |
| Clayton Antitrust Act of 1914 | Outlaws anticompetitive sales contracts, price cutting to force competitors out of business, interlocking directorates for larger corporations, and certain anticompetitive stock acquisitions and mergers. | Labor unions now given limited protection by not being included in definition of combinations in restraint of trade. |
| Federal Trade Commission Act of 1914 | Outlaws unfair competitive practices harmful to business competitors. | Created the Federal Trade Commission (FTC) to enforce this and other laws and regulations protecting competition. |
| Robinson-Patman Act of 1936 | Outlaws *price discrimination* (charging different buyers of the same goods different prices) if such practice tends to lessen competition. | Designed, in part, to protect independent retail stores from unfair competition from chain stores. |
| Wheeler-Lea Act of 1938 | Outlaws any unfair competitive practice harmful to the public. | Broadened the definition of what constitutes an unfair competitive practice (see the Federal Trade Commission Act above). |
| Celler-Kefauver Act of 1950 | Outlaws formal mergers of two or more companies if the merger creates a monopoly or reduces competition. | Significantly strengthened the provisions of the Clayton Act by outlawing anticompetitive mergers. |
| Antitrust Procedures and Penalty Act of 1974 | Increases fines for individuals and corporations that violate the Sherman Act. Makes violation of that act a felony rather than a misdemeanor. | Put added teeth into the enforcement provisions of the Sherman Act. |
| Antitrust Improvement Act of 1976 | Requires companies planning mergers to give prior notice to appropriate federal agencies. Allows state law officials to bring suit at the state level on behalf of injured parties damaged by violations of this act. | Led to a number of lawsuits intended to prevent anticompetitive mergers between companies in unrelated industries (so-called *conglomerate mergers*). |

welfare. The right to own property is basic to private enterprise. The ultimate responsibility to enforce that right lies with the government and its justice systems. The government also helps to define property, as in the case of patents, copyrights, and trademarks.

There are limitations on property rights which are also enforced by the government. The requirement to pay taxes is an important one. In times of war or when special needs, such as building public facilities, arise, the government can actually seize private property. This power is called **eminent domain.** The government must, however, show that the seizure will benefit the public, and it must pay the owner a fair price. The government may also prevent private property from being used in a way that harms others.

A number of regulations to protect the rights of consumers, such as laws that regulate credit practices, have been presented in earlier chapters. There are also many regulations designed to protect the public's health and safety. Some examples of the agencies that administer these kinds of regulations are the Food and Drug Administration, the Consumer Product Safety Commission, and the Occupational Safety and Health Administration. The effects of business activity on the environment are surveyed by the Environmental Protection Agency. The Department of Labor has a number of regulatory powers regarding employment and management-labor relationships, as discussed in Chapter 17.

# CONSUMER CREDIT
*Legal protections for the consumer* ━━━━━━━━━━━━━━━

Credit purchases by individuals are a characteristic of American life. They are so common that they have caused pain to the consumers as well as to business. Collecting bills from delinquent consumers is a major problem, especially for retailers and the loan companies that finance many installment purchases. The problem is so great that there are about 5,000 commercial agencies that specialize in collecting debts from consumers. These agencies are effective in collecting bills that the original seller has about given up on. They recover anywhere from 20 to 50 percent of what is owed, and they typically keep half of that amount. Collection agencies have often overstepped their legal position in the past. To correct this, the **Fair Debt Collection Practices Act** was passed in 1978. Among other things, the law forbids bill collectors to:

- Tell the debtor's employer, family, or neighbors about the debt
- Telephone the debtor at home between 9 p.m. and 8 a.m.
- Use false identification as a lawyer or as any kind of official
- Use obscene, profane, or abusive language

**CONSUMER CREDIT PROTECTION ACT** In an effort to help customers protect themselves in credit transactions, Congress passed the **Consumer Credit Protection Act (CCPA)** in the early 1960s. The Truth-in-Lending Law, as it is often called, requires many different kinds of businesses and organizations to disclose to customers the total interest and service charges on credit purchases and loans. The Credit Protection Act does not establish a maximum interest rate; it merely requires that buyers or borrowers be informed of how much interest they are paying for credit.

In April 1971 the Fair Credit Reporting Act (FCRA, Title VI Amendment of the Consumer Protection Act) became effective. This act specifically restricts the kind and amount of information that may be provided by one organization to another about an individual's credit worthiness. Restrictions are imposed on records of old bankruptcies, arrests, and/or convictions that occurred 7 or more years ago. Furthermore, the act prohibits the distribution of listings of people who are believed to be poor credit risks, regardless of the list's validity. The act also requires that an individual being screened be made aware of the process and be told when his or her application has been denied on the basis of information furnished by credit reporting agencies. The provisions of the act do not apply, however, when commercial credit is being requested. In order to help consumers to more fully understand their rights under the law and to be more prudent in their assumption of debt, the Federal Reserve System publishes useful guidelines, some of which are illustrated in Table 23-3.

# REGULATED INDUSTRIES
## *Establish controlled monopolies*

Monopolies are desirable for providing certain kinds of goods and services. Telephone service is one example. A town with five competing telephone companies would not get efficient service. Service lines would be duplicated all over town. Each user would have to have five different telephones, one connected to each company, in order to be able to communicate with everyone else. Governments have avoided this situation by allowing and encouraging the formation of monopolies to provide certain services. These ***public utilities*** are private companies protected from competition so they can efficiently provide essential public services. Utilities include companies providing electricity, gas, telephone service, mass transportation, and a variety of other products needed by the public. To compensate for their freedom from competition, public utilities are closely regulated by governments. The state, local, or federal government, unlike competitive businesses, can directly control the quality and extent of service a utility gives and the rates it charges.

Direct regulation of many utilities providing service within a state is the responsibility of state governments. Federal regulation of utilities is

---

**TABLE 23-3**
**HIGHLIGHTS OF THE CONSUMER CREDIT PROTECTION LAWS**

1. Lenders must tell you the method used for calculating the finance charge and when your payments begin.

2. Credit advertising must be accurate and not misleading. "Only $2 down," for example, must also state that you will have to pay $10 a week for the next 2 years, if that is the case.

3. All credit applicants must start out on the same footing. Specifically, race, color, age, sex, or marital status may not be used to discriminate against you.

4. You may not be denied credit just because you or your family receive some sort of public assistance, including social security benefits.

5. If you are denied credit, you must be notified within 30 days after your application was completed. If you are dissatisfied, you may seek guidance from a number of federal enforcement agencies. As a starting point, contact your nearest Federal Reserve Bank.

6. The law does not guarantee that you will be given a loan or obtain the credit you seek. Its purpose is to ensure that your application will be treated fairly and equitably within the limitations prescribed by the law.

most important in the areas of interstate power lines and pipelines, transportation, and communications. The Federal Power Commission has broad powers to control rates for electric power transmitted between states and to regulate the operations of interstate power companies. The Interstate Commerce Commission and the Federal Power Commission both have some authority over interstate pipelines, depending on how the lines are used. The Federal Communications Commission can directly control rates and service for interstate telephone and telegraph transmissions. In addition, it licenses and regulates radio and television stations and allocates radio frequencies for specific communications uses.

In some instances, when the public becomes understandably concerned with a particular problem, regulation escalates. This is particularly true of federal legislation dealing with hazardous materials and wastes, as illustrated in Figure 23-3.

## DEREGULATION
### Competition and inconvenience

Significant changes in the public's attitude toward regulation of business, especially transportation and banking, took place during the late 1970s and early 1980s. Most notable has been the impact on the airlines industry, which has been almost completely deregulated so far as routes and fares are concerned. This has led to vigorous, often cutthroat, competition. On the one hand, the public has gained through lower rates. On the other hand, many convenient routes and services previously required by the regulatory agencies have been discontinued. Commercial trucking, too, has been largely deregulated, leading to a complexity of rates but also a level of competition favorable to shippers.

As mentioned earlier in this text, deregulation of banking has led to a number of abuses and a carelessness in management that might not have occurred earlier. In many instances, bank services have declined as a result of deregulation, but the competition in offering a variety of investment packages, usually paying higher interest rates, has greatly increased.

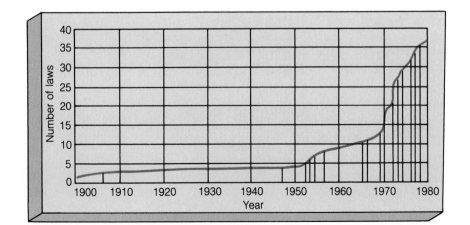

Figure 23-3 Escalation of federal regulation of hazardous materials and wastes.

## OTHER STATE REGULATIONS
*Imposition of laws, fees, and licenses* ▬▬▬▬▬▬▬▬▬▬▬

In addition to controlling the operation of utilities, state governments—and, to a lesser extent, local governments—impose detailed regulation on certain other business and professional activities. They grant charters for the formation of corporations. They often have pollution, safety, property rights, and wage and hour laws supplementing or overlapping federal statutes. They may require direct licensing of businesses and nearly always require a license for the practice of medicine, law, and certain other professions. They often regulate specific kinds of businesses, such as the insurance industry or automobile repair shops. They may independently outlaw certain products, such as disposable bottles or cans, for environmental or health reasons. Local zoning, licensing, advertising, and trade regulations also affect businesses. The interaction of local, state, and federal regulation presents a difficult and complex administrative problem for many companies.

## 5 TAXATION
### All businesses pay in some way

Most businesses are influenced to some extent by government regulation. The government's taxation powers are enforced on all businesses. Governments incur expenses by providing public services and promoting the general well-being. They pay these expenses by collecting taxes from individuals and organizations, including businesses, within their jurisdiction. Establishing a tax structure that provides enough revenue and is fair to all taxpayers is a difficult and complex job. Three different policies of taxation are often combined in a tax program:

■  **Proportional taxation** collects the same percent rate of taxes from every taxpayer. A 10 percent proportional income tax would take 10 percent of everyone's income, regardless of whether the individual made $5,000 or $5 million a year. Real estate and personal property taxes are often proportional.

■  **Progressive taxation** charges an increasing tax rate as the amount of income or property being taxed increases. A person with a small income may pay 15 percent in taxes, while someone with a larger income might pay 33 percent.

■  **Regressive taxation** charges a lower percent rate as the amount being taxed increases. Under this scheme, a person with a higher income would pay a lower rate than someone with a smaller income.

In the United States, most income taxes are meant to be progressive and most other taxes, proportional. Regressive taxation may still occur, however. Obvious examples of this are the sales taxes charged by many state and local governments. Low-income people contribute a far higher percent of their income to the sales tax than the wealthy, and therefore pay a higher tax rate.

The most important purpose of taxation is to raise revenue for governments. In addition, taxation may be used as a regulatory method.

# REVENUE TAXES
## *Designed to provide government support*

Governments gain revenue to support their operations through a variety of taxes. The most important source of revenue for the federal government is a tax on personal and corporate incomes. The general sources of federal revenue are shown in Figure 23-4. Many states and some cities also depend heavily on income taxes.

An *income tax* is a regular payment made to a government. The amount paid is based on how much money an individual earns from employment and investments. *Corporate taxes* are also an income tax based on profits remaining after all costs have been paid.

For most corporations, federal and state taxes are significant expense items, routinely taking up to 34 percent and more of pretax profits. Since corporations in general have no way to pay the taxes except from revenue generated by sales, the taxes are ultimately paid for by raising the prices of goods. It is the individuals and firms that buy these products who actually pay corporate taxes.

Most states and many smaller governments have sales or property exchange taxes to raise revenue. A *sales tax* is a tax payment for which the amount is determined by the value of products being bought. A property *transfer tax* is similar to a straight sales tax, except that it generally applies only to major purchases like cars or real estate. In certain cases, the transfer tax may be paid in part or wholly by the seller.

*Property taxes* are paid at regular intervals, their amount being based on a valuation of real or personal property. Property taxes are a major source of operating revenue for towns, cities, and counties.

*Payroll taxes* are deducted from regular payments of salaries and wages. The most important of these is the social security tax, which is shared by employer and employee. The proceeds are used partly to maintain a retirement and disability fund for United States workers. A further payroll tax—unemployment insurance—is paid by employers. It

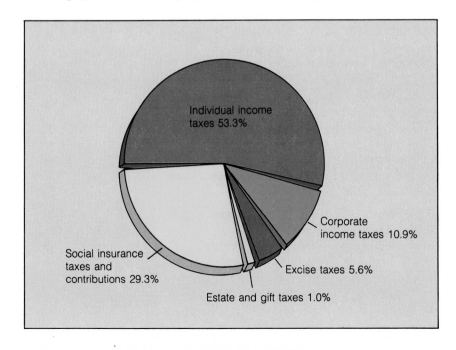

Figure 23-4 Sources of revenue for the U.S. government reported in 1986.

is used by state unemployment commissions to make partial wage payments to workers who are laid off or discharged.

## REGULATORY OR RESTRICTIVE TAXES
*Imposed to discourage undesirable actions* ━━━━━━━━

Though all taxes provide revenue, some are meant to accomplish more than that. A protective tariff, for example, is a tax. Its real purpose, however, is to reduce the amount of goods imported by raising their price relative to domestically produced goods.

***EXCISE TAXES*** *Excise taxes* are collected from the manufacturers, or sometimes from the retail sellers, of certain kinds of goods. One use of such taxes is to provide revenue for special purposes. Excise taxes on tires and motor vehicles, for instance, contribute to highway construction. Excise taxes may also be imposed in an effort to discourage the use of certain manufactured goods. This is part of the rationale behind taxes on tobacco products and alcoholic beverages.

***TARIFFS AND CUSTOMS DUTIES*** *Customs duties* are service taxes collected when goods are imported, either by private travelers or commercially. They provide government revenue and, to some extent, discourage importation. *Tariffs* are sometimes set on certain products to substantially raise the domestic prices of imported goods and protect domestic producers.

***COMMUNICATIONS AND TRANSPORTATION TAXES*** Telephone and teletypewriter services are also taxed. Air travel has a special tax; it is paid directly by airlines and by customers who purchase tickets. Truck transportation companies sometimes must pay a special ***use tax*** for highway use in addition to general licenses. These taxes are often interpreted as a partial compensation for the government's granting of monopoly status (in the case of telephone service) or as partial repayment by private companies for the use of public facilities. However, the taxes are, in fact, all paid by consumers.

***OTHER BUSINESS TAXES*** All levels of government have imposed a variety of minor taxes that apply to businesses in specific situations. Businesses usually need licenses to operate. A large company may need scores of different licenses from different cities, counties, and states. Each license requires a fee. Charters for corporations are usually taxed, sometimes quite heavily. Utilities pay "franchise fees," or taxes for the right to operate within jurisdictions. When new facilities are built, fees must be paid to obtain building permits. Many areas have ***severance taxes*** that must be paid when a natural resource like timber or minerals is used. These taxes encourage conservation and provide further revenue.

## IMPACT OF TAXES ON BUSINESS DECISIONS
*Depreciation and interest are major tax factors* ━━━━━━━━

Taxes are of interest to business managers because they represent an important amount of money that must be paid out. They are also important because the specific ways they are assessed can influence the best choice to make in many business decisions.

A simple example is selecting a site for a new manufacturing plant. If the value of the plant is $10 million, annual real estate taxes could be as low as $60,000 or less in many rural areas with low property tax rates. In many highly developed urban areas, property taxes on the same plant could be $250,000 or higher. If the rural area could provide the utilities, transportation facilities, work force, and other requirements, the factory could operate there at a significantly lower total cost.

The decision of whether to back an undertaking with borrowed money or with equity financing is often influenced by the effect of taxes. Interest paid on borrowed money is a deductible expense for income tax, reducing the amount of tax owed. The deduction, for many companies, is substantial enough to make borrowing significantly less expensive in the long run. In this situation, debt financing may be more attractive than equity financing.

Taxes are often involved in decisions about buying new equipment or building facilities. Production facilities depreciate in value as they are used. The average loss in value each year can also be counted as a deductible expense, and thus can reduce income taxes. Tax statutes, however, set limits on the length of time facilities can be depreciated. A 50-year-old factory, for example, may operate perfectly well. If it can no longer be depreciated, however, income earned from its products will, in effect, be subject to higher taxes than income from a new factory with substantial depreciation expense.

**LEASE VERSUS BUY** Leasing a building or equipment, rather than buying it outright, often offers attractive tax advantages to businesses. Leasing is a form of renting, although the commitment tends to be longer and more binding than ordinary rental agreements. If a company purchases a warehouse, for example, for $1,000,000, it may be allowed by the Internal Revenue Service to charge the depreciation of this building as a yearly expense for 25 years. Each year, the company could deduct 1/25 of the building's cost (or $40,000) from its income as a depreciation expense. If the company were paying income taxes at the 34 percent rate, this would save the company $13,600 each year.

On the other hand, if the company chose to lease the same kind of building from another owner at $100,000 a year, it could deduct this expense from its income before taxes and save approximately $34,000 a year in taxes. That doesn't tell the whole story, of course. In the buy decision, the company has to consider the additional yearly loss of interest-earning power of the $1,000,000 it has invested in the building. When interest rates are at 10 percent, this cost would be $100,000 a year. The net cost of owning would then be $86,400 ($100,000 minus the $13,600 saved on taxes). The net cost of leasing the same building would be $66,000 (annual leasing expense of $100,000 minus the $34,000 saved on taxes). In this instance, tax considerations might lead management to lease the building rather than buy it. (See Figure 23-5 for a graphic demonstration of this example.)

Tax effects such as these are very common. They influence hundreds of decisions such as whether to rent or buy facilities, whether to manufacture components or buy them from suppliers, and whether to expand internally or buy existing operations. Nearly every conceivable business decision can be influenced to some extent by some type of local, state, or federal tax.

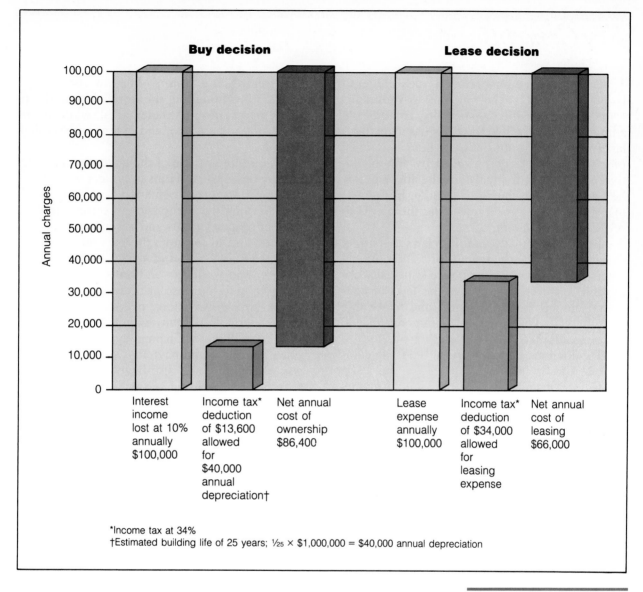

Figure 23-5 Impact of income taxes on lease-buy decisions for a $1 million warehouse.

# Key Concepts

**1.** Law is a collection of formal rules and regulations enforced by the power of government. Laws can be classified as statutory, common, or administrative. Each kind of law has its particular application to business. Under the legal process, laws may be enforced by administrative agencies, individuals and businesses may be prosecuted, or individuals and/or businesses may resort to litigation by asking the courts to settle disputes among them.

**2.** Businesses must conform to laws that affect everyone, such as the law of torts and criminal law. Certain laws, however, are especially applicable to business, such as the laws of contracts, property, sales, agency, and negotiable instruments. The Uniform Commercial Code has been adopted by all but one state as a set of legal guidelines covering most fields of commercial law.

**3.** Businesses often wish to provide customers with legal assurances, or warranties, that goods or services have certain characteristics. Individuals and firms that cannot pay their bills may resort to bankruptcy for specified legal protection from their creditors. The law also offers a method for protecting the ownership of identifying marks (through trademarks), works of the minds (by copyrights), and inventions (through patents).

**4.** An important role of the government is regulating business activities to protect the general welfare of society. Regulation is specifically intended to promote free and fair competition, to protect property rights and the interests of consumers, and to improve the general welfare in such areas as health and safety, environmental quality, and working conditions.

**5.** The main purpose of taxation is to provide the revenue governments need to carry on operations. Some important revenue taxes are those levied on personal income, corporate income, sales, property, and payrolls. Some taxes, while generating revenue, also have the effect of restricting or regulating certain activities. Import tariffs, for example, discourage the importation of certain goods. The way that certain taxes are levied provides options requiring management decisions, such as in lease-or-buy situations.

# Review Questions

**1.** Define, identify, or explain each of the following key terms or phrases, found on the pages indicated.

*agent (p. 535)*
*bankruptcy (p. 538)*
*business (commercial) law (p. 534)*
*common law (p. 531)*
*consideration (p. 534)*
*Consumer Credit Protection Act (CCPA) (p. 542)*
*contract (p. 534)*
*copyright (p. 539)*
*corporate tax (p. 546)*
*criminal law (p. 533)*
*customs duties (p. 547)*
*deed (p. 535)*
*eminent domain (p. 542)*
*excise tax (p. 547)*

*express warranty (p. 537)*
*Fair Debt Collection Practices Act (p. 542)*
*implied warranty (p. 537)*
*income tax (p. 546)*
*interlocking directorate (p. 540)*
*laissez-faire (p. 539)*
*law (p. 531)*
*lease (p. 535)*
*litigation (p. 533)*
*negotiable instruments (p. 536)*
*patent (p. 539)*
*payroll tax (p. 546)*
*personal property (p. 535)*
*precedent (p. 531)*
*principal (p. 535)*
*product liability (p. 537)*
*progressive taxation (p. 545)*
*property tax (p. 546)*
*proportional taxation (p. 545)*

2. With which type of law is a precedent of particular importance, and why?

3. How does the government enforce administrative law?

4. What are the five main requirements that must be met for a contract to be valid and le-

gally enforceable?

5. Why has the Uniform Commercial Code been so important to business?

6. A person buys a bucket and finds out when she gets home that it leaks. She returns it to the retailer, claiming that a bucket should be warranted to hold water. Another person purchases a clock with a written slip attached that assures him that if the clock fails to operate within 90 days, it may be returned for a new one. Which of these situations represents either an express or implied warranty?

7. What have been the main goals of government in regulating business?

8. What is a regulated industry? Provide some examples. Why are they allowed to exist?

9. What is the difference between a revenue tax and a restrictive tax? Give an example of each.

10. Distinguish between proportional taxation and regressive taxation.

# Case Critique 23-1
## Dating Around the Law

You enter a food market or your favorite convenience store. You proceed to the dairy case. There's a deep lineup of your brand of yogurt. Do you take the one in front? Never! You reach to the back to pick what you believe is the freshest carton.

Many state and local statutes try to save you this trouble by regulating the dating of food products. They insist that the manufacturer, food processor, or packer stamp a "sell by" date on the container. So far, the federal government has stayed away from this problem, leaving it up to state agencies or city agencies for enforcement. The trouble is that few authorities can agree on the best way to determine the dates after which spoilage is likely to occur—and/or the most helpful way to declare this to the public. It is small wonder that the federal government has not legislated a dating standard.

Let's go back to the supermarket and examine some of the sanctioned methods of dating food products.

Most popular is the *sell-by (or pull) date*. This is the last day a retailer is permitted to sell this product as "fresh." (The retailer may often be allowed to sell it so long as the fact has been made clear that the sell date has expired.) The sell-by date is the one most commonly used on beef, fish, poultry, dairy products, and bakery products. The sell-by date is determined by figuring in the time for processing, shipping, a reasonable shelf life, and 2 days in the customer's refrigerator at home.

A similar marking is the *best-if-used-by date*. It is applied to cereals, aseptically packaged juices, snack foods, peanut butter, salad dressing, processed meats, and refrigerated dough products. This designation is usually the result of the manufacturer's judgment of how long the product will remain unchanged after packaging. It does not necessarily mean that consumption of the product after that date will harm you. It is an indication that the perceived quality of the product will be affected—taste, texture, color, or smell.

Other manufacturers use a *best-if-purchased-by* designation. This helps to protect the retailer, since no one knows how long consumers may keep the product on their shelves before using it.

Some processors focus on the *expiration date;* others on the *pack date.* An egg carton, for example, marked "EXP Jan 27" means the same thing as a sell-by date. Some over-the-counter drug products use EXP dates to mean best-if-used-by. (EST, which appears on USDA-inspected meat products, refers to something entirely different: An EST number identifies the establishment where packed so that complaints can be traced to their source.) A pack date is often used for canned foods and cake mixes that can be expected to have long shelf lives.

Consumers repeatedly ask for federal agencies, like the Food and Drug Administration, to step in and standardize markings and to establish dating limits for commonly consumed foods and drugs. Manufacturers and retailers try to limit regulation, which is often complex and confusing, especially when the same products are distributed in different states. Businesses would prefer to develop the standards on a vol-untary basis through their trade associations. Nevertheless, as can be expected, even the manufacturers have a difficult time finding a consensus in the matter.

Meanwhile, consumers fend for themselves and try to find the product placed on the retailer's shelf most recently.

1. How would you classify the legal source of dating requirements? Who makes policies and enforces these requirements?
2. What problems must be overcome in establishing standards for dating food products? How might they be solved?
3. Which method of dating do you think is preferable? Those based on "purchase by" or "use by"? Why?
4. In your opinion, which direction should the solution to this problem take? Continue to let the states handle the problem? Ask a federal agency to regulate? Or let the various businesses involved deal with dating on a voluntary basis?

---

*SOURCE:* Carole Sugarman, "Making All Those Numbers Add Up," *The Washington Post,* January 27, 1985, pp. H-1–2.

---

# Case Critique 23-2
## You Didn't Finish the Job

Rockabilly Reggae Company signed a contract with the Bubba Construction Corporation to build a small addition to its record-pressing plant. The contract specified that the building was to be of cinder-block construction, 24 feet by 12 feet and 18 feet high. The roof was to be of corrugated metal. Doorways, window sizes, and flooring were also specified. The contract was signed on February 12 and called for completion of the building within 120 days after signing. The total price agreed upon was $175,000. Rockabilly paid Bubba Corporation $25,000 upon signing the contract and agreed to pay the additional moneys in three equal payments of $50,000 each as the building was one-third, two-thirds, and finally completed.

Construction began as planned and seemed to proceed according to the contract. Rockabilly paid Bubba Corporation $50,000 on March 15, another $50,000 on April 15, and the final $50,000 on May 10. At the time of the final payment there was a slight disagreement between the owners of Rockabilly and the contractors about details regarding the interior finish of the building. Bubba assured the owners that the job would be completed to Rockabilly's satisfaction. Accordingly, the construction company sent in a crew of plasterers from a subcontracting company to refinish the surface of the interior cement blocks. The cost of this work came to $5,996.

From that time forward, the disagreement between Rockabilly and Bubba heated up. The construction company contended that the extra refinishing work went beyond the specifications in the contract and that the company should be paid an additional $5,996. Rockabilly disputed this claim. It said that Bubba had never fully completed the interior finishing. If there was any refinishing, it was the construction company's fault, not the owner's.

To make matters worse, the subcontractor pressed Bubba for payment of its bill. Bubba told the subcontractor that the bill could not be paid until Rockabilly paid Bubba. This became public gossip in the community where Rockabilly operated. Accordingly, Rockabilly paid the subcontractor the $5,996 so that there would be no reason why the company could not occupy the building immediately. Then Rockabilly turned around and sued Bubba Corporation for the $5,996 and another $100,000 for damages to its reputation due to Bubba's "slanderous remarks." Said the firm in its suit, "Rock-

abilly has paid all amounts due on the contract as it has matured." Said the Bubba Corporation, "We finished the job as specified. You never made it clear about the kind of interior finishing you expected."

1. Were all five elements of a contract present at the signing? If so, what was wrong with the contract that Rockabilly signed?
2. Was it wise for Rockabilly to pay the subcontractor? What might have been a better alternative?
3. If you were asked to settle this case, on what factors would you place the most emphasis: Rockabilly's prompt payments as construction progressed or Bubba's claim that the $5,996 represented work not covered by the contract? How would you decide the case?

## CHAPTER 24

# Ethical Behavior
# and Social
# Responsibility

## Learning Objectives

*The purpose of this chapter is to define ethical behavior as it applies to business conduct, discuss the general trend of business's response to the growing demand for ethical behavior and social responsibility, and analyze some of the continuing problems that will affect the future direction of business in the United States.*

*As evidence of general comprehension, after studying this chapter you should be able to:*

1. *Distinguish ethical from legally required business practices.*

2. *Identify the attitudes and expectations of the various groups that are involved with the business community.*

3. *Explain some of the ways in which power groups try to influence business practices.*

4. *Cite evidence of how businesses, collectively and as individual companies, have responded to the call for social responsibility.*

5. *Express considered opinions about continuing problems that confront business, such as problems related to the environment, land use, and opportunities for minorities and women.*

*If your class is using SSweetco: Business Model and Activity File, see Chapter 24 in that book after you complete this chapter. There you will find exercises and activities to help you apply your learning to typical business situations.*

## 1 ETHICAL BEHAVIOR IN BUSINESS

is conduct that is acceptable to those directly involved and to the community at large.

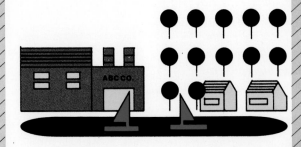

## 2 BUSINESS MUST RESPOND TO ATTITUDES AND EXPECTATIONS

from many influences.

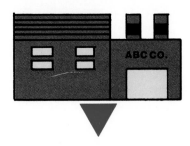

Competitors/Employees/Suppliers/Customers/
Creditors/The community/Investors/

## 3 BUSINESS MUST COPE WITH POWER GROUP PRESSURES FROM MANY SOURCES

Public interest groups/Trade associations
The legal system/Labor unions

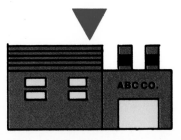

## 4 THERE IS EVIDENCE OF BUSINESS'S GROWING SOCIAL RESPONSIBILITY

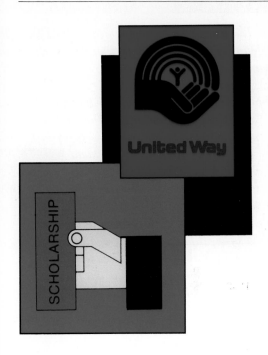

## 5 STILL, PROBLEMS REMAIN

with respect to the environment, economic growth, land use, minorities and women, and multinational operations.

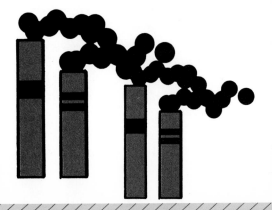

# BUSINESS AS USUAL VERSUS SOCIAL RESPONSIBILITY

*The United States companies justified their presence in South Africa by claiming that they were, in fact, agents of reform. More than 150 of them, for example, were closely adhering to the Sullivan Principles. These were guidelines formulated in 1978 by the Reverend Leon H. Sullivan, calling for equal employment opportunity and fair treatment for South African blacks. Xerox, for example, at the time defended its presence by saying, "We feel that we can do more working in the system, than by just avoiding it completely."*

*For most Americans, gradual change in human relations in South Africa was not enough. Increasingly, citizens' groups pressed the federal government to take economic sanctions and a strong diplomatic stance against apartheid. Many citizens demanded that American companies pull out of South Africa entirely. At first only a few did.*

*Then in October 1986 the United States government yielded to public pressure and passed a sanctions bill against South Africa. The bill severely limited U.S. trade with South Africa by barring imports of iron, steel, uranium, coal, textiles, and farm products. It also forbade new U.S. investments in South Africa and ended commercial air traffic between the two countries.*

*By late 1986, the resistance of American corporations began to crumble. General Motors Corp. and International Business Machines Corp. withdrew from South Africa the same day. Honeywell Inc. and Warner Communications Inc. followed close behind. By the year's end, some 70 companies, including Coca-Cola and Procter & Gamble, had announced their departure. Some large corporations, however, remained. They did so because of the belief that they could make a more positive contribution to South African life by maintaining their presence than by selling out to South African nationals. As a matter of practical fact, many companies that did leave South Africa still had indirect involvement through sales of parts, technology, and brands to international intermediaries, thereby skirting the provisions of the sanctions bill.*

# 1 ETHICAL BEHAVIOR
## What is good for society should be good for business too

*Ethics* is a collection of moral principles and rules of conduct accepted by part or all of the members of a society. Ethics guides behavior based on beliefs about what is right and wrong. The source of these beliefs may be tradition, religion, or reasoned judgments about what is best for the individual and society as a whole. ***Business ethics*** is the group of rules of conduct applied specifically to business situations.

Ethics is not the same as law. Many ethical beliefs are formally reinforced by law, but many are not. Until recently, it was legal to fire almost any employee for any reason, regardless of the length of his or her service. Often the terminated employee was denied any provision for a company pension. Today, this practice is inhibited by federal law.

In practice, ethics is expressed and felt as a combination of pressures that direct one to take or not to take certain actions. Decisions must be acceptable to many different elements of society. First, they must be acceptable to the conscience of the decision maker. A manager may legitimately think, "I could legally take this action, and I could probably get others to accept it, but I ought not do it because it isn't right."

Managers must consider the potential effects of their decisions on the people and companies directly involved with the business operation: customers, suppliers, competitors, employees, investors, and creditors. In addition, managers must consider—and try to control—the possible effects of their decisions on the community at large.

It is only recently that business has become aware of how it affects individuals and the whole society. The laissez-faire business environment of the nineteenth century promoted the belief that almost any practice that increased profits was, in the long run, good for the country. The result was cutthroat competition, fraud, deceptive marketing, price and market manipulation, worthless and dangerous products, exploitation of workers, and other practices that today are considered unethical.

At the same time that so many harmful business activities were being carried on, some companies did abide by the fundamentals of good business ethics. At the height of the ruthless development of the nineteenth century, many managers still believed in producing high-quality products, honestly sold at a fair price. They felt success could be built on hard work, creativity, and genuine customer satisfaction. It is the belief that high ethical standards are in the long run good for profits that is stressed in business today.

In spite of improvements, however, there is evidence that managing a business may involve, at every level, a compromise with an individual's ethical standards. In 1975, a major survey asked 238 managers whether they felt "pressured to compromise their personal standards to attain company goals." About 50 percent of the top-level executives said they did. In 1981, 8,000 first-time supervisors nationwide were asked a similar question: "Are you ever asked to carry out orders or policies that are contrary to your moral beliefs about what is right or wrong?" Half of the supervisors said they never were, 45 percent said occasionally, and 5 percent said frequently. There is little evidence to suggest that conditions are any different today.

# 2 ATTITUDES AND EXPECTATIONS
*Business decisions must take into account many influences*

If a manager accepts the notion that how decisions affect others should be considered, then decision making becomes even more complex than it ever was. A wide variety of individuals and organizations, as well as society as a whole, may be affected by a given business decision. Each of these groups has its own desires and expectations, which may conflict with those of other groups and may also change as various conditions change.

## INDIVIDUALS IMMEDIATELY AFFECTED BY MANAGEMENT DECISIONS
*Consideration of their viewpoint*

Among those who have a high personal stake in management decisions are employees, customers, suppliers, competitors, investors, and creditors.

**EMPLOYEES** Workers were once viewed as being similar to machines—as standard, interchangeable elements to be used at the lowest possible cost with the highest possible productivity. Modern ethics, however, tends more toward the view that the company has a real obligation to provide its employees not only with good pay and good working conditions but also with the opportunity to grow and to achieve their full potential.

In three areas, in particular, employee rights and privileges are being advanced by both legal and voluntary means.

■ *Rights to free speech and to privacy.* It used to be that employees, like children, were supposed to be seen but not heard. Currently, most employees expect to be able to say what they think about their jobs and companies without reprisals being taken against them. Then there is the matter of employee records. Employees want to know what is kept in their files, and they do not want unauthorized people looking at them. At companies like United Technologies, Smith Kline, and Chase Manhattan Bank, there are formal policies limiting what will be kept in company files and assuring employees access to see that the information is correct.

■ *Greater assurances of job security.* During the wave of factory closings and movement of manufacturing operations overseas in the early 1980s, employees, labor unions, suppliers, and communities made themselves heard. Employees were asking for extensive advance notice before a plant shut down or moved. Furthermore, there is growing pressure for companies to demonstrate economic justification before such an action.

■ *Improved quality of work life.* Increasingly, employees cannot see why work should necessarily be boring, hazardous, or demeaning. They are asking employers to provide greater opportunities to share in the decisions that affect their work. And some employers are responding to these expectations because they believe that an improved quality of work life will also improve employee productivity.

**CUSTOMERS** The attitude toward customers is changing too. Business has become increasingly conscious of the importance of fair prices, good quality products, and honest merchandising. This has been helped along by **consumerism,** which refers to organized efforts to protect the users of various products from harmful or deceptive business practices.

Many states and municipalities maintain offices of consumer affairs. These agencies provide information services for consumers, acting as watchdogs over supermarkets, retail stores, and lending institutions. They also provide an avenue through which to seek redress when a consumer feels wronged. Some corporations have added consumer representatives to their boards of directors.

**SUPPLIERS** Ethical considerations also arise in relation to suppliers. The decision of one company to buy from another depends on price, quality, supplier capabilities, shipping costs, and similar factors. The problem is that some unfavorable purchasing decisions can put a supplying company out of business. Opportunities for fraud, "kickback" payments in return for purchase orders, and other illegal activity may often arise.

**COMPETITORS** Even though many business activities that affect competition are strictly controlled by law, ethical questions still abound. The use of industrial espionage to discover trade secrets of competitors is an example, as is the hiring away of key employees by competitors. The central problem of ethical competition is how to compete fairly without losing the aggressiveness and will to win needed for success.

**INVESTORS AND CREDITORS** The traditional view of business's responsibility is to maximize profits at any price. This places the interests of owners and investors above those of consumers and the public. Managerial decisions are understandably influenced by this priority. It is still clearly a manager's duty to operate businesses in such a way that profits will be created for investors. Creditors also deserve protection from fraud and deception on the part of borrowers who refuse to meet obligations.

## THE COMMUNITY AT LARGE
*A concern for the greatest good*

There has been increasing concern about business's commitments to society as a whole. Business obviously plays a central role in the economy. In the United States, private business is still the primary means of converting resources into goods and services the society needs to function. The question arises of whether a company should temper its business decisions with considerations of what is best for the overall economy. Especially in the case of a very large corporation, a decision could be made that would benefit the corporation but damage the economy. For instance, a decision by a large oil company to limit supplies of oil may help the company to increase prices and profits. However, it may also prove damaging to the economy as a whole since industrial growth is dependent on an ever increasing supply of energy sources such as oil.

Similar conflicts occur in business activities that affect the quality of the environment. Efforts to control air and water pollution, for instance, can be very expensive. They can cost individual companies millions of dollars, which means higher prices and a possible decrease in sales volume and profits.

# B·I·L·L·B·O·A·R·D

## CAN CORPORATE BOARDS BE ETHICAL?

In a debate over corporate ethics, three notable people displayed different, but not entirely conflicting, viewpoints. None of the three was fully optimistic about how much the public could rely upon the ability of a corporate board of directors to protect the public's interest.

Ralph Nader, famous consumer advocate, took this position: "The idea that boards can govern corporations the size of Exxon, Lockheed, or Sears by flying to the scene for a few hours of meetings is unrealistic." Nader favors the assignment of special duties to individual board members. One would be held responsible for relationships with consumers, another with employees, and so on. Nader charged that despite "extensive documentation of mismanagement, boards themselves usually escape accountability."

Robert K. Mueller, chairperson of the board of the research firm Arthur D. Little, Inc., also felt that the task of the board was enormous and almost beyond management: "My position is that board governance conditions are 65 percent uncertainty and 20 percent confusion . . . the other 15 percent comprise ritual, legal, and programmable activities."

Ethics is a process of deliberation and debate, said Mueller. "This continuing process of clarification is in response to new values, emerging technological and social developments, or shifing po-

> ### Ethics is a process of deliberation and debate,

litical forces. Today's directors appear to be more relaxed about reasonable disclosure of corporate affairs and more acutely concerned with accountability."

Kenneth R. Andrews, editor of the *Harvard Business Review*, sees other barriers to effective ethical behavior of corporate boards: "To whom is the board responsible and by whom is it held to account?" he asked. "The law says the shareholders. This is not the reality. The shareholder who buys shares one moment and sells them the next is not ex-

hibiting the responsibilities of ownership, ethical or otherwise." He added that corporate boards face "a hopeless profusion" of possible socially desirable programs. They must, suggested Andrews, "identify those non-economic activities in which the company should engage—relating them as closely as possible to the mission of the company."

### QUERIES

**1.** With whom do you agree in this debate?
**2.** How do you estimate the probability of corporate boards acting to ensure ethical conduct on the part of the corporations they represent?
**3.** What other factors may be more powerful than the board in obtaining socially responsible behavior from businesses? ∎

*SOURCE:* W. Michael Hoffman, moderator, "The Role of Corporate Boards in Institutionalizing Ethics," *Business Ethics: Bentley College's Fifth National Conference on Business Ethics,* p. 1, The Center for Business Ethics at Bentley College, Waltham, Mass., 1983.

# PROFILE

CHRISTINE NEVIN works full-time at her paid position as manager of economic development for a major utility. In her spare time and on her days off, she heads a voluntary community organization, BrooklynWorks. Its mission is to stimulate business and create more jobs all over Brooklyn. As president and member of the executive committee of BrooklynWorks, Nevin has many responsibilities. These include supervising the paid staff, conducting outreach sessions to attract exhibitors and buyers, running committee meetings (sometimes on Saturday mornings), and conducting seminars. Consolidated Edison, her employer, encourages and supports such social responsibility. Why? Because new jobs and more people working and living in the community means more gas and electricity sold—the Company's "bottom line."

Before joining Con Ed, Nevin worked for 3 years in a rewarding but poorly paid social service job. She did gain experience in administration, however. When she applied for a job at the utility, Con Ed was impressed with Nevin's social service background and hired her as a lower level (#6) line supervisor. She advanced quickly to a Level 11 branch manager's job, supervising 20 managers in charge of meter readers and customer service reps. She also controlled budgets and administered training for 100 employees. When Nevin was promoted to Manager of Economic Development at the age of 30, she was encouraged to carry her skills outside the company into volunteer work for the community. ∎

**CHRISTINE NEVIN**

SOURCE: Jacquiline Giambanco, "Brooklyn's Public-Spirited Exec," *Working Woman*, November 1985, pp. 155–158.

Businesses usually benefit from a stable and well-managed social and political environment. However, it is not always easy to decide how much business should contribute to improving society. Again, expense is the key. If companies devote large amounts of time and money to reducing poverty and improving public education and health care facilities, the companies may suffer economically. At the same time, both ethical and practical considerations make it important for businesses to make every effort to improve society as a whole. This conflict remains unresolved. The important point is that in recent years, the social and business climate has led to an extended public examination of such issues. It appears likely that in the future, businesses will be more likely to take the community into consideration when making major decisions. Indeed, some progress is already evident. Companies like IBM and the Ford Motor Co. now have board members responsible for promoting sensitivity to community needs.

## BUSINESS AS THE BAD GUY

*Is the general impression accurate?*

Since the time of the first capitalists, it has been a popular theme to portray businesspeople as predatory, greedy, inconsiderate human beings. As the owners and managers of the very large corporations have become further and further removed from ordinary citizens, this feeling about them has not diminished. An observation of the Business Roundtable supports this conclusion. Francis W. Steckmest, speaking for this group in *Corporate Performance: The Key to Public Trust*, said: "Occasional examples of a flamboyant executive life style are a reason for concern about the uses of executives' power. They also act to confirm public suspicions that executives are insulated from many inconveniences and adversities and, as a result, are insensitive to the day-to-day concerns of the citizenry, including the adverse impacts of corporate performance on people. Behavior that fosters the twin beliefs that executives misuse corporate power to advance their own self-interest and that they don't care about what concerns the public holds explosive consequences for the large corporation."

*SOURCE:* Francis W. Steckmest, *Corporate Performance: Key to Public Trust*, McGraw-Hill, New York, 1982, p. 208.

Surveys of public attitudes toward business cycle upward and downward in the extent of their approval or disapproval. During the years from 1968 to 1978, public confidence declined markedly. It turned upward during the early 1980s and then began to fall again.

There is also the publicity associated with the occasional **whistleblower** who discloses a company's fraud or mismanagement to the press or the law and is discharged as a consequence. In one of the most notable cases, three engineers employed by the San Francisco Bay Area Rapid Transit District (BART) revealed to the press conditions of unsafe and mismanaged construction. They were unceremoniously "quickmarched" to the exit by company guards. Three years later, BART settled the engineers' claims of unfair discharge out of court for $75,000.

On the other hand, business is fair game for either criticism or satire. In a study conducted by the Media Institute in 1981, it was apparent that television projects a distorted view of business to the public. Some 200

---

### *Action Brief*

#### QUACKS FIND EASY MARKS

*Every year, thousands of gullible Americans lose more than $25 billion in health frauds. There was, for example, the "moon dust" promoted for the cure of arthritis at $100 for 3 ounces; it turned out to be plain ordinary beach sand. There was also the California company selling a product that promoted weight loss while sleeping; it made $1 million before the FDA stepped in. The quacks that perpetrate these schemes prey especially on the elderly or the infirm. Large, nationally known firms are rarely involved; they are so visible that their products are regularly monitored by the FDA. The agency, however, says that it cannot keep up with the flood of ingenious frauds on the market. The FDA urges caution when considering any product that exploits fear, promises painless treatment or a miraculous scientific breakthrough, relies on anecdotes and testimonials, and carries a price out of line with regular medicine.*

prime-time programs were examined, with 118 businesspeople in important roles. The study concluded that two out of three were portrayed as either foolish, greedy, or criminal. Almost half of the episodes showed businesspeople involved in illegal acts. Typical portrayals ranged from the diabolical J. R. Ewing of *Dallas* to the gracious Mrs. Pynchon, the newspaper publisher in the now canceled *Lou Grant* show. In between, there were the odious Louie, the cab manager of *Taxi;* the familiar proprietor of *Archie Bunker's Place;* and Mel, the tough-talking owner of the diner in *Alice.* All told, the survey concluded, television almost never portrays business as a socially useful or economically productive activity. Since half of the working population in the United States is employed in the private sector, this seems like an unfair picture of the work life of a very great many Americans.

# 3  POWER GROUPS
## *Business can and must fend for itself*

Businesses operate in an environment in which the interests of people and organizations affected by business decisions are aggressively represented by public pressure groups. Business, in turn, has its own organizations representing and working for business interests. It is important to recognize that all of the influences may affect a decision at the same time. The major power groups include:

***LABOR UNIONS*** Many companies on their own initiative are beginning to demonstrate more concern for the development and satisfaction of their employees. At the same time, labor unions remain a strong force working for the rights of employees. Unions have a great deal of influence on wages and fringe benefits, work hours, working conditions, safety efforts, and other issues that affect the welfare of workers. In some cases, unions have also become involved in consumer protection. From management's point of view, labor unions are an important complicating factor in decisions affecting personnel policies and actions.

***TRADE ASSOCIATIONS*** Businesses often create organizations to publicize and promote the concerns of particular industries or of business as a whole. These trade associations influence public opinion on issues affecting the trade; inform businesses involved in a trade of important legal, market, or social changes; lobby for favorable legislation; and carry out research and education in order to further the progress of member businesses. The policies of trade associations are an important influence on the decisions made by managers of individual companies.

***GOVERNMENT AGENCIES*** Government agencies are the means by which government regulations are carried out. These agencies may actually use legal action when regulations have been violated. They are important in business decisions because managers must try to determine ahead of time whether a proposed action will be a violation.

***THE LEGAL SYSTEM*** Apart from the powers of government regulatory agencies, the overall legal system influences the decisions of managers. Competitive pressures sometimes make laws governing business look like obstacles to success. Genuine questions of legality may arise, especially when decisions become very complex as a result of trying to balance other conflicting influences.

**PUBLIC INTEREST GROUPS** Increasingly, formal groups representing the general public are playing an important role in business and government decisions. Ralph Nader's organizations, Common Cause, the Urban League, the Sierra Club, Friends of the Earth, and other organizations strive to protect workers, minorities, consumers, and the environment. They inform, educate, lobby, and carry out research. They may actively confront managers with issues they believe are not being properly handled, such as local air pollution. They may use formal or informal boycotts or other pressure tactics.

# 4 BUSINESS RESPONSE
## *A growing social awareness*

The response of many modern business managers to increasing social pressures has begun to be guided by ***enlightened self-interest.*** This is an ethical concept that calls for acting to further one's own best interests while taking into account the effects of one's behavior on others. The concept also includes the notion that when one helps others, one also benefits in the long run. Business efforts to support public education, for instance, not only help society as a whole but also provide better educated employees for the future. Social unrest caused by racial prejudice and poverty is harmful to business. Companies that work to overcome these problems are improving the overall climate for business in the long run. There have been important responses to the need for social responsibility by the business community collectively and by individual companies.

## COLLECTIVE RESPONSE
### *Gradual commitment*

One way of promoting social responsibility within business and professions has been the adoption of ***codes of ethics.*** Industry and professional organizations may specify standards for ethical conduct. Doctors, lawyers, public accountants, and managers who are members of the American Management Association, radio and television stations that are members of the National Association of Broadcasters, and many other individuals and companies agree to accept codes of ethics. These codes set standards for dealing with other companies or professionals in the field, for honesty, and for service to the public. The codes vary as to the extent to which they have been defined to guide specific decisions and the extent to which they are enforceable. It is generally true, in any case, that when the members of a trade or professional organization publicly accept a written code of ethics, the occurrence of severe abuses decreases.

Business organizations have made positive efforts to help other groups concerned with social improvement. The Advertising Council Inc., for example, prepares advertisements and solicits free advertising space from its members to publicize the programs of scores of charitable and public service organizations. Businesses collectively make large do-

---

## *Action Brief*
### RIGHTING A WRONG

*What's the best way to lodge a complaint when you feel that a business has done you wrong, either with faulty merchandise or sloppy service? First of all, don't write an irate letter to the company president. At least that's what one consumer advocate says. "Nastiness gets you nowhere. Instead, try a moderate approach. Make an appeal, not a demand. Anger and sarcasm put the complaint recipient on the defensive," advises Herb Cohen, author of* You Can Negotiate Anything. *Says another expert: "Try to personalize your complaint by placing it face-to-face, rather than on the phone. And start by going through normal customer-complaint channels. At every level, your first choice should be a personal visit, your second a phone call, your third a letter. All discussions, however, should be followed with a letter of confirmation. Get the first and last names of everyone you deal with and keep copies of everything." When all else fails, head for the small-claims court.*

nations to such groups, and individual businesspeople devote much free time and effort to fund-raising and management counseling. The United Fund, for example, is largely supported by the business community.

The National Alliance of Businessmen is a business-based organization. One of its goals is to create training and employment opportunities for the hard-core disadvantaged who have few job skills. These private efforts, partly funded by the federal government, have actually turned many long-term unemployed people into productive workers with permanent jobs.

## INDIVIDUAL COMPANY RESPONSE
*Taking responsibility for their employees and their products*

Individual businesses also often adopt codes of ethics concerning the behavior of their employees. These codes stress honesty and loyalty and sometimes give quite detailed policies on dealing with suppliers, customers, competitors, and employees. They may also prohibit such practices as accepting gifts or entertainment or entering agreements where a conflict of interest might occur.

Some companies have very aggressive hiring and training programs for minorities and women. Some automobile manufacturers, for instance, seek out potential workers in the community, give them complete prejob and on-the-job training, and actively provide opportunities for promotion and advancement. Hundreds of other companies have similar programs. In addition, many businesses give advisory and financial support to local training and retraining efforts and to educational institutions in general.

Many companies, such as Johnson Wax, have set up special departments to identify and resolve consumer problems with their products. Other companies have become deeply involved with community efforts in developing parks, recreation facilities, wildlife preserves, and similar public-use areas. Certainly, individual businesses have spent many millions of dollars to reduce the extent to which their production facilities or their products lower the quality of the environment.

## POLITICAL ACTION COMMITTEES
*Financial aid for friendly legislators*

A somewhat recent development has been the creation by business of **political action committees (PACs)**. These organizations are formed either within a corporation or by a trade association. Their main purpose is to provide a legal way of making contributions to the political campaigns of candidates whom they look upon with favor. Individuals within a company, not the corporation, make the donations to the PACs. By 1985, there were more than 2,500 corporate and association PACs, and they made campaign contributions of nearly $50 million. Among the largest PACs are the American Medical Association, the National Association of Realtors, the National Automobile Dealers Association, the Associated General Contractors of America, and the Independent Insurance Agents of America. The maximum PAC contribution of an individual allowed by law is $15,000.

PACs have been criticized, due to their business relationships, for the potential of raising funds far in excess of what groups of ordinary citizens could raise. As such, their critics contend, PACs may be able to exert an influence politically and socially in far greater proportion than the number of their members would warrant. PACs have now become popular with labor unions and consumer groups, as well.

# 5  CURRENT AND CONTINUING PROBLEMS
*The cost-versus-benefits dilemma stands in the way of solutions*

Despite the fact that businesses are willing to take greater responsibility, important and complex problems continue to beset relations between business and the rest of society.

## THE ENVIRONMENT
*Catching up is costly*

Remedying the damage done by industry to the physical environment and protecting it from further destruction are severe challenges. Pollution from all sources has become such a serious problem today that it threatens life and health.

Air pollution results from the release into the air of gases or solid matter that may be harmful to various kinds of life forms. Automobiles are the largest single source of pollution. They pour hundreds of millions of tons of pollutants into the atmosphere every year. Many industrial processes also cause severe air pollution. Other offenders include public waste treatment plants and trash disposal incinerators.

Water pollution may be caused by a number of sources. Chemicals from industrial processes, chemical fertilizers carried in runoff water from farms, oil spills from offshore wells and tankers, heat from power plants, human waste from inadequate sewage treatment plants, and many other pollutants reach our lakes, rivers, and streams. Many eventually settle in the ocean, threatening the balance of life there.

The land is polluted by pesticides and industrial chemicals that build up in the soil. Billions of beverage containers and millions of tons of paper products litter fields and roadways. Cities and towns create huge mountains of refuse every year, which is buried, burned, or simply allowed to pile up.

Pollution is, in fact, seriously threatening life. The problem is made critical by the tremendous expense of creating and applying solutions. In some instances, the technology needed to prevent or control pollution has not even been invented. In addition, nearly every pollution control effort has economic effects beyond its immediate cost. A factory with devices to reduce pollution produces goods that are more expensive than those produced by a factory without the devices. A farm using less effective pesticides has lower yields than one using more damaging sprays. Truly effective sewage treatment usually means higher municipal taxes. Nonpolluting automobile engines use devices that make cars more expensive to operate.

Pollution problems are slowly being solved. The government, business, and private citizens must make a concerted effort if pollution is to be significantly reduced. The cost of creating and maintaining a safe and clean environment is ultimately borne by all.

## HAZARDOUS WASTES
*A hidden problem surfaces*

A major problem with an industrial society is what to do with the various harmful and polluting wastes it generates. The most spectacular wastes are from nuclear energy plants. But they make up only a small portion of the hazardous chemical wastes resulting from normal processes in the manufacture of chrome and other metal platings for autos and appliances, insecticides, and other products. It is no small problem: New York State, for example, generates more than 100,000 tons of waste a year. Even the prescribed treatment plants for many pollutants end up with noxious waste to be disposed of. The problem is where to put it.

In less sophisticated days, industrial wastes were used in land fills, dumped in abandoned quarries, taken out to sea, shipped to friendly nations abroad, or buried in salt mines. Few people ever asked the question of what ever happened to the waste after it was dumped. We now know that it remains as a hazard for many years, sometimes forever. Most people believe that the benefits from industry far outweigh the disposal problem. But when it comes to finding a place to dump the waste, it is still a problem. New England, for example, did not (in 1982) have a single commercial hazardous waste disposal facility. Everywhere the typical answer from most countries, states, and communities has been, "Put it in someone else's backyard."

Unfortunately, business has not done very much to relieve the dilemma. In many instances, the companies handling hazardous materials have denied or understated the potential for damage. After the disaster of poisonous fumes leakage at Bhopal, India, for example (some 2,000 people were killed), Union Carbide gave great assurances to its domestic neighbors that such a thing could not happen in the United States. Only a short time afterward, however, a cloud of toxic gases leaked from a Carbide plant in West Virginia, causing the hospitalization of 32 residents. A month later, toxic gas leaks occurred at another Carbide plant.

The chemical industry now acknowledges the danger inherent in its processes, but cites its outstanding record of safety within its plants. It has the fewest on-job injuries in all manufacturing. The industry also calls attention to the dramatic decrease in transportation-related incidents, like a ruptured tank car at a train wreck in Arizona and a tanker-truck fire near the nation's capital, both of which caused massive evacuations of local residents. Such accidents have dropped from a high of 10,070 in 1981 to about half that figure today. Nevertheless, even this number of incidents is alarming.

In the past, industries whose processes harbor potential problems have, perhaps understandably, been reluctant to talk about these dangers. Beginning in 1986, however, a provision of the Occupational Safety and Health Act (OSHA) enforces the so-called right-to-know rule. This requires chemical companies to disclose to OSHA the hazards associated with their products. If the industry fails to comply, not only with the letter of this requirement but also with the spirit of it, harsher regulation can be predicted to enforce a greater social responsibility.

# LAND USE AND QUESTIONS ABOUT GROWTH
*The rights of private ownership are at issue* ━━━━━━━━━━━

As the United States continues to develop, available land becomes scarce and the uses of private property begin to interfere with each other. The problem of controlling the use of land without distorting the concept of private ownership can only grow worse as population increases and industrialization progresses.

The need to manage land use arises from two principal causes:

■   Many areas of the country have developed to such an extent that there simply is not enough land available for all uses. This creates a need to use land more efficiently and with less waste.

■   Different ways of using land do not always work well together. For example, a metal-stamping plant 50 feet away from a hospital may interfere with proper operation of the hospital. In order to prevent such interference, specific uses of land must be restricted to certain areas.

Attempts by governments to manage land use decrease the control individual owners have over their property. This is a source of conflict. However, without control, many areas of the country would rapidly become unlivable. The usual response to this issue is for local governments to enact ordinances giving the government limited control of land use. These *zoning ordinances* restrict the use of land within defined areas to specified purposes. For instance, a zone might be created where only single-family houses are allowed and another, for only heavy industry. Governments also use their powers of taxation to encourage or discourage certain kinds of land uses. For example, a lower tax rate for agricultural land encourages farming.

The problems of real estate development and land use have grown so severe in some areas that a separate issue has emerged: efforts are being made to prevent further growth altogether. In some areas, citizens' groups and governments have made attempts to slow or stop growth. This clearly conflicts with business goals, since growth is nearly always desired by individual companies and by the business community as a whole. However, if the quality of life suffers enough as a result of growth, actions may be taken to restrict such "progress."

# MULTINATIONAL OPERATIONS
*Cultural differences are narrowing* ━━━━━━━━━━━

Many practical and ethical problems that result from international business operations have already been mentioned. Bribery, kickbacks, and other practices have flourished in overseas operations on a greater scale than has been common in domestic operations. Two factors contribute to the problem: (1) the growth of international operations resulting in increased competition and more opportunities for unethical practices and (2) a more widespread acceptance of a common standard of behavior arising from cross-cultural contacts and influences.

In 1977, the United States Congress moved to put a check on bribery by domestic companies abroad by passing the Foreign Corrupt Practices

Act of 1977. This makes it a crime for any individual or corporation to make or promise payments to foreign nationals, agencies, governments, officials, or political parties "in order to obtain or retain business." The law is enforced by the Security Exchange Commission, which can impose fines of up to $1,000,000 on corporations and up to $10,000 and/or imprisonment for up to 5 years on company officials.

## MINORITIES AND WOMEN
*Progress has been made, but there is still a long way to go* ___

Opportunities for minorities and women have been increasingly promoted in the business community in the past decade. Progress has clearly been made in select occupations. For example, in 1972 about 42 percent of all office managers were female. The figure was 53.4 percent by 1983. Just 1.6 percent of all sales managers positions were held by minorities in 1972. By 1983 the figure had risen to 7 percent. However, the problem still remains unsolved. Unemployment is much higher among minorities than among other groups. Educational opportunities are still limited. Prejudice and hatred are still commonplace. Most career opportunities are still very restricted for women. Many vocations, particularly those with a high level of responsibility and large salaries, are virtually closed to almost everyone but white males.

However, progress is in sight. Government-enforced programs, like affirmative action plans, are reducing barriers. Business's growing concern for the development and training of employees is also improving the lot of women and minorities. As managers and other professionals gain experience in working with them, more top-level positions and new occupations are likely to open up for these groups.

## CONFLICT OF VALUES
*The creation of wealth is still business's greatest responsibility* ___

There are several sides to the issue of what business's responsibility to society should be. One viewpoint is that business must subordinate its objective of creating profits to the general needs and interests of society at large. Another viewpoint is that the creation of wealth is still business's greatest responsibility, and concern about ecology, conservation, and society's well-being should not take priority over this primary objective. Still another viewpoint is expressed by people like the late Harold Smiddy, founder of the General Electric Academy of Management at Croton, New York. He believed that it is unrealistic to make business firms responsible not only for the generation of wealth and all the values it brings but also for restricting its own efforts in the pursuit of its goals. It is better, he believed, for a nation that advocates free enterprise to employ the same kinds of checks and balances in business that it does in government. In Smiddy's opinion, the community at large should establish laws that regulate business in the best interests of the people, and the government should enforce those regulations. Regardless of the wisdom of this philosophy or its chance of prevailing in the future, at the present time, and probably for a long time to come, people who wish to move ahead in business can be expected to accept the profit motive as its main impetus.

# Key Concepts

1. Business ethics is a collection of principles and rules of conduct for carrying on business in a way that is fair both to those who deal directly with a company and to the community.

2. Managers today must consider the diverse, often conflicting, attitudes and expectations of employees, customers, suppliers, competitors, investors, creditors, and society as a whole.

3. Business decisions are made in an environment of pressure brought about by groups representing their own interests. These forces include labor unions, government agencies, the legal system, and public interest groups.

4. Business's response to these pressures and expectations is demonstrated by the establishment of codes of ethics, charitable and community leadership efforts, educational support, programs to develop opportunities for minorities and women, pollution control programs, and in other ways.

5. In spite of business's growing social consciousness, serious problems remain. Difficulties with pollution, land use, opposition to growth, multinational operations, and opportunities for minorities and women are still basically unsolved.

# Review Questions

1. Define, identify, or explain each of the following key terms or phrases, found on the pages indicated.

>   *business ethics (p. 557)*
>   *code of ethics (p. 564)*
>   *consumerism (p. 559)*
>   *enlightened self-interest (p. 564)*
>   *ethics (p. 557)*
>   *political action committees (PACs) (p. 565)*
>   *whistle-blower (p. 562)*
>   *zoning ordinance (p. 568)*

2. What is business ethics? What is its relationship to law?

3. Contrast the general ethical beliefs of nineteenth-century business with an equivalent principle in the twentieth century.

4. What three expectations are especially important to employees now?

5. What is consumerism, and why is it important in many business decisions?

6. What two main factors must be balanced when businesses are deciding how much positive action to take toward improving general social conditions?

7. What role do industry trade associations play in business ethics?

8. In what ways do political action committees (PACs) resemble consumer organizations?

9. Do you think enlightened self-interest is better than any other kind of self-interest? Explain.

10. Why do each of the following present a problem for business and for society?
    a. Environmental pollution
    b. Land use
    c. Economic growth
    d. Multinational operations
    e. Opportunities for minorities and women

# Case Critique 24-1
## The High-Living Retail Buyer

This is a true story, and it happened recently. Nevertheless, we won't use the actual name of the person involved. Edward F. Riley was a buyer of jeans and other sportswear for a southwestern chain of retail clothing shops. His employer began to be concerned about Riley's style of living when he bought a 35-foot motorboat. It didn't seem warranted by the nature of Riley's job. When Riley was unable to provide a credible explanation, the company got a court order to have Riley's bank safe-deposit box opened and examined. In it were more than $70,000 in cash, stock certificates, a Rolex watch, two diamonds, an 18-karat gold bracelet, 13 gold coins, and a 6-ounce gold bar. In addition, Riley owned three homes and a Mercedes Sport coupe. He also held many shares of stock in a company that was a major supplier of clothing to his employer.

Investigation showed that the source of Riley's good fortune was a number of bribes received from supplier firms. Here's how it worked. Riley had bought thousands of blue jeans the previous year at $9.75 a pair. The next year, he placed an even larger order but negotiated a lower price with the supplier, $9.00 a pair. That began to look pretty good to Riley's boss. However, the story sours when another clothes maker tells Riley that he can deliver the identical pants for $8.75 each. Riley then goes back to the first supplier and the first supplier, in order to retain his order at $9.00 a pair, offers to give Riley the difference between the two prices. The deal is closed, and the first vendor sends Riley the 25 cents difference for each pair of the 10,000 jeans in the order, or $2,500. The bribe is not detected because Riley sets up a phony company that serves as a paper intermediary in the transaction. The original vendor simply charges the 25 cents on his books as "an agency commission." Riley repeated this kind of negotiation over and over, as did six of the other buyers who worked for the same company. In court, the company claimed that Riley accepted a total of $525,000 in cash and gifts and his colleagues, more than $735,000.

Riley's defense, to himself at least, went something like this. "I negotiated a price that was 75 cents under last year's price. That should make me a hero with my boss. I deserve the 'bonus' for making the deal." Riley's boss disagreed with his view. He said, "When manufacturers feel they have a buyer in their pocket, they'll dump extra merchandise on him because he's afraid to refuse. The retailer then gets stuck with an oversupply of unsalable merchandise and has to discount it at a loss to clear his shelves. Furthermore, dishonest buyers don't demand routine discounts, such as advertising allowances and other considerations, as honest buyers do."

1. Who do you think is more to blame for this practice, the buyer or the vending firm? Why?
2. In what ways can consumers be hurt by such practices?
3. In order to prevent such practices, many retailers ask their buyers to take polygraph (lie detector) tests periodically and also employ private investigators to detect any radical improvements in their buyers' life-styles. Some firms simply fire employees for such dishonesty. Others prosecute them. What is your reaction to the fairness of these preventive measures?

SOURCE: Hank Gilman, "Bribery of Retail Buyers Is Called Pervasive," *The Wall Street Journal*, April 1, 1985, p. 6.

# Case Critique 24-2
## Nature's Way

There's a skyscraper jungle in Maryland. It is perched, literally, on the water's edge. It is Ocean City, once an island of broad, sandy, scenic beaches on the Atlantic Ocean. Today, it is described by environmentalists as a prime example of tax-supported beach destruction. Who are the vandals who have created this monstrosity? They are mainly real estate developers and their construction-company partners who have packed the beach with high-rise condominiums, hotels, motels, and expensive restaurants. The developers have been criticized as greedy businesspeople, and they may be. But their most avid customers are thousands of well-to-do Americans who want to live right on the sea's shore.

Not only do these buildings obstruct the view of the ocean and crowd the narrow strip of beach that remains, but they also create an economic problem from which their proprietors and owners seek federal relief. All over the nation's seacoast, the Ocean City pattern repeats itself, from New Jersey to New Orleans. As the ocean rises at about 1 foot a century, it covers anywhere from 1,000 to 2,000 feet of shoreline. As a consequence, owners of commercial and rental property see their basements inundated and their frontages battered by the high waves of winter storms.

Property owners typically look for protection from massive sea walls to hold back the ocean or from groins (long fingers of masonry extending outward into the sea) to induce sand deposits. Neither system works very well or for very long. In fact, it has been demonstrated time and again during this century that both methods tend to accelerate the ultimate and permanent destruction of a beach. Since such methods are incredibly expensive, the property owners ask for government aid, especially from the federal government. Louisiana, for example, has embarked on a $40 million program to place such armor on its beaches. Ocean City plans to go the same route. Estimates are that the cost of a beach "nourishment" program that moves sand from the ocean shelf onto the shore is upwards of $26 million, and that it would last only until the next major storm. Nevertheless, Ocean City continues to allow, and even to encourage, beachfront construction.

1. Who do you think is most to blame for this condition? The real estate developers and construction companies? The private citizens who purchase or rent these properties? The local officials who issue permits for continued construction?
2. Should taxpayers who do not live near or regularly use oceanfront properties be expected to share the burden of protecting them? Why?
3. What do you think might be the best way to provide optimum use and enjoyment of the nation's coastline with its maximum protection and care?

SOURCE: Orrin H. Pilkey, "The Twilight of Ocean City," *The Washington Post*, May 26, 1985, pp. C1–2.

## Computer security and professionalism

In an information society, the value of a company is often wrapped up in its information—technical information and information related to its customers. This puts computer security at a premium. Security systems must guard against both outside and inside invaders. While a certain amount of insider misuse of a computer system represents unmitigated theft, the majority of cases are rather mundane. According to a Data Processing Management Association (DPMA) survey, nearly half of all cases involve things like game playing, using the computer for personal work, or altering records. *Program abuse*—copying or changing records—accounts for 24 percent. *Data abuse*—diverting information to unauthorized persons—amounts to 22 percent. *Hardware abuse*—damaging or stealing computer equipment—is last with 5 percent.

According to DPMA, motivation for internal abuse was fairly evenly divided among ignorance of professional conduct (27 percent); misguided playfulness (25 percent); personal gain (25 percent); and maliciousness or revenge (22 percent). Much of this abuse could be prevented, says the association, by establishing work rules and professional standards for those who have rightful access to the system. As a last measure, polygraph testing may be needed.

*SOURCE:* Sam Dickey, "Is Getting In Getting Out of Control?" *Today's Office,* August, 1985, pp. 29–34.

## Office automation damaging to your health?

Researchers are accumulating evidence that video display terminals (VDTs) are free from radiation dangers. On the other hand, they identify health problems associated with the stress of regular computer operation. Time spent at a terminal does not seem to be the critical factor. What is more important is the type of work performed by the computer operator. Clerical workers are most disturbed, because of rigid work procedures combined with the demand for high production output. In contrast, professionals are bothered much less because they have greater flexibility in their jobs and more control over their tasks. The key factor in managing computer-generated stress, says one expert, is the degree of control the users have over their jobs.

*SOURCE:* Edward Wakin, "The Jury's Still Out on Office Systems Safety," *Today's Office,* September 1985, pp. 39–40.

# *Choosing and Pursuing a Career in Business*

The study of business can pay impressive benefits. Among other valuable returns, it prepares you to obtain a better, more rewarding job and to look forward to a more promising career. There is often a direct relationship between the extent of your educational preparation and the occupations open to you. Figure A-1 illustrates some of these relationships. In each of the fields examined (service and administrative, for example), the variety and attractiveness of the jobs available increase as the applicant's educational level moves upward. Job choices are fewest at the high school level and improve markedly with a degree from a private business or technical school, or from a community college. The job horizon becomes even more varied and attractive for 4-year college graduates.

## THE BIG PICTURE

### *A growing, but selective, job market*

The United States economy adds about 300,000 new jobs every month. The great majority of these are found in the service sector, although jobs in manufacturing are growing at a faster rate than in the past decade. By looking at a sampling of ten important industries, you can see (from Figure A-2) that retailing continues to offer the most job opportunities (more than 21 million by 1995), with jobs in health care, high-tech industries, and banking and financial fields growing to more than 5 million each. The increase in manufacturing jobs is taking place in high-technology industries, printing and publishing, and computer and electronics fields, not in the traditional American industries like textiles and autos.

**HOT—AND COLD—JOBS** Some jobs are growing in number faster than others. It may be no surprise that computer programmers will be in high demand, but so will data processors, computer operators, and medical assistants. Openings for routine stenographic work are on the decline, however, as are the many relatively un-skilled jobs—like foundry laborer and garment worker. It is apparent that the hot jobs of the future are those that require education and high-level skills. Relatively unskilled work, requiring little education, will present fewer and fewer job opportunities.

**FINDING YOUR NICHE** It may seem like a puzzle as you try to translate the bare statistics about job opportunities to find those that you feel are most appropriate for you. For this reason, it will be helpful for you to first consider a number of general approaches to job selection. These considerations should, in turn, lead you to a selection of more specific opportunities that best suit your interests, attitudes, and capabilities. For example, in searching for your particular job niche, you might give serious thought to any of these six approaches:

1. *Getting your foot in the door.* This approach implies that getting a job—almost any kind of job—is more important early in your career than which particular job you get.

   *Working part-time* in a particular field, like retailing or banking, will help you to improve your skills and provide valuable insights into business. Part-time work will also help to tell you whether or not you like the kind of work available in that field. Many firms advertise for part-time help during peak seasons. If you have already acquired identifiable skills (such as typing, recordkeeping, or data entry), there are a number of service companies that "rent out" skilled people to other firms as *"temporaries."*

   Working during your *holidays and vacations*, wherever you can find employment, also helps to give you a feel for what different kinds of industries and jobs are like. At one major department store, for example, more than 10 percent of Easter and Christmas salespeople are asked to stay on in permanent jobs.

   *Internships* are especially valuable in finding your niche. Internships may be hard to obtain and often go

| | High school diploma | High school diploma or on-the-job training or apprenticeship | Junior college or private business school diploma | Four or more years of college |
|---|---|---|---|---|
| **Service and Administration Occupations** | Building custodian<br>Dispatcher<br>Driver<br>Mail carrier<br>Guard<br>Maintenance worker<br>Receptionist<br>Stenographer<br>Switchboard operator<br>Typist | Administrative secretary<br>Cashier<br>Clerk<br>Data preparation clerk<br>General secretary | Administrative assistant<br>Employee relations assistant<br>Executive secretary<br>Legal assistant<br>Occupational therapy assistant<br>Personnel administrator<br>Personnel assistant<br>Purchasing specialist<br>Record administrator<br>Sales specialist | Career/Placement counselor<br>Corporate lawyer<br>Educational specialist<br>Employee relations specialist<br>Industrial hygienist<br>Industrial psychologist<br>Labor relations specialist<br>Legal administrator<br>Occupational therapist<br>Personnel specialist<br>Public relations specialist<br>Purchasing agent<br>Salesperson |
| **Scientific Technical and Production Occupations** | Electroplater<br>Factory assembler<br>Machinery operator<br>Mechanic's helper<br>Millwright<br>Mobile equipment operator<br>Production painter | Appliance repairer<br>Carpenter<br>Computer operator<br>Electrician<br>Electronics assembler<br>Machine repairer<br>Machine tool operator<br>Machinist, Mechanic<br>Tool and die maker<br>Welder | Computer programmer<br>Computer technician<br>Drafter<br>Engineering technician<br>Industrial artist<br>Science technician | Application engineer<br>Automation specialist<br>Chemist<br>Computer designer<br>Computer scientist<br>Design engineer<br>Engineer<br>Engineering technologist<br>Field engineer<br>Industrial designer<br>Manufacturing engineer<br>Physicist<br>Sales engineer<br>Systems analyst |
| **Financial and Analytical Occupations** | File clerk<br>Stock clerk<br>Typist | Accounting clerk<br>Bookkeeper<br>Business machine operator<br>Data preparation clerk<br>Key punch operator<br>Secretary<br>Shipping and receiving clerk<br>Statistical clerk<br>Teletypist | Accounting technician<br>Computer programmer<br>Financial assistant<br>Research assistant | Accountant<br>Auditor<br>Economist<br>Financial analyst<br>Market research analyst<br>Patent lawyer<br>Statistician<br>Systems analyst |
| **Art, Design, and Communication Occupations** | Composing room worker<br>Printing press assistant<br>Typist | Bookbinder<br>Display worker<br>Electrotyper and stereotyper<br>Lithographic worker<br>Photo lab worker<br>Printing press operator<br>Secretary<br>Typographer | Drafter<br>Illustrator<br>Industrial artist<br>Photographer<br>Proofreader<br>TV & film technician | Advertising copywriter<br>Art director<br>Editor<br>Industrial designer<br>Public relations specialist<br>Technical writer<br>TV & film director |

Figure A-1 Occupational opportunities related to Educational Achievement.

to the better students, but they do provide an inside track to experience and future employment. Internships are usually 10- to 12-week summer programs offered by progressive firms. These programs allow students to work for good pay, often side by side with professionals who help the intern get a "hands-on" feel of jobs in that company.

2. *Mind or body work?* Many people like jobs that stretch the mind—working with numbers or ideas. Other people work best with their hands, using them skillfully to manipulate tools and machinery. The greatest growth in jobs, however, has been in those requiring mind work, or at least a combination of

thinking *and* hand skills. Mind (or knowledge) work typically emphasizes speaking and writing skills, human relations, creativity, planning, and problem solving. In the high-tech industries, especially, even the manipulative hand skills must be supplemented by creative and problem-solving skills.

*Computer literacy* seems to go hand in hand with all the better new jobs, whether mind- or body-oriented. In manufacturing, for example, automation is here to stay, and automation is almost inseparable from the computer system. In construction activities, too, job schedulers now depend almost entirely upon computer-related programs.

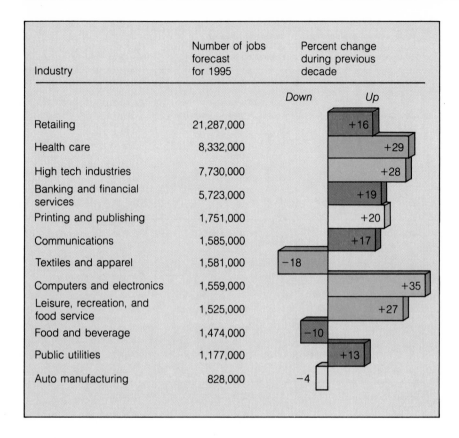

| Industry | Number of jobs forecast for 1995 | Percent change during previous decade |
|---|---|---|
| | | Down / Up |
| Retailing | 21,287,000 | +16 |
| Health care | 8,332,000 | +29 |
| High tech industries | 7,730,000 | +28 |
| Banking and financial services | 5,723,000 | +19 |
| Printing and publishing | 1,751,000 | +20 |
| Communications | 1,585,000 | +17 |
| Textiles and apparel | 1,581,000 | −18 |
| Computers and electronics | 1,559,000 | +35 |
| Leisure, recreation, and food service | 1,525,000 | +27 |
| Food and beverage | 1,474,000 | −10 |
| Public utilities | 1,177,000 | +13 |
| Auto manufacturing | 828,000 | −4 |

Figure A-2 Size and growth of job markets in important industries.

Another aspect of the mind-versus-body choice is the *staff-versus-line* distinction. Line jobs often carry with them more authority and a visibility that leads to advancement. Staff positions, which offer services or advice to the line departments, are growing in importance, however, and also in compensation. Staff jobs are typically associated with personnel, communications, health services, planning, and quality control departments.

3. *Exploring the "unknown" jobs.* There is an understandable tendency for most job seekers to go after popular, visible jobs. These include secretarial and retail sales positions, office clerical and bank telling jobs, airline reservation agent and motel desk jobs, factory assembly and construction supervision jobs, industrial purchasing and retail buyer positions, and a host of others. Less conspicuous, but often just as attractive and well-paying, are the "unknown" jobs, often unique to a particular company or industry. Such positions include production assistants in factories, publishing houses, and advertising agencies, urban planners, legal assistants, and tax preparers, insurance agents, manufacturer's sales representatives, order expediters, and traffic coordinators, construction estimators, direct mail analysts, hotel utility clerks, and hundreds more.

4. *Spreading a broad net.* It's a mistake to narrow down your job choices too soon, or to reject a particular job or industry without giving it a closer look. There are dozens of major, and hundreds of minor, industries. Each has its own set of opportunities and demands. Each of the following industries or occupations, for example, has, at one time or another, been viewed as unattractive or as a "dead end." Yet, any one of these might just be right for you:

■ *Manufacturing.* This downtrodden industry is experiencing a rebirth. It now needs people who can devise better production methods and more flexible production schedules and who can manage people more effectively. There are many new types of jobs being created in inventory control, employee training, quality control, and employee relations.

■ *Banking.* Deregulation caused banking and related financial services fields to grow at an unprecedented pace. The routine and most visible position of bank teller, however, is on the wane. Banking jobs involving computer technology are on the rise. The side of banking other than deposits is becoming more complex and important. This has opened new jobs in credit and loan management. Good jobs there require analytical skills, especially financial ones, an ability to perform calculations quickly, and, surprisingly, persuasion and sales skills in order to attract and hold new commercial borrowers.

■ *Television.* Behind *The Bill Cosby Show*, *Miami Vice*, and *Hill Street Blues* are thousands of nonacting jobs. Off-camera jobs in television include all those people who provide administrative support—programming, sales, marketing, accounting, clerical services, and public affairs. The work in television, however, is fast-paced, varied, and very competitive.

■ *Real estate.* This job market goes far beyond the typical real estate broker, or salesperson. Large commercial properties—like office buildings, apartment houses, and shopping malls—require property managers and their related staffs to supervise these projects while they are under construction and to manage and maintain operations after completion.

■ *Food industry.* This industry is the largest employer in the nation. Its fastest growing segment is food service, which ranges from luxury restaurants to fast-food outlets, vending machines, and institutional services at hospitals, schools, and military bases. While the majority of jobs in food service are semiskilled, jobs for restaurant managers are predicted to grow by 50 percent to 450,000 in the next decade. There are many other attractive occupations in food service, too, such as food purchasing, quality control, and distribution. Since the food service business does not have a tradition of educational preparation, business students with technical or community college educations can often find ready employment there.

5. *Small or large company?* Job security, good working conditions, and opportunities for advancement without changing employers make working for a large company very attractive. There are drawbacks, of course, such as the pressure to conform, reels of red tape to put up with, and jobs that may be narrowly specialized. Work for a small company is likely to present an opposing set of advantages and disadvantages. Pay and benefits are often less attractive, as are job security and opportunities for advancement. On the other hand, small-company work is usually more varied, and thus less monotonous, with a minimum of red tape and a great deal of informality.

6. *To be your own boss.* The dream of many people is to own and operate their own business. Admittedly, *entrepreneurship* is on the rise in the United States. It takes an unusual person, however, often one with unusual financial resources, too, to start and succeed in his or her own business. The risks are great, the hours long, and the pressures heavy. The rewards can be great, of course, in a self-fulfilling way as well as monetarily. On average, however, it would appear that it is wiser to work first for someone else, preferably in a business that is well-run, so as to gain practical experience. If, after that, a capable individual fully understands what it really takes to make a profit—revenues that exceed expenses, month after month—then he or she may be better prepared to try to fly alone in the business world.

# YOUR JOB SEARCH

*A PLAN AND A TIMETABLE* One thing is certain: few jobs will seek you out. Accordingly, you should develop your own unique job-search plan well in advance. It should be accompanied by a firm schedule, or timetable, for implementing the plan. Your find-a-job plan should include the following steps:

1. Check out the employment services offered by your school or college. Its placement office may provide help in locating potential employers or scheduling on-campus interviews with company recruiters, offer advice about preparing a résumé, and conduct practice sessions in job interviewing.

2. Join student organizations that have a vocational orientation so that you can share the ideas of others investigating similar professions.

3. Research five occupations or industries that seem attractive to you. Ask for help from your professors or school librarian. This means reading annual financial reports of companies in the industry, studying the annual *Occupational Outlook Handbook* of the U.S. Department of Labor, and reviewing relevant reports from your local chamber of commerce and your state and national departments of commerce. Try to see whether the information you gather matches your capabilities and interests. If not, investigate another five fields.

4. Visit your library to identify trade organizations that may provide literature and leads about jobs in a particular industry. Study the various trade journals and business magazines serving the industries that might be able to use your knowledge and skills. This will give you a feel for the problems and opportunities in that industry, and familiarize you with the kind of equipment and materials it uses.

5. Prepare your résumé (see the example below). Make it clear, concise, and descriptive of your capabilities and potential.

6. Activate your job search. Do so by (1) reading and earmarking the help-wanted advertisements in your local newspaper, (2) scanning *The Yellow Pages* of your telephone book to identify local firms that might employ your skills, (3) checking out current employment opportunities with your local, state, or federal employment agency, (4) contacting your local chamber of commerce for names and addresses of prospective employers (5) making direct calls at the employment or personnel offices of local firms, and (6) writing letters of application (to which your résumé is attached) to the more distant firms that sound promising.

7. Prepare a weekly search schedule. This should set aside specific days of the week and times of day during which you will (1) update your potential sources and/or (2) apply in person for job interviews. Persistence pays off. You may have to make more than 50 contacts to secure the kind of position you want.

*YOUR UNIQUE JOB CRITERIA* You may not be able to find a job that exactly suits you, but you should begin your job search with a list of go, no-go criteria. That is, you should identify, realistically, those things that you absolutely expect from a job and those things that you would find totally unacceptable. For instance, what are your attitudes toward each of the following?

1. *Pay*.   What minimum will you accept?

2. *Working conditions*.   Must the job be white-collar, at a desk, and in a clean environment? Or are you willing to get your hands dirty, at least for a while?

3. *Benefits*.   How many holidays and how long a vacation do you expect? What importance do you place on paid insurance (health and life), pension plans, etc.?

4. *Variety of work*.   Must you be offered a chance to do many things? Are you easily bored by routine work? Would you rather specialize than be called upon to wear many hats, including sweeping the floor if necessary?

5. *Learning possibilities*.   Do you expect your employer to help you improve your skills and learn other ones? Or doesn't this matter; you'll find a way to acquire knowledge and skills on your own?

6. *Skills transferability*.   Will the skills you learn on this job be valued by other companies and help to make you more employable as a result?

7. *Advancement potential*.   Is this an important factor to you at this time? Will it be later? Do you want to stay with this company, or are you viewing this job as a stepping-stone to something better elsewhere?

8. *Industry*.   Does the job possibility reflect the kind of industry you want to stay with? Which industries hold a great appeal for you at this time and which ones turn you off completely?

9. *People*.   What kinds of people do you prefer to work with? Are there some kinds of people or situations that you find unacceptable?

10. *Location*.   How far will you, or can you, afford to travel each day to work? Are there certain geographic areas, local or nationwide, where you wouldn't work? Will you relocate, if necessary?

**A WINNING RÉSUMÉ**  You should build your résumé with care. Its purpose is to communicate—quickly—your ability to do a good job for a potential employer. If the résumé says enough of the right things about you, it will capture an employer's interest to the extent that you are offered a job interview.

A winning résumé not only reports your capabilities and potential but also demonstrates your ability to communicate what is important to others. It should clearly get to the heart of what makes you tick, what makes you an especially good job candidate. Your résumé should, if possible, contain concrete, credible examples that show that you can produce results. A brief reporting of your educational achievements, accomplishments (if you can document them), and extracurricular activities helps to verify your implied claims that you would make a valuable employee.

A good résumé should be laid out in a businesslike pattern and be clean, brief, and easy to read. There should be no spelling, punctuation, or grammatical errors. Your résumé should contain only information relevant to your job search. It should clearly and honestly represent you. Remember, your résumé *is* you until you have a chance to present yourself in person.

Formats for résumés have not been standardized, but Figure A-3 illustrates a well-designed résumé with all the essential elements included.

**PLANNING YOUR CAMPAIGN**  Experts in job search advise the following:

■  Get in touch with as many employers as you can afford to contact. Do not rely exclusively on the want ads.

■  Answer advertisements promptly. Many openings are filled before the advertisement has stopped running.

■  Do not expect too much from "blind" advertisements; experience shows that the chances of finding a job through them are slim.

■  Be cautious about answering "no experience necessary" ads. They often mean that the job is unattractive and hard to fill because of low pay, poor working conditions, or straight commission salary.

■  Look for unsolicited work. Get a list of firms in your neighborhood from a bank, chamber of commerce, or *The Yellow Pages*. Fill out applications at personnel offices. Let friends, relatives, and others know of your job search. Informal methods like this are often fruitful.

■  Be diligent in making out applications, seeking interviews, and following up. Persistence is a strong tool for prying open job opportunities.

■  Be ready to accept something less than the perfect job in order to get a foothold, especially with a good employer. Most people have to perform work that has its menial, tedious, and unattractive facets so that they can show their potential. Good jobs are obtained by building on a record of sound performance in lesser jobs.

**PREPARING FOR THE INTERVIEW**  Many a job interview is lost before the candidate walks in the door. A successful interview requires planning, research, and rehearsal. Days before your interview, you should:

1. *Find out more about the potential employer*.   Consult your library or chamber of commerce, or someone who works at the interviewing company. Write for a descriptive brochure. You'll want to know a little about the company's history, its products or services, financial condition, marketing policies, and reputation in the community.

2. *Review your own strengths and weaknesses*.   Be prepared to put your strongest values forward—as they relate to the job in question. Be prepared also to defend your weaknesses. You must be ready to acknowledge, for example, that you may have little experience in that particular line of work. If you are prepared, however, you can counter with a reply that this has not been a serious problem in the past since you are a diligent and attentive learner.

3. *Anticipate the kinds of questions you might be asked*.   Generally speaking, interview questions fall into two categories:

| | |
|---|---|
| NAME: | Wilma Kaye Nagel |
| ADDRESS: | 106 North Main Street<br>Valleyville, Virginia 22999 |
| TELEPHONE: | (703) 555-9090 |
| CAREER INTERESTS: | Responsible position in some aspect of retail merchandising. |
| EDUCATION: | **1986 to the present**—Blue Ridge Community College, Weyers Cave, Virginia. Have accumulated 64 credits toward Associate degree in applied science with major in merchandising. Expect to graduate in June 1988. |
| | **1982 to 1986**—Turner Ashley High School, Valleyville, Virginia. Graduated with diploma in general education; electives in retailing, typing, and Spanish. |
| SCHOLASTIC ACHIEVEMENTS: | Graduated in top 25 percent of high school class of 345 students. Achieved grade point average of 3.25 out of possible 4 points. |
| EXTRACURRICULAR ACTIVITIES: | **College**—Chairperson of Spring Festival; member of Phi Beta Lambda; worked an average of 15 hours per week since date of enrollment. |
| | **High school**—Captain of swim team; vice president of junior class; held part-time job as cashier in department store from 1982 to 1984. |
| WORK EXPERIENCE: | **February 1986 to the present**—Part-time assistant merchandise manager, Z-MART Clothing Company, Harrisonburg, Virginia. Duties include checking stock in and out for sportswear department, supervising two salespersons, and displaying merchandise. |
| | **July 1984 to February 1986**—Part-time salesclerk, Rosaline Fashions, Bridgewater, Virginia. Duties included arranging stock, waiting on customers, and taking inventory. |
| | **1982 to 1984**—Part-time checkout cashier during Christmas rush, Mid-Way Department Store, Hainesville, Virginia. |
| | **1980 to 1982**—Self-employed, doing garden and lawn work during the summers. |
| OUTSIDE INTERESTS: | Volunteer, 3 hours per week, at Chilton General Hospital, Bridgewater, Virginia. Hobbies include swimming, interior design, and carpentry. |
| REFERENCES: | Lawrence R. Buxton<br>Instructor, Merchandising Department<br>Blue Ridge Community College<br>Weyers Cave, Virginia |
| | Rhonda F. Feinberg<br>Store manager, Z-MART Clothing Company<br>Harrisonburg, Virginia |
| | Marlene H. Duchamp<br>Coordinator of Volunteers, Chilton General Hospital<br>Bridgewater, Virginia |

Figure A-3 Sample résumé.

■ *Substance questions.* These seek out concrete information about you, your education, and your work history. Reply to them in short, specific sentences. Be concise; you'll want to guard against rambling. Typical questions are, "Tell me about your background," "What are your major accomplishments?" "How does your educational background qualify you for this job?" "Why should we hire you?"

■ *Poise questions.* These are asked by interviewers to judge your personality, your ability to reply under stress, and the extent to which you would fit in with the people at that company and its philosophy. There usually are no "right" or "wrong" answers to these questions, so try to answer directly and honestly. Often, the interviewer doesn't care so much about *what* you say so much as *how* you answer. Obviously, don't get angry. Don't allow yourself to become too negative. Your objective will be to project a pleasant, positive outlook. Typical questions here are, "What kind of people do you enjoy working with?" "What kind of work have you found most unsatisfactory?" "How would you handle a disagreement between you and another employee?" "Tell me about your worst boss."

4. *Rehearse your interview beforehand.* Like an actor before a play, a golfer practicing a swing, or a student getting ready for a test, it will help to rehearse beforehand what your answers and behavior during the interview will be. Have a friend ask you the questions outlined above. Try out your answers by speaking aloud. Record them on tape to see how they sound to you, whether the tone of your voice reflects confidence. Think through what you want to say and revise your answers so that you can make the most concise and effective replies.

**YOUR INTERVIEW STRATEGY** Some authorities describe the job interview as "the 60 most critical minutes of your life." That may be an exaggeration, but it points up the wisdom in having a preplanned strategy for making the most of a brief period of time. You won't be able to control the interview; the employer will. Nevertheless, you can contribute greatly to its success by following a strategy that places you and your capabilities in the best possible light. For example, a winning strategy will be based on the following precepts:

1. *Make a good appearance.* Neatness in dress and care in grooming are absolutely necessary. Generally speaking, your clothing choice ought to be conservative so as not to distract from your person or from what you will be saying.

2. *Be on time.* It is even better if you arrive a few minutes early. This gives you a chance to catch your breath and to become comfortable in strange surroundings. If kept waiting for the interview, don't be impatient or demonstrate nervousness. It's not unusual for someone to observe your behavior while you're waiting.

3. *Take advantage of the "warm up" period.* Most interviewers use the first few minutes to get a "feel" of your personality before they proceed to the substance questions. During this period, try to relax yourself and to tune your ear to the voice and manner of the interviewer.

4. *Be pleasant and cordial.* As in most human exchanges, a smile goes a long way in gaining acceptance. As a job applicant, you are a guest. Your behavior should readily indicate appreciation for the opportunity to present yourself for consideration. Don't approach the interview as an imposition placed upon you or as an opportunity to debate.

5. *Project a positive image.* This can be done in a number of ways. Shake hands firmly. Look the interviewer in the eye in friendly fashion. Listen attentively. If you miss a question or do not understand one, ask that it be repeated: this demonstrates your interest. Don't be afraid to display enthusiasm. Take your time, if needed, to think through what you want to say before answering difficult questions. Try to keep your replies short. Don't smoke, even if a cigarette is offered you.

6. *Ask the interviewer questions.* If you have done your homework, you can ask questions that demonstrate the validity of your interest in the company. Don't dwell on pay and fringe benefits, but do ask about the company's product or service line, its plans for growth, and what the normal promotional paths might be for a person of your qualifications.

7. *Differentiate yourself from other candidates.* Your job-search preparation should help here. Try to focus on the two or three things that you do best. (E.g., "I make few errors. My attendance is nearly perfect. I can handle, and am ready to perform, a variety of assignments.") Show how these can contribute to a solid job performance. In replying to questions, do not be afraid to repeat these qualifications.

8. *Close the interview firmly.* Most personnel interviewers will control the close of the interview. Nevertheless, it is appropriate and it makes a good impression if you also sum up forcefully your understanding of what has transpired and your concluding view of the job opening. (E.g., "I understand that you will be interviewing several other candidates, but I do wish to emphasize how interested I am in filling this job. I believe that my qualifications—by reason of education, experience, and motivation—would enable me to perform the job very well. You would find me an excellent employee.") When the interview is concluded, thank the interviewer, shake hands if possible, and leave in a businesslike fashion.

9. *Follow up.* Regardless of the outcome of the interview, it makes a good business impression for you to write a brief note, thanking the company for the interview and expressing your continued interest in the position. (If the job no longer appeals to you, write anyway, asking that your name be removed from the

active applicants.) It is also appropriate to telephone the interviewer periodically to determine the status of the job opening and to ask that your application be kept active. Don't, however, persist to the point of becoming a nuisance, especially if you are told that the job has been filled. As an applicant, you will "lose" many interviews before you "win" one. Approach each one as an opportunity for improving your job-seeking and interviewing skills, and be appreciative of the company that gave you that chance. Persistence in your job search and maintaining a positive outlook will eventually pay off.

## YOUR FIRST JOB

### Starting out right

The world of work will hold surprises for you. Hopefully, you may find your first job to be a good one—fair pay, interesting work, a decent boss, nice people to work with, a chance to move upward. Unfortunately, not all first jobs turn out that well. There is often a chance that, as a consequence of the job's demands or your lack of preparedness, the job may appear disappointing. Don't despair. You may be suffering only temporarily from what experts describe as "job shock." This is, more often than not, your own reaction to the rather common circumstances that do not live up to your expectations. Most jobs are not completely designed to satisfy the employee. Much work, at almost any level of employment, entails monotonous routines. Furthermore, your boss and your associates may be indifferent to your personal problems. It can be very discouraging. At this stage, there are three things to keep in mind: (1) The job will probably look and feel much better if you give it a few more months; (2) what may appear to be a dead-end job may in fact be a great spot for learning more about the company and your profession; and (3) for most of us, the only way to get experience is to first get a job, learn as much as possible from it, and then manage to turn that experience into a better job.

**A STRATEGY FOR SURVIVAL** You may find it helps to approach your first important job as a survival situation. Therefore, everything you do at work should be based upon (1) making the work itself more enjoyable and (2) moving your performance up to and beyond the level of what your employer judges to be satisfactory. While there is a multitude of sound advice about how to accomplish these twin objectives, a notable employer provides what may be the best guidelines for getting you through the first 12 months of your business life. Renault/Jeep Corporation, in its *Guide to Starting Your Career,* lays down these five simple rules of the workplace.

1. *Work a full day, every day.* You are expected to be on the job during working hours. Working late does not make up for arriving late.

2. *Get the work done on time.* In school, you may be able to turn papers in late, but finishing work assignments continually after the deadline is unacceptable.
3. *Your boss is your boss.* Be respectful and follow orders. When you feel you have special insight that can help solve a problem, by all means speak up. However, don't argue over the small stuff, or you may irritate your boss and get a reputation as a complainer.
4. *No job is fun all the time.* Every job has its share of tedium and frustration. It stands to reason that the newest and least experienced employees will be asked to complete many of the routine tasks. Don't be discouraged. Do your best, as cheerfully as possible.
5. *Be honest.* Everybody makes mistakes. Don't be afraid to own up to yours. Lying or laying the blame on someone else can be damaging to your career, as well as to your conscience.

**DRESSING APPROPRIATELY** Advising women or men about what to wear at work is a sensitive issue, but there do appear to be certain agreed-upon guidelines for business wear. For *women* (for most jobs), advises one experienced counselor, "tailored clothing only. No frills, ruffles, straps, or plunging necklines. Don't affect a 'feminine' style of dress. Try suits and blazers in plain, neutral colors, or understated plaids. Choose dresses in dark colors, worn with or without blazers. Use scarves for accents. Wear dark pumps with medium or low heels. Stud earrings and modest necklaces are all right, but avoid dangling bracelets."

For *men* (for most office, sales, or clerical work) the same counselor suggests "dark or gray suits, solid, pin-striped, or shadow plaid. Navy blazer and gray trousers are popular. Wear dress shirts in solid colors, mostly white, pale blue, or yellow. Choose from a variety of ties in muted colors in contrast to the suit. Solids, stripes, or small patterns are preferred. Wear calf-length hose in dark colors to match the suit, and black or brown 1-inch belts. Tassle loafers, wing tips, or lace-up shoes are fine. Avoid flashy cuff links, rings, or neck chains."

**BUILDING A NETWORK** Networking is now an accepted dynamic of business life. At its simplest, networking is just another name for making friends. Among these friends should be people who are supportive to you vocationally as well as personally. Your work associates will provide an important part of your network. People in other jobs, within and outside your company, should also be included. Most important, you should try to make a business friend of people at higher levels within your own company. The main purpose of the networks is *not* to use their influence in seeking advancement but as a means of exchanging information, contacts, and resources. One of the best ways to expand your network is to join a professional association related to your field and to volunteer your time to it. That way, you establish credibility based upon your performance and can exchange useful information as a result.

# Glossary

The numbers in parentheses following each definition refer to the chapter or chapters in which the terms are introduced and explained.

## A

**absolute advantage** A term used to describe the position of a country in international trade when it is the only country able to make a certain product or when it can make that product at a lower cost than any other country can. (22)

**accounting** A numerical information system whereby the day-to-day monetary transactions of an organization are recorded, classified, summarized, and interpreted. An accounting system monitors the flow of cash and the fluctuations in financial obligations. *See also* **financial accounting; managerial accounting.** (13)

**affirmative action plan** A written plan intended to eliminate discrimination in employment policies by spelling out positive steps to increase hiring and promotion of minority groups and women. An affirmative action plan is required by law of federal agencies and private industries contracted by the government. In most other cases, it is voluntary. (16)

**arbitration** A process in which a third party not directly involved in a labor-management dispute tries to facilitate a settlement. In arbitration, negotiating parties agree to be bound by the decisions of the arbitrator. *See also* **mediation.** (17)

**assets** (1) Any valuable property used for or resulting from a business. Examples of assets are cash, money owed by customers, inventory, and real estate. (2) Those things of value which

a company controls, such as land, equipment, cash, and accounts receivable. (3)

## B

**balance of payments** The total payments by a nation to foreign countries minus the total receipts of that nation from foreign countries. (22)

**balance of trade** The total value of a nation's exports minus the total value of its imports. (22)

**balance sheet** The main report, in summary form, of the overall financial condition of a company, showing assets, liabilities, and equity at a particular time, usually the last day of a fiscal year. (13)

**bankruptcy** A legal procedure in which a court divides up the remaining assets of an insolvent person or company among the people and organizations to whom money is owed; when this procedure is applied, all debts are erased. (20)

**behavioral school of management** The belief that an organization's goals can be met only by first understanding and then consciously dealing with people's psychological needs and interactions. Also called the human relations school of management. (5)

**bona fide occupational qualification** The legal requirement that a job specification regarding age, sex, or other restrictive characteristics be proven to be undeniably related to job performance. (16)

**bond** A written pledge to a lender or lenders stating the intention of the borrower or borrowers to repay a loan and specifying the principal, the date of maturity, and the rate of interest. (18)

**boycott** An organized refusal to buy the

products of a company or industry. (17)

**break-even point** Point at which volume of goods sold at chosen price will exactly equal total cost of production. (10)

**budget** (a) A plan or forecast, often financial in nature, in which data is presented in numerical form. (b) An operating plan expressed in concrete numbers. It, too, is usually financial, showing expected expenditures, but it may also show other factors that can be expressed numerically, such as worker-hours and materials. (14)

**budget variance report** Listings of all proposed expenditures compared with the actual costs that were incurred for each item. An analysis and control tool. (14)

**business enterprise** An activity that satisfies human wants and needs by providing goods or services for private profit. (1)

**by-laws** In corporation management, a group of rules, agreed upon by the owners, describing how stockholders will delegate management control. (21)

## C

**capital** (a) Any kind of wealth that is available to support the activities of producing goods and services, that is, of creating more wealth. (b) Private money and resources which are used to pay for the cost of setting up and running a business. (2)

**capital-intensive process** A production process in which equipment or materials are of primary importance; the activities of workers have a lesser significance. (11)

**cash budget** A budget showing expected cash receipts and expenditures for a particular planning period. (14)

**centralized organization** An organization in which almost all authority is concentrated in a few positions at the top. (6)

**chain of command** The downward flow of authority, responsibility, and channels of communications within an organization. *See also* **Scalar principle.** (6)

**chain store** One of a group of stores which are associated under a common management or common ownership and follow a common policy. Chain store operation is usually characterized by central purchasing and warehousing of products before they are distributed to local retail outlets. (8)

**charter (articles of incorporation)** A state-issued document legally recognizing the existence of a new corporation. The charter states the name and purpose of the corporation as well as stock authorization and other fundamental information. (21)

**classical school of management** The belief that worker and equipment productivity and profits can be increased by applying rational analysis to the production and management functions of a business. (5)

**close corporation** A corporation, usually small, whose ownership is closely held and not traded or offered as stock to the public. The owners are usually directly involved in the management of the business. (21)

**coinsurance provision** A common provision in fire insurance policies which states that if property is insured for less than its total value and it suffers damage that is less than total, the insurance company will pay only a specified portion of the loss. (20)

**collective bargaining** The process of negotiation by a union with the management of a company. This type of bargaining is called "collective" because the negotiators represent all the member-workers as a group. (17)

**command economy** An economic system in which the government plans and controls economic activity by assessing available resources and social needs and then directing the manufacturing and distribution facilities of the country toward certain goals. *See also* **Communism; Socialism.** (2)

**commercial bank** In the United States, a privately owned business that provides financial services to customers but which must obtain a government charter in order to operate. (19)

**commercial paper** A short-term

promissory note that does not have any security. (18)

**committee** A group of people within an organization formally assigned the responsibility to discuss, or deal directly, with a well-defined matter. (6)

**common carrier** Any organization engaged in transporting goods or passengers for hire by land, water, or air. (8)

**Common Market (European Economic Community)** A cooperative trade community of nine European nations acting together to further common interests by promoting the free movement of labor, capital goods, and so on among members. (22)

**common stock** Stock issued by every corporation to its owners in order to provide permanent risk capital. (18)

**Communism** An economic system in which central government control and planning have almost entirely replaced the free market, eliminating private ownership and profit and competition.

**comparable worth** A methodology for equating the worth of various jobs in the organization according to their contribution to the organization. (16)

**comparative advantage** A theory for determining which kinds of production will be most advantageous for a country in international trade: (a) A country with multiple absolute advantages should concentrate on the products in which its advantage is greatest. (b) A country with no absolute advantages should concentrate on products in which its disadvantage is the smallest. *See also* **absolute advantage.** (22)

**conglomerate combination** The joining together into one company of various companies that produce different, generally unrelated goods and services. (21)

**consideration** In law, "something of value." Consideration may be money, personal or intangible property, a promise to perform work, and so on. In contract law, consideration is the impelling influence or "thing of value" that causes a contracting party to enter a contract. (23)

**contingency approach** Uses various aspects of other approaches based upon the situation faced. (5)

**continuous process** Production operations which run for long periods of time with few pauses or changes. (11)

**contract** In law, a voluntary agreement in which two or more parties (individuals

or corporations) bind themselves to act or not to act in a certain way. A contract may be written or oral. (23)

**conversion process** In business, the process of creating or adding value or usefulness to available resources by changing them into an end product or service for which there is a demand. (1)

**cooperative** A form of business ownership in which production, marketing, or purchasing facilities are jointly owned by a group and are operated mainly to provide a service to members of the group rather than to make a profit. (3)

**corporation** An association of individuals, created under the authority of law, which exists and has powers and liabilities independent of its members. (3)

**current assets** Working capital, or the assets used to support the day-to-day operations of a company. Typically, current assets are cash, accounts receivable, negotiable securities, and inventories. (18)

### D

**data processing** All of the operations involved in collecting, organizing, analyzing, and presenting data, or information. Data processing may be, but need not be, associated with the use of computers. (12)

**database** Interrelated data stored in a computer file for easy access, retrieval, and updating. (12)

**debt financing** Funds raised by a business through borrowing, principally in the form of a bank loan or the sale of bonds. (18)

**decentralized organization** An organization in which much authority is delegated to managers who are close to the actual operations. In this type of organization, top management does not usually concern itself with lower-level operating decisions. (6)

**delegation** Assigning specific responsibilities along with related rights and authority to individuals and groups. A function of authority. (6)

**demand** The quantity of an economic good or service that will be bought at a specific price. (2)

**demand pricing** When prices are set in response to shifts in consumer demand. (1)

**depreciation** A loss in value of equipment, buildings, or other fairly permanent assets caused by normal wear and aging. (13)

**differential pricing** Sets different prices for various segments of the market. (10)

**differentiation** A promotional technique which points out the unique features of a product that will make it appeal to the chosen market. (9)

**discretionary income** The amount of money left over after the basic needs of life have been paid for. (7)

**disposable income** Take-home pay, that is, the amount of money available for spending after all taxes and fixed deductions are taken out. The amount of disposable income is a measure of the standard of living. (2)

**distribution** All those activities involved in moving goods from their point of production to consumers or from the seller to the buyer. (4)

**distribution channels** The routes products follow as they are bought and sold on their way to ultimate markets. (8)

**dividend** A portion of the surplus profits of a corporation divided among its owners, or stockholders. (18)

**division of labor** (1) Dividing up all activities, tasks, and responsibilities of a business into specific jobs and then grouping them into departments. (2) Breaking down production processes into separate tasks and assigning one or more tasks to individual workers. (6)

**dumping** Selling surplus goods overseas at less than their market price at home. (22)

### E

**economic indicator** A measure of economic activity which can be used to judge the direction in which the national economy is moving. Examples of economic indicators are employment statistics, consumer spending, the money supply, and interest rates. (14)

**economic order quantity (EOQ)** Best amount to order when replenishing inventory levels. (11)

**embargo** A legal prohibition by a country against trade in certain goods or with certain countries. (22)

**Employee Stock Ownership Plan (ESOP)** Under the terms of this plan, employees, as stockholders in the firm, share in both the profits and the losses. (17)

**entrepreneur** An individual who uses personal initiative to organize a new business. (2)

**equity (financial)** Money invested in a business. *See also* **capital.** (13)

**equity (human resources)** Conditions under which employees believe their rewards are fair. (15)

**equity financing** Funds raised by a business by selling shares in its ownership. (18)

**exchange rate** The amount of currency of one country that is equal to a given amount of the currency of another country. (22)

**expense budget** A forecast in numerical terms showing total amounts planned to be spent for specified purposes during a budget period. (14)

**exporting** Selling goods or merchandise to a company or government in another country. (22)

**express warranty** A statement made by a seller, often in a written form, that the article being sold is of a specified quality and type. The warranty may also state that the seller will repair or replace the merchandise if defects are found. (23)

### F

**Factoring** Providing money in return for accounts receivable, either by discounting or by buying the accounts outright. Factoring is performed by a company. (18)

**FIFO** First in, first out; an inventory accounting system that assumes that the cost at which an inventory was accumulated will be charged to the finished goods when sold. *See also* **LIFO.** (13)

**financial accounting** The maintaining by an organization of financial information which must be reported to, and used in dealing with, the "outside world"—investors, banks, regulatory government agencies, and so on. *See also* **accounting.** (13)

**fixed cost** Operating costs which do not vary according to the amount or type of goods produced or services provided, but remain relatively stable, for example, rent and utilities. (10)

**flexible budget** A budget that is capable of responding to the changing conditions of a business while still fulfilling its purpose. A flexible budget is usually achieved by the adoption of alternate budgets as conditions require. (14)

**FOB (free on board) destination** A term applying to the situation when the seller pays all transportation costs, except for the unloading of the goods at their destination. (8)

**FOB (free on board) factory** A

situation when the buyer pays all shipping costs, except for the loading of the goods at their point of origin. (8)

**follow-the-leader pricing** Setting prices very close to those already established for similar products of competing firms. (10)

**franchise** An independently owned company that pays a parent company a fee for the right to sell a certain product or to use certain methods or brand names. (3, 4)

### G

**general partnership** Co-ownership of a business by two or more people who contribute their private capital, share all profits, and accept individually and as a group all responsibility for satisfying the debts of the business. (3)

**going public** The act of making the first public offering of a corporation's stock. (21)

**grievance procedure** An orderly procedure spelling out the steps by which claims of wrongful treatment of workers by management can be appealed through various levels of union and company management. A grievance procedure is usually included in a labor contract. (17)

**gross national product (GNP)** The total market price of all the goods and services created by an economy, usually measured over a period of one year. (2)

### H

**historical trend forecast** A business forecasting technique based on finding out what consistent trends have occurred in the past and assuming that the ones identified will continue in the future. (14)

**horizontal combination** The joining together of more than one company operating at the same level of production or distribution of the same kind of goods or services, for example, two pharmaceutical manufacturers. (21)

### I

**implied warranty** A warranty, implied by law even when it is not expressed by the seller, that in most sales the buyer is receiving clear ownership of the property and the seller is authorized to sell it, and that the goods are as represented and can be used for their intended purpose. (23)

**importing** Buying goods or merchandise from a company or government in another country. (22)

**income statement (operating statement; profit and loss statement)** An accounting report that shows the revenue received and the expenses paid by a company during a certain period of operations. (13)

**indirect distribution channel** The path to markets followed by goods which pass through intermediaries (wholesalers, distributors, assemblers, brokers, agents, retailers, and so on) to the ultimate consumers of those goods. (8)

**industrial goods** (a) Goods used to make other products. (b) Goods used in the general operation of a business or an institution. (7)

**informal organization** The internal structure of relationships within a business which is assumed by workers and managers to exist without specific planning. (6)

**institutional advertising** Advertising which presents messages from a company, a group of companies, or other institutions without the intent to sell specific products but usually to promote a good reputation or goodwill. (9)

**insurance** A means of protecting businesses from various kinds of loss by sharing the risks. Each participant contributes regularly to a fund which is used to reimburse any contributor who suffers a specified type of loss. (20)

**intensive distribution** Placement of products in as many outlets as possible. (8)

**interlocking directorate** A directorate linked to that of another corporation by placing the same people or some of the same people on the boards of directors of different companies. Establishing an interlocking directorship is a means of controlling competition. (23)

**intermediary** An individual or business that performs some marketing functions in return for discounts from the producer or for markups when the goods are resold. (8)

**intrapreneurship** The innovation and creativity of entrepreneurship within, and with the support of, the formal corporate structure. (21)

**J**

**job analysis** The systematic study of the characteristics and activities required by specific jobs. (16)

**job enlargement** The process of increasing the number and kinds of activities performed by a single worker in order to make his or her job more interesting. (15)

**job enhancement; job enrichment** The process of making a job more satisfying for a worker by increasing his or her involvement in it through any of a variety of means, such as encouraging the worker to improve job techniques or to train others. (15)

**joint venture** A form of business ownership set up by two or more companies to carry out a one-time, short-lived business project, at the completion of which it ceases to exist. (3)

**just-in-time inventory control** Materials arrive just as needed, rather than being held in company inventory. (11)

**L**

**labor-intensive process** A production process in which workers make a more significant contribution to the value of the output than does any other element in the production process, such as equipment. (11)

**law of supply and demand** Supply and demand interacting to determine price and amount of goods and services that will be exchanged. (2)

**leverage** The ability of the owners of a business to control and use the profits from the total amount of capital when part of the capital is borrowed. (18)

**liabilities** Money owed by a company for any reason, for example, borrowing or purchasing on credit. (13)

**LIFO** Last in, first out; an inventory accounting system that charges the latest cost of accumulating inventories to the cost of goods sold. *See also* **FIFO.** (13)

**limited liability** The restriction of the responsibility of an individual owner of a corporation to the amount of money which he or she has invested in the corporation. (3)

**limited partnership** A form of business ownership in which one or more partners are granted limited liability, provided there is always at least one partner with unlimited liability. (3)

**line organization** An internal business structure in which every employee is a member of a direct chain of command from the top executives down through the levels of management. (6)

**liquidity** The ease with which a possession can be turned into cash. (19)

**M**

**make-or-buy decision** The decision process of comparing the total cost of manufacturing a product internally with the price of purchasing the product. (11)

**management** The process of planning, organizing, directing, and controlling the use of a firm's resources to effectively and economically attain its objectives. (5)

**management information system (MIS)** A set of interrelated procedures for collecting, analyzing, and reporting information (past, present, and projected) organized in such a way that the information is directly usable by managers for decision making and planning and controlling operations. The system is closely related to accounting. (12)

**management by objectives (MBO)** An arrangement between superiors and subordinates that enables subordinates to participate in establishing performance goals in such a way as to motivate and guide the subordinates' progress toward these goals. (15)

**manager** A person who performs the unique work of management—planning, organizing, directing, and controlling; an individual who works through the efforts of other people in an organization to enable the organization to meet its objectives. (5)

**managerial accounting** A system which provides managers with information on costs and revenues. This information is used internally in running the company. *See also* **accounting.** (13)

**market** A means by which buyers and sellers exchange goods and services at mutually agreed prices. (7)

**market segmentation** The breaking down of a market into subgroups that are homogeneous in some way. (7)

**marketing concept** A concept that rests on the belief that profits can be maximized by concentrating on the needs and wants of consumers and by creating products for which there is consumer demand. (7)

**marketing mix** The four main ingredients of the marketing process, which are product planning, product placement, product promotion, and product pricing. (7)

**markup** An indicator of a company's profitability. It is the difference between what a retailer pays for merchandise and the price a customer is charged. Computation of markup varies; it is determined by subtracting the cost of goods sold from the net sales and dividing the result by the cost of the goods sold, or by dividing the difference between the cost of goods sold and the net sales by the net sales. (10)

**mediation** A process in which a third party not directly involved in a labor-management dispute tries to facilitate a settlement by clarifying issues, bringing in new information, inducing compromise, and so on. Negotiators are not required to comply with a mediator's suggestions. *See also* **arbitration.** (17)

**merger** The joining together of two or more companies, either by the pooling of their resources and assets or by outright purchase, with the result that only one company exists. (21)

**money market mutual funds** Speculative investments (from which investors can buy shares) made up exclusively of interest-bearing, short-term borrowing instruments. *See also* **mutual funds.** (19)

**monopoly** A company that operates with no competition in producing or marketing particular goods. (2)

**multinational corporation** A corporation that carries on operations in a number of different countries. (22)

**mutual funds** Investment companies in which individual investors pool their money to buy stocks, bonds, and other securities. (19)

**mutual insurance company** An insurance company owned exclusively by policyholders (those insured) and, like a cooperative, operates as a nonprofit organization. (20)

**mutual savings bank** A cooperative bank which maintains savings accounts for depositors and uses part of the deposits for making mortgage loans and other investments. This type of bank may distribute earnings to depositors. (19)

### O

**oligopoly** An economic situation in which only a few competitive businesses supply the same goods or services to the same market, usually without strong competition. (2)

**open corporation** A corporation which offers its stock for sale to the general public. (21)

**open shop** A company or industry that has no officially recognized union. Workers are free to join the union of their choice, and management makes no formal effort to avoid unionization. (17)

**operations** The term generally used for all business processes except those that create physical goods, which are generally called "production processes." (11)

**organization** All the people, their roles, and relationships, that make up the human resources of an enterprise. (6)

**overhead** Expenses that do not add visible value to a product or service during its manufacture or provision. (4)

### P

**participative management (system 4)** One of four styles of management identified and described by Rensis Likert. Highly motivating, it stresses the active participation of employees in the management process. (15)

**penetration pricing** Setting as low a price for a product as possible, with the expectation of achieving profits through volume sales. Penetration pricing is used when new products are introduced. (10)

**performance appraisal** An attempt to judge the quality of the work of the employees of an organization with the intention of keeping general productivity as high as possible. (16)

**plans, strategic** Plans, policies, and procedures for attaining the overall, or long-term, goals of a business. (5)

**plans, tactical** Plans and procedures for attaining the short-term goals of a business that are a year or less away. (5)

**policy** A general guide as to how managers and workers are to decide issues that may occur in the future. Establishing a policy provides a way of shaping the deciding process while allowing discretion to the decision maker. (5, 20)

**positioning** Aiming a product at the specific market segments that would be most likely to buy it. (9)

**preferred stock** Stock which has priority over common stock when the profits of a company are distributed to stockholders. (18)

**prime rate** The interest charged by major banks for short-term loans to their large commercial customers with the best credit standings. (19)

**private nonprofit organization** An organization whose primary goal is to meet needs that cannot or are not effectively or fully satisfied by business. Although financed, established, and operated much like a business, it does not intend to make a profit. Examples of private nonprofit organizations are hospitals and museums. (1)

**product life cycle** The set of stages through which most finished products move, usually identified as introduction, growth, maturity, and decline. (7)

**product line** A group of similar or related products that can be sold by using the same kind of distribution and promotion methods. (7)

**production** The manufacture of physical materials or goods. Production ranges from basic resource extraction, such as mining, through the use of already manufactured materials to produce other manufactured goods, such as television sets. Production comprises all those activities which create goods or services to be sold, including manufacturing, purchasing of raw materials, and supervising production workers. The term is generally used for business processes in which the physical form of materials is changed. (1)

**productivity** The amount of goods or services produced from a given amount of resources. Productivity is a measure of production efficiency. (2)

**profit** The amount of money left from income made by selling goods and services after all the costs of producing the goods and services have been paid for. (1)

**program evaluation and review technique (PERT)** A planning technique for scheduling activities and allocating resources; especially useful for one-of-a-kind projects, such as building a bridge. (11)

**protective tariff** A tax levied on imported goods by a country in order to discourage the importation of certain products or to raise the price of these products so that they compete less effectively with domestic goods of the same type. (22)

**proxy** A legal statement empowering someone else to cast one's own vote. (21)

**public enterprise** An organization, not intended to make a profit, operated by a unit of government and financed by taxes or service charges paid by the public, which produces goods or renders services deemed essential for the public good. (1)

**pulling strategy** A technique used in promoting a product in which attempts are made to stimulate a strong consumer demand, usually by advertising. (9)

**pure risk** A type of business risk. Pure risk refers to the possibility of loss caused by accidental fire, injury, or other damage to property or life. (20)

**pushing strategy** A technique used in promoting a product in which strong promotional efforts are directed toward wholesalers and retailers in an attempt to persuade them to sell the product aggressively. (9)

### Q

**quality circles** Small groups of employees who acknowledge a mutual dependency for quality and productivity and who meet regularly to identify and resolve operating problems. (11)

**quality control** Inspection of products

and services to insure that they meet their designed specifications. (11)

**quantitative approach** A modern theory of management which emphasizes the overall system in which work is done and uses the statistical study of groups of operations, workers, consumers, and so on to permit prediction and to guide decision making. It is derived from systems theory. (5)

**quick ratio (acid-test ratio)** Quick assets (assets that can be used very quickly to pay bills, that is, cash, marketable securities, accounts receivable) divided by current liabilities. The quick ratio is a sensitive indicator of liquidity. (13)

## R

**ratio analysis** A technique for interpreting financial statements in which certain categories of assets, earnings, expenses, liabilities, and equity are compared. Ratio analysis permits a comparison of the performance and condition of a company with its own standards or with those of other companies. (13)

**retailer** A company or an individual who buys products for resale to ultimate consumers. (8)

**return on investment** A measure of how much income has been produced from the capital invested in a business by its owners. Return on investment is calculated by dividing net income by owners' equity. (13)

**return on sales (net profit margin; ratio of net income to sales)** An indicator of the profitability of a company. Return on sales is determined by dividing net income before taxes by net sales. (13)

**revenue budget** A budget that attempts to forecast, in numerical form, the total income from all sources that will be available during an upcoming budget period. Among these sources are sales revenues as well as all others, such as dividends and interest from savings accounts. (14)

**robotics** A form of automation in which mechanical devices duplicate the motions of the human hand. (11)

## S

**safety stock** A minimum supply of materials or goods or an inventory, for example, for one-week's use. This stock is kept on hand in case regular deliveries are delayed. (11)

**sales promotion** The category of promotion that includes all promotional activities except actual selling and advertising. (9)

**Scalar principle** The concept that authority and responsibility should flow in an unbroken line from the top to the bottom of an organization. *See also* **chain of command.** (6)

**self-insurance** The practice, followed by some businesses (usually large ones), of maintaining a reserve fund to be used if a major loss occurs. (20)

**services** Personal, professional, or financial activities that help people or organizations. The creation of a physical product is not a direct outcome of these activities. (1)

**shopping goods** Regularly purchased but comparatively expensive goods for which buyers are willing to "shop around" before making a selection. (7)

**sinking fund** A fund to which a company contributes annually so that, by the maturity date of a bond issue, the fund will contain enough money to retire the issue. (18)

**skimming** The practice of setting the highest price consumers are likely to accept when introducing a new product, with the intent to reduce prices later, when competition is felt. (10)

**Socialism** An economic system in which the government owns and operates the major industries of production and distribution and plays a heavy regulative role in all other business activity, but permits certain freedoms of capitalism to exist in a modified form. *See also* **command economy; Communism.** (2)

**software** In computer technology, (a) the collection of instructions, readable by a computer, that tells the computer what to do (for example, computer programs); or (b) the procedures for gathering, preparing, checking, and distributing data and output. (12)

**sole proprietorship** A form of business ownership in which a single individual assumes the risk of operating the business, owns its assets, and controls and uses its profits. (3)

**span of control** The number of employees or activities directly supervised by one manager. (6)

**specialty goods** Products with unique characteristics—especially a brand name—that make consumers willing to exert considerable effort to locate and buy them. (7)

**standard industrial classification (SIC)** A numerical system which groups specific industries into comprehensive categories. The system was devised by the Office of Management and the Budget. (1)

**standard metropolitan statistical area (SMSA)** A concentrated population of 50,000 or more people that has been designated a SMSA by the federal government for census and statistical purposes. (7)

**statement of changes in financial position (funds statement; sources and uses statement)** An accounting report in summary form showing the sources of funds a business has used during an accounting period and the uses to which the funds were put. (13)

**stock dividend** A dividend paid to the stockholders of a corporation in the form of new shares of stock rather than cash. (18)

**stock split** The procedure of dividing each share of the existing stock of a corporation into two or more new shares in order to reduce the price of single shares. (18)

**strategic plans** Overall guides to long-range courses of action to be taken to meet objectives. (5)

**Subchapter S corporation** A legal form of small business that combines the limited liability of a corporation with the tax advantages of a single proprietorship. (3)

**subsidiary** A company that has merged with one or more other companies and whose assets are mainly or entirely owned by another company. (21)

**system** An organizational form or set of interrelated rules, procedures, and the like. A system can be economic, social, political, physical, and so on. (1)

**systems theory** A group of verbal and mathematical principles that describe how the related parts of a system may be organized. (5)

## T

**tariff** A special tax on imported goods, usually imposed to protect domestic producers from lower priced foreign products. (22, 23)

**technology** The collection of methods a society uses to provide itself with the material needs of life. The processes, methods, and knowledge used to produce goods and services. (2)

**Theory X and Theory Y** Two common managerial views of people and their motivation, described by Douglas McGregor. **Theory X:** The average worker inherently dislikes work and responsibility, must be forced and directed. **Theory Y:** Work is natural; employees will readily accept responsibility and work toward goals that provide self-respect and fulfillment. (15)

**trade credit** A purchase made on credit from the vendor. (18)

**trademark** A brand that is protected by law. (23)

**trust** (a) Any business combination that limits or eliminates competition. (b) Literally, a scheme by which a company gives dividend-paying trust certificates in return for voting control of the stock of another company. (23)

## U

**underwriter** In business finance, an intermediary (such as an investment bank or banker) who buys all or a large part of an issue of the stock of a corporation and resells it to investors, receiving a commission for services rendered. (21)

**Uniform Commercial Code** A large body of commercial laws, written by legal experts, covering every major area of business law that falls under state jurisdiction and designed to make the laws governing business transactions more uniform in application. Of itself, the code has no legal force, but much of it has been made enforceable law by most state legislatures. (23)

**Union shop** An industry or company that requires all employees to join a recognized union within a specified time after they are hired. (17)

**unity of command** The principle that each person in an organization should have only one immediate superior. (6)

**unlimited liability** The responsibility of the proprietor of a business for paying all debts and charges that may arise from its operation. Characteristic of small businesses and farms. (3)

**utility of place** The value or usefulness of a resource or product which is determined by its location—its availability for immediate use by the consumer. (1)

## V

**value analysis** An analysis carried out jointly by the engineers and purchasing agents of a company to examine every part of a product to determine whether less expensive substitutes can be used without impairing its function. Value analysis is a means of reducing the costs of materials and production. (11)

**variable costs or expenses** Costs which rise and fall according to changes in production activity or volume of output. Examples are expenses for materials, labor, and other resources whose use depends on production. (10)

**vertical combination** A method of joining together into one large company a number of smaller companies, all of which contribute at some level to producing and selling a single kind of product, such as gasoline. (21)

## W

**warranty** A guarantee, implied or explicit, of the integrity of a product usually specifying that the manufacturer will be responsible for the replacement of defective parts for a certain period of time. (23)

**wholesalers** Intermediaries who sell goods to buyers who are not the final users. (8)

**word processing** The production of written communications through the combined use of systems management procedures, automated and/or computer technology, and skilled personnel. (12)

**worker's compensation insurance** Insurance carried by businesses to compensate employees for losses caused by physical injury or illness suffered because of their jobs. Worker's compensation insurance is required by law in all 50 states. (20)

## Z

**zero-based budgeting** A budgeting and planning system that requires managers to justify their annual budget requests as if the associated expenses had never occurred before. (14)

# INDEX